"In *War and Peace on the Rio Grande Frontier,* 1 Quiroga shows how reporting and analyzing economic activities can shed light on fundamental historical processes, which are all too often obscured by ideological prejudices. Few more telling examples than those in *War and Peace* can be found to confirm, once and for all, the socioeconomic integration of a space that was both regional and binational and whose development was consolidated after 1850 despite the blindness of those who observed (and still view) this border from the elegant capitals of both nation-states."

Mario Cerutti, Universidad Autónoma de Nuevo León;
author of *Problemas, conceptos, actores y autores:*
La Historia Económica y Empresarial en el norte de
México (y en otras latitudes)

"An important addition to the growing body of historical works which seek to understand and explain that cooperation and conversation among peoples and individuals are as much a part of lived life in the past as confrontation and conflict."

David Cannadine, Dodge Professor of History,
Princeton University, and author of *The Undivided Past*

"*War and Peace on the Rio Grande Frontier* depicts in exquisite detail the counter-vailing forces that shaped life along the U.S.-Mexico borderlands in the nineteenth century: great economic opportunity along with potential for deadly violence. González-Quiroga has mined the literature and documentary sources available to give us a detailed, humane, and perplexing yet realistic portrait of frontier society."

Andrés Reséndez, author of *The Other Slavery:*
The Uncovered Story of Indian Enslavement in America

"*War and Peace on the Rio Grande Frontier* is a sweeping, compelling history of the Texas-Mexico border region in the turbulent nineteenth century. González-Quiroga's incisive binational perspective and narrative make this essential reading for anyone wishing to understand the formation of this unique borderlands. Encyclopedic in scope, *War and Peace* is, without question, a significant contribution to both American and Mexican histories."

David Montejano, Professor of the Graduate School,
University of California, Berkeley, and author
of *Anglos & Mexicans in the Making of Texas*

War and Peace on the Rio Grande Frontier, 1830–1880

NEW DIRECTIONS IN TEJANO HISTORY

Alberto Rodriguez and Timothy Paul Bowman,
Series Editors

War and Peace on the Rio Grande Frontier, 1830–1880

Miguel Ángel González-Quiroga

UNIVERSITY OF OKLAHOMA PRESS : NORMAN

Published in cooperation with
THE WILLIAM P. CLEMENTS CENTER FOR SOUTHWEST STUDIES,
SOUTHERN METHODIST UNIVERSITY

Library of Congress Cataloging-in-Publication Data

Names: González-Quiroga, Miguel A., 1946– author. | William P. Clements Center for Southwest Studies, sponsoring body.

Title: War and peace on the Rio Grande frontier, 1830–1880 / Miguel Ángel González-Quiroga.

Description: First edition. | Norman, OK : University of Oklahoma Press, 2020. | Series: New directions in Tejano history ; volume 1 | "Published in cooperation with The William P. Clements Center for Southwest Studies, Southern Methodist University."—Title page. | Includes bibliographical references and index. | Summary: "Draws on national archives, letters, consular records, periodicals, and other sources to create a sweeping narrative of the history of the Rio Grande borderlands between 1830 and 1880 and the complex relations of violent conflict, cooperation, and economic and social advancement"—Provided by publisher.

Identifiers: LCCN 2019046676 | ISBN 978-0-8061-6498-4 (hardcover) | ISBN 978-0-8061-9095-2 (paper)

Subjects: LCSH: Rio Grande Valley (Colo.-Mexico and Tex.)—History—19th century. | Rio Grande Valley (Colo.-Mexico and Tex.)—Economic conditions—19th century. | Mexican-American Border Region—History—19th century. | Mexico—Relations—Texas. | Texas—Relations—Mexico.

Classification: LCC F392.R5 G66 2020 | DDC 972/.1—dc23

LC record available at https://lccn.loc.gov/2019046676

War and Peace on the Rio Grande Frontier, 1830–1880 is Volume 1 in the New Directions in Tejano History series.

The paper in this book meets the guidelines for permanence and durability of the Committee on Production Guidelines for Book Longevity of the Council on Library Resources, Inc. ∞

For Fernando Jr. and Ariana
Theirs is the future.

Contents

Illustrations

Series Editors' Preface

Miguel Ángel González-Quiroga's masterful study, *War and Peace on the Rio Grande Frontier, 1830–1880*, is the first book in the New Directions in Tejano History series. Most historians interested in the Texas-Mexico borderlands during the nineteenth century have been fascinated with one dominant element of the region's past: its almost extraordinary legacy of violence. Given the history of Indian raids, warfare, revolt, extralegal violence, racial strife, and political conflict, such an overwhelming preoccupation with violence certainly makes sense. This book, however, takes a different approach. A lived reality alongside the region's excessive violence involved cooperation and coexistence between Mexicans, Anglo-Americans, Native Americans, African Americans, and Europeans. There is a growing body of historical literature that deals with either cooperation or conflict among various groups in borderlands settings; *War and Peace on the Rio Grande Frontier* is a stunning achievement of analysis and synthesis, offering a once-in-a-generation narrative that only an eminent historian such as González-Quiroga can achieve.

Meeting here are Anglo-Americans who moved into the region from afar to engage in entrepreneurship, trade, religious proselytizing, and settlement; Mexicans from the south who sought to push the boundaries of opportunity and belonging in *el norte*; Native Americans who plumbed American and Mexican settlements alike for plunder and captives; and Europeans who crisscrossed the borderlands looking for new futures in a distended frontier space. There is no similar study that both synthesizes and analyzes this complex sweep of Mexico-Texas borderlands history over such a long duration during the nineteenth century, which makes this book a much-needed contribution to the literature on borderlands, Texas, Mexico, and Native American histories.

To accomplish this feat, González-Quiroga has spent an entire career scouring archives on both sides of the border, finding sources that help elucidate the long history of conflict and cooperation in the U.S.-Mexico borderlands, many of which undoubtedly had never before made their way into the hands of a professional historian. González-Quiroga relied on national archives, letters, consular records, periodicals, published primary sources, and a host of other materials to give voice to borderlanders' perspectives while weaving their many varied stories together. González-Quiroga tells these stories in a compelling way that will be useful and essential for classrooms, graduate seminars, and professional historians. Of equal (and some might say greater) importance, though, is that this book is written in a jargon-free style that will appeal to a general readership.

In these ways, then, we proudly welcome this important book as the first offering in the series. The book is Tolstoyan in scope. Perhaps an even better adjective to describe this book, though—and one that will make sense to borderlands historians who are reading this preface—would be to call it "Weberian." The late David J. Weber, a noted borderlands historian and a contemporary of González-Quiroga's, left an indelible imprint on borderlands history by offering sweeping and deeply readable works of vast synthesis—his two books, *The Mexican Frontier, 1821–1846* (1982) and *The Spanish Frontier in North America* (1992), instantly come to mind. Given the quality of its research, its scope, and its readability, *War and Peace on the Rio Grande Frontier* belongs in the conversation with Weber's classic works.

It is truly my distinct honor to introduce this book to what will certainly become a dedicated and long-lasting readership.

Timothy Paul Bowman
(series coeditor with Alberto Rodriguez)

Acknowledgments

T his book was possible thanks to the labor of others. Those who wrote the books, protected and organized the documents and made them accessible to me and others, and those who shared with me their knowledge all deserve my recognition and gratitude. Among them are numerous teachers, librarians, archivists, colleagues, students, and friends.

I was born and have lived most of my life in a rural town in Northeast Mexico: General Zuazua, Nuevo León, named after one of the state's greatest military figures. Until recent years, when it was absorbed into the Monterrey metropolitan area, Zuazua was a small town where everyone knew each other. I have many friends and relatives there, as well as in the neighboring town, Ciénega de Flores. As they are too numerous to mention, I want to acknowledge their friendship, which has been a great moral support throughout the years. Zuazua and Ciénega de Flores, like all towns and cities in northern Mexico have been greatly influenced by their proximity to the United States. My personal story of migrating to the United States at an early age is one shared by many residents of northern Mexico since the border was established.

After many years I returned to Mexico in 1982. The Facultad de Filosofía y Letras of the Universidad Autónoma de Nuevo León became my academic home for the better part of thirty years and was always supportive of my research. Special mention goes to Juan Ángel Sánchez, Bernardo Flores, Ricardo Villarreal, Nicolás Duarte, José Reséndiz, and María Luisa Martínez, who directed the institution while I was there. It was there, in the Colegio de Historia, that I had the opportunity to work with Mario Cerutti, one of Mexico's foremost historians. Mario and I collaborated in various publishing ventures, including two books, several articles, and the journal *Siglo XIX*. Mario had a great influence on my thinking, especially the idea that irrespective of the border, Texas and Northeast

Mexico was an integrated region, united by economic, social, and cultural ties. We shared many car rides from Monterrey to Austin to do research in the Center for American History and the Benson Latin American Collection of the University of Texas. What we found there gave support to that idea.

Over the last four decades, I have been fortunate to work and learn from many colleagues and students too numerous to mention at the Facultad de Filosofía y Letras and at various universities in Monterrey and throughout Mexico. I should mention however the Universidad de las Américas in Puebla, where I received my graduate training, because it was there that I developed an inclination for archival research. For that I give credit to my teachers Laurens Perry, Errol Jones, and Stephen Niblo and my fellow students Federico Lobdell and David LaFrance.

Archival research was vital to this study, and I could not have carried it out without the help of the many men and women who did their daily work without notice, often without acknowledgment. In Monterrey I want to express my appreciation to Hector Jaime Treviño, Cesar Morado Macías, Jesús Ávila, and the staff at the Archivo General del Estado de Nuevo León. Artemio Benavides and Romeo Flores Caballero, who directed the archive, also deserve mention. My thanks also to Juana Margarita Domínguez and her staff at the Archivo Histórico de Monterrey and to the diligent staff of the Archivo Diocesano de Monterrey. Catalina Roel of the Santiago Roel Melo Collection generously provided documents for this study.

In Coahuila, I found the Archivo General del Estado de Coahuila in Ramos Arizpe (now located in Saltillo) to be well organized with a friendly and helpful staff under the direction of Lucas Martínez and Francisco Rodríguez. The same applies to the staff of the Archivo Municipal de Saltillo. In Mexico City I was well served by the people at the Museo Nacional de las Intervenciones, the Archivo Histórico of the Secretaría de la Defensa Nacional and the Archivo Histórico Genaro Estrada of the Secretaría de Relaciones Exteriores.

Throughout the years many friends and colleagues have shaped my education. I will not name them because I would inevitably leave someone out, but they can be sure that they are not forgotten. For reasons of space, I will mention a few of the ones who contributed to the making of this book. Roberto Rebolloso and José Roberto Mendirichaga provided works that were incorporated into the bibliography. Sergio Javier García shared insights about his ancestor, one of the Confederate soldiers who made Mexico his home after the Civil War.

A climate of sharing and critical thinking was fostered in a research seminar at the Facultad de Filosofía y Letras that at times included Lidia Rodríguez,

José María Infante, Martha Casarini, Lylia Palacios, Jacobo Castillo, Moisés Saldaña, Rogelio Cantú, Guadalupe Rodríguez, Lídice Ramos, Javier Arizpe, María Eugenia Flores, José Javier Villarreal, Armando González, Rebeca Moreno, Benigno Benavides, Guadalupe Chávez, Ludivina Cantú, Miguel de la Torre, Armando González, Eleocadio Martínez, and other colleagues.

Two great historians of Nuevo León deserve mention: Israel Cavazos Garza and Isidro Vizcaya Canales. Also worthy of mention are historians Gabriel Martínez, Eva Rivas, Juana Idalia Garza, Edmundo Derbez, María Zebadúa, Mario Treviño, José Antonio Olvera, Alberto Barrera, Rocío González Maiz, Javier Rojas, Pablo Ramos, Ahmed Valtier, and Oscar Flores. Leticia Damm aided me in translation efforts throughout the years.

From other parts of Mexico, I want to acknowledge Manuel Ceballos, Cirila Quintero, and Clemente Rendón de la Garza in Tamaulipas; Ricardo León, Carlos González, Consuelo Pequeño, and Raúl García in Chihuahua; Martha Rodríguez and Carlos Recio in Coahuila; Miguel Soto, Marcela Terrazas, Gerardo Gurza Lavalle, Josefina Zoraida Vázquez, Laura Herrera, Mercedes de Vega, María de los Ángeles Pozas, and Carlos Marichal in Mexico City; and Martín González de la Vara in Michoacán. Octavio Herrera of Tamaulipas, who has vast knowledge about Northeast Mexico, was particularly helpful to me.

In the United States the two scholars who had the greatest influence on me were John Mason Hart of the University of Houston and David Weber of Southern Methodist University. Many other colleagues in the United States have shaped my thinking. Among them are Armando Alonzo, José Ángel Hernández, Douglas Brackenridge, Jonathan Brown, Roberto Calderón, John Chávez, Frank de la Teja, Brian DeLay, George Díaz, Francis Galan, Amy Porter, Stanley Green, Paul Hart, Sam Haynes, Sonia Hernández, Gilberto Hinojosa, Rob Jones, Tom McDonald, Ron Tyler, David Narrett, Raúl Ramos, Omar Valerio Jiménez, Andrés Reséndez, Doug Richmond, Terry Rugeley, Joaquín Rivaya Martínez, Michael Snodgrass, Andrew Torget, Roberto Treviño, Bruce Winders, Teresa Van Hoy, and Emilio Zamora.

As in Mexico, the aid of the staff of various U.S. archives was crucial in the making of this book. In Texas, I received courteous and professional assistance at the Dolph Briscoe Center for American History and the Benson Latin American Collection of the University of Texas at Austin. Also in Austin I want to thank the staff of the Texas State Archives and the Austin Public Library. My appreciation also goes to the staff of the Mary and Jeff Bell Library at Texas A&M University, Corpus Christi. In Dallas, the DeGolyer Library at Southern

Methodist University deserves my recognition. In San Antonio I owe a debt of gratitude to the Texana Collection of the San Antonio Public Library, as well as to the Institute of Texan Cultures of the University of Texas at San Antonio and the Daughters of the Republic of Texas Library.

With financial support from the Universidad Autónoma de Nuevo León and the Rockefeller Foundation I was able to make trips to California and Washington for research. I received valuable assistance from the staff at the Bancroft Collection of the University of California at Berkeley. My gratitude goes to Barbara Tenenbaum of the Library of Congress and to the staff of the National Archives in Washington. Three online resources that were invaluable to me and all scholars are the Portal of Texas History, the Handbook of Texas, and the Hemeroteca Nacional de México. I thank everyone involved with these projects and cannot imagine completing this book without them. I am also indebted to the History Department of the University of Texas at San Antonio, which invited me as a visiting researcher and has given me access to the wonderful library resources and databases of the university.

One of the institutions that was vital to the development of this book is the Clements Center for Southwest Studies at Southern Methodist University in Dallas, Texas. My term there as a research fellow was highly rewarding, especially the opportunity to participate with gifted colleagues in various manuscript workshops. My deepest appreciation for those who have been responsible for the operation of the center: David Weber, Sherry Smith, Benjamin Johnson, Andrew Graybill, Neil Foley, Andrea Boardman, and Ruth Ann Elmore. During my stay at the Clements Center, I was invited to live in the home of Bruce and Barbara Mickey, two of the finest physicians and people I have known.

For their kindness and assistance in providing illustrations for this book, I wish to thank Kristy Sorensen of the Austin Presbyterian Theological Seminary, Jerry Thompson of Texas A&M University at Laredo; Mellisa De Thorne of the P. I. Nixon Medical Historical Library at the University of Texas Health Science Center at San Antonio; Mathew C. Martin of the Southwestern Oblate Historical Archives of the Oblate School of Theology in San Antonio; Olivia Strozz Galindo and Iván Vartán of the Archivo Municipal de Saltillo; Tom Shelton and Carlos Cortez of the Institute of Texan Cultures; and Robert G. Rodríguez, who provided a photo from his family collection. I also thank cartographer Ana Gabriela Arreola Meneses for the map that accompanies this text.

Special thanks to the following colleagues who read all or parts of the manuscript and provided valuable observations: James E. Crisp, Stanley Green, James

Nichols, Gilberto Hinojosa, Joaquín Rivaya Martínez, Luís García, Josefina Zoraida Vázquez, David Montejano, and Michael Parrish. Jerry Thompson and Patrick Kelly not only read the manuscript and provided suggestions but have been very supportive of my work. I am also indebted to the two anonymous readers who provided feedback and support for the manuscript.

I wish to mention and thank a few people who are very important in my life: my father and mother who gave me my existence, my wife, Martha, and sons Fernando, Juan Zenón, and Miguel Ángel, and my sisters, Blanca and Aída Margarita. My brother-in-law José Sánchez is a voracious reader and has shared with me many of the books he has read, some of which have made their way into my bibliography. I also want to thank Juan Ángel González, Victor Hugo Garza, Noé M. and María Esther Pérez, John and Pamela Martínez, John and Mayra McMillan, and Gerardo Chapa and his family for their inspiration and moral support while this project was in the making.

Finally, for her skill, patience and good humor, I want to acknowledge the help of my copy editor, Kirsteen Anderson, who has done a great job, and my editors and friends at Oklahoma University Press who made this book possible: Kent Calder, Steven Baker, and the series editors, Alberto Rodriguez and Timothy Bowman.

Introduction

I n October 1878 relations between Mexico and the United States were close to the breaking point. The "prevailing belief" in Mexico, wrote U.S. ambassador John W. Foster, was that there would be war between the two countries. The *New York Times* recognized that the "delicacy of the situation is such that either Government could at any time bring on a war by a single indiscretion."[1] This state of affairs had come about because of the incessant violence along the Rio Grande throughout the 1870s and the unilateral order given to General E. O. C. Ord on June 1, 1877, to pursue Mexican raiders across the border. Conflict had been an oppressive reality in the border region since the 1830s, but the violence of the 1870s was particularly hellish. It included cattle rustling, filibustering expeditions, attacks by armed bands from both sides of the border, Indian depredations, and three major revolts against the Mexican government. One historian has written that a "reign of terror" prevailed in the region.[2]

This state of violence, fueled by racial hatred, national rivalries, lack of government authority, competition for the resources of the region, and an international border that offered refuge to lawless men, has been analyzed in many histories of the U.S.-Mexican border.[3] But the main point of this book is that alongside the conflict, another reality existed in the region, one that is less known but just as pervasive. This was a reality based on coexistence and cooperation among Mexicans, Anglo-Americans, and the other ethnic groups that inhabited the region, including Native Americans, African Americans, and Europeans.[4]

At the same time as diplomats and journalists of both countries were talking of war, Mexicans, converted to Presbyterianism by American missionaries, were crossing the Rio Grande from Matamoros to Brownsville to help establish the first Mexican Presbyterian congregation in Texas in 1877. Milton Faver, married to a Mexican woman, was employing cowboys from south of the Rio Grande and purchasing livestock from breeders in northern Mexico for his cattle ranches near Presidio, Texas. Following a pattern established decades earlier and in spite of the violence, Mexican rural workers were migrating in large numbers across the border to work on farms, ranches, and army posts on the Texas frontier.[5]

In 1877–78, at the height of the diplomatic crisis, American and European business and professional people were in northern Mexico, looking for opportunities to work and invest their money. San Antonio merchants, in tandem with their Mexican counterparts, were purchasing mining and ranching properties in Coahuila, initiatives that preceded the massive American investments in Mexico in the last two decades of the century. Dr. Frank Paschal, who would later become one of San Antonio's most prominent physicians, was winning the admiration and affection of the people of Chihuahua, where he ministered to everyone, even if they were unable to pay for his services. Many other examples can be cited (and will be in the pages of this book), but clearly another history besides the well-known story of conflict and violence was unfolding in the Rio Grande border region.[6]

These parallel histories are reflected in the title of this book, and they share center stage with a silent actor that made both of them possible: the Rio Grande border, which is a secondary theme of this book. In the course of this study I will show that the border generated conditions for violence as well as opportunities for advancement. These disparate scenarios provided fertile ground for cooperation. Importantly, cooperation resulted from conflict as well as from economic opportunities.

Violence was always latent because the border region brought together people of different races and national origins; it attracted lawless men and Indian predators who sought refuge on one side of the boundary after committing crimes on the other side; it generated territorial disputes between opposing governments; and it was far from the centers of power of both countries—where all too often the arm of the law could not reach. All of these elements made the border a particularly conflictive region.[7]

The border was also however a magnet for newcomers because it provided myriad opportunities for social and economic advancement. Freedom from oppression was the goal of runaway slaves, Mexican rural workers, and migrant tribes. Others were attracted by economic opportunities that abounded in areas such as commerce, stock raising, freighting, and mining. Alongside these legal activities, the border also gave rise to a clandestine economy that included land speculation, smuggling, theft of livestock and other property, and bounties for killing Indian raiders or retrieving runaway slaves. This underground economy was pervasive, involved members of all races and classes, and—like the legal economy—often entailed cooperation among different groups. The opportunities offered by the border economy constitute a third important theme in this study because they attracted people to the region and made it a vibrant and viable place, despite the incessant violence.

The study of the period and the region reveals the concurrent nature of conflict and cooperation, because in the midst of conflict, or in spite of it, most inhabitants were engaged in peaceful and mutually rewarding pursuits.[8] This book will focus on this duality and explore the economic and social relations among the diverse human groups that inhabited the Texas-Mexico border region during a period of almost ceaseless violence. Alongside the conflict between and among the different groups, peaceful exchanges, cooperation, accommodation, sharing of hardships and danger, and relations of friendship and marriage also occurred. These associations show that conflict was not the only reality and that the Texas-Mexico border region was also a space for broad interethnic interactions and commercial exchange. Emphasizing cooperation without ignoring the violence, this book offers an alternative view of border history, from a framework of cooperation not conflict.[9]

Along with the politicians and military men that populate more traditional histories, this book discusses other actors who occupied the same stage but played different roles: merchants, ranchers, laborers, freighters, medical doctors, pioneer women, religious missionaries, consular agents, and various everyday people. Some historians have assigned such people minor roles, but they made up the substance of historical processes and movements and shaped the decisions of those in power. These historical actors created a diverse history that has been largely obscured by the focus on violence. They did something more: long before the coming of the railroad, merchants, migrants, and missionaries, through their energy and zeal, integrated the region. The integration of a binational region between 1830 and 1880 is the final relevant theme in this study.

The groups that inhabited the region—which included Mexicans, Anglo-Americans, Native Americans, African Americans, and Europeans—fought each other, but also struggled together to make a living, to gain prosperity, or simply to survive. This book will stress what the members of these groups—particularly Anglos and Mexicans—did together. In a harsh frontier environment they often discovered commonalities in interests, problems, and needs. Theirs was a shared history. Together they traded and smuggled goods; speculated in land; participated in violent acts and wars; worshiped God; enjoyed parties; faced dangers, diseases, and natural disasters; and pursued outlaws and Indians, sometimes with the help of other Indians. Importantly, many of these cooperative actions were not motivated by benevolence or altruism, but by self-interest. No one has stated this idea better than Adam Smith: "man has almost constant occasion for the help of his brethren, and it is in vain for him to expect it from their benevolence only. . . . It is not from the benevolence of the butcher, the brewer, or the baker that we expect our dinner, but from their regard to their own interest."[10]

The perception that violence characterizes the history of the U.S.-Mexico borderlands extends into the present, since many people consider the present border as a place where trafficking in people, arms, and drugs, among other problems, generates violence. This book is intended to revise or balance those perceptions, which are often held by those unfamiliar with the region. Oriented toward a broad reading public, this book is written in a narrative style that tells the stories of people and events.[11]

Centered on the lower Rio Grande, this history covers a transnational region that extends northward to include part of Texas and southward to encompass three states in Northeast Mexico—Tamaulipas, Nuevo León, and Coahuila. (Chihuahua is mentioned occasionally because of its commercial importance to Texas.) This frontier region, on the periphery of two nations and including parts of both, is my unit of study.[12] That is only the physical region, however. David J. Weber, one of the greatest borderlands historians, wrote that a frontier is a social "and not simply a physical or geographical environment." It "is best understood as a social phenomenon, representing an interaction between man, his institutions, and the physical and spatial environments of an area of low population density where two cultures or two nations meet."[13] Of course, one must be flexible with regard to spatial limits because the movements of people, goods, capital, and ideas defy specific boundaries.[14]

These movements occur where "two nations meet," but the border is also a place where two histories meet. Herbert Eugene Bolton wrote that the histories of the American nations are intertwined. This is especially true of those nations that share a common frontier. The great borderlands historian mainly focused on the colonial period, but for the greater part of the nineteenth century the histories of the United States and Mexico continued to merge, enveloped in economic, social, and cultural processes that touched people's lives on both sides of the border. The spread of the capitalist economy, the pacification or elimination of Indian peoples, and the construction of the nation-state in a postcolonial world are but examples of these processes. Borderlanders were shaped by these forces often without being aware of them. Their local histories were "but a thread out of a larger strand."[15] It will also become evident that local events also helped shape the greater world. This, then, is a borderlands and a transnational history.

It is important to address racial terminology. In the usage of the years under study, and to which I will adhere, Mexicans were not commonly referred to as "Tejanos," but as "Mexicans," regardless of the side of the river on which they lived, although Mexicans who lived outside the state also referred to their counterparts in Texas as *mexico-texanos* or *mexicanos de Texas*.[16] Additionally, Anglos often scornfully labeled Mexicans as "greasers." Light-skinned Mexicans were simply Mexicans, even if their color and social position usually differentiated them from Mexicans with Indigenous blood. Anglo-Americans and Europeans in northern Mexico and among the Mexican population of Texas were usually referred to as *norteamericanos* and *europeos*. I will specify the nationality of the many Europeans who inhabited the region when known. Generally, "Anglos," "Anglo-Americans," and "Anglo-Texans" refer to white persons with U.S. or British ancestry, although sometimes non-Anglo white Europeans were included in these labels. "Native American" and "African American" are terms of modern usage. In Northeast Mexico these people were referred to as *indios* and *negros*. Indians who were peaceful were referred to as *indios pacíficos* or *indios mansos*, but the hostile ones were referred to simply as *salvajes* or *bárbaros*. I realize terminology is a complex and contentious issue, but I will try to allow the context (albeit fluid and dynamic in the border region) to determine what term is used.

A word on the periodization is also in order. In the 1830s the Rio Grande was a frontier region without a fixed border, held tenuously by Mexico but coveted by the United States. By 1880 a border separating the two countries (though not necessarily the two peoples) had been firmly established. The general arc of this era, which will serve as the backdrop of this book, is one of substantial change, much of it generated outside the region: the powerful advance of the U.S. economy in the 1820s and 1830s, Mexico's loss of its northern territory and the creation of a border in the 1840s, civil wars in both countries in the 1860s. and consolidation of state power in the two nations in the 1870s. There were also however remarkable continuities in the patterns of commercial exchange, shared economic interests, internal migration, and family linkages across the binational region. These changes and continuities are reflected in the lives of the people who lived or settled in the border region and gave it viability in spite of the wars, rebellions, Indian raids, and random violence that were part of their daily existence. Their stories are told in the following nine chapters and an afterword, which offers some final thoughts on cooperation and race relations, as well as commentary on the Texas-Mexico border region after 1880.[17]

CHAPTER I

Attraction and Rejection

The Beginning of a Pattern, 1830–1836

I n the fall of 1828, Reuben Marmaduke Potter, a native of New Jersey, set out from Matamoros on the Rio Grande with a load of goods to sell at the fairs of Monterrey and Saltillo. The twenty-six-year-old Potter was accompanied by Manuel Márquez, an employee of Lovell, Toler, and Company, a commercial firm in that city. The fair at Saltillo, one of the largest in Mexico, brought together thousands of consumers and merchants from different regions.[1] Besides buying and selling, fairgoers had many options for entertainment, including bullfights, cockfights, card games, singing, and dancing, all of which provided a respite from the rigors of the trip and of life on the frontier.[2] Potter wrote to his brother that after the fair the merchants "and the immense concourse of natives" who had come "to buy, to sell, and to steal" had disappeared "like a snow in March." He returned to the Rio Grande in a convoy with other merchants— many of them Frenchmen—"with their mule loads of money" worth "sixty or seventy thousand dollars."[3]

Potter arrived at Matamoros to find eighteen-year-old Charles Stillman tending store as part of his father's mercantile business. Three years earlier, in 1825, Francis Stillman, a Connecticut Yankee, had disembarked at Brazos de Santiago, near the mouth of the Rio Grande, with a shipload of oats and hay and returned to New England with a cargo of wool. Soon he was operating a transport business between New York and Matamoros. His son, Charles, received a rapid immersion in Mexican economics and culture while managing a store for his father in Durango in 1827 at the tender age of seventeen. Having gained a command of Spanish, Charles Stillman would make a fortune in the Mexican trade and would become one of the most powerful men in the Rio Grande border region during most of the next four decades.[4]

In January 1834, Joshua Davis, an Irish-born merchant who had established a small business based in Monclova, Coahuila, set out from there toward Aransas Pass on the Texas coast to purchase goods from two vessels that had arrived from New Orleans. In the company of two Mexican servants and the famous abolitionist Benjamin Lundy, whom he had recently befriended on the former's tour of northern Mexico, he passed through Laredo with "nine mules and two horses . . . and three thousand dollars in specie." In late February, almost a month after setting out, he had bought his merchandise and was headed back toward Monclova.[5]

Potter, Stillman, and Davis are representatives of a sizable group of foreigners who came to Northeast Mexico in the 1820s after the country had won its independence from Spain. They did not come to introduce commerce to the region; local merchants and Indian tribes engaged in it long before their arrival. In April 1822, three prominent merchants of the province of Coahuila had set out on a long trip that would take them through San Antonio de Béxar and Nacogdoches toward their destination: New Orleans. José Francisco Madero, alcalde of Monclova, asked for a leave of absence in order to make the journey. Madero, great-grandfather of Francisco I. Madero, a leader of the Mexican Revolution of 1910, was accompanied by Victor Blanco, ex-alcalde of Monclova, future governor of Coahuila, and patriarch of one of the state's most powerful families. Blanco owned a store in Bexar and needed to replenish his stock of goods. Along the way they were joined by Ramón Múzquiz, another Bexar merchant soon to become *jefe político* of Coahuila y Texas after the Constitution of 1824 joined the two provinces. Commerce with Louisiana existed in the second half of the eighteenth century, but increased significantly after 1804 when that territory became part of the United States. The goods these merchants purchased in New Orleans would eventually find their way to regional markets as far away as San Luis Potosí and Jalisco.[6]

Many other unnamed traders and freighters participated. We know they existed from obscure documents or through the writings of travelers. On Davis's trip to the Texas coast, for example, his party was joined in Laredo by a group of five persons "with several mule loads of sugar which they had bought at Monterrey . . . at about three cents a pound." Benjamin Lundy reported that it was "good brown sugar, put up in rolls, being better than the inferior qualities produced in the West Indies and Louisiana."[7]

The experiences of these merchants, both foreign and native, reveal a story of movement, of people traveling back and forth, to and from distant places, carrying goods and meeting and socializing with other people. The very act of movement opened people's minds, as Mark Twain well knew when he famously remarked in *The Innocents Abroad* that "travel is fatal to prejudice, bigotry, and narrow-mindedness." The merchants were of various nationalities, including British, American, French, Spanish, and Mexican. The trips also involved *carreteros* (cart drivers), *arrieros* (muleteers) and, when the trip involved the movement of livestock, vaqueros. Long before the arrival of foreigners in the area, native producers and merchants had begun to tie this vast region together. The trails to Louisiana were well worn by the 1820s because much of the commerce was in livestock. Cattle and horses were scarce in the East, so ranchers in Texas and Northeast Mexico rounded up large herds to take to Louisiana in exchange for products such as farm implements, housewares, European wines, and textiles of all kinds. Ignoring the Spanish Crown's prohibition on trade, these merchants connected the Rio Grande region to a broader world because many of the products that eventually reached Saltillo, Monterrey, Monclova, and beyond had their origin in the United States or Europe.[8]

Despite these mercantile activities, the region that encompassed Tamaulipas, Nuevo León, Coahuila, and Texas was a rather sleepy backwater, a subordinate part of a larger world. When asked to analyze the four provinces with a view to their possible unification, Julián de Llano of Monterrey wrote that the "population of the four provinces is made up of rural workers and small producers, simple, honest people without any kind of education; a small number of merchants . . . and an even smaller number of ordinary artisans." The little industry to be found was owned by foreigners (mostly Spaniards), and the region offered "only middling fortunes and much misery." Each province had a number of wealthy landholders. In Coahuila, one family, the Sánchez Navarros, came to own most of the territory of the state.[9]

This region, on the periphery of Mexico, was however at the forward edge of U.S. economic expansion. The *vecinos*, or inhabitants, were about to be introduced to a faster-paced, more dynamic reality with the arrival of many acquisitive and mostly gregarious outsiders. After independence Northeast Mexico became a meeting place where different races and ethnic groups coexisted and interacted with each other in manifold ways, especially in commercial exchange. Local merchants had blazed trails to Louisiana, New Mexico, and the interior of Mexico since the eighteenth century, but the arrival of Anglo-Americans and Europeans in the early nineteenth century intensified interethnic contacts. These trade routes persisted and new trails were opened later, creating an integrated transnational region that existed before and after the establishment of a definitive border.

The purpose of this chapter is to examine the impact that the arrival of Europeans and Anglo-Americans had on the region and its people. Their presence altered local traditions and hastened economic, political, social, and cultural change. Of particular interest are the relations that developed between the newcomers and the local people, relations that were generally respectful and friendly until deformed by forces generated mostly from outside.[10] In order to comprehend these relations, a few comments on the salient characteristics of the region are necessary.

THE PHYSICAL AND HUMAN LANDSCAPE

This region, whose center is the Rio Grande, has a topography as varied as the human groups that inhabited or passed through it. It extends westward from the coastal plains of the Gulf of Mexico to the plateau beyond the Sierra Madre Oriental of northern Coahuila and eastern Chihuahua and the mountains of the Big Bend in the Trans-Pecos region of Southwest Texas (see map). It spreads northward to San Antonio and the Balcones Escarpment in south central Texas and southward to the cities of Monterrey, Saltillo, and Ciudad Victoria, the capitals of Nuevo León, Coahuila, and Tamaulipas, respectively. It includes the forbidding desert of the Bolsón de Mapimí, on the edges of Coahuila and Chihuahua, but also flourishing valleys watered by rivers or natural springs, as in the region of Montemorelos in Nuevo León, where immense fields of corn and sugarcane were cultivated, and Parras de la Fuente in Coahuila, which, according to one source, "was in the centre of the best grain producing country in Mexico, although its immediate vicinity was covered by extensive vineyards producing delicious grapes, from which wine and brandy were manufactured."[11] Yet, much of the region, especially north and south of the lower Rio Grande, is semiarid and uninviting, covered by mesquite, tall grasses, cactus, and scrubland called chaparral. This "wild and vivid land"[12] was more suitable for raising livestock than crops, and that is precisely what many of the inhabitants of the region did during the colonial period and into the nineteenth century.

Spanish colonization of northeastern Mexico and Texas was slow, but it accelerated during the eighteenth century when the Spanish Crown began to fear French encroachment into its northern regions. Missions and presidios in Texas grew into towns. Thus were born Nacogdoches (1716), San Antonio de

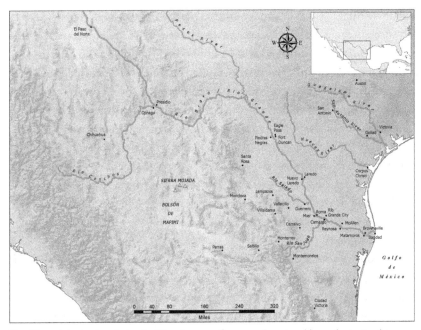

The Texas-Mexico borderlands. The absence of state and national boundaries in this map provides a true picture of how those who lived there perceived the territory. People moved freely throughout the region, which was integrated by social, economic, and kinship networks. Map by Ana Gabriela Arreola Meneses.

Béxar (1718), and La Bahía de Espíritu Santo (Goliad) (1721).[13] Colonization of the area bordering the Rio Grande began in 1749, when José de Escandón, an intrepid Indian fighter who had won fame as a pacifier and colonizer in central Mexico, marched north from Querétaro at the head of 755 soldiers and 2,515 colonists to establish towns on the river. Escandón also invited the vecinos of neighboring provinces to participate, and residents of Nuevo León and, to a lesser extent, Coahuila, constituted the major part of the colonization effort. By 1755 Escandón had founded Reynosa, Camargo, Mier, Revilla (Guerrero), Dolores (later destroyed), and Laredo. Refugio, later renamed Matamoros, was founded in 1784. Together, these seven towns made up the Villas del Norte, which were in the middle of the vast region my study encompasses and where the most intense exchanges, violent and peaceful, took place between 1830 and 1880.[14]

The Villas del Norte were also at the center of a vast ranching country that shaped the economic and social life of the region. The original settlers brought with them some 214,000 head of livestock, and the raising of cattle, horses, mules, and sheep became the principal economic activity.[15] The combined herds of the river settlements were estimated at eight hundred thousand in the last decade of the eighteenth century and at three million on the eve of Texas independence in 1835.[16] These numbers contradict the contention of some observers that the Nueces Strip, the region between the Rio Grande and the Nueces River where many residents of the villas had their herds, was unfit for man or beast. General Egbert Viele characterized the region as a rainless district dominated by thorny chaparral, in a torrid subtropical zone that could never be cultivated nor populated, a zone where "nature seems to be plunged into a sea of despair from which it cannot rise." The harsh terrain and adverse climate did not however discourage the hardy rancheros who established a thriving community and gave life to the region.[17]

Agriculture was limited. In a few places along the river there were fields of sugarcane, cotton, corn, beans, and various vegetables, but many of the inhabitants acquired their foodstuffs through commerce. One historian states that "with impressive profits from stock raising easier to generate, the villas turned to importing corn, wheat, and other farm products from nearby provinces in exchange for salt and livestock."[18] Agriculture was thwarted by cycles of flooding and droughts, as well as the constantly changing course of the river. Moreover, the farm implements used by the *pobladores* were primitive. In the 1820s, Texas colonist Noah Smithwick opined, perhaps with slight exaggeration, that Mexican farmers used plows that "were counterparts of the one Romulus used in laying out the city of Rome, being simply forked sticks . . . tied on to a straight stick . . . lashed to the horns of a pair of oxen."[19]

Some food supplies came from the haciendas that dotted the landscape of parts of Tamaulipas, Nuevo León, and Coahuila to the south and west. In 1819, a particularly dry year, the inhabitants of Laredo and Bexar were saved from starvation because the haciendas of Coahuila provided them with grain.[20] The haciendas were major fixtures of the rural landscape of Northeast Mexico. These *latifundios*, or large estates, were generally owned by an absentee landlord and operated by a local manager. They emphasized stock raising, but also raised crops where conditions were favorable and sold their produce in regional markets. Some haciendas, such as Potosí and Soledad in Nuevo León, were immense, but the largest in the region belonged to the Sánchez Navarro family of Coahuila. It occupied "more than half of the entire state" and included more than eighty thousand square kilometers.[21] Numerous farms and ranches also dotted the countryside. Some were independent while others belonged to the latifundios and were leased to tenant farmers. These smaller units gave rise to a rural middle class of smallholders and self-employed workers. Another segment of the rural population consisted of *sirvientes*, or peons, who labored on the haciendas and were tied to them because they were indebted to the *hacendado*. They bore the brunt of an oppressive system that, in time, would push many of them to seek better opportunities in the developing Texas economy.[22]

Society was dominated by an economic and political elite whose power rested on landownership—and increasingly after independence—commerce.[23] Below them were many small farmers and ranchers who worked, and defended, their own land with their families and a few hired hands.[24] At the lowest rung of the social ladder were rural people without land who worked on the ranches and haciendas. These were the *peones, jornaleros* (day laborers), and sirvientes. Class differences and class structure shaped contacts and interactions with foreigners. Members of the upper class had greater contact with the newcomers, but eventually middle- and lower-class people would experience increased interactions.[25]

Class stratification was tempered by challenging conditions on the frontier: isolation, a hostile environment, and danger from predators and potentially hostile neighbors. These conditions nurtured some sense of egalitarianism. Historian Arnoldo de León's description of Texas residents near the end of the Spanish Empire reflects the broader population of the Mexican North. They "accepted a similar ethos, adapting a familiar ranching culture to the new land, enduring the rigors that accompanied life on the range, devising means of wringing a profit from contraband trade . . . and taking political stands expressing regional desire." Given the conditions of life, "there developed an ethic for self-reliance and the feeling that local needs held priority over crown expectations."[26]

Social and class relations were also conditioned by race. The border region was a fertile field for *mestizaje*, the complex process of racial and cultural mixing that was an integral part of the Spanish Empire.[27] Although race "did not constitute an insurmountable barrier to upward social mobility on the Mexican frontier," many members of the upper class "denigrated others of darker hue, and tended to 'whiten' themselves as they moved up the social ladder by denying their Indian and black ancestry."[28] This was evident in Bexareño society, where many Mexican elites disdained lower-class mestizos. "Men like [José Antonio] Navarro, [José Francisco] Ruiz, and the Seguins moved easily in the Anglo world," and were often closer to their Anglo counterparts than to the lower-class members of their own race.[29] At one time during the 1850s, there was an influx into South Texas

and Northeast Mexico of peaceful Indian tribes and European colonists who
joined African Americans and Mexican mestizos. At that point the region saw
one of the largest concentrations of ethnic and racial minorities on the continent.
Class and race may have socially stratified the population of South Texas and
Northeast Mexico, but the many instances of "everyday intimate interaction" and
the special conditions of frontier life shaped a society that was racially mixed,
ethnically fluid, and culturally diverse.[30]

A Vast Theater of Terror

Northeast Mexico and South Texas cannot be understood without considering
the powerful effect of Indian raids and invasions that were a terrifying part of life
during the first eight decades of the nineteenth century. Numerous Indian groups
inhabited the region before the coming of the Spanish, mostly in the area of the
Rio Grande delta. These hunter-gatherers were gradually displaced by Spanish
colonization and were eventually decimated by disease and conquest until most
of these "Indian groups disappeared from the historical record by 1825." Some,
particularly a subgroup called Carrizos, became integrated into the Spanish
settlements or lived peacefully near the river towns.[31] Delta Indian bands did
not disturb the peace of northern Mexico. The problem came from afar. Apache
and Comanche raiders swept down from the north, devastating the country. The
magnitude of the problem was summed up in a contemporary report:

> Agriculture has been abandoned because the farmer is daily assaulted
> by the Indians; commerce is paralyzed because there is no safety
> along the roads; the inhabitants flee in search of refuge to the interior
> of the country after seeing their homes burned down, their flocks
> destroyed, and their fields ruined, while they weep not only because of
> the death, but the defilement and inhuman mutilation of their wives
> and daughters. . . . [H]alf of the Republic is soaked daily with the
> blood of our brothers; the cries of the victims can already be heard
> in the capital of the Republic, along with the shrieks of the savages.[32]

El Semanario Político, the official newspaper of Nuevo León, condemned the
cruelty of savages who exulted "in the blood of their innocent and defenseless
victims, throwing innocent children into the air and receiving them on the points
of their lances in the presence of their afflicted mothers."[33]

    In part, this state of affairs was brought about because Mexico abandoned
the Spanish Empire's Indian policy during and after independence. In the late

The Apaches Are Coming, by Frederic Remington. One of the most chilling sounds on the Rio Grande frontier was "Vienen los indios" (The Indians are coming). Indian raids were a grim reality for most of the century, bringing desolation and suffering to the residents of Texas and Northeast Mexico. From *Harper's Weekly*, January 30, 1886. No. 074-1333, UTSA Special Collections.

eighteenth century Spain had used what historian David Weber refers to as an iron fist and a velvet glove to deal with recalcitrant, hostile tribes, combining diplomacy, rewards, and gifts with repression when necessary. This policy of inclusion favored accommodation and reciprocal exchange, and contributed to several decades of relative peace in the northern reaches of the empire.[34] However, Spanish Indian policy began to break down during the independence movement when gift-giving and frontier defenses were abandoned, particularly in areas of insurgency, such as Texas and Northeast Mexico. Mexican Emperor Agustín de Iturbide proposed a policy of benign commerce and colonization toward the hostile tribes, but neither the policy nor the empire survived for long. Successive governments were swamped by debt and political anarchy and "could provide neither sufficient direction nor resources to carry out an effective Indian policy on the frontier." The few soldiers who patrolled the northern frontier were usually short of food and adequate clothing, and were simply outgunned by Comanche raiders who possessed better firearms. The pobladores of northern Mexico were often left to defend themselves, which increased their dissatisfaction with and isolation from the government in Mexico City.[35]

According to historian Brian DeLay, Apache and Comanche raids converted "much of the northern third of Mexico . . . into a vast theater of hatred, terror, and staggering loss for independent Indians and Mexicans alike." The violence unleashed by these raids, especially in the 1830s and 1840s, "claimed thousands of Mexican and Indian lives, made tens of thousands more painful and often wretched, ruined northern Mexico's economy, stalled its demographic growth, and depopulated much of its countryside."[36]

The defenders of northern Mexico were principally rural people: small farmers, ranchers, peasants, vaqueros, sirvientes, jornaleros, and arrieros. Since colonial times, writes historian Israel Cavazos Garza, Nuevo León had been a *tierra de guerra viva* (a land of perpetual war) in which "there was not a single vecino . . . that had not participated in military life."[37] Each community formed its own "civilian militiamen," not unlike the American minutemen, to provide defense. According to the bishop of Monterrey their training began early: "Since they are constantly besieged by the savages, the need to defend their property and their lives has made them good shooters and even the children practice daily at hitting targets."[38]

The violent encounter between vecinos and Indian raiders was only one facet of the complex relations between and among Indians, Anglo-Americans, and Mexicans. Behind the Indian raids were trade networks to dispose of the plundered goods, networks which involved members of all three groups.[39] Native Americans had traded for centuries, and they incorporated new arrivals—Europeans, Anglo-Americans, and Mexicans—into their trade channels.[40] Comanche warriors swept into northern Mexico from the southern plains of the United States and returned with captured horses, mules, and humans. Anglo-American traders obtained from them vast quantities of horses and mules to sell to the U.S. army posts on the frontier and to the "thousands of immigrants [who] were buying tens of thousands of animals to pull, pack, and carry them and their families to Oregon."[41] "Wealth in the form of human and animal resources flowed into the southern Plains as it flowed out of the northern frontier," but for the *norteños,* the inhabitants of northern Mexico, there was no comfort in the fact that "one people's loss was another people's gain."[42]

In exchange for plundered goods, Indians received liquor, trade goods, and firearms with which to continue and increase their raids. According to David Weber, "The problem became so alarming that in 1826 Mexico's secretary of state asked the United States minister in Mexico City to stop the 'traders of blood who put instruments of death in the hands of those barbarians.'"[43] The traffic in arms to the Indians was not limited to evil Americans, however—Mexicans were also accused of supplying Indians with weapons. In 1840 General Mariano Arista, military commander of the northern frontier, issued a proclamation threatening soldiers and civilians with execution for trading arms and ammunition to the Comanches.[44]

Arista's threat reflects a reality that has not received the same attention as raids and their attendant devastation. The trade networks of Comanche and Apache raiders were not limited to the southern plains or the Texas frontier. They sprang up wherever there were willing partners. The towns of northern Mexico often provided such accomplices. These relations extended back to the late colonial period, when Lipan Apaches and Comanches raided ranches and stole livestock, which they traded directly or through intermediaries called *tratantes*. These middlemen were often from the northern provinces as well, so the Indians stole from one group of pobladores and sold to another.[45] This practice continued throughout the nineteenth century. In the 1850s vecinos of Nuevo León complained that Mexican residents of the town of Rio Grande in Coahuila traded with Indians and collaborated in their raids; and the town of San Carlos, Chihuahua, near the border with Coahuila, was notorious as a place of refuge and commerce for Comanches and Apaches. In 1854 a group of Mexican traders were discovered at a Comanche camp in southern Chihuahua before a battle with Mexican forces at Espíritu Santo Canyon. Three of these traders were killed in the battle. One eyewitness revealed that "these people were in the habit of visiting the Comanches to obtain livestock in exchange for 'powder and provisions.'"[46]

Americans and Europeans in Northeast Mexico

As in the rest of the continent, the menace of hostile tribes did not impede the arrival of Americans and Europeans. They came riding on the wings of chance, attracted by the powerful magnets of adventure and wealth; some came in search of a new life, others to escape an old one. In the early 1820s many came to Refugio (literally, "place of refuge," later renamed Matamoros). Besides Reuben Potter and Charles Stillman, Daniel W. Smith arrived from New England and James Wiley Magoffin from Kentucky to engage in commerce. Years later, Smith would become U.S. consul in Matamoros and Magoffin in Saltillo. Three Irishmen who settled in Matamoros—John McMullen, James Power, and James McGloin–obtained grants from the Mexican government to settle Irish and Mexican families in the area of the Nueces River. According to historian Graham Davis, "The Irish *empresarios* spoke Spanish, married into high-born Hispanic families, and were well versed in Mexican ways from their time as merchants in Mexico." James Power provides a good example. His marriage to María Dolores Portilla proved highly beneficial because her father, Felipe Roque de la Portilla, a Spaniard who had attempted to establish a colony in Texas in 1809, helped Power to fulfill his colonization contract, which called for half of the two hundred families to be Irish Catholics and the other half, Mexican. From his post in Matamoros, Don Felipe helped persuade Mexican families to relocate to San Patricio on the Nueces River. "The Irish settlers in Refugio and San Patricio," writes Davis, "learned from the ranching practices of their Mexican neighbors." De la Portilla shared his experiences with Powers, who "in turn, passed on the knowledge and culture of ranching to his nephew Thomas O'Connor." This "process of cultural transfer . . . worked through the example of neighbors and was facilitated by language and intermarriage."[47]

So many foreign, and especially American, merchants located in Refugio/Matamoros that even before the city was formally opened to foreign commerce in 1826, U.S. merchants in New Orleans petitioned President James Monroe to establish a consular office there. The population grew from 2,320 in 1820 to about 7,000 in 1829, and by 1837 Matamoros had 16,372 inhabitants. In the early 1830s there were about three hundred foreign residents in the city, most of them engaged in commerce.[48]

Some Americans and Europeans merely passed through Matamoros; others bypassed it as they gravitated toward South Texas or Northeast Mexico. Among them were men of Irish origin such as Dr. James Hewetson and John J. Linn. Hewetson became interested in acquiring Texas land while in New Orleans with Stephen F. Austin. He traveled to Bexar and eventually settled in Saltillo, where he married Josefa Guajardo, a wealthy widow. A well-known medical doctor, Hewetson was also a consummate businessman. He became a Mexican citizen and got involved in the rough and tumble of Coahuilan politics. He remained a prominent member of that community until his death in Saltillo in 1870. John Linn used New Orleans, where he was a merchant in 1822, as a springboard to get to Texas. He established a store in Victoria and seems to have had a special gift for getting along with the Mexican people, who held him in high regard. Linn served the cause of Texas independence, but his identification with his Mexican neighbors was such that he was briefly arrested, along with members of the De León family of Victoria, on accusations of being a Mexican sympathizer.[49]

Northeast Mexico and South Texas were suited for raising livestock, and many Mexicans grew up in ranching families. These vaqueros transmitted their knowledge of ranching to Anglo newcomers. After the establishment of the border, many Mexicans from south of the Rio Grande migrated north to work on Texas ranches and cattle drives. No. 75-138, UTSA Special Collections.

   Scotsman Juan Cameron signed contracts to bring colonists to Texas in the late 1820s. He failed in that endeavor, but he obtained two leagues of land in Texas and had many business and political connections in Coahuila and Nuevo León. In various documents he claims residency in those states, though he settled in the lower Rio Grande Valley after 1836. Cameron was imprisoned with Benjamin R. Milam when the political faction they supported was overthrown in Coahuila in 1835. Both escaped and joined in the fight for Texas independence, where Cameron served as translator between the contending forces. Among the Europeans there were quite a number of Frenchmen, as Reuben Potter discovered at the Saltillo fair. José Rougier arrived in Monclova around 1822, and spent five years bringing goods from Louisiana to sell throughout Coahuila, apparently without permission from Mexican authorities as he admitted that he never had a passport.[50]

   Men with a taste for adventure also arrived in Northeast Mexico by way of military expeditions. One of these was led by Francisco Javier Mina in 1816. Mina, who had fought absolutism in Spain, organized an expedition to help the people of New Spain fight for their freedom during Mexico's War of Independence. He recruited a number of Europeans and Anglo-Americans during stops he made in England, Baltimore, and New Orleans. Mina was captured and executed and his movement crushed, but some of his followers stayed in Mexico. Among them were Carlos Bork and Samuel Bangs. Bork, an Irishman, was involved in land transactions and commerce—not all of it legal—and was manager of the Hacienda Los Hornos in Coahuila. For reasons yet unknown, he was exiled during the government of Santa Anna in 1833. He returned, resumed his business, and in 1841 and 1844 was charged in Coahuilan courts with engaging in contraband. He was married to Francisca Cacho, who inherited his property upon his death in 1852.[51]

Samuel Bangs is credited with introducing the printing press in Northeast Mexico. His skill as a printer is probably what saved him from execution after his capture by royalist forces in the Mina expedition fiasco. He was assigned to work as a printer in Nuevo León, but got into trouble for stabbing a lady friend in the chest after drinking a considerable amount of *aguardiente*. María Estéfana Cárdenas had berated Bangs and broken a cane stalk over his head in an argument. She survived the stabbing to see the twenty-one-year-old Bangs exonerated and herself scolded by the judge because if she had "acted with the decorum of a lady [the incident] would not have occurred."[52] Throughout the 1820s and 1830s Bangs lived variously in Nuevo León, Coahuila and, after he married, with his wife and children in Tamaulipas. Bangs learned Spanish and was baptized into the Catholic Church, which changed his name from Samuel to José Manuel. His integration into Mexican society was shared by his wife, who learned Spanish quickly and had a deep affection for the people of Tamaulipas, with whom she lived. Her death from yellow fever in 1837 was a deep blow to Bangs, who left Mexico with his two children to live in Texas.[53]

The aforementioned Benjamin R. Milam was an adventurer who arrived in Mexico with James Long on their filibustering raid to Texas in 1819. Milam is best known as a hero of Texas independence, but long before that event he lived and worked among the Mexican people, became a Mexican citizen in 1824, and served in the Mexican army. He requested and received a grant of land between the Guadalupe and Colorado Rivers and assumed the obligation to colonize his land with Catholic families and "establish schools in the Spanish language," although the project was largely a failure. With Englishman Arthur G. Wavell and fellow American David G. Burnet, Milam engaged in several enterprises and had mining interests in the state of Nuevo León. He was a close ally of the federalist governor of Coahuila, Agustín Viesca, and he, Viesca, and Cameron were imprisoned together after their political rivals triumphed in the state in 1835.[54]

In addition to the many men who came to the region to engage in commerce, a surprising number of foreigners were—or claimed to be—medical doctors. It is impossible to know the exact number, but their presence is noted in municipal reports and official correspondence regarding their activities. A list of foreigners from an unspecified town in Coahuila in 1828 contains just three names: David Staples and Jorge Davis from England, and Juan Thomais from France. Staples, who entered Coahuila by way of Matamoros, and Thomais, who came through Tampico, were both physicians. A census report for Nuevo León in 1832 lists only six physicians in a population of 98,172. Four were in Monterrey, and one each was in Linares and Montemorelos.[55]

The census report is almost certainly wrong, as the names of other foreign physicians appear in municipal correspondence during approximately the same time, but it is clear that there was a shortage of physicians in Northeast Mexico and that foreign doctors stepped into the breach. The alcaldes knew the people's distress when a physician was needed and there was none to be found. In their communications with the state government, they indicate how much these professionals were valued. Juan Warren practiced medicine in Montemorelos after obtaining his degree from Transylvania University in Kentucky in 1828 and being licensed by the medical board of Leona Vicario (Saltillo) in 1831. Alcalde Refugio García noted approvingly that Warren had taken his exam in Latin. Eduardo Beaviem practiced in Linares, where he lived with his Mexican wife. Benjamin Smith did the same in Pesquería Grande. He was described as "a peaceful young man who does not discuss politics and does not harbor dissatisfaction or revolutionary tendencies."[56] Alcalde José Cayetano de Cárdenas of Cerralvo described Dr. Juan Phincas (probably Hicks) as a model person who was "very accurate in his diagnosis, generous to the poor, and very friendly." He never turned anyone without money away and would gladly surrender his last quarter. He was also described as devoutly religious and respectful of Mexican laws.[57]

Another highly valued physician was Juan Long, who lived in Santa Rosa (Múzquiz), Coahuila, but was in Lampazos, Nuevo León, when he saved the life of the governor in January 1843. What little is known about Long reveals a lot about the process of Americans' integration into Mexican society. He arrived in Coahuila sometime before 1827 and, probably through marriage, became part of the prominent Vidaurri family. He claimed relationship to two governors, referring to Francisco Vidaurri of Coahuila as his father and to Santiago Vidaurri,

the powerful governor of Nuevo León in the 1850s, as a cousin. He apparently
never became a Mexican citizen, though he declared himself a Mexican patriot
and deplored how Americans treated Mexicans in Texas in the 1850s. In one letter
to Santiago Vidaurri, he wrote "with respect to the injustices that are committed
by our neighbor, they are insufferable, and although it is my native country, it is
necessary to say the truth." He lived a modest existence as a farmer in Múzquiz
and tried his hand at mining even as he continued to heal the sick. He was still
in Coahuila in the 1860s.[58]

The humanitarian service that many of these physicians provided to the Mexican population, even at the risk of their own lives, was amply demonstrated during
the devastating cholera epidemic of 1833, which killed 7 percent of the population
of Coahuila y Texas. Englishman Dr. Coley arrived at Matagorda from New
York in 1833, having been commissioned "by a society to write a description of
Texas." While traveling west from Matagorda "he was met by a deputation of
Mexicans who begged him to come into Gonzales and treat the cholera which
was raging there." The good doctor came down with the disease and died. He
was buried by a new friend he had met on his arrival in the town: William L.
Cazneau, a man destined to play an important role in the border region over the
next three decades. Physician Charles Linn, brother of John Linn, was also on
a mission to save Mexican lives from the ravages of cholera when he was struck
down in Coahuila during that fateful year of 1833. During his more than forty
years of living among the Mexican people, Dr. James Hewetson did more than
engage in commerce and politics; he was a very good doctor who, it was reputed,
developed a cure for cholera.[59]

Not all the physicians were model citizens, and some were not even doctors.
José M. Howe, who was at Montemorelos in the early 1830s, had lost his passport
and was mired in poverty. His presence was tolerated out of pity, according to
Alcalde Refugio García. Others were fond of liquor. When Reuben Potter made
his trip to Saltillo in 1828, he wrote of finding his long-lost cousin Santiago in
Cadereyta, about twenty miles from Monterrey. Potter noted "the strangeness
of his dialect; for he minces Spanish and English, like his brandy and water, half
and half." Cousin Santiago evidently sought refuge in Mexico and alcohol, for
he told Potter that "he would never return [to the United States] unless able to
free himself from the obligations he had incurred." It is likely that he never did
either. A note from the alcalde of Monterrey dated 1833 stated that a Dr. Santiago Cullinan had died in Cadereyta. He left his earthly belongings to his friend
Eugenio Serrano.[60]

The lack of trained physicians on the frontier provided an opening for *curand-eros* (healers), who were mainly Mexican, and for quacks, who mostly came from the United States. For example, Ennis Fraser of Kentucky practiced medicine in Marín, near Monterrey, and it was discovered later "that he had never attended medical school nor worked in any hospital as a doctor."[61] An anonymous source stated that Mexicans, though otherwise wary, "would place their lives in the hands of the Americanos when it came to medical matters."[62] The memoirs of Noah Smithwick and John Linn support this assertion. Smithwick was on a smuggling expedition with his friend John F. Webber in San Fernando, Coahuila, and it was taking longer than they had expected to dispose of their merchandise. It was suggested that one of them should pretend to be a medical doctor in order to allay the suspicions of the authorities, so Webber began receiving patients, with Smithwick—who could speak better Spanish—acting as interpreter. Using medicines such as calomel, quinine, and tartar emetic, which the pair had brought on the trip for their personal use, Webber would adopt "an air of importance that would have done credit to a professional" as he "noted the symptoms, shaking his head, knitting his brows, and otherwise impressing the patient with the seriousness of his condition." Smithwick, who admitted that he "looked on the Mexicans as scarce more than apes," greatly enjoyed the farce.[63]

John Linn, who had a more positive and even sympathetic view of Mexicans, had a similar experience. He was present at Candela, Coahuila, when the cholera epidemic that ended his brother's life broke out. The terrified residents and the local government looked to him for assistance and, with medicine provided by James Hewetson, he assumed the role of doctor "in the name of charity." With assistance from the local priest, Linn "devoted [his] whole time to the suffering inhabitants" and was gratified to contribute in "no small degree to the relief of the people." He described his departure: "When I left the town the people lined the streets to bid me adios—the most expressive of farewells, as it is a commen-dation to the protection of God." A youth whom Linn had aided told him: "Don Juan, receive my best wishes, my earnest thanks and prayers. May the good God guard you and restore you once more to your family." Linn was deeply touched, declaring that the virtue of gratitude, rare in most people, "like the diamond among minerals . . . is the most precious."[64]

COMMERCE: THE TIE THAT BINDS

To a greater degree than any other activity, commerce—legal and illegal—brought Anglo-Americans, Europeans, and Mexicans together in many forms of cooperation during those early years. Understanding that commercial exchange was one of the keys to the development of Texas, Stephen F. Austin extolled the virtues of trade with Mexico: "Every one who has any knowledge in regard to the commerce of Texas must know that the Mexican markets are the best in the world for the products of Texas." He gave as examples two Texas staples: cotton and corn. An arroba of cotton (about 11.5 kilos or 25 pounds) could be sold in the United States and Europe for between two and four pesos but in Mexico City, Puebla, or San Luis Potosí for seven or eight pesos. A *fanega* of corn (approximately fifty-five liters) could be sold for four to six pesos in Mexico whereas in Texas and New Orleans it sold for less than one peso.[65] Intrepid foreign merchants and the products they brought began to penetrate the economic and social fabric of Northeast Mexico in the 1820s and 1830s. New ports such as Tampico and Matamoros were opened to foreign commerce, and the entire Northeast began to come alive with economic activity. These merchants fanned out from Matamoros to Nuevo León and Coahuila, creating a network that resembled half of a spider web, enveloping towns and integrating local merchants to serve as partners, middlemen, or buyers for products from the United States and Europe.

Notarial records and contemporary accounts reveal these connections. In 1833 Ricardo Blossman, a Matamoros merchant, sold various pieces of cloth, handkerchiefs, thread, silk and cotton stockings, and other merchandise with a value of 951 pesos to Alejandro Bustamante of Saltillo. In the same year, the firm of Burril and Chapman sold to Toribio Ortiz, a local merchant, various textile products as well as needles, buttons, and ribbon with a value of eight hundred pesos. Other Coahuila merchants served by this firm were Antonio Espinoza, Pedro Santa Cruz, Rafael Vargas, Manuel Pedrero and Dionisio Mancha.[66] H. A. Gilpin, a Yankee trader from Rhode Island who represented a Matamoros firm, used his Mexican contacts in faraway Zacatecas to sell $80,000 worth of merchandise that he received in 1832 off the Texas coast. He later moved to Corpus Christi, where it was reported that he had taken "over 600 mule loads to Zacatecas, at one time" from the Texas Gulf Coast. In the late 1840s he and other merchants were looking to expand their trade by establishing a better route to Chihuahua.[67] John Linn, who "soon learned, by diligent study, to speak the language of the country," established a number of connections in Matamoros to sell merchandise acquired in New Orleans. In 1829, before traveling to the Louisiana port, he asked his friend Bruno García "to purchase another stock of tobacco and an assortment of dry-goods that would be suitable for the trade." Linn depended on his Mexican colleague to help him sell his merchandise and also to supply him with mules for its transportation.[68]

Sometimes foreign merchants collaborated to dispose of their merchandise. Linn sent one of his brothers, Edward, to Saltillo in 1833 to sell goods he had received from New Orleans. Edward Linn was advised by James Hewetson, "who was well posted in Mexican affairs," to sell the goods quickly in Zacatecas as trouble was brewing between the Texans and the Mexican government. Unfortunately, the person they chose to help them in Zacatecas, an American named J. A. Porter, proved to be dishonest and the adventure was a financial failure.[69]

Over the course of many years and in the three states where he resided, printer Samuel Bangs established his own connections. At times he sold directly to his Mexican clients, as when he sold a printing press to a member of the prominent De Llano family of Nuevo León in 1832. Manuel María de Llano used this press to print an antigovernment newspaper, El Antagonista, the first independent paper in the state. At other times Bangs worked in partnership with Alejandro Uro of Monterrey, who found a market for printing presses and accessories in Nuevo León and Coahuila and as far south as Aguascalientes and Zacatecas. The merchandise was "delivered by pack mules, and cash was transmitted by trusted employees or friends."[70]

Foreign merchants were also often middlemen in other business transactions. As a representative of the Hacienda Los Patos, Leon R. Almy leased various ranches to Ignacio Arizpe for two thousand pesos a year. Almy had become a Mexican citizen in 1827 and had received permission to introduce a machine to drill for water. Two years later, he gained permission to introduce pumps to extract water out of the ground, which gave Coahuilan planters the hope of agricultural production in the arid land.[71] Carlos Bork, manager of the Hacienda Los Hornos, granted Cesáreo Figueroa of Viesca, Coahuila, power of attorney to collect all monies owed to the hacienda. The Hacienda Los Hornos was the property of William S. Parrott, whose interests Bork represented. Parrott, an American businessman and diplomat, had been engaged in commerce in Mexico since the early 1820s and corresponded frequently with Stephen F. Austin. He served as U.S. consul at Mexico City in 1834–36, and became an agent of President James K. Polk to the Mexican government prior to the war between the two countries.[72]

The presence of these foreign merchants implied other forms of cooperation with the Mexican population. Commerce obligated them to interact with Mexicans of all classes. John Linn did this naturally with the arrieros and servants that he regularly employed or with the people he attended to in his fleeting role as doctor in Candela. Reuben Potter did the same with fellow merchants and the cart drivers and arrieros who accompanied him on his trips. Joshua Davis regularly employed Mexican servants to journey from Monclova to the Texas coast to buy goods for his store. With or without sponsors, Mexican traders and teamsters were often seen in Texas. An early settler reported in the late 1820s that "Mexicans traded extensively with the Texans, and their trains of burros loaded with silver dollars to be exchanged for tobacco and other commodities were frequently seen and always welcomed at Matagorda." S. Rhoads Fisher, who established a trading post at Matagorda, received many Mexican traders looking for tobacco and salt, and often invited them to dine at his table.[73] However, it was illegal commerce, or smuggling, that brought together Anglo-Americans, Europeans, and Mexicans in more wide-ranging forms of cooperation.

The Allure of Contraband

It is impossible to estimate the extent of illegal trade, but in the period between 1825 and 1850 it probably equaled at least one-third of the value of the legal trade, perhaps more. One historian asserts that at the end of the 1820s "two-thirds of the foreign products sold in the country represented commodities that had eluded custom levies." José María Luis Mora, the most conspicuous Mexican liberal thinker of the first half of the nineteenth century, also gave this estimate in 1834.[74]

During the Spanish Empire the pobladores of the northern provinces were forbidden to trade with Louisiana, but they did it anyway because goods could be obtained there for as much as 400 percent less than from Veracruz and Mexico City, since those goods were taxed heavily and carted hundreds of miles. The Crown's refusal to open ports on the Gulf Coast, which would have considerably lowered the cost of goods, drove the pobladores to engage in contraband. Moreover, the opening of Mexico's ports after independence was accompanied by a protectionist commercial policy. The Spanish were gone, but their restrictive attitude with respect to trade remained in the hearts of Mexican government officials. In 1821, the Iturbide government imposed a 25 percent tax on all imported goods and, according to one historian, this policy "was the most liberal for a decade not only in its rates of duties, but also in its prohibitions and other restrictions."[75] In 1827 the national congress approved a new tariff structure that prohibited imports of fifty-four different products, and in 1829, many other items were added to the prohibited list, including many cloth and cotton products that were very popular in the northern states. Someone commented facetiously that a list of permitted items might have been shorter. Thus, commercial policy conceived in Mexico City would have a profound impact on the border region.[76]

The Mexican government was in a dilemma. "Eighty to ninety percent of its regular income came from import and export duties during the half century after independence," according to David Weber, but it did not or could not change a corrupt and inefficient customs system that kept revenues down. As an alternative, government officials chose to raise tariffs, but "failed to produce more income because they instead encouraged greater smuggling and graft." The ultimate cause, according to another historian, was the "political, financial, and administrative weakness of the Mexican state."[77]

The frontier states tried to promote their local artisans and producers. Manuel Gómez de Castro, governor of Nuevo León, declared in 1827 that revenue from the tobacco monopoly would be "much greater" if not for the "ominous contraband" of foreign tobacco. A year later, he lamented that the operations of local artisans and small textile producers "were completely ruined because foreigners introduce cotton goods cheaper than can be manufactured in this country." Clearly, the national government ban on textile imports in 1829 failed to stimulate local production in Nuevo León.[78]

The inhabitants of the northern states had many incentives to engage in smuggling, including proximity to the United States and the vast supply of assorted articles that could be obtained quickly in New Orleans. Some products, such as cotton goods, shoes, and coffee, could not be readily obtained in northern Mexico so "the natives proved eager to buy them on the black market."[79] Others were highly profitable. One hundred pounds of tobacco, for example, could be bought in New Orleans for $1 to $1.50 and could fetch in Mexico between $50 and $75. Moreover, many frontier officials favored lower tariffs and "lacked the will to enforce those federal regulations that they regarded as detrimental to their region's interests." One official in New Mexico "passionately condemned a new tariff law [of 1829] that prohibited importation of some woolen and cotton goods, nails, locks, and other items."[80]

Authorities in Mexico City were powerless to stem the huge tide of contraband goods from entering the country, especially across the vast expanse of the northern frontier. It did not have sufficient customhouses or officers to do the job. In 1835 "a hapless revenue officer reported that he could not collect duties because he had no soldiers and could not pursue *contrabandistas* because he had no boat."[81] It was useless for the national government to appeal to patriotism because the northern states had become increasingly dependent on foreign goods, and their regional interests mattered more than nationalism. Some local mercantile interests also tried to stem the tide, pressuring states like Nuevo León and Coahuila to pass

Smuggling was a major part of the clandestine economy on the Rio Grande frontier. It involved people of all races and classes, and it promoted interethnic cooperation. This illustration shows men carrying contraband across one of the many fords on the Rio Grande. From *Harper's Weekly*, September 4, 1886. LC-USZ62-119617, Library of Congress.

laws prohibiting foreign merchants from engaging in retail sales.[82] These laws, however, only drove the foreigners to find Mexican middlemen, with whom they established stronger bonds of cooperation.

Another reason why the Mexican government was incapable of stopping the contraband trade is that it was so widespread and involved virtually all sectors of society. This was the message that more than 130 ranchers, farmers, and merchants of Cadereyta, Nuevo León, sent to the federal government in August 1840. They complained that products from Texas—especially tobacco—were inundating local markets. "A multitude of Mexicans" participated in this illegal trade and had "well-established mercantile relations with the enemies of the nation." To Texas, they accused, went "the horses, the mules, hides . . . in exchange for articles of clothing, tobacco, etc." And no amount of vigilance and control was sufficient to stop it.[83]

Mexican and foreign merchants, many with ties to New Orleans and with ships at their disposal, participated in the contraband trade. Some of these foreigners established roots in Matamoros and married into prominent local families. Mexican participants included arrieros, carters, and landowners who "cooperated with smugglers by hiding the contraband on their ranches."[84] Many government officials up to the highest levels were also involved or chose not to prosecute smugglers. Common citizens outside the commercial loop benefited as consumers of contraband goods. The problem was so serious that Nuevo León governor Juan Nepomuceno de la Garza y Evia deplored the "detestable inclination of many of the vecinos of Nuevo León to participate in the illegal traffic of products" and ordered local authorities to report all citizens traveling more than two hundred leagues from home and those who were believed to be in collusion with the Texans.[85]

Whether as participants or consumers, most members of society were involved in smuggling; it was widely accepted even by otherwise honest people, which explains why it was irrepressible. Revealing testimony is provided by Jesús González Treviño, a Monterrey merchant who admitted to participating in the contraband trade in a posthumous document published one hundred years after his death. His parents were known for their integrity and high ethical standards. They instilled in their son the values of honesty, hard work, modesty, and charity toward others. As a young man, Jesús was sent to Matamoros to work in the firm of Clausen y Compañía. He tells of the trains of wagons that arrived in the port laden with silver coins. He and Benjamin Burchard, his boss, made trips to Brownsville almost daily with coins strapped to their bodies and covered by their clothing. They also hid the silver in sacks of grass hauled by mules. In this way, they were able to avoid paying the 8 percent duty. They befriended the customs inspectors, and by regularly giving them presents generally avoided searches. Later in life, González Treviño hired professional contrabandistas to cross into Mexico with merchandise he had purchased in Texas or Europe. They would transport it as far as Parras, Coahuila, where González Treviño obtained documents that legalized the goods in order to send them farther into the interior. He traveled frequently to Texas to buy goods. On one trip he crossed the river at Piedras Negras with 120,000 pesos, but only declared 7,000. Like most people who avoided paying taxes, he reasoned that "those who paid duties in their totality would be ruined."[86]

Two respected foreign merchants of Saltillo, Carlos Bork and Ricardo Blossman, were at various times accused of introducing contraband. In 1829 the customs collector in that city confiscated forty-eight bundles belonging to Blossman, which Matías García had brought from Matamoros. The merchandise included various cotton products, such as stockings and shawls, as well as pieces of lace and suspenders that the customs collector claimed were introduced illegally. Blossman argued there was a mix-up when the merchandise was packed and that

the articles were listed on another bill of lading which reflected the payment of
duties. The judge who tried the case rejected that argument. In a separate case,
Bork, who was based in Saltillo but had extensive contacts all over Coahuila,
was also accused of smuggling, and forty-four packages that belonged to him
were confiscated in the town of Viesca.[87]

Because of its immense profitability, tobacco was the most important product
of the contraband trade. John Linn was one of the most assiduous practition-
ers. In 1829 he and a Mexican collaborator made the arduous trip from Corpus
Christi Bay to the Rio Grande to obtain mules. Returning with the mules, he
loaded them with forty bales of tobacco and headed for Camargo. A Mexican
colleague in that town helped him "materially in making sales" and even went to
the Texas coast at Linn's request to bring another shipment of tobacco.[88] Various
cases of Americans and Mexicans accused of trading in contraband tobacco can
be found in the judicial archives of Nuevo León and Coahuila. In one such case
Rafael Cantú and Faustino de la Garza, vecinos of Topo de los González near
Monterrey, were accused of collaborating with Peter H. Bartelson of Philadelphia and another American, Guillermo Yten, in introducing seven 100-pound
packs of Virginia tobacco. Cantú's house was used as a hiding place. Cantú and
De la Garza, who were both farm laborers, admitted to owning one pack each
and claimed the other five belonged to Yten. The two Mexicans were assessed
a heavy fine, Bartelson was exonerated for lack of evidence and Yten escaped.[89]

Through reading Noah Smithwick's memoirs, it becomes clear that "Guillermo Yten" was really Billy Eaton, and that he was an old hand at this game.
According to Smithwick, Eaton and a partner "were endeavoring to land a load
of tobacco in Laredo during the night when they were surprised by a squad of
soldiers." Eaton was captured with the tobacco, but his partner escaped. While
being taken in, Eaton managed to untie his hands and get away on a fast horse.
The soldiers followed, but "soon relinquished the pursuit and Billy said he heard
them laughing hilariously over the escapade. Had they taken him in they would
have been obliged to produce the contraband."[90]

Smithwick himself seemed proud of his smuggling adventures. He recounts
that in 1828 he sold the merchandise in his shop and "invested the proceeds in
tobacco, and, in company with Joe McCoy, Jack Cryor, and John F. Webber, set out
for Mexico on a smuggling trip." After the group crossed the Rio Grande above
Laredo at Presidio del Norte, Mexican soldiers "found our tobacco and helped
themselves to as much as they could conceal, making no attempt to arrest us. . . .
To have done so would have necessitated the surrender of the goods, which they

had no intention of doing." Smithwick and Webber continued to San Fernando where they received help from John Villars, an American who had gone to Mexico during the War of Independence. Villars helped them to hide their remaining tobacco with Doña Petra, who was the widow of an American "and consequently the steadfast friend of all Americans. . . . Therefore our being domiciled there was quite a matter of course, occasioning no suspicion." It took time to dispose of the tobacco and in the interim, Smithwick and Webber participated in the aforementioned farce in which they played the roles of doctor and interpreter.[91]

Land Speculator's Paradise

Another economic activity that brought together Anglo-Americans, Europeans, and Mexicans was the purchase and sale of Texas land. In the accepted American tradition, this activity turned into speculation on a vast scale.[92] Land speculation motivated by greed combined with the generous land laws of Mexico. It was in the interest of the Mexican government to populate its northern lands, both to protect them from Spain and to help ward off Indian incursions. Because there were not sufficient Mexicans available or willing to settle in Texas, Anglo-Americans were allowed to receive land if they promised to obey the law and adhere to Catholicism. The federal government delegated the colonization process to the various states, and on March 25, 1825, the government of Coahuila y Texas passed a very generous law that allowed settlers to buy a *sitio* (one league, or 4,428 acres) plus a *labor* (177 acres) of land for as little as $100, which could be paid over a six-year period. Additionally, Mexicans could purchase as many as eleven sitios, so many Europeans and Americans, including iconic heroes such as Ben Milam, became Mexican citizens in order to acquire additional land.[93]

The generous law quickly attracted settlers, along with a swarm of speculators. Companies such as the Texas Association of Nashville, Tennessee, were created for the purpose of speculating in Texas land. Prominent American politicians such as Sam Houston participated.[94] Another organization, the Galveston Bay and Texas Land Company, was created in New York with the participation of American and Mexican investors who had received generous land grants. Among them was Lorenzo de Zavala, former governor of the powerful state of Mexico who had fled to New York in 1829 after the government of Vicente Guerrero, whom he had helped put in power, was overthrown. Other participants included Joseph Vehlein and David G. Burnet. In October 1830, they integrated their holdings for the purpose of selling the land they had been granted. The company was modeled "on systems established by earlier land speculators in Kentucky,

Tennessee, and Mississippi" and, according to one observer, it was "the most extensive land Company that was ever known in this or any other Country." Its holdings encompassed some 16,000 square miles in southeastern Texas.[95]

The enterprise was highly rewarding: Zavala reportedly received $100,000 (approximately $2.2 million today) for his cession of land to the company. The partners also enriched themselves by defrauding naïve French, Swiss, and German settlers who were already in the United States and dreamed of owning their own farm in Texas. Not knowing that the state of Coahuila y Texas offered 4,605 acres of land to immigrant families, they entered into a contract with the company and received a 177-acre farm site while signing a release "giving the company the balance of that headright—4,428 acres."[96] The activities of the speculators drove Stephen F. Austin to declare: "I had rather herd with vermin than with that class of human beings."[97]

Among the members of the Galveston Bay Company were Joel Poinsett, the former ambassador to Mexico, and other prominent businessmen from New York. Besides Zavala, there were two Mexican participants: José Antonio Mejía, a Cuban-born naturalized Mexican who was one of the firm's sales agents, and José María de Jesús Carvajal, a native of San Antonio, who became surveyor of the company. Both had large landholdings in Texas. Among his various occupations, Mejía had been a customs official in Mexico, where he seemingly made a fortune. This would explain how he was able to purchase 243,540 acres of land in the name of his children near the Navasota and Trinity Rivers. These lands were surveyed and deeded to him in November 1833. Carvajal had studied in Virginia and Kentucky under the auspices of Stephen F. Austin, who described him as "a sprightly, intelligent youth," whose "principles [were] sound and honorable." His fellow Mexicans referred to him as a "Norteamericano." Carvajal, for his part, wrote that his affection for Austin was limitless. He obtained an extensive property in Southeast Texas as a result of his marriage to a daughter of Martín de León, the empresario who obtained a grant of land on the lower Guadalupe River and founded the town of Victoria. As a representative to the Coahuila y Texas state congress, Carvajal voted for lax laws that would permit the sale of Texas lands to the many immigrants who were arriving in the region. Like Mejía, he was bilingual and bicultural and was the prototype of the borderlander who had extensive business, political and social ties among Anglos and Mexicans. Both men would play important roles in the future events of Texas and the border region.[98]

Traffic in Texas land was promoted in such faraway places as Nashville, New York, and New Orleans.[99] However, the most intense activity took place in

Monclova and Saltillo, the centers of political and economic power in Coahuila. Two networks were deeply involved in land transactions: one made up of foreign and local businessmen, the other composed of Anglo-American, European, and Mexican Freemasons. This "secret society" may seem rather quaint to the modern reader, but it was very important in the late eighteenth and early nineteenth centuries. Before the establishment of political factions or parties, Masonry provided a platform for prominent men to engage in politics. A significant number of political leaders in the United States and Mexico were Masons. So were many of the Americans who came to Saltillo seeking land grants, including Robert Leftwich, Frost H. Thorn, David G. Burnet, and Benjamin R. Milam. Among the Europeans, Juan Cameron and James Power were members. They made common cause with committed federalists in the Coahuilan elite, such as José María and Agustín Viesca and José Francisco Madero, who were also Masons. Agustín Viesca was one of the founding members of the yorkino faction of Mexican Masonry, which favored states' rights and was well disposed toward the United States and toward opening the country to foreign immigration. It was through the Viesca brothers that Stephen F. Austin became a Mason and established a lodge in San Felipe de Austin in 1828.[100] Masonry proved to be an effective bridge in facilitating land transactions. Historian Andrés Reséndez argues that "this vast network of landed interests running from Mexico City, through Saltillo and San Antonio, and to the various colonization projects and land grants throughout Texas is what kept an array of diverse human beings together."[101]

The other network, made up of local and foreign entrepreneurs, shifted easily from traffic in merchandise to traffic in lands. José Francisco Madero, who was appointed land commissioner for Coahuila y Texas, used his connections to amass a large amount of property. Since he was limited to eleven sitios of land, he had his wife, Victoriana Elizondo, acquire eleven more.[102] Madero died suddenly at an early age during the devastating cholera epidemic of 1833–34. In time his son, Evaristo Madero, would become patriarch of one of Mexico's most powerful families, whose economic and political influence extends to this day. Madero left most of his land to his wife and children, but he had sold a part to Henry Prentiss of New York, who with his brother James, formed the Union Land Company for the purpose of promoting Texas colonization. In a similar transaction José María Aguirre, Rafael de Aguirre, and Tomás de la Vega each acquired eleven sitios of land in Texas in 1830, then granted power of attorney to Samuel May Williams, Stephen F. Austin's partner, so that he could take possession of all thirty-three sitios and find a buyer.[103]

A good illustration of the way this commercial network functioned in land sales is provided by the operations of James Hewetson, who moved in Coahuilan business and political circles like a fish in water. In 1834, twelve vecinos of Parras, Coahuila, each of whom had purchased eleven sitios of Texas land, contracted Hewetson to find buyers or hold a public auction to sell their land. Hewetson, in turn, transferred his representation to a Mexican colleague, Juan T. Mazo, to carry out the operation.[104] People from all over Coahuila and as far away as Mexico City hired Hewetson to dispose of their Texas land, and he was also a prolific buyer in his own right. Notarial records show that he purchased properties in Saltillo and other parts of Coahuila, as well as in Texas. In 1835 he granted power of attorney to Henrique Rueg of Nacogdoches so that the latter could take possession of twenty sitios (88,560 acres) of land that Hewetson had purchased. Two years later Hewetson was offered at least six sitios in the area of Bexar by Jesús Vidaurri. He also purchased from José Antonio de la Peña and Miguel Dávila their twenty-two sitios next to the Red River for two hundred pesos apiece.[105]

A WILL TO COOPERATE

From these transactions, it seems clear that the exchanges that occurred and the networks that developed in commerce, land sales, and other pursuits required an environment conducive to cooperation and harmonious relations between foreigners and native Mexicans. There is reason to believe that a relaxed and hospitable atmosphere did indeed exist, at least for a time, until outside forces and pressures began to fray those relations. In 1832 Daniel W. Smith, the U.S. consul in Matamoros, wrote the U.S. State Department that the political instability that had disrupted the rest of Mexico had not affected Matamoros, which "continued to flourish and is now in a state of rapid improvement." He added: "At present there are about 300 foreign residents in this town, a majority of whom are American citizens; and . . . there is every reason to believe that as much, if not more, harmony and good feelings subsist between them and the natives as perhaps at any other part of the republic."[106]

The Rio Grande frontier was a fertile field for cooperation. Complicating the many histories that recount racism, hatred, and conflict between Mexicans and Anglo-Americans in the border region, many Americans and Europeans were quite willing to live among the Mexican people. It is also clear that the Mexican population was receptive to these newcomers. Noah Smithwick, who was not particularly fond of Mexicans, remarked: "Americans were held in high esteem in Mexico at that time, and I could have traveled through the length and breadth of the land without spending a dollar."[107]

The will to cooperate was plainly evidenced by the many interethnic marriages that occurred in the border region, particularly between Anglo men and Mexican women. Perhaps the highest form of cooperation is marriage, even if it is marriage born of convenience and even if it sometimes ends in conflict. Arnoldo de León writes that in San Antonio "a minimum of one daughter from almost every well-to-do family in the city had become the wife of an Anglo suitor. In South Texas, the newcomers not only acquired valuable ranch property by marrying women from landed families but incidentally acquired esteem and economic and political authority."[108] In some communities such as San Antonio, many Mexican families considered assimilation into Anglo society and culture to be vital. This process was not without obstacles, especially in times of nativist hostility as in the 1850s in Texas. One historian writes, "Only the women and children with Anglo surnames, light skins, and wealth had a reasonable chance to escape the stigma attached to their Mexican ancestry."[109] In other communities, particularly those close to the border or with majority Mexican populations, it was Anglo men who saw the need to assimilate into the Mexican community and its culture in order to succeed. The children of these marriages, unlike their counterparts in San Antonio who strove to become Americanized, usually attended school in Mexico and became "thoroughly Mexicanized."[110]

The interethnic marriages between Anglos and Mexicans deserve our attention because they contradict the notion that members of these two races were not made to live together. Historian Rebecca McDowell Craver studied the incidences of mixed marriages on the upper Rio Grande in New Mexico, on Mexico's northern frontier. She discovered that such marriages were common between 1821 and 1846. She asks important questions such as, "If frontier Mexicans suspected, feared, and hated Anglo-Americans, why did the women marry Anglos?" And if the Anglos were the targets of Mexican suspicion and hatred, "why did so many of them remain to make the northern fringes of Mexico their permanent home and become rooted in Hispanic culture?" Her answer is, "It appears that historical literature has exaggerated the animosity between Hispanic native and Anglo newcomer on the Mexican frontier. Far from being wary of the norte-americanos, the native citizenry, both rich and poor, male and female, readily accepted many of the new arrivals as settlers in their midst. The initial contact between Mexicans and non-Hispanic foreigners in New Mexico seems to have been not a clash of cultures but a cooperative fusion."[111]

In the Mexican perspective of these mixed marriages, the concept of cooperation was vital. For Texas Mexicans, according to historian Ana Carolina Castillo
Crimm, "there was danger both socially and economically in having a daughter
marry an Anglo [because] there would be no joining of extended families, no
strengthening of the clan, no betterment for all." Meanwhile, many Anglos
believed that Mexican families were too conservative and paid slight attention
to the "development and recognition of individual abilities that would help ele-
vate the Latin community." Doña Luz Escalera de León, a matriarch of the De
León family of Victoria, expressed the feelings of many Mexicans. She felt that
the Anglo practice of "amassing fortunes at the expense of others and then not
sharing it with the family was selfish. Only when individual abilities were used
for the good of the whole did the families and the community prosper. . . . The
success of one was the insurance which protected all of the members. The family
cared for its own, good and bad, rich and poor. For the Tejanos of Victoria, the
family was the basis for existence."[112] The subject of mixed marriages in the
border region has not received sufficient attention, but it was a natural, perhaps
inevitable, part of life.

Among many liberal thinkers in Northeast Mexico, there was a genuine
acceptance of foreigners, particularly Europeans. A reflection of this attitude is
the colonization law of Tamaulipas, enacted in 1833 under the governorship of
Francisco Vital Fernández. The proclamation began, "The world is a common
homeland and men travel from one nation to another in search of well-being."
Nations that accepted immigrants made rapid progress, the document further
declared, and it was natural for societies to reward their own citizens, but also
to accept in their midst "men of goodwill."[113] In this spirit, the government of
Tamaulipas granted a contract to Johann von Racknitz in 1835, but conditions at
that time prevented its fruition. Von Racknitz, who had served in the military
in his native Germany and tried but failed to join the Mina expedition, had
earlier attempted to establish a German colony in Texas. He "had a clear and
enduring vision of himself working with other similarly motivated Germans to
build a dynamic community first in Texas and then in Tamaulipas that would
be linked with Germany in culture and commerce." Such was the spirit of some
Europeans who facilitated relations between the races in Mexico's Northeast.[114]

Perhaps it was easier to accept new arrivals in the border region because most
of them were not bent on territorial expansion or racial domination. It is also
true however that Europeans and Anglo-Americans were in the minority in
Mexico, so if they had racial prejudices, it was convenient to suppress them.[115]

What's more, the people of the borderlands—natives and newcomers alike—were generally flexible in their views, pragmatic in their behavior, and guided more by self-interest—not to mention self-preservation—than by racial or ethnic considerations. Pragmatism, racism, the very need to survive, all influenced conflict and cooperation in the border region, and it is clear that the attitudes of Anglo-Americans and Mexicans toward each other were not fixed or static. They were constantly changing and contingent upon many factors, and varied according to circumstance.[116] This becomes evident in the events leading up to Texas independence.

COMMONALITY AND CONFLICT IN TEXAS INDEPENDENCE

Relations between the Texas colonists and the local elites of Bexar and Coahuila are a good starting point. These relations were largely characterized by commonalities and shared interests. Although there were obvious differences in ethnicity, language, culture, and religion, natives and newcomers shared certain affinities. To begin with, they were hardened by living in a harsh environment prone to prolonged droughts, occasional lethal epidemics, and deadly Indian raids. Francisco R. Almada, a noted historian of Chihuahua, wrote about the character of norteños: "The tough, strong, brave, and hospitable nature of the men of the northern states" was conditioned by their habitat, which "forced them to devote greater effort to extract less produce from the land than in other regions of the country; to the long struggle of their ancestors against the Apaches and other naturally rebellious tribes; and to the need to depend on each other."[117] The native norteños developed a strong and independent spirit, not unlike that attributed to the Texans by T. R. Fehrenbach. They were self-sufficient and disposed to seek local autonomy, an attitude shared by the Texas colonists, who were imbued with federalist principles. These sentiments were at the heart of a long chain of separatist movements in Northeast Mexico, beginning with the independence of Texas.[118]

There was competition between local and foreign merchants, but also cooperation. Historian Randolph B. Campbell asserts that "Anglos gave their Hispanic counterparts contacts with suppliers in the United States and, in turn, received assistance in dealing with Mexican officials and regulations."[119] According to David Weber, the Mexican leaders of San Antonio "saw the economic growth of Texas, its security from Indians, and their own fortunes, as inextricably linked to the well-being of the Anglo-American newcomers and their slave-based, cotton-growing economy." They protested vigorously when the Mexican government abolished slavery in 1829 and once again when it attempted to ban further Anglo immigration to Texas with the law of April 6, 1830. José Francisco Ruiz, one of the town's principal leaders, famously declared: "I cannot help seeing advantages which, to my way of thinking, would result if we admitted honest, hard-working people, regardless of what country they come from . . . even hell itself."[120]

Another commonality was the attitude toward slavery. The local elites understood that slavery was decisively bound up with the cotton economy and prosperity. Mexican leaders in San Antonio became "full-throated supporters of slave-based agriculture as practiced by U.S. immigrants."[121] When the state government of Coahuila y Texas banned slavery in its constitution of 1827, José Antonio Navarro used his position in the state congress to bulldoze through a law that permitted colonists to continue bringing in their slaves as indentured servants under contracts signed before they crossed the border into Texas. And when President Vicente Guerrero decreed the emancipation of slaves throughout the republic in 1829, Ramón Múzquiz traveled to Saltillo and petitioned for an exemption for Texas. He was aided in his mission by the Viesca brothers whose connections to Guerrero—all were Masons—were crucial in excluding Texas from the prohibition.[122] Many Coahuilan elites were not averse to slavery. Victor Blanco acquired slaves in 1820 for his cotton-ginning operation. Melchor Sánchez Navarro, a powerful Coahuilan hacendado, was disagreeably surprised in 1827 when he traveled to San Luis Potosí with three of his slaves. The state had recently passed a law banning slavery, and he was told that they were freemen the moment they crossed the state line.[123]

A final commonality between the local elites and the Texas colonists was their shared opposition to many policies of the Mexican government. On issues of ideology, commerce, immigration, and—to a lesser degree—slavery, many local leaders in San Antonio and Monclova shared the views of Texans. They were in the same predicament and were inclined to unite to face a common foe: the Mexican government. The notion of a common enemy is a recurring theme in the history of the border region, whether in the form of a faraway government, Indian predators, or other enemies.[124]

Historian Samuel H. Lowrie argues that "the relations between the Mexicans of Texas and the American colonists were generally, until 1832 at least, based on cooperation and mutual interest." Brian DeLay writes that there were good relations between Coahuilan politicians and the Texas settlers, but "changes in national politics began tearing this web apart."[125] In the early 1830s the common ground between the Coahuila y Texas elites and the colonists began to fracture, battered by two external forces: the incessant and growing immigration of Anglo-American colonists, particularly from the slaveholding South, and the response of the Mexican government to that invasion. The Mexican population of Texas at the time of independence was about five thousand, half of whom resided in or around San Antonio de Béxar, with the rest distributed among Nacogdoches, La Bahía, and the Rio Grande settlements. The decision to accept Anglo-American colonization opened the floodgates to a steady stream of immigrants, and by 1835 "an estimated 1,000 Americans a month entered Texas by way of the Brazos River alone." The Anglo population of Texas swelled to about thirty thousand, greatly outnumbering the Mexican inhabitants.[126] The Mexican government was cognizant of the threat this imbalance posed. During a tour of inspection in Texas, Manuel Mier y Terán wrote of the steady, silent method of Anglo occupation: without armies or wars, they assumed certain rights, then applied diplomatic pressure and threats, followed by incitements to revolt to take possession of the occupied land. One of Mier y Teran's lieutenants, José María Sánchez, observed this process on the same trip to Texas in 1828. He wrote that the Anglo-Americans had "taken possession of practically all the eastern part of Texas, in most cases without the permission of the authorities. They immigrate constantly, finding no one to prevent them . . . without either asking leave or going through any formality other than that of building their homes."[127]

After independence, Mexico needed time to define and build a strong nation-state. It did not have that time; Anglo-Americans were rushing toward the frontier. Events were moving with breathtaking velocity, but the reaction of the Mexican government was slow. The Fredonia revolt of 1826–27, in which Haden Edwards and others rose up to separate Texas from Mexico, was a wake-up call. That experience and the warnings about losing Texas in Mier y Terán's report moved authorities in Mexico City to pass the Law of April 6, 1830, banning further American immigration to Texas. This attempt by Mexico to control its borders was also part of a conservative, centralist tide that was sweeping the country and would capture the national government in the mid-1830s. In Texans' eyes, it became one of the precipitating causes of the war for Texas independence, but it also damaged relations between Anglo-Texans and Mexicans in the Rio Grande region.[128]

The war for Texas independence strained the generally harmonious relations between Anglo-Texans and the Mexican population, though it did not shatter the common ground that had been built. The fact is that Texans—most of them in any case—made war not on the Mexican people but on the Mexican government, in the same way that the Mexican inhabitants of Zacatecas, Yucatán, and other rebellious provinces did. A discussion of the causes of Texas independence is not within the scope of this study, but relations between Anglo-Texans and Mexicans is central to this study. Therefore, because some scholars have claimed that the war to separate Texas from Mexico resulted from growing ethnic and cultural differences between these two groups, a few observations are in order.

Racism and cultural differences undeniably played a role in provoking the war. Many authors concede this point, though not all of them claim that such issues were at the heart of the conflict.[129] Unlike the early colonists, many of the later immigrants to Texas came from southern slave states where the society was steeped in bigotry and had a belligerent attitude toward Mexico and Mexicans.[130] Yet contemporary observer Reuben Potter asserts that the "lower order of the Anglo-American element" was mainly responsible for racism against Mexicans: "In no people are race antipathies liable to be more bigoted and mean than in those of Anglo-Saxon blood; and of the under strata of that breed the low American is perhaps the worst sample."[131]

However, a case can be made—and historian James E. Crisp does indeed make it—that "the Texas Revolution was less a consequence of racial friction than a precipitating cause of it." Crisp writes that not long before the conflict, officials from the *ayuntamiento* (town council) of San Felipe de Austin wrote to their counterparts in Bexar: "if the people of Béxar are Mexicans by birth, we are so by adoption. . . . We repeat it, we are one and the same people." Crisp concludes, "This kind of statement would not be made again by Anglo-Texans after their defeat of Santa Anna at San Jacinto."[132] Even as late as 1835, after his imprisonment in Mexico City, Austin insisted that in their efforts to gain separate statehood within the Mexican federation, the Texans had assembled peacefully and petitioned respectfully "in harmony with republican institutions." Moreover, they "believed that they were acting as faithful Mexican citizens who understood their duties and aspired to fulfill them and as honorable men who were seeking their individual welfare and happiness."[133]

It seems clear that racial attitudes hardened during the war, especially after the barbarity Santa Anna displayed at the Alamo and Goliad. In the heat of the revolution, racist rhetoric intensified. This change in attitude can even be seen in Austin, a longtime defender of Mexico. When he explained the situation to eastern listeners, he "declared that the conflict . . . was 'a war of barbarian and of despotic principles, waged by the mongrel Spanish-Indian and Negro race, against civilization and the Anglo-American race.'"[134] Historian Paul Lack agrees that "the war left a core of uncompensated losses, mutual suspicion, and festering hatreds that poisoned relations between Mexicans and Anglos during the period of the Republic and beyond."[135]

The degree of poisoning, as will be seen, was not enough to impede coexistence and cooperation between the two races. This may be due to a perception among many borderlanders that other issues besides race were involved. James E. Crisp is convinced that "the Texan revolt did not center on the culturally sensitive issues of race, language, or religion." The war, he asserts, "was prompted by questions that divided other frontier areas from the Mexican metropolis: disagreements over states' rights and local autonomy, exorbitant tariffs and the haphazard suppression of smuggling, inefficient and arbitrary administration of the laws, and the weakness and corruption of the army."[136]

The disagreement between the Texans and the Mexican government over states' rights is particularly relevant with regard to the issue of slavery. The promise of prosperity based on cotton cultivation with the use of black slaves drew thousands of Anglo-Americans to Texas. These settlers came from a society where slavery was constitutionally accepted and they believed that it was the province of each state to regulate it. Initially they sought separate statehood within the Mexican federation in order to draft a constitution tolerant of slavery. When they saw that this was impossible, they rebelled. Thus, "the Texas Revolution was not a defense of . . . American ideals of liberty." It resembled more "an outright defense of slavery."[137] Historian Neil Foley expresses this argument bluntly: "the famous trio of southern-born whites, Jim Bowie, Davy Crockett, and William Barrett Travis, gave their lives at the Alamo for the freedom of white men to own slaves."[138]

Randolph B. Campbell contributes a final observation that because most Anglo-Texans did not have much contact with the Mexican population, "ethnic and cultural differences . . . do not completely account for the revolution." Moreover, there were generally good relations between Texans and Mexicans prior to 1835 and "the fact that a sizable minority of Tejanos fought alongside the Anglos in 1835–36 indicates that ethno-cultural conflict alone cannot explain the revolution."[139]

COOPERATIVE VIOLENCE DURING TEXAS INDEPENDENCE

Campbell's point that "a sizable minority" of Mexicans fought with the Texans leads us to one of the pillars of this study: Anglo-Americans and Mexicans forged bonds of cooperation in a broad range of endeavors. It should not surprise us that they also cooperated in the realm of violence. They not only fought against each other, but also fought side-by-side for a common cause, against a common foe, or to remove a common obstacle. They struggled together when they had similar interests or when their particular interests converged. For the sake of brevity, I refer to this scenario as "cooperative violence." I am not referring to random or individual acts of violence, but to cases of conspicuous cooperation in which Anglos, Mexicans, and other racial groups such as Indians or Blacks, for whatever reason, fought on the same side.[140]

Cooperative violence is a constant throughout the half century covered by this study, beginning with the series of events in the early 1830s that led to the final break between Texas and Mexico.[141] This cooperation was often related to the common causes of federalism, local autonomy, and resistance to centralism. The complexity of these relations is exemplified by a curious fact: in 1832 Anglo-Texans embraced Santa Anna and his movement against the government of Anastasio Bustamante. When Texans rebelled against Juan Davis Bradburn, the arbitrary customs collector of Anahuac who represented the Mexican government, they took up the *santanista* banner against oppressive centralist policies. In the Turtle Bayou Resolutions of June 1832, the Anahuac rebels "expressed opposition to the Bustamante administration because of its violations of the Constitution of 1824 and called on all Texans to support the patriot opposition led by Santa Anna."[142]

A significant number of federalist leaders in Northeast Mexico chafed under the centralist direction being taken in Mexico City. They also identified with some of their Texas neighbors on a personal level. The imprisonment of Stephen F. Austin is revealing in this regard. Because of his prudence and conciliatory nature, Austin had many friends in Northeast Mexico. After staying at the home of Victor Blanco, Austin described him as a "warm and sincere friend." He wrote to his assistant, Samuel M. Williams, to help Blanco obtain a tract of land near the Trinity or San Jacinto River, which he required, not for speculation, but for a family of ten children. Austin added, "a more promising family I have never seen."[143] Austin was arrested in Saltillo on January 3, 1834, as he was returning to Texas from Mexico City. His letter "recommending action on separate statehood without the approval of the national government" became known to the authorities, and he was taken to the Mexican capital.[144] En route, Austin befriended General Pedro Lemus in Monterrey, whom he described as "a man of high honor and liberal principles and a Gentleman." He also received kind treatment from the governor of Nuevo León, Manuel María de Llano, and from Colonel Domingo de Ugartechea, who was assigned by the army to that state. During his yearlong imprisonment Austin wrote to friends in Texas about individuals like Victor Blanco and Ramón Múzquiz, who aided him in his ordeal.[145]

Creeping centralism in Mexico led some norteño federalists to look to Texas for support. In 1834, Manuel María de Llano, Nuevo León's liberal governor, suggested to Agustín Viesca a plan that would separate Texas from Coahuila, "set up a federalist state government in Texas, and then get Anglo-Texan colonists to uphold the newly established state government."[146] This suggestion was made at a time when Coahuilan federalists were declaring their opposition to Santa Anna's turn to centralism and seeking help from European and Anglo-Texan federalists in Northeast Mexico and Texas. Diego Grant, a naturalized Mexican of Scottish origin and one of the biggest landowners in Parras, Coahuila, headed the local militia and gave them his support.[147] In their desperation, the Coahuilan federalists, who dominated the state congress in May 1835, took the extreme measure of granting Samuel Williams and his associates twelve hundred leagues of Texas land (some five million acres) on the promise that they would "raise a militia of one thousand men, supply them with arms and ammunition, and keep them in the field for one year." Williams put his concession in his pocket and returned to Texas, where he began to mobilize troops, not for his Coahuilan benefactors, but to fight for Texas independence.[148]

While some Mexican federalists looked north for assistance, they, in turn, were being courted by Anglo-Texans. In late 1835, with centralism firmly established in the capital and after Santa Anna had suppressed a federalist uprising in Zacatecas, Texans began the revolt that would lead to their separation from Mexico. In their struggle they looked for support from Mexicans on two essential fronts: internally from Mexican Texans and externally from Mexican federalists. Two expeditions, one to Tampico and the other to Matamoros, exemplify the second strategy. The Tampico expedition, launched from New Orleans, was led by an ally of the Texans, General José Antonio Mejía, whose role in the Galveston Bay Company was described earlier. After arriving from Cuba in 1823, Mejía had entered the Mexican army and become involved in Mexican politics with the yorkino faction of Freemasonry, where he established many ties to politicians sympathetic to federalist and liberal principles. He also served as secretary of the Mexican Legation in Washington, where he formed valuable alliances with American politicians and businessmen.[149]

Mejía was supported in his plans by a Mexican exile community in New Orleans that included former vice president Valentín Gómez Farías. He also found support in the Committee of Texas Affairs, a group of merchants more interested in separating Texas from Mexico than in defending federalist principles in Mexico. Mejía gathered some 150 men in New Orleans, and on November 6, 1835, set out for Tampico, where he counted on the support of fellow federalists with whom he hoped to start an uprising that would spread throughout the country. His goal was to help Texas by diverting Santa Anna from attacking the province. Unfortunately for Mejía, the expedition was a dismal failure. Thirty-one of its members were captured and most of them were executed, while Mejía and the rest escaped and sailed for Texas.[150]

Early in November Texan delegates to the Consultation at San Felipe de Austin established a provisional government but refused to break with Mexico altogether. In an appeal to Mexican federalists, they demanded a return to the Constitution of 1824. The governing structure included a provisional governor and a general council. When General Mejía returned from his failed Tampico expedition and offered assistance to the Texans, a division emerged between the provisional governor and the general council. Mejía had the complete confidence of Stephen F. Austin, who described the Mexican federalist as "one of the most honest and best men" in Mexico. However, Henry Smith, the provisional governor, did not trust Mejía and refused to authorize support for him. The general council strongly disagreed with that position and tried to oust Smith. In this climate of suspicion, Mejía returned to New Orleans. One historian argues that this "signaled the beginning of the end of the cooperation between Texian leaders and Mexican Federalists."[151]

Even though it was the beginning of the end, it was not quite the end. James Grant (referred to earlier as Diego Grant, as he was known in Coahuilan business and political circles), joined with Francis "Frank" W. Johnson, one of his former partners in land transactions, in heading an expedition to take the strategic town of Matamoros. Born in Scotland and naturalized in Mexico, Grant now appeared to assume the role of Texas patriot. The expedition, organized in January 1836, recruited Mexican Texans under the leadership of Plácido Benavides of Victoria with the aim of establishing contact with the federalist leader Antonio Canales of Tamaulipas. It was also believed that General Francisco Vital Fernández, the military leader of that state, would unite his forces with the Texans to defend the Constitution of 1824.[152] Like the Tampico adventure, The Matamoros expedition ended in failure. The anticipated unity with the federalists of Tamaulipas never materialized. Grant and Johnson never even got close to Matamoros. They divided their force and were easy prey for the troops of General José Urrea. Johnson was defeated at San Patricio, though he managed to escape. Grant was less fortunate;

he lost his life in the battle of Agua Dulce, near San Patricio on March 2, 1836, just four days before the battle of the Alamo.[153]

Grant was betrayed by his optimism and by the federalists he had counted on to rise up against Santa Anna. However, the issue goes deeper. The Tampico and Matamoros expeditions reveal the possibilities and limits of cooperative violence. First, it is clear that the Texans and Mexican federalists sought unity to further their particular interests. The Texans wooed federalist support in Mexico until December 1835, though by then most Texans wanted a complete separation from Mexico. "By this time, most Texian leaders had independence as their ultimate goal," writes Randolph B. Campbell, "but they saw the need to build strength before making an actual declaration."[154] Mexican federalists also worked in pursuit of their interests. Tamaulipecos such as Francisco Vital Fernández and Antonio Canales were guided by an instinct for survival. They appeared willing to side with the Texans on the issue of federalism until the approach of Santa Anna's sizable army made them reconsider their priorities.

These events also demonstrate that unity based on deception and suspicion cannot prosper. Some Texans treated all Mexicans with suspicion. Henry Smith, the head of the provisional government, said that they should not be trusted because "we will in the end find them inimical and treacherous."[155] The Texans hid their true intentions from Mexican federalists, who began to suspect their motives when the Texans refused to lend support to leaders such as Valentín Gómez Farías, Agustín Viesca, and José Antonio Mejía. Even more discouraging was the discovery that that the Texans were bent on separating Texas from Mexico. Federalist leaders, wrote historian Joseph M. Nance, "lost interest in the Texan revolutionary movement for they had no desire to assist in the dismemberment of their homeland."[156] However, these men also suffered from self-deception. They thought they would receive ample federalist support in Mexico at a moment when the majority of the country was embracing centralism and turning its back on federalism because of the anarchy and chaos of the first decade of Mexican independence.[157]

Still, the attempt to forge a Texan-Mexican alliance was not a total failure. The Texans chose Lorenzo de Zavala, perhaps Mexico's most prominent federalist, as their first vice president, essentially saying: "our fight is not with Mexicans, but with the Mexican government." Moreover, the presence of men such as Zavala and Mejía on the side of the Texans was not lost on decision makers in Mexico. Vicente Filisola considered it risky to attack Texas because these rebel federalists knew Mexico's situation and resources perfectly and were in a position to advise the Texans. Finally, and in spite of initial failure and frustration, future events would confirm that many Anglo-Texans remained willing to unite with Mexican dissidents, especially after centralism proved to be as divisive as federalism and within a few short years generated a host of uprisings in Mexico.[158]

Even as they sought external support for their movement from Mexican federalists, the Texans also looked to the Mexican population in Texas for help. Most Mexicans remained neutral, but some cast their lot with the Texans and participated actively in the struggle that led to independence.[159] The most significant participation of Mexican Texans in support of the Texan separatists occurred at the siege of Bexar at the end of 1835. A force led by Stephen F. Austin and later by Edward Burleson attacked San Antonio, which was occupied by the troops of Martín Perfecto Cos, Santa Anna's brother-in-law. In a prelude to the battle, a skirmish occurred at Concepción, just outside the town. Mexican rancheros under the command of Juan N. Seguín and Plácido Benavides joined a force led by James Bowie and James Fannin and defeated a larger body of troops commanded by Colonel Domingo de Ugartechea. The stage was set for the battle for Bexar. The initial assault began on December 5, directed by Benjamin Milam and Frank W. Johnson, who knew the Mexicans well. About 160 Mexicans participated in the siege, which lasted several days. They were led by Juan Seguín, and included Salvador and Manuel Flores, Juan M. and José M. Zambrano, José A. Rendón, and Sylvestre de León. Other Mexican Texans contributed outside the field of battle. Juan Seguín's father, Erasmo, put his ranch at the service of the Texans, who utilized it as an important source of supplies. Mexican women also participated. They "cooked for the Americans and brought them water from the river until Mexican soldiers started shooting at them."[160]

Perhaps more important to the Texans were the desertions and defections in Cos's ranks provoked by Mexicans sympathetic to the Texans. José María González, an army colonel with federalist sympathies, "distributed leaflets within San Antonio, exhorting Cos's troops to desert and join the fight for freedom. His efforts succeeded: Some 250 cavalrymen sent out to escort reinforcements simply did not come back."[161] Before returning to New Orleans, José Antonio Mejía contributed to the Texan victory. In a strongly worded proclamation, Mejía urged Cos's troops to lay down their arms because they had been deceived into thinking the Texans wanted to separate Texas from Mexico. All they wanted, according to Mejía, was a return to the Constitution of 1824 so "that the nation may enjoy liberty and that the power of a dictator should not impose upon us the yoke of slavery."[162] Mejía may have been deluding himself with respect to the Texans' intentions, but the fact is, his exhortations and those of González contributed to the desertion of several hundred of Cos's men and the defection of some to the Texas ranks. It was these defections, in the words of historian Vito Alessio Robles, that provoked so much "disorder and discouragement" in the ranks of the santanista general. The last straw was when Cos ordered four cavalry companies to the Alamo and they failed to show up. He surrendered shortly thereafter.[163]

Two aspects of the siege of Bexar deserve mention. One is that if it had not succeeded, the battle of the Alamo, which occurred three months later, might never have taken place. Cos would have remained in possession of the town. However, it did succeed, in good measure due to the support of Mexican Texans. This raises the second point: It is likely that most of the Mexican Texans who participated in the siege did not know they were fighting for Texas independence. Their fight was against the despotism of Santa Anna, and Cos, his brother-in-law, was a vivid symbol. Moreover, the Texans had not yet revealed their hand. If Mejía suspected by early December that they were fighting to separate Texas from Mexico, he did not say so to his fellow Mexicans. He continued to think—or at least to say publicly—that they were fighting for federalism and the Constitution of 1824.

After the siege of Bexar, Mexican participation in the rebellion was considerably more limited. Eight Mexicans, including Gregorio Esparza, died alongside their Anglo comrades defending the Alamo on March 6, 1836.[164] A few days earlier, on March 1, three Mexicans, Lorenzo de Zavala, José Antonio Navarro, and José Francisco Ruiz, had signed the Texas Declaration of Independence at the tiny settlement of Washington on the Brazos. Juan Seguín supported his Texan allies and, with a company of men, provided valuable services to the Alamo defenders. He and his company, some twenty-five men, also fought with Houston's troops at San Jacinto.[165]

Mexican cooperation with the Anglo-Texans in their struggle for independence should not be overemphasized. Most Mexicans had conflicting loyalties. The Esparza family is a good example: Gregorio died in the Alamo defending the Texan cause, while his brother Francisco fought with Santa Anna against the Texans.[166] Mexican Texans, like many of their kinsmen of Northeast Mexico typically fought for freedom and federalism; only a few were committed to Texas independence. They opposed the despotic government of Santa Anna, but were increasingly uncomfortable with the Anglo numerical superiority that was rapidly converting them into an unwelcome minority in their own homeland. What was worse, many of the recent Anglo newcomers were adventurers and extremists motivated by racial hatred and the desire to seize Texas from Mexico's grip. With each approaching step of Santa Anna's army, Mexican Texans were faced with what David Weber describes as two "unhappy alternatives—domination by Anglo-Americans or domination by the centralist dictatorship." Because of these conflicting loyalties many Mexican Texans did not take sides. They sought to protect their families, remained neutral, "cooperated with the group in charge at the moment, and hoped for an end to the nightmare."[167] This neutrality provoked the hostility of many Anglo-Texans, who used it as a pretext for committing abuses against the Mexican population after independence.

～

Early in the nineteenth century, after Mexico's independence, Anglo-Americans and Europeans in search of opportunity began to settle in the region of the lower Rio Grande. Many of them were merchants who established themselves in the newly opened port of Matamoros; others ventured into interior towns such as Monclova, Monterrey, and Saltillo. With their energy and enterprise, these traders contributed to opening the region to a broader world. Among the foreigners were medical doctors who melded easily into a racially mixed population that was socially stratified but culturally unified by language and religion. This northern province was under constant siege by hostile Indigenous tribes—Comanches and Apaches—that swept down from the southern plains of the United States in search of mules, horses, and human captives. Because Mexico's central government was far away and largely incapable of defending its northern territories, the task of frontier defense was left mostly to the pobladores. Indian raids were largely motivated by a market for plundered goods, part of the clandestine economy that involved Native Americans, Anglos, and Mexicans.

The province of Texas received a steady stream of Anglo settlers who established common ground with the local Mexican population but experienced growing differences with the Mexican national government, especially in the areas of slavery and commerce. Most of the vecinos of the frontier rejected Mexico's restrictive commercial policy, and they responded by joining their Anglo and European neighbors in lucrative activities such as contraband and land speculation, two facets of the vast clandestine economy that became a hallmark of the border region. These activities intensified the contacts and exchanges between the native population and foreign immigrants at a time when the Texas colonists were growing increasingly restive under Mexican rule and moving steadily toward a confrontation with the government.

The differences sharpened with the influx of thousands of new Anglo settlers into Texas, many of them hailing from the southern states and committed to a slave economy. The efforts of the Mexican government to stop the increasing violation of its borders were met by resistance that ended in the separation of Texas. Racial and cultural differences between Anglos and Mexicans were factors in the separation of Texas from Mexico, but more important were issues of local autonomy. As Santa Anna's army marched north to crush the rebellion in Texas, Mexicans in the province faced a difficult choice. Some joined with the Texans in resisting the Mexican government and played an important role in the movement, especially during the siege of Bexar in December 1835, in one of the many instances in border history of Anglos and Mexicans joining together to fight for a common cause. Most Mexicans, however, remained neutral, especially when they discovered that the revolt was aimed at separation from Mexico. This neutrality, coupled with Santa Anna's excessive cruelty in the execution of Texas prisoners at the Alamo and Goliad hardened racial attitudes and heightened persecution against Mexicans in Texas after the war.

CHAPTER 2

Conflict and Cooperation

1837–1848

T he movement for Texas independence culminated in the battle of San Jacinto on April 21, 1836. The end of the war was not the end of the warfare, however. Armed conflict between the Mexican government and the Texans continued off and on until 1845, when the former Mexican province was annexed to the United States. During that period, Mexico and the breakaway Republic of Texas engaged in numerous skirmishes and battles that kept the Rio Grande region in turmoil. The Santa Fe, Somervell, and Mier expeditions carried out by the Texans between 1841 and 1843 and two attacks on San Antonio by the Mexican army in 1842 were the most visible episodes in a continual state of conflict. This violent period is hardly an auspicious setting in which to render an account of cooperation between Anglo-Americans and Mexicans, but that is one of the aims of this chapter. The pattern of mutually beneficial relations and interactions that had been established since the 1820s across a broad expanse of territory, especially in commerce, could not be obliterated by the political dismemberment of part of that territory or even by the continuing racially fueled violence. Many histories of the period focus on the violence and ignore or downplay the multiple forms of interethnic exchange and cooperation that took place. This section will explore both, along with the role that the border played in their development.

UNENDING VIOLENCE

A brief explanation of the conflict between Mexico and Texas will help to set the stage for the period of the Texas Republic (1836–45). In general terms, Mexico was determined to recover its lost province and Texas was just as determined to maintain its independence. This in itself was sufficient to generate conflict, but other elements were also involved. The Texans claimed all land as far south as the Rio Grande on the basis of the Treaty of Velasco signed by Santa Anna, a treaty that the Mexican government rejected. So the issue was framed in simple terms: Would Mexico accept Texas's independence? And, was the boundary the Rio Grande, as Texas wanted, or the Nueces River, as Mexico insisted? Moreover, the hostility and hatred generated by the war, coupled with the neutrality most Mexican Texans maintained in that conflict, led many Anglo-Texans to persecute them and to use fraud, coercion, and violence to despoil them of their land. A Texas army that included many rowdy and fractious volunteers arrived in Goliad in 1836 and began to evict Mexican families from their homes. The story was repeated in Nacogdoches, where Mexican families were "robbed of their livestock, grain, and belongings." Throughout most of Texas, according to one historian, "Anglos flooded in and took the ranches, the livestock, and indeed the livelihood" of the Mexicans. Some Mexicans fled to Louisiana, others to Mexico. The state of Coahuila received many of these emigrants and petitioned the Mexican government for relief on their behalf.[1]

Some Mexicans chose to stay and fight. Vicente Córdova, who had been alcalde of Nacogdoches, gathered a force of Mexicans and Cherokees, about four hundred in strength, and rose up against the Texans in August 1838. The Córdova rebellion, it became clear later, had been supported by the Mexican government. Córdova was incited to revolt by santanista general Vicente Filisola, perhaps because the latter had a huge land grant in Texas that was now threatened by the loss of Mexican sovereignty over the region. However, Córdova was also responding to the Anglo attacks on Mexican property and the shrinking opportunities for Mexicans in the new order. Whatever caused it, his movement was crushed, and the Mexican population of the region was compelled to submit to Anglo domination.[2]

The Córdova revolt had another effect: it stoked Texans' fears of an attack from Mexico. The president of Texas, Mirabeau Buonaparte Lamar, faithful to his middle name, struck first. Desirous of consolidating his claim to the far northwest reaches of Texas and extending its dominion to the Pacific Ocean, Lamar organized an expedition of 321 men to march to Santa Fe, in the Mexican province of New Mexico, in the middle of a hot summer in 1841. A large group of merchants accompanied the expedition, seeking to extend Texan trade to the region and to give the venture a veneer of legitimacy. After tramping through rough country; getting lost and finding their way again; and suffering Indian harassment, hunger, and thirst; the Santa Fe "Pioneers" finally arrived in New Mexican territory, where the forces of Governor Manuel Armijo promptly captured them. The prisoners were subjected to a long and painful march to Mexico City and received brutal treatment from some of their captors.[3]

One of the participants in the Santa Fe expedition, George Wilkins Kendall, a reporter for the New Orleans *Picayune*, wrote a book that was widely disseminated. Kendall's account stressed the cruel treatment of the prisoners and fomented hostility against Mexico in Texas and the United States. One of his stories concerns fellow prisoner John McAllister, a young man from Tennessee who had sprained his ankle, was in terrible pain, and could not continue at the pace of his fellow prisoners. His tormentor, a Captain Salazar, described by Kendall as a bloodthirsty savage, shot him down in cold blood when the man refused to march. This account and many others like it pictured the Mexicans as cruel and savage.[4]

Lamar's objectives were thwarted, but his actions provoked a cycle of violence that caused more bitterness and hatred. Joseph M. Nance affirms that the Texas president's "poor judgment . . . unleashed a chain of events that brought the first significant body of Mexican troops into Texas since the battle of San Jacinto." Nance refers to two Mexican invasions that occurred in 1842.[5] Mexicans were indignant that filibusters had invaded their territory and Texans were incensed over the treatment of the Santa Fe prisoners. As antagonism was growing on both sides, Santa Anna returned to power in 1841 and vowed to reconquer Texas. In March 1842, General Rafael Vázquez led several hundred troops into Texas and held San Antonio less than a week before retreating to the Rio Grande. A few months later, on September 11, Mexican General Adrián Woll headed a larger invasion. He encountered armed resistance, particularly at the battle of Salado Creek, which forced him to abandon San Antonio on September 20. Woll brought back to Mexico fifty-two captives who were imprisoned at the infamous Perote jail, a flea- and rat-infested dungeon where the Santa Fe prisoners were also held. Among those prisoners were San Antonio civic leaders and businessmen such as Samuel A. Maverick, John Twohig, and Duncan C. Ogden who, despite their terrible experience, would play important roles in promoting commerce with Mexico years later.[6]

The two Mexican invasions of 1842 provoked outcries for swift and energetic revenge against Mexico.[7] Historian Sam W. Haynes asserts most Texans wanted war with Mexico in order "to settle the matter once and for all. Recklessly, impulsively, they howled for war."[8] Hundreds of armed volunteers quickly gathered at San Antonio and President Houston ordered General Alexander Somervell to lead an expedition to the border to punish Mexico. This was the beginning of the Somervell expedition, which metamorphosed into the Mier expedition.

Somervell and his 750 men descended upon Laredo, whose Mexican population was probably not aware that they had become Texas citizens in 1836 by virtue of Texas's territorial claims. The inhabitants welcomed the expedition on December 8 and "declared themselves to be friends of the Americans." What they received in return was the sacking of the town by discontented soldiers who were more interested in plunder than vindicating the honor of Texas. Somervell apologized to the townspeople, but a pattern of insubordination of his men had been set. Some of his troops abandoned the campaign at that point and Somervell continued downriver, crossed the Rio Grande, and occupied the town of Guerrero. Short of rations and unable to obtain provisions from the Mexican population, he decided that his expedition was heading for disaster and ordered his troops to return to San Antonio. This order provoked a mutiny because the majority of the adventurers insisted on continuing. Somervell returned home with some 189 men, while another 308 men, led by William S. Fisher, continued on to the town of Mier. Thus began the Mier expedition.[9]

By the time Fisher and his men reached Mier from the west, a large Mexican force led by General Pedro de Ampudia was arriving from the east. The Texans attacked the town on Christmas Day 1842, and fought from noon of that day until the following day, when they were overpowered by sheer numbers. They were forced to surrender and marched under guard to Matamoros and thence to Monterrey and Mexico City. Something occurred along the way that made the trip infamous. On February 11, 1843, beyond Saltillo, at a place named Salado, which means "salty" in Spanish and also "unlucky" in popular jargon, most of the Texans made their escape. In their effort to reach the Rio Grande, they became separated and got lost. Only three succeeded in reaching the river, while 176 were recaptured. As punishment for their escape, they were subjected to a terrifying lottery in which each man drew a bean from a pot. Most of the beans were white, but one out of ten, seventeen, were black. If a man chose one of the black beans, he was marked for death. This gruesome event became known as the Black Bean Episode and was broadly publicized in Texas and the United States as another example of Mexican barbarity.[10]

The violent events that followed the Santa Fe expedition: the Mexican incursion into Texas, the Somervell and Mier expeditions, and the Black Bean Episode, had a poisonous effect on race relations. Moreover, these events occurred at a time when Texas, like most of the United States, was suffering from the lingering effects of the Panic of 1837. James E. Crisp argues that the renewed conflict with Mexico at a time when Texas was bankrupt and weak militarily "also contributed to a reemerging Texan self-image as a besieged bastion of white civilization surrounded by barbarians."[11] In Mexico, anti-Texan sentiment had been growing since 1836. The separation of that province provoked nationalist outcries in government publications. The *Semanario Político*, official newspaper of Nuevo León, called the Texans "ungrateful, immoral, and alien riffraff, bereft of conscience and devoid of honor." The Mexican public was told that these "vagabonds, adventurers, and cannibals" sooner or later would try to take over the whole country, and the people were encouraged to mobilize to defend the nation.[12]

Despite the heated rhetoric there is no evidence that anyone except political and military leaders took seriously the possibility of going to war against the Texans. On a personal level many Texans and Mexicans continued to cultivate friendly relations, even within the context of the ongoing violence. The treatment of the Santa Fe prisoners is a case in point. The story that was disseminated in Texas and the United States and which has been passed down to us in the present day is a narrative of Mexican cruelty and barbarism. Largely hidden in the interior pages of a Mexican newspaper is a different version, known to only a few participants and readers, and ignored by a broader American public, swept away by the eloquent tale told by the master publicist George Wilkins Kendall. Two of the Santa Fe prisoners, Commissioners Richard F. Brenham and William G. Cooke, wrote a letter to the governor of Chihuahua, Francisco García Conde, which was published in the Mexico City daily *Siglo Diez y Nueve*. Brenham and Cooke expressed "sincere feelings of gratitude . . . for the generous manifestation of kindness and courtesy" that was extended to them by the government and people of Chihuahua. "The liberality which has been displayed to our destitute soldiers, in supplying them with the comforts and necessaries of life and the kind hospitality that has been extended to us all, individually and collectively, has almost caused us to forget the misfortunes that have assailed us since we left our country."[13]

The two commissioners also expressed the hope that "our relative situation as national enemies, will be changed by the establishment of peace and amity between Mexico and Texas; when an intimate social and commercial intercourse may arise between our respective countries, that will remove the prejudice and animosity that do now, and have heretofore existed mutually among our people, and cause feelings of friendship to be substituted for those of hostility."[14] Governor

García Conde thanked the two commissioners for the "gratitude and recognition" they expressed toward the people of Chihuahua. Chihuahuenses, he wrote, "have done no more than that which is inspired by humanity and that which is expected from its spirit of philanthropy and civilization, as they are convinced that a prisoner is no longer an enemy and . . . deserves the same consideration as a stranger or someone in misfortune." The exchange of letters occurred in late October 1841, but was not published until May 1842, after the New Orleans *Picayune* published reports of the brutal treatment meted out to "citizens of the United States [who were captured] traveling peacefully and legally from Texas to Santa Fe." The editor of *Siglo Diez y Nueve* declared his intention of refuting the lies and slander propagated by American newspapers about the Santa Fe prisoners.[15] This little-known episode reveals that beneath the visible surface of hostility, members of both races—Anglo-Texans and Mexicans—desired to get along and to explore avenues of friendship and mutually beneficial exchange. It also helps explain why little effort was required to get the two peoples interested in resuming their commercial relations.

INCESSANT COMMERCE

Scarcely more than a year had passed after Santa Anna's humiliating defeat at San Jacinto when a revealing proclamation appeared in the Villas del Norte. It was signed by Vicente Filisola, the Mexican general who oversaw the withdrawal of the Mexican army from Texas after the battle. Filisola declared that he had become aware of the "scandalous traffic" that the vecinos of the border region were carrying on with the inhabitants of Texas. They received tobacco, merchandise, and foodstuffs and exported horses, mules, and other provisions in what he perceived as "a criminal and treasonous violation of the law." He prohibited Mexicans from crossing to the other side of the river unless they had a ranch on the left bank and then only with authorization from local authorities. And he warned violators that they would face the death penalty if they shared any kind of information with the enemy.[16]

Filisola had cause for concern. The Mexican government and its emissaries in northern Mexico were still at war with Texas and bent on subjugating and reincorporating the breakaway province, but these were not issues that mattered to the majority of people in the border region. At the close of 1838, the *Matagorda Bulletin* announced that "trading parties of Mexicans from Laredo and other Rio Grande towns were beginning to arrive daily, first, at San Antonio and, later, at Goliad, Victoria, Matagorda, Lamar, San Patricio, Houston, and other points, bringing in specie, horses, sugar and flour which they exchanged for tobacco, various items of merchandise," and other goods, including firearms.[17] A Houston newspaper reported that the traders were patient and friendly, and "showed that they were desirous to renew their former intimate connections with our citizens. There was a cheering prospect that a friendly intercourse would gradually extend into the interior of Chihuahua and Tamaulipas, and eventually pave the way for a lasting peace."[18] These expressions of friendship and trade with Mexico appeared less than two years after the battle of the Alamo, the massacre at Goliad, and the hatred against Mexicans that these events engendered. The resumption of friendly relations would be repeated time and time again in the border region. In the face of wars, racial hatred, and many other obstacles, commercial exchange at times suffered temporary interruptions, but always resumed.

During the Texas Republic this pattern is amply demonstrated in the development of commerce on three fronts: Santa Fe–Chihuahua, Matamoros, and the Villas del Norte. Much as Francis Stillman and Daniel Smith used New Orleans as a springboard to arrive at Matamoros, William Becknell, Charles Bent, and other merchants used Saint Louis as a platform for extending their commercial operations to Santa Fe, New Mexico, in the early 1820s. The governor of the province, Facundo Melgares, welcomed Becknell in 1821 and told him "that he welcomed trade with the Americans" and had no objections to their settling in the region. It became clear that the "Americans were as eager to sell as Mexicans were to buy." By the following year, Becknell and other merchants set out from Missouri and established the Santa Fe Trail. Among them was Charles Bent, who built a fort near Taos and married a Mexican woman. The Anglo-American merchants took with them "cargoes of textiles, lead, hardware, cutlery, glassware, and similar goods" and brought back "silver, mules, pelts and hides, blankets, and other items in demand on the East Coast." By the 1830s the Santa Fe Trail had become perhaps the most important overland commercial circuit between Mexico and the United States.[19]

Like a relentless wave, Anglo-Americans did not stop at Santa Fe. In their drive to find bigger markets they "began to look southward toward . . . Chihuahua, Durango, Zacatecas, and Sonora." Offering many more potential clients than Santa Fe and located in the center of a rich silver-mining region, Chihuahua became the preferred destination of these determined traders. "By the 1830s, over half of the goods entering New Mexico over the Santa Fe Trail continued to Chihuahua and points beyond." The Anglo-American traders found more than markets, however; they discovered silver, a commodity that, because of its scarcity, was highly valued on the U.S. frontier. David Weber asserts that in "the early 1830s the silver peso, which was roughly equivalent in silver content to the United States dollar, had become the chief medium of exchange in Missouri and had helped to stabilize the monetary system of all of America's western states and territories." In time, a constant stream of silver flowed from the mines of Chihuahua and was conveyed toward the United States. It could well be said that those were the mines that launched a thousand wagons.[20]

The Santa Fe–Chihuahua trade attracted a hardy breed of men, accustomed to hardship and danger. Josiah Gregg, Henry Skillman, James Wiley Magoffin, and many others plied the lonely roads and faced the ever-present risk of hostile Indians and other predators. Some of these merchants established stores in Chihuahua. Magoffin, who had lived in Matamoros and served as U.S. consul at Saltillo, made Chihuahua his base of operations by the late 1830s. He was there in time to meet the Santa Fe prisoners on their long march south to Mexico City. "Don Santiago" shared with them "coffee and tobacco, and gave them food and champagne."[21] The profits to be made were a major incentive for these men. The value of the trade in the 1830s and early 1840s has been estimated at $150,000 to $250,000 a year, and by 1846, it may have been as high as $1,000,000.[22]

From an early date this lucrative trade drew attention in Texas. Stephen F. Austin knew that Chihuahua was much closer to Texas than Missouri and he expressed the hope that "the whole trade of the Chihuahua and Sonora and New Mexico regions must ultimately enter in one of the ports of Texas."[23] Juan Almonte shared Austin's vision. After his inspection of Texas in 1834, he wrote that "if the road between Cópano [on the Texas coast above Corpus Christi] and Bexar were to be extended as far as Chihuahua, there would be undoubtedly an immense trade between this department and the states of Durango, Chihuahua, and New Mexico."[24] Texas merchants, among them H. A. Gilpin and John Linn, reached out to Chihuahua. As early as 1834, Linn made a trip to that state and sold his entire stock to men working the mines, for which he was paid in silver bars. Few others emulated him because of the lack of an adequate road. Years later, San Antonio and Austin merchants financed various exploratory trips in search of an adequate route to Chihuahua by way of El Paso.[25]

Merchants of Chihuahua were also reaching out to the east to extend their trade. In 1839 the citizens of Shreveport, Louisiana, were startled to see a large group of Mexican traders, who had traveled north from Chihuahua to El Paso del Norte then headed east across Texas to Fort Towson, Arkansas, a journey of six hundred miles, in forty days. These daring Mexicans navigated this route without guides, relying only on a chart and compass. They "brought with them nearly a half million in silver bullion which was transported partly on mules and partly by wagons." Most important, they demonstrated that a direct route from Texas to Chihuahua was feasible, which spurred the desire of many Texans for a direct commercial connection to that state.[26]

At about the same time, an Anglo-American merchant residing in Chihuahua believed that he could shorten the route to Texas and Louisiana even further by bypassing El Paso and cutting across Presidio del Norte, in the Big Bend region. Henry C. Connelly, who had received his medical degree in Kentucky, ventured to Chihuahua, where he became a merchant and freighter. Having married a Spanish woman and lived in Chihuahua for twenty years he "was accepted as a Mexican businessman of acumen and good repute."[27] In 1839 Connelly and two other merchants formed a caravan that "included about a half dozen proprietors, fifty dragoons furnished by the governor as a military escort, and enough cart drivers, herdsmen, foragers, and servants to round out over a hundred men altogether." Some seven hundred mules were used to carry about $300,000 in silver bars and coins (approximately $6.6 million in today's dollars) to the United States and return with manufactured goods. Connelly obtained permission from Chihuahuan authorities for his venture. Since Presidio del Norte was not an official port of entry, Governor José María Irigoyen de la O assured him that he would facilitate his reentry into Chihuahua at that point and would charge only a nominal duty.[28]

The caravan arrived at Red River in 1840, and it is interesting to observe how the people there treated the party of Mexicans. Connelly wrote that "our Mexican friends, notwithstanding the hostile attitude in which the two countries stood toward each other, were treated with a kindness which they still recollect with the warmest feelings of gratitude." It seems clear that "the spending of a quarter of a million dollars in hard silver among those money-starved communities" was a strong incentive for cordial relations. Connelly's role is also notable. Like other Anglo-Americans and Europeans who ventured into the borderlands, he served as a bridge between the different ethnic groups of the region.[29]

When Connelly returned to Chihuahua, he was at the head of sixty to eighty wagons and about two hundred people, including even a circus. He ran into bad luck, however. A new governor—more nationalistic and less indulgent toward the Americans—impounded the goods until the requisite duties were paid, making the business unprofitable.[30] This occurred in 1840–41 when a state of war existed between Mexico and the Texas Republic, and the fact that so many people were willing to join Connelly and venture into a territory of a nation whose army was sworn to combat the Anglo presence was either the triumph of hope over reality or a sober assessment that matters were not that bad and could be worked out to the satisfaction (and benefit) of everyone concerned. Moreover, the fact that the undertaking failed does not alter the reality that cooperation for profit was the goal and such cooperation could be established despite ethnic and racial differences.

The second commercial front of importance during the Texas Republic was the port of Matamoros, which had prospered in the decade before Texas independence. After 1836, however, Matamoros ceased to flourish. One historian writes that "the decade from 1835 to 1845 was a period of economic stagnation and even retrogression." Exports declined from $625,515 in 1828 to $481,277 in 1842. Income from duties had been more than a million pesos in 1834–35, but by 1842 was only 262,227 pesos. This blow to the finances of the national government aggravated other problems, such as defense against Indian depredations in northern Mexico. The population also declined from a high of 16,372 in 1837 to only 7,000 by 1846. The decreasing trade had an important effect on the Anglo-American presence. Only about twenty Anglos remained by November 1837.[31]

The commercial decline of Matamoros during the decade of the Texas Republic had many causes. The protectionist policies established by the Mexican government in the 1820s were reinforced after centralism was imposed in the mid-1830s. The authorities closely watched ports such as Matamoros, and although there was evasion, corruption, and contraband, the high tariffs and prohibitions acted as a brake to commerce. This situation was compounded by specific events. The recent war and a brief blockade by the Texans in July and August 1836 caused antagonism toward Anglo-Americans. In turn, many Anglo-Americans, who were among the most active merchants, abandoned the port. Trade through Matamoros suffered another setback when the French navy blockaded the port in the last six months of 1838 because of the "Pastry War" between France and Mexico. In 1844, a devastating hurricane leveled brick houses in Matamoros and caused about seventy deaths in the region. Internal wars in Mexico between federalists and centralists also had a deleterious effect because they disrupted silver production in the mining regions and exposed merchants and shippers to confiscations. To this dreary list must be added Indian raids, which were a constant until the 1870s. As will be seen though, the raids made commerce more dangerous but did not prevent it.[32]

Although commerce declined in Matamoros, this does not mean the town was lifeless. It continued to be a vital component of the economic life of Northeast

Mexico. This was evidenced in 1841 when General Mariano Arista, the regional military commander, obtained permission from the central government to introduce a sizable cargo of cotton thread for which he hoped to obtain urgently needed funds from local merchants. Producers and merchants in Mexico City howled in protest that this shipment posed a "threat to the prevailing economic rules"—meaning that it threatened their monopoly. A year later, as a result of pressure from the same merchants, the government considered closing the ports of Matamoros, Mazatlán, and Guaymas. When word of this proposal reached Saltillo, the ayuntamiento protested energetically. The measure, it declared, "would effectively cause the ruin of a considerable part of the commerce of many towns." It would also provoke "an extraordinary increase in the price of goods" and an escalation of the contraband traffic. The proposal was finally withdrawn.[33]

Trade through Matamoros, while diminished, did continue, and what was lost through this vital artery was offset by a third commercial front which included routes that originated in or crossed the Villas del Norte. These interior routes became important circuits for commerce between Texas and Northeast Mexico during the Texas Republic. Filisola's order of 1837 banning trade from the Villas del Norte, like all orders of this nature, was ignored by the residents. By the following summer, two government officials reported to Filisola, now minister of war and navy, that exchange with the Texans continued unabated. General Francisco González Pavón, military chief of the Tamaulipas border, wrote that the vecinos "carried on a commerce so bountiful that it was sufficient to fill them with riches." The absence of hard money was not a problem. They obtained Texas merchandise through "an exchange of horses, mules, and cattle, which are abundant in these lands."[34]

By December 1838 and through the early months of 1839, commerce increased and became more open. Mexican traders arrived at San Antonio, Matagorda, "and other points farther east, [with] beans, flour, leather, piloncill[o]s, shoes, saddles, and specie, which they exchanged for calico, bleached and unbleached cloth, tobacco, American hardware, and other commodities."[35] One of the points farther east was a new and growing town on Buffalo Bayou. In April 1839, "a large caravan departed from Houston to the west with some ten to fifteen thousand dollars' worth of goods, while another came into town the next day to obtain supplies for the Mexican market."[36] Much of the trade emanating from or passing through the Villas del Norte was bartered. However, barter was soon augmented by specie that merchants brought in from Chihuahua, most of it probably through Presidio del Norte. The Houston *Telegraph and Texas Register* reported the arrival of "large quantities of silver . . . from Chihuahua. One trader arrived with $17,000 in specie, and it was estimated in May 1839 that goods valued between $100,000 and $150,000 could be sold immediately at Béxar for specie or bullion."[37]

Two developments that contributed to the growing trade between Texas and northern Mexico were triggered from far away: one was the deplorable economic situation in Texas as a result of the national Panic of 1837; the other was a federalist uprising in Northeast Mexico provoked by the imposition of centralist policies in Mexico after 1835. The severe economic crisis after 1837 left Texas "virtually impoverished." Henry Smith, the treasurer appointed by newly elected president Sam Houston, found that "the treasury was empty, the new nation's credit was in low repute, money was scarce." Smith had no money even to buy official stationery with which to perform his duties.[38] The Texas government recognized that gold and silver from Mexico could revitalize the economy. Accordingly, the third congress adopted a resolution on January 26, 1839, "providing that the president be authorized to give every encouragement and support, consistent with the nation's safety, to trade between the western settlements of Texas and those of Mexico on and beyond the Rio Grande." The new president, Mirabeau B. Lamar, quickly signed a proclamation on February 21, opening the commerce of Texas with Northeast Mexico.[39]

If Texans needed the trade, the federalists of Mexico's Northeast who rose up against the central government desired it even more. The uprising originated in Tampico, where General José Urrea, perhaps the only Mexican military man admired for his role in the Texas war, led the revolt in October 1838. It quickly spread northward to the Villas del Norte and included towns in Nuevo León and Coahuila. Caudillos, or regional leaders, such as Antonio Canales and José María González, were joined by other political leaders in a rebellion that kept the region in a state of upheaval throughout 1839 and 1840. Jesús Cárdenas, another organizer of the movement, issued a decree in June 1839 that appealed deeply and directly to the interests of the border communities. He accused the national government of instigating their ruin by prohibiting trade with Texas. Alcaldes of the region under federalist control would grant passes allowing merchants and producers to travel to Texas with their goods. Through this policy, federalist leaders hoped to achieve two goals: gain the support of border residents; and gain access to arms and economic support in Texas for their movement. Antonio Canales wrote to President Lamar, expressing his desire to work together toward peace and mutual support and proposing a system of free trade with the Texans. Part of that mutual support included joint combat against Indian raiders.[40]

The revolt in Northeast Mexico, often referred to as the Federalist War, pro-
pelled commerce through interior routes extending from Presidio to the Villas del
Norte in the lower Rio Grande Valley. In December 1838, merchants "continued
to pour in from northern Coahuila and Tamaulipas." With a "friendly disposition
toward Texas and Texans," these traders reported that "the whole country along
the Río Grande [had] declared in favor of Federalism, as if this were a better
reason than ever why they should be kindly received in Texas." Dr. Horace A.
Alsbury, whose Mexican wife had survived the siege of the Alamo, reported that
these men shared the federalist propensities of the Texans. Moreover, since the
Mexican government had failed to eliminate the Indian menace, they were ready
"to make common cause with our citizens against the savages."[41]

By December 1839, Mexican traders had reached the city of Austin in central
Texas, taking cattle and *piloncillo*, a cone-shaped piece of compacted, unrefined
brown sugar that was consumed all over northern Mexico. The following year
the *Austin City Gazette* reported that merchants had arrived "with 170 head of
cattle and a number of mules and some specie, the whole of which they have left
among us, purchasing goods and groceries in exchange." In early 1841, fifty-seven
traders from Chihuahua were in Austin, prepared to trade 50,000 silver pesos
for merchandise.[42] Some of these traders passed through Laredo, a key link in
the interior trade, connecting Bexar, the most populous commercial center in
Texas, with Mexico's Northeast.

The commercial axis that connected Laredo and Bexar was complemented
by a route that crossed the arid Nueces Strip and linked the Villas del Norte—
including Laredo—with the region around Refugio and a trading post established in September 1839 by Henry Lawrence Kinney and William P. Aubrey
that was destined to become the city of Corpus Christi. Refugio County was
home to many merchants who had lived or traded in Mexico. These men were
sympathetic to the federalists, many of whom they had known for years, and
they were more than willing to help them, especially if doing so could further
their own interests. Kinney and Aubrey were newcomers, but they built their
ranch and trading post on the south side of the Nueces River (a circumstance
that was used later to justify Texas's claim to the disputed region between the
Nueces and the Rio Grande) and proceeded to expand a growing contraband
trade that had been carried out before them by John Linn, Noah Smithwick,
and others. Kinney soon bought out Aubrey's share of the business. In a dangerous territory in a time of war, it took courage just to survive, but Kinney
did more than that.[43]

Aware that his trading post was on a precarious legal footing, Kinney traveled to Matamoros and met with General Mariano Arista. The military commander apparently gave him permission to engage in commerce because Kinney began to make improvements at his ranch. Since Arista was a sworn enemy of the Texans, we can only admire Kinney's special talent in persuading him to allow an Anglo-American to engage in commerce at a place hotly disputed by the Mexican government. There may however be another explanation. It is believed that Arista and Kinney cooperated in the contraband trade. If true, this may explain how on a soldier's salary Arista amassed extensive landholdings in Nuevo León and a palatial mansion in Monterrey, which impressed the American soldiers who conquered the city in the U.S.-Mexican War. Alessio Robles includes Arista among "the plague of deal-making, profiteering generals who carved out fortunes at the expense of the misery of officers and soldiers or by use of shady speculations in the customhouses."[44]

We may never know whether Arista was in fact engaged in smuggling. What is known is that he took a firm public stand against it. On April 13, 1841, he issued a scorching proclamation that inveighed against "the scandalous commerce that the *vecinos* of the border were carrying out with the Texans, who were enemies of the Republic" and warned offenders that, if caught, their goods and beasts of burden would be confiscated and they would be forced to serve for ten years in a frontier company of the army.[45] Threats that those who traded with the Texans would be punished with forced military service were common, but General Adrián Woll, the military commander who had invaded Texas in 1842, went even further. He "decreed that any individual found more than one league north of the left bank of the Rio Bravo would be arrested—or shot on the spot." This ridiculous order would have made it impossible for landowners to visit their ranches north of the river.[46] Official documents reveal that these threats did nothing to impede the trade. After citizens of Laredo ignored the military's threats and traveled to Texas to exchange their cattle for badly needed goods, the local military commander angrily accused residents of treason because "forgetting the label of *mexicanos*, they continued trading with the enemies of the nation, protecting them with clandestine commerce . . . and in fact, recognizing the independence of Texas."[47]

Smuggling to Survive

Faced with the threats and prohibitions of the central government, norteños responded in the usual manner: by resorting to smuggling. If it was pervasive in the period prior to 1836, it became even more widespread during the years of the Texas Republic. Based on information from observers and the government officials who had to deal with it, historians have tried to estimate the number of people involved. Historian Joseph B. Wilkinson believes that "over 15,000 Mexicans, operating all along the river and deep into Mexico—as far south, probably, as [Ciudad] Victoria and San Luis Potosi—were engaged in the smuggler's trade." Another estimate is that by 1844 some 16,500 Mexicans were involved in the contraband trade.[48]

The involvement of so many people is not surprising considering that contraband was an important part of their livelihood. This is what Miguel González Taméz told the judge at his trial for smuggling three packs of tobacco. He left his home in Cadereyta, Nuevo León, "to traffic in this product to help him to subsist," but he was caught and taken before the revenue collector of Marín, the town where he was taken. González Taméz complained to the judge that the collector, Juan González, not only confiscated the tobacco, he also kept the man's horse, saddle, and weapons. González Taméz's appeal succeeded only partially. Everything was returned to him except the tobacco, which was sold at public auction. José María Castro and Alejos Cadena suffered a similar fate. After their two barrels of tobacco were confiscated in Vallecillo, they returned to Agualeguas, where they were known as "vecinos who were notoriously poor."[49]

A much bigger shipment was seized in Vallecillo, near the Texas border. Luciano de la Garza and Waldo González of Villaldama were imprisoned for having in their possession twenty-one packs of tobacco, articles of clothing, raw cotton, and other items that they had obtained in Texas. They appealed to the judge to allow them to go free on bail because their incarceration was causing great hardship to their families. From their declarations it is clear that they were common rural people who were simply trying to augment their income by engaging in the contraband trade.[50]

Court records also demonstrate that women had a role in smuggling. In December 1843, Juan Othon, revenue collector of Monterrey, reported that he had levied a fine of 1,200 pesos on Faustino Villarreal, Alejandro García, and the latter's wife, Prudencia. They had confessed to having in their possession about six hundred pounds of tobacco "that was confiscated at Puerto de la Gacha [and] that they had hauled from the border." Another case was that of María del Rosario Pérez of Cadereyta. She was fined forty-eight pesos and five reales when she was discovered in possession of twenty-four pounds of tobacco in a chamois suitcase. Another case involving a woman caused a public uproar when agents of the national government tried to confiscate contraband tobacco hidden in various houses in Linares, Nuevo León. Of the four houses searched in Linares, three had contraband tobacco. Lázaro Villarreal and his wife, María, won over the crowd when they defied the agents, flaunting a tobacco leaf at them and claiming that there were nine hundred kilos inside the house. The crowd cheered the woman after she yelled at the hated agents that they were thieves.[51]

One of the most celebrated cases in Nuevo León involved Lucinda Griggi. The case began with the confiscation of more than twenty-four thousand spools of cotton thread found in the store of Valentín Rivero, a prominent Spanish merchant. Rivero denied that the merchandise was his, declaring that "it was public knowledge that Mrs. Griggi had brought it into the city." Griggi, who was thirty-something years of age, was a native of France and had connections in high places. Sources differ on whether she was the wife or concubine of the Franco-Mexican general Adrián Woll, but it was public knowledge that Woll provided the lady with an armed escort instructed to evade the customs guards. Griggi defended herself, stating that Rivero was in fact the owner of the merchandise, but he had not paid for it yet. Moreover, she argued that it wasn't contraband because it had entered the country as part of the special permit that Mariano Arista had obtained from the federal government to import cotton thread. The judge declared both parties guilty, stating that the prohibition on that type of merchandise was still in effect.[52]

The contraband from Texas that entered cities of the interior such as Monterrey usually passed through the Villas del Norte, where government officials were either complicit or powerless to stop it. Rancho Las Tortillas, upriver from Guerrero, was one of the most important crossing points during the Texas Republic. Rafael Uribe, an official of the Guerrero ayuntamiento and one of the town's most distinguished citizens, complained bitterly of the "scandalous smuggling that the bad Mexicans are carrying on with Texas" and threatened to punish the local magistrate for his absolute lack of action against smugglers. However, the same Uribe entered into an agreement with Juan N. Seguín of San Antonio to introduce contraband goods into Mexico. Seguín was associated with various businessmen in San Antonio, including the commercial and shipping firm of Howard and Ogden, and resorted to the contraband trade to recover from economic losses incurred in the Federalist War. General Mariano Arista believed Uribe was guilty of smuggling, but he also suspected the same of many other local officials and military officers.[53]

Another concern was the revenue that was lost due to smuggling. General Francisco González Pavón complained that there was no money to pay for sufficient soldiers and customs officials to police the region. What rankled military commanders the most however was the fraternization of the Mexican population with the Texans. González Pavón wrote that the frequent contact between the vecinos and Texans as a result of the trade was "creating relations and even sympathies that, because they are criminal, should be cut off at the root because they [the vecinos] will give the enemy information on the state of the army, its resources, movements, and dispositions."[54]

A Dangerous Enterprise

As if Mexican traders did not have their hands full defying their government, enduring threats from the military, and evading customs inspectors, they had to contend with the dangers of traveling through arid country peopled by hostile Indians and bands of thieves. In February 1845, the alcalde of Agualeguas, Nuevo León, reported that forty Mexican smugglers traveling near the Nueces River were attacked by a large body of Indians numbering almost one thousand. The smugglers were killed and their merchandise seized.[55]

To the traders the thieves were no less a menace than the Indians. According to historian LeRoy Graf, "the revolution had left behind a roving, lawless element which all too quickly saw its chance to get easy plunder by raiding the ox-cart and mule trains which traversed the disputed country." They were organized in bands and numbered up to three or four hundred. From Victoria County, John Linn wrote that these predators were horse and cattle thieves who stole the animals and drove them out of the region. They increasingly extended their operations to include all kinds of property, however, so in Goliad, Refugio, and Victoria Counties nobody's possessions were safe. Oftentimes, Mexican freighters and traders were victims of these predators.[56] A Texas newspaper reported that the citizens of Victoria were organizing a force of 125 volunteers to go in search of an outlaw named Córdova who had "been committing murders, depredations, and robberies along the Rio Grande, and between that river and the Nueces." Córdova's band was described as a motley group of "between fifty and a hundred men, chiefly Indians, but with them are mixed up Mexicans, mulattos, negroes, and desperate renegade Americans." Volunteers were promised a share of the spoils taken from the band. The inducement for local merchants was "to protect the Mexican trade from ruin."[57]

The situation grew considerably worse in the summer and fall of 1841. The Texas government received anguished notices from the lower Nueces that Texan depredations of Mexican caravans were paralyzing commerce. Companies of volunteers that had been organized to combat the ruffians began preying on the traders instead. One such letter to President Mirabeau B. Lamar was from S. L. Jones, who had gone to Corpus Christi Bay and with some friends had "made considerable shipments" to that place with the intention "to enter extensively into the Mexican trade." Their project was thwarted by Texan raiders and volunteer companies. Jones stated that these thieves were "exasperat[ing] the frontier settlers of the Rio Grande who are otherwise the friends of this Country."[58]

In June 1841, one of these companies robbed and killed eight Mexican traders. Anger spread through the Villas del Norte and a force of two hundred men led by Colonel Enrique Villarreal was sent to the Nueces to capture and punish the murderers. They found the band of killers led by Captain John Yerbey and proceeded to execute them. This infuriated the Americans, who retaliated, setting off a cycle of reprisals from both sides that interrupted commerce for the remainder of the year.[59] This cycle was an eerie harbinger of a phenomenon that would plague the Nueces Strip for most of the next four decades, reaching a climax during the cattle wars of the 1870s.

The road between Laredo and Bexar was only slightly safer. A band of thieves led by Agatón Quiñones preyed on the merchant caravans along that route. Numbering between one hundred and three hundred men, the band at times ventured as far south as the area of Corpus Christi. However, "the majority were bands of Americans," according to LeRoy Graf. The "robbers were usually army deserters who roamed the country in gangs of ten to one hundred men attacking all parties which seemed to promise profitable plunder."[60]

The constant threat to commerce reveals interesting examples of interethnic cooperation, both among the robber gangs and among those who combated them. It was not uncommon to see Mexicans collaborating with Anglos and Indians in criminal acts. Yerbey's band on the Nueces Strip, for example, included a Mexican guide, Tom Ca[v]azos, who was "notorious for his guiding the Americans in such enterprises." In mid-1841 a motley group of Anglos, Mexicans, and Lipan Apaches descended on Mier with the intention of plundering the town. Several of these looters were captured, including Francisco Granados and Leonardo and Agustín Garza. A fourth criminal, Melitón Contreras, was accused of spying for the Texans and executed.[61]

Oftentimes Mexicans and Anglo-Americans joined together against the robber bands. In 1836, the provisional government of Texas commissioned Jesús Cuéllar as a captain in the Cavalry Corps, whose mission was to provide frontier defense. Cuéllar had served in the Mexican military in Tamaulipas and fought with the

Texans during independence. Other Mexicans served in the Texas Rangers under John Coffee "Jack" Hays. In 1841 a group of twenty-five rangers rode out of San Antonio toward Laredo in search of Agatón Quiñones and his band. The group was mixed: twelve were Anglo-Americans and thirteen were Mexicans, led by Captain Antonio Pérez. Historian Jerry Thompson writes that "although illiterate, Pérez was well known to San Antonians as an Indian fighter." Oftentimes these forays were ineffective in combating the thieves, but quite effective in generating fear and hatred of the rangers among the Mexican population, especially the "lower class citizens of Laredo and the lower Rio Grande Valley [who] were often arrested, assaulted, and on rare occasions hanged by Rangers for what in others would be the most petty of crimes."[62]

Trade Prevails

In spite of the best efforts of law-enforcement officials on both sides of the Rio Grande, merchants and teamsters faced omnipresent danger, and it is amazing that trade continued under such conditions, but it did. This commercial activity was evident to one observer who toured the country in 1840 and wrote that although Mexico and Texas were at war, this did not appear to hinder commerce with "the states bordering upon Texas," which "were entirely friendly, and in consequence, a considerable trade was carried on with them."[63] The favorable disposition of the Texas government was a vital component, but President Lamar recognized that after the federalist revolt fizzled out at the end of 1840, the Mexican government would tighten the reins on the northern states and attempt to suppress the trade that had flourished, which is precisely what General Mariano Arista was attempting to do. Lamar took advantage of a note Arista sent him proposing that they join forces against Indians and, in June 1841, sent two emissaries, Cornelius Van Ness and John D. Norris, to Monterrey to meet with the general. The mission had various objectives: one was to agree on a strategy for ending the state of warfare and violence in the border region; another was to attempt to "establish on a firm and . . . lasting footing a safe and friendly commerce with that portion of the Mexican territory bordering on and to the westward of the Rio Grande." The third objective was strategic in nature and would be revealed later.[64]

As the commissioners neared Monterrey, they reported that the Mexican population was "anxiously praying for peace and the reopening of a safe and direct trade with Texas." Arista, however, was more cautious. He did not have the authority to enter into any kind of agreement with the Texans. Moreover, the interior trade had seriously diminished legal trade through Matamoros, severely reducing the government revenues that supported his army. Arista did assure the commissioners that no hostile movement was planned against Texas for the present and that no Texans would be interfered with east of the Rio Grande.[65]

The Texas government's promotion of trade with Northeast Mexico was a calculated strategy. Lamar hoped to promote commerce by placing a military force on the Rio Grande frontier which, aside from providing protection to commerce, would embolden federalists in Chihuahua, Coahuila, Tamaulipas, and adjoining states. In addition, it was hoped that this military force could tame Indian marauders. A Houston newspaper predicted that secure conditions would allow merchants of Northeast Mexico to trade with Bexar, Aransas, and other towns, and take back goods and manufactured items that had been prohibitively expensive due to high duties. Since "the population in those states [was] three or four times greater than that of Texas," customs duties would be voluminous and "more than sufficient to defray the expenses of the troops requisite to protect the trade."[66] The reasoning was that the trade would "prove so lucrative" that the region would be quickly settled and these settlements "would prove an impregnable rampart to Mexico." Texas thus sought to promote trade with Northeast Mexico as a strategic element in its struggle for survival. This apparently was Lamar's third objective in sending envoys to Monterrey to see Arista.[67]

Independent of the strategic interests of their government, most Texans who lived near the border region were in favor of continued commerce with the northern Mexican states, according to General Hansbrough Bell. When Lamar sent him to make an inspection of the frontier in October 1841, Bell learned that recent depredations by raiders from south of the Rio Grande had provoked general hostility toward Mexicans. As a result there was a group of Anglos that favored expulsion of the Mexicans and their commerce. He reported however that there was another, larger group who could distinguish between predators and friendly Mexicans desirous of peaceful coexistence. This second group considered that "the friendly rancheros and others of unsuspicious character engaged in trade should be permitted to continue that trade, while all others should be annihilated or expelled beyond the Río Bravo."[68] Bell explained that many of the frontier citizens had developed a certain dependence on commerce with Mexico: "Most of them ride Spanish horses and mules, with Spanish Saddles—wear Mexican Blankets, and it is not unusual to see and handle Mexican *Plata* [silver]; all procured in the way of Trade." He concluded that the deployment of a military force on the frontier would protect and increase commerce and would offer various advantages that would help dissipate the remaining opposition to the trade.[69]

The growing interdependence of Anglo-Texans and Mexicans of the border region was part of a much larger process that began in the late colonial period when Anglo-Americans moved into the Louisiana Territory and began trading with Mexico's northern provinces. Through commercial exchange, these northern regions were swept into the irresistible magnet of the market revolution that was propelling the U.S. economy in the first half of the nineteenth century. David Weber has stated the case clearly: Mexicans of the border region were gradually pulling away from the weakening centripetal force of the Mexican central government and gravitating toward the much stronger "American commercial orbit." This movement accelerated after Mexican independence, particularly due to the opening of ports such as Tampico and Matamoros, but also through a multitude of "highways of commerce" that developed all along the frontier.[70] Thus, Andrés Reséndez likens Mexico's Northeast in the first half of the nineteenth century to a fault line that was simultaneously pulled "in opposite directions" by two competing forces: the U.S. economy and the Mexican state.[71] The stresses caused by these external forces produced a fracture in 1839–40 in the form of a regional rebellion known as the Federalist War.

THE FEDERALIST WAR

The Federalist War is one of the most important events that transpired in the border region during the Texas Republic. The war is well known in Texas, particularly because it generated the notion of a breakaway nation called the Republic of the Rio Grande. Rather than retelling that story, I wish to focus on one of the least understood facets of the episode: the military cooperation between Anglo-Texans and Mexican federalists. The rebellion originated in Tampico and extended to the Villas del Norte in November 1838. One of the roots of the uprising is to be found in Mexico's turn to centralism in the mid-1830s, which enjoyed brief popularity. That popularity lasted only until the promulgation of the new constitution, the Seven Laws, which went into effect in 1837. The Seven Laws immediately began to "upset the operational system of the former states [now departments], leaving them without funds and affecting the interests of local commercial and bureaucratic elites." Among the changes, governors were to be designated by the central government and protectionist policies reinforced. Regional elites, who had grown accustomed to relative autonomy under federalist governments, now felt threatened.[72] Moreover, residents of the northern states were deeply offended that the government failed to defend them against Indian raids while imposing upon them a series of oppressive exactions and an onerous military presence in order to continue the war against the Texans. General Vicente Filisola wrote to his superiors about the effect that the military presence had on the border residents: "the hatred toward the military here is very great and each day it grows more as long as they are weighed [down] and injured with the exactions" required to maintain the army.[73]

Federalist movements erupted in various parts of Mexico in the late 1830s, most notably in Jalisco, Sinaloa, Sonora, and Yucatán. However, the movement in Northeast Mexico had a singular feature not shared by the others: its proximity to Texas, which the federalists could turn to for support. The Federalist War of 1839–40 is also unique in the cooperation that it generated among Texans and Mexicans. It gave rise, if only ephemerally and in a limited way, to a sense of solidarity among people of different races fighting for freedom from economic and political oppression. The study of the revolt also reveals the limits and hazards of that cooperation.[74]

The revolt began on November 3, 1838, when Antonio Canales, a former deputy to the Tamaulipas state congress, issued an anti-centralist manifesto. Joining Canales were other local leaders from Tamaulipas, Nuevo León, and Coahuila. Prominent among them were Antonio Zapata, Jesús Cárdenas, and José María Carvajal. A military and political figure from outside the region, Juan Pablo Anaya, also joined the revolt. He had participated with Miguel Hidalgo in the Mexican War of Independence and with Andrew Jackson in the War of 1812 against the British, and had served briefly as minister of war in 1833. Because of his fluency in English he was commissioned to seek men, arms, and money in Texas. The federalist leaders counted on the participation of rancheros and rural people and had the sympathy of many residents of the region.[75]

Ideology was not the dominant force of the revolt, although federalism, with its emphasis on local autonomy, was a natural fit for the leaders of the movement, who were above all pragmatic men. Juan Pablo Anaya told the Texans that the aim of the movement was to restore the federalist principles embodied in the Constitution of 1824. Jesús Cárdenas, however, was more forthright, declaring that the people of the northern frontier had raised an army for the "defense of their liberty, property, and interests."[76]

Antonio Canales, the principal leader of the revolt, was born and raised in Monterrey, where he studied law before settling in the Villas del Norte. Described as a "small man of brown complexion" with a high forehead and obvious intelligence, he was a charismatic leader with a "magnetic personality" but limited capacity in military matters.[77] The other emblematic figure of the federalist revolt was Antonio Zapata of Guerrero. A mulatto from a poor family, Zapata raised sheep in his youth and, through uncommon energy and hard work, became a ranchero and "accumulated a fortune in sheep and land." He was also a successful merchant and a renowned Indian fighter. His bravery and fearlessness in combating Indians made him one of the most admired and respected men of the Villas del Norte.[78] The relations that Canales and Zapata developed with the Anglo-Texans during the Federalist War provide a study in contrast. At the end of the conflict Zapata was widely admired whereas Canales was reviled for what the Texans perceived as cowardice and duplicity.

The Federalist War began in November 1838 and ended exactly two years later, in November 1840. Events in Nuevo León reflect one of the glaring contradictions of the revolt. The federalists were accompanied by a contingent of Texans, but the Texans' presence was repudiated by most of the Mexican population. This became evident when the federalist force commanded by Zapata—which included a large number of both Texans and Carrizo Indians—ran wild through the northern towns of Nuevo León in August 1839. A town official of Salinas Victoria wrote to the governor that Zapata's men carried off the horses and took all the weapons, ammunition, and money they could get their hands on. In Cerralvo the federalists "took twenty-six rifles from the municipal office despite pleas not to take them because they were needed for defense against the savages." In the eyes of many townspeople, the federalists were behaving in the same way as the centralists.[79]

What occurred in Nuevo León was part of a larger pattern. The war with the French was settled in March 1839, which freed the national army to combat the federalists. By the summer of 1839, it was clear that the centralists had the upper hand. This is when Juan Pablo Anaya appeared on the scene, reaching Monclova in August, where he met with Canales and Zapata. They appealed to him to travel to Texas and obtain all the help he could get to bolster the federalist cause.[80]

Accompanied by Colonel A. Nelly, Anaya traveled to San Antonio and then to the capital, Houston, arriving on September 11, 1839. His mission was to obtain loans, arms, and volunteers, and he was reportedly authorized to offer the Texans recognition of their independence with the boundary at the San Antonio River in exchange for 1,500 volunteers. This proposal was clearly at odds with Texas's pretension of possessing all land to the Rio Grande. Anaya set up a "recruiting station on the grounds of the Texas capital" and drew a lot of attention.[81] A Houston newspaper reported that many Texans were sympathetic to the federalist cause. Some felt disdain for centralism; others desired a republic in northern Mexico to serve as a buffer between Texas and her hostile neighbor; and still others sought an alliance with the federalists to combat the Indians.[82]

This first round of recruitment in Texas—the second would come in the spring and summer of 1840—netted the federalists more than two hundred Texans led by two experienced military men, Colonels Reuben Ross and Samuel W. Jordan. Several dozen Carrizo Indians also joined the force, along with several hundred Mexican rancheros. They had no difficulty defeating the local militia of Guerrero on October 1, 1839, at the beginning of a renewed offensive. Two days later they won a resounding victory against a large centralist force at the battle of "El Cántaro" (known in Texas as Alcantra) near the town of Mier. In this engagement Carvajal suffered a bullet wound that broke his arm, which caused him pain for the rest of his life.[83]

Flush with success, the federalists headed for Matamoros in December. Canales, who led a force estimated at 1,700 troops, called on military commander General Valentín Canalizo to leave the city and fight in the open. He added that he and Canalizo were both Mexicans; their disputes were of a political nature; and the population need not be sacrificed. Canalizo responded that he would fight wherever he chose, adding that although they were both Mexicans, "in me exists the very recommendable circumstance of not being a traitor."[84] Canales lifted the siege on December 16 and decided to march to Monterrey in hopes of capturing the Nuevo León capital. This action infuriated some of the Texans in his camp. Fifty of them, led by Ross, returned to Texas while the rest, led by Jordan, continued with Canales to Monterrey.[85]

Canales believed the city was poorly fortified and could be easily taken. What he did not know was that General Mariano Arista, who had been named military commander of Coahuila and Nuevo León just three months earlier, had arrived on December 24 with about 1,600 men, just in time to head off Canales, who now led a force of a little more than a thousand troops.[86] In an exchange of letters, Canales asked Arista to settle their differences by fighting out in the open so as not to bring destruction to his native city. Arista wrote a scathing reply. What was Canales doing? "Begging for protection from a band of thieves" who had stolen Texas? "Bringing strangers to thrust a dagger into his Mexican compatriots"? He declared that the government was taking steps to resolve the problems of the region, including "restructuring presidial companies to combat the barbarous Indians." He admonished Canales, "there is no pretext . . . for continuing to be the scourge of these Departments."[87]

These arguments did not persuade Canales, but Arista's superiority in troops and firepower did. Instead of fighting, the federalist leader retreated toward the Rio Grande with the centralists in pursuit. The military fortunes of the federalists continued to flounder. They reached the Rio Grande on January 7, 1840, and eventually made their way to Presidio del Rio Grande (near Laredo, not to be confused with Presidio del Norte in Chihuahua). Canales sent Zapata with a small force to Santa Rita de Morelos in Coahuila to obtain money and supplies, but Arista's troops continued their relentless pursuit. At Morelos Zapata and about twenty-three men—including twelve Texans—were captured. Arista offered Zapata amnesty if he would renounce his federalist allegiance, but the proud warrior refused. The centralist general then proceeded to execute the rebel leader and his Mexican and Texan soldiers. Zapata's head was cut off and placed in a cask of *mezcal* so that it could be preserved long enough to be placed on a pole opposite his house in Guerrero as an object lesson to those who rebelled against the government.[88]

If the federalists were discouraged by their failures, they did not show it. On January 18 they held a convention on the east bank of the Rio Grande opposite Guerrero and established a governing structure for their movement. Some considered this action as an attempt to break away from Mexico and establish a separate republic like the Texans had done. Apparently the Texans thought so. They invented a name: the Republic of the Rio Grande, and even a flag for the proposed new nation. The Mexican federalists were not however ready for such a step. They proposed that the northern states of Chihuahua, Zacatecas, Durango, Nuevo León, Tamaulipas, and Coahuila, along with the region of Texas extending to the Nueces River, unite in an administrative unit called the Frontera del Norte de la Republica Mejicana, which explicitly attached it to the Mexican republic. The principal federalist leaders of Nuevo León, Coahuila, and Tamaulipas were on the governing council, with Jesús Cárdenas as president and Canales as chief of military operations. José María Carvajal was named secretary. Sixty Texans led by Captain Jack Palmer were assigned as a special guard to protect the council.[89]

Did the federalists intend to separate from Mexico and form a new nation called the Republic of the Rio Grande? Historians do not agree on the subject,[90] but there is an underlying question that is more applicable to this study: If norteños wanted to break away from Mexico, was it because they did not have faith in the Mexican nation? Did they not share a national identity as mexicanos? To whom or to what did the norteños owe their loyalty? Two military men who knew them well were convinced their loyalty was not to the nation. Writing from a prison cell in Perote, General José Urrea addressed former vice president Valentín Gómez Farías in April 1840, urging him to lead a movement to save the nation. Mexico, said Urrea, was in danger of losing her northern provinces, just as it had lost Texas. The people of California, New Mexico, and the periphery of the Río Bravo were fed up with a national government that did not respond to their needs. In those regions, "the North Americans were welcomed and some of them have married into the most prominent families."[91] This sentiment was shared by the centralist general Francisco Mejía, who was scandalized by the independent thinking and separatist tendencies of the Mexicans of the border region. He was persuaded that they nurtured "an exaggerated sympathy for the United States and Texas" that led them to harbor schemes of independence that would be supported by these enemies of Mexico. He declared: "they do not care about our nationality, but only about getting whatever they are after."[92]

Mejia's complaint reveals the sense of alienation that border residents felt toward a government that promoted economic policies inimical to their interests while failing to carry out the most basic task of government: the protection of its citizens. It is little wonder that many norteños did not identify with the Mexican state. As Brian DeLay eloquently wrote: "when raiders came and attacked a family in northern Mexico, what good was Mexican citizenship?"[93] El Patrono del Pueblo, a federalist newspaper, complained that while a thousand soldiers lazed around in Monterrey oppressing the population, the towns in the northern part of the state were being devastated by Indians. Just as important was the material well-being of norteños, which was often "more dependent on commerce with foreigners than on loyalty to the Mexican state."[94]

Throughout the Federalist War the central government resorted to nationalist appeals to win the loyalty of border residents. It branded the three groups that composed the federalist force with denigrating epithets: the Texans were thieves and assassins, the Indians were brutal savages, and the federalist leaders were dupes and traitors pursuing their own selfish interests. By combating these forces of evil, the government was defending Mexican women, children, and, above all, national honor.[95] Centralists also raised the specter of falling prey to an alien power. The deluded federalists, warned General Valentín Canalizo, would be swallowed up by their Texan allies who were out to "conquer our departments in order to unite them to their so-called Republic."[96]

While the centralists were attempting to use the Texas presence to turn the borderlanders against the federalists, the leaders of the revolt, Canales, Cárdenas, and Carvajal, were drawing even closer to the Texans in an attempt to keep their movement alive. By early April 1840, they were in San Antonio and then in Victoria and Refugio. In each town they found enthusiastic followers. San Antonio mayor Samuel A. Maverick backed their movement, as did many of the prominent Anglo-American and Mexican families, including the Menchacas, the Navarros, and the Seguíns. Samuel G. Powell provided a loan of "upward of $3,000" for the cause.[97] There was also encouraging support in Victoria, where Samuel A. Plummer, Lamar's attorney, had offered to organize a company to fight the centralists and had urged the Texas president "to send one thousand Texans to aid the Republic of the Rio Grande."[98]

At a large dinner on April 10, Cárdenas, who was described as "a handsome noble-looking man of about thirty-four," spoke about the movement and "the sympathy which ha[d] always existed between Texas and the people of the northern frontier" of Mexico. He alluded to "the uniformity of the interests of the inhabitants of both countries" and assured his listeners that they were all—Texans and norteños—fighting "for the cause of liberty." Cárdenas reminded his Texas listeners that the enemies of the federalists were also the enemies of the Texans: they were "the same who shed the blood of Texians in the Alamo and at Labahía [Goliad]." By using these symbols so dear to Texans, Cárdenas was performing a bit of manipulation to advance his cause.[99]

Merchants of Refugio, some of whom had lived in northern Mexico and had traded with the Mexicans, aided the federalists in hopes of making a profit. Among them were James Power, an empresario; Philip Dimmit, whose marriage to María Luisa Lazo brought him into Martín de León's extended family in Victoria; Richard Pearse, who had engaged in commerce in Matamoros since the early 1820s; and Edward Linn, brother of John J. Linn. Daniel Driscoll's tavern in Refugio became a "headquarters and refueling station" for the Texan forces that fought with the federalists.[100] Merchants new to the region also benefited. Henry L. Kinney and William P. Aubrey, who had established their trading post on the Nueces a few months earlier, "soon gained a monopoly of the contraband trade" with the federalists.[101] New York native John P. Kelsey was in Galveston in December 1839 when he heard of the federalist revolt. He quickly gathered up "a stock of arms, munitions, and other supplies" and headed for Corpus Christi to sell to Canales's army. Kelsey would later move to the Rio Grande and continue his involvement with Mexico for more than half a century.[102]

Word got around that recruits were again needed to fight in northern Mexico. Lieutenant John McDaniel wrote an open letter in the *Colorado Gazette* in April 1840, asking his countrymen to support the federalists, who were combating a priest-ridden and despotic government. For helping to rescue the Mexican people from slavery the Texans would be rewarded with "a bounty of half a league of land" and exclusive rights to the spoils of war.[103] Predictably, many of the volunteers were not exactly of the virtuous variety. Most were adventurers at best and cattle thieves at worst. Some had served in the Texas army, others were former rangers. In the wake of the prolonged economic crisis caused by the Panic of 1837, they were lured by the promise of land and money.[104] Many "had been the very cattle thieves or so-called cowboys that had preyed on the Mexican cattle herds that ranged the ranches on the north bank of the Rio Grande."[105] In the words of one historian, "for twenty-five dollars a month and a share of the spoils, they temporarily put aside their hatred of Mexicans." By summer Canales was at San Patricio with a force of about 300 Mexican rancheros, 80 Carrizo Indians, and 140 Anglo-Texans.[106]

This force was woefully inadequate to wage war against several thousand centralist troops commanded by Arista, but with an optimism that could only have been born of arrogance or the illusory notion that the people of the Northeast would rise against the government, the federalists rode toward the Rio Grande for another confrontation. Samuel Jordan, who had returned to lead the Texas contingent, joined Juan Molano at the head of a column bound for Ciudad Victoria, the capital of Tamaulipas, while Canales led another group toward the interior of Nuevo León. Molano and Jordan met with little resistance and with their 250 men, 115 of them Texans, they took Ciudad Victoria without a fight on September 29.[107]

The army was then supposed to head for Saltillo but a dispute broke out between Molano and Jordan. The Texans were committing abuses and depredations against the Mexican population in the towns through which they passed. When Molano demanded that Jordan keep his rowdy troops in line, the two men feuded. Molano knew that Texans' abuses would play into the hands of Arista, who astutely used such occurrences to turn public opinion against the federalists. In mid-October en route to Saltillo, Molano received a letter from Arista offering him and his troops guarantees of safety and forgiveness. He accepted, and the stage was set for what the Texans would deem a great betrayal at Saltillo. When the federalists reached the city on October 23, their forces numbered about 335, including 110 Texans. Suddenly, the Mexicans, except for a couple of dozen troops led by Colonel José María González of Laredo, went over to the centralists. González and his men fled to Texas while Jordan's men tried to make a stand against a vastly superior force that now included their former federalist allies. Finally, they were forced to flee toward the Rio Grande, aided in their escape by a group of thirty to forty Mexican fighters sent by Juan N. Seguín.[108]

Meanwhile, Canales, heading about three hundred men, one hundred of them Texans, could not advance because he was cut off by a much larger force, so he had to return to Camargo on the Rio Grande. He began to receive conciliatory overtures from Arista even as he realized that Molano's defection had left him abandoned. He could not seek refuge in Texas after the events at Saltillo, so he decided to surrender. In early November he signed an agreement to end the conflict, which Arista ratified. A few days later, Canales and Arista met at Cadereyta with a fraternal embrace, and the two marched together to Monterrey, where they were met with music and cheering crowds.[109]

The federalists lost the war because they underestimated the strength of the centralist forces and overestimated the support they would obtain from Texas and their own people. The national government was able to send several thousand troops to quell the revolt and chose as their leader a man who was conciliatory but firm. Along with his military campaign, Arista waged a propaganda campaign portraying the federalists as traitors for embracing the Texans and endangering Mexico's sovereignty. This message resonated among Mexican families being despoiled by Jordan's troops.[110]

The consequence of this little war should not be underestimated. It contributed to a trend of militarizing the border region that had begun during Mexican independence. The military buildup placed another burden on border residents without providing the defense they required against Indian raiders. It had unintended benefits for both the Texans and the political elite of Tamaulipas, however. According to Nance, the federalist revolt "secured for Texas a long interval of peace after the failure of the Mexican campaign in Texas in the spring of 1836."[111] The political leaders of Tamaulipas, in turn, skillfully used the implicit threat of a potential alliance with Texas to apply pressure on the central government and obtain concessions. Historian Octavio Herrera argues that their pact with Arista allowed them to recover the positions of power they had lost with the introduction of the centralist regime. Canales, Molano, and Cárdenas would occupy important positions in the state after the revolt. They had played the Texas card effectively, "acquiring . . . a capacity to negotiate the peace from a position of strength."[112]

The Federalist War shows that Anglo-Texans and Mexicans of the border region could cooperate, although based not on true friendship or solidarity but on shared or convergent interests. It was essentially a marriage of convenience. The flexibility displayed by the federalist leaders was a useful weapon within the internal power struggles of Mexico, but this malleability infuriated the Texans, who came to see Canales as a sniveling coward and opportunist and Molano as totally unscrupulous, and to believe both had used the Texans to further their own ends. Ironically, it was the most inflexible of the federalist leaders who won the respect and admiration of the Texans. Antonio Zapata fought bravely at the head of his men and led an integrated force of Anglo-Texans and Mexicans into battle. The conservative press accused him of letting his men ransack the towns for weapons and horses, but he always expressed concern for his soldiers' well-being. He saw the "bare feet and tattered clothes" of the Texans and asked the people of Villaldama, Nuevo León, to donate used clothes for these men who had joined the Mexicans in "fighting for liberty." Through such actions, the mulatto Zapata attained great stature among the race-conscious Texans, who named a county in his honor a few years later.[113]

The camaraderie and mutual respect that developed between Zapata and his Texan soldiers contrasts sharply with the relations engendered by Canales and Molano. In fact, many Texans' most lasting memory of the Federalist War was Canales's duplicity and Molano's defection at Saltillo, which embittered many Texans toward Mexicans. This disenchantment was soon followed with anger over the treatment of the Santa Fe and Mier prisoners and the Mexican invasions of 1842.[114]

TEXAS MERCHANTS AND THE REVIVAL OF TRADE

These episodes generated ill will against Mexicans, a sentiment which reached a peak in 1842. The anti-Mexican feelings apparently did not extend to commerce, however, perhaps because "trade has [the] facility to survive when all other means of communication cease."[115] Moreover, in 1843 the governments of Mexico and Texas signed an armistice that had an immediate effect on trade. Throughout the border region and along the coast as far as Corpus Christi and Galveston heightened activity was visible. The *Houston Morning Star* foretold "a new era of peace between Texas and Mexico," sustained by "an immense and valuable trade." The two nations would thus "be inclined to view each other in a very different light, from that dimed [sic] by the cloudy atmosphere of war."[116] San Antonio was one of the biggest beneficiaries of the renewed trade as "business flourished once more. Mule trains arrived from the south, bringing sacks of gold and silver. During the summer of 1843, Mexican traders put $50,000 of the precious metals into circulation. Bishop [Jean M.] Odin described the city as 'bustling with activity.'" This revival occurred scarcely one year after the Mexican invasions of Texas and while the Mier prisoners were still in Perote and fresh in the collective memory of Texans.[117]

The revival of trade in 1843 is exemplified by the actions of various merchants who were intimately tied to commerce with Mexico. After his participation as a supplier in the Federalist War, John Kelsey became acquainted with the Spanish merchant Mateas (probably Mateo) Ramírez, who introduced him to Mariano Arista. The New Yorker and Arista probably came to an understanding because Kelsey obtained merchandise in New Orleans and established a store at the future site of Corpus Christi. That is where he stayed until the end of the U.S.-Mexican War, when he moved to Rio Grande City. He would live in that town and across the river in Camargo until the end of his life in 1898. Kelsey is one of those little-known figures who lived through all of the vicissitudes of the region—hurricanes, epidemics, Indian raids, and wars—and who mediated between the various ethnic groups along the Rio Grande. According to Marieta Kelsey, he won the respect of Mexicans by fair dealing and was "held in highest regard on both sides of the river."[118]

Another merchant whose experiences serve as a barometer of life in the border region was William Neale. A native of England, Neale arrived in Mexico as a teenager in 1821. At San Juan de Ulúa, Veracruz, he met a young military officer, Pedro de Ampudia, with whom he established a lifelong friendship. He went back to England where he was married in 1827, but returned to Mexico and settled in Matamoros in 1834. By this time Ampudia was a general. When Neale baptized his son in the Catholic Church, he asked the Mexican general to stand as godfather and named William Pedro Neale in his honor. Neale established a prosperous business hauling freight between Matamoros and Port Isabel, at the mouth of the Rio Grande. When the Mier prisoners were at Matamoros, Ampudia allowed Neale to give them money. A few years later, during the opening shots of the U.S.-Mexican War, Ampudia used Neale's wagons to carry out wounded soldiers from the Palo Alto battlefield. Neale lived through Texas independence, the U.S.-Mexican War, the War of Reform in Mexico, the Civil War in the United States, and countless border conflicts from the 1830s to the 1870s.[119]

In the same mold as Kelsey and Neale, Henry Clay Davis came to Texas as an adventurous youth from Kentucky in the late 1830s and settled in San Antonio.

He was one of the participants in the Mier expedition who survived the debacle. Back in San Antonio, he accepted the invitation of Antonio Reséndez, a wealthy young Mexican, to visit his home in Camargo, and while in that town he met and fell in love with Hilaria Garza. In order to gain her parents' permission to marry her, he agreed to settle on the northern bank of the Rio Grande across from Camargo so that they could see her often. That was the beginning of Rancho Davis, which became Rio Grande City. With his wife and six children, Davis established a trading post and built a life among the Mexicans of the region.[120]

Perhaps no one exemplifies these frontier merchants better than Henry L. Kinney. A native of Pennsylvania, Kinney had been engaged in land speculation in Illinois but was cleaned out in the Panic of 1837, so he drifted to Texas. He was described as "a tall man, strongly built. He had dark hair, hazel eyes, and a complexion browned by the sun and the winds. He spoke Spanish 'like a native' and conversed with ease among the different Indian tribes." His ability to communicate with Mexicans and Indians in their own languages was one of his many gifts. He was courageous in battle, but engaged in battle only after diplomacy had failed. His success was also due to "his uniform cordiality in meeting strangers and dealing with them, whether they were Indians, Mexicans, or non-latins."[121] Kinney firmly believed that in order to survive on the frontier it was necessary to "make our common enemy our friends."[122] He is an emblematic figure among the Texans who traded with Mexico because his experiences reflect a willingness to subordinate national, ethnic, and racial prejudices to a pragmatic attitude necessary to survive in a hostile environment.

Kinney, Davis, Kelsey, and other merchants of the Rio Grande frontier, who had knowledge of the terrain and extensive contacts in the Villas del Norte, were strategically placed to supply Zachary Taylor's army when it arrived at Corpus Christi in September 1845, in preparation for the U.S. invasion of Mexico. Despite the specter of war, Mexican traders continued to arrive at Corpus Christi with silver and other products while the "contraband trade and the barter of mustangs and beeves still were the town's chief businesses."[123] Taylor's army generated a great demand for large quantities of provisions as well as mules and horses. Many of these were obtained in the Villas del Norte and the towns of Northeast Mexico through the trade networks developed by Texan and Mexican merchants and also through informal channels that sprang up to meet the demand.

This commerce was illegal and, according to Mexican authorities, immoral. José María de la Garza, a revenue collector in Lampazos, wrote to the state government in September 1846 that "bad Mexicans . . . without concern for the

Henry Lawrence Kinney exemplified pragmatic Anglo-American frontier merchants who were willing to get along with people of any race and nationality in the interest of trade. In 1839 he established a trading post on the site that would become Corpus Christi, which city he founded. LC-USZ62-110031, Library of Congress.

state of war that exists between our nation and the United States and lacking in honor and dignity are in league with the Americans, engaging in commerce and making trips to Texas."[124] The inhabitants of the Villas del Norte were closer to the emerging market and moved quickly to provide what Taylor's army required. The prefect of the district reported that "by December 1845 some of the vecinos . . . had traded three thousand head of cattle in Corpus Christi." Many of these transactions were facilitated by middlemen such as Kinney, Davis, and Kelsey. General Francisco Mejía, commander of the Fourth Division of the Northern Army of Mexico, was enraged and ordered that these merchants be captured and taken to Matamoros.[125]

Once in Corpus Christi, Mexican traders sold their horses at prices that ranged from $8 to $30. Ulysses S. Grant, the quartermaster of Taylor's army, "purchased horses and 1,000 wild mules from the Mexicans for the anticipated invasion of the traders' own country." The Mexicans also offered "blankets and fabrics of beautiful patterns and colors, priced at $10 to $50." They also brought silver bars, and it was reported that by January 1846, they were arriving "daily, coming from as far as Monterrey" for this purpose. The merchants were doing a brisk business and apparently expressed satisfaction in dealing with the U.S. troops. Perhaps believing that all Mexicans would welcome the invading army with open arms, the *Telegraph and Texas Register* reported that the traders "wished the army would move at once to the Rio Grande."[126]

THE U.S.-MEXICAN WAR IN THE BORDER REGION
The U.S.-Mexican War (1846–48) put in sharper focus the relations between Anglo-Americans and Mexicans in the border region and their perceptions of each other. Since the 1820s the vecinos of the Northeast had experienced the many faces of American expansion. They had received in their midst foreign merchants and doctors, mostly peaceful and hardworking people who shared their knowledge and experiences. They had also known the brutal pillage of filibusters and adventurers. They had endured racial hatred and violence but also beneficial exchanges. The war brought a much bigger challenge, however. The army of the United States had entered their territory on a mission that most could not comprehend. What follows is not a thorough explanation of the impact of the war on northern Mexico, but a few observations on how the people of the Northeast reacted to the American invasion and occupation. As in previous experiences, there were two faces of the American presence: one essentially benign and one extremely negative.

The war offered diverse opportunities to the people of Northeast Mexico. Political leaders, producers, merchants, and rural people tried to make the best of an unfortunate situation. Merchants benefited from the opening of trade as tariffs on imports were reduced by one-half or more and "many articles of daily use, that had previously been prohibited, became available."[127] Jesús Cárdenas, who had been one of the leaders of the Federalist War, expressed great misgivings over the U.S. presence, but he found some solace in the arrival of more ships because "we can get things cheap, like a blanket for one real."[128] Producers from the farms, ranches, and haciendas of the region also profited from selling their products to the U.S. army. This is reflected in the production statistics of various rural towns such as Montemorelos, Nuevo León, located about forty-five miles south of Monterrey. Montemorelos almost doubled its production between 1843 and 1848, from 70,393 pesos to 134,703 pesos. Production declined to 111,775 pesos in 1849 after the U.S. army had left.[129] Some rural people accepted work as scouts or arrieros for the U.S. army. John Salmon "Rip" Ford, who served in the war, wrote of two Mexican scouts: "No two men connected with our command did more efficient service than Miguel and Vicente . . . these men were faithful to the United States."[130] To solve the problem of transportation, Taylor's army obtained hundreds of men and mules from the Mexican countryside.[131]

The attitude of norteños toward the invading army was by no means uniform but, at least at the beginning of the invasion, it was not intensely hostile. Both President James K. Polk and his military commander, Zachary Taylor, had received information that public reaction in northern Mexico would not be antagonistic. Polk had received information from Delphy Carlin before the start of the war. Carlin, a merchant, "had traveled . . . more than thirty thousand miles in northern Mexico, and believed that most of the people had the true American spirit." Taylor got word from a confidential agent that he had sent to Matamoros in September 1845. The agent informed him that "should war be declared, Tamaulipas, Coahuila, and Nuevo León would probably pronounce for independence, and establish friendly relations with us."[132] Perhaps these statements reflected wishful thinking, but it is clear that the people of the Northeast felt at least a certain ambivalence toward the United States. While they "feared [the country's] territorial ambitions, and could sense the Americans' racial prejudice," they had grown dependent on U.S. trade networks. Moreover, according to historian Joseph B. Ridout, "many northeasterners associated the United States with the ideas of liberty, federalism, and political institutions that had disappeared in Mexico in the mid-1830s. Prior to the war, and even in its early stages, tamaulipecos and others bore much optimism and goodwill toward their yanqui neighbors."[133]

On July 9, 1846, Secretary of War William L. Marcy wrote Taylor, instructing him to continue his policy of a "just and honorable conduct towards the people" in the civilian population. Marcy reminded him that "in a country so divided into races, classes, and parties . . . there must be great room for operating on the minds and feelings of large portions of the inhabitants." Taylor should persuade the people that the invasion was not directed against them but intended to overthrow an oppressive government, which would be beneficial to the entire population.[134] This policy, which was imparted to all other military commanders in the field, bore fruit in some of the towns that witnessed the arrival of the invading army.

In early October 1846, an American steamboat, the *Major Brown*, cruised up the Rio Grande and docked at the town of Guerrero. The townspeople, who had never witnessed such a spectacle, were welcomed aboard the vessel and expressed their "wonderment at everything connected with the machinery of the boat." The alcalde of Guerrero declared that the "Americans can do anything they like, and it is no use fighting against them" because they can "make iron into any shape they please." Many of the Americans "expressed themselves highly gratified at the beauty and courtesy of the women, and at the cordiality of the men. The strongest desire was manifested by very many of the citizens, that peace might be soon established . . . between Mexico and the United States."[135]

While the *Major Brown* was docked at the town, a party of Lipan Apaches attacked the ranches nearby, "carried off five little boys, killed several men, and wounded others. Two of the wounded men passed the night of the attack on board of the boat," where their wounds were dressed, and were later carried to town. "The citizens generally evinced much gratitude for the kindness shown their unfortunate friends, and begged . . . the Americans [to] send troops for their protection." On October 8, "an immense crowd of all ages, sexes, and conditions, thronged the shore" to say goodbye to the *Major Brown*. The Americans received "acclamations, waving of scarfs, handkerchiefs, shawls, and blankets, with wishes for a prosperous voyage, and a speedy return."[136]

Upriver, a U.S. detachment commanded by Mirabeau B. Lamar occupied Laredo. The former president of Texas—who had been ordered there by Taylor—found the town in a deplorable state, "exposed to the ravages of the Indians" and victim of a recent deadly epidemic "attended with great mortality." Lamar provided the citizens with medicine "from a spirit of humanity, as well as conciliation."[137] He also worked to rid the region of Indians and outlaw bands that preyed on commerce. Several of the alcaldes of the nearby towns requested the presence of U.S. soldiers to combat a group of about 150 robbers that operated on the road between Laredo and Bexar. In March 1847, Lamar wrote to Texas governor J. P. Henderson, conveying his impression that "good feeling prevails between our people and the Mexicans. Our coming amongst them has given a new impulse to every thing and they seem fully to appreciate the protection our presence affords."[138]

One of the soldiers in Lamar's unit, Hamilton P. Bee, came aboard as a second lieutenant. He had come to Texas in 1837 with his mother at the age of fifteen. His father, Barnard E. Bee, had served in a number of government posts, including as secretary of war in Houston's government and secretary of state in Lamar's administration. Hamilton served the Texas Republic in its war against the Indians and later entered politics, being elected to the first senate of the new state of Texas. He vacated his seat to join Captain Ben McCulloch's company in the war against Mexico in 1846 and participated in the battle of Monterrey. After the battle he was assigned to Lamar's company at Laredo. Bee stayed in Laredo after the war, and from 1849 to 1856 represented Webb County in the Texas legislature. During his last two years of service he was elected speaker of the state house. Bee also owned a stock ranch and engaged in commerce. He shared the hardships of his mainly Mexican neighbors and would have an enduring relationship with Mexico (where he lived for a decade) and Mexicans until the end of his life.[139]

According to one observer, General John E. Wool assiduously practiced the policy of conciliation and good conduct toward the Mexicans. On his march from Bexar to Saltillo to meet up with Taylor's army, Wool stressed to his men that the war was not against the people of Mexico, and he was implacable with his troops "in all matters relating to discipline." At Parras he "conciliated the good will of the people by his kind treatment and forbearance." Francis Baylies, who reported on the march, recounts a pause at Patos, the hacienda of Jacobo Sánchez Navarro, where Wool and his staff were "received with the most cordial hospitality" and invited to dinner. Baylies adds derisively that the Mexican officers who were invited that evening "relieved [Don Jacobo] of his silver plate!"[140] Wool also stopped to rest his troops at the hacienda of Miguel Blanco, son of Victor Blanco, who "was profuse in his hospitalities." In Monclova, Wool encountered ill feeling among the populace, but he "succeeded in conciliating the inhabitants, and Mexicans and Americans freely mingled in the festivals and balls which followed the occupation of the city."[141]

Many U.S. soldiers believed that they were doing an immense service to the Mexican people by invading their country. Lieutenant John J. Peck wrote of the magnanimous policy of paying for everything the army consumed, instead of taking it by force from the population. "We distribute more money than they ever dreamed of and it goes to the poorer classes for labor, vegetables, chickens, eggs, and so on." Peck boasted of the virtues of the occupation: "Many are glad we are here, for the harvest of ready money. They have never seen so much gold and silver before, notwithstanding they have the richest mines in the world."[142] George Wilkins Kendall, the chronicler of the Santa Fe expedition, accompanied Taylor's army and was also surprised that the Mexicans were not more appreciative of the humane American presence. They received protection from Indian raids, fair compensation for their products, and liberation from an oppressive government, and "yet in not a single instance did any portion of them even hint at a desire to throw off the oppressive yoke they had so long borne, or express a willingness" to live under the liberal institutions of the United States.[143]

There was, however, one negative aspect of the American presence that reared its ugly head in Matamoros at the beginning of the U.S. occupation. Taylor's army included several thousand volunteers, many from Texas and other southern states, who came to Mexico filled with racial hatred and a desire to avenge the events in Texas ten years earlier. The literature on the racial attitudes and abuses committed by these irregular American soldiers is extensive,[144] and I will not cover it exhaustively here, but a few observations will illustrate how the people of Northeast Mexico experienced the racial antipathy of many Americans firsthand, which served to solidify their identity as Mexicans.

The generally favorable attitude toward the invading army that existed in Northeast Mexico was understandable, given the Mexican government's neglect of the region over several decades. This positive view was however quickly shattered by the actions of the volunteers, some of whom were Texas Rangers who had fought with and against Mexicans for many years. "Their ferocious hatred for Mexicans" prompted non-Texans to refer to the rangers as "packs of human bloodhounds."[145] They unleashed their murderous fury first at Matamoros and later at Monterrey. General George Gordon Meade wrote that the volunteers acted more like "hostile Indians than . . . civilized whites," and "inspired the Mexicans with a perfect horror of them."[146]

Because of its location far from the coast, the town of Mier did not receive much attention, but the cruelty of the war was eloquently expressed in a report by the ayuntamiento in 1852. Most of Mier's territorial jurisdiction was north of the Rio Grande, land that was ceded in the Treaty of Guadalupe Hidalgo. It was left with 106 out of its former 848 leagues. The Anglo-Texans, according to the report, descended upon the ranches in bands numbering from five to one hundred. They "ordered their owners to vacate those properties [because] they were theirs by right of conquest." They murdered in cold blood some of Mier's most respected citizens, among them Gil Moreno, Manuel Barrera, Romualdo Vela, and Leocadio Naranjo. The report also documented that since 1835 residents had lost livestock valued at more than one and a half million pesos.[147]

The residents of Nuevo León were forewarned as Taylor's army began its march toward the interior. The Semanario Político reported on the "abuse and violence" perpetrated at Matamoros by the "most immoral and depraved elements of the United States."[148] However, this did not prepare them adequately for what occurred. In 1847 at a ranch near Agua Fría on the road to Monterrey, a

Texas force led by Mabry "Mustang" Gray "rounded up all the male inhabitants old enough to bear arms, tied them to posts, and shot them through the head. Thirty-six were executed during a gruesome half hour."[149] The male inhabitants of Guadalupe, a small settlement in the town of Marín, were rounded up one day because they happened to be near the site of a guerrilla attack against U.S. wagons. Twenty-four "unarmed and peaceful" farm laborers were massacred by the volunteers in "one of the darkest passages in the history of the campaign."[150] What undoubtedly inspired the greatest fury among the Mexicans were the attacks on their women. Lieutenant Napoleon J. T. Dana wrote: "Many outrages have been committed on respectable females," some of which were "hellish . . . and heart-rending in the extreme." In one incident a group of volunteers "entered the house of a very respectable family [and] obliged the husband to leave the room. Some held him outside whilst two remained inside. One held a pistol to the lady's head whilst the other fiend incarnate violated her person."[151]

These acts hardened norteños' attitudes against the United States. If they had earlier entertained the idea of breaking away from Mexico and accepting incorporation into the United States, this notion quickly dissipated under the weight of the atrocities committed by American volunteers in the early part of the war. Hilario Mesa, who had discussed with other norteños the possibility of forming a separate republic, admitted that the "outrages perpetrated at Matamoros . . . had chilled sympathy with the Americans." After that experience "his fellow citizens were determined to remain Mexicans."[152]

This calls attention to a larger issue: the effect of the war on the rise of Mexican nationalism, which has played a major role in defining U.S.-Mexican relations to the present day. Lorenzo Meyer, a Mexican historian and political scientist of great distinction, has argued that the war "was a disaster that left a profound mark on the conscience of the ruling classes" and finally filtered down to the popular classes.[153] His general proposition may be right, especially in reference to those of the popular classes who did not come into contact with the American invaders. However, what occurred at Patos, the hacienda of Jacobo Sánchez Navarro in Coahuila, shows that the war left no less profound a mark on the popular classes who were directly affected. Not long after Sánchez Navarro hosted General John Wool at dinner, Patos was the scene of a violent massacre of Mexicans by rangers assigned to Wool's forces. After the battle of Angostura (Buena Vista) a ranger got drunk, went into a church, and pulled down a wooden crucifix, which he proceeded to drag through the streets. Then he trampled over the elderly priest who tried to stop him. The outraged citizens caught the ranger and proceeded to torture him in the center of town. The ranger's friends appeared and "charged into the crowd, killing indiscriminately." The scene was described as "carnage." Sánchez Navarro complained to Wool, but the affair was kept secret so as to avoid embarrassing the army. The hacendado remained on good terms with the Americans and even supplied the invaders with products from his haciendas, but he also provided the Mexican army with money and supplies and managed to stay on good terms with both sides. In contrast, his workers and their families maintained a sullen hatred for the norteamericanos.[154]

The Treaty of Guadalupe Hidalgo in 1848 demarcated a formal border dividing the region, bringing changes but also continuities. One thing remains clear, a political boundary agreed upon by two distant governments could not separate a region that had been united by affinities and multiple relations of exchange. These ties continued to unite the region and have done so until the present day.[155]

～

The decade between 1836 and 1845 witnessed a fundamental shift in the relations between Anglos and Mexicans in Texas. Both groups adjusted to the new order: Anglo-Texans were no longer circumscribed by the Mexican government and Texas Mexicans were forced to submit to Anglo domination. The decade was replete with violent episodes, some related to the despoliation of Mexican lands in Texas, others to the issue of Texas independence as the Mexican government fought to recover its lost province and the Texans to preserve their separation. Racial hatred against Mexicans, exacerbated by the Texas war, intensified with the supposed or real mistreatment of Texas adventurers captured in the Santa Fe and Mier expeditions and the two invasions of Texas ordered by Santa Anna in 1842.

Amidst the violence however there were growing forms of cooperation and interdependence. Not long after the battle of San Jacinto, the Texans and Mexicans of Northeast Mexico reached out to one another to continue the trade that had become a vital component of their daily lives. In Texas the conviction grew that trade with its southern neighbor was vital to the new republic's survival. In addition, there was a growing dependence on Mexican products such as silver. In Northeast Mexico, the vecinos ignored threats of reprisals from their government and danger from Anglo, Mexican, and Indian predators in order to continue trading with Texas. Much of the commerce was in contraband and required cooperation of people on both sides of the disputed boundary. Three important trade routes connected the region, running through Matamoros, Presidio, and the Villas del Norte. These commercial linkages bound Northeast Mexico even more firmly into the expanding economic orbit of the United States.

Despite interethnic violence, Anglos and Mexicans joined together in criminal activities either as outlaws or in pursuit of outlaws. The most conspicuous act of cooperative violence during the decade occurred in the Federalist War, when several hundred Anglo-Texans participated with federalists of Northeast Mexico in a revolt against the central government. Among other motives, Texans hoped Mexico's northern states would separate and form a buffer state between Texas and Mexico, so they conjured up a Republic of the Rio Grande that may have existed only in their imaginations. This experiment, in which differing interests converged, did not have a happy ending. It culminated with ill feelings and accusations of betrayal, revealing the limits of cooperative violence.

To most merchants the bitter feelings engendered by the Federalist War and the subsequent expeditions and invasions by both governments were mere inconveniences, and some even prospered by supplying Mexican federalists during the revolt. Commerce resumed with vigor in 1843 after the turbulence produced by the federalist revolt and the military incursions had died down. The contacts that Texas merchants had established with Mexican producers and middlemen facilitated their provisioning of the U.S. army when it arrived in the border region in preparation for the invasion of Mexico.

The U.S.-Mexican War had important repercussions for the region. Northeast Mexicans were initially encouraged by the open ports and ready market provided by the American army and the hope that its presence would keep marauding Indians at bay. At first, hostility against American troops was muted and some norteños even entertained the notion that the region would prosper if it were annexed to the United States. These hopes were dashed by the volunteers attached to Zachary Taylor's army. The abuse and violence they perpetrated against the Mexican population caused much bitterness and killed any idea of accepting annexation. Norteños gained a stronger identity as Mexicans as a result of the war.

CHAPTER 3

The Permeable Border

1849–1860

*T*here is an unforgettable passage in Gunter Grass's novel *The Tin Drum*. Russian soldiers enter a cellar in Danzig and shoot Alfred Matzerath, a member of the Nazi Party. In the same cellar a small army of ants—unaffected by the violent intrusion of the Russian troops—had created a trail between a sack of potatoes and a torn bag of sugar. The German falls heavily over the trail disrupting their work, but the ants, "undismayed by the detour, soon built a new highway round the doubled-up Matzerath; for the sugar that trickled out of the burst sack had lost none of its sweetness."[1] This image is a good metaphor for Northeast Mexico after the U.S.-Mexican War. The war had created disarray among the inhabitants, but they adjusted to the new situation and continued to do what they had always done: maintain the ties to Texas that were essential to their survival and well-being.

Continuation of Commerce and Development of Texas Border Towns

U.S. troops marched out of Northeast Mexico in the summer of 1848, and immediately following the war, intense activity could be observed all along the river, on the roads, and in the towns of the surrounding region. New towns were springing up on the Texas side, founded by merchants engaged in commerce with Mexico. Cities farther in the interior such as Corpus Christi, San Antonio, Austin, and Houston were all vying for the Mexican trade. The population of Texas grew at a phenomenal rate of 325 percent between 1847 and 1860, from 212,295 to 604,215. This population growth increased demand for certain products while generating many more commodities for export. New projects were in motion everywhere.

For example, Mifflin Kenedy had arrived on the Rio Grande during the war and begun operating a steamboat, hauling men and supplies for the U.S. Army. In December 1848 he set out for Mexico on a commercial venture, joined by Samuel A. Belden and James Walworth. They had intended to reach the famous fair at San Juan de los Lagos in Jalisco, but they never made it that far because they sold their goods in Zacatecas. On a journey reminiscent of Reuben Potter's trip twenty years earlier, Kenedy gathered up another load of merchandise and headed for Monterrey.[2]

Other merchants were busy founding towns to capitalize on the Mexican trade. Under the leadership of Henry L. Kinney, Corpus Christi grew into a town and immediately began to look toward Mexico for its economic prosperity. A group of prominent merchants that included Kinney and H. A. Gilpin, who had long traded in Mexico, were appointed in 1850 to a committee to determine the best way to build a road from Corpus Christi to Eagle Pass, on the Rio Grande across from Piedras Negras.[3] Underlining the importance of Mexico, in September 1848, a bilingual weekly newspaper began publication. The *Corpus Christi Star* reported the same month that a train of wagons had arrived from Laredo "loaded with wool and hides" and would soon "return loaded with merchandise."[4] The *Star* declared that Corpus Christi should be the main entrepot for the Chihuahua trade because it was the closest port to Chihuahua on the Gulf of Mexico. The writer reminded readers that merchants from that Mexican state had arrived before the war "to open this route, deeming it the most feasible of all others, and had not the friendly relations been interrupted between the two countries, the road ere now would have been covered with pack mules and wagons laden with goods landed here from New Orleans."[5]

The *Star* also reported that William L. Cazneau, who had a profitable business in Laredo, had gone to New York in order to buy "a large stock of goods" to sell in Chihuahua. Cazneau had been in the region for almost two decades. He had fought in the Texas war for independence and had represented Travis County in the Texas congress.[6] The *Star* praised his value to the region: "This section of country requires men like Cazneau, who are not afraid to adventure, and who . . . often realize a rich harvest."[7] Other merchants were invited to join the expedition to Chihuahua, and on July 21, 1849, they set out. Cazneau's caravan was composed of about one hundred men and fifty wagons and carried about $90,000 in goods. One of its objectives was to open "a trade thoroughfare through El Paso from the Texas coast" that could successfully compete with the route to Chihuahua from faraway Independence, Missouri.[8] Within that larger goal,

Cazneau hoped "to form two trading posts . . . , one at Presidio del Norte and one at El Paso, where the Mexican traders will buy goods and themselves convoy them into Mexico."⁹ A contemporary observer who witnessed the departure of the huge caravan described the streets of the small village "filled with oxen and teamsters." He made mention of the "motley crowd . . . men of many complexions and languages—the fair skinned German, the ruddy Irishman, and the swarthy Mexican, contrasted with the bronzed faces of the keen Yankee and the rough but ready son of the Texas prairies."¹⁰

A month later, in August, another caravan laden with goods left Corpus Christi for the Rio Grande. "This merchandise was destined for river towns and the interior as far south as Monterrey." The party consisted of about thirty men who were well armed and prepared to defend themselves from robbers.¹¹ A participant in many of these events was Henry Clay Davis. He joined with three other merchants in opening a "transportation line" of wagons and ships that connected the Rio Grande to New Orleans by way of Corpus Christi. Davis was desirous of finding the best route from Rio Grande City to Corpus Christi. The *Star* predicted that Corpus Christi "will not only have the trade from the Presidio, Laredo, and Mier, but we will even have it as low down as Camargo."¹²

As Cazneau made his way to Presidio he could not have known that a trading post like the one he envisioned for that settlement had been established months earlier by John W. Spencer, Ben Leaton, and J. D. Burgess. Spencer had served in the U.S.-Mexican War and then, with Leaton and Burgess, participated in the Santa Fe–Chihuahua trade. He established a ranch and trading post, which became the town of Presidio. Spencer raised horses and later obtained cattle from Chihuahua to supply Fort Davis, an army outpost built to defend travelers on their way to the goldfields of California. His trading post "came to be known as a supply station for traders, freighters, and Indians" and became an important location on the trading route between Chihuahua and the interior of Texas.¹³

Cazneau returned to a place that he had seen on the Rio Grande, a crossing commonly used by smugglers called Paso del Águila, "because of frequent flights of Mexican eagles from the wooded grove along the Escondido [River]." He joined James Campbell, a merchant who had arrived shortly before from San Antonio, and together they founded the town of Eagle Pass.¹⁴ Cazneau had a diversity of interests, including land speculation. He and his wife, Jane McManus, stayed in Eagle Pass for two years and bought more than a thousand acres of land. He was however particularly interested in Mexican silver. He discovered that through Piedras Negras he could access the silver mines of nearby Santa Rosa. He obtained a special permit to supply these and other mines, and beginning in 1851, "silver bullion trains out of Mexico passed through Eagle Pass to Indianola for transshipment to New Orleans and the United States Mint—some shipments were as much as three hundred thousand dollars." The cargo was hauled in "processions of 150 wagons pulled by six mules or oxen, or trains of 250 Mexican carretas."[15]

Two other merchants who would develop extensive ties to Mexico had a decisive influence on the early development of Eagle Pass. John Twohig, one of the prisoners captured by the Mexican army during the invasion of San Antonio in 1842, bought several thousand acres in the area of Paso del Águila north of the river, and in April 1848, had a part of that land surveyed for the future construction of Eagle Pass. German-born Friedrich Groos became a supplier to Fort Duncan, a military outpost built to defend the frontier located just above Eagle Pass on land bought from Twohig. In order to fulfill his contracts with the military, Groos persuaded seventy families from Mexico to migrate north of the river and work as freighters. These families would form the base of the town's population.[16]

Among the towns founded by merchants engaged in trade with Mexico—including Corpus Christi, Presidio, Eagle Pass, and Rio Grande City—one stands out: Brownsville. Charles Stillman founded the town at the site of Fort Brown, built by the U.S. army on the Rio Grande opposite Matamoros. Stillman had considerably increased his capital during the U.S.-Mexican War, and in March 1850, joined Mifflin Kenedy, Richard King, and two other investors in establishing a steamship company that dominated traffic on the lower Rio Grande for the next two decades. Most important, after the war Stillman bought an extensive property across the river from Matamoros from the children of José Narciso Cavazos and his first wife. However, Cavazos had remarried and transmitted that land to the children of his second wife, who fought the sale in court. The second wife's children eventually lost, and the bitterness of that experience made a deep mark on the eldest son, Juan N. Cortina. Stillman moved ahead, forming a company in 1848 with other investors and selling lots for a town that he named Brownsville. Cortina's implacable hatred of land-grabbing *gringos* would maintain the border region in a state of turmoil for almost two decades.[17]

The zeal to trade with Mexico coincided with a larger fever: the rush for gold in California. Many of the travelers chose to go through Texas and northern Mexico en route to the west coast, then continue to the goldfields by ship. Consequently producers and merchants found a market supplying the many travelers passing through the region. Through his many contacts in the border ranches, John P.

Kelsey obtained pack animals to sell to the emigrants at Rio Grande City. He offered California travelers "150 gentle saddle mules and 50 pack mules."[18] In Corpus Christi, Henry L. Kinney also obtained from the Mexican ranches in the Nueces Strip and Northeast Mexico large quantities of mules and horses, intending to outfit the emigrants; instead he unwittingly benefited the Comanches. A local newspaper reported that Indians drove off many of the horses and that "the largest number taken from Col. Kinney's ranchos happened a few days after their arrival from Mexico."[19]

Some gold seekers crossed into Mexico at Eagle Pass, resupplying themselves at James Campbell's store. The commander of Fort Duncan wrote to the state authorities of Coahuila, requesting information on the rules that must be followed by the "American companies that wanted to pass through Mexico on the road to California."[20] According to one source, "Some Mexicans found lucrative employment in manufacturing leather canteens and packsaddles used by the wagon trains." Offering another economic opportunity, in March 1850, an agent from San Antonio traveled to Coahuila to purchase more than six hundred oxen, mules, and horses needed to haul provisions for a large group headed for California.[21]

A greater number of forty-niners probably passed through northern Mexico by way of Matamoros and Monterrey. U.S. consul Thomas Stemmons informed his superiors that about three thousand emigrants "utilized Matamoros as the gateway to the Pacific coast." Stemmons stressed the advantages of shorter distance and lower costs for travelers to California.[22] The passage of many Anglo-American travelers through northern Mexico so soon after the bitter war between the two countries reveals perhaps unexpected attitudes of both Anglos and Mexicans toward each other. From Monterrey, John E. Durivage, a correspondent for the New Orleans *Picayune*, wrote that "there have been no complaints made against emigrants passing along this route to California. They have behaved themselves and respected the Mexicans, and have consequently left a most favorable impression wherever they have passed." Durivage also reported that there were "quite a number of Anglo-Americans" living in Monterrey, "toward whom the Mexicans are all very well disposed" because "the Americans are respected if they are respectable."[23] This passage was written in 1849, when one would assume that resentments and ill feelings from the war would still be strong.

Various cities in Texas competed to gain a larger share of the Mexican trade and to entice the forty-niners to pass through their communities en route to California. The key to success was to offer the best possible route to Mexico. As early as 1848 John Coffee Hays and a force of Texas Rangers and San Antonio merchants set out from San Antonio in search of a good route to El Paso. They never reached their destination. Their trek was "an almost disastrous fifty-seven day ordeal" in which the men were "reduced to eating their mules and horses, a panther, cactus tunas, and bear grass." They got only as far as Presidio, where they spent ten days at a private fort and trading post owned by Ben Leaton, Spencer's former partner.[24] In February 1849, a more formal attempt was made to connect San Antonio to El Paso. Two topographical engineers, Lieutenants William H. C. Whiting and William F. Smith, led a group of emigrants heading for California. They passed through Presidio and reached El Paso in April. Whiting and Smith returned to San Antonio by a more southerly route that became one of the principal roads between the two cities.[25]

These expeditions commonly employed Indian or Mexican scouts who knew the region and how to survive in the wilderness. Whiting and Smith hired José Policarpo Rodríguez, who had been born in Zaragoza, Coahuila, and had a reputation as a tracker. "Polly," as he was called by those who wished to avoid complications, once explained to General Persifor Smith how to find water on the plains by studying "the trees, the trails, the doves, the butterflies, and the wild animals."[26] Irrespective of racial differences, men on the frontier were valued for their worth.

Austin merchants did not want to be left out. At about the same time as the Whiting-Smith expedition, they financed a trip of exploration to El Paso led by Major Robert S. Neighbors and Rip Ford. Neighbors was one of Texas's most successful Indian agents. Ford was an Indian fighter, ranger, newspaper editor, political leader, and one of Texas's best-known public figures. Relying on guides from several Indian tribes, Neighbors and Ford set out for El Paso in March and returned in early June, a few days after Whiting's return. On their way back, with the help of a Mexican named Zambrano, they discovered a route that would become the Upper (or Northern) Road to El Paso.[27]

Interest in the Chihuahua trade was also expressed in the bustling new city of Houston. In 1851 the *Telegraph and Texas Register* exhorted local capitalists to "make an effort to divert a portion" of the trade to Houston. The writer reasoned "that goods could be transported from Houston to Chihuahua, at as cheap a rate, or cheaper, than they could be transported from any point on the Gulf coast." He further informed readers that "a new road ha[d] been opened by Matagorda bay to El Paso, by way of Bexar" and lamented that due to the "apathy of our capitalists," other towns were monopolizing the lucrative trade.[28]

Corpus Christi merchants were still seeking the construction of a good road to El Paso in 1854. A local paper continued to insist that Corpus Christi would "offer such facilities for transportation, as are not, and cannot be possessed by any other route."[29] It seems clear however that in the 1850s San Antonio, with its connection to the Gulf at Matagorda Bay, was winning the competition for the Chihuahua trade. A local newspaper reported on the many merchants "who will leave our city during the coming summer, taking our new and justly celebrated route to El Paso." It declared the trade route between Independence, Missouri, and Chihuahua–Santa Fe was moribund and heralded a new order in which the route connecting Matagorda to El Paso by way of San Antonio would reign supreme.[30]

CONTRABAND, REPRESSION, AND REVOLT

While Texas cities were vying for the Chihuahua trade, the lower Rio Grande was, more than ever, a paradise for smuggling. Scarcely three months after the departure of U.S. troops from Mexico, Nicolás de Arredondo, in charge of the rural police of Coahuila, reported to his superior on the "scandalous commerce" in Texas goods that were entering at unauthorized points along the river.[31] Antonio María Jáuregui, a federal military commander assigned to Northeast Mexico, wrote to the minister of war and navy that "since the evacuation of Monterrey by American troops, it has been common to observe large shipments from the border making their way to diverse points of the interior." He calculated the value of the goods at several million pesos and claimed that "the republic acquired most of the merchandise that it consumed" via smuggling. These goods, complained Jáuregui, were often paid for with silver taken clandestinely out of the country by traders who obtained permits from almost any alcalde. Thus, the contraband flowed in both directions across the border.[32] Consul Stemmons at Matamoros corroborated this situation when he informed the State Department that "smugglers from Texas operated along some 350 miles of the border, upstream from Matamoros." In the first six months of 1849 "their forbidden commercial activities had resulted in the removal of an estimated $1.25 million in specie, along with significant amounts of hides and wool, from south of the border."[33]

Although smuggling was mostly done at night, visitors to the region had no difficulty spotting it. Major William H. Emory, sent to survey the new boundary, wrote of smuggling's pervasive nature: "As might be reasonably expected in any country where the duties on foreign goods amount almost to prohibition, smuggling ceases to be a crime and identifies itself with the best part of the population, and connects itself with the romance and legends of the frontier."[34] Another visitor, the French priest Abbé Emmanuel Domenech, wrote incisively that Henry Clay Davis's former ranch, now Rio Grande City, was a collection of

"American stores and Mexican huts, where smuggling progresses on an extensive scale." The inability of the Mexican government to stop the contraband enabled "American dealers at the Rancho Davis [to] realize immense fortunes."[35]

The Mexican government could not possibly police every ford and flatboat down the long river. One popular crossing place was at Rancho San Pedro, at Roma and across the river from Mier. Roma played the same role as Rio Grande City, farther downriver. With its "fine houses and warehouses" owned by American merchants, Roma was a haven for smugglers. Mexican authorities could not stop the contraband, but they did eventually establish a customhouse at Mier.[36] However, the smugglers were getting bolder. When customs officials seized a cargo of merchandise at a ranch called Guardado de Arriba and sent it toward Camargo under armed guard, a party of Americans disarmed the guards and took the cargo across the river. General Francisco Ávalos, the military commander at Matamoros, was aware that bands of adventurers, joined by Mexican collaborators, were "disposed to defend the fraudulent importation of merchandise" into Mexico.[37]

This situation was well known to Mexican national authorities. In July 1850 Mexico gained a new secretary of the treasury, Manuel Payno, who had lived in Matamoros and knew the northern frontier well. Payno also knew that the Rio Grande was a sieve through which illegal merchandise flowed into the country. This not only dampened legal commerce but also cut sharply into government revenues that were highly dependent on customs duties. Determined to stop the illegal traffic, Payno issued a regulation creating a fiscal police force called the Contraresguardo, stationed in the states of Nuevo León and Tamaulipas. Its purpose was to prevent smuggling by vigorously patrolling the border and stationing armed inspectors in various towns of these states. Like all previous anti-smuggling measures by the national government, the Contraresguardo provoked angry letters to fiscal authorities from many towns of the Northeast.[38]

The merchants of the Rio Grande—Anglo-Americans, Mexicans, and Europeans—did more than write angry letters. They jointly financed a revolt against the government, headed by José María Carvajal, one of the leaders of the Federalist War a decade earlier. The genesis of this conflict goes back to the U.S.-Mexican War when U.S. authorities had eliminated high tariffs and prohibitions. For the first time, norteños discovered the value of free trade. As Tamaulipas governor Francisco Vital Fernández eloquently expressed: "Our ports tasted the satisfying spectacle of [commercial] freedom."[39] Just as border residents were getting used to the freewheeling trade policies of the American occupation, however, the war came to an end and so did free trade. The Mexican government reimposed its authority and its stifling protectionist policies, to which the vecinos responded by smuggling on a larger scale. When the Mexican government created the Contraresguardo and initiated extensive confiscations, the latent discontent ignited into revolt. This was an eerie echo of the Federalist War ten years earlier, which had also been provoked when a centralist government tried to tighten the reins on the border region.

The Carvajal Revolt, also referred to as the Plan de la Loba or the Merchants War, because it had the backing of many Rio Grande merchants, started out as a protest by border residents against national government policies and somehow became transformed—especially under the weight of American involvement—into a separatist movement that called for the establishment of the Republic of the Sierra Madre. The revolt may have been inspired by the merchants of Matamoros or Brownsville or by Carvajal, who declared that he aspired to be the George Washington of his country. There is no question that some sectors of the border community were in favor of separation, but this was not a popular position among the majority of people in Northeast Mexico after the war.[40]

In this climate of rumors and speculation about a separatist movement, Carvajal began his revolt in September 1851 at Guerrero, where the vecinos laid out their demands in a document called the Plan de la Loba. They called for an end to high tariffs and prohibitions; the elimination of duties on foodstuffs for the next five years; and the abolishment of excessive penalties for smuggling. Significantly, in two articles that Texan sympathizers of the movement apparently forgot to read, the signers explicitly rejected the idea of separating from Mexico. Article 10 stated that the plan was "eminently national and liberal" in nature, while Article 12 declared that "the states that adopt this plan may organize a provisional government, though any thought of separation or annexation is discarded."[41]

Rio Grande merchants including Richard King, Mifflin Kenedy, Charles Stillman, and Henry Clay Davis supported the movement and provided financial support to Carvajal because they opposed the trade restrictions of the Mexican government. Moreover, there was a pool of men who were looking for adventure and good pay after the war ended. The *Corpus Christi Star* proclaimed that many Americans were willing to join the movement: "Should the citizens of the Sierra Madre ever deem that [their] interest or happiness requires a change of government, they may count upon the sympathy of gallant spirits in the United States, without whom, Texas would have still been a part of Mexico."[42] Two features in this text are noteworthy. One is the reference to the "citizens of the Sierra Madre," who were probably unaware that they were prospective citizens of a new country. The other relates to those willing to save them. William Neale, who knew the people and the region as well as any contemporary observer, was more realistic about the "gallant spirits" who inhabited the region: "more men of desperate character, desperate fortunes, and evil propensities, were congregated here on this frontier from 1846 to 1848, than ever got together in any other place . . . on the earth since the deluge."[43]

Despite skepticism in some Texas newspapers, most of the press justified the movement and fanned the fire of revolt. The *Telegraph and Texas Register* explained that the "trade of Brownsville, Roma, and of most of the towns on the east bank of the Rio Grande [had] been almost ruined by the Mexican revenue officers, who have endeavored by the most tyrannical impositions to prevent Americans from trading with any of the towns or settlements in the interior."[44] Clearly, the Contraresguardo was beginning to irritate the merchants. To other Texans the issue of slave flight was of even greater importance, however. The *Texas State Times* published a letter from a reader in Laredo who proposed raising $600,000 (approximately $16.8 million today) to ensure the success of Carvajal's revolt because his movement was the only guarantee of getting their slaves back. The editor—Carvajal's friend Rip Ford—agreed with the letter writer: "To the people of this State it is a question of vital importance, involving no less than the security and the perpetuation of one of our social institutions." To Ford, at issue was nothing less than "self-preservation," because without the work of slaves "our vast bodies of cotton and sugar lands will remain uncultivated—our resources undeveloped, our growth and prosperity retarded and crippled." In other words slave owners would not develop the region near the border for fear of slave flight, and the Carvajal Revolt was seen as a means to increase their confidence.[45]

After initiating the revolt, Carvajal called on Rip Ford for help and made him a colonel in his rebel army. Ford enlisted about four hundred Texans, who provided their own guns. The movement offered Ford and his men a special inducement: many black slaves had fled to Mexico, and there was an active individual and group campaign to return them to Texas for bounties. Carvajal offered slave catchers the right "to seize and transport into Texas any fugitive Negroes, in return for service in the revolution."[46] Rip Ford described Carvajal as a man fighting for freedom and against tyranny; in reality, he was fighting for the freedom of slaveholders to exercise tyranny over their slaves.[47]

Carvajal made several incursions into Mexico, but the most important action occurred between October 1851 and February 1852. After defeating a few

José María de Jesús Carvajal. A native of San Antonio and protégé of Stephen F. Austin,
Carvajal lived most of his life along the Rio Grande and played a major role in many of the
regional wars from the 1830s to the 1860s. Bilingual and bicultural, he had extensive business,
political, military, and social ties among Anglo-Americans and Mexicans. LC-USZ62-123471,
Library of Congress.

government troops in Camargo, Carvajal and a force of about seven hundred
men, including some four hundred Anglo-Americans, advanced toward the city
of Matamoros. During the last ten days of October, Carvajal put Matamoros
under a brutal siege, but he was beaten back by the forces of General Francisco
Ávalos, who relied on more than military force to defeat the rebels. He followed
the advice of the city council and reduced import duties by more than 50 percent,
eliminating one of the rebels' complaints and winning over many among the
merchants and the general population to his side.[48]

The brutality of the siege was mirrored in the destruction and pillaging of
many homes and buildings of the city. U.S. Consul James F. Waddell excoriated
Carvajal for having "shed the blood of his brothers . . . for no higher purpose than
the accomplishment of the miserable scheme of the artless speculators."[49] The

residents of the Northeast repudiated Carvajal for inviting American mercenaries to invade and kill Mexicans, but the Texas press continued to report on his heroic struggle against oppression. The *Telegraph and Texas Register* recounted a battle at Cerralvo between the rebels and government forces led by General Antonio María Jáuregui in which several officers among the would-be liberators "were killed while gallantly leading their men in the assault." The newspaper praised both Anglo and Mexican freedom fighters for performing "their duty with such chivalry and courage." This example of cooperative violence was more than matched by Jáuregui's unit, which included "Indians and negro auxiliaries." Moreover, the latter were the real freedom fighters in this conflict because they were struggling to maintain their freedom against the slave catchers in Carvajal's army.[50]

Carvajal's defeat came swiftly and from an unexpected source. Antonio Canales, his former ally in the Federalist War, had mobilized a large force that included local militias and a large body of Seminoles and Maroons (fugitive slaves who had intermarried with Seminoles) that had recently settled in Coahuila. Canales routed the rebels in February 1852, at Paso del Azúcar on the banks of the San Juan River near Camargo. By this time Carvajal's force had been reduced to 438 Anglo-Americans and eighty-four Mexicans who "in their escape, abandoned all of their war materiel." Carvajal had to be rescued by Henry Clay Davis and a war party of Indians, who crossed the Rio Grande to return him to safety in Texas.[51]

The persistent Carvajal tried to revive his movement in 1853, but it had degenerated into a shameful series of forays by his Anglo and Mexican supporters. Carvajal and some of his collaborators were finally imprisoned and tried in Brownsville, although they were later exonerated. Carvajal's revolt failed because the vecinos of the border region did not rally to his cause and because he relied on Anglo-Americans. The norteños became convinced that this was not a Mexican revolt but a foreign invasion. Moreover, grim reminders of atrocities during the recent U.S.-Mexican War convinced the residents of the Northeast that they were better off under Mexican rule. They were willing to trade and work with Anglo-Americans, but they did not want to live under Anglo domination and end up like their fellow Mexicans in Texas.[52]

The border region was just getting over the Carvajal disturbances when a large-scale rebellion against the government of Santa Anna in central Mexico sent shock waves reverberating throughout the border region. The movement began with the Plan of Ayutla in March 1854, which was backed by a broad coalition of liberals that included Juan Alvarez, Ignacio Comonfort, and Benito Juárez. By the summer, liberals in Tamaulipas led by Juan José de la Garza had joined the movement. On August 10, they issued their own plan at San Lorenzo de la Mesa on the banks of the Rio Grande. In addition to calling for the ouster of Santa Anna, it included a list of local demands, including lower import duties, an effective regional military force to combat Indian raids, and less stringent immigration laws that would allow the entry of honest, hardworking immigrants to help populate and modernize the state.[53]

The movement in Tamaulipas did not advance militarily until the summer of 1855, when a larger regional rebellion led by Santiago Vidaurri toppled the santanista governor of Nuevo León. Vidaurri, an experienced Indian fighter from the military bastion of Lampazos on Nuevo León's northern frontier, gathered a large force from his hometown and the surrounding area in May 1855, and marched toward Monterrey. He had served the state government for more than twenty years and had lived through all the wars since Texas independence. He knew the border region as well as anyone and possessed extraordinary administrative and leadership qualities. His organization of the Nuevo León National Guard in 1850–51 provided him with a network of friends and allies in towns throughout the state. He shared the borderlanders' disdain for the central government, especially its tariff policy, which had been reinstated in 1852 after Carvajal's defeat.[54]

Vidaurri took Monterrey almost without a fight on May 22, 1855, then sought to extend his movement to Tamaulipas and Coahuila. By early July he was at Mier on the Rio Grande, where he forged an alliance with Juan José de la Garza and other liberal leaders of Tamaulipas. Vidaurri and De la Garza agreed to work together to liberate the Northeast from santanista rule. De la Garza was named governor of Tamaulipas and second in command of the Ejército del Norte, Vidaurri's Army of the North. De la Garza marched to Matamoros, defended by General Adrián Woll, while Vidaurri set his sights on Saltillo.[55]

The capital of Coahuila had been reinforced, and Vidaurri realized that he would need more firepower to take the town. One historian has written that he looked to Texas for help, asking the merchants of the Rio Grande to provide resources for his movement. It is not clear how much support he received, but *El Bejareño*, the Spanish-language newspaper of San Antonio, reported that some three hundred Anglo-Americans had crossed the border at Brownsville to join the rebel army. The battle of Saltillo began on July 22, and by the following day the city fell to Vidaurri's forces. His army, composed largely of rancheros skilled in Indian warfare, had no experience in operating artillery, so Vidaurri relied on Anglo-American and European artillerymen, who played an important part in the victory. Among them were Edward Pendleton and Edward H. Jordan.

Pendleton was an American who had served in Carvajal's army during the Plan de la Loba. Jordan's nationality is unclear, either British or American depending on the source. He was a merchant at Laredo before the revolt so he was likely of British origin, although perhaps he had become a naturalized American citizen. Vidaurri wrote that at Saltillo, Jordan "fought with determination" and "unusual valor." The success at Saltillo placed most of Northeast Mexico under Vidaurri's control and drove another nail in the coffin of Santa Anna's government, which fell the following month.[56]

Vidaurri's movement attracted a large following in the Northeast and Texas because of his promise to lower customs duties and open new ports for commerce. In Texas the embers of separatism began to glow again and Vidaurri was seen as a new messiah who would successfully liberate the northeast region from Mexico and establish the Republic of the Sierra Madre. A movement in support of the revolt immediately got underway in Texas in the summer of 1855. A group calling itself the Directing Committee was formed in San Antonio and elected as its chairman Hanson Alsbury, a real estate broker and brother of Horace Alsbury, who had supported the Mexican federalists in 1840. The committee named Bennett Riddells as agent to deal with the leaders of the uprising. As a merchant living in Chihuahua with a Mexican wife, Riddells had a history of dealing with Mexicans. "He owned the American hotel in Chihuahua and served from time to time as the American consul there."[57] Alsbury instructed Riddells to procure funds from the revolutionary chiefs to support a Texas auxiliary force, which the committee promised to mobilize. He was also ordered to assure those leaders that the committee was not "prompted by mercenary motives" but "by a sincere desire to aid in the cause of brave men justly struggling for the maintenance of their liberty against the oppressions of a tyrant [Santa Anna]."[58]

Another movement headed by Captain W. R. Henry appeared at the same time, though it is not clear whether it was related to Alsbury's group. Henry, who would be elected sheriff of Bexar County a year later in 1856, issued two proclamations. One, intended for the people of northern Mexico, declared that "our only wish . . . is to see reestablished the federal system, and to secure treaties by which the interests of both countries shall be protected, and which will allow us to exchange our products . . . without fear of molestation, under the protection of just and equitable tariffs." The other proclamation—intended for Texans' consumption—was more candid about Henry's intentions: to "displace the far-famed Santa Anna, and establish . . . a government more favorable to the interests of Texas, enlightened in its views, and with the final intention of extending the proud American Eagle over its protection." Henry wisely omitted mention of the eagle to his Mexican audience. He did mention that men were arriving in large numbers to Uvalde County and were soon expected to cross the Rio Grande and begin disseminating his proclamation among the Mexican population. Henry, who had earlier been accused of leading a band of "robbers, outlaws, [and] filibusters," took pains to remind his readers that he was at the head of a group of volunteers who would be respectful of Mexicans and their property "and will behave as becomes men of honor."[59]

These movements of support went nowhere. Even though Vidaurri called on Brownsville merchants for assistance and accepted foreign artillerymen in his ranks, it is clear that he wanted nothing less than unilateral control of his movement and was unwilling to share glory or power with anyone. A strong-willed leader such as Vidaurri would not accept subordination to his own government, much less to a foreign one. Accordingly, he rejected most offers of aid from foreign sources and accepted only those he could control. His domestic policies spurred unprecedented economic growth in Nuevo León. He took over the ports on the Rio Grande and opened new ones to international commerce, drastically reducing import duties and filling his coffers to build a powerful army with which to challenge the national government.[60] In defiance of the national government, he incorporated Coahuila into Nuevo León on February 19, 1856—an unprecedented action in Mexican history—and tried but failed to do the same with Tamaulipas. He attracted to his side brilliant military men such as Ignacio Zaragoza, Mariano Escobedo, Miguel Blanco, and Juan Zuazua, all of whom attained national fame; and he built an army made up mostly of rancheros and rural workers of the Northeast, which allowed him to exercise hegemony over the region for almost a decade, from 1855 to 1864.[61]

Many Texans would not easily let go of the notion of making common cause with Mexican liberals or republicans to form a separate nation in northern Mexico. In 1856, one year after the raid known as the Callahan expedition, which caused much ill feeling in northern Mexico, W. R. Henry heard a rumor that Vidaurri had proclaimed in favor of creating the Republic of the Sierra Madre. Henry wrote immediately to wish him success and offer his services. Texans would rise as one "to your call in favor of liberty," he wrote, adding that "hundreds of young and honorable men of Texas are but awaiting the call . . . to join in with the sons of Liberty and assist in hoisting and sustaining the Flag of Sierra Madre."[62]

There were many men like Henry in Texas, deluded into thinking that norteños were anxious to break away from Mexico. They did not know what

John Forsyth, U.S. ambassador to Mexico, explained to Secretary of State Lewis
Cass; namely, that the mistrust and fear of Americans in northern Mexico "has
prevented the states bordering on the United States . . . overrun by savages and
receiving no protection from the Mexican government . . . from breaking their
feeble ties with the central government, and seeking, in annexation with us, that
security for life and property of which they are now wholly destitute." He went
on to state that the expropriation of land belonging to Mexicans in Texas and
California had convinced northern Mexicans that their "proper titles, especially
to land, would not be respected by their new rulers." Indeed, he was convinced
that "this circumstance alone has saved to the republic of Mexico the fidelity of
Tamaulipas, New Leon, Chihuahua and Sonora."[63]

Vidaurri's case appeared to be different, however. His constant disputes
with the national government nurtured Texans' hopes that he would someday
lead a separatist movement and create a nation more agreeable to U.S. interests.
Vidaurri, however, showed no interest in separating from Mexico. He most
emphatically rejected that idea in a letter he sent to the *Southern Intelligencer*
in February 1859. In response to an anonymous letter published in that newspaper, Vidaurri blamed a "brainless foreigner" (probably Manuel Payno, who
was neither brainless nor a foreigner) of accusing him of authoring a plan to
separate northern Mexico and create the Republic of the Sierra Madre, a project he deemed "criminal and foolish." Vidaurri challenged anyone to prove that
his policies were anything but radically Mexican, and promised to pay the cost
of traveling to Mexico "to the person who possesses those proofs of infamy and
treason" in order to eradicate the vain hopes of those in Texas who still pined for
a separate republic in northern Mexico. He concluded that the state of Nuevo
León y Coahuila, which he governed, was a "zealous defender of the honor and
independence of the [Mexican] nation" and would be "the first in combat the day
that the security of the border was threatened by external machinations against
the interests and the indissoluble union of the Mexican Republic."[64]

A PERMEABLE BORDER
Although Vidaurri vehemently opposed U.S. expansion into his domain, he was
not averse to the settlement of outsiders in Nuevo León y Coahuila. Foreigners,
especially Anglo-Americans, continued to come to northern Mexico in spite of
the instability in the country. Monterrey, which, according to one eyewitness,
resembled a cemetery after the U.S. attack in September 1846, experienced
remarkable recovery and growth in the 1850s. This renaissance was fueled in part

by the establishment of the border on the Rio Grande, which made Monterrey the chief beneficiary of many of the commercial enterprises springing up on the left bank of the river from Brownsville to Eagle Pass. In the eight-year period after the war, "the population of the city doubled, the value of its urban buildings tripled, and the mercantile and industrial capital rose to six million pesos."[65]

Doctors and merchants continued to arrive and settle in the region, and by 1858 hundreds of Anglo-Americans were living in Mexico, according to Peter Suzeneau, U.S. consul in Matamoros. From Laredo, Santos Benavides wrote to his good friend Santiago Vidaurri, recommending a Dr. Malone, who wanted to relocate to Monterrey after providing valuable service in the former community. Another of Vidaurri's friends, Ángel Navarro, son of José Antonio Navarro of San Antonio, wrote that Dr. George S. C. Todd of Kentucky wanted to practice his profession in Saltillo and that he promised to "avoid mixing in political issues." Navarro also recommended a Dr. Laurent, who wished to practice medicine in Mexico. Laurent was accompanied by his wife.[66]

Foreign merchants—some of them Anglo-Americans—traveled to Monterrey in greater numbers in the 1850s. One of these was William Glover. Following a pattern established in most of the towns of northern Mexico where the United States chose its diplomatic representatives from the merchant class, he was named U.S. consul in that city in February 1850.[67] Frontier merchants routinely moved on to new towns or settlements in their quest for markets and greater profits. New Orleans was a prolific platform for launching merchants toward Texas and Mexico. Some of the foreign merchants in Monterrey maintained ties to or a part of their operations in New Orleans, as well as in Brownsville and Matamoros. Daniel Wolf, who at times identified as Prussian and at other times as American, imported 100,000 pesos in merchandise for his store in Monterrey. He ran a business in Brownsville worth 60,000 pesos and owned properties in New Orleans from the days when he operated in that city. In Monterrey Wolf's reputation as a businessman was stained when he threatened to kill a fellow merchant over the sale of a carriage.[68]

Vidaurri's drive to pacify and modernize Nuevo León y Coahuila led him to embrace the idea of populating his vast state with docile Indians, runaway slaves, and German colonists from Texas.[69] The Indians and former slaves would serve as a bulwark against hostile Indian raiders, while the Germans—with their intelligence, discipline, and exemplary work habits—would help bring progress to the state. In November 1855, Miguel Blanco, whose family had a lengthy relationship with Texas, wrote to Vidaurri about a large group of Germans who wanted to immigrate to Mexico. They were disgusted with the nativist turn in Texas, reflected in the rise of the Know-Nothing Party, and wished to "devote themselves to their peaceful endeavors and live in peace." Blanco asked Vidaurri to receive two German representatives, Carlos N. Riotte and Gustavo Frauenstein, and facilitate their objective by eliminating bureaucratic obstacles. He cited as a reason for supporting the project: "you know better than I how much we need that kind of colonization for our own security against the usurpation of the Americans and the progress of our towns."[70]

German colonization was also promoted by Colonel Emilio Langberg, a native of Denmark who had served in the Mexican military since the 1830s and had been sent to defend the northern frontier from Indian attacks. The multifaceted Dane was an expert violinist, horseman, and surveyor, as well as a keen observer of the differences on the two sides of the border. He compared U.S. soldiers with those under his command and reflected that the former "behave with decorum and respect, with their discipline and instruction, their cleanliness and order." He was hopeful that they would "stimulate our troops and officers to imitate them by finding a respectable way to live." Contrary to the policy makers in Mexico City, obsessed with centralizing control, Langberg declared that "civilization will come from the frontier. Contact will make people on the border more hard working and industrious as they come to know the comforts of life."[71]

In that spirit, he addressed the German colonists of Texas in a letter published in one of their newspapers in San Antonio. Langberg, who had studied in Göttingen and had an affinity for the German people, assured them of "favorable conditions" and a "most friendly welcome on the part of the people."[72] Langberg's negotiations were approved by Santiago Vidaurri, who offered the Germans twenty-nine leagues of land in the jurisdiction of Lampazos where they would live together with Mexican families. The newcomers would be exempt from paying taxes for three years and would enjoy religious freedom. The latter concession shows Vidaurri was aware that the lack of religious freedom had torpedoed previous attempts to attract European immigration to Mexico. He was ahead of his liberal colleagues at the national level, who would not take that step until 1860, during the War of Reform. Regardless, the project never materialized. The *New York Daily Times* had already anticipated that "so sagacious and intelligent a people as the Germans" would not go and "live in a country like Mexico, among a debased population, and where popular freedom is at the mercy of a bigoted priesthood, and life and property are subject to the vicissitudes of military adventurers who aim at the rule of the country."[73]

However bad conditions may have been in Mexico, African slaves and some Indian tribes decided it would be better than living in the United States. In fact, from the moment that slaves set foot in Texas they began to abandon their masters and flee toward the interior of Mexico. They often took with them property, particularly animals that they sold in Mexico. Archival records in Nuevo León show that from the 1820s onward through the 1830s escaped slaves were being reclaimed by their owners in Texas. A U.S. official wrote in 1839 of the "frequent escape of slaves from the American side of the Rio Grande into Mexico" and the likelihood that Texas travelers would run into their "own property in Matamoros."[74] Despite Mexico's caste system, blacks enjoyed freedom and could aspire to a higher social status in Coahuila, Nuevo León, or Tamaulipas, where they were welcomed and treated like human beings rather than a form of property. This is what one black fugitive discovered when Rafael Jiménez found him near Laredo in the heat of summer in 1841, dying of hunger and thirst. He was cared for until he recovered his health. David Thomas, another refugee, arrived in Allende, Coahuila, with "one daughter and three grandchildren in order to save his family from slavery."[75]

The makeup of the population of northern Mexico contributed to the acceptance of blacks. There were blacks in the region in the eighteenth century, perhaps survivors of the shipwreck of a slave ship. They mixed easily and intermarried with the Indian population. Almost 6 percent of the population of Tamaulipas in 1853 had African ancestry. General Thomas J. Green, one of the prisoners of the Mier expedition, "encountered [Sam] Houston's ex-slaves, Tom and Esau, outside the town of Matamoros" and observed their acceptance in society. He recalled that Tom treated the group of prisoners with respect and told them of his plans to get married. He also informed them proudly that General Pedro de Ampudia would be his godfather at the wedding. In Texas the privilege of having a prominent general serve as godfather to a black person would certainly be unthinkable and, aside from the liberty, it was this kind of distinction that made many slaves choose to escape to Mexico.[76] One former slave, Felix Haywood, declared, "In Mexico you could be free, they didn't care what color you were, black, white, yellow or blue." Rip Ford, a keen observer of those times who was also a strong proponent of capturing and returning escaped slaves, recognized that blacks were popular in Mexico, although he accused Mexicans of hypocrisy for reviling American slavery while enslaving their own people for debt.[77]

When Frederick Law Olmsted made his celebrated tour of Texas and northeastern Mexico in 1856–57, he observed thousands of "Mexicans of mixed negro blood" in "respectable social positions whose color and physiognomy would subject them, in Texas, to be sold by the sheriff as negro-estrays who cannot be allowed at large without detriment to the commonwealth."[78] Information is scarce on black individuals or families who fled Texas to live in Mexico. Ben Kinchlow was one individual who did not have to flee. His master sent him and his mother to Matamoros, probably on some kind of work arrangement with a Mexican rancher. Kinchlow worked as a ranch hand and "reported having a friendly and cooperative relationship with Mexicans on both sides of the river." He spoke of a supportive and sharing community: "When any of the neighbors killed fresh meat we always divided it with one another . . . and when people wanted to brand or do other work, all the neighbors went together and helped without pay."[79] Interactions between races must have been interesting in Matamoros. Benjamin Lundy reported an incident in which Anglos in a dance hall objected to "the admittance of a group of young Blacks." The blacks stayed while the Anglos were invited to leave the premises.[80]

The number of slaves who escaped to Mexico will never be known. There was a steady flow of black refugees through the Eagle Pass and Laredo regions. W. Secrest, a visitor to Eagle Pass in 1851, reported that more than eighteen hundred blacks were living at a nearby settlement.[81] Rip Ford estimated that there were about three thousand living between the Rio Grande and the Sierra Madre in 1851. Slave flight intensified in the 1850s, and by 1855 another "contemporary observer estimated the number of former slaves in northern Mexico at about 4,000." Historian Rosalie Schwartz, states in her book on the subject that "most likely there were several thousand fugitive Negroes in Mexico in the 1850s."[82]

Mexicans generally sided with the slaves. The Mexico City newspaper *Siglo Diez y Nueve* declared: "If we are enemies of slavery, it is because the Negro is a man, because the Negro is our brother."[83] It is hard to tell whether this statement reflects toleration or just U.S. baiting, but without doubt many Mexicans sympathized with the plight of escaped slaves. The national government refused to cooperate with Texan officials who sought the return of slaves and incorporated into the Constitution of 1857 a provision that fugitive slaves could not be extradited. This sentiment extended to some officials at the local level. Manuel Flores, the alcalde of Guerrero, Coahuila, warned the blacks in his district to relocate farther into the interior to avoid problems with slave catchers. He also kept a close watch on Anglo-Americans who requested passports to engage in business because some of them were in the business of trapping slaves. The justice of the peace at Piedras Negras instructed his subordinate in the Rio Grande district to take strict measures to ensure the safety of blacks in the event that Anglo-American slave catchers arrived: "if they wish to use force you will detain them and send them to this command."[84]

In Texas it was widely believed that Mexicans helped black slaves escape to Mexico. One of the delegates to the Texas convention in 1845 denounced the "peons of the west [who] have come in and enticed our negroes away."[85] When slave flight increased greatly in the 1850s, that belief was elevated to the point of hysteria against the Mexican population. In 1852, authorities at Matagorda "caught a group of Mexicans stealing horses and running three slaves off to Mexico. The population reacted swiftly and severely, expelling the entire population of Mexicans from the town."[86] Throughout the 1850s, several Texas counties, including Uvalde and Colorado, expelled Mexicans or restricted their movement because they blamed them for luring slaves to Mexico. As in the Texas war for independence, this is another example of historical circumstances that intensified racial hatred against Mexicans, who more and more were referred to as "greasers."[87]

Ironically, while Mexicans were being vilified for contributing to slave flight, some actively collaborated with Anglo slave catchers to retrieve runaways. This form of cooperative violence was motivated by the promise of profit. Rewards of up to $500 were offered for the return of each fugitive. Carvajal's approval of cooperation with slave hunters during his revolt of La Loba has been noted. When slave flight intensified in the 1850s, some of the vecinos of Laredo, recently incorporated into the United States, "began to capture escaped slaves and send them back in servitude."[88] The collaboration between Anglo-Americans and Mexicans required teamwork because the former had the description of the slave and the latter the knowledge of the region. In January 1850, two Mexicans, José María Nuncio and Marcos Mariscal, joined four Anglo-Americans and set out from Eagle Pass toward the interior of Mexico in search of an escaped slave. They arrived at the ranch of Ramón González in the Rio Grande District, where the fugitive had found protection. When the ranchero and his family refused to give up the slave, both men and women were brutally beaten. The four Anglos escaped across the border with their prey, but the two Mexican collaborators were captured by military authorities.[89]

In March 1851, the alcalde of Guerrero, Manuel Flores, received word that an Anglo-American and a Mexican were on their way to the border after capturing a slave. Flores set out with a group of men, caught up with the slave catchers, and ordered them to surrender. The American went for his gun, but Flores fired first and put a bullet in the man's chest. The alcalde sent for an American physician living nearby, but the doctor, Benjamin Thomas, arrived too late. The American slave catcher had died, while his Mexican partner in crime had wisely escaped into the woods upon the arrival of the alcalde.[90]

These individual forays into Mexico in search of runaway slaves clearly had limited success. Slave owners began to consider organizing slave-catching expeditions into Mexico. The notorious slave hunter Warren Adams organized one such venture, but it was thwarted when the commander at Fort Duncan alerted military authorities in Piedras Negras. Another group of slave hunters was organized in 1859, and again the authorities at Fort Duncan tipped off their counterparts across the Rio Grande.[91]

Vidaurri's success in the summer of 1855 encouraged slave owners in Texas to hope that a successful revolt would enable them to recover their runaway slaves. These concerns were at the heart of the aforementioned movements led by Hanson Alsbury and W. R. Henry. Their lofty rhetoric about helping brave Mexicans to cast off the chains of tyranny masked their primary interest, which was the prompt recovery of their property; namely, runaway slaves. In turn, Alsbury and his group offered to return fugitive peons from Mexico who had escaped their debts by fleeing to Texas. They declared that because the governments of the United States and Mexico had not signed an extradition treaty, "the duty of self preservation impels the co-terminous States" to provide "protection to the persons and property of all concerned." In the absence of state power, local authorities and groups arrogated to themselves the right to take measures in defense of their interests.[92] Henry's movement had the same impetus. In the weeks prior to Henry's proclamation, an Austin newspaper reported on the increasing numbers of runaway slaves and opined that "by aiding the liberal party in Mexico we can accomplish an arrangement which will make Slavery as secure in Texas as any State in the Union."[93]

Vidaurri's apparent indifference to Alsbury's and Henry's groups led slave-holders in Texas to seek another approach. Faced with a significant increase in Indian raids against Texas from Mexico, they decided that they could kill two birds with one stone: they would mobilize an expedition to enter Mexico, punish the Indians, and bring back runaway slaves. They sought to enlist Mexican authorities in order to ensure the success of the mission, contacting Colonel Emilio Langberg, the military commander of Coahuila, "about the possibility of negotiating the return of fugitive slaves living in Mexico, offering to pay for each one delivered to the river." Langberg was willing to accept the offer if the

Texans collaborated in returning to Mexico the sirvientes who had been escaping their debts and their haciendas by fleeing to Texas. His boss, Governor Vidaurri, however, vetoed any deal involving private citizens and instructed Langberg to repel any force that crossed the border.[94]

Meanwhile, James H. Callahan, representing a group of investors whose properties suffered continuous Indian raids, led a force of more than a hundred men into Mexico in late September 1855. Langberg's troops, led by Manuel Menchaca and Miguel Patiño and including Indian fighters, met and defeated this force at Río Escondido, a skirmish that Mexican newspapers portrayed as a new symbol of the defense of Mexican sovereignty. In his retreat, Callahan put Piedras Negras to the torch.[95]

Whether the Callahan raid had as its primary objective the return of runaway slaves or the punishment of Indian raiders based in Mexico, it convinced Vidaurri that he needed to cooperate more closely with his Texas neighbors in order to avoid future invasions of the territory he zealously controlled. In late November, two months after Callahan's incursion, he wrote to Hamilton P. Bee, the then-president of the Texas legislature. In another example of transborder networking, Vidaurri had heard of Bee from his friend and military collaborator Edward Jordan, who had been Bee's neighbor in Laredo. Vidaurri learned that Bee had presented a resolution condemning the sacking of Piedras Negras; offering compensation for those who lost property; and promoting "a treaty of extradition of runaway slaves and sirvientes of both countries." Vidaurri praised Bee for his noble intentions and asked him please to inform him of the outcome of his efforts.[96]

Bee responded, professing his "regard and admiration" for Vidaurri and informing him of his legislative efforts. He had "introduced a series of measures, providing for an amicable arrangement of all questions pending between the two countries, including the mutual delivery by Texas, on the one hand of fugitives from labor in Mexico, and by Mexico on the other of fugitive slaves from Texas." The measure was stalled, but Bee was hopeful it would be approved in the next session. He assured the Nuevo León governor of "the warmest feelings of respect for yourself and good wishes for your cause" among the people of Texas. Their continued collaboration, he wrote, would "strengthen the bonds which ought to unite two neighboring countries whose interests are identical, for they are based upon the principles of liberty and justice."[97] This exchange of letters reveals Vidaurri's willingness to get involved in the legislative processes of his foreign neighbor if it served his interests.

IMMIGRANT TRIBES

When black people arrived in Northeast Mexico, they became part of a broader community of exiles that included Indians from various peoples: Cherokees, Kickapoos, Caddos, Lipan Apaches, Seminoles, and black Seminole maroons, known as *mascogos* in Mexico. Members of these tribes began to migrate to northern Mexico at various times beginning in the period after Texas independence. An initial group of Cherokees who were expelled from Texas arrived in Coahuila in 1839 accompanied by about eighty Kickapoos. This group was followed by another band of Cherokees and Caddos in 1839 and 1840. An additional group of 330 Caddos entered Coahuila in 1841. Their arrival in Mexico was promoted by General Mariano Arista, who wanted them to "form a barrier against Texans and the 'ferocious incursions' of raiding Indians from the west."[98]

After the U.S.-Mexican War, Arista, in his role as minister of war and with his personal knowledge of the border, set out to militarize the frontier and protect it from Indian raiders. He encouraged the immigration of docile Indians who would be given land and resources to develop their communities in exchange for helping to defend the northern settlements. His plan moved a big step forward when about seven hundred Seminoles arrived in 1850. About a hundred mascogos and a like number of Kickapoos were also part of that migration. The leader of the Seminoles was Coacoochee, better known as Wild Cat or Gato del Monte, a charismatic leader who traveled to Mexico City in 1852 to petition for a grant of land in the Hacienda Nacimiento near Santa Rosa, Coahuila.[99]

The mascogos, led by John Horse, or Juan Caballo, were descendants of slaves who had escaped bondage and had acquired Indian customs through living with the Seminoles in Florida. They adapted to Mexico better than the Kickapoos or Seminoles because they had a greater interest in farming than fighting and adopted Catholicism more willingly than the others. They established their own colony at Nacimiento de los Negros, very close to the Seminole settlement. Their colony grew impressively, replenished constantly by arriving runaway slaves from Texas.[100]

A second prong of the strategy of frontier defense was the establishment of a chain of *colonias militares* on Mexico's northern border, a defense system similar to the presidios of the Bourbon period and designed to defend the region against Comanche and Apache raiders. Mariano Arista, one of the few men in Mexico City who knew the northern frontier, was the driving force behind this strategy. In command of these colonias was Inspector General Antonio María Jáuregui, who praised the decision to utilize Seminole and mascogo warriors because "these tribes . . . are hard-working, industrious, and combative and because they . . . will be the bulwark that will smash the savages that ravage our fields and afflict our inhabitants."[101] The Seminoles and mascogos were fierce fighters and fulfilled their role superbly. They participated in more than forty operations against Comanche and Lipan Apache raiders. Rosalie Schwartz writes that "Mexican authorities were generous in praise of the industriousness of the colonists and lauded their effectiveness in checking the destructive activities of warlike Indians in the area."[102]

Lipan Apaches were the most problematic of the immigrant tribes. Their culture was grounded in mobility and the liberty that came from raiding and nomadism. They had inhabited the Rio Grande region before the arrival of the Spanish, but after the separation of Texas they made various treaties with the government of the new republic and used Texan sanctuaries to launch raids on northern Mexico. They were seen frequently in San Antonio trading hides, and relations between them and the settlers of Gillespie County in Central Texas were described as "harmonious." Their presence, however, began to displease many white settlers desirous of occupying their lands and for that and other causes, relations between Apaches and settlers began to deteriorate. By the mid-1850s, most of the bands migrated to Northeast Mexico while a scattered few drifted to Texas's western frontier. They used the establishment of the border to their advantage, raiding on one side and seeking refuge on the other. In 1852, the Lipans sought to make peace with the Mexican government, but Arista, who was president at the time, knew they would never accept "the trappings of civilization and dedicate themselves to labor and sedentary agriculture." He decided to make total war on them.[103]

When Santa Anna returned to power in 1853, the government made peace with the Lipans, perhaps thinking that, as historical enemies of the Comanches, they could be induced to help protect the frontier. That did not occur, however. The Lipans used the truce with Mexico to increase their raids in Texas. These raids, according to historian Nancy McGown Minor, were "tacitly sanctioned" by the Mexican government. "Raids in Texas brought large numbers of stolen horses and cattle. The animals were driven across the Rio Grande and sold in the marketplaces of Zaragoza and Santa Rosa [Coahuila], bringing a boon to the Mexican economy and a steady supply of guns, ammunition, and trade goods to Lipan Apaches."[104] Months after the santanista government granted peace to the Lipans, a "spate of raids . . . occurred around Laredo in Webb County in the

A Lipan Apache. Lipan Apache raids in Mexico and Texas in the 1850s led Santiago Vidaurri to unleash a war of extermination against them. A few continued raiding into the 1870s, causing many problems between the United States and Mexico. Lithograph by Arthur Schott. No. 070-0142, UTSA Special Collections.

spring of 1854" attributed to them. The Texans were incensed and threatened to exterminate them, wherever they were found. These were the raids that served as a prelude for the Callahan expedition of 1855.[105]

Lipan intransigence was only one of the many problems posed by the policy of accepting immigrant tribes. Another was the scarcity of resources on the frontier and the extreme poverty in which Indians were forced to live. The Mexican government, always beset by political upheavals and a bankrupt treasury, did not keep its promise of providing the immigrant tribes with resources. Their repeated calls for food and supplies went unanswered. In desperation some of them began raiding, either in Texas or within Mexico. Moreover, the vecinos of the Northeast were wary of these Indians from the start. They had fought Indians for decades and could not get used to the idea of a friendly or docile Indian. Disputes between some of the tribes and their

Mexican neighbors intensified, and in 1851 many of the Kickapoos, disgusted with Mexico, returned to the United States.[106]

Conditions for the immigrant tribes worsened in 1856–57 when a deadly smallpox epidemic struck hard at the Seminole community near Santa Rosa. Dr. Juan Long, who had lived in Coahuila since the 1830s, rushed to the area and vaccinated the Indians, but many of them died, among them their leader, Wild Cat. In the following years the Seminoles began drifting back to Texas and the Indian Territory of Oklahoma.[107]

Vidaurri continued to count on a steady flow of escaped slaves who generally settled near Santa Rosa, close to the mascogos. He offered them land and they reciprocated by joining the fight against Comanche and Apache raiders. Vidaurri was determined to keep these groups satisfied. He encouraged the mascogos to move farther into the interior near the grape-growing region of Parras, out of reach of the persistent slave hunters. To these refugees, as well as to his Indian allies, Vidaurri offered more than land, he "appointed salaried instructors in agriculture, reading, writing, and religion." In the spring of 1856, Vidaurri also established a "chapel and a school for the children."[108]

The loss of most of the Seminoles was made up in part in 1865 by the arrival of several bands of Kickapoos from Kansas and Oklahoma. On their way to Mexico through Texas, these bands were attacked by a detachment of Confederate cavalry at a place called Dove Creek. Their hatred for Texans from that day forward would have an important effect on the border region. Once in Mexico they became excellent allies against Comanche and Apache raiders but, using the Dove Creek ambush as justification, they began to make deadly forays against the hated Texans. These raids became a major source of friction between the Mexican and U.S. governments until the Kickapoos were decimated in the devastating transborder raid of Ranald S. Mackenzie in 1873.[109]

With the abolition of slavery after the Civil War, the black Seminoles considered returning to Texas. Lured by the promise of land and jobs as army scouts, John Horse led a group of mascogos to Texas in 1870, where they settled on land north of Eagle Pass. General Zenas R. Bliss employed them at Fort Duncan and proclaimed that they were "excellent hunters, trailers, and brave scouts" who provided a valuable service to his unit.[110] Bliss put a premium on skill and the ability to perform tasks instead of the color of a man's skin, but many among the Texan population did not share those values. Conflict broke out between the mascogos and Texans, resulting "in the death of several men and the serious wounding of John Horse. When it became evident that they would not be given title to land in Texas, John Horse led a group of his people back to their original settlement in . . . Mexico."[111]

Among the immigrant tribes the Lipans continued to provoke conflict. The Callahan expedition of 1855 had failed in one of its objectives, which was to punish them and dissuade them from raiding Texas. It did however set in motion a determined strategy by Vidaurri to combat all predatory Indians, both those who entered Mexico from Texas and those who used Mexico to raid in Texas. He would not countenance these raids because they disrupted the harmonious relations he sought with the Texans. Much less would he accept Lipan raids on Northeast Mexico, which were carried out from remote hideouts in southwestern Texas and isolated areas of Coahuila and Chihuahua. Vidaurri tried in many ways to win over the Lipans, but finally lost his patience and ordered their extermination if they continued to attack the ranchos and towns of Coahuila.[112]

He sent Captain Francisco Treviño to the inhospitable Bolsón de Mapimí on the border with Chihuahua to seek them out in one of their strongholds. On the way west, one of Treviño's subordinates asked him to reroute their journey in order to protect the ranchers of Coahuila. Treviño responded with frontier stoicism: the ranchers should defend themselves as best they could; if they died they could take solace in the fact that "we are all mortal, and anyway, we all must die."[113]

In March 1856, Vidaurri sent two armed groups to search out the Lipans in Coahuila, one headed by Pablo Espinoza and the other by his right-hand man, Juan Zuazua, one of the fiercest Indian fighters in northern Mexico. Both operations were deadly effective. More than 130 Lipans were rounded up, and many of them murdered in captivity under various pretexts, including attempts to escape. Historian Isidro Vizcaya Canales is persuaded that the massacre of the Lipans was premeditated. Vidaurri boasted to the minister of war and navy that the "complete destruction" of the Lipans was an "urgent necessity . . . so that the settlements of the frontier could live in peace." Vidaurri had struck a deadly blow against the Lipans, but he did not eliminate them. Those who survived continued their raids until the 1870s.[114]

Vidaurri's policy of extermination included cruel measures. He sent Jesús Carranza of Cuatro Ciénegas, Coahuila, a bottle of poison accompanied by a letter instructing him to pour it "in the water holes of the desert, making sure that they are the farthest and most frequently used by the Indians and where the water does not flow." Certain that "it was impossible to punish the Indians in any other way," Vidaurri advised Carranza to inform the inhabitants of the surrounding country of the location of the water holes to be poisoned "in order to avoid a tragedy." Carranza seemed to be appalled by the measure and looked for a way out. He later informed Vidaurri that the water holes were empty because of the drought, and that he would wait for winter before taking further action. In another exchange of letters, Carranza wrote that Mescalero Apaches wanted to negotiate peace. Vidaurri responded that it was useless to deal with them because they were "very wicked and only asked for peace to rest" in order to strike again.[115]

The War against the Hostile Tribes

Vidaurri's struggle against Indian raiders complemented the war that the national government had begun immediately following the U.S.-Mexican War. The establishment of the colonias militares came after national authorities realized that more active participation from its armed forces was required to defend the northern border. Each colonia would have between 100 and 150 fighting men in addition to local citizens who might wish to participate. The system was largely ineffective however, because the colonias were usually undermanned and too far apart to be truly effective against the highly mobile Indian raiders.[116] Aside from the establishment of the colonias and the employment of Indian and African American allies, Mexican officials at both the national and regional levels sought the collaboration of U.S. and Texas authorities in combatting hostile Indians. Cooperation became a necessity once the establishment of the border precluded Mexican pursuit of raiders across the Rio Grande. In December 1849, the Ministry of Foreign Relations instructed regional military leaders in the northern states to contact their counterparts on the other side of the border and "express to them the need to cooperate to contain the incursions of the bárbaros or to punish them when they returned from Mexico to their camps [in Texas]." The minister pointed out that Article 11 of the Treaty of Guadalupe Hidalgo obligated U.S. officials to combat Indian incursions into Mexico.[117]

General Antonio María Jáuregui, the inspector general of the colonias, was sensitive to the need for cooperation with American authorities. In March 1850, he was informed that the commander of Fort Duncan had alerted a body of his troops that a band of Comanches was heading into Mexico. He reminded his officers of the need to constantly maintain the "good relations that exist with the commanders of the U.S. military posts on the left bank of the Río Bravo" because they offered "great benefits to the service of the nation, especially in the war against the bárbaros."[118]

Besides sharing information, American military commanders delivered to Mexico captives and captured animals that had been recovered from Indian raiders. In early 1851, Hamilton P. Bee reported from Laredo that a ranger force had fought a party of Indians and had taken from them an eighteen-year old Mexican boy and seventy-five mules and horses. The boy was returned to his family, to their great relief, and the animals to their Mexican owners.[119] On another occasion an official of the colonias militares stationed at Villa de Rosas, Coahuila, sent to Jáuregui a list of seventeen captives that were returned to Mexico by Colonel D. J. Morris, commander of Fort Duncan. All of them were boys. One of these, Narciso Herrera, was about eleven years old. He had been tending a wheat field when he was taken captive in Chihuahua five months earlier. Another lad, José María Rocha, was seven years old. He had been taken from Rancho de los Ballesteros in Sabinas Hidalgo, Nuevo León. He could not remember his father's name but recalled that his mother was named María de Jesús Valle.[120]

U.S. military authorities in Texas realized that it was in their interest to collaborate with their Mexican counterparts in combating Indian incursions into Mexico because they needed Mexican cooperation to combat raids into Texas by tribes that used Mexico as a refuge. In reference to Lipan Apaches, Colonel Albert Sydney Johnson, who was stationed in San Antonio before his memorable participation in the Civil War, wrote that the Lipans, "tho' contemptible in number, cannot be put down without the simultaneous action of the troops on both sides of the border."[121]

Some U.S. military men were willing to cooperate with their Mexican colleagues even beyond the scope of their normal duties and restrictions. In May 1851, Juan Manuel Maldonado, the sub-inspector of the colonias militares, informed Jáuregui that General Arney of the Eighth Military Department based in Bexar had granted Mexican troops permission to cross the Rio Grande into Texas in pursuit of Indian predators. Maldonado wrote that the American general was "very desirous of cooperating with Mexican forces in order to prevent the raids of the savages into Mexican territory." Maldonado added that it was expected that "in similar circumstances, U.S. troops would be allowed to enter Mexican territory." Jáuregui replied that while he concurred with the spirit of the proposal, he would not authorize it until and unless the national government authorized it.[122]

In spite of Jauregui's reservations, informal agreements to allow transborder raids against marauding Indians were not uncommon. The commander of Fort Duncan authorized Nicandro Valdéz to cross the Rio Grande to hunt down an Indian force that had crossed the border near Piedras Negras. On another occasion, William Stone, a merchant and sheep rancher in Eagle Pass married to a Mexican woman, mobilized a force to go after Apache raiders south of the

Rio Grande. He obtained authorization and was joined by citizens of Piedras Negras.[123] In another instance of cooperation, Major T. M. Anderson of Ringgold Barracks informed his superiors that "General José Cabellos, commanding the line of the Bravo, [had] returned a drove of cattle driven from this side, and arrested the purchaser of the stock on the Mexican side."[124] There are many examples of transborder cooperation in response to raids. Most of these cases have never made it into the history books.

To combat those Indians beyond his area of authority, Vidaurri also reached out to military chiefs in Texas to lead a joint effort against the nomadic tribes. He wrote letters to the commanders of Forts McIntosh, Duncan, and Clark, exhorting them to cooperate with him in stamping out the Indian threat. In a letter of March 1856, to Lieutenant Colonel Daniel Ruggles, commander of Fort McIntosh at Laredo, he deplored the "barbarous tribes that in large numbers cross the Río Bravo to rob and plunder in Mexican territory and sell or exchange the fruit of their spoils to American citizens." Vidaurri decried the U.S. authorities' tolerance of "shameful and inhuman traffic" against "the fortunes and properties of a friendly nation." In a follow-up note to Ruggles, Vidaurri claimed (incorrectly, it turned out) that his forces had decimated the Lipan Apaches. Most of the tribe was imprisoned and the warriors killed so that they were no longer a threat. The Nuevo León governor wrote that he was not concerned with the welfare of his citizens only, but also that of his Texan neighbors "with whom we are united by ties of friendship."[125]

By the end of the 1850s the Comanche raids began to diminish for a combination of reasons. The contribution of the Seminoles was important, as was the expansion of U.S. military power in Texas and the southern plains. Moreover, the Mexican Northeast was struck by cholera in 1849 and smallpox in 1856–57. The captives taken by the Comanches spread these epidemics among the Indians, severely reducing their population.[126]

Migration of Mexican Workers to Texas

The conflict that enveloped the Northeast in the 1850s involving different Indian groups did not deter the mobility of another marginalized people: Mexican rural laborers, whose trek to Texas in search of work more than matched the southward march of Indians and blacks. Labor migration from Northeast Mexico to Texas began early in the nineteenth century and accelerated after 1848 when the boundary between the two nations was fixed on the Rio Grande and the Texas economy began to expand. Moving northward from Mexico into Texas came naturally, for it was deeply ingrained in the historical psyche of the norteños. Successive waves of colonists had pushed the boundaries of New Spain ever northward, as "pioneers from the most recently settled areas usually spearheaded the further expansion of the frontier."[127]

Although few records exist, the impetus to find work in Texas began to develop among residents of Mexico's Northeast in the 1830s and 1840s, before the establishment of the border. Merchants such as John Linn and Joshua Davis hired sirvientes from the Villas del Norte and Coahuila to aid them in their commercial journeys to the Texas coast. After Texas separated from Mexico in 1836, sirvientes discovered that one way to escape their indebtedness to their *amos*, or masters, was by fleeing north. Between 1836 and 1849 the towns of Morelos, Nava, Guerrero, San Fernando, and Allende in northern Coahuila all reported incidents of sirvientes escaping to Texas, although in small numbers. A report from Allende revealed that eight of these—six men and two women—had escaped to Texas between 1845 and 1847. They left owing a total of 1,137 pesos. In Tamaulipas, General Adrián Woll reported that there was a steady flow of people from the Villas del Norte to South Texas.[128]

The presence of these sirvientes in San Antonio was derogatorily noted by a citizens' group that met in 1841 to demand greater frontier protection. The group called for the creation of a force to restrict the movement "of pilfering Mexicans and escaping Peons of Mexico."[129] Aside from individual sirvientes, a slow but steady movement of Mexican families flowed into the Victoria-Goliad area throughout the 1840s. This migration contributed to linking the region "with the Rio Grande frontier into a cultural salient which stamped an indelible Mexican character throughout the south of Texas."[130]

In one of the many ironies of border history, the U.S.-Mexican War, which generated so much ill feeling, promoted labor migration in various ways. Many rural people of the Northeast were displaced when the invading forces torched their ranchos and haciendas. Others, bound by debts, simply availed themselves of the American presence to walk away from their haciendas. According to one historian, cotton was being produced along the river before 1848. The production came to an end, however, "as soon as indebted workers saw the U.S. army arrive . . . they began to leave the Mexican cotton plantations in droves." Some of the hacendados wrote to Taylor "in the hopes that he would oversee the return of their sirvientes, but he refused to turn them over and even employed a good number of them in his own camp."[131] The letter that José María Girón of Matamoros sent to Taylor is revealing. He wrote that some sirvientes who had "received their wages in advance in accordance with the customs of the country," were shirking their responsibilities to their amos by "finding protection in the camps of the U.S. Army located on both sides of the river . . . mistakenly assuming that the judges no longer have authority to punish them and compel them to return to the service of their masters." In fact, the workers were not mistaken; they assumed correctly that the jurisdiction of Mexican judges did not extend to Texas.[132]

The invading army created jobs that Mexicans could fill. Some were employed on the steamships along the Rio Grande as *fogoneros* (stokers), while others served in the military camps as mule drivers and cowboys at salaries several times higher than they had made before the war.[133] Taylor's army needed teamsters and arrieros to drive the wagons and handle the pack animals that carried provisions from Camargo to Monterrey. Many of the animals—some nineteen hundred mules—as well as between three and four hundred arrieros were recruited from the local population, a task carried out by a future U.S. president: Ulysses S. Grant. The arrieros were paid twenty-five dollars a month, much more than the four to six dollars that rural laborers received.[134] When the war ended, the U.S. government sought to retrieve equipment that had been left in Mexico north of the Sierra Madre. Thirty Mexicans were hired at Brownsville and Matamoros at twenty-five dollars a month to help in that task. Among them was Juan Nepomuceno Cortina, who had fought against the Americans during the war and would fight them again many times.[135]

The establishment of the border in 1848 did not alter the historical trend of northward movement for the residents of the Northeast; instead, it accelerated migration and added a new dynamic. Sirvientes could now escape across the border and be beyond the reach of Mexican law. The hacendados of northern Mexico were now in the same fix as the Texas slave holders because the border provided a safe haven for runaways.[136] Governor Jesús Cárdenas of Tamaulipas expressed this reality clearly in 1849 when he pointed out "the difficulties that Mexican [landowners] had with the U.S. justice system." Even worse, some of these sirvientes took with them "the cattle and other property of their masters." Thus, the new border created a situation that "leaves us without sirvientes and exposes us to frequent robberies because the fugitive sirviente continues to cross the [Río] Bravo to steal, taking advantage of his knowledge of local conditions."[137] One historian asserts that runaway peons "were the conduits for a tremendous transfer of resources and laboring men from one side of the Grande/Bravo to the other."[138]

There is ample reason to believe that most sirvientes and other migrants who sought work in Texas in the 1850s did not venture far from the border region.

Most of them probably found employment in the farms and ranches owned by Mexicans between the Rio Grande and Nueces Rivers, and a few ventured as far north as San Antonio or east to Victoria. The reason they went no farther is simple. The 1850s were not a good decade and Texas was not a friendly place for Mexicans. The bones of migrants, or crosses built in their memory, were strewn alongside the paths and roads leading to Texas. They had fallen victim to Indian predators and the many lawless men—Anglo-Americans and Mexicans—who inhabited the border region preying on travelers. Many of the predators, according to the *Corpus Christi Star*, were "unprincipled Mexicans from the other side, united with worthless Americans," former soldiers of the U.S.-Mexican War who stayed in the region and who were better suited for a life of plunder than one of honest pursuits. The newspaper called for a strong and permanent police force to eradicate the problem "and leave American and Mexican citizens to pursue their avocations in quiet and in safety."[139]

The danger inherent in traveling to Texas did not necessarily deter Mexican laborers, but they faced another threat: the pervasive racism and hatred directed at them by many Anglos. The Comisión Pesquisidora, a Mexican government commission established to investigate the origins of the border conflict between the United States and Mexico in 1872, concluded that Anglo-Americans considered Mexicans an inferior race and an enemy to be combated, which justified depriving them of their property and expelling them from Texas.[140] Not all Anglos felt this way, of course, but there is little doubt that racism against Mexicans was widespread. It was exacerbated in the 1850s by the rise of nativism, a national movement which spawned the American, or Know-Nothing, Party and had a brief but significant influence in Texas politics. The Know-Nothings railed against Catholicism, and thus German and Mexican immigrants of that faith became targets. They were also opposed to cheap Mexican labor and the displacement of Anglo-American workers.[141]

The accusation that Mexicans were responsible for slave flight, which provoked the expulsion of Mexicans from Texas, contained a strong dose of nativism and exclusionism. An occurrence in Austin illustrates the dynamic. A group of Mexican laborers arrived in Austin in the fall of 1854, when the issue of slave flight was hot. Anglo citizens, most of them with roots in the slave South, held a meeting on October 7 and "adopted a report that warned all 'transient Mexicans' to leave within ten days or face forcible expulsion." They also agreed not to employ Mexicans and to restrict the foreigners' presence in the city. Only "good" Mexicans, those recommended by an Anglo, could remain in Travis County. About twenty Mexican families were expelled, and by 1860 "only twenty persons with Spanish surnames resided in Travis County, and their position clearly rested on the uncertain toleration of Anglo residents."[142] Notably, slave flight continued after the transient Mexicans were gone, making it clear that the problem was not of their making. Once set in motion, however, racial hatred quickly translated into savage violence against Mexicans, eleven of whom "were reportedly lynched near the Nueces River in 1855." This climate of violence had as one of its ugliest manifestations the so-called Cart War of 1857.[143]

Between July and November 1857, Anglo bands in Goliad and Karnes Counties, where there were still bitter memories of the massacre of Fannin's men during the Texas Revolution, began to attack Mexican freighters who transported cargo between San Antonio and the Gulf coast. The merchants and transport companies of San Antonio used Mexican freighters almost exclusively, which provoked the ire of Anglo teamsters who complained of a Mexican monopoly on the transportation of cargo. It is not clear if the attacks were motivated by competition for jobs or racial hatred, or both. It is also unclear how many Mexican teamsters lost their lives.[144]

The episode generated a lot of newspaper coverage in San Antonio that reveals the importance of Mexican teamsters to the commerce of the Alamo City. One writer to the *San Antonio Ledger* wrote that "communication with the coast has been almost, if not entirely, put to a stop, and not only commercial ruin, but absolute starvation stares us in the face."[145] This bit of hyperbole was repeated in the *San Antonio Daily Herald*, which rejected the idea of replacing the Mexicans with Anglo teamsters. "To admit that our people will ever give up the employment of Mexican carts and Mexican cartmen would be equivalent to signing the death-warrant to the prosperity of San Antonio." The newspaper refuted the notion that there was general hostility toward the Mexicans and argued that the abuses against them were the product of a group of worthless men who had come to Texas and who were too lazy to do hard work, but not to steal from honest Mexicans.[146]

Prominent men of San Antonio, such as T. S. Paschal and Samuel Maverick, supported the Mexicans, and the most important transporters hired them almost exclusively to guide their wagons. These included the firms of Howard and Ogden and C. L. Pyron. George T. Howard had fought against Mexicans for a good part of his adult life during the Santa Fe and Somervell expeditions and the U.S.-Mexican War, but he did not hesitate to engage in many business enterprises with Mexicans nor to hire them to drive his wagons after he and

Ogden established their transport company in the 1850s. In time they became the largest carrier in San Antonio, with about eight hundred teams and profits of up to $50,000 a year. Charles L. Pyron also participated in the U.S.-Mexican War and fought in the battle of Monterrey. Yet, like Howard, he relied on Mexican teamsters for his company. Most of the Mexican cart drivers who were victims of the attacks worked for Howard and Ogden or for Pyron.[147]

A lot of ink has been dedicated to the Cart War, but basic questions have not been answered, such as how many carters were killed, what motivated the attacks, and who the perpetrators were. After a tour of Goliad and Karnes Counties, Samuel Maverick wrote to Governor Pease that he believed the Know-Nothing Party and the climate of hatred and exclusion it promoted were behind the attacks. The problem was attenuated when the cartmen were given protection by a U.S. army escort that was supplemented by a group of volunteers from San Antonio.[148]

To escape the racism and hatred directed against Mexicans in eastern Texas and parts of Central Texas, most Mexicans migrated to a stretch of land that bordered on the Rio Grande through south central, southern, and western Texas. Extending to the Nueces River and a little beyond and encompassing San Antonio, it continued westward from the Gulf region across the Big Bend country and toward El Paso. Historians Arnoldo de León and Kenneth Stewart have referred to this expanse as the "Mexican settlement region," or simply the Mexican region; because the majority of the population there was Mexican, it was a relatively hospitable area for those migrating from south of the border in search of work.[149]

During the 1850s the Mexican region was largely populated by Mexicans and a few Anglos willing to live alongside them. Many residents owned their own farms or ranches and were in constant need of extra labor. In 1851, a Texas newspaper reported: "The country between Roma and Brownsville is steadily improving and many new farms have been opened along the river. Great numbers of cattle and sheep have been driven into the country between the Rio Grande and Nueces, from Mexico, and large stock farms have been established in that section." Improvement was also reported in the region around Corpus Christi and San Patricio, areas "well adapted to sheep husbandry." The regions around Eagle Pass and Presidio, passageways to Chihuahua and the goldfields of California, were soon dotted with farms and ranches that managed to survive in spite of the Indian menace.[150]

Many Mexicans of Northeast Mexico were not deterred by the risks and dangers of migrating to Texas. They had many and powerful reasons for leaving their homes and heading north. To begin with, life in Mexico was no bed of roses. Local and national wars, such as the Carvajal Revolt (1850–52), the Revolution of Ayutla (1854–55), and the War of Reform (1858–60) kept northern Mexico in turmoil for a good part of the decade. These conflicts and the ever-present Indian attacks caused much suffering and displacement. Internal political struggles also shattered the stability of the northern states from Chihuahua to Tamaulipas. Santiago Vidaurri justified his usurpation of Coahuila based on the chaos produced by three warring factions in that state and on the "iron tyranny" of the Sánchez Navarro family, which resulted in the "oppression of the poor, the promotion of division in the state and its march toward ruin and destruction." Tamaulipas, according to Vidaurri, was in a worse condition because it was mired in political anarchy.[151]

Political instability gave rise to regional strongmen, caudillos who needed an army to claw their way to power. The local and federal governments also required armed forces. Thus, forced conscription into military service was common, and just as frequent was flight across the border to avoid it. According to one historian rancheros "escaped across the river to avoid conscription by local caudillos." Those already trapped in a military unit—especially one located close to the border—took advantage of the opportunity to escape to Texas. In October 1852, José María de la Garza and José María Rodríguez, who were stationed at the military colony of San Vicente, were ordered to visit nearby ranches to obtain meat. They never returned. Neither did Guillermo Rodríguez, another soldier who failed to show up for daily muster. Their commanding officer suspected that they had fled for Texas.[152]

People flocked to the east bank of the Río Bravo in search of better economic conditions. In 1857, prominent citizens of Matamoros sent the national congress a petition for a *zona libre*, a zone for the free importation of goods. They stated that the people of the border region lacked what they needed for a decent life. Thus, "they seek in another country an occupation and so many other things that are lacking in ours." Towns on the Texas side offered all kinds of concessions, which "kept them flourishing, vigorous, prosperous, and happy."[153]

In 1856, the official newspaper of Chihuahua, *El Eco de la Frontera*, editorialized that fifty Mexican families had relocated to the northern side of the border in a forty-five-day period. They left because they were tired of harassment and extortion from customs officials every time they returned from the U.S. side with needed goods that they could obtain at much cheaper prices than in Mexico. This source also calculated that more than five thousand persons had abandoned Mexican soil in previous years in search of a better life north of the

Rio Grande.[154] A Corpus Christi newspaper also decried the "lack of security of property and the continuous exactions imposed by [the Mexican] government" that drove many norteños to "seek asylum on this side of the Rio Grande, where they know that not only is there a stable government, but that they will receive greater protection of life and property."[155]

It is safe to say that most of the migrants during this period were peons or sirvientes, many of whom labored under debt peonage. The slow trickle of these rural workers heading for Texas in the 1830s and 1840s, before the establishment of the border, became a steady flow in the 1850s as more began to flee north to escape an oppressive system. In a petition to the national congress, the Matamoros citizenry lamented that hacendados in desperate need of farm labor had paid big advances to sirvientes, who consequently saw their chance to escape, taking their advances and whatever they could steal.[156]

The sirvientes left because they were fed up with a system that exploited them. Several contemporary observers compared debt peonage unfavorably to slavery. Emilio Langberg, the Danish-Mexican military commander of Coahuila, told Vidaurri that slaves in Texas were treated better than Mexican peons. Sirvientes "found themselves in a state of slavery worse than that of beasts; they suffer every type of terrible treatment and they never receive the money that is the fruit of their work." They had no possibility of paying their debt, so their only hope of escape was to flee "in bands" across the border.[157]

Jane McManus Cazneau, who spent two years in Eagle Pass as wife of William Cazneau, also believed that peonage was worse than American slavery. She wrote that almost all of her servants had lived under debt peonage in Mexico, and she described their suffering in vivid detail.[158] I should point out, however, that peonage differed from slavery in one fundamental respect. In the former condition "the labor embodied by the peons' debt . . . was a commodity, not the peons' physical body itself." Moreover, civil and religious authorities in Mexico often acted to ameliorate the lot of the peons.[159]

In addition to being crushed under debt, many sirvientes worked for cruel masters, indifferent to their problems or needs. Rudesindo Jiménez complained to the authorities of Nuevo León that his amo, Melchor Villarreal, had him dragged behind a horse because he had stayed at home to take care of a sick child rather than reporting for work. He demanded action "against an inhuman and barbarous master who has no consideration of any kind for his servants and who sees them as beasts and not as men who have the misfortune of living in a form of slavery in order to obtain a miserable subsistence."[160]

Jiménez was trapped in a system that he labeled as a form of enslavement. Like his black brothers in Texas, he might find refuge by crossing the border, or he might become a hunted man. Mexican bounty hunters, much like Texan slave catchers, roamed the border region on both sides of the river in search of escaped peons. At Eagle Pass Manuel Ríos became one of their victims. He was "kidnapped by Mexican bounty hunters in broad daylight and returned to peonage in Mexico." His case outraged the local citizens, who sent a letter to Secretary of State Daniel Webster, demanding action against this violation of American sovereignty. Distrustful of border residents, whom he believed "were anxious to provoke a new conflict with Mexico so that they might grab more land," Webster responded that Ríos should find redress under Mexican laws.[161]

No one knows how many sirvientes fled to Texas. A conservative estimate is that almost three thousand escaped between 1848 and 1873, and some took their families with them.[162] The flight of the sirvientes had a clearly negative effect on the agrarian economy of the region. The large landholders of Montemorelos, Nuevo León, demanded a solution to the "constant and terrible flight of servant labor to the neighboring republic." They complained that "by the simple act of crossing the Río Bravo, [the sirvientes] parade brazenly before one's eyes without the possibility of bringing them back even if they are reclaimed."[163] In Coahuila the situation was worse. The emigration was partially responsible for the population decline, from 73,000 in 1840 to 66,000 in 1852. In 1848, the year the war between the United States and Mexico ended, the governor of Coahuila "ordered the municipalities to report on the flight of servants in order to recover them because agriculture was being paralyzed."[164] The ink was barely dry on the treaty of peace before Mexican laborers were heading resolutely to the country that had invaded their homeland. Indifferent to national pride, they wanted a decent life in exchange for their work.

The attraction toward Texas (pull) was even more powerful than the forces of expulsion (push) from Mexico. Migrant laborers were easily accepted in the Mexican region, where the Anglo minority coexisted with the Mexican majority. In the 1850s the demand for Mexican labor was nowhere near as intense as it would be in later periods, but there were still many opportunities in an economy that was growing rapidly. Commercial expeditions employed many Mexican teamsters who drove their own carts and wagons. In 1850 Benjamin Franklin Coons, a prominent Santa Fe trader, had difficulty finding teamsters (of any race) to transport supplies from Indianola to El Paso.[165] Other towns that simply wanted to grow found that the arrival of Mexican families strengthened their communities. In September 1848, the *Corpus Christi Star* reported that "many Mexican families are crossing to this side of the Rio Grande, and building temporary jacales [huts] on the river. At San Antonio, too, we hear that families are arriving from the upper Rio Grande, with the view of settling." Corpus Christi civic leaders wanted to attract some of these families who were hardworking and responsible. The editor, John H. Peoples, declared: "We will insure them protection in life and property and a hearty welcome. Our country has been and is now the asylum of the misgoverned of every land, and the children of our near neighbor can never be an exception."[166]

In some communities, families from Mexico were not only welcomed but actively recruited because of the shortage of labor on the Texas side of the border. The seventy families that Friedrich Groos took to Eagle Pass were a "colony of dependable, hardworking families" that "formed the nucleus of what later became a decent, law-abiding community."[167] In the Big Bend region, ranchers such as Milton Faver and John Davis married Mexican women and actively recruited families from south of the border to work on their ranches. The King Ranch also got its start with the recruitment of Mexican families. Richard King went to Cruillas, Tamaulipas, and "offered to settle the entire population of the village on his Santa Gertrudis rancho." As a result, "more than one hundred men, women, and children with all their possessions piled on yoked oxen, donkeys, and carts started north to the Wild Horse Desert and their new home." These were the families of the King Ranch that became known as kineños.[168]

Higher wages were another attraction that drew Mexicans north to Texas. At mid-century rural workers in Coahuila were paid between three and five pesos a month plus rations, which usually included corn. The rate was similar in Zacatecas and slightly higher in Nuevo León. In Texas, vaqueros in the Nueces Strip were paid six dollars a month plus a ration of corn, though historian David Montejano has written that Mexican farm and ranch workers could earn as much as fifty cents a day. Those engaged in transport could earn more, depending on the weight of the cargo and the length of the trip.[169]

Mexicans in Texas found diverse employment. A few became guides, scouts, and interpreters, especially for law enforcement agencies and the army. José María Flores, who brought his family to the Eagle Pass region, was frequently employed as a guide by the military commanders at Fort Duncan. José Morales, whose brother had been killed by Comanches, rode with Rip Ford's ranger company, as did Lorenzo, a muleteer, and Roque Maugricio [sic], who was half Indian and half Mexican and had been taken by the Comanches as a young boy. He spoke the Indian language and knew the country well, was an expert in finding a trail, and had a great sense of smell. He "was indefatigable, never appeared to flag, never complained of being tired or hungry. He was in the habit of reporting the truth, and had nothing sensational about him," wrote Ford.[170] Morales and Maugricio, like many other Mexicans of the border region, had been personally harmed by the Comanches, and they may have joined Ford's company to find a measure of revenge against the hated enemy. If so, this is another way in which the war against the Indians brought Anglo-Americans and Mexicans together.

It is likely that many Mexicans found employment as domestic servants in the homes of Anglo ranchers and farmers who discovered that it was not feasible to bring slaves close to the border because they would flee to Mexico. A planter discovered this in the late 1850s, when he attempted to grow cotton in the area around Corpus Christi. He traveled to South Carolina to bring a group of African Americans to work his land. Some of the slaves quickly saw their opportunity and escaped to Mexico. A U.S. official wrote that as a consequence of slave flight, "all the household drudgery and menial services [were] performed by Mexican servants."[171]

There was plenty of work transporting goods, especially to and from San Antonio, which was fast becoming a major distribution point for the Texas frontier and for trade with Mexico. The rise of new communities in central and western Texas, many of them peopled by German immigrants, demanded a military presence to protect them, thus the Eighth Military Department was established in 1849, based in San Antonio. The immigrant communities and military presence generated a substantial volume of trade, much of it hauled by Mexican freighters.[172] Mexican involvement in the freighting business made an impression on Frederick Law Olmsted, who wrote in 1857 that they did not seem to have occupations other than hauling freight. It has been estimated that 50 percent of the Mexican population of south central Texas was so employed.[173]

Working with animals such as oxen and mules came naturally to Mexicans, who were raised in a largely pastoral society. The important merchants and carriers of San Antonio preferred to hire Mexicans because of their skill and dexterity, as well as their discipline and work ethic. August Santleben, who freighted between Texas and Mexico for almost three decades, declared that "Mexicans made the most expert drivers, and those of other nationalities whom [he] employed never gave equal satisfaction." He admired their reliability, stating "they were always ready, night or day, to attend to any duty that was required of them."[174]

Commerce depended on the movement of freight. Before the coming of the railroad, much of the freight in South Texas was transported in carts or wagons, such as the ones pictured here. Hauling freight became the main occupation of Texas Mexicans in the 1850s and was crucial in moving the massive volume of trade during the Civil War. No. 91-47, UTSA Special Collections.

Many of the Mexicans who went to Texas in the 1850s probably found jobs in the cattle and sheep ranches of South and West Texas. They were skilled in roping, branding, shearing, and handling livestock. According to historian Robert C. Spillman, "the development of stock raising on a large scale in South Texas after 1850 gave rise to the importation of the services of the Mexican vaquero or cowboy, who was readily adapted to the raising of stock in the hostile South Texas environment."[175]

The care and handling of sheep was not a job for everyone, because the life of *pastores* was difficult and lonely. Burr G. Duval captured this reality in his diary while traveling in West Texas. In one entry, he wrote: "I went to a Mexican sheepherder's camp to beg a bucket of water and found Mr. Greaser as usual polite and hospitable. He very cheerfully gave me as much as I wanted out of his small stock and with many 'adioses' we parted." Aside from the racist condescension, it is revealing that Duval expected the Mexican pastor would be "polite and hospitable," as if it were the natural state of things (as indeed was the case here). He then proceeded to describe their lot: "O what a life these herders must lead. Each one has charge of a thousand or two sheep which he accompanies at all times ... week after week, year in and year out, solitary and alone, with no company except his sheep, one is appalled at such a life of utter isolation."[176]

Whereas most Mexicans worked with livestock on farms and ranches, a few chose, shall we say, "self-employment" in this activity. They were the rustlers and cattle thieves who crossed the river and made forays into the Nueces Strip. A Brownsville newspaper condemned the criminals that came "from the interior of Mexico" to prey "upon the fat steers of the Nueces country."[177] Some of these outlaws may have deluded themselves that they were striking a blow at the hated Americans. Rip Ford pointed out that they "came from considerable distances in Mexico to engage in stripping those who had conquered them." The problem with this interpretation is that they raided both Mexican and Anglo ranches. They were driven less by national pride and vindication than by the lucrative market that allowed them to "sell their plunder to a steady supply of customers on both sides of the border."[178] Actually, ranches on both sides of the river were targets. A case in point is Antonio González Sepúlveda of Tamaulipas, who was caught after he and his criminal band murdered Mariano García, "an honest citizen who was killed ... while he was asleep in his ranch, without any object nor cause than that of stealing his property, and crossing over to Texas some of his cattle."[179]

The vast majority of both Mexicans and Anglo-Americans were engaged in peaceful and productive pursuits, the kind that do not draw attention or make headlines. In the Victoria area a steady flow of Mexican migrants, some with their families, arrived in the 1850s "at a time when the founding families among the Mexican Americans were winning back their lands in court cases and reestablishing themselves as ranchers." According to Ana Carolina Castillo Crimm, they "needed and evidently hired the day laborers who came looking for work since [they] were profiting from the rise in cattle prices."[180] Those laborers probably landed employment through the assistance of a family member or friend as there were extensive family and friendship networks in Northeast Mexico and Texas. Pedro Ansualdo arrived in Victoria in the 1850s with two oxcarts and later acquired two more in order to trade between Victoria and the coast. "As his business expanded, he brought the Lara family from Mexico to help on the small farm and with the carting business."[181] When Toribio Lozano, a native of Agua Fría in the state of Nuevo León, established a sheep ranch in the Nueces Strip, he went back to his hometown and persuaded a group of pastores to travel to Texas to work for him.[182]

Although many migrants sought work on Mexican-owned farms and ranches, by the middle and latter part of the 1850s more and more could be found working in areas that brought them into contact with Anglos who lived in the Mexican region or with Anglo society on the fringes of that region. Their transition was eased by fellow Mexicans who had gained a respectable position in that society or by Anglo or European ranchers and businessmen who had no qualms about hiring Mexicans. In March 1850, José Francisco Ruiz, an agent for a Bexar capitalist, traveled from San Antonio to Río Grande (presently Guerrero), Coahuila, in search of draft animals for the forty-niners crossing Texas on their way to California. He requested permission to recruit 115 sirvientes to drive the carts and wagons at least as far as El Paso del Norte at a rate of ten pesos monthly. It is not clear how many he was able to employ because the Coahuila authorities, already alarmed by the flight of sirvientes to Texas, considered that the departure of even more would be highly prejudicial to the producers of the state.[183]

The transportation of goods offered many opportunities for Mexicans to interact with Anglos. Friedrich Groos's Mexican families at Eagle Pass were mainly employed in freighting for Fort Duncan and other frontier forts of the U.S. army. "Each head of household received four carretas or ox carts along with four oxen."[184] The San Miguel and Alderete families were among those recruited by Groos. Refugio San Miguel was born in Tamaulipas, but relocated to Eagle Pass. He was described as a "man of great energy and perseverance," who "forged his way from obscurity and poverty to a position of local prominence and influence." According to John Henry Brown, "opportunities in Mexico for young men to advance were not good and, being ambitious to accomplish something in the world, young San Miguel became restless and decided to try his fortune in Texas."[185] He "was a diligent worker, and before long he had built up his freighting line to twenty carts and forty yoke of oxen. His trade extended to towns well into the interior of Texas and Mexico." In 1854 he married Rita Alderete, and together they built one of the biggest ranches in Maverick County with "thousands of cattle and sheep, and hundreds of horses on a great unfenced range." Rita was not yet thirty when her husband was killed in 1868. She managed to raise six children while operating an extensive ranch and freighting business. Rita Alderete is one of many hardy Mexican pioneer women who are seldom mentioned in histories of the border region.[186]

In the area around Victoria, on the periphery of the Mexican region, arriving Mexicans had many opportunities to interact with Anglo society. In addition

Rita Alderete with a granddaughter. Mexican pioneer women have not been studied extensively, yet many played key roles in their communities. Through talent and hard work, Rita
Alderete and her husband, Refugio San Miguel, built a large ranch and freighting business
in Maverick County. After Refugio's early death, Rita ran both operations while raising
their six children. Family photo courtesy of Robert G. Rodríguez, a great-great-grandson
of Rita Alderete.

to working as farmworkers or freighters, some turned to commerce or became
"cattle brokers," who would "buy cattle in Victoria or Goliad or along the San
Antonio and Guadalupe River valleys and move the herds to the coast for sale."[187]
In 1852, forty-year-old Prudencio Espetia arrived in Victoria from Mexico. Six
years later he "had saved enough money to buy a small farm . . . three miles south
of town on the Guadalupe River." His success was due to hard work and also
to the generosity of Doña Luz Escalera de León, widow of Fernando de León,
who sold him a 242-acre property for the modest sum of $140. Doña Luz and
her family were supportive of new immigrants such as Espetia, who "became
automatically part of the large extended families, whether through marriage or
through godparenthood."[188]

The examples of Ansualdo, Espetia, and San Miguel show that through hard work, thrift, and a measure of opportunity, Mexicans could be successful and climb socially in Texas. According to Castillo Crimm, they "do not fit the picture presented by the Anglo diaries which depict them as peons with little drive or ambition. Over the years, many of them saved their money and eventually bought land and became farmers in their own right."[189]

Mexican workers were not mindless brutes, content to take whatever was offered to them. The American owners of the flourishing Jesús María silver mine in Vallecillo, Nuevo León, recognized that Mexican workers were keenly aware of what was in their best interest. In an internal document of 1855, workers were described as "proverbially very sagacious in these matters—they run from a bad mine as sailors desert a sinking ship: they are now coming in squads from various parts, even as far as Zacatecas, to our mine."[190]

The Mexicans who immigrated to Texas usually did so for greater opportunities or higher wages. Some, however, sought to get away from the seemingly endless internal conflicts in Mexico and find a more stable environment in which to raise their families. Comparing life in Texas and Mexico, *El Bejareño* of San Antonio declared that the differences were profound. North of the Rio Grande there was liberty and general prosperity under a system of moderate laws. In Mexico there was "military despotism, poverty, edicts, [and] political upheavals . . . that continuously irrigate her soil with blood." Despite the hard conditions in Texas, Mexicans would have a better future there than in their own country. The Rio Grande, according to the editorial, "is more than the boundary between two nations; it is also the line that separates . . . progress and ignorance, the future and the past."[191]

It was this favorable setting that political refugee Manuel Múzquiz was looking for when he packed up his belongings and headed for Texas. Múzquiz settled with his family about six miles from Fort Davis in 1854. He built an adobe ranch house and, with his servants and ranch hands, began to raise cattle to provide the fort with beef and other products. One historian writes that Múzquiz was perhaps "the largest operator in the Fort Davis area before the Civil War." His experiment lasted only about a decade, however. During the Civil War the fort was abandoned and the region was overrun by Indians. Múzquiz and his family were forced to return to Mexico.[192] His eventual failure was due to circumstances beyond his control and did not erase the decade-long relationship he had with the military men stationed at Fort Davis. They were dependent on him for supplies and he on them for protection from Indian attacks.

COEXISTENCE IN THE MEXICAN REGION

Arnoldo de León has written that in Central, South, and West Texas, Mexicans "coexisted with unneighborly Anglo-Americans who judged them to be a people of a lower caste. White society contemptuously thought Mexicans to be undeserving of equality with the white race, and mechanisms to ensure Anglo supremacy abounded."[193] De León's statement is undoubtedly true, and he has studied this issue extensively. However, it is also true that not all Anglo-Americans were unneighborly. For many Mexican migrants integration was easier in communities such as Eagle Pass, San Antonio, Laredo, and Brownsville, where there was relative harmony between the races. Between Piedras Negras and Eagle Pass, wrote Consul Joseph Ulrich of Monterrey, who was not sympathetic to Mexicans, "there is harmony, arising principally from a community of interests, between the populations on both sides of the river."[194] In Eagle Pass there was an inclusive community where "Euro-Americans, mestizos, and 'civilized' Indians lived and worked together." Even Jane McManus Cazneau, who believed in white racial superiority, felt that Mexicans and Indians could assimilate. She wrote: "Workingmen and mechanics come over to us from Mexico with their families, and women and children begin to flit about the prairies." Historian William Kerrigan claims "Cazneau considered the non-Anglo residents full members of the community."[195]

Another Anglo woman who came to the border region and lived alongside Mexican families in Rio Grande City was Teresa Viele, wife of then Lieutenant Egbert L. Viele. She shared her husband's low opinion of Mexicans, but was somewhat less racist and rather more condescending. She was disgusted by Mexicans' acceptance of blacks, but admired their self-sufficiency: the Mexican "is his own shoemaker and tailor; the leather of his garments and of his sandals is made from the skins of the animals he has himself killed. He makes his own carts, hewing the wheels out of the solid wood." As Teresa began to know the Mexicans better, she "finally commenced looking upon them as a new circle of friends and acquaintances. They [were] an amiable, smiling, innocent race of people, utterly unconscious of the higher emotions of civilization save the feeling of sympathy in misfortune, which pervades all classes of Mexicans."[196] Teresa Viele personally witnessed the difficult conditions under which Mexicans of the border region lived. She wrote of a drought that made food scarce. "Starvation seemed staring us in the face. . . . Even frijoles became scarce, and butter, milk, bread, and other such small but necessary items, were utterly unknown to us for weeks." She added that food was "flavored with red ants, which were so thick that it was impossible to eat without devouring them by scores." After a while, she said, they did not taste that bad.[197] Shared hardships among diverse people forced to live together on the frontier tended to attenuate racial prejudice.

Military men who came to the frontier from other parts of the United States had various opinions of the Mexican population. Egbert Viele was uncompromisingly hostile, but many others were more moderate in their judgments. One of these fair-minded Anglo-Americans was General Zenas Bliss. Whereas others referred to Mexicans as dissolute and lazy, Bliss wrote in his diary, "The men are very temperate in their habits and, although they make delicious wine at many places on the Rio Grande and distill brandy and mescal, it is seldom that a Mexican is seen intoxicated and it is as seldom that a lady can be persuaded to taste wine."[198] Just as Bliss was not obsessed with racial or ethnic differences, neither was Randolph B. Marcy, a West Point graduate who had a distinguished military career. He was stationed at Fort McIntosh (Laredo) in the 1850s, where he worked arduously to learn the customs and language of the native Mexican population.[199]

Many border communities had Anglo and European residents devoid of racist sentiments. Jesse Sumpter lived among Mexicans at Eagle Pass over more than half a century. After he was discharged from the army at Fort Duncan in 1852, he stayed in the region, working at a number of different occupations, including as saloon keeper, rancher, freighter, merchant, peace officer, and customs inspector. He married Refugia Ramírez in 1859 and had two children. His descendants "still reside in Eagle Pass, as well as in other parts of Texas and northern Mexico." He judged men on their merits and often hired Mexicans for his various enterprises. One of these was Agustín Flores, whom Sumpter considered "a truthful and upright man." They faced danger together when they were attacked by Indians and managed to defend themselves. On a less fortunate occasion, Flores was traveling by himself toward Sumpter's ranch when he was killed by Indians. Sumpter received a report that a man had been attacked; he went out with a group of men to investigate and "found my old companion butchered. I took his body to my ranch . . . and buried it."[200]

William Stone, one of Sumpter's neighbors at Eagle Pass, became a great friend of many Mexicans, although his association with Mexico began during his participation in the U.S.-Mexican War. Stone went into business supplying Fort Duncan with hay and wool. He invested his profits in land and became a successful rancher with more than 100,000 acres of land and 30,000 sheep.

In 1858 he married Josefa Martínez, a native of Rio Grande, Coahuila, whose father, Severo Martínez was a prominent citizen of Eagle Pass. Stone had many friends and associates in Coahuila, among them Evaristo Madero, son of José Francisco Madero. He and Evaristo became partners in a mercantile business for many years. He was described as an "open-hearted, generous" man who was always "considerate to the poor and unfortunate." These qualities won him the loyalty of Anglos and Mexicans alike. They explain why Mexican authorities readily assented to his request to pursue Lipan Apaches in Mexico and why the citizens of Piedras Negras volunteered to join him.[201]

San Antonio likewise harbored many Anglos and Europeans sympathetic to the Mexican people. One of these was Xavier Debray, who joined with A. A. Lewis to found the Spanish-language newspaper *El Bejareño* "dedicated above all to the interests of the Mexican-Texan population." The two editors proclaimed that one of their objectives was the establishment of bilingual public schools so that "without losing the language of Cervantes, Mexican-Texan children will acquire the national language and be taught the obligations of citizens . . . worthy of belonging to a free country." These lofty goals were mixed with more earthly concerns, as they also declared their aim to "carry out their enterprise, launching our bark in the ocean of publicity." No doubt they were intent on capturing an important market segment.[202]

Debray, a distinguished academician of French origin who was greatly respected in San Antonio, was also a professional translator. He and José Agustín Quintero, who would have a prominent diplomatic role during the Civil War, advertised their services as "Interpreters and Translators of the Spanish and French language" and offered to "attend to all business entrusted to their care." A. A. Lewis was a lawyer who served the Anglo and Mexican communities. He translated official Spanish documents into English and also offered nighttime Spanish classes.[203]

Another resident of San Antonio for many years was a famous character in Texas history: Judge Roy Bean, the "Law West of the Pecos." A little-known facet of his charismatic personality was his affinity for Mexico and Mexicans. He felt very much at home in San Antonio, where "everybody picked up the Spanish language and slid into Spanish ways." According to one historian, Bean "liked the people—the proud men and the beautiful girls. . . . He liked the Mexican view that every man had a right to his own vices. And so he left the Frenchmen and the Germans and the Americans to enjoy their own society while he went Mexican." Long before he settled in the Pecos region, he married the daughter

of a San Antonio rancher, eighteen-year-old Virginia Chávez, and had four
children, although the marriage eventually failed.[204]

~

After the shock of the U.S.-Mexican War, the Texas-Mexico border region
quickly returned to normalcy as producers and merchants on both sides of the
new border sought to continue the mutually rewarding exchange that had been
growing since before Texas independence and that was vital to their survival.
Towns in Texas vied with one another to find the most suitable routes to reach
their southern neighbor, and new towns were founded by merchants anxious to
benefit from the Mexican trade. Contraband trade continued as a mainstay of
the region's economy despite efforts by the Mexican government to prevent it.

The 1850–60 period witnessed many episodes of violence, including filibustering and slave-catching expeditions, Indian cross-border raids, and the Cart
War of 1857. Two major revolts—one led by José María Carvajal and the other
by Santiago Vidaurri—were provoked by regional demands for greater autonomy and fewer restrictions on trade with Texas. Some of these violent episodes,
particularly the Carvajal Revolt, involved alliances among diverse racial groups
pursuing their individual interests. Military men on both sides of the border
cooperated in combating Indian raids far more commonly than most histories
indicate. Combat against hostile Indians reflects how the struggle for survival
led to violence as well as cooperation. Indians carried out raids in order to survive. For the same reason non-Indian inhabitants of the region joined together
to fight them.

Despite their differences, groups in the border region shared various commonalities. Occasionally, they shared certain values or ideals, but more often their
commonalities revolved around needs for security or material things. Jointly
engaging in commerce or combating Indians helped fulfill those needs. They
also shared certain qualities such as pragmatism and adaptability. Pragmatic
people did not let their attitudes or ideology get in the way of their self-interest.
Newcomers had to accept prevailing practices, such as the widespread smuggling
in the border region. It was not a suitable place for rigidly honest or moralistic
people. Similarly, pragmatic Mexican rural workers shunned patriotic appeals (not
to speak of a miserable life on the haciendas) in search of a better life in Texas.

During the decade of 1850–60 the border was a major passageway for migrant
people because "mobility across the border expanded life possibilities."[205] American and European merchants and doctors, peaceful Indian tribes, and runaway

slaves all streamed south into Northeast Mexico, while Mexican rural people migrated north to Texas, in search of a better life. In Texas Mexicans found racial hostility but also opportunities for advancement. Some Anglos and many European immigrants to Texas accepted Mexicans and lived in relative harmony with them. The harsh realities of life on the frontier often made people come together and depend on one another, regardless of racial or ethnic differences.

The study of migrant peoples is one of common men and women struggling for survival in adverse conditions. Their stories are seldom told, but taken collectively they reflect some of the most important processes in borderlands history. Migrants' existence and activities played an important role in shaping the relations between the United States and Mexico. These people gave life to a "region grounded in local relationships of social and economic exchange." They inhabited "interconnected communities, economies, and ecologies that could not be divided simply by proclaiming that a linear boundary ran through them."[206]

If the Texas-Mexico border region can be considered a "middle ground," or an "area of interaction between two or more cultures in which neither culture is assumed to have an altogether superior position," it is because these common people made it so.[207] Historians Jeremy Adelman and Stephen Aron recognized that "borders formalized but did not foreclose the flow of people, capital, and goods" until a later period when borderlands became bordered lands. On the Rio Grande frontier, some historians, including myself, would argue that the permeability of this particular border has endured until the present.[208]

CHAPTER 4

Commercial and Religious Expansion

1849–1860

Throughout the 1850s, violence associated with theft of livestock, Indian raids, and runaway slaves plagued the Texas-Mexico border region. Three wars—the Revolution of Ayutla, the War of Reform, and the Cortina War—also shattered the peace of the region. The strife did not, however, deter the peaceful endeavors of merchants, missionaries, or migrants who continued to integrate the region.

PROTESTANTISM IN A CATHOLIC WORLD

Opportunities for interracial and interethnic coexistence and cooperation were enhanced by religion. Religion has the dual capacity for bringing people together or driving them apart,[1] but as Anglo-American Protestant preachers and European Catholic priests and nuns began to arrive in the border region in the late 1840s and the 1850s, opportunities for mutually rewarding exchange between these religious people and the Mexican population increased considerably. In the 1820s the Mexican government had made it a condition for Anglo settlers to adopt Catholicism, but the entry of Protestantism into Texas went largely unchallenged because the authorities could not enforce that provision and the Catholic Church was weak on Mexico's northern frontier. Zebulon Pike observed this weakness in 1807, long before Texas colonization, when he wrote that religion in the region was "Catholic, but much relaxed."[2]

After Mexican independence, the Catholic Church faced many problems, including a severe shortage of priests to cover the periphery of Mexico. "By 1828," writes David Weber, nearly half of Mexico's parishes "lacked resident priests and a disproportionate share of empty parishes existed in rural and remote areas such as the frontier." In 1831 the government of Coahuila y Texas received a petition from San Antonio to send clergy to baptize the Indians willing to accept the sacrament. Officials responded that the government did "not have the resources with which to console their afflictions."[3] In the 1850s the Abbé Emanuel Dome-nech wrote that "families and entire ranchos along the international boundary had not observed a minister for twenty or thirty years."[4]

American Protestant missionaries willingly stepped into this vacuum. Baptists, Methodists, and Presbyterians ignored the ban on religions other than Catholicism and preached freely throughout Texas, although "formal religious services were rare events before the separation from Mexico."[5] Perhaps the first Anglo-American missionary to reach out to the Mexican population was Sumner Bacon, a member of the Cumberland Presbyterian Church.[6] In 1835, Bacon reported that he had accomplished his objective: "I have succeeded in placing a Bible or Testament in the hands of every Mexican I have met that could read, and when they have money they willingly pay for them."[7] At least some of his religious literature was prepared especially for the Mexican population. In 1832 the American Bible Society sent to Texas "seventy-five Bibles and one hundred Testaments, some of which were printed in Spanish."[8]

Presbyterians such as Daniel Baker and John McCullough were in the forefront of missionary efforts to evangelize the Mexican population. Before coming to Texas in 1848, Daniel Baker, a Georgian educated at Princeton, had been pastor at a Washington, D.C., church, heading a congregation that included John Quincy Adams and Andrew Jackson. He preached in most of the state and "ascended the Rio Grande River as far as Roma" in order to investigate "the condition of the country for evangelical work." One of his successors wrote that Baker "represented the Mexicans as accessible, and many of them manifesting the desire for instruction in the Bible."[9] The diffusion of Protestant ideas began to be evident in the Villas del Norte. When the bishop of Monterrey visited Camargo in 1854, a bystander caused a public scandal when he heckled the bishop and his retinue. The authorities warned municipal officials to be on the lookout for those who "traveled the roads spreading the doctrine of the Protestant sects and using Bibles and books to further that end."[10]

The drive to spread Protestantism in San Antonio, the heart of Catholicism in Texas, was spearheaded by John McCullough, another former Princeton student. A religious newspaper reported in 1847 "that there [were] two organized Protestant churches, a good Sabbath School, Bible class, and female prayer meeting in San Antonio."[11] McCullough labored arduously to put a roof on his church and obtain funds for his school. In 1847 he had about fifty students, two-thirds of whom were Mexican. He reported that if he could afford to offer a free school, he "could have at least five hundred Mexican children in daily attendance." This not only reflects the intense drive of the Presbyterians to convert Mexicans to their faith, it also speaks eloquently of the desire of many Mexican families to educate their children.[12]

When Baker traveled to the Rio Grande in 1849, he became aware that local patrons in Brownsville had established a Sunday school less than a year after Charles Stillman founded the town. Interested citizens requested donations and books from the American Sunday School Union, which responded positively, and they began their conversion efforts. Some said it was a useless effort because the population of the Rio Grande was mainly "composed of renegadoes [sic], refugees from justice, and of the filth and off-scouring of the world." Yet by 1850 the school had "nearly one hundred scholars, and a library of almost seven hundred volumes."[13] The school had as one of its goals to "train the youth on the east bank of the Rio Grande, that they will be to their Roman Catholic neighbors on the western side of the river correct specimens of Protestantism."[14] Significantly, the school reached out to invite the youth of Matamoros to participate, and a ferry service was provided so they could cross the river free of charge. According to one source, "from that city of Romanism, many came to be taught in the principles of the holy Bible."[15]

The push to convert the Mexican population of the lower Rio Grande to Protestantism was greatly intensified with the arrival of Melinda Rankin in 1852. Born and raised in New England, Rankin traveled west as a young woman to do missionary work for the Presbyterian Church. She was in Mississippi in 1846 when soldiers returning from the U.S.-Mexican War told her of their experiences in a country where all religions except Catholicism were banned. Imbued with the religious and nationalistic principles of Manifest Destiny, Rankin resolved to make it her life's work to take Protestantism to Mexico and "vindicate the 'honor of *American* Christianity' against a 'tyrannical priesthood.'" She moved to Texas in May 1847 to be closer to Mexico, and for several years "spent her time teaching, establishing schools, writing for periodicals, and publishing a book, *Texas in 1850*."[16] By 1852 she made her way to Brownsville, where she was rapidly introduced to frontier solidarity. She obtained a room, but "had no bed to sleep on and nothing to eat. She quickly received a cot from a Mexican woman, a pillow from an American woman, and meals from a German woman."[17]

She set to work, opening a school for Mexican girls, but at the same time a group of Catholic priests and nuns arrived from France to open a convent and school. A spirited competition ensued between Protestantism and Catholicism to win over the people of the border region. Rankin realized that without resources to expand she was at a disadvantage, so she decided to return to New England and solicit funds to build a school in Brownsville. Risking everything, including her life in a perilous storm at sea, Rankin pursued her goal relentlessly. Many rejected the idea of investing money in trying to convert Mexicans, saying that they "were a people just fit to be exterminated from the earth." She discovered that even "ministers of the gospel" told her that it was "better [to] send bullets and gunpowder to Mexico than Bibles." Rankin persevered and obtained enough funds to establish the Rio Grande Female Institute in 1854. A board of trustees was established, headed by Hiram Chamberlain, whose daughter married Richard King later that year.[18]

Rankin's goal of working in Mexico was stalled by the lack of religious freedom in the country. She invited her sister Harriet to come and help her, not knowing that a deadly yellow fever epidemic was about to descend on Brownsville. Her sister succumbed to the disease in 1858 and Rankin herself was struck shortly afterwards. She came close to losing her life and had "resigned herself to dying, but an elderly Mexican woman, the grandmother of some of her pupils, stayed with her and nursed her back to health." This poor woman received generous offers "of money to nurse other people, but she . . . stayed with Rankin." The generosity of this old woman confirmed for Rankin the "basic goodness and nobility in the Mexican people that many of her contemporaries did not see."[19] Throughout the 1850s she faced many trials and tribulations, but these were merely a rehearsal for her experiences during the Civil War and her long-awaited entrance into Mexico in the 1860s.

CATHOLICISM EXPANDS

While Melinda Rankin and other Protestant missionaries were making inroads among the Mexican population of the border region, the Catholic Church did not stand still. The separation of Texas from Mexico in 1836 fractured Catholic organization in the province. Texas had been administered by the Diocese of Linares in Monterrey since 1777, but after Texas independence, communication broke down. Only one Catholic priest was to be found north of the Nueces River in San Antonio, although the towns and settlements along the Rio Grande still under Mexican political control were served by the diocese. This untenable situation was addressed in October 1839, when Rome established the Prefecture Apostolic of Texas. A prefecture was an administrative unit of lesser stature than a diocese, but from that time forward, the Catholic Church of the United States would minister to souls in Texas. In December of that year, a group of Vicentian priests arrived in Texas and their work led to the foundation of the Diocese of Galveston in 1847, under the leadership of Bishop Jean Marie Odin, a native of France who had served in the United States for many years.[20]

After the war between the United States and Mexico, the area south of the Nueces to the Rio Grande became U.S. territory and the Diocese of Galveston assumed the role of serving the Catholic population of the region. The leading citizens of Brownsville asked Bishop Odin to send Catholic missionaries because they were anxious "to induce Mexican and American Catholics of position and respectability to establish themselves in that city, and thus contribute to its mercantile and social importance."[21] Odin arranged for several Oblate priests to relocate from Canada to Brownsville in 1849. Their work was fraught with adversity; when they arrived, "they found a miserable shed to serve as a temporary chapel." There were only ten people at the first mass, but attendance increased rapidly. Soon, they had to give up their "chapel" because the landlord of the property on which it stood put the land up for sale.[22] Additionally, given the constant immigration of Mexican and a few German Catholics to the Rio Grande region, Bishop Odin wrote that it was becoming necessary for "all our priests . . . to speak English, Spanish, and a little German."[23]

While the Oblates were serving the Rio Grande Valley, Bishop Odin recruited Marianist priests and Ursuline nuns in the early 1850s to establish schools in San Antonio. Odin purchased a property from his good friend John Twohig in order to build a school "for the multilingual male youth of San Antonio."[24] The Ursuline sisters began their work in San Antonio in 1851. Odin built a convent for them, but even before it was completed they opened their school. Historian James T. Moore writes that "soon over three hundred students were enrolled, and when facilities for boarding students were completed, the number increased even more as families in other parts of Texas as well as Mexico began sending their children to the school."[25]

It is important to underline the amount of European involvement—especially French—in Catholic missionary work in South Texas. Odin traveled to Europe on various occasions to recruit religious people. In his reminiscences, Father Pierre Fourrier Parisot writes that in March 1852, "six Oblate Fathers and one Lay Brother, accompanied by four Nuns of the Incarnate Word, two Ursuline Sisters, four Brothers of Mary, and eighteen Seminarians, bade adieu to 'La Belle France' and went aboard the sailing vessel 'La Belle Assise,' at Havre, en route for

Texas." The school and convent of the Church of the Immaculate Conception in Brownsville reflected this international flavor. It was run by fourteen Ursuline nuns, two of them from Mexico, nine from France, and three from Ireland.[26]

In his criteria for priests, Bishop Odin asked not only that they be able to speak several languages, but also that they be "ready to live a life of privations and hardships" because the "vast majority of Catholics in the diocese of Galveston lived in scattered villages of five, ten, or fifteen families." Arduous and oftentimes dangerous travel to visit these communities was an imperative. It was truly a "ministry on horseback."[27] The lot of the Oblate priests was not an easy one. They "braved bandits and marauders, flash floods, and seemingly interminable droughts; and suffered infestations of ticks, chiggers, fleas, and rashes of all kinds. They abided extreme hunger, thirst, fatigue, and loneliness."[28] Even in the urban areas, they had no luxuries. On a visit to the Marianist brothers in San Antonio, Bishop Odin discovered that they were dying from hunger. He asked Twohig for help and the generous merchant "ordered a supply of potatoes, bread, and meat" and thereafter "helped them with groceries and provisions."[29]

The missionary zeal and indifference to adversity of the Catholic missionaries was more than matched by their leader, Bishop Jean Marie Odin, one of the most extraordinary churchmen ever to come to Texas. He was born in France in 1800 to a family of respectable economic and social status. In 1822, while studying in the seminary, he responded to a call for missionaries in America. He spent many years in Missouri, where he became a Vicentian priest. Odin arrived in Texas with three Spanish Vicentian priests and was named second in charge of the Prefecture Apostolic of Texas. He "worked tirelessly; his efforts produced such outstanding results that he has been acclaimed the founder of the modern Catholic Church in Texas." Because of his outstanding qualities, Pope Pius IX named Odin bishop of the newly created Diocese of Galveston on May 4, 1847.[30]

In 1850, Odin started out from Galveston on a trip to the Rio Grande Valley, but he followed a roundabout route, going first to San Antonio, then to Eagle Pass by way of Castroville. While at Fort Duncan he made contact with Mexican civil and military authorities to let them know that he wished to travel to Nuevo Laredo on the Mexican side of the river. His request caused quite a stir because people in those parts had never seen a bishop. He was received with great fanfare and ceremony by the people and the civic, religious, and military leaders of Piedras Negras and Guerrero before he set out for Nuevo Laredo, joined by an escort of soldiers and vecinos from that place. One military chief was impressed with Odin's "humility, poverty, and evangelical morality."[31]

The news of Odin's brief entry into Mexico even reached the Mexican president, who, through his secretary of war and navy, Mariano Arista, instructed local authorities to receive the bishop "as an illustrious traveler."[32] He reached Nuevo Laredo shortly after a large band of Comanches had murdered one man and injured six others in the area. His presence brought solace to the population, although one person, probably an Anglo male, was disappointed that the traditional fandangos had been suspended. He expressed the hope that the bishop would leave shortly and "we will then make up for lost time. The Senoritas will dance none the lighter for having been confessed, [pardoned], and confirmed."[33] Odin then continued his journey along the southern side of the Rio Grande toward Guerrero. In that town the local pastor asked him to administer the sacrament of Confirmation. Recognizing that he was outside his jurisdiction, Odin wrote to the bishop of Monterrey and received immediate authorization. He attended to the population on both sides of the river and later "recorded that he confirmed about 11,000 people in the towns and cities of the Rio Grande Valley: in Guerrero, Mier, Camargo, Reynosa, and Matamoros in the Mexican state of Tamaulipas, and in Laredo, Roma, Rio Grande City, and Brownsville in Texas."[34]

Odin returned to the Rio Grande in 1854. On this trip he had the opportunity to meet Francisco de Paula y Verea, the newly appointed bishop of Monterrey, who "had quickly gained the reputation of being an excellent pastor and administrator." Verea was on a visit to the towns on the southern side of the river and "the two prelates met at a rancho when their confirmation visits brought them together." The meeting was constructive because "they were able to work out jurisdictional problems resulting from the flood-induced shifting of the Rio Grande, which left small isolated pockets of Texas and Mexico on the 'wrong' side of the river." Following the meeting with Verea, Odin accepted an invitation from the alcalde and local pastor of Reynosa to visit their town. After four grueling months, "riding a mule and wearing a tattered suit spattered with mud," the bishop returned to Galveston in November 1854.[35] Odin's final visit to the Rio Grande Valley was in 1858, accompanied by Father Pierre F. Parisot, one of the Oblate priests. He conducted confirmations from Port Isabel to Laredo. "By that time he was fifty-eight years old and had been on the Texas frontier eighteen years. His strength in the face of harsh existence still held, according to Father Parisot "who accompanied him one day on a thirty-mile trip over a muddy trail." During this journey "Odin traveled almost two thousand miles and confirmed 3,413 people."[36]

Odin's visits to the Rio Grande underscore the basic truth that religion knows no political boundaries. The European-born priests sent to the region reached out to the Mexican population on both sides of the border, and there was ample cooperation between Catholic religious leaders on both sides of the river. The Reverend Robert Cooke wrote that although "the Rio Grande was the boundary line of the Oblate Missions in Texas . . . the zeal of the Fathers at Brownsville was not to be confined to its northern banks." They gladly accepted the invitation of the parish priest of Matamoros "to give missions in several parishes in Tamaulipas." Bishop Verea of Monterrey did not hesitate to call on the Oblates to shore up his diocese. At his request, they "established themselves at Victoria, the capital of the State of Tamaulipas. They also undertook the pastoral care of Matamoros and of the sanctuary and Mission of our Lady of Agualeguas in the State of Nuevo Leon."[37]

One of the missionaries recruited by Odin in Europe was Emmanuel Domenech, who came to the United States in 1846 and was ordained as an Oblate priest in San Antonio in 1848. The fastidious Domenech had unkind words for Austin, "a small dirty town," and Houston, a town "infested with Methodists and ants."[38] His view of Anglo-Texans in the mostly lawless frontier was no better. They were "the very scum of society," rough men with dubious pasts in search of "adventure and illicit gains."[39] Assigned by Odin to Brownsville, Domenech had to take a crash course in Spanish in order to communicate with the largely Mexican population. He immediately offered his support to his Catholic colleagues on the southern side of the Rio Grande and visited the ranches and towns on both sides of the river. He wrote that the region around Reynosa "was left almost entirely to itself in the matter of religion. It had hardly ever a visit from a priest," and oftentimes people "died without sacraments."[40]

Domenech was succeeded in the Brownsville mission by Fathers Jean-Maurice Verdet and Pierre Keralum, both skilled in construction. These two priests built the imposing "Gothic-style church" in Brownsville that "became the architectural pride of the town, its most imposing building."[41] Keralum helped build churches in Roma and Laredo as well as other church buildings in Brownsville but, according to one source, he was best known for his "genuineness, simplicity of life, generosity, and affability. He was a model of religious poverty, obedience, and unpretentiousness, as he tirelessly made his missionary rounds among the scattered ranches."[42]

Verdet and Keralum worked extensively with the Mexican population, especially in remote ranches where they "carried on their mission, not waiting to be

sought after but living out their lives among the people." Verdet heeded Bishop
Odin's request to "continue their friendly relations with the priests on the Mexican
side of the river" by paying a visit to Bishop Verea in Monterrey, which Odin
applauded because it helped to cement the ties between Catholics on both sides
of the border.[43]

The close ties that were developing among the leaders of the churches in Texas
and Monterrey were enhanced considerably by the 1858 arrival in Brownsville of
Father Pierre Fourrier Parisot. He had come to Texas from France in 1852 with a
large group of missionaries recruited by Odin. Within a month of his arrival and
after intensive courses in English and Spanish, he "was able to preach in English
in the cathedral." He helped found a seminary-college in Galveston, where he also
taught classes in Greek, Latin, and mathematics. In 1857 Parisot was appointed

Father Pierre Fourrier Parisot was one of many Oblate priests who came from France to
serve on the Rio Grande frontier. In 1858 he was assigned to Brownsville where he served
for thirty-six years. The Oblates endured privations and dangers and were instrumental in
conserving and strengthening the adherence to Catholicism among Mexicans on both sides
of the border. Courtesy of Southwestern Oblate Historical Archives. San Antonio, Texas.

chaplain at the Ursuline Convent in San Antonio, and the following year he was in Brownsville, which became his base of operations for the next thirty-six years. "Working incessantly through yellow fever epidemics, border conflicts, conflicts in Mexico, and Civil War obstacles, he covered on horseback a vast mission ground on both sides of the Rio Grande."[44]

Parisot adhered strictly to Odin's instruction to collaborate with the Diocese of Monterrey in providing Catholic services in the border region. He wrote that there was "a large community of Oblates" in Brownsville who "were able to go to the assistance of their brother Priests on the Mexican side of the river when necessary." Four of his fellow Oblate priests "were the Pastors of Matamoros and of the country around within a radius of thirty miles."[45] At the request of Bishop Verea, Parisot himself took charge of the parish in Reynosa, which he found in a deplorable state of neglect. It required "fifteen days with two men to restore the edifice to a decent appearance. The spiritual work was slower."[46]

While at Reynosa in 1860, Parisot faced one of his greatest challenges. A religious leader with supposed miraculous powers to cure people and a great following had emerged in Nuevo León and was preaching heretical notions, among them, "that God had decided to eliminate most of the sacraments of the Church," which, of course, would have put the priests out of business.[47] Pedro Rojas, better known to his followers as "Tatita," was described by a Laredo merchant as "a man about sixty years of age, very dark and vulgar looking, with a long white beard reaching half way to his waist." He wore sackcloth pants and a coat over a "dirty white shirt open down the bosom" and "sandals on a pair of very dirty feet." The merchant added that Tatita "wields a rod of iron over about two thousand human beings," who kiss his feet and consider "him to be the God of Hosts."[48] Rojas had been expelled from Nuevo León and was making his way to Mier, Tamaulipas, when Parisot decided to go there and confront him.

As Parisot got nearer to Mier he "saw crowds of pilgrims on their way to visit Tatita" and "invalids carried to him, in vehicles of every description." When he reached the town, "the streets were crowded with strangers, and the principal plaza of the city was packed with human beings, all on their knees, reciting the Rosary with this singular personage, who was looked upon as a Saint." It was believed that the "impostor" was protected by three hundred armed guards "who [drew] their share of the profits," and that "an American [was] the manager of the whole affair." In a fateful encounter Parisot accused Rojas of "doing the devil's work, feigning sanctity under the cloak of religion, deceiving the weak and the ignorant." Furthermore, he denounced Rojas's "false doctrine," which "cast odium on religion and Priests." The Catholic prelate dressed down Rojas for more than an hour before addressing a multitude of several thousand people. Among shouts of "angry disapproval," Parisot called Rojas "a hypocrite and an impostor." As the crowd grew angrier, Parisot was whisked away while Tatita took the stage and whipped the crowd into a deadly frenzy. At that moment the alcalde of Mier stepped in to protect Parisot and offer an armed guard to see him safely out of town. Ironically, Pedro Rojas was killed a few days later by fellow Mexicans. "A young man from a neighboring village gathered a certain number of comrades and resolved to go and meet Tatita on the road and kill him because he said, such a man as that would bring shame and dishonor on religion and our country."[49]

The good relations that the Oblates and the Mexican clergy of Monterrey had cultivated throughout the 1850s became of crucial importance at the end of the decade, when many clerics were forced to leave Mexico because of their opposition to the Constitution of 1857. Among these was Bishop Verea, who was expelled from Nuevo León on September 10, 1857, after a bitter dispute with Governor Santiago Vidaurri over the application of the law confiscating church property. Odin, who regarded Verea as a "good and saintly bishop," offered him sanctuary in his diocese, and Verea stayed in Brownsville as "the guest of the Oblate Fathers for nearly three months prior to his departure for Europe." In the interim Verea was not idle; he preached the Lenten sermons and regaled the Oblate priests with his many adventures as a priest and bishop in Mexico. "During one of his Pastoral visits, he was attacked by a band of robbers, who very respectfully demanded his money or his life. The Bishop and his secretary gave them what money they had, then the highwaymen knelt down and religiously asked the Bishop for his blessing."[50] Mexican clerics from other states, such as San Luis Potosí, made their way to Brownsville, and "the Oblate Fathers did all in their power to mitigate their sufferings and their exile."[51]

During the War of Reform Mexican liberals expelled Catholic priests and sent them to Texas, where it was hoped that they would learn to comport themselves differently under the direction of a civil government. Mexican liberals such as Santiago Vidaurri knew about Bishop Odin and held him in high regard for his austerity and dignity. When thirty priests were exiled from San Luis Potosí, the official newspaper of Nuevo León y Coahuila hailed the measure, declaring that they would find Texas Catholic clerics "models to be imitated." They would also see that "pure Catholic religion was perfectly compatible with liberal institutions," and would learn to subsist without seeking enrichment or charging exorbitant fees for their services.[52]

Ironically, two years after Vidaurri expelled the priests, he was searching for replacements in Texas to come to Nuevo León and administer the sacraments. In July 1859, he wrote to his good friend Santos Benavides of Laredo, asking him to help him in a special mission. Would Benavides "utilize his influence . . . to determine if the bishop of Texas would consider an official request" to send "Catholic priests to fill with Christian hands the spiritual needs of the towns in my charge?" Knowing that this could take time, Vidaurri asked Benavides if he could please spare one or two priests from Laredo to come to Nuevo León. Perhaps the caudillo of Nuevo León thought priests could be moved like pawns on a chessboard. Or perhaps he was unaware of the close ties between Catholic prelates on both sides of the border and that the Texas clerics were harboring the very priests he had expelled. In any case, he had become painfully aware of the vital importance of these holy men to the population under his control and was desirous of obtaining docile priests from across the border.[53]

Mining Ventures in Northeast Mexico

While these events were transpiring, the economy was accelerating on both sides of the border in the 1850s, which promoted greater cooperation among the various ethnic groups in the region. Three areas of economic activity reflect this trend: mining, the raising of livestock, and commerce. Silver mining had been the principal economic activity of New Spain. The independence movement and the departure of the Spaniards—and their assets—in the 1820s deeply affected the industry, although Zacatecas and Chihuahua suffered less than states in the center of the country, such as Guanajuato.[54] In the Northeast, there were few mines and virtually no native capital to revive the ones that existed. A few Anglo-Americans and Europeans arrived to invest in the industry. They may have entertained dreams of replacing the Spaniards as the chief beneficiaries of Mexico's vast deposits of gold and silver, but they would be disappointed because Northeast Mexico was not Zacatecas, and the exploitation of the mineral wealth of the region—especially in Coahuila—would not reach its potential until half a century later during the Porfiriato.

The mines of Nuevo León illustrate the problems faced by the industry in the region. There were three mining areas, centered on the towns of Cerralvo, Villaldama, and Vallecillo. An 1827 report from Cerralvo states that mining operations had ceased for lack of investment capital, though in years past those mines had "yielded considerable bonanzas." In Villaldama, where lead and silver were produced, only five of seventeen existing mines were being worked by "poor individuals"; and in Vallecillo, reports from the 1820s and 1830s indicate that there were thirty-four mines, but they were plagued by lack of investors, workers, and wood, which had to be brought in from afar.[55]

The mines required capital that Americans or Europeans could provide, but the unrest of the 1830s and 1840s was too convulsive to attract investments. The war over Texas, the conflict during the Texas Republic, and the war between the United States and Mexico came in rapid succession during those two decades. These events, coupled with internal revolts and the constant Indian attacks made long-term investments inordinately risky.[56] Some investors were waiting for conditions in Mexico to improve. In January 1841, the *Austin City Gazette* reported that there were eight mining towns in Chihuahua and one thousand mine shafts, but "the mines are very ineffectively worked, and the full extent of the Mexican mineral beds will probably never be developed until American or Texian . . . enterprise carries steam into the bowels of the earth to drag its untold treasures into light."[57]

After the U.S.-Mexican War, conditions in Mexico showed signs of improvement, and Anglo-American capitalists renewed their drive to acquire mines in Mexico. Many political leaders of Northeast Mexico recognized that the country needed to modernize, which American investment could facilitate. In his annual report on the state of the Nuevo León economy in 1848, Governor José María Parás declared that Mexican industry was a "pygmy" compared to that of other western nations. It needed to apply technological advances, utilize machinery being employed in other countries, and replace human power with steam engines or we "will not have escaped the backwardness in which we find ourselves in all branches of industry."[58] American mining entrepreneurs were interested in doing just that. In 1849 a group of investors tried to revive the Jesús María mine in Vallecillo, Nuevo León. They entered into an agreement with a local miner, Patricio Flores, who would supervise the machinery that was being transported from the United States. Flores reported that he had already received nine wagons and two carts that contained part of the steam engine and pumps to extract the water from the mine. The rest of the equipment was still at Camargo on the border, some seventy-five miles from Vallecillo.[59]

After a short time the investors decided to pull out and sold their interest in the mine to another group that included Charles Stillman. The new firm, named the Vallecillo Mining Company, continued to extract water from the mine while sending a German engineer to evaluate its potential. His report revealed that two rich veins of silver had been discovered where the previous Spanish owners had discontinued their operations many years earlier. One of the veins, he wrote, was soft and did not require the use of gunpowder. Moreover, it "yields larger quantities of ore than most of the other mines of the country." The ore was of such richness and abundance that it gave "the absolute certainty of great returns for the capital invested."[60]

The investors were pleased, and so was Governor Juan Nepomuceno de la Garza y Evia. He reported that the current owners of the Jesús María mine in Vallecillo had brought in additional machinery to extract the water and had recruited mine workers from the interior of Mexico and "soon this source of riches will be open to the benefit of the state."[61] In November 1852, Charles Stillman ordered Julio M. Prevost, who had been hired as superintendent, to report to the mine. Prevost, born in Philadelphia of French parents, was a military surgeon who had served with Generals Taylor and Wool in the U.S.-Mexican War. After the war he decided to stay in Mexico, but not to practice medicine. Instead, he became interested in mining and determined that the best place to learn about it was in Zacatecas. He met a Mexican girl, fell in love, and proposed marriage to Mariana Cossío, daughter of Severo Cossío, who would later become governor of San Luis Potosí. She accepted, but there was one problem. Prevost was a Protestant, and the Catholic Church would not consent to marry them. They resolved the issue by traveling to Brownsville, where Hiram Chamberlain performed the ceremony at Fort Brown on May 28, 1850.[62]

With the support of the Nuevo León administration, Prevost imported almost four hundred thousand pounds of machinery free of customs duties in 1854. He left the company, probably sometime in 1855, to return to Zacatecas. He must have left on good terms because he was praised for his "capacity, integrity, and energy in the prosecution of an important and honorable trust."[63] By the time Prevost left, the Stillman group's mines in Vallecillo were a huge success. Throughout the 1850s they produced "over $4 million in silver and lead exports." Stillman also "sold shares . . . on the New York Stock Exchange."[64]

One of the stockholders was Major Samuel P. Heintzelman, a mining engineer who had graduated from West Point. Heintzelman, who had served in the U.S.-Mexican War and would go on to have a brilliant military career as a Union general during the U.S. Civil War, was assigned to Texas in 1859, after serving as president of the Sonora Exploring and Mining Company in Arizona. He arrived in time to lead the attack on Juan Cortina, whom he defeated on December 27, 1859, near Rio Grande City in the decisive battle of the Cortina War (which will be discussed later in this chapter). Less than a week after the battle, Heintzelman was in Vallecillo visiting the mine in which he had invested $10,000. He was careful not to wear his army uniform and was joined by a merchant from Roma because, he said, "it would hardly have been safe to have met a party of Cortinas's men under the circumstances. I passed for one of the proprietors of the Vallecillo mines, who only understood a few words of Spanish." Heintzelman noted that enormous quantities of lead were extracted. Little did he know that shortly after, much of that lead would be sent to fortify his enemy, the Confederate army.[65]

Other capitalists were exploring the once-rich mines of nearby Villaldama and those in the region of the legendary Real de Catorce in the neighboring state of San Luis Potosí. Juan Cameron, a fellow prisoner with Ben Milam, had filed his first mining claim in the 1820s. He joined an American investor in 1856 to file a claim to a copper mine near San Antonio de Yguana in Villaldama, famous for its fabulous mineral output during the colonial period. Old hands such as Cameron were joined by new investors, such as Juan Weber, a German American friend of Santiago Vidaurri who would become a prominent merchant of Monterrey and a member of the economic elite of the city during the Porfiriato. Weber took another step on his climb up the economic ladder when he joined a group of investors in filing a claim to a different mine in Villaldama in 1857.[66]

The activity of foreigners was also apparent at Catorce (in San Luis Potosí, near the border with Nuevo León), where a group of investors from New York and New Orleans had purchased a silver mine in 1855. An enthusiastic writer to the *New York Daily Times* stated that assuming peace was maintained in the country, these investors "expect to put up their machinery and commence work next Fall."[67] The hope for peace was overly optimistic, however. Soon the War of Reform broke out and shortly thereafter the War of French Intervention, plunging Mexico into a state of upheaval for nearly a decade, from 1858 to 1867. More than these conflicts, however, it was the Civil War in the United States that postponed most investments in Mexico in the first half of the 1860s.

STOCK RAISING IN THE BORDER REGION

Stock raising was another activity that brought together the diverse people of the border region, and while it would not acquire vast proportions until the 1870s, it grew steadily in the 1850s. Most of the farms and ranches in South Texas and the Nueces Strip, writes historian Armando Alonzo, belonged to Mexicans who held on to them until near the end of the century. These Mexican rancheros "played a leading role in the commercialization of ranching and participated in other economic activities" that brought them into contact with Anglo society. Mexican ranchers drove their cattle to ports on the Gulf and either directly or through agents sold them to buyers from as far away as New Orleans and New York.[68]

These hardworking rancheros had business sense and, under difficult conditions, sought ways to improve their herds. An American traveler who passed through the Nueces Strip in the late 1850s described what he saw at the ranch of Cecilio Valerio. There were "about 400 head of horses, mares and mules." Valerio had acquired "a powerful dark bay American stallion with which he ha[d] crossed his Spanish mares, and produced large and likely colts." The visitor opined that the Mexican's success "shows what can be done by ordinary attention and perseverance on a stock farm in this favored country. A few years ago he had hardly a dollar. Running mustangs and trading them off to advantage . . . reserving some likely animal to breed from, the old man is now very independent."[69]

Besides applying their knowledge and skills to their own ranches, Mexican ranchers shared their expertise with the Anglo-American and European newcomers to the region from their first encounters in the 1820s on. When the Irish arrived in Texas to settle the McMullen-McGloin colony in San Patricio in the late 1820s, they found a land very different from the one they had left. They learned from the rancheros and vaqueros "the techniques of cattle care and Mexican horsemanship. . . . They learned to use the *silla de campo* which was a forerunner of the Western saddle, the *lazo* and the *reata* for roping, the 'cutting out' of an animal from the herd for branding, the roundup, and the drive." They also "learned how to battle the droughts, how to gather and singe the prickly pear [cactus] for the cattle to eat." These and many other examples of cultural borrowing and transculturation were common on the frontier.[70]

The exchange of livestock across the border offered other opportunities for interaction between people. Northeast Mexico was both a market for and a supplier of livestock for Texas ranchers and merchants. In times of drought or scarcity of beef, the inhabitants of Monterrey could rely on imported beef from Texas. Authorities called this a "constant" commerce. Satisfying this market with exported beef was however expensive. Esteban and Policarpo Garza petitioned local authorities to allow them to sell beef at a higher price because it had been brought from Texas at great expense.[71] Although at times cattle were scarce, the Northeast produced horses and mules prolifically. Evaristo Madero raised large quantities on his ranches in Coahuila and obtained even more from other sources, then sent them to his business partner, William Stone in Eagle Pass, to be sold in Texas.[72]

Another large-scale producer of horses was Santiago Vidaurri, who leveraged his political power to amass land and capital. Vidaurri and his son, Indalecio, raised horses and mules on their hacienda at Catujanes near Lampazos. This huge and forbidding 80,000-acre tableland with 1,400-foot perpendicular walls served as a mountain fortress to resist Indian invasions.[73] Santos Benavides of Laredo helped Vidaurri find clients in Texas. In one letter the Nuevo León governor lamented that he had so much stock that he didn't know what to do with it and asked Benavides to find buyers for him. When Vidaurri did not have stock available, he helped his clients in Texas find other sources. For example, his friend Ángel Navarro of San Antonio wrote Vidaurri requesting that the latter give Gabriel Abrams assistance on his trip to buy horses in Linares, Nuevo León.[74]

Stock buyers were always at risk of attacks from Indians or bandits. Three Texan buyers ventured from Roma into the interior of Mexico to buy animals during the unsettled conditions provoked by the Cortina War. They were reportedly killed by Cortinistas for the mere reason that they were gringos.[75] On another occasion in the early 1850s, George H. Giddings, who would later operate a mail route from New Orleans to California through Texas, was attacked by a party of close to one hundred Indians after he bought three hundred mules at Saltillo. Giddings was with a party of twenty-five men, five of them American and the rest Mexican. His group sought refuge at a nearby ranch, where they found nine victims—mostly women—who had been killed by the Indians. During the night Giddings "sent out a courier to the Mexican officer commanding at Monclova [who] sent a large force of troops" that drove the Indians away.[76]

The purchase of horses and mules in Mexico brings to light one of the most remarkable characters in the history of South Texas. Sally Skull was a flinty, weather-beaten woman with "steel-blue eyes," who swore like a sailor, packed a six-gun; and was not afraid to use it. It is said that she shot one of her five husbands as well as a man at a fair organized by Henry L. Kinney in Corpus Christi in 1852. Rip Ford, who witnessed the latter incident, wrote later that she "was famed as a rough fighter, and prudent men did not willingly provoke her in a row."[77] She grew up in Austin's Colony and was still in South Texas at the time of the Civil War. In the 1850s she ran a ranch at Banquette and traveled often to Mexico in search of horses. Newspaperman John Warren Hunter described her as follows: "Sally Skull spoke Spanish with the fluency of a native, and kept in her employ a number of desperate Mexicans whom she ruled with the iron grasp of a despot." Together they "would make long journeys to the Rio Grande where, through questionable methods, she secured large droves of horses. These were driven to Louisiana and sold." Hunter added that when the Civil War broke out "Old Sally fitted out a mule train of several wagons, with Mexican teamsters, and engaged in hauling [cotton] to the Rio Grande."[78]

Those "questionable methods" were the methods preferred by many border-landers and were a prominent feature of the clandestine economy on the border. Horses were rustled in Mexico, and cattle rustled in Texas, in massive quantities. In August 1859, a circular from the governor of Nuevo León called attention to the "disgraceful traffic" in cattle and other livestock stolen in Mexico and sold in Texas. His circular followed on the heels of the capture of four individuals who had stolen twelve mares and three colts and sold them in Texas.[79] But this arrest was a drop in the bucket. LeRoy Graf writes that a thousand head of mules and horses passed through Rio Grande City en route to the interior of Texas in a two-month period in 1852.[80] In Cameron County, the Lugo brothers stole animals on both sides of the border. They worked with A. Werbiski, an Anglo-American who sheltered the stolen livestock on his ranch.[81]

Mexico's Comisión Pesquisidora accused several prominent persons of running large-scale horse-stealing operations. Adolphus Glaevecke, a native of Prussia, was the most notorious. He came to the Rio Grande in 1836, married Concepción Ramírez, a cousin of Juan Cortina's, and bought a large spread along the river in Cameron County. After hearing numerous witnesses and reviewing judicial records the comisión declared that Glaevecke headed a band of horse thieves that included Florencio Garza, Juan Vela, Marcos Guerra, and several others. In another example, Thaddeus Rhodes, a North Carolinian who arrived on the border with Taylor's army, settled in Hidalgo County and married Rafaela Hernández. He was accused of heading a band that preyed on the ranches of Reynosa and the towns of northern Nuevo León. According to the comisión, the organizers or instigators were Texans and those who executed the operations were Mexicans from both sides of the border. Richard King was one of those Texans, according to the comisión, and among his principal operators were Thomás Vázquez and Atilano Alvarado.[82] The theft of livestock, especially of cattle stolen in Texas and taken to Mexico, would reach epic proportions in the 1870s.

MERCHANTS INTEGRATE THE REGION

Trade was the crucial element in the continuing integration of the vast Rio Grande binational region, so it is useful to focus on some of the towns and a few of the merchants who drove this integration. San Antonio, Matamoros, and Monterrey continued to play key roles, now joined by towns such as Eagle Pass, Laredo, and

Brownsville (which grew rapidly after its founding in 1848). Established merchants, such as Charles Stillman and John Kelsey, were joined by newcomers including Joseph Kleiber and José San Román. Kleiber, a native of the Alsace-Lorraine region in Europe, arrived in New Orleans in the 1850s and eventually moved to Brownsville, where he bought a drugstore in 1860. He began to contact the clients of the former owner, many of whom were in Mexico. He also wrote to Casa Sepúlveda in Monterrey and proposed maintaining the same business relationship and traveled up the Rio Grande, meeting with many Mexican merchants willing to buy his products. Kleiber requested one thousand business cards in Spanish from a firm in New Orleans in order to attract greater business in Mexico.[83]

No other merchant, not even Stillman, had more contacts in northern Mexico than the Spaniard José San Román. Like Kleiber and many others before him, San Román used New Orleans as a stepping stone to Matamoros. He arrived on the Rio Grande during the U.S.-Mexican War and opened a store near the main plaza where he sold clothing, shoes, hats, and other goods. He quickly branched out and expanded his business throughout the 1850s, so that by the time of the Civil War he had established connections with fellow merchants in Tamaulipas, Coahuila, Nuevo León, Zacatecas, Durango, San Luis Potosí. and Chihuahua. In particular San Román established ties to Spanish merchants in Monterrey, such as Valentín Rivero and Mariano Hernández. From them he obtained wool, hides, and silver in exchange for a broad range of products that included farm implements, machinery, wagons, firearms, glass, paper, furniture, wine, and food products. San Román connected Mexican merchants not only with Texas, but also with the entire Atlantic world. This network would become increasingly evident during the American Civil War.[84]

Farther up the Rio Grande, John Z. Leyendecker, a native of Germany, opened a commercial establishment in Laredo. Leyendecker had arrived in Texas with his family in 1845 and lived for a number of years in Fredericksburg. Shortly after settling in Laredo, he married Juliana Benavides, sister of Santos Benavides and member of one of the most powerful families in South Texas. Leyendecker served as an intermediary to connect San Antonio merchants with their counterparts in Monterrey. When Francois Gilbeau, a French merchant in Bexar, wanted flour and other food products from Mexico, Leyendecker obtained them from the Spaniard Mariano Hernández in Monterrey. When, in turn, Hernández required cotton for his newly opened textile plant, Leyendecker obtained it for him from Gilbeau.[85]

Besides strengthening the San Antonio–Northeast Mexico connection through Laredo, Leyendecker's operations gave new life to a road between

Laredo and Corpus Christi (previously improved in 1848). Leyendecker commonly used that route to send hides and silver to New York and to transmit goods from New York and Europe to Northeast Mexico. In New York, Perkins, King, and Company was one of several firms that traded with the Laredo merchant. Like San Román, but on a much smaller scale, Leyendecker added another link in the chain that tied Mexico's Northeast to the Atlantic economy.[86]

Another native of Germany, Friedrich Groos, made Eagle Pass his base of operations, and his success mirrored the growing significance of the Eagle Pass–Piedras Negras trade route. With his brothers, Carl and Gustav, and with the collaboration of families he had brought from Mexico, Groos opened a mercantile firm, F. Groos & Company. Established in 1854, it soon had branches in San Antonio, New Braunfels, and Matamoros. On November 27 of that year Friedrich married Gertrude Rodríguez, and they would bring nine children into the world. His business connections in Texas and northern Mexico would serve him well during the commercial boom of the Civil War period.[87]

The two centers of this developing transnational region were the inland cities of San Antonio and Monterrey. Fueled by commerce with the military posts on the frontier and with northern Mexico, the Alamo City (San Antonio) grew rapidly. A local newspaper boasted that "there is not perhaps in the United States an inland town of the same size as San Antonio that is possessed of as much wealth."[88] Its location made San Antonio an ideal platform for commerce with northern Mexico. Many of the merchants who settled there had come to Texas from Europe. One was John Twohig, a sagacious Irish-American merchant known for his charm and amiability. Described as "short and thick set," he "was fond of fun and frolic as a man could be."[89] In his younger days he was a daring risk taker. In order to stock his store, he went to New Orleans in July 1840 and purchased ten thousand dollars' worth of merchandise on credit. He returned to San Antonio from the coast in a wagon train organized by Father Odin. When General Rafael Vázquez attacked San Antonio in 1842, Twohig offered safe haven to Juan N. Seguín, who some Texans considered a traitor. When Gen. Adrián Woll attacked a few months later, "[Twohig] coolly blew up his store—declaring that no man should rob him of his goods."[90] Twohig lost more than his store, he also lost his freedom, being confined for several months at the prison at Perote beginning in July 1843, before he managed to escape. Despite his suffering, he became a steadfast friend of the Mexican people.

Jean Baptiste LaCoste was another merchant who developed close links to Mexico. A native of France, LaCoste came to San Antonio in 1848 after a brief stay in New Orleans. In 1851 he opened a bar and billiard hall on Main Street that was "well furnished with a supply of choice liquors." The following year he married Manuela Menchaca, daughter of José Antonio Menchaca, one of the Mexican soldiers who had fought on the Texan side at San Jacinto. They had six children. LaCoste joined James R. Sweet as a partner in a copper mine at Santa Rita in New Mexico, which opened the way for extending their mercantile operations to Chihuahua. In 1861 while Sweet was serving as mayor of San Antonio (1859–62) for the second time, he informed LaCoste, who was in Chihuahua, that business was languishing in San Antonio (the U.S. army had pulled out due to the secession crisis) and he was considering moving to Chihuahua permanently, a move that other San Antonio merchants had already made.[91]

The other center for commerce between Texas and Northeast Mexico was Monterrey. Its merchant class, like that of Texas, was heavily laced with Europeans, especially Spaniards. Most had extensive relations with their Texan counterparts, and the operations of three merchants are sufficient to illustrate those ties. Patricio Milmo, whose birth name reportedly was Patrick Mullins, arrived in Mexico from Ireland and found a job in Monterrey as a commercial agent in 1848 or 1849. Throughout the 1850s he engaged in commerce and made a great leap up the social and economic ladder in 1857, when he married Prudenciana Vidaurri, daughter of the Nuevo León y Coahuila governor. His commercial firm, Patricio Milmo y Compañía, greatly expanded its operations during the Civil War with a branch in Matamoros and agents along the border to coordinate the trade in cotton. In time Milmo amassed a fortune and owned land in Nuevo León, Tamaulipas, Coahuila, and Texas. He established ties with most of the major merchants in Brownsville and San Antonio and, with his brother Daniel, founded the Milmo National Bank of Laredo in 1882.[92]

Another Monterrey merchant, Evaristo Madero, was not originally from that city; he was born in Coahuila and at the age of five watched his father, José Francisco Madero, die in the horrific cholera epidemic of 1833. He made his home in Rio Grande until he established his firm in Monterrey in the early 1860s. Born to wealth, Madero chose not to live a life of ease but to achieve success through his own efforts. He worked for a friend of the family, a local transporter, hauling freight to Texas until he made enough money to buy his own team. He began making trips throughout Texas as far as Nacogdoches, and though he was possessed of a pale complexion and blue eyes, he was well aware of the pervasive racism against Mexicans. He learned to dodge problems by avoiding vices and dedicating himself to his job, stating that the authorities "do not mistreat those who attend to their business and are not looking for trouble." He quickly branched out into commerce and established close ties with Texas merchants such as Friedrich Groos, William Stone, and William Schuchardt of Eagle Pass and John Twohig of San Antonio. He also had business ties with Santiago Vidaurri, whom he assisted with selling livestock in Texas.[93] Like many merchants of the period, Madero did not hesitate to deal in contraband. In 1858 the customs collector at Piedras Negras complained that Madero had exported *caudales* (probably silver) through the ford at Pacuache without paying duties. He asked the alcalde of Guerrero to inform the judge so that he could "undertake the investigations to clear up such a serious and scandalous crime."[94]

Unlike Madero, Jesús González Treviño had humble beginnings. Born in 1838 in Monterrey, he was barely nine years old when U.S. forces conquered the

Evaristo Madero, grandfather of Francisco I. Madero, leader of the Mexican Revolution, began freighting between Mexico and Texas in the 1840s and branched out into commerce. Like several other frontier merchants, he made a fortune in the Civil War trade and built a business empire based on ranching, mining, banking, and manufacturing. He became the patriarch of one of Mexico's most powerful families, a family whose presence is still felt today. Courtesy of Fototeca del Archivo Municipal de Saltillo, Saltillo, Coahuila.

city. His family left temporarily but soon returned and made the best of the occupation. Jesús took care of the horses of the American soldiers and received coins that he took to his mother, who saved them for her son. On an excursion with other schoolboys he went to the camp of Zachary Taylor, where he received a pat on the head from the future president of the United States. His elder brother, Manuel, died suddenly and his father went blind so Jesús and his brother, Lorenzo, at very tender ages, had to assume responsibility for supporting the family. Jesús served as a clerk in a commercial firm for five years in the early 1850s, then in 1857, before the age of twenty-one, he partnered with the Spanish merchant Emilio Zambrano to form a commercial firm. Jesús was a daring merchant who traveled broadly in Mexico, Texas, and Europe to buy and sell his merchandise. On more than one occasion he defended his property at gunpoint. When he married Rosa Zambrano he became part of one of Monterrey's most prominent and prosperous families. His brother, Lorenzo, became a partner of Evaristo Madero and married one of his daughters. Both brothers had extensive ties to Texas, establishing personal relationships with merchants such as Friedrich Groos, John Kelsey, and Charles Griesenbeck.[95]

The merchants of Texas and Northeast Mexico had many things in common. They were pragmatic men who largely abstained from public expressions of dogmatic positions or ethnic or racist attitudes that might affect their business. Many were Europeans, and their presence in the border region may have helped to soften the anti-Mexican racism that was pervasive in parts of Texas where Anglo-Americans formed the vast majority.[96] Many of these merchants married Mexican women and mixed easily in their new communities. Most circumvented the law or engaged in contraband when the opportunity arose, which was often. And, most importantly, in pursuing their interests with zeal, at times with ruthlessness, these merchants played a fundamental role in uniting Northeast Mexico and Texas, converting a vast region into an integrated economic zone.

Contraband, the Zona Libre, and a Conflict-Fueled Economy

The Rio Grande served as a unifying element at the center of this region. A good illustration of this unification is the trade dynamics that led to the creation of the *zona libre* in 1858. After the renewal of Mexican commercial restrictions and high tariffs, towns that depended on trade with Mexico sprang up on the left bank of the river. Brownsville, Rio Grande City, Roma, and other towns became storehouses for goods that were much more expensive in Mexico. Mexican merchants and ordinary citizens began crossing the border regularly to purchase items and smuggle them back across the river. Meanwhile, businessmen on the Texas side did more than wait for customers. They took their goods across the river in search of Mexican buyers. Francisco Landeros, the head of the customhouse at Matamoros, declared in 1854 that merchants "along the Texas side of the Rio Grande continued to gather merchandise that they intended to slip into Mexico without paying any duties, as contraband."[97]

While towns on the northern bank of the river flourished, those on the southern bank languished. At about the same time the political situation in Mexico was turning chaotic. In December 1857, General Félix Zuloaga launched a conservative movement that plunged the country into civil war and essentially cut the states loose from the center. At this juncture, on March 17, 1858, the interim governor of Tamaulipas, Ramón Guerra, decreed the establishment of a zona libre "where goods could be sold without duty or tariff." This was an extraordinary example of state sovereignty, surpassed only by Vidaurri's audacious incorporation of Coahuila two years earlier. Guerra's stated aim was to "prevent the complete depopulation of the Mexican border towns, whose residents were 'constantly emigrating to the neighboring country.'" His decree was not specific about the area encompassed by the zona, but it included the frontier towns extending from Matamoros to Monterrey-Laredo (Nuevo Laredo) and "encompassed a narrow strip of territory six to eight miles wide along Tamaulipas's northern border."[98]

The response was immediate. There was a sudden surge in population and commerce. The border towns of Matamoros, Reynosa, Camargo, and Mier had registered annual imports totaling 1.4 million pesos between 1848 and 1857. In 1858 and 1859 "imports registered 3.5 and 4.5 million pesos respectively." People began returning to the region. The population in the border towns of Tamaulipas increased from 18,000 in 1858 to 50,000 in 1862.[99] The zona libre was later ratified by the federal government and expanded as far as El Paso. It caused much friction between the United States and Mexico because Washington complained that it was unfair and provoked contraband, but the people of the border region and most of the merchants quickly adjusted to the new situation.

Curiously, a good part of the transborder commerce was stimulated by states of war on both sides of the border, against Indians or internal enemies. Historian Richard J. Salvucci has argued, "The costs of remaining on a nearly permanent war footing were severe. Peasants pressed into armed service could not plant or harvest, a major source of disruption to an agrarian economy." Moreover, "moving armies around the countryside required huge numbers of horses, mules, and oxen to drag artillery and to carry supplies." He concludes that the diversion of these resources from peaceful pursuits was detrimental to the economy.[100] Historian Mario Cerutti has a different perspective, claiming, "The myriad necessities generated by military conflicts on both sides of the river augmented commercial activity . . . and stimulated production in areas and regions suited to supply the insatiable demands of war." He analyzes the voluminous documents from the Vidaurri administration to show that, on average, 80 percent of its expenditures were war-related.[101]

Wars undoubtedly reoriented trade patterns and routes. The War of Reform (1858–60), for example, was fought largely in central Mexico, making travel there dangerous and forcing merchants and consumers to look north for supplies. Those sectors in northern Mexico that still depended on goods from Mexico City and Veracruz now had to look for products in northern markets. Jacobo Sánchez Navarro found that he could no longer reliably obtain cloth and wines from Mexico City, so he began to purchase these and other goods through Matamoros and Monterrey.[102]

The Indian Wars required a military presence, which made demands on suppliers and merchants of the region. After the colonias militares were established in Northeast Mexico, it quickly became evident that they needed certain products, such as foodstuffs and articles of clothing, that they could best obtain in Texas. Beginning in 1851, just three years after the U.S.-Mexican war, the colonias began purchasing goods from merchants in Eagle Pass. At first they paid promptly and in cash, which enabled them to begin buying goods on credit. Later, when the colonias were beset with funding shortages, they began defaulting on their payments. In June 1853, one of the principal suppliers, Dionisio Meade, wrote to General Pedro de Ampudia, governor of Nuevo León and military commander of Northeast Mexico. On behalf of his fellow merchants, Meade requested payment for goods supplied to the colonias. Meade represented that there had always been "willingness on the part of the merchants of [Eagle Pass] to satisfy the needs of the military authorities of Mexico."[103] In support of Meade's letter, Juan Manuel Maldonado, the sub-inspector of the colonias, reported that Meade "with the best good faith . . . because of the sympathy that he has for Mexico, where he has lived for many years, did not hesitate to continue selling his provisions on credit, knowing that he would be paid when the money arrived." Maldonado blamed Carvajal's revolt for disrupting prompt payments to the Eagle Pass merchants.[104]

Although Ampudia had fought the Americans on many occasions, he had no qualms about buying from them. As head of the government of Nuevo León in 1853, he utilized an agent in Brownsville, R. J. Lawlor, to purchase arms in the United States. These purchases became a routine practice because modern weapons could not be found in Mexico. In 1848 the minister of war and navy instructed the government of Coahuila to buy one thousand rifles and nine hundred carbines for use by the local militias and colonias militares. The weapons were to be distributed in Tamaulipas, Coahuila, and Nuevo León because those states had "an urgent need to arm themselves to resist the incursions of the bárbaros."[105]

The acquisition of arms in the United States was one of the principal pillars of Santiago Vidaurri's regional power in Northeast Mexico. His control of the customhouses on the Rio Grande provided him with the resources to buy weapons, pay his soldiers, and provide for their families, essential steps for recruiting a citizen-army.[106] In his rise to regional power, Vidaurri worked closely with local merchants or sometimes directly with Texas merchants to obtain arms. In 1856 he relied on Valentín Rivero, Juan Clausen, and other Monterrey merchants to purchase two thousand Mississippi rifles and five hundred carbines, as well as percussion caps and other munitions. From Thomas A. Dwyer of Laredo, he acquired arms, gunpowder, and uniforms. In compensation, Vidaurri allowed these merchants to import goods at lower rates through the customhouses under his control.[107]

During the War of Reform, the ability to acquire weapons was a crucial component of Vidaurri's success. In May 1858, near the beginning of the war, the state government had contracted with Charles Stillman and one of his associates in Brownsville for more than ten thousand firearms and various pieces of artillery. The weapons were reported to be Sharps and Minié carbines and Mississippi rifles. In August, "an enormous shipment of American-made arms" arrived in Monterrey, destined for Vidaurri's army in the interior. It required fifteen wagons and two companies of soldiers to carry these arms and munitions to the theater of war in San Luis Potosí.[108]

Vidaurri sent one of his most able lieutenants, the lawyer Ignacio Galindo, to the United States to negotiate with arms dealers and oversee the huge volume of arms flowing across the Rio Grande. In August 1859, he spent 130,000 pesos on arms to be delivered in Brownsville by Stillman and R. J. Lawlor, who received 5,000 pesos for their services. The armament, wrote Galindo to Vidaurri, "is of a superior class, I am sure you will like it very much."[109]

The importance of arms for Vidaurri's Army of the North cannot be measured only in numbers. Historian Luis Medina Peña argues that the Sharps rifle, due to its size, precision, and maneuverability, was "the state of the art for the soldier on horseback." Vidaurri's infantry used the longer Mississippi rifle, but far more numerous was his cavalry, which used the smaller Sharps. His army employed guerrilla warfare in quick lightning strikes, and the Sharps rifle—which could only be obtained in the United States—was ideally suited for that kind of warfare. It was a perfect symbiosis of tactics and weapons.[110]

Constant flows of arms moving south and silver to pay for them moving north were two of the principal items in a growing array of commodities that passed through Brownsville and Matamoros. Silver and hides were the principal Mexican exports across the frontier in the 1850s, while Mexico received a broad range of items that included clothing, machinery, firearms, tools, paper, furniture, food-stuffs, farm implements, and cotton for Mexico's growing textile industry. The volume of trade was such that Mexico's minister of the treasury, José Urquidi, complained that "the entry of American and European merchandise across the border . . . made itself felt in the markets of Mexico City."[111]

Brownsville was one of the great beneficiaries of this conflict-fueled commerce. In just a few years the town that Stillman had founded was basking in prosperity, according to two prominent people who were there. Rip Ford wrote that the late 1850s were "the palmy days of Brownsville" because the "trade of many of the northern states of Mexico came in by the way of the lower Rio Grande. The quantity of goods entering by way of Brazos de Santiago and the mouth of the Rio Grande was enormous. They represented $10,000,000 a year and sometimes $14,000,000 a year" (approximately $363.6 million in today's dollars). Ford knew personally most of the major merchants of the city and was certain "that the businessmen of Brownsville and their friends in Matamoros could raise a million dollars on short notice."[112] Gilbert Kingsbury, merchant and postmaster of Brownsville during this period, estimated the value of goods that passed through the customhouse at Brownsville at about two million dollars a month in 1860. He wrote that in proportion to its size, Brownsville had more millionaires than any other town on the continent.[113]

The War of Reform and Its Impact on the Rio Grande

Before I draw the 1850s to a close, I should mention two events that significantly affected the border region and promoted multiethnic cooperation: the War of Reform (1858–60) and the Cortina War (1859) in the lower Rio Grande Valley. The Army of the North, Vidaurri's army of citizen-soldiers, played a conspicuous role in the War of Reform. Military and political leaders in central Mexico wondered how Vidaurri could mobilize an army from the vast emptiness of the Northeast. Vidaurri once boasted that "in four to six hours he could raise . . . some 800 battle-hardened troops" from the Rio Grande district alone. Many rancheros and rural people hearkened to his call so that he was able to marshal an army of five thousand troops, most of them tempered by years of fighting Indians.[114] In a letter to Benito Juárez, Vidaurri stated that his soldiers were "landowners [who] knew their rights and who wished to put an end to the fighting so that they could go back to their work and families."[115]

Vidaurri could easily have augmented his army by accepting foreign mercenaries, but he did so only sparingly. The presence of foreign mercenaries in the War of Reform has not been fully studied.[116] Benito Juárez accepted the offer of American economic aid in order to buy arms, but he was reluctant to accept the offers of American and European mercenaries who wished to fight in his army. He eventually accepted a few, but only on his own terms. Vidaurri followed the same pattern. Colonel Samuel A. Lockridge, who had fought with the notorious filibuster William Walker, wanted the governor to open a port in northern Mexico that would serve as a platform for attacks on Cuba. To achieve that end, he offered to support Vidaurri with men and arms. The Nuevo León governor replied "that he had no need for them, and that it would not be proper to permit them to interfere in the affairs in Mexico, saying that men without a flag would inspire distrust."[117]

Vidaurri eventually hired small numbers of American and European mercenaries, mainly to operate his artillery. Edward Jordan, who had served Vidaurri in his rise to power in 1855, once again took charge of the artillery unit when the Army of the North took the field against the conservatives in 1858. Under the command of General Juan Zuazua, Jordan's thirty pieces of artillery, operated mostly by Mexican gunners, were decisive in the battle of San Luis Potosí on June 30, 1858. This victory and another at Zacatecas shortly thereafter, gave Vidaurri national stature as a military leader who could defeat the vaunted armies of the conservatives. Jordan's star was on the rise as Vidaurri personally marched south to lead his army against the brilliant conservative general Miguel Miramón. Vidaurri was no military genius, however. He replaced the injured Zuazua and put Jordan in charge of a vital component of his forces as they prepared to meet Miramón's army at Ahualulco, a few miles northwest of San Luis Potosí. On September 29, 1858, Miramón crushed Vidaurri's army, and in the recriminations that followed, Jordan was scapegoated and blamed for the defeat.[118]

Vidaurri ordered his agent in the United States, Ignacio Galindo, to locate J. K. Duncan, an American artilleryman who had offered his services to Vidaurri three years earlier, but had been rejected. Duncan was still somewhat resentful, but agreed to serve when he was asked to bring with him enough officers and engineers of his choosing for three or four batteries. Duncan was also enthusiastic about sharing his knowledge of artillery with young Mexican soldiers. Galindo told Vidaurri that in the United States "there was ample willingness to help us," but "it had not been exploited because of apathy and ineptitude."[119] For the remainder of the war, Vidaurri's army counted on an effective artillery unit "made up of Mexicans, except the officers, who were Americans." The number of Americans and Europeans who served in Vidaurri's army and with the liberals is not known, but it was small. However, in the words of historian Lawrence Taylor, "it was indicative of a trend that would be much more pronounced . . . during the last years of the French intervention."[120]

CORTINA ERUPTS ON THE SCENE

The Cortina War was not really a war; it was the brief occupation of Brownsville by a band led by Juan Nepomuceno Cortina, known as Cheno to his supporters, and a series of skirmishes that followed in late 1859 between Cheno and the forces that mobilized against him. These included Anglo and Mexican citizens of Brownsville, the Texas Rangers, the U.S. army, and Mexican military forces from Matamoros. The contours of this brief conflict are well known. Throughout the 1850s, Cortina developed a hatred of Americans as he observed the way corrupt lawyers, judges, and politicians in South Texas took possession of Mexican properties, including those of his own family. When he witnessed Marshal Robert Shears beating a former servant of his in the streets of Brownsville, Cortina snapped and shot the law officer. He returned to the city on the morning of September 28, 1859, looking for revenge. His men, about seventy in number, terrorized the populace, shouting "viva México!" and "Mueran los Gringos!" When the rampage ended, five people lay dead.[121]

Cortina made it clear that his fight was not with other Mexicans. At Alexander Werbiski's store, where Cheno stole arms and ammunition, he told Werbiski's sobbing Mexican wife not to be afraid because it was "no night for Mexican tears." His war was with corrupt Anglos such as Adolphus Glaevecke, who robbed Mexicans of their property. He thundered, "Our personal enemies shall not possess our lands until they have fattened it with their own gore."[122]

The uprising provoked a firestorm in the Texas press as fears of a race war swept the state. The *San Antonio Ledger and Texan* published a letter from "F. F. Fenn" of Brownsville, a pseudonym used by merchant and postmaster Gilbert

Juan Nepomuceno Cortina was one of the most polarizing figures in Rio Grande border history. Anglos accused him of being the main perpetrator of cattle rustling in South Texas. His fight against land-grabbing lawyers and politicians made him a symbol of Mexican resistance to Anglo oppression in the nineteenth century. From *Frank Leslie's Illustrated Newspaper,* April 9, 1864. LC-USZ62-119579, Library of Congress.

Kingsbury. Kingsbury wildly exaggerated Cortina's force at between 500 and 1,200 men, declared that the rebel leader had "the sympathy of the whole Mexican race with very rare exceptions," and claimed the situation was becoming "a war of races."[123] Rangers were dispatched, but were insufficient to quell the revolt so U.S. troops under the command of Major Samuel P. Heintzelman arrived on the scene, and by December, Cortina and his forces had been vanquished. By the time the conflict was over, the region between Brownsville and Rio Grande City had suffered great destruction as most of the ranches, Anglo and Mexican, had been razed. According to historian Jerry Thompson, "151 of Cortina's men were killed and perhaps twice that many wounded. Fifteen Americans and eighty Mexicans not affiliated with Cortina also lay dead." Heintzelman stated that it would "be a long time before the ill-feeling engendered by this outcome [would] be allayed."[124]

The Cortina revolt has generated a lot of attention among historians and the general public (though curiously not in Mexico). This coverage is justified because the war is a prominent example of conflict between Anglos and Mexicans and the way in which the latter defended their property and dignity, which were increasingly under attack in nineteenth-century Texas. There is however another story within the story that few historians emphasize and of which the general public is largely unaware: Some Mexicans were opposed to Cortina's uprising and a number of them collaborated with Anglos in combating him. Immediately after Cortina's raid on Brownsville, a group of men formed The Committee of Public Safety to defend the city. The so-called Brownsville Tigers were led by Mifflin Kenedy, who was named commander of part of the group, composed of Anglos. The other part, made up of Mexicans, was led by Francisco Yturria, a sometime partner of Charles Stillman and one of the most important merchants of Brownsville and Matamoros. Members of the upper class, including Cortina's half brother, Sabas Cavazos, sided with the Anglo establishment against the rebel leader.[125]

The majority of the Mexican population however sided or sympathized with Cortina, believing that his struggle was also theirs. Identifying with his statement that "the plunder of Mexican land and property was the fundamental cause of the revolt," they were persuaded by his argument that a "conspiracy of lawyers and local authorities" was involved in "confiscating Mexican possessions." Notwithstanding this substantial Mexican support, some sixty Mexican rancheros of the region, led by Antonio Portillo, joined the fight against him.[126]

The Anglo population of Brownsville not only counted on the support of a small part of the local Mexican population, it also received men and arms from Mexicans on the other side of the border. On September 28, 1859, the very day of the raid, Sheriff J. W. Brown sent an urgent message to Joaquín Arguelles, commander of the military garrison at Matamoros. The message stated briefly: "I appeal to you as a friendly authority to send a force to this side as we are without troops." Arguelles responded the same day that the troops and good citizens of Matamoros "are ready and willing to aid the inhabitants of Brownsville and, if necessary, will cross the river when you or other competent authorities consider it convenient." Arguelles promptly informed his superiors, and a few days later reported that he had sent a hundred men and a quantity of arms for the defense of Brownsville.[127]

Aside from these official requests for aid, the Committee of Public Safety appealed to General José María Carvajal, who had influence over the authorities in Matamoros. Carvajal used that leverage to persuade the National Guard of Tamaulipas to send fifty troops to help defend Brownsville. Jerry Thompson writes that Brownsville citizens "watched in awe as Mexican soldiers crossed the Rio Grande to protect United States citizens from an irregular army of Mexicans led by a man [Cortina] who considered himself a United States citizen."[128] One Brownsville resident expressed the sentiment of many: "We feel somewhat humiliated at the necessity of calling on the Mexican authorities for protection."[129]

Three weeks after the initial emergency, Mayor Stephen Powers of Brownsville again appealed to Matamoros for aid in the hunt for Cortina. A force from the National Guard of Tamaulipas with a twenty-four-pound cannon crossed the river. This force, about seventy-five in number, joined the Brownsville Tigers, and they set out after the rebel leader. They found him at Rancho del Carmen but he defeated them. This all transpired before Major Heintzelman and his troops arrived and defeated Cortina in a bloody battle near Rio Grande City on December 27, 1859. In January 1860, Heintzelman met with General Guadalupe García, commander of the Mexican military on the Río Bravo, who offered his cooperation in eliminating Cortina from the border region. García and other Mexican leaders were probably sympathetic to Cheno, but "they were apprehensive that [he] would provoke an invasion of their country."[130]

As in the Carvajal revolt and the Federalist War preceding it, the Cortina uprising displayed the strategic alliances between members of different races and nationalities. These alliances were becoming a hallmark of the border region and would play a significant role in the tumultuous 1860s, when civil wars inflamed both sides of the Rio Grande.

~

In the 1850s, religion flourished on the Rio Grande frontier as missionaries, both Protestant and Catholic, competed for souls in a previously neglected area. Protestant missionaries courageously ventured into a Catholic world, using education as a means to draw closer to the Mexican population. Melinda Rankin and others worked arduously to convert Mexicans to Protestantism. In response, the Catholic infrastructure expanded quickly to meet the needs of a growing population of Mexicans and European Catholic immigrants in Texas. Many prelates were of European origin, particularly French. Priests led a Catholic surge in South Texas, and reached out to the Mexican Catholic Church, working closely with their counterparts below the Rio Grande to provide services and sacraments to a population long ignored. Oblate priests traveled deep into the chaparral of the

Nueces Strip in search of souls to save. When priests were expelled from Mexico they found support in Texas among their fellow Catholic clerics.

Economic expansion throughout the 1850s in areas such as mining, stock raising, and commerce enhanced cooperation between people on both sides of the Rio Grande, and these connections helped to integrate the region more firmly. American businessmen invested in mines in Northeast Mexico that for lack of capital had been largely left undeveloped since the departure of the Spaniards during Independence. However, wars and political instability in Mexico, as well as the U.S. Civil War limited investments until the 1870s. Livestock, one of the principal resources of the region, was moved, both legally and illegally, across the international boundary. Anglo and Mexican sellers and buyers established a pattern of trade in which cattle were usually moved south while mules and horses were driven north.

Commerce and contraband continued to dominate the regional economy. Texas merchants, many of European origin, reached out to Mexico to expand their businesses. Merchants in Northeast Mexico, operating mainly out of Monterrey, also reached out to Texas. Commercial linkages and smuggling networks involving Anglos, Europeans, and Mexicans grew quickly and endured firmly, even in the face of cultural differences, ethnic mistrust, and racial hatred. This is one of the constants of border history. The contraband trade attracted many Mexican merchants and consumers to the towns on the Texas side of the border. These towns flourished while those on the Mexican side stagnated. This slide was halted when, without legal authority, the government of Tamaulipas created an economic free zone, a local initiative that the national government initially opposed but later accepted.

The supply needs of military forces on both sides of the border generated a market for regional producers and middlemen. Wars in Mexico also generated a demand for arms that could be best obtained from the United States, with Texas merchants serving at times as intermediaries. Episodes of cooperative violence were again in evidence in the War of Reform and the uprising of Cortina.

As the 1850s came to an end, a decade had transpired since the establishment of the border on the Rio Grande. The residents of the region had no role in its establishment, but as the preceding two chapters have shown, they moved quickly to leverage it in pursuit of their interests. On the Texas side, African American slaves saw opportunities to escape to freedom in Mexico and enterprising merchants founded cities to profit from the Mexican trade. On the southern side, diverse groups availed themselves of the new jurisdictional structure to promote their objectives in ways oftentimes inimical to Mexico's interests. Smugglers intensified their unlawful activities; Kickapoo and Lipan raiders adapted rapidly to an area of opportunity by carrying out raids in Texas; regional officials took matters into their own hands and decreed a zona libre to protect local merchants and consumers; sirvientes fled their life of drudgery on the haciendas in search of a better life for their families north of the river. An unintended consequence of the border was a world of opportunities for a growing population of inhabitants. The border became a major protagonist in the events of the period, and its importance would only intensify in the following decades.

CHAPTER 5

The U.S. Civil War and Its Impact on the Rio Grande

1861–1867

I n early November 1863, about six thousand Union troops commanded by General Nathaniel P. Banks landed at Port Isabel, intensifying the Civil War in the lower Rio Grande Valley. The federal troops moved swiftly toward Brownsville, and on their approach they could see smoke billowing toward the sky. General Hamilton P. Bee, the commander of Confederate forces in the region, had set fire to Fort Brown along with hundreds of bales of cotton that could not be carried off. At the head of "a train worth $1,000,000, which [he had] brought away from the smoking ruins of Fort Brown," Bee marched into the interior of Texas toward the King Ranch, where he hoped to regroup and reestablish the movement of cotton, vital to the Confederacy, toward the neutral port of Matamoros for shipment overseas. With Brownsville cut off, the Confederacy would have to depend on alternate routes to reach Matamoros. Bee wrote to José Agustín Quintero, the Confederate agent at Monterrey, that the cotton traffic would have to be rerouted through Laredo and Eagle Pass toward Monterrey and then Matamoros. He stated his case simply: "It is, therefore, on General Vidaurri that I rely in this emergency. If he will protect the trade to Eagle Pass through his territory, the trade will be as beneficial to his people as essential to ours."[1]

Bee's letter underscores the importance of collaboration between Texas and Northeast Mexico during the 1860s, when civil wars broke out in both the United States and Mexico. Regional and transborder cooperation that had developed over four decades multiplied during that period as merchants, producers, freight-

Hamilton P. Bee had a distinguished public career. He participated in the U.S.-Mexican War and represented Webb County in the Texas legislature. As commander of Confederate forces on the lower Rio Grande during the Civil War, his gift for diplomacy was essential in maintaining the flow of commerce across the Rio Grande. After the war, Bee and his family lived in Coahuila for a little more than a decade and he maintained a constant connection to Mexico throughout his life. No. 85-701, UTSA Special Collections.

ers, and inhabitants of Northeast Mexico and South Texas reoriented their lives and occupations to meet the demands created by wars—not of their making—on both sides of the border. The Confederacy needed to export its cotton and import war matériel, but the Union blockade of its ports forced it to depend on the neutral port of Matamoros for trade with Europe and northern Mexico to supply a vast array of articles needed to fight the enemy. This is a well-studied history and my aim is not to repeat it but to focus on the people of different races and nationalities who came together on the field of battle and in the realm of trade. Wars and commerce also generated an immense transborder labor market, particularly in the transportation of cargo, that further integrated the region.[2]

CIVIL WAR AND THE EXPLOSION OF COMMERCE

At a state convention on February 1, 1861, Texas delegates voted to secede from the Union, and shortly thereafter they joined the Confederate States of America. As a belligerent state, Texas suffered the blockade of its ports and it became imperative to find a way to export its vast wealth in cotton and import an immense array of materials needed for survival and to wage war. Confederate authorities and enterprising merchants quickly discovered that Matamoros, as a Mexican—and thus neutral—port, was not subject to the blockade. This situation was made manifest early in 1862 when the *Portsmouth* and two other Union vessels arrived at Brazos de Santiago "creating a 'panic in the market' and paralyzing the cotton trade." When they seized a British ship carrying cargo for José San Román, two warships, one British and the other French, appeared. The British vessel, the fifty-six-gun *Phaeton*, was there "to keep the mouth of the Rio Grande open to the trade of the world." This "European gunboat diplomacy," writes David Montejano, "effectively ended the Union attempt to extend the blockade to the Rio Grande. The Lincoln administration did not desire to engage in hostilities with the English or the French."[3]

Merchants such as Charles Stillman, Richard King, Mifflin Kenedy, and José San Román moved part of their operations from Brownsville across the river to Matamoros and continued to trade, but now on a much larger scale. The mouth of the Rio Grande became a huge two-way funnel that received and shipped cotton from Texas, Louisiana, and Arkansas, as well as all kinds of merchandise from northern Mexico and as far away as New England and Europe. Merchants who had operated in the border region for years and who had business contacts in and knowledge of the region were ideally positioned to handle the vast volume of trade generated by the Civil War.

Confederate authorities recognized the strategic importance of Brownsville-Matamoros. From Brownsville, Major Charles Russell, the quartermaster in charge of obtaining supplies, wrote to one of his superiors: "negotiations can be made in this city and Matamoras [sic], with reliable and responsible mercantile houses, by which every article required in each one of the departments (quartermaster's, subsistence, ordnance, and medical), can be obtained on reasonable terms, in quantities sufficient to supply the entire Trans-Mississippi Department."[4] A key component of the Rio Grande shipping infrastructure was the fleet of steamboats of M. Kenedy and Co. that plied the river from its mouth to Brownsville-Matamoros and as far as Roma. This company, formed in 1850, was operated by Mifflin Kenedy, Richard King, and Charles Stillman. When the war began, the partners began to haul Confederate cotton and put their fleet of steamships under Mexican registry so that they could not be detained by Union vessels. Rip Ford wrote that the company's ships played an important role in the cotton trade "and the boats reaped an unusually rich financial harvest."[5]

Kenedy, King, and Stillman also became suppliers for the Confederate government. General John Bankhead Magruder, commander of the District of Texas, informed the Confederate officials at Richmond, Virginia, that he had decided to purchase supplies through the house of King, Kenedy, and Stillman of Brownsville because they were reliable and offered lower rates than the houses in Matamoros.[6] The success of these and other Brownsville merchants was due to their proximity to Matamoros and their propensity to use that port with the same ease and security that they felt on American soil.

This extraterritorial prerogative was a source of frustration to Union officials. Joseph P. Couthouy, one of the Union naval officers in charge of enforcing the blockade, spoke from experience in May 1863, when he explained to Secretary of the Navy Gideon Welles "that nine-tenths of the cargoes" consigned to Matamoros within the past year "were, in fact, destined to supply the rebels in Texas, and were securely stored in the warehouses of Brownsville within twenty-four hours after their simulated sale on the Mexican side of the river." Couthouy had worked in the Brownsville branch of the Commercial and Agricultural Bank of Texas and was "well acquainted . . . with all the leading merchants and traders on both sides of the Rio Grande." It was clear, he pointed out, that "Matamoras is but the Mexican synonym of Brownsville so far as this trade is concerned. The merchants and the warehouses of the one city are those of the other also."[7]

Stillman ranged far beyond the Rio Grande in his operations, buying and renting vessels, placing them under foreign flags, and using other business associates, especially ones with Spanish surnames, to camouflage his transactions. Thus Jeremiah Galvan, José Morrell, and Francisco Yturria became willing partners in Stillman's machinations.[8] Couthouy informed his superiors that the *Alice Tainter* had sailed from New York to Matamoros with a cargo valued at about $80,000, "consisting of 700 bags coffee, 1,700 barrels flour, 400 boxes crushed sugar, 400 barrels ship bread, a large quantity of assorted provisions, and several thousand gunny bags." On board was a passenger bound for Matamoros, by the name of Jerry Galvan of Brownsville, who claimed to be part owner. On the *Mystic Valley*, another vessel boarded by the blockaders, a letter was found addressed to Charles Stillman from one of his agents in New York. The letter implicated

the Brownsville founder in a cargo on another ship, the *Kibby*, also bound for
Matamoros. Stillman's cover-ups did not fool Couthouy, who referred to him as
a "notorious partisan of the rebels," whose activities were "illegal, dishonorable,
and traitorous to the last degree."[9]

José San Román participated in the cotton trade on an even larger scale than
Stillman did. With agents, suppliers, and buyers in Cuba, New Orleans, New
England, and many parts of Mexico and Europe, he was in a unique position
to take advantage of the cotton boom. Like Stillman, San Román had moved
part of his business to Matamoros and had all his cargoes consigned to that
port to fool the Union blockade squadron. They were not fooled, though they
were powerless to stop the shipments. Joseph P. Couthouy, Stillman's nemesis,
captured the vessel *Teresita* on its way to Matamoros from Havana. The cargo
consisted of machinery used on steamboats, including two boilers. Also aboard
were forty-seven boxes of the finest quality steel, "well suited for the manufacture
of swords and bayonets." Although the ship was under a neutral flag and was
bound for Matamoros, Couthouy smelled a rat. He knew that San Román had a
store in Brownsville, and on board the *Teresita* he found a copy of the *Brownsville
Flag* featuring an ad in Spanish promoting the store in Brownsville. According
to Couthouy, this evidence made it clear that the Spaniard was "a merchant of
that place, and renders it almost equally certain that the cargo of the *Teresita*
was really destined to the use of those waging war against the Government of
the United States."[10]

Couthouy and his Union sailors were outmatched in this cat-and-mouse game
with the wily Spaniard. It is highly probable that no other merchant in America during the Civil War period handled a greater volume of cotton and silver
shipments overseas than San Román did. In October 1864 alone, his company
shipped 4,435 bales of cotton from Matamoros. In August 1862, his firm recorded
shipments of silver valued at 106,365 pesos.[11]

San Román's voluminous correspondence reveals the numerous merchants
who collaborated with him in the expanding commerce. Some were new to the
border region, others were old hands who had arrived years earlier. Joseph Kleiber
worked for himself as well as in collaboration with San Román. In February 1863,
he sent the Spaniard more than eighteen thousand pounds of rope needed in
Texas to tie cotton bales. Kleiber's brother Emile worked between Camargo and
Piedras Negras, receiving cotton and shipping it to San Román in exchange for
medicines and other goods destined for the interior of Texas. One shipment
involved two hundred bales of cotton. Another merchant who collaborated

with San Román was John P. Kelsey, who had been in the border region since 1840, when he was a supplier in the Federalist War. Kelsey used his base in Rio Grande City and Camargo to receive and ship cotton to San Román's storage facility in Matamoros. For example, in the three-day period of October 10–12, 1864, Kelsey sent San Román eighty-seven bales of cotton.[12]

Many merchants who had no alliance with the Confederacy got involved in the cotton trade when they saw its great potential for profit. The merchant Colonel Charles Power traveled from Texas to Monterrey to see Governor Vidaurri with a view to selling cotton. Power, described as an "English gentleman" with "a large wealth" went armed with a letter of recommendation from a surprising source: Sam Houston. The old warrior had been forced out of the governorship when he opposed secession, but he had stayed in Texas and led a quiet life. Power happened to be his brother-in-law. Houston had known Vidaurri years before and addressed him as an "admired friend." Despite the passage of time, he wrote, "my memory has often recurred to you with best wishes for your fame and happiness. Though we are distant from each other, I offer my heart to embrace you." Power was accompanied by his nephew, Houston's son. Houston recognized that he "could place these gentlemen under no other auspices so favorable to them in Mexico" as that of the Nuevo León governor. This anecdote illustrates how transborder networks forged years earlier were a vital component of doing business, not only for established merchants such as Stillman and San Román, but also for newcomers to the border region such as Power.[13]

The intense commercial activity in Brownsville and Matamoros contributed to a reduction in political, racial, and ethnic strife in the area. Rip Ford witnessed the change. He recognized that many Union and Confederate merchants were in Matamoros, but politics was subordinated to trade. "Goods were sold to anyone having money or cotton. There was little thought of politics in the trading circles."[14] The war, according to one study, "served to overshadow local disputes and differences between Mexicans, Europeans, and Americans living there. The cotton boom attracted a flood of strangers who paid little attention to local prejudices or feuds. Their main concern was making money."[15] While the war generated hatred and violence in most of the United States, on the lower Rio Grande it also had the paradoxical effect of promoting coexistence and cooperation among those whose only ideological devotion was to get rich.

The economic boom also transformed Matamoros and for a brief period converted it into one of the busiest ports in the Americas. The town played a crucial role in supplying the Trans-Mississippi Department of the Confederacy, which encompassed Texas, Louisiana, Arkansas, Missouri, and the Indian Territory (Oklahoma). Since Matamoros is about thirty-five miles from the mouth of the Rio Grande, a provisional town, Bagdad, was erected overnight on the Mexican side to receive and send on cargo that moved through Matamoros. It rapidly became an international community with representatives of many countries and a multitude of foreign languages spoken on its dusty streets. In March 1863, it was reported that between 180 and 200 ships were anchored off Bagdad waiting to receive or deliver cargo.[16] At about that time a Union correspondent estimated that the Confederates were receiving four million dollars' worth of supplies each month through Matamoros.[17]

The town's importance was stated eloquently by S. S. Brown, a Union refugee who had fled to Monterrey. In an often-quoted statement, he wrote to General Lew Wallace: "Matamoras is to the rebellion west of the Mississippi what New York is to the United States—its great commercial and financial center, feeding and clothing the rebellion, arming and equipping, furnishing it materials of war and a specie basis of circulation in Texas that has almost entirely displaced Confederate paper." Brown was convinced the impact of Matamoros was felt beyond the Trans-Mississippi Department and that the "entire Confederate Government is greatly sustained by resources from this post."[18] Although the extent of the commerce cannot be quantified, estimates are that during the war, between 250,000 and 300,000 bales of cotton passed through Matamoros.[19]

One of the critical items obtained in exchange for cotton was lead, which was crucial for making ammunition. The U.S. vice-consul in Monterrey commented to Secretary of State William Seward "that it would be better to stop the trade of Matamoros than to have an army of ten thousand men, since the only lead the rebels west of the Mississippi received came from Mexico."[20] In fact, most of the lead being shipped to Texas was produced in Northeast Mexico and probably did not go through Matamoros at all, but rather through the other ports that Vidaurri had opened up on the Rio Grande. Northeast Mexico became a great supplier not only of lead, but of numerous other products required by Texas and the Confederacy. A good idea of its importance can be derived from the actions of two men who carried on a war of their own, which mirrored the larger war. One sympathized with the Union, the other with the Confederacy, and both made Monterrey their home throughout most of the war. The Union representative was U.S. Vice-Consul Myndert Mynderse Kimmey, who wisely used only his initials. He dedicated his energies to stopping the voluminous trade that helped to sustain the Confederacy. In support of that trade was José

Agustín Quintero, whom the Confederate Government sent as a confidential agent to the government of Santiago Vidaurri.

A War within a War: Kimmey Versus Quintero

José Agustín Quintero, a brilliant and energetic Cuban American, became the Confederate agent to Vidaurri's government when the war broke out. Born in Havana in 1829, he was the son of a tobacco planter and an English lady. At age twelve, it is said that he was sent to Harvard, and while he was there his father died and he stopped receiving funds. Though only a boy, José Agustín went to work giving Spanish lessons. He returned to Havana around 1848 and became a journalist and an activist for Cuban independence. After several arrests and one death sentence, he escaped to New Orleans and finally settled in Texas, where he edited the Spanish-language newspaper *El Ranchero* in San Antonio. He acquired further journalistic experience in New Orleans and New York, then returned to Texas where he worked as a translator for the General Land Office. Quintero became a fervent disciple of secession, enlisted in the Quitman Guards, and traveled to Virginia with his unit. At Richmond he met Jefferson Davis, who quickly recognized his value and approved his appointment to serve in Monterrey as a confidential agent of the Confederacy.[21]

Quintero was ideally suited to represent the South. In addition to all his other qualifications, he knew Vidaurri personally, having met him in Texas in 1859. In June 1860, he congratulated Vidaurri on his appointment to a new term as governor of Nuevo León y Coahuila. A few months later Quintero wrote to inform him of his impending move to New York to edit a Spanish-language newspaper with a broad circulation in Hispanic America.[22] In the summer of 1861, Quintero presented himself to Vidaurri with letters from Robert Toombs, secretary of state of the Confederacy, and Edward Clark, governor of Texas. Both leaders professed their friendship and willingness to work with Vidaurri to promote harmonious relations.[23]

Quintero's objectives were to obtain as much information as possible on all issues affecting the Confederacy and to explore "the possibility of purchasing small arms, powder, lead, sulphur, saltpeter, and all other articles necessary for the Army of the Confederate States."[24] The Confederate agent sought to win over Vidaurri through various means. He wrote a laudatory biographical article on the Nuevo León governor in a Brownsville newspaper and sent him a copy. He also sent Vidaurri a chess set to use on long, tedious stagecoach rides. The special agent explained to Vidaurri that this set was designed for bumpy roads:

by "pressing the buttons on the sides of the case, you can move the pieces." Quintero also kept Vidaurri informed of Southern advances in the war against the North, a way of assuring the latter that he was betting on the right horse. "The news from inside the Confederacy," wrote Quintero, "was very promising. We have won the great battle for Richmond. . . . From all quarters we receive news of great joy. The enemy will have . . . to recognize our independence."[25]

The Cuban American skillfully played on Vidaurri's desire to modernize his province by promoting the idea of a transcontinental railroad that would bring prosperity to Northeast Mexico and, by extension, bind the region more tightly to the Confederacy. After a series of talks with the Nuevo León governor, Quintero reported to Richmond that Vidaurri was interested in joining Nuevo León y Coahuila to the Confederacy. Though this claim seems far-fetched, Quintero wrote that Vidaurri's interest in annexation was genuine and that many people believed it to be true because it was rumored all over Texas and northern Mexico. It should be stressed that this was written by Quintero, who should have known better. As editor of the San Antonio newspaper *El Ranchero* in 1856, he had rejected rumors that Mexicans of the frontier desired separation because they "place even before their very existence, their quality as Mexicans."[26] Vidaurri may have mentioned annexation to Quintero, but he was too astute to put anything like that in writing. More likely, Vidaurri was hedging his bets in case his regional power was threatened by his enemies in Mexico. In any case, the government of Jefferson Davis rejected any idea of annexation, but insisted on close ties to the caudillo.[27]

Quintero did everything in his power to establish conditions for the secure passage of cotton to Matamoros so that it could be shipped to foreign ports and all the items necessary to sustain the Confederacy could be obtained in northern Mexico. He worked with zeal and great energy in cooperation with Vidaurri and the merchants of Monterrey. In August 1862 he wrote, "Everything with the exception of small arms can be obtained here." Though arms were not available, materials to make ammunition, such as lead, were abundant.[28] General Hamilton P. Bee expressed what the trade with northern Mexico meant to the South: "With the glittering attraction of our cotton the whole available resources of Mexico are being brought to us. Shoes, blankets, cloth, powder, lead, saltpeter, sulphur, etc., are now coming in quantity which will soon supply our wants." Bee's "etc." included foodstuffs such as flour, coffee, rice, and salt, as well as leather goods and other products.[29]

Among the merchants of Monterrey who supplied the Confederacy was the firm of Lorenzo Oliver and Brothers, a company with "contacts all over northern

Mexico and considerable experience in Texas and New Orleans."[30] Quintero was instructed to obtain from that firm "200,000 pounds of cannon powder . . . to be delivered as soon as possible" and to "procure such further quantities of powder, lead, etc. . . . for their delivery in Texas." The special agent reported that he had also signed a contract with Oliver Brothers that guaranteed delivery of 90,000 pounds of lead per month from mines that had recently been discovered near Monterrey. So anxious was Oliver Brothers to become the main supplier of the Confederacy that José Oliver traveled to Richmond to deal directly with the government and offer a wide range of articles, including blankets, shoes, sulfur, and salt. By August 1862, the firm was running sixty wagons between Monterrey and San Antonio.[31]

One of the most prolific suppliers of the Confederacy was Patricio Milmo, Vidaurri's son-in-law. Milmo established a branch office in Matamoros, and associated with Thomas Gilgan of Brownsville, J. B. LaCoste of San Antonio, and Evaristo Madero of Coahuila to supply the Confederacy with a wide range of products from Europe and northern Mexico in exchange for cotton. One of the men he hired to haul cotton from Harrisburg to Eagle Pass was Roy Bean, the future "law west of the Pecos." When the *William Peel*, a steamer laden with cotton and consigned to Milmo, was detained by Union authorities, Milmo, a naturalized Mexican, declared himself a British subject and appealed to that government for redress. Some of Milmo's biggest contracts involved the sale of flour, which reportedly "was impossible to procure from the wheat-growing districts of Texas." He and one of his agents, A. Urbahan of San Antonio, agreed to deliver a million pounds of flour to Simeon Hart, the quartermaster at San Antonio, in exchange for 850,000 pounds of cotton. Milmo later claimed that he had sold to Confederate officials almost 500,000 pounds of flour for which he had not been paid.[32]

Evaristo Madero, who worked in association with both Milmo and Vidaurri, also supplied the Confederacy. He received cotton in return for flour from his haciendas. In partnership with Vidaurri, Madero also supplied the Confederacy with mules and horses from Vidaurri's hacienda at Catujanes. In mid-November he informed the Nuevo León governor that he required eighty to one hundred mules within fifteen days because he had obtained a price of 125 pesos for each animal, payable in cotton. Madero used part of the cotton to have Confederate Army uniforms made at La Estrella textile mill in Parras, Coahuila, which he would later purchase.[33]

Quintero kept a close watch on events in Brownsville-Matamoros, and spent part of his time in those ports resolving problems and ensuring the flow of trade.

He was in Matamoros when the *William Peel*, the ship consigned to Milmo, was detained by a Union steamer near the mouth of the Rio Grande. Quintero appealed directly to Governor Manuel Ruiz of Tamaulipas, who appealed to "the commander of the United States vessel. After a delay of forty-eight hours, the *William Peel* was released. Her cargo was safely landed."[34] On another occasion, Quintero had to soothe the ruffled feathers of Confederate Secretary of State Judah P. Benjamin, who had replaced Robert Toombs. Benjamin complained that Vidaurri was charging onerous taxes that were hostile to the Confederacy. Quintero asked Vidaurri for a reduction, arguing that the benefit "would be mutual, because by increasing the exportation of this article the income of the custom houses would necessarily rise."[35]

Vidaurri acceded to this and other requests by Quintero, whose stock in Texas soared. The Austin *Texas State Gazette* credited the special agent with lowering tariffs on "Mexican products exported to [Texas] from Matamoros." It declared that the friendliness of Mexican officials on the frontier was largely due to Quintero, "who is personally one of the most popular men with Governor Vidaurri and all his cabinet, and who is at the same time a most accomplished diplomatist. The people on this frontier owe Mr. Quintero a heavy debt of gratitude, for he has smoothed many complications."[36] An indicator of Quintero's presence and influence in Monterrey is a bust of Jefferson Davis that was sculpted in the city by Matteo Mattei. Most Monterrey residents knew little of U.S. politicians and probably could not tell the difference between Abraham Lincoln and Jefferson Davis. So they did not commission the bust. It was surely the product of Quintero's unflagging work in popularizing the rebellion and its leader in Mexico.[37]

While Quintero was diligently serving the Confederacy, M. M. Kimmey was performing a similar, if less visible, mission for the Union. A native of New York and loyal Union man, Kimmey was working in a commercial firm in San Antonio when the secessionist wave drove him out of the city. Along with many other Union sympathizers, he decided to move to Monterrey for the duration of the war. Kimmey assumed the post of vice-consul in June 1862, about one year after Quintero had arrived in Monterrey. In October, Kimmey described the extent of Northeast Mexico's involvement in the commerce with Texas: "Large trains are daily leaving for the different points on the Rio Grande though most of them go to Eagle Pass loaded with blankets, shoes, leather, cloth, cotton goods of all kinds, coffee, rice, sugar, powder, salt peter, sulphur, medicine and in fact almost everything needed to supply the armies of the Rebels."[38]

Kimmey informed Secretary of State William H. Seward that the trade had been growing steadily since the beginning of the war, but had reached great proportions during the preceding three or four months. Confederate agents were "scattered through the country contracting for all the flour and corn that can be had." They were even purchasing wheat in advance. He concluded that in exchange for cotton, "goods suitable for the Army are sent back, and from the great amounts it would seem that enough goods go from and through [Monterrey] to supply the whole Rebel Army." What most distressed Kimmey was the Union's inaction: "An order came here a few days ago for six hundred thousand blankets suitable for soldiers. They will be sent in a short time if no force is sent on the line of the Rio Grande River to stop them." The Union, however, would not act until a year later when it landed troops on Brazos Santiago in preparation to occupy Brownsville and the lower Rio Grande Valley.[39]

The frenzy among merchants to supply Texas with breadstuff from northern Mexico at a time when a severe drought was assailing the region led Vidaurri to decree on November 2, 1862, that exports "of corn, wheat, flour and beans" were prohibited.[40] The effect was immediately felt in Texas. A Confederate official wrote of the scarcity and high cost of food in San Antonio because "mostly all subsistence for Texas troops has been drawn last year from Mexico . . . to such an extent has New Leon and Coahuila been drained, that Governor Vidaurri has prohibited, under severe penalties, the exportation of any more breadstuffs, etc., from those states."[41] Quintero, aware of the worsening situation in Texas, appealed to Vidaurri to continue the exportation of grains to that state. What followed is not entirely clear. Vidaurri modified either the decree or its implementation, because he responded to Quintero that the decree was applicable to the Mexican states, but not to the Confederacy. Historian Gerardo Gurza Lavalle affirms that Vidaurri and Madero were partners in the sale of flour to Texas, so it was in his interest to resume the shipments.[42]

Madero carried out his operations mainly through Piedras Negras and Eagle Pass, which, even before the Union occupation of Brownsville, was handling a large volume of trade. Kimmey captured this reality in an October 1863 letter to General J. R. West, the commander of the Arizona District for the Union Army: "Large quantities of cotton are now crossing at Eagle Pass; in fact, more than at any time since the war began. The increase is on account of the danger in crossing at Brownsville and other points."[43] Two months later, on Christmas Day, Kimmey reported data on the volume of cotton that had passed through that port. Throughout 1861 the number of bales—each weighing about 460 pounds—averaged about five hundred per month. Shipments accelerated rapidly, and from April 1862 to November 1863, the total number of bales was 57,467. An even greater amount would pass after the Union invasion.[44]

The Union occupation of the lower Rio Grande Valley in November 1863 set off a complex chain of events: it forced Bee to move his military operations to the interior of Texas; it compelled most of the prominent Brownsville merchants to relocate with their families to Matamoros; and it shifted the movement of cotton to a greater degree toward interior routes, especially Laredo–Nuevo Laredo and Eagle Pass–Piedras Negras, which made the Confederate government even more dependent on Vidaurri's good graces. The reliance was mutual because at this time the regional caudillo was intensifying his dispute with Benito Juárez, which made him more dependent on the Confederacy. The Union presence also intensified the clash between Kimmey and Quintero, for reasons that will become apparent later.

Prior to the Union invasion of the lower Rio Grande Valley, much of the cotton was shipped from Alleyton through the King Ranch on its way to the border at Brownsville. Alleyton, on the Colorado River west of Houston, was connected by rail to East Texas (and to other parts of the Confederacy) so many producers sent their cotton there. From that railroad terminus the cotton was hauled on carts and wagons across the parched sandy plains of South Texas to the border. With the Yankees now in Brownsville, the lower end of the route had to be modified in order to send the cotton farther upriver to Mier, Camargo, Laredo, and Piedras Negras, ports under Vidaurri's control. There was however a danger that Union troops would move up the Rio Grande and occupy those ports, so Piedras Negras, which was farthest away, became the preferred destination. A newspaperman who was sent to the region reported that "unless the Yankee force in Brownsville was largely augmented, the trade with Mexico could be kept open by way of Eagle Pass. The roads to Matamoros, via Eagle Pass and Monterey, are said to be splendid."[45]

Before November 1863, most of the cotton that passed through Eagle Pass came from Central Texas, through San Antonio. Once it crossed the border, it was taken downriver to Matamoros or Monterrey and from there to the coast. A central figure in this movement was Major Simeon Hart, Confederate quartermaster at San Antonio. Hart, married to a Mexican woman, had extensive experience in the Mexican trade as a leading merchant in Franklin (El Paso) before he was forced out by Union soldiers. He informed Secretary of War James A. Seddon at Richmond, that, due to the occupation, he was sending all cotton "by way of Eagle Pass, where it will be crossed into Mexico and proceed to Matamoros." He stated that this change would cause delays, but he was "using every possible exertion . . . to surmount the new difficulties."[46]

Another Confederate quartermaster scrambling "to surmount the new difficulties" was Major Charles Russell, who had been stationed at Brownsville. After the Union invasion led by General Nathaniel P. Banks, Russell informed his superior, Major B. Bloomfield at Richmond, that he could count on two Mexican leaders to help keep the flow of cotton moving toward Matamoros: Santos Benavides of Laredo and Santiago Vidaurri. "Benavides is below with about 150 men and is doing fine service. He says he will protect the Rio Grande. . . . I hope he will be reinforced." With regard to the governor of Nuevo León y Coahuila, Russell wrote: "Vidaurri has placed at my control a sufficient military force for my protection as well as the protection of all the public property under my control and has facilitated me in every possible way."[47]

One of General Hamilton Bee's first actions after his flight from Brownsville was to write to Benavides at Laredo. He instructed him to ensure the protection of the wagons laden with cotton that had been rerouted toward Roma, Laredo, and Eagle Pass. Because he would be facing superior forces, Bee instructed Benavides to engage in "guerilla warfare" and he emphasized the importance of his mission: "The whole country looks to you and your gallant, faithful men, and I am satisfied that the expectation will be more than realized."[48] Back in Monterrey, Kimmey was hopeful that the Union troops would sweep westward through the river country and occupy all of the major crossing points on the Rio Grande. This is exactly what General Banks proposed to do. He sent a small invasion force that moved toward Laredo, occupying Rio Grande City and Roma on its march. Part of this force—about two hundred men—continued to Laredo where they were met by a smaller force led by Santos Benavides. After a fierce battle the Yankees were driven back on March 19, 1863.[49]

The Union retreat from Laredo did not mean that the danger had passed, but as time went by and no further attacks occurred, the town continued to receive great amounts of cotton. Laredo experienced a boom and there was plenty of work. A junior editor of the *Galveston Bulletin* reported that at "Laredo, on the Mexican side, we found some 2,500 to 3,000 bales, which had all been on the road to Brownsville, and [were] turned off by the teamsters and crossed at that place."[50] Months later, in July 1864, the *Weekly State Gazette* reported that the "Laredo route to the Rio Grande is gaining in importance, being now regarded as safe against Yankee raiders from below." The following month its readers learned, "Cotton in quantities, has been received here of late so much so that the labor resources and facilities for crossing the staple to the Mexican side, are inadequate to meet the emergency. Ten times the old prices for boating over the river are being paid."[51]

A key figure in moving Confederate cotton through Laredo was Benavides's brother-in-law, John Z. Leyendecker. He was appointed assistant quartermaster and charged with providing the 33rd Texas Cavalry with provisions, a task that he performed with diligence and ability. He also served as an effective conduit in the flow of foodstuffs from Northeast Mexico to Texas. His account books show that between February and August 1863, Leyendecker handled 469,380 pounds of flour from Evaristo Madero bound for San Antonio.[52]

If the Eagle Pass–Piedras Negras crossing had been important to the Confederacy before the Union invasion of the lower Rio Grande Valley, it became crucial after November 1863. Kimmey wrote that Eagle Pass was "now the only point on the Rio Grande considered safe by the Rebels to cross cotton." He estimated that no less than seven thousand bales would cross through that port to Mexico in the month following the occupation. Kimmey elaborated on this theme in May 1864, after six months of Union occupation, when he informed Seward that Confederate traders in Monterrey had "taken new life and are sending enormous quantities of goods to Texas through Eagle Pass and Laredo." He added that the "occupation of Brownsville has no effect in stopping the trade," because "goods find their way into Texas as well by the upper River crossings as they formerly did through Brownsville."[53] The vice-consul was particularly incensed by the massive shipments of lead which, he wrote, "is the most important article the rebels now get from this country. Since the advance of our forces into Arkansas, the rebels west of the Mississippi River have drawn all the lead they have needed from here."[54]

A familiar cast of characters from the previous decade were on hand in Eagle Pass and Piedras Negras to facilitate the movement of Confederate cotton in exchange for handsome profits. Jesse Sumpter had been appointed customs inspector at Eagle Pass and he reported on the hundreds of bales that passed almost daily through the port, including cargoes from as far away as Arkansas. Friedrich Groos and his brothers were in Piedras Negras during the early part of the war. His firm took out an ad in a Houston newspaper that appealed to planters: "A large quantity of Shoes, Blankets, and Woollen stuffs suitable for negro clothing and other purposes, will be disposed of for cash, or exchanged on favorable terms for cotton, at Piedras Negras, opposite Eagle Pass." Perhaps

Cotton press at Piedras Negras. Commerce through Eagle Pass and Piedras Negras was vital to the Confederacy during the Civil War, especially after the occupation of the lower Rio Grande by Union forces in November 1863. Meanwhile, revenues from the customhouse in Piedras Negras helped to sustain Santiago Vidaurri's regional power in Northeast Mexico. Commerce through this trade route contributed to the integration of Texas and Northeast Mexico. From *Frank Leslie's Illustrated Newspaper*, September 3, 1864. LC-USZ62-119594, Library of Congress.

due to the increased hostility of Texas Confederates toward Germans, Groos later took his Mexican wife and children to Monterrey and then to Germany, where they spent the last two years of the war.[55]

Despite Friedrich's departure, F. Groos and Company continued to operate. One of the Groos brothers, Carl Wilhelm August, was briefly arrested in San Antonio in 1862, and on his release went to Piedras Negras. The following year he relocated to his company's branch office in Matamoros to process the cotton being sent from Piedras Negras.[56] In 1863 the firm took on a young German American to run its cotton yard in Piedras Negras. August Santleben, from Hanover, Germany, had arrived in the United States with his family in 1845 when he was three-and-a-half months old. As a boy he learned to drive one of his father's wagons, hauling supplies for the army. While still in his teens, he began hauling freight from Port Lavaca on the coast to San Antonio. During the first year of the Civil War, Santleben hauled cotton between Columbus and Eagle Pass, but then he moved to Mexico. He worked at odd jobs in Matamoros and Piedras Negras before hiring on with the Groos brothers at a monthly salary of $75, which was a considerable amount for the time. He also gained experience in traveling through northern Mexico. After the war Santleben would spend the remainder of his life carrying freight and people between Texas and Mexico. His life story mirrors those of many other borderlanders who moved with ease from one side of the border to the other. Santleben, like Evaristo Madero, got along with everyone by sticking to his work and doing it well.[57]

Another town greatly affected by the Union occupation of the lower Rio Grande Valley was San Antonio and its acquisitive merchants. Many of these businessmen became involved in the Civil War trade, but the two best examples are John Twohig and Jean Baptiste LaCoste, who left written records of their activities.[58] Twohig, the tough and high-spirited Irish American, had been imprisoned by General Martín Perfecto Cos during Texas independence in 1835 and had been sentenced to hard labor after falling prisoner to General Adrián Woll during the Mexican incursion into San Antonio in 1842. He spent the 1850s building up his commercial and landholding interests and, in 1861, when the question of secession was raised, he was faced with the same dilemma as his fellow merchants. A pragmatic man, Twohig knew that if he sided with the Union he would have to leave the state and could end up losing all that he had gained. He decided to cast his lot with the Confederacy and accepted a position in the Nitre and Mining Bureau, which was concerned with the acquisition of mineral products necessary to manufacture military supplies.[59]

Throughout the 1850s, Twohig had built up an extensive network of contacts in Mexico that served him well during the Civil War. His principal trading partner was Evaristo Madero, from whom he obtained hundreds of thousands of sacks of flour (many of them through Leyendecker of Laredo), as well as other products. Twohig also counted on several agents and middlemen: O. H. Cavender in the cotton-growing region of Texas, his brother-in-law Thomas Johnston in Matamoros, and Daniel Murphy in Monterrey. Murphy's presence in the capital of Nuevo León deserves special mention because it reflects the way merchants— and people in other occupations—changed their activities to take advantage of the new reality imposed by the Civil War. Murphy owned a store in the area of Fort Davis in western Texas on the California road. Intimately acquainted with Chihuahua and its potential for trade with Texas, he opened a stagecoach line between Chihuahua and San Antonio on November 6, 1860.[60] He apparently shifted gears, however, when it became clear in the spring and summer of 1861 that many opportunities for trade—and personal enrichment—would open with the imposition of the Union embargo and the cotton trade through Northeast Mexico to Matamoros. So Murphy put his project on hold and moved eastward toward the flow of cotton. He was one of the agents Kimmey disdainfully referred to as scouring the countryside "for all the flour and corn that can be had."[61]

However, Murphy was busy sending other articles as well. Records show that he shipped more than 171,000 pounds of lead over a period of eleven months, and another 121,988 pounds of nitrate over an unknown period.[62] The importance of these shipments for increasing Confederate firepower should not be underestimated. On the other end of the connection, O. H. Cavender operated for Twohig in Leon County, obtaining from planters all the cotton available. Cavender informed Twohig that he could control much of the cotton shipments from East Texas if he had sufficient bagging and rope.[63] These modest items were essential for the entire movement of cotton and, for practical purposes, as important as lead. Moreover, Murphy could obtain them in Mexico. In January 1863, Murphy sent Twohig forty-eight packets or bales of rope and bagging at a cost of $823.75. Between April and May, he sent another thirty-eight packets of rope. Cavender was thus able to stay ahead of many of his competitors in the purchase of cotton. In August 1863, he asked Twohig for $200,000 to pay for a thousand bales of cotton and negotiate for another 1,700 bales the following month. Twohig also counted on Friedrich Groos in Piedras Negras to provide him with many needed articles. Between January and July 1863, Groos sent him flour, saltpeter, rope, tin, lead, and bagging.[64]

Jean Baptiste LaCoste was another San Antonio–Chihuahua merchant who moved his operations eastward toward the scene of the action. He began a partnership with Henry Attrill, an Englishman who owned a ranch in Fredericksburg, where he raised horses. The two developed a working relationship with Patricio Milmo. LaCoste agreed to supply the Confederacy in exchange for cotton, which he shipped to Milmo in Monterrey, who forwarded it to Attrill, who then sold the fiber to the textile industry in Manchester. Attrill then bought articles LaCoste requested for the Confederacy and shipped them back via the same route. At the end of 1862 and in August 1863, J. F. Minter, Confederate quartermaster for Texas, Arizona, and New Mexico, signed contracts with LaCoste totaling $287,000. The French native claimed that at one time he possessed merchandise in Mexico totaling $432,000. He moved to Matamoros at a time when Maximilian was consolidating his government in Mexico and, as a Frenchman, was an enthusiastic supporter of the Empire, which, in turn, awarded him a medal and recognition for services rendered.[65]

The Union occupation of Brownsville had other consequences. In a note that referred to merchants such as LaCoste, Attrill, Milmo, and their ilk, the Houston

Weekly Telegraph reported: "Since the arrival of the Yankees on the Rio Grande, the contractors and speculators have become quite alarmed."[66] Their anxiety arose from the fact that they had provided the Confederacy with hundreds of thousands of dollars' worth of goods on credit, and with the Union invasion they feared they would never be paid. Attrill and LaCoste decided to cut their losses by selling their claims to Milmo. Major Simeon Hart, the Confederate quarter-master at San Antonio, had promised to pay the merchants in cotton, but due to disorganization and mismanagement, he could not comply with the speed Milmo demanded. And now the Yankees were at the gates. With the apparent backing of Vidaurri, his father-in-law and business partner, Milmo took matters into his own hands and began seizing cotton belonging to the Confederacy. He also confiscated Confederate treasury notes worth $15,000,000 that were being carried by two agents who passed through Nuevo León on their way to San Antonio.[67]

Quintero was mortified. He appealed to Vidaurri to fix the problem, stating that the Confederate notes were worthless to Milmo unless endorsed in Texas, and their seizure was a tremendous blow to the Confederacy. He also stated that quartermaster Hart was willing to pay and had four hundred bales of cotton in Camargo and another three hundred in Laredo "with which to satisfy part of the debt that he had incurred with Milmo." In a follow-up letter Quintero warned of the irreparable harm that Milmo's actions might have on the cordial relations between the two governments and on the flourishing commerce that was beneficial to both.[68]

Vidaurri's response to Quintero was that he should seek a solution in the courts. Apparently, the warm friendship was turning cold. The Confederate agent wrote to General Kirby Smith, military commander of the Trans-Mississippi Department, to inform him of what was occurring and to recommend the cessa-tion of all cotton shipments through Eagle Pass, in order to deprive Vidaurri of his "major source of income, the customs house at Piedras Negras." Smith followed Quintero's recommendation.[69] In a clear reference to Milmo and his associates, a Texas newspaper lashed out at the "miscreants who care more for their pockets than for the success of the Confederacy." Kimmey observed these events with delight, but his satisfaction at the Confederate self-imposed blockade of the Rio Grande did not last long. Vidaurri was under enormous pressure in the first two months of 1864. Benito Juárez and his army were marching toward Monterrey, and the governor desperately needed the revenues from the customhouse at Piedras Negras in order to field a sufficient force to drive him off. Moreover, because of his own business interests, Vidaurri had a personal stake in the continuation of the commerce. "Under these conditions," writes historian Ron Tyler, "a solution was quickly agreed upon, with the Confederacy promising to pay Milmo in full, and Milmo releasing the seven cases of treasury notes."[70]

As the relations between Quintero and Vidaurri began to fray, the dispute between the Confederate agent and Kimmey, the Union representative, sharpened considerably, another consequence of the Union invasion of the lower Rio Grande. Union occupation brought to the fore an issue that had been brewing since the war began. Texans who sympathized with the Union or who simply refused to serve or be conscripted into the Confederate army sought escape through northern Mexico.[71] The region also served as a refuge for deserters of that army. Kimmey and his fellow consul, Leonard Pierce of Matamoros, provided assistance to the refugees and channeled many of them into the Union army in the early part of the war. In October 1862, Kimmey wrote to Seward that he had sent sixty refugees to Matamoros and that Consul Pierce told him that they had "all been sent to New Orleans as recruits in the U.S. Army." Kimmey also reported that there were about a thousand men "scattered about this frontier . . . ready to join the first U.S. Forces sent to the Rio Grande. A few are occasionally leaving for New Orleans to join the army there, but most of them prefer to go back into Texas and revenge themselves for the barbarous acts of the Rebels."[72]

The actions of the Texas refugees and the U.S. consuls who gave them succor made the usually unflappable Quintero livid. The Union invasion of the lower Rio Grande emboldened many refugees to join Northern forces to avenge themselves on Confederate Texas. On November 23, Quintero complained to Vidaurri that Kimmey "was organizing a military company with the object of attacking the state of Texas." He cited as proof the testimony of Tomás Flores, a native of San Antonio, whom Kimmey had offered "the commission of second lieutenant in one of the regiments of General Banks." He requested Vidaurri's immediate action to prevent "such a flagrant violation of Mexico's neutrality."[73]

Quintero had to deal with many such problems while simultaneously coping with an increasingly volatile situation in northern Mexico. A bloody battle for the city of Matamoros broke out in mid-January 1864 between supporters of Governor Manuel Ruiz and the forces of Jesús de la Serna, who was supported by Juan Cortina. The fighting was so fierce that U.S. Consul Leonard Pierce appealed to General Francis J. Herron, commander of Union troops in Brownsville, to rescue him and his family from certain death. After furious house-to-house fighting the city fell to Cortina.[74] Cheno's hatred of the Confederates and his open support for the Union did not bode well for Quintero and the Confederacy.

Meanwhile, in Nuevo León y Coahuila the dispute between Vidaurri and Benito Juárez reached a crisis when the Mexican president arrived in Monterrey to confer with the caudillo in February 1864. The conflict was provoked by Vidaurri's refusal to subordinate his regional power to the will of the government at a moment when the nation was under attack by an external enemy. The center of the issue was Vidaurri's refusal to turn over the customs revenues from Piedras Negras and the other border ports. The exact amount is not known, but both Quintero and Kimmey calculated that Piedras Negras alone provided Vidaurri with $40,000–$50,000 monthly. Quintero added that "since the beginning of the war against the United States, the trade with Texas has brought this state a circulation in cash of close to $3,000,000." These revenues were vital to both Vidaurri and Juárez.[75]

The dispute between the two strong-willed men erupted into armed conflict, and the Nuevo León governor was forced into exile in Texas in April 1864.[76] Quintero now had to deal with a government that he had disparaged for its sympathy with Lincoln and the Union. He summoned all of his diplomatic skills for the effort. In January 1864 he had written a letter to Pedro Santacilia, Juárez's son-in-law and personal secretary. Santacilia was also a native of Cuba, and the family references in the letter reveal that they knew each other well. Quintero was bitterly critical of Vidaurri, whose conduct "has not been that of a statesman, because in supporting the unjust claim of a single citizen [Milmo], he has sacrificed the broader interests of Nuevo León." Then Quintero made a remarkable statement: "I brought this commerce to Mr. Vidaurri more than two years ago and now I can take it to Tamaulipas if peace is restored in Matamoros and the government of Mr. Juárez protects our interests." He told Santacilia that he was willing to meet with the president at any time and asked that the letter be revealed only to Juárez.[77]

If Quintero was concerned that the Juárez government might take steps that would harm the commerce vital to the Confederacy, he need not have worried. The beleaguered president desperately needed the income from the customhouses and was not about to take measures that would disrupt the trade. Indeed, Quintero received "very cordial treatment from the president, who, on the very day of his arrival in Monterrey, invited him to a dinner with the members of his cabinet."[78]

Quintero's efforts to draw closer to Juárez turned out to be ephemeral because the Mexican president, under pressure from the advancing imperialist army, could not defend Monterrey and had to abandon the city after only a four-month stay, from April to August 1864. Kimmey watched as French forces under the command of General Armand A. Castagny marched into Monterrey on August 26. He had no illusions about their mission, writing earlier that the French army was "levying contributions on the citizens for its support and instead of bringing peace as they offer in every instance in advance they bring misery on the people wherever their army goes."[79] Nor did Kimmey believe that French authorities would do anything to upset the lucrative Confederate trade. He was right. Quintero immediately came to an understanding with Castagny that led him to inform Confederate Secretary of State Benjamin enthusiastically: "we have never before been in such a favorable condition . . . in regard to our intercourse with Mexico."[80]

Because French forces also occupied Matamoros, Northeast Mexico was completely under their control. This coincided with the Union retreat from Brownsville, which the Confederates retook on July 30, 1864. The cotton trade was now unfettered and would remain so until the end of the Civil War in April 1865. By the following month when the last skirmish occurred at Palmito Ranch near Brownsville, the cotton boom, known in Mexico as the period of *los algodones*, was over. It had been a wild ride for many of the inhabitants of Northeast Mexico and South Texas.

The War and Its Economic Impact

This extraordinary commercial boom was but a fleeting moment in border history, but it had a lasting impact in various ways. It helped to integrate the region and bring it closer together. The Matamoros-Monterrey axis continued strong, while interior routes that passed through Laredo and Eagle Pass strengthened the connection between San Antonio and Monterrey. These two cities became the twin poles of an increasingly integrated economic region. Civil War commerce also made some of its participants fabulously rich. Brownsville postmaster Gilbert Kingsbury wrote that the war had created a breed of millionaires, some of whom amassed immense fortunes. Historian Marilyn McAdams Sibley has written that Charles Stillman "laid the foundations for one of the nation's major fortunes during the course of the war." His partners, "Richard King and Mifflin Kenedy, parlayed their profits into feudal ranching domains in South Texas, while George W. Brackenridge, sometime Stillman employee, sometime United States treasury agent, earned the stake that formed the basis of a San Antonio banking fortune."[81]

On the other side of the border, Monterrey merchants Evaristo Madero, Patricio Milmo, Mariano Hernández, Valentín Rivero, and others channeled their wealth into various interests that included real estate, banking, mining, and manufacturing. These capitalists and their heirs became members of an oligarchy that was destined to transform Monterrey into Latin America's most important industrial city.[82]

While capital accumulation by the upper classes helped to stimulate future economic development, at least a small part of the wealth generated by the cotton traffic filtered down to other classes of society. This was the judgment of José Eleuterio González, Nuevo León's greatest doctor, who was also a distinguished governor and man of letters. He referred to the Civil War years as "the most brilliant period in the commerce of the frontier states," a time when "the commercial movement was propagated to all classes of society."[83] This trickle-down effect happened in at least two fundamental ways. The transfer of massive amounts of cargo demanded the movement of trains of wagons, carts, and carretas, as well as the animals to drive them, through many of the towns of Mexico's Northeast on their way from Piedras Negras to Matamoros. The provisions that these towns supplied in the way of water, wood, pasturage, and food—combined with municipal taxes and road tolls—reinvigorated the economy of these localities. This became especially true after the Union occupation of the lower Rio Grande moved much of the commerce westward. Quartermaster Simeon Hart reported that he circumvented the danger of Union attack by agreeing to an "extensive arrangement with the house of Marks and Co., Matamoros, to deliver supplies at Villa Aldama, a point in Nuevo Leon about 180 miles from Eagle Pass, on the direct route between the latter place and Matamoras." Perhaps without knowing why or from where it originated, the vecinos of Villaldama, as well as many other towns, were greatly affected by the movement of cotton through their region.[84]

The other way in which a part of the cotton wealth was distributed to the lower classes was in the form of wages paid to the men who transported the cargo. Thousands of rural people from Mexico's Northeast were drawn into a huge, hastily improvised labor market to serve as arrieros, carreteros, and freighters. They perpetuated the tendency of Northeast Mexico's rural people to migrate north to Texas in search of labor opportunities and contributed to forging a stronger bond within the binational region.

Labor Migration in Times of War

The unprecedented volume of trade called for the employment of thousands of men to transport cotton and other goods. Since all the commercial routes to Matamoros passed through the Mexican region and most of them also traversed

Northeast Mexico, Mexicans were mostly hired to do the job. Confederate authorities actively promoted their entry into this promising field. In December 1862, General John B. Magruder ordered that "Mexicans and other foreigners, bringing supplies into the country, will not be interfered with in any manner whatever, but, on the contrary, it is hereby made the duty of every officer, or agent of the government, to afford them ample protection."[85]

The need for transport was so great that Mexicans and their teams, carts, and wagons were sought all over Mexico's Northeast, especially in Monterrey, which became a recruitment center. In September 1861, a Galveston newspaper declared as probable a rumor that "an immense number of carts in Mexico" were being contracted. This proved more than a rumor. Quintero reported to Richmond that there was a shortage of carts and teamsters in the city because most of the carreteros had emigrated to Texas, lured by the high freighting charges being paid.[86] One of the most active agents in Monterrey was Daniel Murphy, John Twohig's representative. In September 1863, he received an urgent request from Major S. L. James to send teamsters with thirty carts to San Antonio. They were needed to haul cotton to Monterrey and would be paid $120 for each trip. Murphy received a commission of $10 for each cart he obtained.[87]

Twohig also relied on Friedrich Groos to hire Mexican freighters in the area around Piedras Negras and send them to San Antonio to haul cotton. In a six-month period in 1863 Groos hired twenty-seven carreteros, all but one of them Mexicans.[88] Another merchant on the border who contracted large numbers of Mexican freighters was John Leyendecker who, as quartermaster for the Texas 33rd Cavalry, hired teamsters and new arrivals seeking work in the Laredo area. Leyendecker also worked in association with the firm of Attrill and LaCoste of San Antonio to provide those merchants with transportation. His records indicate that during the first quarter of 1863, he employed forty-three men to provide transport; all but two were Mexican.[89]

For his extensive commercial operations, José San Román required transportation on a vast scale. Two of his agents on the border, Joseph Kleiber of Brownsville and John Vale of Roma, provided him with carts, wagons, and teamsters. Most of the freighters in San Román's employ were from the towns of Nuevo León and Tamaulipas.[90] Texas planters looked to San Román for help in moving their cotton. John W. Lang of Houston wrote that he had sent Charles Nanwald to the border in search of men and carts to move his cotton. Lang had 450 bales on the Colorado River that he was unable to move to the border. He asked San Román to pay the teamsters an advance and charge the cost to his account.[91]

Little information has been found on the men who participated in this bur-geoning transport. The "González brothers of Saltillo," according to historian Santiago Escobedo, "got their start as a result of the Civil War. They owned a train of twenty-five carts each with five mules." Other carriers included "Rocke Garady" (probably Roque Garay), and the Sada brothers, David and Daniel, of Monterrey. Garay was known to venture as far as Colorado in his freight operations.[92] As a young man, José María Serrano of Santa Isabel headed for Matamoros to enlist in San Román's small army of carriers. His father had written to the Spaniard that he was sending his son to drive a train of carts because the pay was good and there was no fear of suffering embargoes as in Mexico.[93]

Mexican freighters went far afield in their Texas travels. The Galveston *Civil-ian and Gazette* reported, "Long caravans of Mexican carts pass through here almost daily, bound to the railroad for supplies. The cartman, as he flourishes his whip and saunters gaily along, smoking his cigarette, seems alike oblivious of war and hard times." Mexicans were a permanent fixture at Alleyton, near Houston, where the railroad line ended and the long road to the border began. A correspondent for the *Tri-Weekly Telegraph* described the hectic scene at the depot: "It is interesting, composed principally of Mexican teamsters, their carts, teams, dogs and wives, cotton buyers, cotton Sellers, merchants, pedlars [*sic*], speculators, foreigners and soldiers."[94] Condescension gave way to racism in other descriptions. An Austin traveler in Alleyton wrote of seeing "Mexican carts in charge of swarthy greasers, clad in buckskin, with their gaudy colored blankets, shouting in their mongrel Spanish, to their half starved oxen."[95]

The great demand for transportation drove wages to unprecedented levels. Common laborers in Texas typically made fifty cents a day in the 1850s, but on the eve of the Civil War they were making about seventy-five cents. Little wonder that many laborers forsook their tedious, backbreaking jobs in favor of hauling cotton. The payment for transporting goods in the 1850s had remained static at about a dollar per one hundred pounds for one hundred miles. As the Civil War progressed this rate rose considerably so that by mid-1863, teamsters could obtain five or six dollars under those terms. Even teamsters who did not own their teams could earn up to forty dollars per month in Confederate notes, plus rations. During the following year, John Twohig was paying up to 10 percent of the value of the cotton to his carriers. Historian Arthur Mayer affirms that by the middle of 1864, depending on the size of his wagon, a teamster could earn between $600 and $1,500 for taking a shipment of cotton from San Antonio to Matamoros. This figure sounds far-fetched, but the payroll records of John

Leyendecker of Laredo show that quite a number of carreteros were making several hundred dollars, though it is not specified what they were carrying or for how long. In January 1864, one carrier, Benito González, was paid $714.20. Three others, Eleuterio Quintero, Bernardo Mendiola, and Félix González, were all paid more than $300. To many rural people and their families, these were fabulous sums that perhaps allowed some to climb out of the appalling poverty that engulfed them. Spiraling rates also gave Mexican freighters greater leverage. Joseph Kleiber discovered this when he faced a group of freighters who refused payment in Confederate notes. They demanded and received two thousand dollars in silver coins for transporting merchandise to San Antonio.[96]

COTTON, WAR, AND INTERDEPENDENCE

The extraordinary commercial boom that produced riches for a few and a short period of decent wages for many others ended in the spring of 1865 with the conclusion of the Civil War. During that four-year period a modest but important agricultural product brought together people of various races and nationalities. Cotton produced a synchronization of sorts between white planters and the middlemen who owned it and traded it, African American slaves who picked it, and Mexicans who carried it to distant markets. War conditions favored cooperation and obligated people to work and face obstacles together, contact that oftentimes engendered greater understanding and tolerance. This is not to say that racial, ethnic, and national antipathies magically ceased. Indeed, they would escalate again in the 1870s and at the turn of the century, but they were temporarily held in abeyance while more important, life-and-death issues were being sorted out. Moreover, much of the hatred and energies of the majority of Anglo Texans who favored secession were now directed at the Yankees, a new enemy that threatened their way of life. The war years produced many situations that reveal a greater willingness to coexist by many of the diverse populations of the border region. Several occurrences illustrate the point.

While in Monterrey buying goods and recruiting transport as John Twohig's agent, Daniel Murphy took time on April 15, 1863, to write a letter that was published the following month in a Texas newspaper. Murphy addressed his dispatch to his fellow Irish Americans, explaining to them why he supported the Confederacy. He wrote from the viewpoint of an Irish Catholic who deplored the oppression of the Irish, first by the Puritans in England and more recently in New England. He asked them if they had "forgotten the countless wrongs and insults heaped upon them and their religion, and their ancestors for the last three hundred years, by the fanatical Puritan?" Murphy further asked, "Have not the people of Massachusetts permitted mobs to burn churches and convents erected by Roman Catholics to the service of God in one of their principal cities?" He reminded his fellow countrymen that the Know-Nothing spirit was alive and well in the North, where Massachusetts Governor John A. Andrew decreed that regiments from that state "must be officered and commanded by *native Americans*." Murphy's letter is the testimony of one man, but it reflects the complexities of the place and period in which he lived. His experiences in Chihuahua and later in Monterrey led him to have a greater affinity for Mexicans than for the northerners of his adopted country, the United States.[97]

The commonalities of political and military leaders of Confederate Texas and Northeast Mexico during the Civil War period led to alliances that would have been difficult or impossible to forge in ordinary times. A few examples of how those leaders gave voice to those interests reveal how the war brought those men of different origins together and converted them into strange bedfellows. In 1861, Rip Ford, newly appointed commander of the Rio Grande Military District, wrote to his counterpart, General Guadalupe García, Mexican commander of the *línea del Bravo*. His instruction from Governor Edward Clark was to avoid friction with Mexico. The governor, wrote Ford, wanted "a continuance of most kind and friendly relations" with Texas's southern neighbor because "the interest of Mexico, at least of those States adjacent to us, is to favor the Southern Government." Ford too declared his commitment to maintain "friendly relations with Mexico."[98]

When Santiago Vidaurri was forced to leave Monterrey in April 1864, he went first to Laredo, where his friend Santos Benavides received him, then headed for Houston, where General Magruder warmly received him. According to the pro-Union *New Orleans Era*, the Confederate commander met Vidaurri at the railroad depot with these words: "For your noble efforts to serve the people of Coahuila and Nuevo Leon you are now an exile. For your patriotic exertions to . . . free them from any dependence on the most faithless and barbarous of all people [those of the United States], you have offered up yourself as a sacrifice." Vidaurri responded that "he had always felt the greatest sympathy for the Confederate States, as they had battled for their rights and for the poor privilege to be left alone." He was now an exile for fighting for the same rights. So here were two leaders who had rebelled against their government and now shared common ground. The *New Orleans Era* added, with sarcasm, that the "absquatulating ex-governor" and Magruder shared another commonality: they had "fought and

bled for their country, and made enormous fortunes by stealing cotton from
defenceless [sic] citizens, selling it to meet the requirements of the public service,
and pocketing the proceeds."[99]

Wartime inflation affected all sectors of the population and was especially hard
on the working poor, which included many Mexican families. Historian Bill Winsor documents how basic consumer items rose in price as the war advanced. Beef,
which sold for two cents a pound before the war, rose to twenty-five cents. Rice
increased from eleven cents to six dollars; sugar and coffee increased similarly.[100]
These increases caused hardship but also generated a sense of solidarity. Citizens
of Bexar County established supply associations and mutual aid organizations
to purchase foods in great quantities and offer them to the families of soldiers
and indigent families at low cost. The San Antonio Mutual Aid Association
had "over ten thousand persons on its list of beneficiaries and stockholders." The
association obtained some of its products from Mexico. One article was flour,
which sold on the market for forty dollars per hundred pounds. The association
obtained flour for fifteen to sixteen dollars per hundred pounds.[101] A similar
association selling meat at lower prices also appeared. The *San Antonio Herald*
decried the "tyrannical rule of a few butchers" who hoarded meat in order to sell
it at twenty-five to fifty cents per pound. The meat association was able to sell
meat at from five to fifteen cents a pound. The *Herald* concluded: "the poor of
our city are considerably benefitted by procuring their food at prices that they
can pay."[102] The supply and mutual aid associations were mainly operated by
Anglo businessmen while many of the beneficiaries were Mexicans, a topic that
merits further study.

The need for greater cooperation in facing adversity as well as the dependence
of Texas on northern Mexico contributed somewhat to softening the harsh lines
of discrimination against Mexicans. A good illustration is provided by the experience of Vicente Hernández. A native of Zacatecas, Hernández built a modest
bakery in San Antonio after a few years of hard work and saving money. When a
conscription law was passed, he obtained an exemption because he was a citizen
of Mexico and planned to return to that country someday. This exemption was
challenged in a civil case by a prosecutor who argued that Hernández's nationality
did not excuse him from serving in the army. The judge, according to a local newspaper, ruled in favor of the Mexican, stating that it was "inexpedient to force aliens
into the army as it might exasperate other nations toward us." This circumstance,
stated the judge, "was particularly so with regard to citizens of Mexico, which
government had afforded us every facility for obtaining munitions of war, which

we so much needed, whilst other nations had shown an unfriendly disposition." Texas was "still dependent" on Mexico and "should cultivate friendly relations with her."[103] There was an unacknowledged competition between the Union and the Confederacy to gain Mexico's friendly disposition. The Houston *Tri-Weekly Telegraph* reported that in "Monterey there is the best of feeling towards Texas, though Yankee agents are doing all in their power to alienate it."[104]

It is difficult to know how Texan dependence on Mexico might have affected race relations. Ángel Navarro, a graduate of Harvard and son of José Antonio Navarro, had a quarrel with Confederate authorities and decided to leave Texas for Mexico. He wrote to his friend Santiago Vidaurri that in Texas "those of Mexican extraction do not share . . . the same privileges as the natives." He expressed his wish to "live in Mexico among my own kind." It is not known if or for how long he stayed in Mexico or if his grievance reflected a broader collective sentiment.[105]

There are however indicators of greater acceptance of Mexicans. After the cannons ceased their roar and Texans resumed their prewar activities, the issue of Mexican carts on the road from San Antonio to the coast again came to the fore. The *San Antonio Ledger* reminded its readers of the Cart War of 1857, when Mexican cartmen "were run off from this route by a villainous set of men." Things had changed and the people along the route wanted them to return, the article claimed. The report included an extract from the *Goliad Intelligencer* that summarized the issue: "Years ago the San Antonio Mexican carts passed through this place to and from the bay. They were diverted from this route by . . . the work of desperadoes." The cartmen wanted to return "but fear they will again be interrupted. There is no good reason for such fear. We are satisfied they will be as free from danger as any other persons traveling the road. . . . Let them all come this way."[106]

Mexico: Sanctuary for Union and Confederate Refugees

Another testimony of greater acceptance of Mexico and Mexicans was the willingness of very many Texans—both Unionists and Confederates—to go to Mexico during and after the war. They went to Mexico out of necessity and because of its proximity, but in the case of the Confederates, it is ironic that they migrated to a land that many of them had referred to disparagingly as "greaserdom." Union sympathizers abandoned Texas for Mexico when the state joined the Confederacy and life north of the border became difficult for them. Most were single men who would later join Union forces, but some traveled to Mexico with their families and stayed there, forming a community of exiles hostile to the Confederacy. One

Union official reported that Tamaulipas and Nuevo León, "particularly the latter, have large numbers of Union families, who escaped, residing in them."[107] One such family was that of Franklin L. Paschal, whose brother, George Washington Paschal, was editor of the *Southern Intelligencer* in Austin. Ángel Navarro had written to Vidaurri about Paschal, whom he described as an "honest and hard-working" lawyer who "had lived for many years in San Antonio." Paschal was joined by his family, which included his sixteen-year-old son Frank, who would spend many years in Mexico and go on to become one of San Antonio's most prominent doctors.[108]

Among the arrivals to Northeast Mexico during the Civil War period were the Baptist missionary James Hickey and two doctors, James Fakenson Hatchett and William R. Robinson. Hickey left Texas due to the stifling secessionist environment. His presence in Mexico would be strongly felt, as he was one of the pioneers in introducing Protestantism to the country. The two doctors were approved by a professional board in Monterrey and went to Saltillo to begin their practice in 1863. Hatchett (whose Mexican patients were probably unaware of the meaning of his last name), had graduated from the College of Atlanta in 1859 and was thirty-two years old when he went to Saltillo. Records describe him as a married man; six feet, two inches tall; with a white complexion, brown hair, and thick beard.[109] Most of the exiles were probably apolitical, but one Texas newspaper reported that these "Yankee emissaries . . . infest every village and neighborhood of Northern Mexico . . . stirring up hostility to both the Confederacy and the French."[110]

Many of the families settled in Monterrey, to the discomfiture of the Confederate representative Quintero. The Union presence in Monterrey drew sneers in Texas. The *Brownsville Flag* stated that, because of the Confederate victories in the early part of the war, "the Abolition Hall in Monterey has been abandoned by its conclave of niggers, dutch and yankees and the proprietor has fled to parts unknown." All that was left for Union refugees, reported the paper, was "'Uncle Tom's Cabin,' a hotel kept by a nigger under the direct protection of the Yankee Consul Kemmey [*sic*]."[111]

After the war, most of the Unionists returned to Texas, and it was now the Confederate partisans' turn to flee to Mexico. To be sure, there were Confederate sympathizers in Monterrey during the conflict, many of them probably involved in the task of supplying the Confederacy. Some had sought refuge there after the Union occupation of Brownsville. General N. J. T. Dana wrote, "Monterey is now the rebel headquarters on this frontier, and many officers are there, including some of Kirby Smith's staff."[112] Confederate refugees formed part of a small but vocal foreign community in the city, founding their own newspaper, which did not hesitate to voice an opinion, even with respect to Mexican affairs. During the conflict between Vidaurri and Juárez it loudly supported the former. As Juárez built up his forces in Saltillo to attack Monterrey, publisher John S. Swope, the editor of *The Morning Star*, wrote in March 1864 that any attack on Monterrey would be repulsed by Vidaurri, so "there is nothing to fear for the safety of *our* city." It is interesting to speculate on how these Confederates got along with their Unionist neighbors and how they reacted when the hated Juárez took the city the following month.[113]

Confederates migrated to Mexico on a much larger scale after their armies were defeated. It was logical that military men and politicians would want to emigrate to avoid being jailed or living under the domination of the hated Yankees. In fact, historian Todd William Wahlstrom argues that many of the emigrants were "small to middling ex-slaveholders. . . . Rather than fleeing from the threat of punishment and Republican Reconstruction, they largely went across the border into Mexico after the Civil War to pursue new economic opportunities."[114] General Philip Sheridan, who was appointed to head the Military Division of the Southwest, wrote that white Southerners were predisposed to going to Mexico because, during the Civil War, Southern newspapers had constantly expressed sympathy for Maximilian and what he was attempting to do in Mexico. Many adventurers may have assumed that Maximilian's government would be hostile to the United States and that they would find an anti-Yankee haven in Mexico.[115]

Maximilian's government was not hostile to the United States, but its very presence was inimical to Washington, which opposed French designs on Mexico. The new emperor set out to build a strong government and determined that opening the country to immigration was essential to his plan. The Confederacy was defeated one year after Maximilian's arrival in Mexico, and many of its adherents were looking for a place to go, so their situation meshed perfectly with Maximilian's open-door policy toward immigrants. In June 1865, a "Virginia-born scientist of world renown," Matthew Fontaine Maury, went to see Maximilian and informed him that "there were 200,000 families in the South who 'had had enough of Republics' and would come to Mexico if proper inducements were offered."[116]

Maury and Maximilian embraced a common cause, and by September the Confederate emissary was appointed to head the Office of Colonization. Newcomers were offered cleared land at low cost or uncultivated land for free. Immigrants could bring their household effects without paying duty and could even bring their former slaves, though they would have to hire them on a contract basis, which resembled debt peonage. The latter provision provoked an outcry among Mexican liberals, who accused the Empire of introducing a new slave system. Maury actively promoted the colonization scheme in the United States. In June 1866, *DeBow's Review* published a letter from Maury that painted a generally glowing picture of Mexico. In particular, Maury reported that Maximilian assured him Protestants would be free to practice their faith.[117]

The list of Confederates who fled to Mexico reads like a who's who of political and military leaders of the trans-Mississippi region, although some came from as far away as Missouri and Kentucky. The list included the principal military commanders of the district, Generals Kirby Smith and John B. Magruder. General Joseph Shelby led a large group to Mexico. Among the political leaders were former governors such as Edward Clark and Pendleton Murrah of Texas, Henry W. Allen and Thomas O. Moore of Louisiana, and Thomas C. Reynolds of Missouri. Allen seemed pleased when he wrote from San Luis Potosí that he was "in fine health and spirits," had been kindly treated in Mexico, and found the climate "delightful." Murrah had a much different experience. He died in Monterrey from consumption, a malady that had afflicted him since 1861.[118]

General Philip Sheridan was convinced that many of the Confederate emigrants would join Maximilian's army, and he was determined to use the 52,000 troops at his command to stop the flow. He wrote to one of his superiors in Washington that he "had to take strong grounds against this emigration, and finally broke it up by refusing to permit emigrants to embark from the sea-ports within the limits of [his] command."[119] The unrepentant Rebels avoided the seaports and followed the same route that was used to ship cotton during the war, from San Antonio through Eagle Pass–Piedras Negras and on to Monterrey. Sheridan could take comfort in the fact that the route was not easy: the "Rio Grande frontier is nearly a desert, and soldiers and emigrants will find it hard to live on frijolis and tortas, which is all the country can afford, and these not in abundance." Most of the emigrants used the Piedras Negras route, and it is said that when General Shelby's large group crossed the Rio Grande, the general, in a solemn ceremony, buried a Confederate flag in the middle of the river.[120]

On the same day that Shelby sank his flag—July 4, 1865—General John B. Magruder was hosting a grand banquet in Monterrey to celebrate the independence of the country he had abandoned. Vidaurri was not there to toast with his old friend, and the French were in control of the city. Although the official newspaper reported that there were some four thousand Confederate immigrants in Monterrey, the figure was probably closer to one thousand. Nevertheless, there had not been that many Americans in Monterrey since the occupation in 1846–48. Some of them brought dictionaries to help them learn the Spanish language.[121]

Monterrey became a sort of stepping stone for Confederate immigration, though for most refugees it was not a final destination. Colonies were established in different parts of the country, but many Southerners settled in a colony in Veracruz named Carlota, after Maximilian's wife. The project was however doomed to failure from its inception. The Southerners tied their fortunes to those of Maximilian's government, which had little to no chance of survival after the French military withdrew and Juárez's republican army began to conquer province after province on its march toward Mexico City. The United States was also threatening Maximilian with intervention while providing support to Juárez. According to one source there was another reason for the failure of the Confederate colonies: the immigrants "were none too popular with the Mexicans." Their colonies became "islands of foreigners in a native sea with which they had nothing in common." General Sterling Price, a prominent Confederate of the Carlota Colony, was quoted as saying: "We have around us some rich and intelligent families but we do not take as companions other than the ones who establish themselves among us and speak our language." It appears that white Southerners wanted to live in Mexico, but without Mexicans. This racist, exclusionary attitude could not prosper in a country where a full-blooded Zapotec Indian was leading the struggle for republicanism.[122] By 1870, Thomas H. Nelson, U.S. ambassador to Mexico, informed Washington that the "large number of citizens of the Southern States of the Union who came to Mexico immediately after the rebellion [had] almost all returned to the United States."[123]

~

The 1860s witnessed civil wars on both sides of the Rio Grande. While Union and Confederate soldiers battled for supremacy in Texas, liberals fought against conservatives backed by French bayonets in Mexico. These wars provided many opportunities for transborder cooperation, particularly in the area of commerce. After its ports were blockaded by the Union navy, the Trans-Mississippi Confederacy became dependent on trade with and through Northeast Mexico. What followed was a commercial boom unlike anything the region had seen before or would see again until late in the twentieth century with the implementation of the North American Free Trade Agreement (NAFTA). Texas merchants with ties to northern Mexico and Monterrey merchants with experience in the Texas trade moved quickly to supply the Confederacy and transfer its cotton to Europe via the free port of Matamoros.

In recognition of the importance of Northeast Mexico, the Confederate government sent special agent José Agustín Quintero to Monterrey; there, he worked with diligence and diplomatic skill to ensure the continuation of trade. Working in opposition to cut the flow of trade was M. M. Kimmey, the Union vice-consul in Monterrey. These two men carried on a minor war within the larger conflict.

The occupation of the lower Rio Grande by Union troops in November 1863 pushed the movement of trade westward toward interior ports such as Laredo and Piedras Negras, making the support of Nuevo León governor Santiago Vidaurri even more vital to the Confederacy. The Union attempt to stop the trade by marching upriver and taking Laredo was rebuffed by Mexican Texans led by Santos Benavides. The occupation also accelerated the recruitment of Union refugees and Confederate deserters who had fled to Mexico.

Early in 1864, Vidaurri engaged in a power struggle with Mexican president Benito Juárez. He lost and went into exile in Texas. The arrival of the Imperialist army in the border region forced Juárez to march with his government to Chihuahua. Despite these changes, commerce continued because it was in the interest of all the participants and because Quintero skillfully navigated between these competing power structures to defend the interests of the Confederacy.

The Civil War caused appalling destruction and loss of life, but in the Texas-Mexico border region it spawned a cotton boom that brought prosperity to many merchants on both sides of the border, who later channeled their wealth into a broad array of economic activities. Some of the wealth found its way to rural towns in Mexico's Northeast, located on the routes of the cotton trade. Mexican rural people found themselves drawn into a commercial vortex that demanded huge numbers of carts, wagons, and animals, with the men to drive them. Mexicans began hauling freight and for a fleeting moment took advantage of the unprecedented wages paid for transportation. The Civil War revealed that the needs of various groups could be different yet compatible. The need of Confederate Texans was to keep commerce flowing, while the need of many Mexicans, especially those from rural areas, was to access opportunities not available in Mexico.

The Civil War also established new priorities, not the least of which was survival in a struggle with a bitter foe. In these conditions, racial animosities cooled somewhat as the demands of war drew diverse people together and relegated race to a secondary plane. Finally, the antipathy toward Mexicans did not deter Union and Confederate partisans from fleeing to Mexico and living among Mexicans during and after the conflict. Many if not most Confederates who migrated had a distaste for Mexicans, but apparently their dislike of Yankees was greater. They stayed in the country only until they discovered that conditions did not favor permanent residence. Maximilian's defeat at Querétaro practically sealed their fate, and most returned to a forgiving United States.

CHAPTER 6

Cooperation in Times of War

1861–1867

T he massive commercial boom in the Rio Grande region generated by the Civil War, and the interdependence and integration it produced, was only one of the salient aspects of the 1860s. The period was fraught with complexity because wars raged in both countries and because different factions in Tamaulipas engaged in continuous political conflict that resulted in terrible violence. The region was often in disorder that at times descended into chaos. The only reason commerce continued was that it was in everyone's interest to keep it going. The swirl of events and the shifting alliances made for an extremely intricate situation, one not easy to sort out. This chapter focuses on how the state of conflict promoted alliances and cooperation among the diverse actors of the border region.[1] A word on the timeline is pertinent. The Civil War in the United States lasted from April 1861 to May 1865, while the War of French Intervention in Mexico began early in 1862 and ended in June 1867. The U.S. war had an immediate impact in the border region because of the Union blockade, while the French intervention had little impact until August 1864 when the imperialists occupied Northeast Mexico. Thus, the two wars were concurrent on the Rio Grande for only about a ten-month period, from August 1864 to May 1865.

CORTINA AND THE ALLIANCE AGAINST HIM

Before exploring the Civil War, I want to mention a series of violent events that occurred in early 1861 along the Rio Grande between Brownsville and Laredo and that are sometimes referred to as the Second Cortina War. Although this conflict involved at most a few hundred men, it was a kind of herald of things to come because it involved some of the leading protagonists of the larger conflict, among them Santos Benavides, Rip Ford, Juan Nepomuceno Cortina, and Guadalupe García, all military men. It also foreshadowed the sides that they would represent, with Benavides and Ford on the side of the Confederacy, with support from the Mexican García, while Cortina would support the Union. It presaged the role of Benavides as defender of Laredo and the Rio Grande, and finally, it promoted transborder cooperation, which would be commonplace in the following years.

The so-called Second Cortina War can be viewed as an extension of the first revolt because Cortina's defeat by Major Samuel P. Heintzelman in December 1859 did not end the fighting nor quell the underlying bitterness and hatred. Throughout early 1860 violence was rampant. Cortinistas continued raiding and Texas Rangers continued hanging and shooting Mexicans and burning their ranches.[2] Then Cortina left the Rio Grande and joined the liberals in the War of Reform against the conservatives, which kept him occupied for the rest of the year and ameliorated the violence. The Rangers were also withdrawn, so that in July 1860, an American officer wrote that "everything on the Rio Grande was 'perfectly quiet . . . since the departure of the Rangers.'"[3]

Cortina returned to the border in early 1861 at a time when the secession movement in Texas was polarizing the population. His enemies in Zapata County, including the Englishman Henry Redmond and Judge Isidro Vela, ruled the county with an iron hand. They operated a *patron* system that kept the majority of the impoverished and landless Mexicans subjugated, but bitter and resentful. The judge threatened the poorer Mexicans with fines if they did not vote for secession and the vote came in at 212 to 0 in favor of separating from the Union. In early April, Antonio Ochoa, "at the instigation of Cortina, pronounced against the Confederate government."[4] Although some believed that Cortina and Ochoa were inspired by sympathy for the Union, Jerry Thompson argues that the movement was "a reaction to the repressive political oligarchy and boss rule in [Zapata] county." Moreover, since the Zapata County oligarchs favored the Confederacy, it was logical that Cortina would cast his lot with the Union.[5]

In May about seventy of Cheno's troops surrounded Redmond's Ranch near Carrizo, which was defended by a small force led by then-captain Santos Benavides of Laredo. Benavides had been receiving information on Cortina's movements from the alcalde of Guerrero, Juan G. Garza. He managed to get word to Laredo for reinforcements, and they arrived on the morning of May 22, 1861, "after a fifty-five mile ride in thirteen hours." These troops, some thirty-six in number, were led by Refugio and Basilio Benavides, the brother and uncle of Santos Benavides, as well as by Lieutenant Charles Callahan. Santos Benavides went on the offensive and led a counterattack that routed Cheno's force. The rebel leader lost seven men in the fighting, while eleven others were captured and shot or hanged.[6] After the battle of Carrizo, Benavides received expressions of gratitude from all over Texas, including Governor Edward Clark, who wrote: "Whenever our enemies have appeared on our soil, you and your brave men have been present and driven them back, with great honor to yourselves and the gratification of your state."[7] Like Antonio Zapata before him, Benavides won the admiration of Anglo-Texans for his leadership and bravery in battle.

TRANSBORDER MILITARY COOPERATION

The battle at Carrizo brought Texan and Mexican military leaders closer together in their struggle to pacify the border and create stable conditions for the massive commerce that would soon flow through the region. In the aftermath of the battle, General Guadalupe García met with Colonel Rip Ford at Fort Brown and "agreed to not only assist the Confederates in apprehending Cortina, but also to take the field against the revolutionary himself." The two leaders went even further. In violation of national protocols, they agreed that Santos Benavides would be allowed to cross the border in pursuit of Cortina without impediment from Mexican authorities.[8] Ford then wrote to Santos Benavides about the meeting, stating that García expressed "his intention to cooperate with our troops in pursuing and arresting Cortinas [sic] and his followers." He also informed him of the agreement to allow pursuit across the border, but cautioned Benavides to "avoid molesting peaceable citizens who have not participated in the affair. . . . You must go as a friend to Mexico and as an enemy to the followers of Cortinas and Ochoa."[9]

Years later, after Porfirio Díaz had extended his rule to the border region, Ford wrote in his memoirs: "The action of General García indicated a desire on his part to aid the Confederate troops in suppressing the insurrectionary efforts of Cortina and Ochoa." Since the Mexican government was weak during those years, "General García had to treat such men as Cortina with more indulgence than would be evinced now." One can only imagine García's difficult position. Most Mexicans sided with Cortina against the Anglo-Americans, so any action against the guerrilla leader would alienate them. Failure to pursue Cortina, however, would risk provoking war with Texas at a time when Mexico was struggling with profound internal conflicts.[10]

Lieutenant Colonel John R. Baylor was another Confederate officer who sought to enlist Mexican cooperation. Baylor was a Kentuckian charged with defending a string of forts on the Texas frontier. Described by Jerry Thompson as a "man of considerable vigor and magnetism," Baylor had as one of his life's obsessions to combat the Indians. He had fought them for many years and had "even edited an anti-Indian newspaper, the *White Man*."[11] His obsession was energized by an increase in Indian raids due to the unsettled conditions brought about by the Civil War. In June 1861, he wrote to Santiago Vidaurri from Fort Clark, proposing a joint effort in combating Lipan Apache raiders. Baylor stressed "the importance of maintaining friendly relations" between two peoples who shared a common border and growing commercial ties. He argued that this comity was being threatened by Indian raiders because of the "amount of property destroyed . . . [and] the inhuman and indiscriminate butchering of helpless women and children in both Texas & Mexico."[12]

Baylor stated that by "uniting our forces, they will increase twofold and impede the Indians from seeking refuge in one of the two countries after committing their depredations in the other." Though recognizing that the proposal to join the troops of the two nations "may seem strange and rare," he hoped Vidaurri would be persuaded of its merits.[13] Vidaurri responded that Baylor should direct his proposal to the national government, which was responsible for border security. This was an evasion that the caudillo used when he wanted to avoid doing something that might weaken his regional power. He had already warned the national government not to send the army to the border to combat Indians, a role he had arrogated to himself as a justification for retaining the revenues from the customhouses. If he refused to join his forces to those of Mexico's national government, it is not likely that he would have accepted uniting them with a foreign power. Though he collaborated with the Texans in many ways, Vidaurri politely rejected Baylor's suggestion of a binational military force.[14]

Without question, the Confederate officer on the border who was most assiduous in cultivating friendly relations with Mexicans was Hamilton P. Bee. His efforts to work together with leaders south of the border in the achievement of common goals were matched only by those of José Agustín Quintero. Bee had an easy manner with Mexicans, a characteristic that would serve him well during the many years he spent in Coahuila after the Civil War. However, in dealing with them his main attribute was common sense. As Confederate commander at Brownsville, he decided not to enforce conscription because it "would drive Mexican Texans across the border and convert them into enemies of the Confederacy."[15] He was also preoccupied with cultivating a positive image of Confederate forces among the Mexicans. After the Union occupation of Brownsville

Bee learned that Governor Ruiz of Tamaulipas had accused him of setting fire to the city during the Confederate evacuation and of ordering his soldiers to shoot anyone trying to put out the fire. Bee hastily sent a letter to Vidaurri proclaiming his innocence and giving this version of events: "I fired the buildings of the garrison, and burned such cotton as could not be saved, to prevent their use and appropriation by the enemies of my country, and in obedience to superior orders." He reiterated that the accusation that his soldiers fired on those trying to put out the fire was "horrible" and that he was "incapable of such conduct." He asked Vidaurri to insert his version in the official newspaper of Nuevo León y Coahuila for broader dissemination.[16]

CARVAJAL CONTINUES TO AGITATE THE BORDER REGION

Bee assumed his post as commander of the Western District of Texas in charge of defending the Rio Grande in April 1862. The circumstances surrounding his appointment reveal the extent to which Confederate authorities relied on Santiago Vidaurri and other Mexican leaders to maintain the peace and order that was essential to commerce in the border region. Bee's arrival at Brownsville was preceded by months of political turmoil and military clashes among rival groups in Tamaulipas. Two of these factions, the *rojos* and the *crinolinos*, disputed the governorship and fought for control of Matamoros. José María Carvajal was at the center of this dispute and, at the head of the rojos, led the attack on Matamoros in November 1861. General Guadalupe García sided with the crinolinos and defended the city. The siege lasted weeks and extended into 1862.[17]

A reporter from the *Brownsville Flag* paid visits to the two contending generals. He described Carvajal as "a medium sized, heavily built man." The rojo leader "is a very intelligent gentleman, and the fact that he is poor argues that he is honest. He speaks English 'like a book,' and claims to be a man of modern and progressive principles. He was almost unattended at the time of our visit and was too democratic to need a guard." Carvajal spoke of his attachment to Americans and their principles. His children were "now being educated in the same Virginia college where he himself received instruction." Carvajal declared that his intention to take Matamoros was unwavering and he was certain he would succeed.[18] Also convinced of success was García, who impressed the reporter as "an agreeable gentleman and a most popular officer." Behind "entrenchments almost impregnable to assault," García's men "manifest an earnest disposition to fight until the bitter end."[19]

After fierce fighting, the military commander at Brownsville, Lieutenant Colonel Augustus Buchel, brokered a truce so that the beleaguered civilian population could flee to safety and save as much of their property as possible. The *Flag* reported that as a result, "every nook and corner of Brownsville is filled with the poor and desolate people who have been driven from their homes in Matamoros." They left behind a scene of desolation; the "lately flourishing city now looks like a graveyard." One foreigner who had come to Matamoros in the 1820s and had prospered in commerce and land speculation was killed "defending his store." This is how Juan Cameron, the Scotsman who had escaped a Mexican prison with Ben Milam in 1835 on their way to fight for Texas independence met his end. Besides Cameron, there were forty or fifty killed on each side and dozens injured.[20]

As the battle continued, other actors from the larger stage were drawn in. Sensing that the rebellion in Tamaulipas was weakening the northern frontier at a moment when three European nations were threatening Mexican ports, President Benito Juárez appointed Santiago Vidaurri as military commander of the state in January 1862. Although loath to give the northern caudillo a greater power base, Juárez had little choice. Vidaurri was the only leader with a regional military force sufficient to forge peace in the region. Vidaurri sent his principal military officer, General Julián Quiroga, to Matamoros with about eight hundred troops to quell the violence. According to one source, they "were received by the people with great friendship and enthusiasm." An observer wrote that commerce was being restored. In early March "an immense train of carts came down from Monterey, and the river bank seemed to be lined with the articles which the war had pent up in the interior, and which took advantage of the first lull on land to make their way towards the sea."[21]

Even before the arrival of Vidaurri's troops, the battle for Matamoros had been winding down, as Carvajal came to the realization that he could not take the city. He made his most violent attack on February 24 and was defeated. The crinolinos were in control, but the conflict now evolved into a bitter struggle between Carvajal and Vidaurri, which was complicated by the fact that the rojo leader was carrying out his operations from Texas soil and relying on his friend Rip Ford for support. Confederate authorities, who needed Vidaurri's support, were not pleased.[22]

The Nuevo León governor began to pressure Confederate authorities to put a stop to Carvajal. While Quintero personally traveled to the border in March 1862 to try to resolve the problem, Vidaurri was writing angry letters to the governor of Texas and to General John B. Magruder, commander of the District of Texas. Throughout March and April, Quintero worked to disarm Carvajal in order to pacify Vidaurri, but his task was made difficult by Ford's intransigence. At one point Quintero threatened to resign over the issue. Progress was finally achieved when the military commander of San Antonio, General Henry E. McCulloch (brother of Ben McCulloch), ordered Ford to confiscate Carvajal's arms and "disperse all the parties of armed Mexicans found on the Texas side of the Rio Grande." McCulloch sent a copy of the order to Vidaurri. He then decided to remove Ford from command of the forces on the Rio Grande, which is when Hamilton P. Bee entered the picture. On April 25, 1862, McCulloch chose Bee, a "man of considerable tact and knowledge of Mexican character" because maintaining harmonious relations with Mexican leaders was crucial to ensure the flow of commerce.[23]

One of the first persons Bee informed of his appointment was Vidaurri, with whom he had corresponded previously. He wrote to the Nuevo León governor of his president's "great desire to maintain the friendly relations which ought to exist between the Government of the Confederacy and that . . . [over] which you so ably and generously preside." Reminding Vidaurri that as a resident of Laredo for many years he knew the border region well, Bee offered to combat those fugitives from Mexico who used Texas to perpetrate attacks on Mexico. He assured Vidaurri that those fugitives "shall not be allowed to desecrate our soil by using it for purposes of rendezvous and attack on you." He wrote that Santos Benavides had conveyed Vidaurri's views to him and he offered to work together to "facilitate and encourage the commercial relations now growing up between the States of your Government and Texas. It will prove of great benefit to us and make your people rich. It will . . . cement and make forever firm two peoples who can be so useful to each other."[24]

Quintero also applied his diplomatic skills, but Vidaurri was adamant that Carvajal be arrested and extradited. He wrote to Quintero: "I do not doubt your good faith and that of the citizens of Texas. I consider them all my good friends, who desire to preserve friendly relations with Mexico." Because Carvajal and his men continued mounting raids, however, Vidaurri insisted that the only means to maintain harmonious relations was by "apprehending and delivering those criminals; it is the only way to reestablish order, peace and tranquility."[25]

By May 1862, matters had improved considerably. Vidaurri had delegated the role of military commander of Tamaulipas to Ignacio Comonfort, a former president of Mexico who had had a falling-out with Benito Juárez. Comonfort used his considerable tact to pacify the warring factions in Tamaulipas. Simultaneously, Santos Benavides reported to Vidaurri that he had just returned from

Santiago Vidaurri was the archetype of the nineteenth-century Mexican regional strongman, or caudillo. He established hegemony over much of Northeast Mexico for almost a decade between 1855 and 1864. He had many friends in Texas, including Sam Houston. After he lost an epic struggle against Mexican president Benito Juárez, Vidaurri found sanctuary and friends in Texas. LC-USZ62–22170, Library of Congress.

Carvajal's ranch, where he had dispersed a force of about two hundred men who were in the rojo leader's camp. Many of them fled across the river into Mexico. Soon thereafter Carvajal abandoned the border region and joined Juárez's forces in fighting the French invaders, but he was bitter. Quintero wrote that Carvajal had tried to persuade the Confederacy to help him take Matamoros, a proposal that the Confederate agent said "would make even the dead laugh." Carvajal stalked away, stating that the Confederacy "had lost its best friend."[26]

MEXICANS FOR THE CONFEDERACY

The Mexican-Confederate collaborative efforts in combating Cortina and Carvajal were important, but they were mere sideshows to the two main events, the wars between the North and South in Texas and between republicans and imperialists in northern Mexico. These conflicts incited cooperative violence on a much larger scale, as some four thousand Mexicans and a like number of Americans crossed the border to participate. I will cover the Civil War first, in order to explain how Mexicans of the border region responded to the war and how some of them decided to fight for one or the other of the warring factions.

According to Jerry Thompson, who has covered this ground more exhaustively than anyone else, some three thousand Mexicans joined the Confederate army and another thousand fought for the Union. However, the U.S. Civil War did not stir passions among the Mexicans. Secession was an Anglo affair. The secession convention of January 28, 1861, attracted only white delegates. When a conscription law was passed in April 1862, many Mexicans fled across the river. Conscription agents fanned out all over South Texas with varying degrees of success. I. W. Engledow visited the settlements between Corpus Christi and the Rio Grande, where many of the people responded that they were Mexican citizens and thus exempt from conscription. He wrote, "I was perfectly astonished to find such a small number of American citizens—the history of past elections being fresh in my memory."[27]

Although the original law exempted workers engaged in freighting, conscription agents were enrolling them too, so General Magruder intervened to avoid paralyzing commerce. Hamilton P. Bee's position with respect to conscription was noted earlier. He "sought other means of enlisting the services and sympathies of these people, who are useful to us and would be dangerous against us." He sought "to protect them in their rights and immunities as citizens and thereby attach them to our cause."[28]

Despite many Texas Mexicans' indifference to or rejection of the war, an important number of them participated in the Confederate army or the local militias. Some got a taste of the larger world by joining units that fought in Virginia and other faraway places. At the very beginning of the war, in March 1861, Clemente Bustillo organized a company of ninety-three of his Mexican neighbors in San Antonio. Philip N. Luckett's regiment included a company composed entirely of Mexicans, commanded by F. J. Parker. Many Mexicans preferred to enlist in local militia units in order to stay close to home. Most counties of South Texas had militia units led by Anglos with a Mexican presence.[29]

The participants in these army and militia units were not necessarily Mexican Texans; many were Mexicans who happened to be in Texas, which indicates the steady migration of the previous years. F. J. Parker's company, for example, had sixty-two members. Of these "only three had been born in Texas." Most were from Mexico, some from states as far away as Jalisco and Puebla. Many did not speak English and did not always understand orders and regulations; thus, desertions were high. Another cause of desertions was the racism of many Anglos, who continued to commit atrocities against peaceful Mexicans. Why should they fight, Mexicans reasoned, for a cause that did not recognize their basic human rights? Still others deserted because they had entered Confederate service expecting a monthly wage, and when it was not paid, they felt justified in leaving, as they would with any other job.[30]

One Confederate unit that was led and manned by Mexican Texans stands out: the Thirty-Third Texas Cavalry commanded by Santos Benavides, which initially formed part of Colonel James Duff's Regiment. After the Second Cortina War ended in July 1861, Benavides was asked to enlist his men into the Confederate army and help defend the Rio Grande region. However, his men refused to enlist for three years, a condition established by the high command at Houston. The Texas government sent Charles Grimus Thorkelin de Løvenskiold, a Danish American lawyer from Corpus Christi, to persuade Benavides and his men to enlist. After several weeks of observations he wrote to Benavides: "I have passed several weeks amidst your company, and sobriety, good behavior, and excellent discipline characterize them at all times and in all places."[31] Løvenskiold successfully lobbied military and political leaders to grant an exception and allow the Laredoans to sign up for only one year. Finally, eighty men were persuaded to enlist in Santos Benavides's company and a few months later, his brother Refugio enlisted another eighty-five.[32]

Santos Benavides won steady promotions, reaching the rank of colonel, the highest-ranking Mexican in the Confederate army. Union leaders were prepared to offer him the rank of general to serve their cause, but his inclination was always toward the Confederacy. He had no problem with slavery and had even participated in the pursuit of runaway slaves. Thompson contrasts the leadership styles of Benavides and Cortina. The former "represented the more aristocratic Tejanos, or those who had been able to retain much of their land and wealth in the years following the Treaty of Guadalupe-Hidalgo." Cortina, on the other hand, "had become a leader to the poor vaqueros, campesinos, and the generally illiterate persons of Mexican descent on both sides of the Rio Grande, who had never known anything but poverty, exploitation and suppression."[33] Benavides had the esteem of other leaders, such as Rip Ford and Hamilton P. Bee. He and Bee had become close friends during the 1850s when they fought together against the Indians in Laredo. "Mutual respect between the two officers," writes Thompson, "added greatly to the effectiveness of the Confederacy on the Rio Grande during the early stages of the war. Bee's daughter, Lamar, named for his Mexican War commander, was to marry Cristobal Benavides in 1867."[34]

Mexicans for the Union

While Confederate leaders were conscripting and recruiting Mexicans, strong-willed men who favored the Union used Matamoros as a recruiting center to bring Mexicans into their cause. Edmund J. Davis, Leonard Pierce Jr., and John L. Haynes were the three most prominent recruiters. Davis was described as a "tall, slender, graceful sort of man, measuring six feet two and a half inches, of fair complexion." He had been born in Florida, was a cadet at West Point, and served as a volunteer in the U.S.-Mexican War.[35] Davis settled in Texas in 1848, became a lawyer, and served on the Laredo City Council, then as district attorney for a region that included Laredo, Corpus Christi, and Brownsville. He knew Santos Benavides and Hamilton Bee well, and even invited the former to join the Union. Pierce was a "fiery thirty-four-year-old . . . [who] had spent one year in Chihuahua where he had learned to speak Spanish, before moving to Texas in 1857." As U.S. consul in Matamoros, he collaborated with Kimmey, his fellow consul in Monterrey, in channeling refugee Texans into Union ranks. John L. Haynes, a native of Virginia, had served as a newspaper editor in Mississippi and as an officer in the U.S.-Mexican War. He lived for a time in Camargo, Tamaulipas, and became a prosperous merchant at Rio Grande City. He also served in the Texas legislature in the late 1850s. He spoke Spanish fluently, which facilitated his recruiting efforts.[36] Haynes relied on some of his Mexican contacts, such as the locally prominent Antonio Abad Díaz, to help him recruit.[37]

One man who needed no encouragement to fight for the Union was Octaviano Zapata, a close ally of Cortina's, who claimed he had been harassed by Confederates. Owner of a small ranch near Carrizo, he had an unsavory reputation as a "notorious thief and assassin." Union authorities encouraged Zapata to enlist men on both sides of the river. "By 1862," writes Thompson, "Zapata had recruited between sixty and eighty men in and around Guerrero." Throughout that year Zapata continued his recruitment while carrying out raids on Confederate targets in Texas. He traveled to New Orleans in early 1863, where the Union army provided him with arms.[38] He told a friend that he had been made a colonel in the Union army and was asked to "make invitations to all those persons who wished to join me in defending that just and sacred cause." Those who accepted would be provided a uniform, provisions, and a wage of thirteen dollars a month.

They would also have "a free hand with all Confederate interests [property] and after the war will be compensated with 50 acres of land for single men and 150 for married men besides one hundred pesos for each soldier." Many of the recruits were poor peons or *labradores* who accepted because of the material inducements. Others also saw it as an opportunity to get revenge on Texans who had wronged them.[39]

Beginning in late 1862, Zapata carried out his mission to attack Confederate "interests" with zeal. Cheered on by U.S. Consul Pierce, Zapata attacked a Confederate convoy in December. In the same month "a train of three wagons en route from Fort Brown to Ringgold Barracks, escorted by five Confederate soldiers, was attacked at Rancho Soledad near Las Cuevas, and all but one of the Confederate escorts were killed." These raids, combined with the depredations committed by Anglo refugees supported by Kimmey and Pierce, tried Bee's patience. He complained to Governor Albino López of Tamaulipas that action must be taken to stop the raids.[40]

This is when Quintero entered the picture at Bee's invitation. Bee and Quintero traveled to Matamoros to help resolve the issue with the Tamaulipas governor. The three men held a series of meetings and reached a wide-ranging agreement in February 1863. Henceforth, persons crossing to either side of the river would require a passport; permits would be needed in order to move cattle; criminals could be pursued beyond the river upon informing the authorities of the other side; criminals would be extradited; and troublesome Texas refugees would be relocated by the Mexican authorities to at least thirty leagues from the border. A Confederate newspaper considered this a "very important treaty [*sic*]" because it would help "to prevent raids into Texas, by allowing thieves, murderers, etc., to be pursued into Mexico and brought back to be dealt with according to their crimes." It was virtually impossible to enforce all these provisions and the agreement did not function perfectly, but it reflected the willingness of leaders on both sides to collaborate.[41]

An embarrassing incident happened shortly after the agreement was signed. In the early-morning hours of March 15, 1863, a group of Confederates crossed near the mouth of the river and carried off Edmund J. Davis, William Montgomery, and several others who had been active in recruiting Texan refugees and Mexican nationals. Governor López was outraged at the flagrant violation of Mexican sovereignty and demanded the immediate return of the prisoners. Bee, who claimed to have had no part in the incident, "had little choice but to surrender the prisoners when it was demanded of him . . . , but it was too late for Montgomery. He had already been hanged. Feeling ran high in Matamoros against the Confederacy, but the quick return of the living prisoners quieted the city." One historian writes that "it must have been difficult for a Confederate commander to give up such a prisoner as Davis, no matter what the circumstances of his capture." However, "Bee's action was fully supported by his superiors. Mexican neutrality could not be traded for E. J. Davis."[42]

Throughout the spring and summer of 1863, Octaviano Zapata continued to make raids into Texas, but he made a mistake when he got too close to Santos Benavides's territory. Benavides learned of the location of Zapata's band from the alcalde of Guerrero. He summoned forty-two men from his brother Cristóbal's company and thirty-seven more from Thomas Rabb's company and crossed the Rio Grande. His multiethnic force located Zapata's camp near Mier on the morning of September 2, 1863, and a fight ensued. When the smoke cleared, Zapata and nine of his men were dead and the rest had fled through the chaparral. With great pleasure Bee reported the battle to Confederate authorities. The Confederacy, he wrote "shall be no more troubled with this emissary of the Lincoln Government, who has for so long disturbed the peace of this frontier, and at one time actually crossed the Rio Grande into Texas with the flag of the United States." Bee suggested that the military command in Houston "recognize officially the distinguished services of Major Benavides, and the firm, unyielding support which the companies of Laredo, commanded by Captains Refugio and Christobal Benavides (all Mexicans), have ever given to our cause." He was not reticent about adding a feather to his own cap, stating that Zapata's defeat "was the legitimate result of my labors here, which gave the right of our troops to cross into Mexico for just such purposes."[43] This episode leaves the enduring image of a Mexican crossing the border into Texas waving a flag of the United States, a reflection of the complexity of the border in the 1860s.

After the Union occupation of Brownsville on November 2, 1863, recruiting accelerated, with E. J. Davis and John Haynes taking the initiative to integrate more Mexicans into their ranks. By February 1864, Davis reported that his First Texas Cavalry had 943 men, 443 of them Mexicans. Haynes, now a colonel, set out to organize the Second Texas Cavalry, made up entirely of Mexicans. By December 26, he "had about three hundred men in his regiment."[44] Thompson writes that "some of the first recruits to join the regiment were men who had either fought with Juan N. Cortina in 1859–60 or were in sympathy with the elusive 'Cheno.'" It is another of the many ironies of border history that "the United States government was now recruiting men which the army had fought four years earlier."[45] Cortina formalized his alliance with the Union when General John A. McClernand took command of Union forces on the Rio Grande in April 1864. The wily guerrilla leader proclaimed war against the Confederates and was rewarded by McClernand with "an elegantly engraved sword" and, more importantly, "ten artillery pieces in a formal ceremony on Plaza Hidalgo in Matamoros."[46]

Union recruiters had no qualms about accepting in their ranks individuals who had deserted from Confederate service. Adrián J. Vidal is a good example. He was born in Monterrey in 1840, the son of Luis Vidal and Petra Vela. After his father's death he spent his boyhood years in Mier until his mother married Mifflin Kenedy and moved to Brownsville in 1852. Thompson writes that "Vidal learned to pilot steamboats on the Rio Grande with his stepfather but gained a reputation as a habitual gambler and drunkard." At age twenty-one the advent of the Civil War gave him an opportunity to make something of his life. He enlisted in the Confederate army and rose through the ranks to become the captain of a militia company. He won recognition for valor, but became disillusioned and led his men to mutiny in October 1863, just days before the Union invasion of Brownsville.[47]

Vidal's exit from the Confederacy was violent. He was accused of killing several persons in cold blood and threatening to attack Brownsville, though he desisted when the town was reinforced. After the Federal army occupied Brownsville on November 2, Vidal wasted no time, formally joining their ranks on November 10. He took many of his men with him and began to recruit more all along the river. Referring to the surge of Union recruitment, Confederate quartermaster Charles Russell wrote bitterly: "They are recruiting among the Mexicans, and have succeeded in raising about 400 under the traitor Vidal."[48] A reporter on a visit to the Rio Grande wrote, "The Mexican towns of Camargo, Mier, Guerrero, and Laredo were almost deserted by the male population, they having crossed the river and organized in bands for the purpose of robbing and murdering all Confederates."[49]

Vidal maintained the rank of captain, leading a company of partisan rangers that numbered eighty-nine men. His knowledge of the region and the people was valuable to the Union, but his service was brief. He experienced many of the same problems he had faced while serving the Confederacy, including discrimination and a language barrier that was made more onerous because of "his inability to keep the records required of a company commander."[50] In May 1864 he asked to be discharged but did not wait around for the answer; he simply crossed the border with most of his men. There he joined another army: the republicans at war with the imperialists. According to Jerry Thompson, he "quickly gained a reputation for summarily executing captives." When captured, he met the same fate, despite his stepfather's efforts to save him. "Kenedy brought his body back to Brownsville for burial."[51]

Most of the Mexican enlistees in the Union army, like those of F. J. Parker's Confederate company, were born in Mexico. Only about 25 percent were originally from Texas, while about 60 percent came from the border states of Tamaulipas, Nuevo León, and Coahuila.[52] Another similarity with their Confederate counterparts is that most were from the lower class and were drawn to service for economic reasons. Still another parallel was the high rate of desertions and the lower-than-expected rate of enlistments. E. J. Davis recognized that "the bounty promised them has not been paid, nor have they received any of their monthly pay, and . . . there is among them an impression that they have been badly treated." Davis believed that internal conflicts in Mexico were siphoning off some of the possible recruits, but he emphasized the deficiencies of Union military administration, which failed to provide them with decent clothes and shoes. He also believed that cultural differences contributed to the problem: "They soon become dissatisfied with our manner of making payments, and being of Indian blood and nature, the discipline and restraint of this camp, and the value of their horses, arms, and equipments proving too much of a temptation, they take an opportunity to desert and carry them into Mexico."[53]

Davis failed to mention the racism that many Mexicans found to be common among Union officials. Thompson cites the difficulty that Colonel John Haynes had in getting his Second Regiment paid. The paymaster, Benjamin F. McIntyre, refused to pay the new recruits, stating that they were "dishonest, cowardly, and treacherous and only bide their time to make good their escape."[54] The compensation withheld "included the men's bounty money which Haynes had used to lure men into the regiment." Haynes wrote to Davis of the "many difficulties to contend with in the organization of [his] command." Almost three hundred, or about 32 percent, of Haynes's regiment deserted by war's end.[55]

MEXICANS DEFEND LAREDO AND THE CONFEDERACY

The efforts of Davis, Haynes, and the Union strategists were directed to the same goal pursued by M. M. Kimmey: to shut down the commerce that was vital to the Confederacy. That is why they had invaded Brownsville and why they were determined to march upriver to seal off the frontier.[56] Union troops, consisting of Anglo, black, and Mexican soldiers, marched westward, taking the towns of Rio Grande City and Roma. Their next target was Laredo. Santos Benavides was aware of the danger and of his responsibility to defend the town and its surroundings. He could count on only a limited force of about seventy men, so he needed reinforcements. Henry Clay Davis, a fervent Confederate supporter, traveled from Laredo to San Antonio to seek support for Benavides. He reported that of the two thousand Union soldiers in Brownsville, "four hundred regular troops, three hundred of whom are negroes, have been sent up the river to take possession of the country." Benavides, wrote Davis, "should be promptly sustained. He has proved himself a true patriot, and a brave, skillful and successful officer. With a reasonable force . . . he can drive the enemy into Brownsville, and probably into the Gulf."[57]

Benavides himself made a passionate appeal for help in a letter that was published in Austin and Houston, key centers of the Anglo-Texan Confederacy. That letter revealed much about his personality and his prejudices: "This frontier is now invaded, the enemy have advanced and taken the line of the Rio Grande, as far as Roma. They have armed all the Mexican thieves on both sides of the Rio Grande. . . . The chief force of the enemy consists of niggers, renegades and Mexican banditti." He informed his Anglo-Texan readers that he had 150 soldiers, and with another 350 he could drive the enemy back to Brownsville. He argued that supporting him was a matter of patriotism and pragmatism: "I appeal to every man on the frontier, old and young, to come to the protection of his country. If you stay at home, and my small force be unable to check the advances of the enemy, you will either be murdered by the banditti, or be ruled over by niggers and renegades."[58]

What kind of man was this to remind Anglos of their duty? Other letters reveal additional facets of his character. He was generous and loyal to friends, but unsympathetic and ruthless with enemies. When he learned from his brother-in-law, John Z. Leyendecker, that three assassins were thought to be in the region, he instructed him "to keep a sharp lookout on all persons passing from the interior of the State into Mexico, and to arrest all who are not known as good men travelling on legitimate business. If by good fortune you should get hold of either one of the three murderers . . . you will hang them immediately." This directive was also applicable to lesser crimes. "Should you at any time take prisoner any thief or murderer, no matter of what nation, hang him."[59]

As a resident of a city and member of a family that had been Mexican, but was now American, Benavides harbored mixed loyalties. He was proud of his

Santos Benavides was a central figure in the history of Laredo and the border region. A descendant of the founder of Laredo, Benavides became a rancher, merchant, Indian fighter, and politician. As the highest-ranking Mexican in the Confederate army, he led the defense of Laredo against Union forces in 1864. Benavides was mayor of Laredo and served in the Texas legislature. His life reflects the lives of many Mexicans of the border region who identified as Texans while valuing their Mexican heritage. No. 070-0381, UTSA Special Collections.

Mexican heritage and was always at pains to show that Mexicans were as good as Anglos, while remaining faithful to his new American identity. These attitudes are revealed in a letter he addressed to Santiago Vidaurri. Responding to a query from the Nuevo León governor about his availability to fight against the French invasion if required, Benavides informed Vidaurri that he and his company had been called to serve the Confederacy and were fully committed to that enterprise.

> For that reason I am unable to give you my personal help on this occasion as it would be most gratifying for me to die at your side in the field of battle, but you can be sure that although these difficulties burden me at this moment, I will not abstain from giving you

all of my help in all that is possible, that is, in all that will not bring
hardship to the country to which I belong.

My small fortune will always be at your disposal. It is impossible
for me to leave the country in the present circumstances without
bringing dishonor to our race. I take pride in being Mexican and I
wish to prove to all the world that Mexicans are loyal wherever they
are found and have the same worth as the best men of any nation.[60]

Vidaurri was sincerely touched by these sentiments, which revealed "a true
and sincere friend, a man of honor, and a commendable patriot." He praised
Benavides for being true to his responsibilities: "Your behavior does honor to
you and I am proud to have your friendship." The bond between these two men
was evidenced in December 1863, when in the face of a possible Union attack,
Benavides sent his family to the protection of Vidaurri in Monterrey.[61]

In March 1864, as the Union force neared Laredo, Benavides marched to the
outskirts to meet the enemy. He left orders for his brother Cristóbal, in charge
of defending the town: "There are five thousand bales of cotton in the plaza. . . .
If the day goes against us fire it . . . so that not a bale of it shall fall into the hands
of the Yankees."[62] The attack came on March 19. A multiethnic Union force
composed of about two hundred soldiers attacked a Confederate force of about
seventy Anglo and Mexican defenders. After three hours of fighting, the Federal
army withdrew, but stayed close to make another charge on the following day.
That charge never came because Benavides received reinforcements during the
night. The Union force retreated back to Carrizo in hopes of mounting a larger
attack later. On March 21, Benavides sent a report of the battle to Rip Ford, who
was camped near the King Ranch. He praised his men and all of the citizens of
Laredo who "rallied gallantly for the defense." He also called on Ford to send
men and arms in anticipation of another attack.[63] When writing of Benavides
and his men, Ford wrote: "With the odds of more than three to one they drove
off the Unionists, without cotton, without plunder, and without success."[64]

Ford praised the military exploits of Benavides and his men, "whose bravery
and noble bearing on this occasion, caused victory to perch on the banners of
Texas, and who hurled from their firesides an enemy famed for his achievements
by land and by sea."[65] Jerry Thompson, whose knowledge of Texas-Mexican
border history is unsurpassed, writes that the war on the Rio Grande would have
been much different if the Laredo colonel had sided with the Union: "Benavides,
especially in late 1863 and early 1864, was the Confederacy on the Rio Grande, and

without the loyalty of that element of the Mexican-Texan population, which [he] represented, the entire southwestern flank of the Confederacy might have been exposed." For this reason, Benavides and his Thirty-Third Cavalry "performed a record of border defense unprecedented in Texas history."[66]

Despite this victory, Benavides knew that the danger had not passed. Union strategists devised a plan to cross Northeast Mexico to reach Laredo without obstruction. The plan seemed viable because on April 3, Juárez entered Monterrey while a fleeing Vidaurri was on his way to sanctuary at Benavides's home in Laredo. Another Union mission, which included the bilingual John Haynes, went to Juárez requesting passage through Mexican territory. Ford had reached Laredo when he received this news and promptly wrote to General Magruder. Authorization, he stated, "would almost be tantamount to a declaration of war on the part of the Juárez government against the Confederate States." Juárez was not a man to act recklessly. Although he made no secret of his preference for the Union, he was mired in his own predicaments, so he was not about to alienate either of the two warring parties and diplomatically refused to grant authorization to the Union agents.[67]

As it turned out, Laredo and the upper Rio Grande were no longer in danger. For strategic reasons Lincoln's government transferred most of its troops to Louisiana and began to pull back its remaining forces to the lower Rio Grande Valley. General Francis J. Herron, in command of Brownsville, was not optimistic about defending the city. He reported that Ford had about 1,800 men and was receiving reinforcements. He also declared, "I am sorry to state that the Mexicans on this side of the river are co-operating heartily with Ford. Two Mexican officers are traveling with him. They undoubtedly intend attacking this place shortly."[68] Herron was probably referring to Cristóbal and Refugio Benavides, who were with Ford's forces, preparing to lay siege to the city. Several skirmishes and a minor battle occurred on the periphery of Brownsville during the last days of July, which ended unfavorably for Union forces, and they evacuated the city by the thirtieth of the month. Ford and his troops reoccupied the town while the Union was forced back to Brazos de Santiago, where its troops—some fifteen hundred in number—maintained a tenuous toehold until the end of the war.[69]

WAR COMES TO THE NORTHEAST

While these events were transpiring, French troops were advancing by land and sea toward the border region. The focus of conflict now shifted to Northeast Mexico. The French advance had begun when Napoleon's troops returned to

Puebla one year after their stunning defeat at the battle of Cinco de Mayo in 1862. This time the result was very different. Ignacio Zaragoza Seguín, a native of La Bahía, Texas, and one of Vidaurri's best generals, who had defeated the French in the earlier battle, was no longer present, having lost a different battle—to typhoid fever. The French commander François Achille Bazaine defeated the Mexican army at Puebla on May 17, 1863, and marched toward Mexico City, which Benito Juárez and his government abandoned at the end of May. French troops and Mexican soldiers led by conservative generals such as Miguel Miramón, Leonardo Márquez, and Tomás Mejía formed an imperialist army that set out in pursuit of Juárez and sought to conquer Mexico's vast territory. The beleaguered president marched first to Querétaro, then to San Luis Potosí, before arriving at Saltillo in January 1864. His government, according to one historian, resembled more "a flying squadron than a governing body." After a short but bitter struggle with Vidaurri, Juárez decreed the separation of Nuevo León y Coahuila and occupied Monterrey in April. However, he was forced to flee to Chihuahua in August as the imperialists began their invasion of Nuevo León and Tamaulipas.[70]

During his brief stay in Monterrey, Juárez became acquainted with the Texas-Mexico border region. His government received a badly needed injection of cash from the customhouses on the Rio Grande. His uncompromising struggle to defend Mexico's sovereignty stiffened the backbone of many norteños. His imperturbable serenity in the face of calamity and his modesty and sobriety won many adherents to his cause. Vice-Consul M. M. Kimmey, who was attuned to the pulse of the region, wrote that Vidaurri was popular, but when he turned his back on Juárez, his power eroded and most people abandoned him.[71] Juárez was surrounded by danger however. Vidaurri still had supporters in the region, waiting for word from their exiled leader to take up arms. The president looked on in dismay as General Tomás Mejía took San Luis Potosí and prepared to march toward Saltillo and Monterrey. In mid-April he was discouraged by news from Tamaulipas, where a force led by Carvajal, which included "a large number of Americans, was routed by [Charles] Du Pin and thrown back across the Río Pánuco." It did not help that Cortina and Carvajal, his two leading military men in Tamaulipas, were engaged in a bitter struggle for power in the state.[72]

While in Monterrey, Juárez was keenly aware of events in the United States. Kimmey reported that the president and his cabinet read all the U.S. newspapers and were concerned about the fate of the Union in the Civil War. It was clear that Juárez had cast his lot with the North in its struggle against the South. Kimmey stated that most of the Mexican people felt the same way. In late April, Juárez was heartened by news from Washington. His young, brilliant ambassador to Washington, Matías Romero, informed him that the House of Representatives had passed a resolution strongly opposing "the establishment of monarchical governments, backed by European powers, on the ruins of republican ones." Juárez then "dispatched an entire team of secret agents to the United States to secure financial and military aid and to begin recruiting American soldiers of fortune."[73]

While Juárez was looking north, toward the United States, events in the center of Mexico would soon impact the border region. Maximilian landed at Veracruz on May 28, 1864, and entered Mexico City on June 12. The Empire immediately sought to extend its authority to the entire country, and the drive to occupy the Northeast intensified. With the imperialist general Tomás Mejía closing in on Monterrey, Juárez was forced to abandon the city on August 15. One week later French troops under Admiral A. Bosse were landing at Bagdad. Attention was directed toward Matamoros, which had fallen to Cortina in January. Accepting the political reality of Tamaulipas, Juárez had made Cortina a general and appointed him governor and military commander of the state on March 2, 1864. His decision was facilitated by the fact that Cortina was sending money from the customhouse to the federal government.[74]

Between the French occupation of Bagdad on August 22 and the arrival of Mejía in Matamoros on September 26, military authorities on both sides of the Rio Grande scrambled to sort out the new reality. The Union commander at Brazos Island, Henry M. Day, and the Confederate commander at Brownsville, Rip Ford, both sent representatives to see A. Veron, the head of French forces at Bagdad. Veron was careful to maintain a neutral position, but it soon became clear that French preferences were with the South. He assured Ford "that I shall see that all persons and property covered by the flag of your nation [will be] duly respected."[75] Ford also succumbed to realism and sent a diplomatic note to Cortina in Matamoros. He acknowledged that the guerrilla leader turned governor had treated Americans with decency and respect during his occupation of Matamoros. "The immense trade existing between Mexico and the Confederate States was the prevailing reason." Confederate and Union sympathizers shared the same space, but they coexisted peacefully because everyone's focus was on commerce. In his note, Ford stated that he would "do all in my power to render our intercourse officially, commercially, and otherwise, pleasant and mutually advantageous."[76]

The French invasion presented a real dilemma for Cortina, who was now faced with fighting two wars, against the French and against his Confederate enemies. He hatched a fevered plan to join with Union forces to attack Brownsville, but

succeeded only in alienating his own officers. One of those generals was Servando
Canales, who as son of the old federalist leader Antonio Canales had a large
following in Tamaulipas. As the imperialist army neared Matamoros, Canales
and several other military men departed for Brownsville and left Cortina alone to
face the enemy. Under intense pressure and without a practical means of escape,
"Cortina made a decision that would haunt him for the rest of his life. He declared
for the Empire and gave up his hold on Matamoros." Cortina surrendered the
city to Mejía on September 26.[77]

Ford established an immediate rapport with Mejía, whom he described as "an
Indian of rather rugged features who had fought his way up from a low position to
the top of the ladder. He was honest, sincere, and truthful. . . . He was kind and
generous to his friends and was considerate and gentle to his enemies." He was a
capable strategist, fearless in battle, and devoted to Maximilian, Ford continued.[78]
After exchanging visits with Ford, Mejía set out to strengthen the fortifications
around Matamoros and the fortress of Casa Mata. He received valuable assistance
from Confederate Major Felix A. Blucher. The Prussian-born Blucher had served
in the military of his country before coming to Texas, where he participated in
the war for independence in 1836 as well as the U.S.-Mexican War.[79]

The months that followed the takeover of Matamoros were a dark period for
the Northeast and all of Mexico as the Empire reached the height of its power.
The French occupation deepened the political divisions that were already endemic.
Cortina, now serving the imperialists, marched to Guerrero, where Canales, who
was now his bitter enemy, had begun recruiting men to continue the fight. After
a brief battle, Cortina's force routed Canales, intensifying the hatred between
them. After Cortina's submission to the Empire, Juárez appointed José María
Carvajal as provisional governor, but throughout 1865, five different men proclaimed themselves governor, as Tamaulipas sank deeper into political chaos,
"without a visible head to organize a legitimate local government."[80]

In Nuevo León, Vidaurri's followers, under the leadership of Julián Quiroga,
collaborated with French authorities until the caudillo's return from Texas in
September 1864. By that time Vidaurri had lost his regional power. The French
demanded his loyalty but were not about to make the mistake of giving him any
position of authority in the region. Nuevo León was divided between those few
who supported Vidaurri and the French invaders versus the many who either
supported Juárez or waited passively until the outcome became clearer.[81]

Political divisions also afflicted Coahuila and Chihuahua, paralyzing republican efforts to organize an effective resistance against the French. The U.S.

consul in Chihuahua, Reuben Creel, eloquently described the problem. Regional leaders, he wrote, "have interposed themselves between the national Government and the people. They have fostered and developed a State feeling at the expense of national patriotism, and the result of such conduct is being felt in the present lamentable degradation of this Republic." Divisiveness, according to Creel, permits "a few French soldiers [to] run over and occupy so much of the country almost without military opposition."[82]

This, then, was the situation in northern Mexico in the latter part of 1864 and the beginning of 1865, but in the spring of 1865 a ray of hope began to illuminate this dark landscape. Mariano Escobedo, a native of Nuevo León and one of Juárez's best generals, arrived at Nuevo Laredo in March and began to organize the Army of the North. At the same time General Miguel Negrete marched from Chihuahua to Coahuila and took Saltillo without much resistance. In April, Escobedo and Negrete joined forces to attack Monterrey, which was poorly defended. Both cities would soon return to French rule, but the liberals had given notice that they were alive and disposed to take back any region that the imperialists could not adequately defend or occupy. Meanwhile, Cortina escaped the stifling confines of Matamoros and, on April 1, 1865, "reasserted his loyalty to Juárez and the Mexican republic." In the same month, José María Carvajal was on his way to the United States in search of arms for the *juaristas*.[83]

The spring of 1865 also brought news of the Confederate surrender at Appomattox Court House on April 9. During May, Union forces began to move from their refuge at Brazos Santiago toward Brownsville. They were temporarily halted at the battle of Palmito Ranch, the last land battle of the Civil War (which occurred on May 13, more than a month after Appomattox), but finally reached Brownsville on May 29. On the same day, General Philip H. Sheridan arrived at New Orleans to take command of the Military Division of the Southwest, which included Texas. Under his command were about 52,000 mainly black, battle-hardened troops, 30,000 of whom were sent to the Rio Grande to serve under Major General Frederick Steele. Troops were demobilized rather quickly, so that by November most Union soldiers were gone. In 1866, while the War of French Intervention was still raging in Mexico, there were only about 1,500 U.S. soldiers on the Rio Grande. Thus, the thousands of American troops stationed there during the Civil War were no longer around when the fiercest fighting of the Intervention was occurring in Mexico.[84]

Nevertheless, the Union presence was a menace to the imperialists and made itself felt in various ways. To begin with, it gave hope to the republicans. Juárez

knew that the crucial task of procuring men and arms from the United States
would be greatly facilitated by Union control of the Rio Grande. Sheridan toured
the region in the summer of 1865. He shared with his superior, Ulysses S. Grant,
a deep resentment of the French presence and a sense of solidarity with the
Mexican republicans fighting for their freedom. Both generals lobbied for a U.S.
fighting force in northern Mexico. According to one historian, "Grant worked
with American and Mexican leaders to create a private but legal army of recently
discharged veterans to cross the Rio Grande and fight for the Liberals."[85] Grant
wrote to Sheridan: "I would like to see any amount of assistance given to the
Liberals, and if I had my way I would use U.S. forces to give to them the Rio
Grande country as a base to start from; that is, I would clear out the south bank
for them."[86]

The Union occupation of the Rio Grande had other salutary effects on the
republican war effort. It facilitated the recruitment of Union veterans who were
being mustered out of service and enabled men such as Cortina to use U.S.
territory to organize raids against imperialist targets across the border. Cortina
began recruiting men in Brownsville, the city he had attacked six years earlier.
According to Jerry Thompson, "Cortina not only recruited large numbers of
African Americans but also men with experience in the artillery." With U.S.
support, "Cortina began to launch raids against Imperial supply lines from
camps in Texas." French authorities protested vigorously, but they were mostly
unheard or ignored.[87]

The French were dismayed that their Confederate former ally had been
replaced by a new and hostile neighbor. General Philip Sheridan was convinced
of the existence of a Confederate-Imperialist alliance.[88] His principal concern
was that fleeing Confederate soldiers would join up with Maximilian's army, then
after jointly defeating the liberals, would set up a government hostile to the United
States. He wrote of a plan whereby Jefferson Davis would lead fifteen thousand
men to invade Mexico. The plan was thwarted when Davis was captured, but
that did not prevent "numerous bands, squads, and parties, numbering perhaps
3,000 or 4,000 men" from crossing into Mexico.[89]

AMERICAN ARMS AND SOLDIERS IN THE WAR
OF FRENCH INTERVENTION

Whether or not there was a Confederate-Imperialist alliance, many Southern
men did seek to join Maximilian's army. After sinking the Confederate flag in the
waters of the Rio Grande at Eagle Pass, General Joseph Shelby's group passed

into Mexico and into the ranks of the imperialists. It is not known how many rebels signed up with the Empire. Several historians have accepted Sheridan's estimate of two thousand. It is assumed that in the main, "ex-Confederates gravitated to the imperial forces, while northern veterans supported the defenders of the republic of Mexico."[90] There were however exceptions. Rip Ford and some of his men agreed to fight for Juárez under Carvajal's command after being paroled by the magnanimous General Frederick Steele. He expressed his reasoning in his memoir: "While the Confederate war lasted we had been friendly with the imperialists, with the hope of benefiting our cause." After the Civil War the choice was to support Maximilian or a republic. Ford decided "in favor of a government for the people and by the people."[91] Ford's justification expresses with clarity the pragmatism that was the hallmark of the borderlanders, but it is ironic that in his adherence to the army of Juárez, he was now on the same side as his archenemy Cortina.

The Union victory released a strong expression of support for Juárez and his government in the United States, which translated principally into the procurement of arms and men for the juarista cause. The Mexican ambassador in Washington, Matías Romero, was at the center of the drive to mobilize support, meeting with many of the leading U.S. political and military leaders. Juárez sent a team of agents to all corners of his neighbor's territory, from California to New York. Three generals were chosen to lead this team: Plácido Vega, Gaspar Sánchez Ochoa, and José María Carvajal. Vega sent "over 20,000 rifles and a substantial amount of ammunition to Mexico. He also recruited and sent several companies of American volunteers." Carvajal played fast and loose with his commission and was accused of exceeding his orders, but he managed to channel an important quantity of arms and supplies to Mexico.[92]

Prominent military men worked actively in support of Mexico. General Philip Sheridan reported that thirty thousand muskets were sent to the republicans from the arsenal at Baton Rouge. General Lew Wallace received a commission as a major general in the republican army and helped Juárez by "giving legal, financial, and military counsel and recruiting volunteers for duty in Mexico."[93] Wallace also enlisted the help of General Herman Sturm. A native of Germany with training in chemistry and civil engineering, Sturm joined the Indiana state militia at the start of the Civil War, and by 1865 reached the rank of brigadier general, specializing in ordnance. Historian Robert Ryal Miller has documented his contributions, which included over twenty thousand rifles and more than one million cartridges, as well as other provisions. Altogether, Sturm obtained "about two million dollars' worth of military hardware in exchange for the Juárez government's future promise to pay." Miller states that Sturm "was by far the most efficient and productive" of Mexico's agents abroad. "In the history of that period," he writes, "it is difficult to find a similar example of loyalty and friendship to the Mexican republic, especially by a noncitizen of that country." Regrettably, that loyalty was not compensated in what Sturm considered a just manner. He struggled to get paid and was never fully repaid.[94]

Most of the military men who came to the aid of Mexico were driven by more than idealism. They represented business interests that sought to invest in Mexico. Examples are Generals Grant, Schofield, and Wallace, as well as Colonel George Earl Church, a civil engineer who served Rhode Island in the war. After sending from New York "enough munitions and supplies to outfit 7,000 soldiers," Wallace and Church traveled to Chihuahua to confer with Juárez. They "represented business interests in New York which wanted concessions in Mexico for mines, railroads, telegraph lines, and banks."[95] Wallace came away from Chihuahua with great admiration for Juárez as a president. He wrote, "I wish we had as good a one at the head of our government." He was also impressed by the men who surrounded the Mexican leader, stating that his cabinet "was composed of abler men than ours."[96]

American arms played an important role in the republican capability to wage war against the Empire. The participation of U.S. soldiers was less important but not insignificant. Unlike during the earlier War of Reform, Juárez invited the participation of American soldiers. The life of the Republic was on the line. He issued a decree in August 1864 that was published in many major U.S. newspapers. It spelled out the terms for enlisting in the republican army: a monthly salary of 15 pesos for enlisted men and attractive rates for officers ranging from 45 pesos for lieutenants to 500 pesos for generals. These salaries were comparable to those paid by the Union army. In addition to their pay, volunteers would receive a grant of land. These generous conditions attracted many men, especially ones seeking employment after the end of the Civil War.[97] As with Confederate veterans who fought for the Empire, the number of Union soldiers who enlisted in republican ranks is not known for certain. Matías Romero, who was best informed of all the disparate recruitment efforts, calculated the number at three thousand.[98]

It would be interesting to focus on some of the individuals among the American participants in the French Intervention, but information is scarce. One of these Americans was Colonel George M. Green. He was sent to California to "purchase and ship munitions of war; and, if possible, to enlist in the Mexican service a sufficient number of American file-officers to command a brigade of Mexican troops." He returned to Mexico "accompanied by twenty-seven American officers, all of whom had served in the Union army during the War of the Rebellion."[99] Green participated at Querétaro and wrote to his brother about the siege: "My small command, with sixty American officers, which composes the Legion of Honor, captured the Carlotta Regiment of Cavalry, 500 strong, with 80 officers, among them several chiefs."[100]

Lieutenant Colonel J. J. Fisher and Captain Joseph Hopper-Clearwater also served the republicans. Fisher, who translated for President Juárez, was unusual in that he first enlisted in the republican army and later defended the Confederacy. Clearwater, a native of New Jersey, was raised in Orizaba in the state of Veracruz. He served with the liberals for two years and stayed in Mexico after the war. After his marriage he settled with his wife, Theresa, in Tampico and worked for a steamship company. His life ended tragically in a storm in 1879. "With her two children the widowed Theresa returned to Point Isabel and the teaching profession." She taught school in Brownsville from 1882 to 1938.[101]

Several Americans who lived in the border region also fought for the republicans. Lieutenant Eduardo Hale of Coahuila "offered to cross the Bravo to recruit American soldiers willing to provide their services in Mexico in favor of the constitutionalist cause." Dr. Ambrosio Kellogg provided medical services to the soldiers of Coahuila during the Intervention. Emiliano Laing (probably Lang) Gutiérrez of Nadadores, Coahuila, served as a colonel in the republican army. He was born in Parras in 1838, son of Julio Laing, who had come from New Jersey to settle in Mexico.[102]

During the slow injection of men and arms from the United States, the Empire was extending its power. After retaking Monterrey and Saltillo, French forces marched to Chihuahua and, in August 1865, forced Juárez to move his government once again, this time to far-off Paso del Norte on the border with Texas. In this, one of the remotest corners of the country, Juárez continued to direct the war against the Empire. He also had the opportunity to interact with officers and civilians from Franklin and Fort Bliss. One of these individuals wrote years later of his presence at a banquet and ball to celebrate Mexican independence. After dining and conversing at length with Juárez, the author wrote, "We departed very greatly prepossessed in favor of the Mexican president. We agreed in thinking that there was a simplicity and honesty of purpose about him which made him the best man for the difficult position of chief magistrate of the struggling republic in her great hour of trial." Expressions such as these served to illuminate an American public, which was largely unaware of or indifferent to events in Mexico, about the country's leaders. In a nation steeped in racial prejudice, praise for a full-blooded Indian as head of state was not a common occurrence.[103]

The Tide Turns against the French in Northeast Mexico

In the fall of 1865, it appeared to some that the Empire was invincible. Juárez was on the run, many of Mexico's regions were divided, and the people were weary of war. In the Northeast, the heavy imperialist yoke was compounded by political division and fratricidal conflict in Tamaulipas. Maximilian's advisers informed him that the country was largely pacified, that resistance was sporadic and limited. Under these assumptions, the emperor signed a decree in October 1865 ordering the summary execution of supporters of Juárez caught with arms in their hands. This was probably the darkest stain on the well-intentioned Habsburg prince, but it proved to be a damning piece of evidence against him at his own trial less than two years later. While the picture looked bleak, it was evident that republican forces roamed at will throughout the country, especially in Mexico's Northeast, where only the principal cities of Matamoros, Monterrey, and Saltillo were under control of the Empire. It was also becoming clear that Mexico's territory was too vast to be ruled by a foreign army without the consent of the people. Thus, the tide was beginning to turn, albeit slowly, in favor of the Republic. It was not yet the beginning of the end of the French occupation, but it was the end of the beginning.[104]

To preserve its domination over Mexico's Northeast, the Empire needed to maintain control of its principal port, Matamoros. To break the Empire's hold, Juárez ordered his most trusted general, Mariano Escobedo, to proceed to the Villas del Norte, strengthen his forces there, and prepare for a siege of the port. Escobedo began by patching up a temporary alliance of military leaders that included Servando Canales and Juan Cortina. He began his attack on October 25, and throughout the siege his army received support from the U.S. side of the border. The nature of that support was summarized in a harsh letter from G. Cloue, the commander of French naval forces in the Gulf of Mexico, to General Godfrey Weitzel, who had replaced General Frederick Steele as commander of U.S. troops on the Rio Grande. "The mess stores and munitions of war," Cloue wrote Weitzel, "are furnished by persons under your command. Escobedo's pieces are worked by gunners from your army. . . . The wounded are received in the Brownsville hospital. . . . In a word, Brownsville seems to be the headquarters of the Juarists." Cloue argued "that neither Escobedo nor Cortina could undertake anything if they did not have these continually renewed resources from Texas to sustain them." He also reminded Weitzel that France had maintained strict neutrality during the U.S. Civil War and lectured him on his obligations under international law. Weitzel did not conceal his anger, responding that he would not countenance such a "disrespectful" missive and that if Cloue had a valid complaint, he should make it "in proper tone and couched in proper language."[105]

Another sharp exchange took place when General Mejía complained of an attack on the French steamer *Antonia* from the American side of the river. Weitzel responded that there was no evidence the attack had been launched from U.S. territory. Even if it had, Weitzel was powerless because it would "require all the cavalry of Europe and America combined" to adequately patrol the river. To Mejía's complaint that the Americans sympathized with the liberals, Weitzel responded: "This is not strange. The liberals claim that they fight for their freedom. Their cause, then, is one that has awakened the warmest sympathies in every American breast."[106] Escobedo maintained the siege for more than two weeks, but the fortifications built by Mejía and Blucher resisted the fierce onslaught. He withdrew his troops in the second week of November, but stayed in the region, continuing to harass Mejía's forces.[107]

While the battle for Matamoros was playing out, actors on a larger stage were discussing U.S. strategy in Mexico as if it were a huge chessboard. In November 1865, Secretary of State Seward stepped up pressure on the French government to withdraw its troops. He made it known to French authorities that the imposition of a foreign and imperial government in Mexico was inimical not only to the Mexican people, but to the United States as well. Washington would not recognize anything other than a republican government in Mexico. In December, Seward instructed his ambassador in Paris to reiterate American opposition to a foreign monarchy in Mexico. By the following month the French foreign minister, Edouard Drouyn de Lhuys, announced that his government would withdraw its troops beginning in the fall of 1866.[108]

Back in the border region, Escobedo was maintaining pressure on the imperialists. A plan was conceived to strangle Matamoros by capturing imperialist-held Bagdad, which would cut the city off from the sea. The plan required the assistance of U.S. officials, so talks were initiated with General Godfrey Weitzel. These actions materialized in an episode called the Bagdad Raid. It is not clear whose plan it was or who did the negotiating. Some sources stress Escobedo's role, others state that Cortina was behind the plan. What is clear is that it was an attempt at Anglo-Mexican cooperation that went sadly wrong, leading to one of the border's darkest incidents, an event that Jerry Thompson (following one of his sources) refers to as "disgraceful in the extreme."[109]

The episode originated in December 1865, when R. Clay Crawford, "a blustery adventurer" and ex-Union officer from Tennessee, was chosen to mobilize men and lead a raid against Bagdad. Crawford recruited some of the most degraded characters in the region and proceeded to Clarksville, across the river from Bagdad. The attack commenced in the early morning of January 5, 1866. Crawford's adventurers, joined by more than 150 black troops from Clarksville, had no difficulty subduing the small imperialist force that defended the post. In the fighting "the raiders lost four men killed and eight wounded while the Imperial losses were placed at eight killed and twenty-two wounded." Matters quickly got out of hand. The invaders began drinking and went on an orgy of pillage and destruction. "Stores, warehouses, saloons, and even private residences were ransacked as a terrified populace fled into the sand dunes for safety." The plunder lasted two or three days; while some engaged in stealing, others hauled the booty across the river. Everything that could be carried off was taken.[110]

When he heard the news, Escobedo was horrified and immediately dispatched Colonel Enrique A. Mejía and a small force to the besieged town. Mejía, son of José Antonio Mejía, who had supported the Texans in their war for independence, was a professional soldier who had fought for Mexico in the war against the United States and in the War of Reform. He arrived at Bagdad after the damage was done. Mejía engaged in bitter quarrels, first with Crawford, then with Cortina, who with forty men had ridden down from Brownsville on the U.S. side of the river. Mejía thwarted Cortina's attempt to take over the town and use it as a base for his operations, but this made little difference because the imperialists returned in force on January 25 to retake the town. The juaristas withdrew across the river to Clarksville, but the arms and artillery they had captured from the imperialists were seized by American authorities.[111]

The outcry was great. Escobedo wrote to Weitzel that one million pesos would not begin to cover the property stolen. He sent the Brownsville commander a list of the names of persons involved who had fled to Texas and demanded that they be sent to Mexico for punishment. General Tomás Mejía demanded and received the artillery that the juaristas had taken. Colonel Enrique Mejía protested that the artillery belonged to the liberals and should have been returned to them. He wrote to Romero in Washington, who in turn asked Secretary Seward to explain "how arms and artillery taken from a Republican officer who sought refuge in the United States could be given to an enemy of the Mexican Republic the United States did not diplomatically recognize." Seward, Secretary of War Edwin Stanton, and the entire chain of command were mystified by the whole affair and "anxious to put the incident in the past."[112]

The spring of 1866 arrived without major advances as the war dragged on. Internal fighting among the liberals of Tamaulipas continued. Carvajal returned from New York, was appointed governor and military commander of Tamaulipas by Juárez, and resumed his struggle against Canales and Cortina for local domination of the state. The imperialist General Mejía, entrenched in Matamoros, benefited from this disorder, while Escobedo despaired. Americans became involved in these internal struggles, some joining Cortina, others, such as Rip Ford, siding with Carvajal. On May 1, General Andrés Viesca of Coahuila defeated French troops in the battle of Santa Isabel, but the pattern continued: the imperialists controlled the major cities and the republicans for the most part roamed freely throughout the countryside. Then suddenly in June there was a major breakthrough, as the war switched from low intensity to high.[113]

Escobedo learned that a heavily guarded convoy had left Matamoros on its way to Monterrey. It was immense: "two hundred large wagons pulled by two thousand mules . . . with three million dollars in merchandise." The caravan, which stretched for some six miles, was defended by eight artillery pieces and 1,400 well-armed soldiers—most of them Mexican—under the command of General Rafael Olvera. Escobedo massed his troops on the road between Matamoros and Camargo near the Mesa de Santa Gertrudis, and at 4:00 A.M. on the morning of June 16, began his attack. After three hours of furious fighting, the imperialist force was demolished. Losses were heavy. While the republicans lost 155 men, casualties for the imperialists included 396 dead and 165 wounded. Several hundred more were taken prisoner. The republicans appropriated the merchandise and "seized more than a thousand muskets . . . , eight pieces of artillery, and a large amount of ammunition and military equipment, including gun carriages, lances, and sabers."[114]

The battle of Santa Gertrudis was a decisive blow to the French occupation. The Brownsville Daily Ranchero considered it "a death blow to the reign of [the] Empire in Northern Mexico." Morale in the imperialist ranks plummeted and desertions increased. The losses incurred and the changing tide of war convinced Mejía that the occupation of Matamoros was no longer tenable. Just six days after the battle the imperialist commander agreed to surrender the city to José María Carvajal. Escobedo's army entered Matamoros on June 24.[115]

Mariano Escobedo was one of several prominent military leaders from Northeast Mexico who fought against the French intervention. With the aid of American arms and artillerymen, he won the decisive battle of Santa Gertrudis and was commander of Juárez's republican army in the victory over Maximilian at Querétaro. Northern Mexico played a vital role in the defeat of the Empire and the defense of the nation. LC-USZ62-131323, Library of Congress.

What was the American contribution to Escobedo's victory in this crucial battle? Historian Robert Ryal Miller writes that Escobedo's army of five thousand men "included hundreds of volunteers from the United States." He cites a French source that estimated the number at between 1,200 and 1,500.[116] Mexican historians say this is a ludicrous claim, made by the French to belittle the Mexican triumph. Historian Barry M. Cohen admits that "nobody knows the true extent of American involvement," though he cites a source who "personally knew more than fifty Americans who handled the Liberal artillery at Santa Gertrudis." American firepower was probably more important than American manpower. The steady flow of armaments from the United States helped to level the playing field, giving Escobedo and his troops the strength and confidence to face the imperialists in open battle and not merely in guer-rilla operations.[117]

Though less important than American arms, the presence of American and other foreign soldiers in the republican army created interesting cultural exchanges. A glimpse of this phenomenon appears in the memoirs of Edelmiro Mayer, an Argentine of German ancestry who served in the army of his coun-try before commanding a unit of black soldiers in the U.S. Civil War. At the end of that conflict he came to Mexico and was commissioned as a colonel in command of the prestigious Zaragoza Battalion in Escobedo's army. He led one of the columns at Santa Gertrudis and later, after his promotion to general, participated in the siege of Querétaro and the taking of Mexico City. Mayer was greatly admired by his troops for his professionalism and generosity of spirit. In Santa Gertrudis, for example, he gave water to a wounded Austrian soldier when others ignored his plight.[118]

Mayer was accompanied by Captains Francisco Meier, a Hungarian Amer-ican, and Juan P. Encking, an American son of Danish immigrants. Both men spoke Spanish as well as English and served on Escobedo's staff.[119] Encking, also in charge of artillery, was a twenty-seven-year-old with blond hair and blue eyes. Mayer portrays him as a "model for humanity," writing that Encking was fervently nationalistic, believed strongly in the superiority of American institu-tions, and was a firm believer in progress. Mayer recounts some of the exchanges between Encking and his Mexican soldiers, usually around the campfire. When asked who had the greater discipline, American or Mexican soldiers, he replied, "Everything favors the Yankees, except the qualities of resistance and modera-tion, which are exceptional in the legitimate sons of this land. My countrymen would break down if they attempted to carry out the forced marches of Mexican infantrymen." They would "die if they faced half the hunger and thirst endured by the Aztec soldier."[120]

When asked why Union troops would abandon their regiment in the middle of a battle when their terms of enlistment expired, as happened in the Army of the Potomac, Encking replied that the law is clear on that point and the law is strictly observed in the United States. No one can keep a soldier beyond his time of service. "It is true that on the second day of a battle there was an entire division that refused to take up their arms because the terms of their contract had expired, but the commanding general recognized their rights and asked them to honor their commitment for another eight days. They did so, fighting with valor in that battle, which was lost by the Union army." In the United States, he reiterated, "law and property are respected."[121]

The imperialists' surrender of Matamoros sowed the seeds of greater internal strife in Tamaulipas. Mejía, reported the *Dallas Herald*, "evacuated the city, with all the honors of war, taking with him his men, baggage, arms and ammunition." He was afforded American steamers to carry his troops and equipment and was joined by many of his officers, some with American or English names. As with most sudden changes in the port, most of the big merchants crossed the river to safety in Brownsville and began returning days later when they felt safe from reprisals. The *Herald* printed a proclamation from Juan José de la Garza directed to the population of Matamoros in which he extolled the role of the norteños in the national struggle: "The frontier has at all times been the constant defender of liberty; they were its sons who obtained the glorious triumph at Santa Gertrudis."[122]

Santa Gertrudis was a catalyst for a changing tide that swept northern Mexico then continued southward toward the center of the country. During the summer of 1866 republican forces recaptured many cities they had lost earlier in the war, including Tampico, Durango, Saltillo, and Monterrey. The capture of Chihuahua City by Luis Terrazas allowed Juárez to return to that capital from Paso del Norte. With each new triumph, more and more Mexicans rallied to Juárez, supporting further victories and turning the conflict into a war of national liberation. The turn of events caused desperation among the ranks of the imperialists. One French officer in Monterrey wrote of the deplorable situation: "all is anarchy; everything totters and tumbles on all sides . . . and of late fortune has gone against us. We take no prisoners now, and the wounded are dispatched; it is a war of savages, unworthy of Europeans." The French officer condemned the "Americans and niggers who often join the rebel bands, to the number of two or three thousand and sometimes more."[123]

In this context of growing republican victories, Matamoros was like an open wound. After the departure of the imperialists, political chaos enveloped the port. Carvajal was deposed as governor for allowing Mejía to escape; Cortina proclaimed himself governor, but it was Servando Canales who held the upper hand. He mobilized a strong force—augmented by Austrian troops that had fought in Santa Gertrudis—and captured Matamoros. Carvajal, with his foreign advisers, Rip Ford and Lew Wallace, fled across the river while Canales instituted a reign of terror against his enemies. The city may have fallen to the liberals, but it remained outside juarista control.[124]

Canales controlled a port that was vital for the flow of arms and other supplies needed by the liberals. Escobedo was determined to recapture Matamoros and forged an alliance with Cortina to attack the city. The merchants of Matamoros apparently prevailed upon the military commander at Brownsville, Colonel Thomas D. Sedgwick, to come to their aid. They feared for their lives and property, but they had an additional motive. It was reported that Canales owed the merchants $600,000, so their fortunes and those of the obstinate general were intertwined. On November 23, Sedgwick's engineers hastily built a pontoon bridge across the Rio Grande and 118 U.S. troops with artillery crossed over to Matamoros and occupied the main square, Plaza Hidalgo. As a justification, Sedgwick declared that his forces were there to protect American lives and property and raised the U.S. flag over the plaza. Canales did nothing against the American presence, but on the following day he sought out Escobedo and offered to surrender the city if Escobedo would pay the merchants the money owed to them. The republican commander vigorously refused and demanded that Canales surrender and Sedgwick's forces be expelled.[125]

On November 25, Sedgwick met with Escobedo to try to explain his actions. The republican general replied that he had orders to occupy Matamoros and that the Americans should turn over the city to him. Anything less, he told Sedgwick, would be to acknowledge that the city "has been invaded by you with forces of the United States." In response to Sedgwick's argument about protecting U.S. citizens, Escobedo assured him that he would guarantee the safety of all the citizens. Finally, he asserted that "neither international law, nor existing treaties between the United States and Mexico allow a course of action of this nature." If Sedgwick wished to protect Canales, he could do so on his side of the river.[126]

Talks broke down and Escobedo began his attack on the twenty-seventh. Matamoros had seen some bloody battles, but this was perhaps the worst. Escobedo attacked from the east and Cortina from the west, and the fighting was fierce on both fronts. Met with withering artillery fire from heavily defended fortifications, they were forced to fall back. Canales counterattacked and republican bodies began to litter the landscape. Thompson summarizes the bitter results: "In three hours of bloody fighting, Escobedo lost several hundred men killed, four hundred wounded, and between three hundred and four hundred taken prisoners. The defenders lost seventy-five men killed." While the battle was raging, Sedgwick received a telegram from General Philip Sheridan to withdraw his troops immediately. In a stinging letter after the battle, Escobedo blamed Sedgwick for contributing to his defeat by favoring Canales in multiple ways while claiming neutrality.[127]

In the aftermath of the battle Escobedo made it plain that he would not go away. He called for reinforcements to make another attack on Matamoros. Gerónimo Treviño, a rising young military leader from Nuevo León who would play a decisive role in the pacification of the border in the next decade, set out from Monterrey toward the border. When Canales realized he could no longer defend the city, he reportedly showed up at Escobedo's camp with his father, Antonio Canales, the legendary leader of the federalist movement more than two decades earlier. In a teary meeting, he asked for forgiveness and delivered the city to Escobedo unconditionally. On December 1, Escobedo and Cortina entered the port.[128]

The Sedgwick incident could well have caused a rift in U.S.-Mexican relations. Romero protested this violation of Mexican sovereignty to Seward, who disassociated his government from the actions of one maverick officer. The reason the incident did not escalate dangerously was because two prudent military leaders, Escobedo and Sheridan, resolved it at the local level. The Mexican general wrote to Juárez that Sheridan had arrived from New Orleans to confer with him on the matter. The American commander stated that Sedgwick had exceeded his orders, which were simply to give assistance to duly constituted Mexican authorities if requested to do so. Sheridan was convinced that his subordinate "was duped by Canales and most of all by the merchants." Sheridan concluded by assuring Escobedo that, when called on, American forces would come to the assistance of whoever the Mexican leader left in charge of the border. Escobedo declared himself fully satisfied with Sheridan's explanations.[129]

Escobedo concluded his operations on the border in early December and headed south on a journey that would take him to Querétaro, the scene of the Empire's last battle. At the same time the French began removing their troops from Mexico, a process that concluded in March 1867. According to historian Lucas Martínez, the republican advance toward central Mexico was facilitated by American arms and military supplies.[130]

The siege of Querétaro, which began on March 6, 1867 (the first battle began on the fourteenth), lasted seventy-one days. Several prominent *fronterizos* were in the republican ranks, among them the commanding general Escobedo and Gerónimo Treviño, both from Nuevo León; Juan N. Cortina from Tamaulipas; and Miguel Blanco from Coahuila. Two other leaders from the border region were in the opposing army, Santiago Vidaurri and Julián Quiroga. Both left

Querétaro with General Leonardo Márquez to seek reinforcements in Mexico City. Maximilian had traveled to Querétaro to lead his army in person, but he found himself surrounded, with supplies of food and water dwindling, so on May 15, he surrendered, delivering his sword to Escobedo. On June 19, he was executed at Cerro de las Campanas, along with Miguel Miramón and Tomás Mejía. Meanwhile, in the Mexican capital, an era in Mexican border history was coming to an end. Vidaurri found himself trapped by the onrushing army of Porfirio Díaz. He tried to hide, but was discovered and ordered shot. During his brief detention he asked to see Díaz, then Juárez, then his son, and was refused on all three counts. It was reported that Díaz ordered he be executed in a particularly humiliating way: on his knees and with his back turned to his executioners, the mark of a traitor. His remains were returned to Nuevo León for burial in the Mesa de Catujanes.[131]

I close this chapter with a few words on the Americans and their role in the war. Most of them were discharged in August 1867 and returned to the United States. Many accepted the Mexican government's offer of a $300 cash bonus in lieu of land. A few left dissatisfied with their pay and bonuses and filed claims before the Claims Commission of 1868.[132] More research is needed on the way American soldiers interacted with their Mexican peers during the French intervention. After all, only two decades had transpired since the U.S.-Mexican War. Some Mexicans had fought in both wars, one against and the other with the Yankees. It does seem clear that American soldiers were impressed with Juárez. Historian Robert Ryal Miller writes of a meeting between a group of American officers and the Mexican president. One officer wrote:

> The President won our hearts at once. He warmly thanked us for our services in behalf of Mexico. . . . He said that for Mexicans to fight for Mexico was natural; but for foreigners who had no other ties except the love of liberty and a desire to assist a brave people who were struggling against fearful odds, to make every sacrifice and to suffer every privation for the republic, was a spirit so noble that it could not be put in language.[133]

The American contribution to the victory should also be addressed. In a widely used textbook, historians Michael C. Meyer and William L. Sherman argue that "the United States had helped in a small way but it had been Mexicans who drove out the French." General Philip H. Sheridan expressed a similar sentiment in November 1866, when he downplayed the American contribution: "in less than a year this hardy people" had driven the imperialists back toward "the Valley of Mexico, with a fair prospect of their speedy extermination." A final comment comes from Lawrence Taylor: "American mercenaries constituted a small but significant strategic, tactical, and psychological factor in the long, painful road to the eventual constitutionalist victory because they initiated battle plans, operated artillery pieces and fought side by side with their Mexican companions." Most historians agree that arms and munitions from the United States were an important factor in the Mexican victory. It is a curious irony that Mexican nationalism was strengthened in its struggle against a foreign enemy (France) with the aid of a former enemy (the United States).[134]

Although the preceding discussion may have taken us into Central Mexico, the digression is justified by the fact that the border region played an important role in the War of French Intervention: as a place of refuge for a retreating president; as the scene of important combats; as the principal conduit for the entry of men, arms, and supplies; and as a seedbed for some of the war's greatest military leaders, from Zaragoza at the beginning to Escobedo at the end. In short, the frontier, which had always been accused of separatist tendencies, played a vital role in the survival of the nation.

~

A broad array of alliances and episodes of cooperative violence occurred in the border region during the two civil wars. Americans and Mexicans fought with and against each other in one war, while Mexicans and Americans fought against Mexicans and their French allies in the other. The boundary between Tamaulipas and Texas was the center of much of the violence, and Matamoros was a battleground where local caudillos fought for supremacy.

Texas Rangers fought Cortina with collaboration from Mexican officials, while Mexican military forces combated Carvajal, who was aided by the Texans. Confederate officers reached out to Vidaurri and other Mexican caudillos to solve together the problems generated by the Civil War. Some four thousand Mexicans participated with Confederate or Union forces in the Civil War, and a like number of Americans participated with the liberals or imperialists in Mexico's War of French Intervention.

The Mexicans who accepted service in the warring factions of the U.S. Civil War did so not out of a sense of loyalty, but because they were promised good wages. Desertion rates were high when these soldiers were not paid. The strange nature of the alliances fostered by the Civil War is reflected in the case of Cortina, who was recruited by the same government that had tried to exterminate him earlier. Meanwhile, a unit of Mexican troops led by Santos Benavides served the Confederacy with distinction. It checked the Union advance on Laredo and contributed to the recapture of Brownsville in July 1864.

U.S. troops arrived on the Rio Grande in large numbers after the Civil War, but they did not stay long enough to intimidate the French. Nevertheless, the Union triumph in 1865 contributed to changing the tide of the war in Mexico. In June 1866 Mariano Escobedo, aided by a small number of American soldiers and a large supply of American arms, won a smashing victory over the imperialists at the battle of Santa Gertrudis, spelling the end of the French occupation of Mexico's Northeast and propelling Escobedo toward the siege of Querétaro and the fall of Maximilian's empire the following summer.

The fact that American soldiers fought for Juárez reflects loyalty to a common cause among different racial groups. Mexican republicans did not question artilleryman John Encking's nationality or his blue eyes when they fought together against Maximilian. Nor did Confederate Anglos question Santos Benavides's *mexicanidad* when he held the Union at bay. The paramount consideration was that they were on the same side.

Mexico's Northeast was important throughout the War of French Intervention because of the military leaders it produced and because of its strategic importance to both armies. The vecinos of the frontier, who for decades had been critical of the national government, now supported the war against the French and thereby strengthened their ties to the nation.

CHAPTER 7

A Most Violent Decade

1868–1880

T he period from the end of the Civil War and the War of French Intervention to 1880 witnessed almost uncontrolled violence, probably the worst in the history of the border region, but also growing and multifaceted forms of cooperation. It was a period of reconstruction from devastating wars and of nation-building in both countries. It was also a time of transition: from a violent environment to a relatively peaceful one; from primitive means of transport to the arrival of the railroad; from traditional to capitalist forms of production that transformed the Texas labor market; from an emphasis on commerce to a diversification of economic activities; from American dreams of additional territorial conquest in Mexico to the realization that economic invasion was preferable and could achieve many of the same goals. These processes were linked to one further development: both nations began to have greater control over their borders. These issues will be explored in the remaining chapters.

First, it is essential to address the violence because it is the most salient characteristic of the Texas-Mexico border region in the 1870s. It has been the principal focus of many historians and, though this focus is not misplaced, it needs to be adjusted to include a broader reality. To begin, a review of the major sources of violence is in order. It is useful to start with a characterization, widely accepted by scholars of the period, which accentuates the violence but has a great deal of truth. Later I will contrast this perception with a more complex reality. Joseph Wilkinson writes:

> The Border had been accustomed for some years to the violence attendant on Indian warfare, revolution, civil war, and the presence

of men who lived outside the law. But in many ways the years that
began with Reconstruction and extended to about 1880 were the
most violent the region had ever experienced. . . . Banditry on both
sides of the river attained professional status. Indian depredations
were endemic. There was so much killing—legal, quasi-legal, and
outright Murder—so much danger of larceny and rapine, so much
total risk to life, liberty, and the pursuit of happiness, that Captain L. H. McNelly, a Texas Ranger with a reputation for intrepid
bravery, told a Congressional committee he would not expose his
family to the hazards of life on a Border ranch.[1]

An observer of those turbulent years agrees with this assessment. Lucius Avery,
the U.S. commercial agent at Camargo, wrote in 1875 that during all the years
he had spent on the Rio Grande he had never seen so many "frequent acts of
wanton murder and daring robbery as are now taking place."[2]

What were the sources of this violence? Competition for the region's
resources—land, cattle, salt, and so on—among the various inhabitants was
the principal cause.[3] Contributing factors are mostly tied to the inherent nature
of the border: Among them are the makeup of the border population, which
contained many lawless individuals; the lack of government authority or official
complicity in the commission of violent acts; the presence of a long and open
border that offered refuge to Indian raiders and lawbreakers; the promotion of
violence by some Texans hoping to provoke a war that would allow for annexation of additional Mexican territory; racial hatred and a desire to avenge real or
imagined wrongs; and, interestingly, market forces, because one of the region's
greatest resources—livestock, especially cattle and horses—offered relatively easy
opportunities for plunder with a ready market for sale. One or more of these
factors is present in the events that justify—at least in part—the characterization
of the 1870s as a very violent decade.[4]

The reader might ask: Why did violence increase in the 1870s? After fighting
in the wars of the 1860s many men accustomed to violence stayed in the region,
but in the wake of the Panic of 1873 there were few opportunities for honest
employment, so many drifted into contraband and banditry.[5] This process was
not new, but it was accompanied by a breakdown of government authority. In
the words of one contemporary observer, there was a "natural gravitation toward
barbarism which seems inherent in human nature when left unrestrained." In
Northeast Mexico, gone were the days when Vidaurri's regional power imposed

a semblance of order in the region.[6] On the northern side of the border, wrote historian J. Fred Rippy, "Texas was suffering grievously from the disorders of reconstruction and establishing an appalling record for crime."[7] The failure of both nations to impose their authority created a vacuum that was filled by criminals, smugglers, Indian raiders, filibusters, and other disreputable men that a Brownsville editor called "waiters on providence" who were "ready for any enterprise . . . lawful or unlawful that [presented] itself to their attention."[8] Law-abiding people were also obliged to use violence to defend themselves, their families, and their property.

THE CATTLE WARS

To provide order to a disorderly topic, my first focus will be on the violence associated with the theft of livestock. Not surprisingly, some historians have referred to this decade as the "Cattle Wars" or the "Skinning Wars." A subsequent section will explore the continuing Indian raids.

Cattle were bountiful in Texas, and an estimated three million were feral, without owners. Historian Tom Lea states that the severe winter of 1863–64 drove many of these cattle south of the Nueces River. Their proximity to the border was "an open invitation to theft; a traffic in stolen livestock sprang up. . . . A spawn of border ruffians, operating mostly from lairs south of the Rio Grande, began to raid and terrorize the ranches of the border country as far north as the Nueces."[9] In 1872 a U.S. grand jury for the Eastern District of Texas investigated "the invasions . . . and depredations committed upon the people by persons from the Mexican side of the Rio Grande." In a model of hyperbole, it declared that a "reign of terror" existed "between the Rio Grande and the Nueces. Mercenary bands of marauders, Mexican officers and soldiers, and Mexican outlaws and bandits, have been, for about seven years, holding a saturnalia of crime, violence, and rapine upon the soil of Texas." Apart from the pecuniary losses, the grand jury declared that "the loss of life, the sense of insecurity, the decreased value of property, the paralyzation of business, and the moral effects resulting from this war cannot be estimated."[10]

The grand jury was headed by John S. Ford and included twenty of the leading men of South Texas, all of them white and prosperous. Ford was certain that these depredations could be traced to the influence of Juan Cortina. "Mexicans ambitious to acquire riches without work saw a man make a predatory war upon a neighboring state and people, commit murder, perpetrate robberies [and] carry his feloniously-gotten property into Mexico." That man was later awarded civil

and military power in Mexico and held positions of authority. "Under these circumstances it was very natural for him to have imitators." After a hiatus during
the civil wars of the 1860s, wrote Ford, "the depredations were renewed . . . and
robbers held high carnival in the region between the Nueces and the Río Grande.
These atrocious deeds were the legitimate fruits of Juan Nepomuceno Cortina's
infernal labors."[11]

Historians and observers such as Tom Lea and Rip Ford assume that Mexicans in general and Cortina in particular were the principal sources of cattle
theft and its attendant violence. Though it cannot be denied that Cheno and
his followers played an important role in the cattle raids, the story is not that
simple. In "Predator War," a chapter in his book on Cortina, Jerry Thompson
shows how Cheno's raids provoked desperation among Texas ranchers and caused
much friction between the governments of the United States and Mexico. After
1867, Cortina found himself without a war to fight so he turned to an activity
that enabled him to strike back at his Texas enemies and that proved to be very
lucrative. He had the sympathy of many Mexicans on both sides of the border.
Many shared the belief that cows and everything else between the Rio Grande
and the Nueces "originally belonged to Mexicans [and] that they had every right
to take back their own."[12]

Cortina was motivated by personal animosity toward those Texans who
robbed Mexicans of their lands. He also waved a nationalist banner against the
American appropriation of Mexican territory. These sentiments had wide popular support among Mexicans of the border region. However, there was also an
economic incentive. Thompson argues that "Cortina grew rich from the cattle
raids, accumulating a fortune that amounted to as much as $800,000." He had
not been a rich man, yet he "purchased as many as twenty ranches, large and
small, on the frontier."[13] Cortina's market extended well beyond the border;
hides were at a premium in international markets and were one of the principal
exports through Brownsville. It was widely believed that Cheno sold cattle to
Cuba. Though records of these transactions have not turned up, George W.
Mieler, a customs inspector based in Clarksville, across the river from Bagdad
on the mouth of the Rio Grande, reported that "he saw General Cortina super-
intending the loading" of cattle "to a Spanish ship lying off the Mexican shore."[14]

Whether or not Cortina was the main culprit, Texas cattlemen complained
loudly about their livestock losses. John McAllen had fourteen hundred head
of cattle stolen in 1871. Mifflin Kenedy reported more than one hundred thousand head stolen between 1866 and 1869, for which he blamed Mexican raiders.

The abundance of cattle in the Nueces Strip, the proximity of a border that offered refuge, a vast market for cattle hides, the presence in the region of lawless men, and the absence of government authority led inevitably to the cattle raids in Texas in the 1870s. This was part of a larger struggle among various groups for the resources of the region. From *Appleton's Journal, A Magazine of General Literature* 9, no. 210, March 29, 1873. Courtesy of Jerry Thompson.

Kenedy and other ranchers estimated their losses at four hundred thousand head of cattle and twenty thousand horses between 1865 and 1871, at a market value of about $6,500,000.[15] The clamor from Texas cattlemen was so loud that the U.S. government sent a three-man commission headed by Thomas P. Robb to the border in July 1872. The commission heard testimony and received more than four hundred claims totaling $48,496,235.25. The commissioners accepted without question the testimony of claimants that the thefts originated in Mexico and that Mexican civil and military authorities were either incompetent to stop the raiders or openly collaborating with them. They also recognized that greater government authority in the form of an effective cavalry force was needed to halt the raids.[16]

The Mexican government countered immediately with a commission of its own, charged with undertaking a more comprehensive study of the causes of border violence. The Comisión Pesquisidora, which included Ignacio Galindo, a brilliant lawyer who knew the United States well after years of purchasing arms for Vidaurri, did more than interview witnesses. Through Mexican consuls in Texas it obtained court records, government documents, and newspapers in order to complete a deeper and more objective review of the situation on the Texas-Mexico border. The findings were published in Monterrey in 1873 and an English translation was distributed throughout the United States. The Comisión Pesquisidora rebutted most of the conclusions of its American counterpart. To the charge that the border region was a scene of immorality, ostensibly because of the large Mexican presence, the comisión conceded that the extensive contraband by the people of both nations was a source of lawlessness. However, it cited Texas newspaper reports and Governor Richard Coke's own annual message to show that criminality was not a matter of race nor exclusive to the border region, but was a permanent feature of the entire Texas landscape. Most of the heinous crimes committed in the state were perpetrated in counties without a significant Mexican population. In pungent prose the *comisionados* wrote that to look for the "causes of the predominant depravity of Texas" in the border region was "to totally invert the laws of nature."[17]

The Comisión Pesquisidora charged that the Robb Commission's focus on the theft of cattle in Texas ignored the theft of horses in Mexico. By 1872 most of the horses of the Villas del Norte had been stolen, so thieves from Texas ventured deeper into the interior of Coahuila and Nuevo León to raid them. As mentioned in chapter 4, these operations were headed by many well-known Texans, such as Adolphus Glaevecke, Thaddeus Rhodes, and Richard King. Other names surfaced: Thomas Marsden of Beeville, the Wright brothers of Banquette, Patricio Quinn, Federico Mathews, Billy Mann, Charles Kahr, Green Melstaed, and William Thomas, dubbed Tomás Colorado for his red hair. These men usually had Mexican associates. The comisión concluded that "as a general rule, though allowing for exceptions, the organizers and instigators of the theft in Mexico are Americans from Texas; the operators are mainly Mexicans naturalized in the United States or residents of Texas . . . and in part vecinos of Mexico or without a fixed residence." In other words, there was cooperative crime on a large scale.[18]

One of the most interesting findings of the comisión was the extensive collaboration between Anglos and Mexicans in the theft of livestock. Most border predators were not particularly choosy about the racial background of their partners in crime. The Anglo-American horse thief Neil Millstead was, according to a Brownsville banker, "the aider and abettor of thieves coming over from Mexico."[19] Raids that originated in Mexico also often involved interracial cooperation. One source wrote, "Bands of Mexicans, often under the leadership of some white outlaw, made frequent raids from Mexico into Texas." It was not uncommon for Cortina—who was accustomed to recruiting Anglos for his military campaigns—to include them on his raids. Rangers identified Jack Ellis, one of the thieves they killed, as an associate of Cortina's.[20] August Santleben, who knew the border region as well as anyone, wrote that "thieves generally were organized to operate in gangs on both sides of the river and acted in collusion with each other by exchanging stolen property brought from Mexico for other property acquired in a like manner in Texas."[21]

Another interesting finding was that many of the Americans directing the horse-stealing operations were public officials. In a direct response to the charge that Mexican authorities colluded with cattle thieves, the comisión countered that both Glaevecke and Rhodes held public office, the former as an alderman in Brownsville and the latter as a justice of the peace in Hidalgo County. Thomas Marsden was sheriff of Beeville. The Estapá brothers, León and José, two Texas Mexicans associated with horse theft, also held public office. José was collector of customs and León, sheriff of Hidalgo County.[22]

The comisionados then reviewed the issue of livestock theft, tackling the key question of who was stealing cattle in Texas. To the charge that most of the thieves were Mexicans, they responded that this was inevitable because Mexicans were the overwhelming majority in the region. Nine out of ten of the twenty-seven thousand inhabitants living between the Rio Grande and the Nueces River in 1870 were Mexican. While acknowledging that Mexican bandits who brought discredit to the nation formed part of the bands that pillaged the ranches of the Nueces Strip, the comisionados argued that most of the Mexicans involved were not citizens of Mexico, but residents of Texas and largely out of the reach of Mexican authorities. Among those they named were José María Sánchez Uresti; Santiago Núñez; Julián Rocha; Zeferino García; Macario Treviño; Santiago Sánchez; Pedro Cortés; Gerónimo Pérez; and the notorious Lugo brothers, Pedro and Longinos, who had been born in Tamaulipas but lived in Texas.[23]

To the charge made by Texas ranchers that their cattle herds in Cameron and Nueces Counties had been depleted by Mexican rustlers, the comisión cited statistics in the *Texas Almanac* to demonstrate that there was in fact no reduction. It also cited data from the Texas government on the number of proprietors and cattle in the eleven counties close to the border with Mexico: Cameron, Hidalgo, Starr, Webb, La Salle, Encinal, Duval, Zapata, Live Oak, McMullen, and Nueces. The number of ranchers had increased from 1,202 in 1866 to 2,367 in 1872, while the number of cattle had grown from 192,497 to 368,352 and their value had increased from 977,105 pesos to 1,361,217 pesos during the same period. The comisión thus concluded: "the amount of cattle in the eleven referenced counties, far from having decreased to a third or a fourth with respect to the amount in 1866, as alleged by Texas claimants . . . on the contrary, had doubled." There was a sharp decrease in 1871, which the comisión attributed to the extraordinary production of hides and a devastating drought in that year.[24]

Like its U.S. counterpart, the comisión made use of statistics (which can be made to say almost anything) on the export of hides through Brownsville, though using a different methodology and time frame and adding exports from the mouth of the river. It determined that during an eighteen-month period when Texas claims of livestock theft reached a shrill pitch, only 4,156 hides, or 4 percent of the total exported, were from Texas cattle. This represented a loss to Texas ranchers of 41,560 pesos rather than the millions of dollars they were claiming. The comisión ridiculed the pretensions of Texas claimants, arguing that "eighty-two persons presented damages for more than twenty-five million [dollars], that is, for three-quarters of the value of all Texas horses and cattle in 1870." Based on tax rolls, the comisión demonstrated that some of the claimants had tried to commit fraud. Albert Champion, for example, had established his herd in 1857 and reported seven hundred head in 1859. After that year, in order to pay less in taxes, he reported lower numbers and was down to one hundred in 1872. His two brothers reported similar numbers, never having more than three hundred head, and in most years fewer than one hundred. These paltry numbers did not deter the three brothers from filing a claim for close to a million dollars in losses.[25]

Although some Texans who held public office were found to be complicit in the raids, ranchers and government officials north of the line blamed Mexican authorities for harboring and protecting cattle raiders in Mexico. Major Lowery, who managed American mines in northern Nuevo León, declared that the mayor of Vallecillo charged fifty cents per head in exchange for importation documents that gave the stolen stock a thin veneer of legality. The same source stated that another Vallecillo mayor actually "financed raids into Texas and paid the raiders a commission on a sliding scale with a minimum guarantee." Lowery was certain that entrepreneurs from central Mexico had some of these raiders in their employ and managed their operations like a business.[26]

Lucius Avery at Camargo made a distinction between federal versus local Mexican officials. The former wished to "see justice done, [but] they are in nearly every instance thwarted by the perverseness or stupidity of the local authorities

who care little for the law or government when they come in conflict with their
interests or narrow prejudices." Avery believed that local Mexican authorities
approved of the raids and murders carried out in Texas because of the many
wrongs perpetrated against Mexicans north of the Rio Grande. The commercial
agent also differentiated these venal authorities from "the more peaceable and
industrious portion of the inhabitants," who were "overawed by desperados, who
can ride through this country from Laredo to Matamoros on either side of the
river with no fear of molestation."[27]

The comisión investigated the conduct of Mexican authorities and declared
that "in some cases it had been found wanting, in others culpable, but in general
in adherence to their obligations." The report cited cases of joint American and
Mexican cooperation in combating the bands of José María Martínez and Cipri-
ano Flores and Cortina's eradication of the Lugo brothers. However, it condemned
Mexican judge Trinidad González Doria for pardoning known Mexican rustlers
and found sufficient evidence to suspect that Dionisio Cárdenas, the alcalde of
Matamoros, had collaborated with Patricio Quinn in the theft of livestock.[28]

Since the Robb Commission—following the lead of Texas ranchers—had
blamed Cortina for most of the border violence, the comisión addressed this
issue directly, reminding the Americans that Cheno was a U.S. citizen and citing
General Winfield Scott's statement that the Cortina revolt was an internal problem among Texans. Moreover, it was false that Mexican authorities failed to act
against Cortina. The comisión cited numerous efforts to combat him, beginning
in 1859 when troops from Matamoros crossed the border to rescue the citizens
of Brownsville from his attack. Many of the crimes attributed to Cheno, wrote
the comisión, were committed by some of the men who had formerly fought in
his army and were associated with him in the public mind. The report cited the
Daily Ranchero, which speculated in 1872 that perhaps Cortina had been blamed
for crimes committed by others. Finally, the comisión declared that the issue of
Cortina was largely overblown and was another pretext for attacking Mexico.[29]

Many Texans believed that Cortina got away with his crimes because he was
a powerful man. The comisión brought to light similar uncomfortable truths
about prominent Texans. It was well known that Richard King appropriated
all of the unbranded calves his men could round up, many of them belonging
to Mexican ranchers. King was never punished. Francisco Yturria, prominent
merchant and landowner of Brownsville, was also accused of using his ranch for
rustling operations and—along with King—of shielding known outlaws such
as Patricio Quinn from the law. The comisión also recalled an incident in which

Charles Stillman falsely accused Juan Chapa Guerra of stealing horses from him and organized a vigilante group that hanged the man. Because of his power and connections Stillman escaped punishment.[30]

Cattle theft, concluded the comisión, was used like a hammer to hit Mexico and the Mexican people. The Americans were fond of referring to cattle theft as "cattle wars" and converting a criminal activity into a political issue. By doing so, they stoked public opinion and generated hatred and hostility, which suited the purpose of those who desired a war with Mexico in order to acquire more territory. The comisionados recognized that the border region played a crucial role in the relations between the two countries. Stating that criminal activity had to be combated, they proposed the establishment of a strong federal force for that purpose. They also proposed federal tribunals on the border and speedy action by the courts to halt the impunity that fanned the flames of crime. Finally, they proposed greater cooperation with American authorities by strengthening extradition laws and adding cattle theft as an extraditable crime. These proposals were largely ignored by a Mexican government that suffered two large-scale revolts in 1872 and 1876, led by Porfirio Díaz. Meanwhile the border region continued to burn in violence.[31]

The Border Region: A Magnet for Violence

The focus on Cortina in many border histories has largely eclipsed the role of Anglo predators who did their share to terrorize the population. One of these was John King Fisher, who established a ranch in Dimmit County, between the Nueces and Rio Grande, and rustled cattle and horses on both sides of the border. George Durham, a young recruit who joined Leander McNelly's Rangers in 1875, wrote that Fisher's band was "made up of men who have committed crimes in other states and fled for refuge here, where they go to robbing for a living. They are organized into parties of twenty-five to forty men each. . . . They pass stolen horses along this line and sell them up north."[32] In October 1876, it was reported that McNelly's Rangers had killed a number of Fisher's band who "had about fifty head of stolen horses, and twenty-two yoke of work oxen . . . taken from Mexicans on the Rio Grande."[33] McNelly arrested Fisher on various occasions, but he usually paid bail and eluded prison. When carrying out his raids, Fisher did not necessarily single out Mexicans, though they were more numerous and more likely to own horses, which were his usual target.[34]

Another Anglo predator was a man that Mexican and American authorities referred to as McWeber (possibly Weaver). Some of the common people shortened the name to "Make" (with a Spanish pronunciation). In 1872, this ruffian, unknown to history but well known to the Mexican population in the region of Piedras Negras, led a band "of about 15 men composed of Americans, negroes and Mexicans from the Texas side" on a raid against the village of Resurrección, located about forty miles northwest of Piedras Negras and about two miles from the border. The attack was directed principally against the alcalde, Francisco Aguilera, and his family. The aggressors caught the family "sleeping outside of the house in the open yard." Aguilera's wife hurried their children to refuge while her husband engaged in a desperate fight for his life. For two hours he held off his attackers, firing from the kitchen of his house until it was burned down. He continued the fight from the next house, which was also set afire, until the roof fell upon him. His charred body was found later with ten bullet holes. The band of killers also mortally wounded Aguilera's wife and burned three houses. They did not escape unscathed, however. Two of McWeber's men, "John Pulliam and Evans, were mortally wounded and died soon after they had recrossed the Rio Grande."[35]

McWeber was another of those violent men whom the border seemed to attract like a magnet. He had killed an army officer in East Texas and escaped to the border region in 1869. He had lived in Resurrección and had also served as a scout at Fort Clark. The U.S. commercial agent at Piedras Negras, William Schuchardt, informed Washington: "It is reported that McWeber is now organizing another band in the frontier country" for another raid.[36] Schuchardt also made interesting observations about McWeber's intended victims: "The population of the Resurreccion were known at all times as a hard working honest living people who never did consent bad men in their town." They notified American authorities when they found stolen livestock on their ranches. Clearly, they wanted to avoid problems with the Texans. Schuchardt described Aguilera as an "upright hard working man and appreciated by all he had transactions with."[37]

Three years after these events McWeber was still causing problems. The jefe político of the Rio Grande District, Vicente Galán, informed Schuchardt he had received an official notice that the outlaw had convened a clandestine meeting at the head of the Nueces River, which was attended by "more than one hundred armed and mounted individuals." Fearing that McWeber was planning a raid on Mexican territory, Galán was giving forewarning because he wished to avoid "the interruption of the amicable relations that exist between two friendly nations." It is interesting that McWeber's aggressions in this part of the border region generated not the hatred of Americans, but a mature willingness among the people and their authorities to cooperate with American officials in combating the problem.[38]

The 1870s saw so many violent events in the Texas-Mexico border region that it is impossible to recount them all, but it is instructive to comment on a few instances in order to better understand the nature of the violence. On November 28, 1873, seven Mexican shepherds, all natives of Agua Fría in present-day Apodaca, Nuevo León, were hung near San Diego in Nueces County. They were part of a group of about twelve who worked on a ranch owned by Toribio Lozano, who had taken a considerable number of sheep and goats from Agua Fría to Texas and established a ranch there in 1861. Lozano left these men in charge of his ranch, which he visited once or twice a year from his residence in Nuevo León. In early December 1873, he "received a telegram from Corpus Christi informing him that seven of his shepherds had been hung . . . and that the rest had been frightened away, leaving the rancho and the animals without any guard, for which reason the animals had become scattered and lost."[39]

At first local people tried to blame the Indians, but a boy who had escaped the killers said that the perpetrators were landowners and other residents who stole and skinned the animals for their hides. Santos Méndez, another native of Apodaca who worked at a nearby ranch, testified that Lozano "had been for twelve years an owner and breeder of sheep and goats in Texas. The people employed by him were always Mexicans, and were very honest. He always gave them good pay." Méndez continued that "it was well known in Texas that armed bands of American stock-raisers . . . were the persons who committed those horrible murders." Lozano gathered other testimonies that placed the blame on a band of stock-raisers, but he was also convinced that local authorities were negligent or complicit in the criminal activity.[40]

Lozano filed a claim for damages totaling $28,221 and asked for $20,000 for each of the families of the slain shepherds. The Texas government refused to pay and the case was taken up by Ignacio Mariscal, Mexico's minister of foreign relations, who wrote to U.S. Secretary of State Hamilton Fish. Fish responded that his government could do nothing in the matter and added an observation that expressed eloquently the lack of government control of the border region: "Mexicans in Texas and Americans in Mexico who engage in business near the border must not at present, or perhaps for some time to come, expect either government to insure them against all the risks inseparable from such enterprises."[41]

In the summer of 1874 the people of Refugio County were stunned by the brutal murder and dismemberment of Thad Swift and his wife. It was described in a local newspaper as "a crime unsurpassed by the diabolical butcheries of the savage Comanche."[42] Historian Hobart Huson writes movingly of this episode: "No one knew who the guilty persons were, so practically every Mexican of the laboring class in the surrounding country was regarded as a likely suspect." Improvised vigilante groups set out "with a view of exterminating all Mexicans in the section commencing at Goliad." The cattle raids that originated on the Rio Grande led people to assume that Mexicans were guilty of the crime. They were persecuted indiscriminately and many were killed. "Most of the [rest] then began an exodus into Mexico. The roads were lined with ox-carts and wagons headed west." Long-established families, such as the Aldretes "sold their lands and moved to Mexico."[43]

The year 1875 was probably the most harrowing of the decade. A federal grand jury was convened and found that in the region between the Nueces and the Rio Grande "all American ranchers have been ordered to leave their homes by Mexican raiders on pain of death and that one hundred thousand head of stolen cattle are driven to Mexico annually by American [sic] marauders." It reported so many deaths, robberies, and acts of destruction that "a general insecurity of life and property prevails on the border."[44] J. Fred Rippy writes that raids, murders, and outrages were commonplace and that "a reign of terror held sway in a vast section extending from the banks of the lower Rio Grande to Corpus Christi."[45]

The most audacious raid carried out by Mexicans occurred in late March when a band of between fifteen and thirty raiders led by Alberto Garza attacked the farms and ranches on the outskirts of Corpus Christi. This became known as the Nuecestown, or Corpus Christi, Raid of 1875. According to a Texas newspaper, the raiders "came within seven miles of Corpus Christi, robbed several stores and houses, and took a large number of Americans prisoners [sic]."[46] The raiders were bent on plunder, but killed anyone who resisted them. The accounts of robbery and murder were magnified by the time they reached the citizens of the port city. Some residents, terrified, boarded boats and sailed out to sea while others formed a company of armed citizens to repel the raiders. Those who sailed to sea, writes one historian, "Were more in danger of drowning than robbery."[47]

The Nuecestown Raid was devastating for the Mexican population of the Nueces Strip. Because they comprised the majority of the population in the region, Mexicans were the principal victims of the predators. Some residents, such as Julian Rita and his son of Nueces County, were killed, while others, such as Manuel Paredo of Laredo, were robbed. It was reported that due to the danger, "Rancheros are moving into town, traveling is almost stopped and business very much depressed."[48] The Mexican population suffered even more in the aftermath of the raid because, in the words of one historian: "Anglo residents of South Texas retaliated with a vengeance." In all the counties between the Nueces and the Rio Grande, armed companies "proceeded to hunt down Mexican outlaws, peaceful rancheros, and merchants; the avengers looted property and burned homes." Most of the victims "were farmers and stockraisers."[49] Historian and folklorist J. Frank Dobie estimated that the "number of Mexican Texans killed in the months following the raid . . . exceeded the number of Mexicans who died at San Jacinto."[50] It is not clear what motivated the raid, perhaps plunder or the indiscriminate killing and driving off of Mexicans from their Texas lands or both. What is clear is that Texas Mexicans paid a terrible price.[51]

Beset by a resurgence of Indian depredations in West Texas and Mexican raids into the Nueces Strip, in 1874 the Texas government reestablished the Texas Rangers, a body that had been largely nonexistent since the Cortina War of 1859. Leander H. McNelly was appointed commander of one of the two units created, and with about thirty men, was "sent to South Texas to stop cattle theft and to return the South Texas counties to law and order." McNelly became famous in Texas and infamous in Mexico when he crossed the border in November 1875 in pursuit of raiders who had herded more than two hundred cattle across the river. The rustlers were believed to be at Las Cuevas Ranch, which Texans were sure was a launching pad for raiding expeditions into Texas. In the early morning of November 19, the rangers crossed the river and came upon a small camp where men were chopping wood and women were cooking breakfast. They began firing indiscriminately but after killing several men discovered that they were at the wrong ranch. They had attacked Las Cucharas instead of Las Cuevas. They proceeded to Las Cuevas, but were met by a large force of rancheros and local militia and were forced to retreat toward the river. They were rescued by a U.S. cavalry force led by Captain James Randlett, but before crossing the river McNelly was able to obtain the return of seventy-six of the stolen cattle.[52]

This flagrant violation of Mexican sovereignty did not escalate into a confrontation between the two countries because U.S. government officials disavowed McNelly's actions and diplomatically diffused the hostile situation. Meanwhile, the perception of a Mexican military officer on the border reflects the attitude of the Mexican government. Captain Diego García wrote to Lucius Avery that he had taken steps to pursue the cattle raiders and that American forces on the other side of the river should know that if they crossed the border again he would have to make his authority respected. He continued, "it is not desirable that between friendly nations as are ours, there should be a disagreement [over] a few criminals."[53]

The Salt War of 1877 at San Elizario, near present-day El Paso, falls somewhat outside the purview of this study because of its geographic location, but I mention it briefly because it is another violent event resulting from the competition for resources and involving Anglos and Mexicans. Since the colonial period, residents and freighters of the region had extracted salt freely from the deposits at the base of the Guadalupe Mountains for personal use or to sell in regional markets. When the Anglo Charles Howard attempted to privatize what had always been public property, Mexican residents from both sides of the border rebelled. Historian Paul Cool calls the revolt a popular insurgency and states the rebels were willing to fight and die to defend their lives and property.[54]

The revolt turned bloody and several Anglos, including Howard, lost their lives. Mexican insurgents forced a detail of Texas Rangers to surrender their guns before state troops restored peace. In the aftermath of the revolt one of the local authorities, Sheriff Charles Kerber, mobilized a posse in Silver City, New Mexico, described by a ranger as "bad men" who "didn't appear to be under any restraint." This force, along with some of the humiliated rangers, went on a rampage against the Mexican community, killing several peaceful citizens and causing many others to flee south of the border.[55] This story, like those of the Nueces Strip, did not have a good ending for the Mexican residents. Historian Manuel Callahan writes that "salt began to symbolize the diminishing access and loss of control of the political process and the subsequent reduction in economic opportunity that Mexicanos faced as Anglos established their dominance in the region."[56]

REFLECTIONS ON VIOLENCE ALONG THE BORDER

Some of the incidents just described may have been motivated by competition for land. Historian Andrés Tijerina argues that stockmen such as Richard King were particularly adept at using violence against neighboring Mexican ranchers in order to drive them away and take their land.[57] The *New York Times* expressed the issue bluntly: "Mexican stock-raisers own nearly all the lands from the Nueces to the Rio Grande, and they allege that many of the American stock men do not own enough land upon which to pen their cattle." The Americans used violence to drive "Mexican land-owners out of the country and to buy up their lands for a song."[58]

Other incidents were fomented by men who desired territorial expansion. In a lengthy report the *New York Times* recounted the aggressions against Mexico beginning with the Carvajal revolt in the early 1850s through the violence of the 1870s. "Those who are at all familiar with the border Texan will laugh at the assertion that the Mexicans have been the only aggressors in all these recent disturbances," the writer stated. Calling Mexicans essentially a lawless people, the writer still accused Americans of perpetrating much of the violence in order to provoke a war and annex more of Mexico's territory.[59]

A plausible argument can also be made that Texas society in the nineteenth century had a tradition of violence and what occurred in the Nueces Strip was nothing out of the ordinary. "One fairly impartial account states that 'a reign of terror and dread of impending evil spread themselves like a nightmare over the land.' From ambushings, hangings, and house-burnings, the 'war' moved into a phase of armed camps and general engagements, none of which were decisive." This description is not of the Nueces Strip, but of East Texas during the Regulator-Moderator War of the early 1840s. This dispute, which involved only Anglo Texans, was one in a long chain of events that contributed to Texas's reputation for "lack of law and order."[60]

Most of the violent episodes of the 1870s, especially the Swifts' murders, the Nuecestown Raid, and the Salt War, have a common denominator: they were followed by a brutal retaliatory response against innocent Mexicans. To most observers it was clear that a racial dimension was involved. M. M. Morales, the Mexican consul at San Antonio, declared: "for many years we have observed, with authenticated and public acts, that the American people wish to eliminate the Mexican race." Over time, crimes against Mexicans were getting worse and state authorities were doing little to "prosecute and punish the perpetrators of such crimes."[61] General Frederick Steele, who was sent by Governor Richard Coke to report on the Nuecestown raid, stated that there was "a considerable [Texan] element in the country bordering on the Nueces that think the killing of a Mexican no crime."[62]

General Egbert L. Viele, who had served on the Rio Grande and later expressed his views in national publications, wrote that along the border "two widely distinct races confront each other . . . distinct in color, language and religion, and . . . under no possible circumstances could these two peoples commingle together." Given these attitudes, many Texans were only a step away from perpetrating violence against Mexicans.[63] It is only fair to point out that Anglo hatred was not restricted to Mexicans but was pretty evenly distributed among a host of enemies.

When Martin Culver, heading a posse that was hunting lawbreakers, rode up to ranger Leander McNelly, the first thing he said was: "Captain, we got about a hundred men. All white men. Nary a Yankee, nigger, or Mexican amongst us."[64]

It is easy to say, as one Texan did, that Anglos "hated Mexicans like a human hates a rattlesnake."[65] However, not all of them did. The rangers were perceived to be declared enemies of Mexicans and did contribute to killing them, but it seems that in the 1870s most Mexicans in the Nueces Strip died at the hands of Anglo posses and vigilantes. Ranger N. A. Jennings described these groups as "large parties of mounted and well armed men . . . committing the most brutal outrages, murdering peaceful Mexican farmers and stockmen who had lived all their lives in Texas."[66] Governor Richard Coke expressed similar sentiments: "The Mexican population on this side of the Rio Grande, are usually a tractable, docile people, perfectly submissive to lawful authority. . . . There are a great many most excellent citizens among them, indeed the great majority of them are of that character." In a statement that reflected not racial hatred but condescension, the governor then referred to the accusation that the Mexican population of the Nueces Strip was aiding and abetting the raiders from below the Rio Grande:

> The Texas Mexicans who are simple people—many of them very
> ignorant . . . have been led to doubt the ability of our government to
> give them protection, and through ignorance, and fear for the safety
> of themselves and property, rather than sympathy for the maraud-
> ers, have in some instances given them aid and comfort. If assured
> of protection against the vengeance of these bandits they are well
> disposed and loyal to our government and will perform their part
> in expelling them from the country.[67]

The historians who claim the worst offenders were the Texas Rangers have a lot of evidence to back them up. Rodolfo Acuña is particularly critical, referring to rangers as "brutal men who used Gestapo-like tactics." Acuña especially condemns Leander McNelly for murdering innocent Mexican workers during his raid on Las Cuevas. He refers to the ranger captain as "McNeely," a man who "tortured Mexicans and shot them down in cold blood."[68] What he fails to mention however is that a Mexican working for McNelly also tortured Anglos and finished them off by hanging them. His name was Jesús Sandoval and he was one of several Mexicans who worked for McNelly, along with Macedonio Longoria, Lino Saldaña, Timoteo Solís, and Matías Serrata. Sandoval had "lost a wife and daughter to the bandits and . . . now lived for the sole purpose of killing them." His value to the rangers was that he knew every cow trail and river crossing. Apparently, McNelly gave him free rein to torture both Mexicans and Anglos. On one occasion he tortured a captured Anglo outlaw then hanged him after extracting the information he needed. The fact of a Mexican treating an Anglo-American in this manner while in the presence of other Americans reflects a broader reality that should make us reconsider the nature of racial hatred and violence in the border region.[69]

What many Mexicans have read about McNelly is not good. Daniel Cosío Villegas, Mexico's preeminent historian, wrote that before moving on Las Cuevas the ranger captain harangued his troops to give the Mexicans a "Texas lesson," because they had forgotten what was taught to them in 1847. Furthermore, he ordered them to "kill all living persons, except old men, women, and children," before proceeding to kill innocent men in Mexican territory.[70] There is another side to McNelly, however. George Durham knew him well, because he served under him. He and his fellow rangers received from McNelly the following instructions: "There are only two kinds of people for us—outlaws and law-abiding. Treat these law-abiding folks with all respect, regardless of color or size. . . . If his dog barks at you, get away from it. Don't shoot it."[71] A measure of the man is provided by an incident in which McNelly administered last rites to a wounded enemy bandit in the middle of a battle because the dying man was asking for a chaplain. The captain had been a Virginia minister. "He was bent over reading the Scriptures to him when the man went out."[72]

McNelly not only combated Mexican rustlers, he also went after Americans who attacked Mexicans. He informed General Steele that he had broken up a mob in Corpus Christi which had "virtually admitted the killing of 11 citizens of Mexican descent." On this occasion his rangers put a halt to a deadly feud between Anglos and Mexicans. "McNelly made no distinction between the two groups; to him they were all Americans and quarrelling between them was not to be permitted." He also deplored the killing of so many peaceful and innocent Mexicans, writing: "I do not know of any Mexican who owns a ranch on this side (of the river) and who lives in Texas whom I do not consider to be a good citizen."[73] The ranger captain has been glorified by some and demonized by others. His actions in combating lawbreakers were extreme, as extreme as the conditions in which he worked. Manichean labels of good and evil should not be applied without an understanding of the context and complexity of the space and time in which he lived.

CONTINUING IMPACT OF INDIAN RAIDS

The other important source of violence in the border region, the one that strained relations between the United States and Mexico almost to the breaking point, were Indian raids. From the 1830s to the 1850s, northern Mexico bore the brunt of the attacks, but the rural areas of Texas were no less affected. Two eyewitnesses to these events show that life on the Texas frontier was as harrowing as in northern Mexico. August Santleben, who spent three decades traveling the dusty roads of southwestern Texas, declared that Indian depredations left "ruined homes, aching hearts, tearful eyes, and frightful memories as evidences of their dread reality. The history of Texas for almost forty years," he wrote, "shows an almost continuous state of warfare between her people and the blood-thirsty devils of the . . . Indian race along her western and southern borders."[74] General Zenas Bliss, who served as commander of several frontier forts, wrote: "Trains and travelers were attacked on roads, mules stolen, people killed frequently, and the troops were busily engaged all the time, yet the Indians seemed as plenty and as bad as they were twenty years before." Bliss added that Indians now attacked in smaller parties "but they were heard from just the same and just as often."[75]

The 1870s witnessed the consolidation of a change in the historical pattern of Indian raids in Mexico's Northeast, which had commonly occurred from north to south. Beginning in the 1850s, many raids began to have a south-to-north trajectory, originating in Northeast Mexico and destined for Texas. The pattern was not very visible during the Civil War period but gained strength after the conflict. The principal protagonists of these raids were Kickapoos and Mescalero and Lipan Apaches, declared enemies of the Texans. It is impossible to measure the scale of the raids, though historian Sherry Robinson affirms, "Hardly a week passed without a raid by Lipans, Mescaleros, or Kickapoos, separately or together and often joined by Mexicans."[76]

This shift in the pattern of raiding coincided with a reduction in Comanche raids, a process that also began in the 1850s when Texas settlers began to occupy western Texas and frontier forts were established to protect them. The relentless pressure on the Comanches by the U.S. military was an important factor. This pressure was reflected in the treaties at Medicine Lodge, Kansas, in 1867 that forced Comanches and other Plains Indians onto reservations, and in a devastating attack led by Colonel Ranald Mackenzie on Comanches at Palo Duro Canyon in Texas in 1874. The pattern of Indian raids from Northeast Mexico to

Texas now took center stage in the border conflict that shaped relations between the two countries.[77]

The Kickapoos were blamed for many of the raids. They had settled on land provided by the Mexican government in a place called El Nacimiento where the Río Sabinas is born near Santa Rosa, Coahuila. They were an important part of the defensive strategy to defend the region against Comanche and Apache raiders, but they also became willing partners in trading with Mexican residents for stolen Texas livestock. This arrangement was facilitated by the Kickapoo hatred of Texans, which extended back to the Dove Creek Massacre of 1865, when their tribe was attacked by a Confederate force as they were on their way to Mexico. Beginning in 1869, the U.S. government began to apply pressure on Mexico to suppress the Kickapoos. Coahuilan government officials were sent to inspect the Kickapoo villages in search of stolen goods, but found nothing. In 1870 William Schuchardt, the U.S. commercial agent at Piedras Negras, accompanied Major Frank W. Perry, the commander at Fort Duncan, to the Kickapoo camp to interview their chief and discern his views on relocation to the United States.[78]

Schuchardt is one of the best sources on the Kickapoos, because they operated in his district and he sent to Washington many detailed reports on their activities. In one of these he wrote that Kickapoo and Lipan warriors "make constant raids into Texas to steal and murder, and returning boast of their exploits and dispose of their stolen property to Mexicans, who in turn fit them out for fresh raids." So frequent were these raids "that few horses are left within eighty miles of the river on the Texas side."[79] He estimated that there were about eight hundred Kickapoos in Mexico and that some three hundred of these were involved in the raids. After the Indians returned with stolen property "the stock is delivered to the contractors and from there forwarded by them to the city of Saltillo, the capitol of the State of Coahuila, where it is finally disposed of." This may explain why the Coahuilan officials sent to inspect their camp for stolen property found nothing.[80] Schuchardt declared that local government officials, among them the customs collector at Piedras Negras, promoted the raids for their own economic benefit. Texas ranchers were "growing desperate from repeated losses," he wrote and "are talking of entering Mexico to exterminate these tribes."[81]

Schuchardt also included the Lipan Apaches in his reports on raiding in Texas, though he recognized that this tribe was much smaller and had no fixed place of residence. Nancy McGown Minor argues that, like the Kickapoo raids, "Lipan raids were part of an organized economy, where stolen horses and cattle were driven into Mexico and sold, in collusion with Mexican citizens, in border marketplaces." Residents of various Coahuilan towns, including Zaragoza, Santa Rosa, San Carlos, and San Vicente, had trading arrangements with the Lipan.[82] Interestingly, the Lipans and the Kickapoos—following a market logic—were doing in Mexico what the Comanches had done for more than a century on the southern plains with stolen goods from New Spain and Mexico. This, of course, provided no comfort to Texas ranchers.

Not everyone in Mexico was content with this "plunder capitalism." Schuchardt wrote that "many good and honest men living in this district" were "mortified and ashamed to witness such things carried on nearly publicly." These men "attempted for the sake of the honor of their country to put a stop to these outrages, but they very soon found out that . . . they were fighting the state Government and all they carried for their good will was persecution."[83] Schuchardt blamed the Mexican government for its inaction and was certain that many Mexicans would not object to the incursion of U.S. troops to extirpate the cancer in their midst. Moreover, "he reasoned that the Indians, knowing they could no longer use the Rio Grande as a shield, would then agree to cross back into the United States and enter a reservation." This thinking set the stage for Mackenzie's raid.[84]

Colonel Ranald S. Mackenzie, first in his class at West Point, had a brilliant military career before and after his famous foray into Mexico. At the head of the Fourth Cavalry, Mackenzie was fighting Comanches in North Texas when he was transferred to Fort Clark with the mission to stop the raids from Mexico. On May 18, 1873, after riding eighty miles in forty-eight hours, his force attacked three camps near the town of Remolino, Coahuila, which were home to Kickapoos and Lipan and Mescalero Apaches. Mackenzie's troops burned the villages, killed nineteen warriors, and wounded many others. Forty women and children were taken prisoner as hostages to apply pressure on the rest of the tribe to surrender and accept relocation to the United States.[85]

The success of the mission was due in good measure to the thirty-four Black Seminole scouts that accompanied Mackenzie's four hundred–man force. According to Minor, the raid "would not have been possible without their knowledge of northern Coahuila and their assistance in locating Lipan and Kickapoo camps."[86] These Seminole Maroons were a small part of the contingent that had left Mexico in 1861. They were incorporated into the U.S. army for duty on the frontier. One historian says that they "possessed qualities that made them extremely useful to the frontier army, and they were recruited heavily as scouts." Fluent in English and Spanish, they had unsurpassed knowledge of "the terrain and the Indian bands that inhabited or frequented the area." These battle-hardened warriors were considered "the best body of scouts, trailers and Indian fighters ever engaged in the Government service along the border." They served Mexico without fanfare and now served the United States with equal distinction and no apparent sense of contradiction.[87]

Mackenzie's raid has been condemned in Mexico as another act of American aggression, but it put an end to Kickapoo raids, eliminating one troublesome problem in U.S.-Mexican relations. In northern Mexico the immediate reaction to the raid was mixed. C. C. Augur, the commander of the Department of Texas, wrote in 1873 that the "excitement on the frontier . . . was very great for a few days, but when it was clearly understood that it was simply a deserved punishment inflicted upon persistent murderers and thieves the better class of Mexicans were satisfied." Once they understood that the Texans had acted in the absence of action by the Mexican government "the excitement soon died away."[88] This theme was repeated in Schuchardt's correspondence. The Piedras Negras commercial agent wrote that even Mexicans who were unfriendly to the United States recognized that the problem required cooperation from both sides so that U.S. and Mexican troops could cross the border after predators. At Fort Duncan he introduced Mackenzie to an influential politician who represented the Piedras Negras District in Coahuila's state congress. Although this man was "greatly opposed to all interference by Americans in his country, he agreed in every respect with General McKenzie in regard to the way of protecting the frontier of both countries." Two things become clear: this was a vexing local problem that required a practical and local solution without nationalistic complications; and consular agents such as Schuchardt played a role in bridging the divide between U.S. and Mexican authorities on both sides of the line.[89]

After Mackenzie's raid many Kickapoos, joined by a group of Pottawatomies, accepted repatriation to the Indian Territory of the United States. The principal architect of their removal was Henry M. Atkinson, who traveled to Coahuila with Colonel Thomas G. Williams of San Antonio in order to enlist the cooperation of Mexican authorities. Atkinson, who had distinguished himself as an Indian agent, wrote about the cooperation as well as the hostility he faced. On May 16, 1873, he met with Governor Victoriano Cepeda, who was committed to establishing peace on the border that would ensure friendly relations with his Texas neighbors. Cepeda appointed Lieutenant Colonel Antonio Montero to join the U.S. commissioners and sent out a directive to all the citizens and local authorities of the state to facilitate their work. The commissioners then traveled to Monterrey, where U.S. consul Joseph Ulrich introduced them to Governor José Eleuterio González, who gave them his complete support. On the road to Santa Rosa, where they hoped to establish contact with Indian representatives, they learned of Mackenzie's raid and realized that their mission had suddenly become more complicated.[90]

Atkinson also discovered that "influential citizens" of Santa Rosa were working to convince the Kickapoos to kill the commissioners or capture them to hold "as hostages for their women and children captured by General Mackenzie." Consular agents on the border such as Schuchardt were convinced that the opposition to the Kickapoo relocation came from Mexicans who benefited from the clandestine economy that was propped up by plunder.[91]

Despite these obstacles, Atkinson and Williams finally sat down to negotiate with the Kickapoo chiefs. The Mexican commissioner, Montero, who was described as "a high toned gentleman and brave soldier," assured the Indians that they would be protected and would be better off in the United States. After intense negotiations that included providing the Indians with supplies, the Kickapoos accepted relocation. It cannot be doubted that Mackenzie's raid hastened their decision. Atkinson wrote that it demonstrated to the Indians the long reach of the United States and proved to them "that Mexico could no longer afford them a safe harbor after their raids into Texas."[92]

On August 28, 1873, about four hundred Indians set out for Texas. Approximately three hundred remained behind, but Atkinson hoped that at a future date they would also be persuaded to leave Mexico. Instead, they decided to stay in Coahuila, devote themselves to hunting and agriculture, and abandon their forays across the border.[93] Atkinson wrote of the support he received from "Governor Victoriano Cepeda, of Coahuila and the Mexican commissioner, Señor Antonio Montero, [who] were unremitting in their efforts to help us, and by the judicious exercise of their authority gave us most important assistance."[94] Cepeda was grateful for the recognition and assured Atkinson that he was always in the "best disposition to conserve and renew the friendly relations that united Mexico and the United States."[95]

Atkinson and Williams tried to convince the Lipan and Mescalero Apaches to relocate to Indian Territory, but were not successful. After Mackenzie's raid, these bands moved their base of operations to the Bolsón de Mapimí on the border between Coahuila and Chihuahua. They later resumed their raids into Texas, provoking further tension between the United States and Mexico. Their raids became another pressing issue in the agenda of pacification at the end of the decade.[96]

~

It is not a simple matter to characterize the decade of the 1870s in the Texas-Mexico border region. One of its salient features was violence, which reached a level unmatched by anything that happened before or since. Lawless men with bad intentions abounded. Livestock was plentiful and invited plunder. Indians continued their deadly raids. Two nations preoccupied with reconstruction after devastating wars took little action to solve the region's problems. In short, there were grievances aplenty among the region's groups, coupled with a lack of restraint, a sure formula for violence. The governments of the United States and Mexico sent commissions to report on the violence, but for several years their recommendations lay dormant.

Much of the violence originated from the theft of livestock in the Nueces Strip, which Texans blamed on Cortina and his men, though Mexico's Comisión Pesquisidora concluded that many of the Mexican raiders were Texas residents outside its jurisdiction. The Mexican commission claimed that many of the accusations against Cortina and others were a pretext to attack Mexico.

The border region was a magnet for violence because of the ease of committing a crime on one side of the boundary and escaping to the other side. Mexicans did not have a monopoly on transborder raiding. King Fisher and other Americans carried out raids into Mexico. Violent events scarred the region in the mid-1870s. One crime provoked another in a seemingly endless spiral of violence where each group had "the need to maintain a hair-trigger propensity for retaliation." In the absence of state power, argues Steven Pinker, violence is common "in zones of anarchy, such as frontier regions, failed states, collapsed empires, and territories contested by mafias, gangs, and other dealers of contraband."[97]

Much of the violence had a racial component, although a case can be made that racism only aggravated extant competition among various groups for the resources of the region. The struggle for resources helps explain the Indian raids, which constituted another important source of violence. With the decline of the Comanche menace, much of the raiding was now carried out in Texas by Kickapoos and Lipan Apaches who had found refuge in Mexico. After Mackenzie's devastating attack in 1873, Kickapoo raids in Texas came to a halt and most of the tribe accepted relocation to the United States. A commission from Washington, aided by Mexican officials, convinced them that it was in their best interest to return to their reservations. This reflects another commonality shared by Texans and Mexicans: the need for security. The Kickapoos were relocated because they threatened the security of the inhabitants of both sides of the border.

Neither the violence associated with cattle and horse theft and Indian depredations, nor the suspicions, negative attitudes, and ill feelings that many Americans and Mexicans had toward each other throughout the 1870s halted the constant arrival of people to the border region. In a seeming defiance of logic, they came to take advantage of its abundant opportunities. The violence, moreover, was not a major obstacle to increasing cooperation during the decade. These mutually advantageous exchanges are the subject of the last two chapters.

CHAPTER 8

Between Hate and Harmony

1868–1880

I
n September 1873 a prospectus announcing the creation of a Spanish-language newspaper in the border region arrived in Monterrey. The newspaper was to be published in Texas under the name *El Centinela Mexico-Texano*. The proposed publication would address "the urgent necessity of a stable newspaper in the Spanish language, which will protect and sustain the interests of our numerous border population." This printed sentinel would be independent and moderate in tone, but would tell the unvarnished truth about "the strained relations and the distressing and poisoned animosity, with which in recent times the people of our race have been treated, not only by the ignorant classes of the country, but also by the same press, which is violent, arrogant, and impassioned."[1] Four months later, the "arrogant" press in Texas, which apparently had received a very different prospectus, announced that "[a] new Spanish journal will soon make its appearance in Austin. It will be called the El Centinela Mexico Texana [*sic*], and be edited by one of our well-known Mexican-American citizens, Col. Rafael Cabañas." The article added that "correct information on Spanish and Mexican affairs, so badly needed, will thus be supplied by Col. Cabañas, who has our best wishes for the success of his enterprise."[2]

It is not known whether Cabañas ever published his newspaper. The project may have ended in good intentions, but these intentions and the way they were presented to the public of both countries is revealing of Anglo-Mexican relations in the border region in the 1870s, with bitter hatred on one extreme and friendly cooperation on the other. Also instructive is the propensity of many border-landers to tailor their discourse to the particular audience they were addressing. The need in Texas to have "correct information on Spanish and Mexican affairs" came at a time when many Texans were coming face-to-face with Mexicans for the first time, either because more and more newcomers were arriving in areas of Texas outside the Mexican region of South Central Texas, or because many American businessmen and professional people were seeking opportunities in Mexico, and Texas was the logical platform to enter the country. In contrast, the feelings expressed in the prospectus circulating in Monterrey reflected the grim struggle that was playing out in South Texas, especially in the Nueces Strip, and echoed the preoccupation of many thoughtful Mexicans: how to survive and maintain their identity and sense of dignity in the face of the growing American presence and domination.

These issues are important because the 1870s witnessed a considerable increase in the Mexican presence in Texas and the American presence in northern Mexico. The fact that the newspaper would be published in the state capital of Austin, outside the Mexican region, is in itself significant. It signals a time of greater social, economic, cultural, and religious exchange and cooperation. I will explore the increasing contact in this chapter.

Labor Needs in Texas

The northward flow of Mexican laborers to Texas, so evident in the 1850s, accelerated considerably during Reconstruction in step with the expansion of the Texas economy. Texas's infrastructure did not suffer the massive Civil War destruction of other southern states and was able to grow quickly, fueled by a surge of immigrants that almost doubled the population from 818,579 in 1870 to 1,591,749 in 1880. Immediately after the Civil War, Texas was largely an agrarian and ranching economy, but this began to change during the 1870s as railroad lines began to extend to the far corners of the state. In 1870 there were fewer than five hundred functioning miles of rails. Twenty years later, eight thousand miles had been added, creating a network that linked most of Texas and sent tentacles reaching down into Mexico. As in the rest of the United States, railroad expansion was a catalyst that transformed the Texas economy and this is best illustrated in the extension of cotton cultivation to regions once used only for grazing livestock. With the railroad, farmers could get their product to market more quickly and at less cost. All these processes generated a labor market that attracted greater numbers of Mexicans from south of the border. The northward flow of migrant labor was unimpeded by border guards or restrictions, which did not exist until well into the twentieth century.[3]

Mexican laborers were actively recruited for the expanding Texas economy, despite the admonitions of some who were convinced that Mexicans were unemployable because they were inherently lazy. General Egbert Viele, who had been at Ringgold Barracks in the early 1850s, wrote in a national magazine that the Mexicans were a "degraded people," impervious to change. He described the population of Matamoros: "The men are lolling around during the day and spending the greater part of the night in silly amusements, petty gambling and dancing, too lazy almost to breathe, and too knavish to earn an honest living." The women, in contrast, were "always busy, always cheerful, either washing by the riverside or preparing food for their lazy lords."[4]

Apparently the stereotype that Mexicans were generally slothful was more myth than reality because the "lazy lords" were eagerly sought after in Texas. As early as 1867, advertisements began to appear in San Antonio newspapers calling for Mexican laborers to work in the cotton plantations of the region. That workers were wanted in the area east of San Antonio is suggested by an 1870 announcement in an Austin newspaper, signed by the same man who three years later proposed to publish El Centinela, Colonel Rafael Cabañas. The notice offered to procure "One Thousand Mexicans, both for Laborers and House Servants," and "Those wanting good reliable Mexican labor are advised to send in their orders . . . as early as possible." Such a notice would have been unthinkable in the nativist 1850s.[5] In the 1870s Mexicans were not yet poised to displace African American laborers, who continued to enter the state in superior numbers. However, they were beginning to take jobs beyond the Mexican region in areas with majority Anglo populations.

Guillermo Prieto, Mexico's great literary figure and public servant during the Age of Juárez, was mystified that Mexicans would go where they were despised. After a visit to Texas in 1877, he returned to say that he had never "felt as humiliated as he had among those people," referring to Anglo Texans. He warned his countrymen that if they went to Texas they would be met with "scorn, humiliation, misery, and a long train of enmity and calamity."[6] His words fell on deaf ears. Mexicans continued to migrate to Texas for many of the same reasons that had impelled them twenty years earlier: continuous warfare and abusive landowners in Mexico and greater opportunities for advancement in Texas. Commercial agent William Schuchardt wrote of how two large-scale revolts led by Porfirio Díaz in the 1870s had disrupted the region around Piedras Negras. In 1872, during the revolt of La Noria, he wrote, "Besides the soldiers there is not a soul in this town, all families have emigrated to Eagle Pass, and many of them will become permanent residents in Texas, probably because they cannot see an end to the troubles of their country." In 1877, during the Tuxtepec uprising, he repeated a similar story: "There . . . is now a considerable emigration of Mexicans from this side to Texas on account of the unsettled state of political affairs in their own country. Thus the population on the Texas border, principally the Mexicans, has greatly increased."[7]

Sirvientes and rural laborers continued to lead the exodus to Texas. Unknown numbers migrated from the four states of Northeast Mexico: Tamaulipas, Nuevo León, Coahuila, and Chihuahua. The small town of Allende, Coahuila, mentioned in a previous chapter, reflects this trend: forty-six sirvientes escaped to Texas between 1860 and 1872, leaving debts totaling $6,766. The landowners of Monclova demanded legislation and vigilance by the state government to stanch the bleeding. They deplored the emigration and "the facility with which the sirvientes elude their personal obligations and the payment of their debts." When this appeal was passed to the state congress, a curious thing occurred. Deputies responded that although they deplored the flight of sirvientes, the constitution protected the right of transit. They went even further, stating that it was unjust for the debts of the father to be passed down to his children. This was exactly what the landowners did not want to hear.[8]

Upon seeing his countrymen flee in droves to the United States, the famous poet, lawyer, and politician Ignacio Ramírez, known as El Nigromante, wrote that in a couple of centuries Mexico would recuperate the territory lost to the United States. "There will be so many Mexicans in Upper California, Texas, and the annexed territories, that, without violence or war, and in a legal way and through a public movement, they will obtain a tacit reincorporation [into Mexico]. . . . Two centuries in the life of a nation is but an instant. Mexicans, have patience and procreate!"[9]

Jobs were plentiful in Texas, particularly in cattle and sheep raising. One newspaper reported that "the great stock region" was in western Texas and extended from the Colorado to the Rio Grande. "There is no grass to compare with *mesquit* in all its varieties, which covers, as with a dense carpeting, its immense prairies. Horses, cattle, and sheep keep fat on it all the year round."[10] The period after the Civil War was the golden age of cattle. Hundreds of thousands of animals were herded on legendary cattle drives to railheads such as Wichita and Abilene, Kansas, on their way to eastern markets. In 1870–71 alone, it is estimated that about a million head of cattle were driven north to Kansas. About a third of the cowboys who participated in the cattle drives were black or Mexican. This is not surprising, given that many of the drives originated in the Mexican region, where Mexicans were recruited.[11] Ranchers such as John Chisholm, Richard

King, Milton Faver, John Davis, and William Waugh recruited Mexicans to herd their cattle. Waugh stated that vaqueros came and went regularly from northern Mexico to Texas in search of work. Whenever he required hands for his drives, he recruited them from south of the border.[12] In the Nueces Strip most ranches were still owned by Mexicans in the 1870s. It is likely that they employed fellow Mexicans since most Anglos were not disposed to have a Mexican boss.[13]

Mexicans were also recruited for the sheep industry, which saw spectacular growth in the 1870s. Conditions in Texas were favorable: good climate, plenty of pastureland and an abundance of workers, particularly from south of the border. By 1886, Texas had almost 4,750,000 sheep, second in the nation only to California. Nueces County exemplified this growth. In 1860 it had 40,000 sheep; by 1876, the number was 650,000.[14] The town of San Diego in Duval County reveals clearly the growth of sheep raising and the concomitant increase in the Mexican population. It became one of the country's greatest producers of wool in the 1870s. Its population in 1860 consisted of thirty-eight inhabitants, only three of whom were non-Mexican. In 1875 there were about five hundred Mexicans and fifty Anglo-Americans. By 1880, "the town counted 1,000 residents and included a bank, three churches, and a Spanish-English weekly newspaper."[15]

Sheep grazing extended into new regions of Texas. George Wilkins Kendall, the chronicler of the Santa Fe Expedition, had predicted before the Civil War that "Texas was destined to be the greatest sheep country in the world." He became a pioneer sheep raiser in the region around San Antonio and hired Mexicans to tend his flocks.[16] Farther south in Encinal, Webb, and Maverick Counties sheep grazing proliferated. The Callaghan Ranch in Encinal County, just north of Laredo, was reputed to be the largest sheep ranch in Texas "and probably the largest in the United States" with more than one hundred thousand sheep.[17] The productive capacity of the Callaghan Ranch and other smaller operations was demonstrated in the early 1880s when "Laredo handled in excess of five million pounds of wool annually destined for eastern milling markets around Boston."[18]

The *esquiladores*, or shearers, of that wool were overwhelmingly Mexicans from Texas and south of the border. One eyewitness observed about four hundred esquiladores transiting through Eagle Pass in a one-week period, heading for the sheep ranches of South Texas. These workers established a migratory pattern, entering the United States between April and June and again between August and September when their services were required. This presaged the seasonal migratory flows associated with the production of fruits and vegetables toward the end of the century.[19] Mexicans who worked with sheep had little contact with

Anglos. Those on cattle ranches and cattle drives had more extensive association with Anglos. Rancho El Rincon, one of the units of the vast Coleman-Fulton Pasture Company (later commonly called the Taft Ranch), initially established near Corpus Christi in 1871, had workers of different ethnicities and races, though the majority was of Mexican origin. Historian Nora Ramírez writes that there were occasional disputes, but also harmony and cooperative work.[20]

Freighting continued to occupy many Mexicans in the 1870s before the coming of the railroads. Commerce was dependent upon them and the U.S. army employed them regularly to supply its frontier forts. The major freighting companies hauling between Texas and northern Mexico, such as those operated by the Gil brothers of Laredo, Santleben of San Antonio, the González brothers of Saltillo, and the Sada brothers of Monterrey, all employed Mexicans. John Twohig was able to continue his cotton shipments to Mexico with the collaboration of freighters that he or his agent contracted in Piedras Negras and its surroundings. Among the freighters who were employed in 1867, Francisco Ramón had only two carretas, while Gregorio Treviño and Mariano Pérez had ten or more. Santleben employed between eighteen and twenty workers for his freighting business to Chihuahua. Besides a wagon master, he required herders, drivers, and *caporales* who oversaw the operation, for which he paid salaries ranging from $15 to $30 a month.[21]

If merchants were reliant on freighters, freighters were dependent on *cargadores*, or stevedores, to load and unload the merchandise. Santleben was amazed by their resiliency and strength. "The fact that a man weighing not exceeding one hundred and sixty pounds, will place five hundred pounds, or more, on his back and trot off with it, seemingly, without the slightest inconvenience, is certainly remarkable." This weight may be an exaggeration, but he did not inflate their trustworthiness: "No transfer company in the United States could assure greater safety or more prompt delivery of property than these humble carriers of Mexico, who never strike for higher wages and are always ready to work."[22]

More than other occupations, freighting was dangerous in the 1870s. The violence in the Nueces Strip made travel unthinkable unless accompanied by a strong armed escort. In the western region Indian attacks were still common. Santleben and his drivers were fortunate in avoiding attacks, but on one return trip from Chihuahua, he stopped at a waterhole called Howard's Springs, about 120 miles from Fort Clark. As he was leaving, Anastacio Gonzales and his train of wagons arrived from San Antonio. Before departing, Santleben warned him about a band of Indians that had been following his wagons. He learned later that

Gonzales's party had been attacked and many of his teamsters killed, along with some of the family members who accompanied them. The Clarksville *Standard* reported that the attackers "rolled the wagons together, carefully tied their victims under them, piled wood around, and set fire to the pile. The fiends remained till the death throes of the tortured teamsters ceased to greet their ears."[23]

Mexicans contributed to the structural transformation of the Texas economy by providing labor for the construction of the railroads and then for the many economic activities that were transformed by the locomotive, such as cotton cultivation. In March 1870, a Houston newspaper reported "an urgent demand in Texas for labor." Specifically, the Central Railroad, which had an agent in San Antonio, was "authorized to procure three hundred Mexican laborers for their road." Later in the year an Austin newspaper reported that "Mexican labor [was] chiefly employed in the reconstruction of the Railroad from Indianola to Victoria."[24]

Cotton picking had been the province of black slaves in Texas since the 1820s and continued to be the main occupation of free blacks in the 1870s. However, as the railroads opened new areas for cultivation in the Mexican region and its periphery, more and more Mexicans were employed to work in the fields. This trend was observed in the 1870s, but did not become widespread until the following decade. The area around Corpus Christi provides a good example. The local farmer and businessman S. G. Borden declared, "I have employed in cultivation almost entirely Mexican laborers, who I find work well, and readily learn to use our improved tools. Such labor is abundant along the Nueces River and can be secured at 75 cents a day, boarding themselves, and paying only for days of actual work."[25] Beyond the Mexican region, Mexicans were beginning to establish a distinct presence. Arnoldo de León writes that in the 1870s, they "had become daylaborers on farms around Travis County and the Brazos district. The massive movement of Texas-Mexican farm hands into Central Texas would not occur, however, until the 1890s."[26]

As Mexicans continued to migrate to Texas from northern Mexico, they probably became aware that they were escaping from one exploitative labor system and entering another. The major difference was that in Texas they were paid a little more. The arrival of the railroads and the spread of cotton cultivation were part of a larger process of capitalist development that transformed South Texas and heralded the advent of agribusiness enterprises at the turn of the century. Managers of the Taft Ranch applied capitalist rationality to stock raising even before a large part of its operation converted to agriculture, especially cotton cultivation. Historian Josef Barton argues that "the move toward efficiency, and especially the search for new management and technology, caused managers to intensify piecework demands and to step up the pace of work." As in Mexico, laborers were also forced to buy their food at "company stores." Workers became indebted and soon discovered that they had exchanged the prison of Mexico's haciendas for that of the Texas plantations. Barton adds that "county courts did a brisk business enforcing the debts of laborers to company stores in Nueces and Cameron counties."[27]

Mexicans engaged in freighting or stock raising had a certain level of specialization, which gave them a degree of freedom and independence. As the century progressed these opportunities declined and they were relegated to a "general labor pool," which largely limited them to "Mexican work," which "included cotton picking, grubbing, sheepherding, working cattle, laundry work, food service, and other low-grade tasks." According to Arnoldo de León and Kenneth Stewart, by 1900 these unskilled and service jobs occupied 65.5 percent of Mexican workers in the region where they traditionally lived.[28] David Montejano describes how Mexican migrants became proletarians: "In the midst of a ranch society based on paternalistic work arrangements, there emerged and grew a farm society based on contract wage labor and business rationality." By 1920, the Mexican population "had generally been reduced, except in a few border counties, to the status of landless and dependent wage laborers."[29]

Little is known about the lives of Mexican migrants. Most traveled to Texas seasonally or for a short period then returned to Mexico. For the few who stayed, we can get an idea of their backgrounds from questionnaires completed when they were seeking naturalization as U.S. citizens. A sample of 296 such applications in Bexar County between 1848 and 1880 reveals that most respondents had lived in Texas for more than ten years—some as long as thirty years—before applying for U.S. citizenship. Most of the applicants (80 percent) were from the Mexican states bordering on Texas, but in the 1870s natives of Zacatecas and San Luis Potosí became more common. They were overwhelmingly young, with 82 percent being less than thirty years of age (an optimal age for workers) when they entered the United States. Most of the applicants (63.5 percent) were unable to write their names and signed with a cross. They came primarily from rural areas with scant opportunities to obtain an education. More than 50 percent stated that they entered Texas through Laredo or Eagle Pass, thus skirting the region of greatest violence between Laredo and Brownsville.[30]

Most migrants gravitated to the farms and ranches of rural Texas, but a few settled in towns such as San Antonio. Those who did usually "lived amidst poverty and urban blight." Arnoldo de León writes that Mexican barrios in the cities "received a lack of attention from city officials, including the police, disregard from civic leaders, and disrespect by the common citizenry." Nevertheless, "the Mexican quarter acted as a focal point for Tejano life." Both on ranches and in barrios these immigrants "retained components of Mexico's culture. After all, Mexico-born people constituted a majority of the overall Tejano population as late as 1880. Gradually, however, a fusion of Mexican and Anglo ways within Tejano culture occurred."[31]

Most of these immigrants did not leave written records, but thanks to the work of various historians, the stories of two of these men have been brought to light. Valeriano Torres and Luis G. Gómez are not typical of the majority of immigrants because they had a degree of education; Gómez even left a written memoir. Torres was born in Monclova in 1844 and, as a child, moved with his family to San Antonio, where he received an education. He found work as a vaquero hunting stray cattle "in the river bottoms and in the cactus and mesquite-infested brush of southwest Texas." He passed most of his life in a region extending from San Antonio to the Rio Grande and across the Nueces River toward Eagle Pass and south of Laredo. He was a good singer and taught music as well as "basics such as reading, writing, and arithmetic." His was a life of hard work, but he found time to help others by teaching and doing work for the community and the Catholic Church.[32]

Luis G. Gómez was a native of Linares, Nuevo León, who went to school in Matamoros. He crossed the Rio Grande in 1884 and worked at various occupations, finally ending up in the Houston area. "With business skills, he became a partner, the bookkeeper, and a contract procurer for the Tamez-Gómez Company, one of many such contracting operations that at that time supplied Mexican labor to help create the infrastructure that developed the Texas economy." He had many experiences with Anglos in both work and social settings. When he was not working, a big part of his life revolved around listening to and telling stories. Through his interactions with and the stories about Anglos, Gómez recognized the nobility and kindness of some Anglos.[33] Torres, Gómez, and countless others who did not become important public or historical figures and will never be recognized, did their part in transmitting their language, culture, religion, and values to future generations of Mexicans down to the present day.[34]

The arrival of thousands of workers from south of the border in the 1870s had multiple consequences. It increased the Mexican population fivefold, from an estimated fourteen thousand in 1850 to about seventy-one thousand in 1880. "Immigration," according to Arnoldo de León, "accounted for much of the increase; migrants from Mexico comprised some 40 percent of the population total in 1850, 64 percent in 1860, and 61 percent in both 1870 and 1880." Moreover, until 1900 most of the Mexicans who went to the United States had Texas as their destination. As early as 1872, the Mexican government discovered this fact, establishing four of its seven U.S. consular posts in that state.[35]

The migrant flow constantly revitalized the Mexican communities of Texas, giving an injection of energy needed to withstand the challenge of living under Anglo domination, which ranged from benign to oppressive, depending on individual circumstances. Through their northward migration these Mexican workers helped to extend Mexico's history beyond her borders to encompass Texas. Similarly, the Texas labor market transcended its borders and reached down into Mexico to attract the workers it needed to develop its economy. However, something occurred that complicated the process. In the words of Swiss writer Max Frisch, "Workers were called, and human beings came." And their arrival infused a continuing measure of mexicanidad into the social and cultural life of Texas.[36]

Growth of Protestantism among the Mexican Population

Religion continued to bring people together, though at times it also provoked conflict. The competition between Protestantism and Catholicism continued in the 1860s and 1870s amidst the ongoing conflict in the border region. Protestant missionaries now had the support of the Mexican government. The crucible of two wars against Catholicism had forged among the liberals a conviction that religious freedom was essential to Mexico. Juárez is quoted as saying that "the future happiness and prosperity of my nation depend on the development of Protestantism."[37] He decreed religious freedom in December 1860, and the government of Maximilian ratified that fundamental right. Anglo-American missionaries intensified their efforts to convert Mexicans to evangelical Christianity and began to extend their operations to the northern part of the country. This process can best be explained through the missionary work of various Protestant sects in Northeast Mexico and Texas.

Presbyterians were prominent because Melinda Rankin carried their banner in northern Mexico. She had bided her time working with Mexican children in

Brownsville while waiting for conditions in Mexico to change. As the U.S. Civil War ended, the war against French intervention was still raging in Mexico, but Maximilian's government had proclaimed religious freedom, so the impatient Rankin decided it was time to make a move and she headed resolutely for the interior of Mexico. She decided to establish her mission in Monterrey, but had to return to the United States in order to raise funds. She traveled back to Matamoros through a guerrilla-infested region, and she and her party were captured by one of Cortina's bands. During her brief captivity Rankin remained active, providing food and words of religious comfort to the tired and hungry soldiers. The rebel leader himself came into camp at the head of a group of musicians. Rankin recorded her first impression: "He was the complete personification of a guerrilla chief" with his "Indian face and evil eye." Cortina contemplated the prisoners for a while and then declared that he was hungry. Rankin and her traveling companions quickly prepared a meal and refreshments and thereby won their freedom. The missionary continued her journey to New England, where she was able to obtain about $14,000 in donations, with which she bought a building in the center of Monterrey to serve as a chapel, school, and residence.[38]

By 1869, Rankin had raised enough funds to hire and train Mexican religious workers and send them as missionaries to the neighboring states of Zacatecas, Durango, Tamaulipas, and San Luis Potosí. All this activity aroused the hostility of the Catholic Church and lay Catholics in the population. U.S. consul Joseph Ulrich declared that "public opinion was 'universally against the operation of the missionaries.' From the beginning, locals threw stones at the windows of the mission and painted the walls with insults."[39]

Another major problem faced by all missionaries was Mexico's continued instability and political violence. Just four years after the French intervention, Porfirio Díaz's La Noria revolt shattered the peace of Nuevo León. Mission work was interrupted because Bible sellers and teachers had to hide to avoid being conscripted by either of the warring factions. Forced loans were exacted, which missionaries were obliged to pay along with the rest of the population. The revolt kept the state in turmoil during the latter part of 1871 and the early part of 1872. Nevertheless, in the midst of the struggle, Rankin was able to write to her supporters in New England: "We have some eight or nine schools, where the rising generation are taught the principles of the Bible." Rankin departed Mexico in the fall of 1872, after helping to lay the foundation for a permanent Protestant presence in Northeast Mexico. That foundation was reinforced by Brígido Sepúlveda, an early convert to Presbyterianism who oversaw the development of an organized congregation in the 1880s and the erection of a church in the 1890s. Rankin wrote of her experiences in Texas and Mexico in *Twenty Years among the Mexicans*.[40]

Protestantism in Monterrey and Northeast Mexico was also advanced by the work of three Baptists: James Hickey, Thomas Westrup, and W. D. Powell. Hickey, a native of Ireland, studied theology in England, then immigrated to North America and lived and preached successively in Canada, the United States, and Mexico. He was in Texas doing mission work among the Mexican population when the Civil War erupted. His Union sympathies led him to Mexico, where his knowledge of Spanish and his love for humanity allowed him to blend easily into the population. In late 1862, he began to preach and distribute Bibles in Monterrey and the surrounding region. His humility and kindness won him many adherents, who referred to him as "Don Santiago." One of his followers was Thomas Westrup, an Englishman who had arrived in Monterrey in 1860. Westrup embraced the Baptist faith and Hickey ordained him as a minister in an unofficial ceremony that was later formalized in New York. In 1864, one year before Rankin's arrival, Hickey and Westrup founded the First Christian Church in Monterrey. Hickey's life among the Mexicans was cut short by his death in 1866. His last request, to be buried in the United States but facing Mexico, was granted when he was laid to rest in Brownsville in December 1866.[41]

The combined work of Rankin, her successors, Hickey, and Westrup resulted in a growing Protestant presence in Nuevo León. By 1880 the municipal government of Monterrey reported that the Presbyterians had eighty-four followers and one minister, while the Baptists had sixty-one adherents with two ministers.[42] These results did not impress consul Joseph Ulrich. He admired the tenacity of the missionaries, but considered that the outcome of their work was insignificant. He concluded that trying to Christianize people who were already Christians was like "taking coals to Newcastle."[43]

The Baptists greatly strengthened their presence in Mexico through the activities of W. D. Powell, who worked in Texas for several years before being sent to Coahuila to do mission work in 1882. He arrived at Saltillo at a propitious moment. Evaristo Madero had become governor in December 1880, and he and Powell struck up a friendship based on both men's desire to promote education. Their collaboration was reflected in the 1883 Annual Meeting of the Baptist Church at San Antonio, where it was revealed that Powell had "been tendered lands and buildings by Governor Madero . . . for the purpose of establishing and endowing orphanages and an institute for higher education of women." These institutions would be operated by the Baptists but open to members of all religions. The Baptist Assembly also resolved to raise $20,000 for the two projects.[44] Within two years the school for women became a reality and it was named after the Coahuilan governor. The school's founding also attracted Texas Baptists. A Dallas newspaper reported, "The Madero institute for girls, at Saltillo, will soon be opened and a large excursion of Baptists will leave Texas for Saltillo on the 29th instant to witness the opening ceremonies."[45]

Years later, Powell proudly reported that he had opened two schools, one for boys and one for girls. In six years of operation, the latter had prepared seventy girls to be teachers, an achievement unmatched by any other school on the frontier. He declared with confidence that he had "the best ladies college in the country outside the City of Mexico."[46] Powell stated that there was a genuine popular interest in education and that most of the funds for the schools had been collected in Mexico. The incentive to study was great. "The teachers are well paid. Every woman graduate taking a school receives at least $60 per month. . . . The men are paid as high as $100 per month. The children are all furnished text books by the government, a provision rendered necessary by the general poverty of the masses." Powell gave much of the credit to the visionary governor, Evaristo Madero, who "is one of our most liberal patrons" and "president of our board of trustees."[47]

The Society of Friends (Quakers) was represented by the extraordinary husband-and-wife team of Samuel A. and Gulielma M. Purdie. Establishing a mission in Matamoros in 1871, they stated that one of their goals was "to make our mission the publishing centre of evangelical literature for all the Mexican missionary centres." Their aim was to send their bulletin, "El Ramo de Olivo" (The Olive Branch) to every state in Mexico. They relied on Mexican women, such as Elizia and Emiliana Flores, for assistance in setting type, translating, distributing copies and other activities related to publication.[48]

Samuel Purdie wrote of the dependability, friendliness, and hospitality of Mexicans, as well as their basic honesty: "We have yet to learn that there is more thieving in Mexico than in New York in proportion to the population."[49] He described the Mexicans as "a mixed people, Spanish, Indian and Aztec and all grades of admixtures with an addition of negro blood . . . all mingling together pleasantly and peaceably."[50] His son wrote of his parents: "The contact with this mixture of races must have expanded in their hearts the sense of universal brotherhood, one of the great fountains of missionary zeal."[51] Perceptive Mexicans could observe the basic goodness of these Anglo missionaries who yearned for their salvation and wonder why only a few miles away in the Nueces Strip other Anglos hated Mexicans and sought their destruction.

Compared to the Baptists, the Presbyterians, and the Society of Friends, the Methodist Church was slower in getting a foothold in northern Mexico. In 1880 a small group of Methodist women in Laredo began a school for Mexican girls that eventually became the Holding Institute, for many decades one of the most important educational institutions of that city. It was named after Nannie Emory Holding, a Kentucky missionary who became superintendent in 1883 and directed the institution for thirty years. In an effort to extend their influence, Texas Methodists convened the Border Conference of the Methodist Church in Monterrey in 1885. All Protestant sects stressed education and established schools as the foundation of their missions. Education was central to the Methodists in accordance with the teachings of Joseph Bellamy, who believed that evil in human nature arose from ignorance, and the way to combat evil was through education. Perhaps spurred by the conference in Monterrey, Methodist pastor John B. Laurens opened a school in that city offering bilingual education to Americans and Mexicans. It began as the Colegio Fronterizo and later became the Instituto Laurens, a school still in operation today and known for its excellence and for educating the political and economic elite of the city.[52]

It is impossible to know how many people were drawn to Protestantism. Jean Pierre Bastian, who has studied the Protestant experience in Mexico more than any other scholar, writes that 68,839 people were converts in 1910, out of a population of about 15.2 million.[53] Irrespective of numbers, the new religious denominations promoted diversity in a society unaccustomed to change. Protestant missionaries worked to change traditional Mexican values in order to build a new society based on individualism and not corporatism. This new way of viewing the world introduced concepts "centered not on the natural order pre-established by divine right, but on the individual as a subject of religious and political life." In this respect, missionary institutions "were genuine laboratories for inculcating democratic traditions."[54]

The propagation of Protestantism among the Mexican population of Texas is a vivid example of transborder religious cooperation, as converts in Mexico and South Texas were recruited to aid in evangelizing the ever-growing Mexican population in the state. The major Protestant churches had few Anglo missionaries who could speak Spanish, so these converts helped fill that void. Two men, both named Hernández, illustrate this phenomenon. Alejo Hernández had an interesting, though very short, life. Studying in a Catholic seminary when the

French invaded Mexico, he became embittered by the Church's support for the invaders. He left the seminary, joined the republican army, was captured, and ended up on the Rio Grande. During a visit to Brownsville he wandered into a Protestant religious service and was captivated by the serenity and joy of the worshipers. He converted to Methodism, traveled to Corpus Christi, and in 1870 was "licensed to preach" in the Methodist faith. He preached to the Mexican population around Corpus Christi and in Laredo. In 1872, he was ordered to Mexico City to head a newly organized church. After a year and a half in the Mexican capital he suffered a stroke that left him semi-invalid. He returned to Corpus Christi, where he died in 1875. He was barely thirty-three years old.[55]

The other Hernández, Vicente, was born in Zacatecas around 1850. At the age of twelve "he was drafted into the Mexican army to fight against the French forces under Emperor Maximilian, and was present in Queretaro, Mexico, when Maximilian was tried . . . and shot." Returning to the border region, he moved to Corpus Christi and then to San Diego "where he was converted and baptized into the Methodist church by Reverend Felipe Cordova in the year 1877. From San Diego he went to Monterrey, Mexico, and attended the Presbyterian Mission School, studying for the ministry." After a two-year stay in the Nuevo León capital, he returned to San Diego, where he served for more than half a century as the minister of the Methodist church in that town.[56]

Because the Texas Methodist Church grew faster than other Protestant denominations, it needed more Spanish-speaking missionaries, and recruited them from among the converts in Monterrey. In 1874 William Headen, a prominent Methodist and city leader of Corpus Christi, traveled to Monterrey and brought back three men, Doroteo García, Fermín Vidaurri, and Felipe N. Córdova. They became missionaries and were named to head districts in Texas: García in Corpus Christi, Córdova in San Diego, and Vidaurri in Laredo. It was Córdova who ordained Vicente Hernández a few years later.[57] The Assembly of the Southern Methodist Conference of West Texas reported in 1879 that there were fifteen Mexican preachers holding prominent seats in its annual assembly, all of whom had been accepted in the previous five years. The presence of these Mexican preachers facilitated Methodist expansion. When a Methodist church was built in San Antonio in 1881, an enthusiastic supporter wrote: "We rejoice! A Methodist Episcopal Church almost on the very borders of Mexico. The Methodist Episcopal Church in the United States and the Methodist Episcopal Church in Mexico will soon shake hands across the Rio Grande."[58]

The Presbyterian Church, according to historians R. Douglas Brackenridge and Francisco O. García-Treto, was "the pacesetter in Mexican American missions in nineteenth-century Texas." Expanding out of its "missionary activity in Mexico the first Mexican Presbyterian congregation in Texas was organized in Brownsville in 1877. Mexican Presbyterian converts from Matamoros were instrumental in forming the Brownsville Church." In 1884 that church "became part of the newly formed Presbytery of the State of Tamaulipas, Mexico." This relationship continued into the twentieth century, and the Brownsville congregation "remained a 'foreign church' on Texas soil." One of the religious workers trained in Matamoros, José María Botelló, joined with Reverend J. W. Graybill in establishing a Presbyterian presence among the Mexican population of San Marcos.[59]

The success of Presbyterian missions among Mexican Texans over "nearly half a century" was in part the work of Walter Scott. Scott's "mother was a descendant of the French Huguenots and his father was a staunch Scottish Calvinist." Like Santiago Hickey, they emigrated to Canada, then the United States, and finally Mexico when the Civil War came to Texas. Scott "was born near Monterrey, Mexico in a small adobe hut on August 6, 1865." His father "raised his family to appreciate both Anglo and Mexican cultures." The bilingual and bicultural Walter came under the influence of the Presbyterian mission in Monterrey.[60] After his family returned to San Antonio in 1878, Scott prepared himself for the ministry and in 1892 was ordained as "evangelist to the Mexican people," which according to Brackenridge and García-Treto, "marked the beginning of a new era in Mexican American evangelism in Texas."[61]

According to Brackenridge and García Treto, Scott "went on an extensive tour of southwest Texas covering some nine hundred miles in six weeks." He "gathered together small groups of potential church members, distributed Spanish Bibles and tracts, and began to acquire land in various communities where small but substantial churches could be built. . . . Many of the church buildings were erected in part with his own hands." This European American preacher "identified with Mexican Americans to a much greater extent than any who had preceded him and most who followed him."[62]

It is clear that Scott's commitment to the Mexican community came from deep inside, but his father, Walter Scott Sr., also likely instilled in him an admiration for the work of Santiago Hickey. Hickey profoundly influenced the senior Scott, who lived in Monterrey and collaborated with the Baptist missionary in his work of evangelization. He wrote that Hickey had visited almost every "house, mansion or

Walter S. Scott (seated in the middle) was a Presbyterian minister who worked tirelessly among the Mexican population of South Texas. In this photo he is surrounded by young Mexican associates. R. Douglas Brackenridge Research Papers, 1886–1975, Austin Seminary Archives, Stitt Library. Courtesy of Austin Presbyterian Theological Seminary.

hut" in the region: "many were the privations that he suffered, the heat, the cold, hunger and thirst, and through it all he traveled on his horse with his sixty-five years as if he was a young man of twenty, riding forty or fifty miles a day under a burning sun."[63] The spirit of Santiago Hickey and his service to the Mexican people survived in the lives of Walter Scott and his son.

Religion was a bridge that united Anglos and Mexicans, but that bridge was narrow. Despite the best efforts of Protestant missionaries most Mexicans in Northeast Mexico and Texas remained Catholic. The few who accepted conversion risked rejection or, at the very least, incomprehension by members of their community and even of their own family. One of the few early converts to leave a written record was José Policarpo Rodríguez, who not only accepted Methodism, but became a preacher and wrote of his conversion. Rodríguez was a guide and tracker for the Whiting-Smith expedition to find a suitable route from San Antonio to El Paso in 1849. In the 1870s, he was operating his ranch along Privilege Creek in Bandera County. A friend, James Tafolla, who had been educated in Georgia, had converted to Methodism and worked diligently to convert Rodríguez. In 1876 he finally succeeded. Rodríguez's conversion to

Methodism caused a sensation among his neighbors and friends. He wrote that "the report that I had gone crazy was believed by many." His family was adamantly opposed, but he was undeterred and, not content merely to adopt a new religion, he became a preacher, exhorting others to do the same.[64]

Rodríguez carried out his new role with missionary zeal: "I had two good horses and a complete camping outfit, and lived among the people. I visited them wherever I found them, and used all kinds of methods to reach them with the gospel." One of the methods was through medicine. Rodríguez offered his knowledge of how to cure various ailments to people who often had no access to a doctor. He wrote, "Medicine has opened many a closed door to me, and . . . I gained an entrance that seemed securely closed against the gospel." Missionaries in Mexico used schools effectively to open doors among the Catholic population. Rodríguez used medicine to equal effect. He also wrote about his experiences with hostile Catholic priests. A man who had scalped an Indian and had shown the scalp to a horrified Anglo woman was not one to back away from aggressive priests. His life experiences had made him tough, a quality required for his new line of work. [65]

He required resources to venture farther afield, so he called on his friends, including the Mavericks of San Antonio, for support. He joined the Reverend A. H. Sutherland on two trips to Eagle Pass to preach among Mexicans there. Sutherland, who became one of the principal Methodist missionaries in northern Mexico, encouraged Rodríguez to work south of the border as well as in Texas, and soon Rodríguez was visiting communities in Guerrero and Zaragoza, Coahuila. His religious work, like that of many other missionaries, was not limited by geographical, racial, or class boundaries. For the sake of Christ, he wrote, "I talked to everybody I came in contact with—Americans, Mexicans, and negroes."[66]

The Defiant Response of Catholicism

The growing Protestant presence among Mexicans in Texas and Northeast Mexico posed a challenge to the Catholic Church. Its response depended on the location of the battlefield. In Northeast Mexico Catholicism competed on its home turf with overwhelming support, or at least acquiescence, from the majority of the population, but an uneasy relationship with the government. In Texas it had no advantages, but struggled fiercely to maintain and increase its sway among the Mexican population. The Catholic hierarchies in Texas and Northeast Mexico faced the Protestant challenge in a complex and changing environment where transborder connections continued to be important.

The liberal assault on the Mexican Catholic Church, embodied in the Reform laws and carried out through two bloody wars, left that institution battered, but it continued to have the support of the majority of Mexicans, who for three centuries had known no other religion. Relations between the Church and the government are exemplified by what occurred in Nuevo León. In 1857 Santiago Vidaurri expelled the bishop of Monterrey, Francisco de Paula y Verea, who found refuge in Brownsville. By 1864, Vidaurri had been removed from power and Verea returned. Throughout the 1860s and 1870s government-Church relations were ambivalent. The state sought to impose its authority and the Church to maintain its prerogatives. One of the Reform laws required citizens to register births, marriages, and deaths with the government, but many citizens ignored this obligation and continued to record life events with the Church. The Nuevo León official newspaper editorialized: "Here in the state . . . the civil registry has been established in all of the municipalities." It failed to gain traction however due to "the indifference of many persons whose wrongly understood religious sentiments outweigh their social obligations."[67]

In the tense rapprochement between the state government and the Church, the Church was vulnerable because it was chronically short of funds. It could not continue to defy a government that authorized the celebration of public events and fiestas that were an important source of the Church's income. The government also realized that it could not provide all the services that the people required, so when the Church asked for authorization to collect contributions in all towns for the construction of an orphanage to be administered by the Sisters of Charity, the government could hardly refuse.[68] The state government also recognized that religion was an essential element of social control, so it acceded to requests by the Church to use funds from public celebrations to build or renovate church buildings, a prerogative that was not available to Protestants.[69]

The Church in Nuevo León faced a severe financial crisis in the late 1860s and early 1870s, which coincided with the initial period of Protestant activity in the state. In February 1867, Church officials in Monterrey lamented the sad financial state of the cathedral. Its resources had dwindled "to the point that the day is not far off when mass will be suspended for lack of resources."[70] Bishop Verea was especially concerned about the deplorable condition of the seminary, which was "in its most extreme level of misery and neglect." The seminary was his main priority because without new priests the Church had no future: "In the diocese there are more than sixty parishes that only have one priest," many of whom were old and sick. The thirty-one seminarians set to study in a seminary operating in a rented building were inadequate to meet the need.[71]

Verea proved to be an extraordinary prelate. He recognized that the world was changing and that his church had to adapt to new circumstances. In a pastoral letter he called for a spiritual renewal of the clergy. Like the first Christians, they had endured abuse, public ridicule, expropriation of their property, and exile, but this should only make them stronger in their faith. They had been accustomed to living in abundance and now their poverty would purify them. His goal was to develop a clergy that was "chaste, pure, pious, devoted to its duties, and detached from the vanities and pleasures of the earth." Verea no doubt remembered his experiences with the simple Oblate fathers who lived a Spartan existence in the rough and rugged border region.[72]

Bishop Verea was succeeded in 1879 by a man who had been Maximilian's personal chaplain. Ignacio Montes de Oca was a brilliant but phlegmatic and difficult man who demanded blind obedience from those who served him. Perhaps his most distinguishing feature was his profound aversion to Protestants. In his sermon at the benediction of the imposing church of Nuestra Señora del Roble, he stated that the building was made of stone, built to last, not like the flimsy wooden churches of the United States. Like the church founded by Christ, it would resist all its enemies. He referred to the Protestant missionaries as "vicious men," who came "to a Christian land that neither called them nor wanted them." Instead of doing productive work "they only know how to denigrate the beliefs of a country that gives them undeserved hospitality."[73]

On one occasion a lowly carpenter discovered the new bishop's vindictive nature. He "built benches for some foreigners who turned out to be Protestants and used them for their church." Montes de Oca promptly excommunicated the poor man. The carpenter remained barred from the church until the arrival of Archbishop Jacinto López, who "reinstated him and contracted him to build the doors of the cathedral." Montes de Oca's biographer described a self-important man: "The bishop, who excommunicated his parishioners for trading with heretics, proceeded like a prince through the streets of Monterrey on his horse, with green Episcopal colors on his harness and with a coat of arms embroidered in gold on the raw leather of his saddle."[74]

Montes de Oca's dogged defense of the Church led him into a bitter conflict with Evaristo Madero, who became governor of Coahuila in December 1880. Madero promulgated a law that prohibited priests from baptizing or marrying anyone whose birth or marriage had not been registered with the government. Priests who failed to obey could be assessed a fine or land in jail. Montes de Oca undertook a vigorous defense of his besieged Church. He did not succeed. Madero's law was upheld by the Supreme Court and the Coahuilan governor was vindicated for making an important contribution to defining the spheres of church and state in Mexico.[75]

The rivalry between these two powerful men was further sharpened by Madero's support of Protestantism. When the Baptist-sponsored Instituto Madero opened in early 1885, Montes de Oca called it an "aberration" that propagated "Anabaptist propaganda" and threatened to censure all families that sent their daughters there. Madero, he accused, "summoned the Anabaptists, [and] gave them a home and property for their school. He gave them large amounts of money . . . that came from Catholic taxpayers." The bishop's accusations may or may not have been true.[76] What is certain is that he was opposing a man with a progressive spirit who truly believed in religious toleration. As governor, Madero did use public money to print and distribute in Spanish four books of Benjamin Franklin's writings. He believed that Franklin embodied the national essence of the United States, based on values of hard work, frugality, commonsense, honesty, and modesty, among others. It is impossible to know how many people, especially young people, were influenced by these books, but their circulation, as well as the presence of missionaries and other Americans, gave norteños a more benign image of their neighbor than the image forged by war and plunder of their territory.[77]

CATHOLIC EXPANSION IN THE MEXICAN REGION OF TEXAS

North of the Rio Grande the Catholic Church did not carry the burden of the church-state conflict that was rocking Mexico. Its major challenge was to keep pace with the expanding population, which included many Catholics of German, Irish, and Mexican origin. The Catholic population outgrew the Galveston Diocese, so a new one was established in 1874, centered at San Antonio and led by Bishop Anthony Dominic Pellicer. In the same year, Father Pierre Parisot wrote that "immigrants, especially from the neighboring land of revolutions, came in such numbers" that it was also necessary to establish a vicariate at Brownsville.

Bishop Dominic Manucy was appointed to the Brownsville vicariate in February 1875 and took possession that month.[78]

Bishop Pellicer was greatly loved and he served his diocese well. By the time of his death in 1880, it "contained forty-seven thousand Catholics, forty-five priests, fifty churches, and eight chapels." He was succeeded by Bishop Jean Claude Neraz, who "lived a Spartan existence, often having only the corn his people donated for him to live on."[79] The egalitarian community that one usually associates with a religious congregation evidently had its limits. Faced with ministering to a heterogeneous population, the San Antonio Diocese, in a display of adaptability, and perhaps to avoid discord, separated congregations by language and culture. Thus, St. Mary's Church "ministered to those of Irish extraction, St. Joseph's ministered to the Germans, San Fernando to the Spanish-speaking, and St. Michael's to the Polish." Mexico, which did not have large numbers of European immigrants, did not have the same issue, though even if it had, given its history of mestizaje it is unlikely that it would have followed the same policy.[80]

In the Nueces Strip and the lower Rio Grande Valley, Bishop Manucy established a highly authoritarian style of leadership not unlike that of Montes de Oca in Monterrey. An ill-tempered man, Manucy was not to be crossed. Parisot phrased it delicately: "Bishop Manucy was a profound thinker, an interesting conversationalist, but a man who was somewhat melancholy and this made him unpleasant when under the influence of discouragement."[81] No one can deny however that he was a skillful administrator. By 1882, he had "seen nine new churches and chapels built and four priests ordained and the erection of three large chapels in the country and convents in Rio Grande City and Roma." Forty thousand Catholics resided in his jurisdiction. "Bishop Manucy, despite his negative attitude, had served his people well."[82]

Oblate priests, the Catholic cavalry, continued to travel the dangerous trails of South and West Texas and northern Mexico. They "braved bandits and marauders, flash floods, and seemingly interminable droughts; and suffered infestations of ticks, chiggers, fleas, and rashes of all kinds. They abided extreme hunger, thirst, fatigue, and loneliness." Due largely to their efforts, people in many ranches and isolated communities were united through the bond of religion.[83] On rare occasions these settlements received visits from higher clergy. In 1879 a reception was given for the bishop at Los Federales Ranch. Father Parisot described the great piety of the Mexican population, but also their partial assimilation to American culture. In one home, pictures of Andrew Jackson and Robert E. Lee hung on the two sides of an altar.[84]

Europeans continued to dominate the composition of the Catholic clergy. Bishop Claude Marie Dubuis, who succeeded Bishop Jean Marie Odin as head of the Galveston Diocese in 1862, continued his predecessor's practice of traveling to Europe to recruit priests and nuns. In 1866 he persuaded a group of Sisters of Lyon to come to Texas and establish a hospital. They were sent to San Antonio, and in 1869 the first Catholic hospital there opened its doors under the auspices of the Sisters of Charity of the Incarnate Word. The hospital was available to "all persons without distinction of nationality or creed."[85] For their part, the priests hailed from various orders and national origins. There were Franciscans, Benedictines, and Carmelites from Germany; Resurrectionists from Poland; Vicentians from Spain and Ireland; and Jesuits from Spain, Italy, and Mexico, among others. Marianists had a German-French origin while the Oblates "were overwhelmingly French. Yet due to their borderlands ministry, they became, for the most part, fluent in Spanish, the common language of the border country, while their English usually remained halting."[86]

Women made a huge contribution in providing education and social services for the Catholic Church. The Sisters of the Incarnate Word, the Ursuline Sisters, and the Sisters of Charity, among others, "gave, in the majority of cases, a great impetus to education and social institutions like universities, hospitals, schools, orphanages, asylums for the old, etc."[87] In many of the schools "the majority of the students were Mexican or Mexican American children." The Sisters of Charity of the Incarnate Word established the first school for girls in 1875. It was located at San Fernando Cathedral in a predominantly Mexican neighborhood.[88]

Transborder cooperation among Catholic clerics, which had been common under Bishops Odin and Verea in the 1850s, continued in the 1870s. In March 1878, St. Mary's College, at that time San Antonio's "most prominent educational institution" and destined to become St. Mary's University, was the scene of a "courtly public reception with an address in Spanish and orchestral and vocal music" organized by Bishop Pellicer for the visiting Bishop Verea of Monterrey.[89] In November 1882, with Pellicer and Verea gone from the scene, Bishop Montes de Oca of Monterrey and a group of priests visited Corpus Christi for the dedication of St. Patrick's Church.[90] On another occasion, Montes de Oca was invited to visit San Antonio and, in view of his feud with Madero and other problems, he accepted eagerly.[91] While in the Alamo City he became aware of the pioneering educational work being done by the Sisters of the Incarnate Word and in 1885, at his request, "the Sisters were called to teach in the College of La Purisima, in the City of Saltillo." According to María Luisa Vález, the establishment of that school "was due to the efforts of Jesuit Father Maas, who . . . left Texas to become superior of the College of San Juan in Saltillo, where he and the bishop became friends and conceived the College of La Purisima."[92]

Priests and nuns crossed the border as duty or circumstances required. In 1874, Father Francis Henry Andres, who had served as the first pastor of St. Joseph's Church in San Antonio and who was fluent in Latin, Greek, German, English, and Spanish, "was called to Mexico, serving first in a small town on the Rio Grande, and then in Linares, Ramos Arizpe, Monterrey, and later at Musquiz [sic], Coahuila."[93] The vecinos of Eagle Pass/Piedras Negras were variously served by Mexican or American priests. Oftentimes one or the other town was without a permanent priest, so the void was filled by a cleric from across the border.[94]

Political events in the heart of Mexico contributed to the transborder movement of Catholic priests and nuns. In the mid-1870s, President Sebastián Lerdo de Tejada stiffened the government's religious policies. Tensions rose and Lerdo expelled all religious orders from the country. The Sisters of Charity were forced to leave in early 1875 and some of them found refuge at least temporarily in Brownsville. In March, writes Parisot, "there came the last batch of twenty two Sisters of Charity. . . . They were accompanied by Father Frias, Lazarist, of Mexico, and the Rev. Fr. Planchet, a French Priest of Monterrey." The Sisters were invited to share the convent of the Sisters of the Incarnate Word until their departure for New Orleans.[95]

Reminiscent of colonial times, the Jesuit order was once again expelled from Mexico in 1873, even before the nuns. A group of these priests, including Europeans, Americans, and Mexicans, arrived in San Antonio. The Jesuits established "an informal seminary for the benefit of their own members." Bishop Pellicer "began sending a few men to them for training, and in 1876 arranged for them formally to open a seminary as well as a men's college in Seguin, near San Antonio."[96] The men's college opened in the fall of 1876 under the name El Colegio de Nuestra Señora de Guadalupe. Bishop Verea of Monterrey was one of the patrons. A pamphlet described the college as located "in a beautiful setting, with a study plan at a high school level, which included 'reading, writing, elements of English grammar, calligraphy, history, geography, arithmetic and Christian doctrine.'" The colegio was a multiethnic and multiracial institution. Teachers of various nationalities gave classes to students from the United States, Mexico, and other countries.[97]

The goal was for the college to attain a sufficiently large enrollment to sustain the seminary, but it failed to do so, remaining in operation for only four years.

As early as 1878, when Porfirio Díaz relaxed Lerdo's restrictions on the Catholic Church, some of the Jesuits began to trickle back to Mexico and by 1880 the school closed. Texas's loss was Coahuila's gain because Bishop Verea invited the Jesuits to open the Colegio de San Juan Nepomuceno in Saltillo, which became one of the most prestigious educational institutions in northern Mexico.[98]

Another form of transborder cooperation promoted by Catholicism was schooling. Upper-class Mexicans of Texas and Northeast Mexico had diverse reasons for sending their children to educational institutions across the border. When Vidaurri was still in power in Nuevo León, he received a letter from his friend Santos Benavides in Laredo asking for a favor. He wanted to know "which areas of study were available to girls in the convent [at Monterrey], as well as the conditions for payment. I want my daughter to go to that city to stay for a year in the convent because she has lost her capacity to write in Spanish as it is not studied in San Antonio."[99]

Some of northern Mexico's wealthier citizens wanted their children to master English, preferably in an American setting. They discovered that by attending Catholic schools in Texas their children could learn both English and American values while maintaining traditional religious and cultural values embodied in Catholicism. The correspondence of Evaristo Madero provides a glimpse into this process. Not only did he send his children to study in the United States and Europe, but several of his nieces studied at St. Josephus Academy at San Antonio. One of these, Isabel Navarro, wrote to him often and kept him informed about his other nieces at the school, Carolina, Jovita, and Rafaelita. In May 1872, Isabel wrote of being anxious for summer to arrive so that she could go home to see her family. Her English was progressing, she wrote, though it still lacked polish: "I cannot write you more longer because I can not express myself in this language well."[100]

A man as open-minded as Madero could easily reconcile his support of both Baptist schools in Coahuila and Catholic institutions in Texas. His philanthropy toward the Ursuline Sisters in San Antonio was well known. August Santleben wrote, "The Sisters of the Ursuline Academy . . . have good reasons for holding him in grateful remembrance because of the aid he extended to them during and after the Civil War in the United States."[101] He was also a benefactor of their convent in Laredo, where a relative of his, Sister St. Pierre, was mother superior. After hearing that Madero was to send a young woman to study in Texas, St. Pierre wrote and asked him to consider the convent at Laredo. "I know more than anyone else what she needs to learn. First of all to be a good house keeper, which is very important for a young lady."[102]

Madero's friends in San Antonio often helped him to make the necessary contacts. Friedrich Groos, who had transferred many of his operations to the Alamo City, responded to Madero's inquiry about St. Louis College, a school operated by the Christian Brothers. Groos said he knew little of the school, but that four of his nephews had studied at San Antonio Academy, directed by William B. Sealey, and that it had an excellent reputation. One of those nephews entered Princeton after completing high school. Only English was spoken at the school, but other languages were taught. San Antonio Academy, wrote Groos, accepted only twelve interns and had filled its quota, but he offered to ask his brother, Gustav, to write to Sealey to see if he could make room for Madero's two sons. The institution had the backing of some of San Antonio's principal financial leaders, who established the school in 1886 to provide young men with a quality college preparatory education.[103]

BALANCING HATE AND HARMONY

There is ample testimony in the historical record that many Anglo-Texans hated Mexicans and that some, if not most, rangers treated Mexicans in a brutal manner. For every expression of ethnic or racial hatred, however, we can point to an opposite expression of admiration and respect. For every act of violence there are many instances of harmony and sharing. Unfortunately, the hatred and the violence—still the focus in today's news media—have attracted the attention of historians. Who wants to know about everyday people working or celebrating together? Historical documents and narratives by historians who do want to know about those people allow us to piece together a fairly convincing pattern of interracial sharing, mutual help, collaboration, and even friendship that is not unusual in a frontier society where cooperation in fighting common enemies such as Indians or disease might mean the difference between life and death.

As their correspondence amply attests, U.S. consular agents did not hesitate to aid Texas Mexicans when they suffered abuse in Mexico.[104] Of course, it was the duty of consular agents to do so. Other Anglo-Americans, such as William Stone and Bethel Coopwood, were under no obligation to represent the people of Piedras Negras in their restitution claims against the United States for the destruction caused by the Callahan raid of 1855. Both of these men acted either out of solidarity or self-interest, but the end result is that they provided legal support to the claimants before the U.S.-Mexico Claims Commission of 1868.[105]

August Santleben documented various acts of solidarity among Anglos and Mexicans. On one occasion the supervisor of his wagons, George Holiday, was camped at Sabinal Creek when, suddenly, "a young man from East Texas, who was looking for trouble, rode into his camp with a pistol in his hand, swearing that he intended to kill a Mexican and dared them to show themselves. Holiday did not want to see his men killed, and . . . he advised them to open fire on the foolish fellow." They merely wounded the troublemaker and he went off "crying out that he was shot and was afraid that he would die."[106]

Women played a vital though largely unacknowledged role in the Texas-Mexico borderlands, and one of their principal contributions was in bridging the divide between Anglos and Mexicans. A comprehensive study has not been attempted, but various sources give an idea of their worth. On one of his many travels, August Santleben met Sister St. Stephens of San Antonio, who traveled to the military forts on the frontier caring for orphans. Many years later, he wrote, "Many helpless orphans have been sheltered, nourished, and trained partly through her efforts in the forty years since I first became acquainted with her."[107]

Caring for others on the frontier was not precisely characteristic of most men other than doctors, but it was common in many women. In November 1869, the American community in Saltillo laid to rest a woman they truly loved and admired. Josefa Guajardo had died at the age of sixty-two after thirty-seven years of marriage to James Hewetson, the Irish empresario and friend of Stephen F. Austin. Hamilton Bee, who was living in Saltillo with his family at the time, wrote the obituary. The foreign residents, he wrote, wished to express "their appreciation of the services, rendered by this estimable lady to . . . the sick and distressed foreigners of all nationalities, who have required assistance when in this place." Doña Josefa fed starving prisoners, "ministered to the sick and dying, of our countrymen, and passed a long life in doing good to her fellow beings." Bee praised the "charity, the kindness, and the virtues of this Mexican lady" and expressed to Hewetson that "the name of his wife [would be] held as blessed in the hearts of hundreds in Texas, and elsewhere, who have been the recipients of her goodness."[108]

Salomé Ballí and Petra Vela exemplify the role of women in the Texas-Mexico border region. Both belonged to the upper class and married Anglo men, but adhered faithfully to their Mexican culture. Salomé Ballí married John Young, the founder of Edinburgh, Texas, and after he died, married his business partner, John McAllen, one of the founders of the city of McAllen. In 1860, she was one of the wealthiest people in Texas. The social life she established on the Santa Anita Ranch reflected her cultural roots. She and her second husband "supported their employees like an extended family, caring for their health and well being."

Every June 24, during the celebration of the Día de San Juan (Saint John's Day), "McAllen brought in provisions, liquors, and a band of musicians . . . the vaqueros and their families would assemble at one of the water wells to enjoy food, drink and dancing in the cool shade."[109]

Petra Vela was a widow with several children by her first husband, Luis Vidal, when she married Mifflin Kenedy in 1854. She was described by contemporaries as "notably handsome of tall and commanding figure, united with [a] grace in bearing and winning manners." A highly intelligent woman, she was also described as "warm and energetic with a spirit of love that dominated her nature." Two features stand out: her fierce devotion to her family and her generous nature. Her family was large; in 1860 it consisted of six girls and five boys. Her charitable acts, according to her biographers, were "often done in secrecy and silence." She supported the struggling Catholic Church with her donations, contributing to the school of the Ursuline Sisters and the construction of the Church of the Immaculate Conception in Brownsville.[110] The land she had inherited from her father combined with Kenedy's business acumen to amass a family fortune. They made a good team. Her knowledge of Spanish and Mexican culture helped Kenedy navigate the complex social and cultural life of the region, much as he had navigated the Rio Grande with his steamboats.[111]

Petra Vela and Salomé Ballí were such great friends that they referred to themselves as sisters. They exemplify many other women whose stories remain hidden. Women were the principal protagonists of cultural transmission and of adherence to family and the Catholic faith. Thousands of them married Anglo-Americans or Europeans or joined with them in informal unions and contributed to the construction of a multiethnic and multicultural society in the border region.[112] Petra and Salomé lived in a society that had been conquered militarily and politically by Americans, but culturally it stood unbowed. Historian Patricia Nelson Limerick has argued that in the American West "the contest for property and profit has been accompanied by a contest for cultural dominance. Conquest also involved a struggle over languages, cultures, and religions." In the Texas-Mexico borderlands women such as Petra Vela and Salomé Ballí were in the front lines of that struggle. They formed a bulwark for the protection of Mexican cultural values even as they integrated into Anglo society.[113]

The sharing of danger and the rigors of the frontier was accompanied by the occasional sharing of gaiety. While some Anglos were hunting down and killing Mexicans in the Nueces Strip, others were fraternizing with them at parties, balls, and other festivities elsewhere. To mitigate the rigors of his arduous journeys,

Petra Vela, wife of rancher Mifflin Kenedy, was an intelligent and generous woman who contributed to many worthy causes. Mexican women like Vela who married Anglo husbands were on the front lines of a struggle to preserve Mexican culture in the U.S.-Mexican borderlands. No. 098-0306, UTSA Special Collections.

August Santleben attended social functions when the opportunity arose. In 1866, there was a Fourth of July celebration in Eagle Pass. The customs officers at Piedras Negras and their families joined their Eagle Pass neighbors to celebrate. Almost a year later, a grand ball was held at Piedras Negras to celebrate the republican victory over Maximilian. Writes Santleben, "All foreigners in Eagle Pass were invited, and many, including Thomas B. McManus, Charley Groos, and myself, were in attendance, together with all the best people in that part of the country."[114]

Other social events occurred spontaneously. In 1874 Santleben was traveling from Chihuahua to San Antonio with his wagons loaded with goods. Just outside Presidio del Norte he made camp. That night he was joined by James Clark, the customs officer at Presidio, with his wife and two other young ladies. Hugh Kelly was also there with six men who joined the party. They had supper then a dance.

Also present, wrote Santleben, was the Loza family of San Antonio. Professor Manuel Manso "and his orchestra troop, comprising several members, also from Chihuahua, were with our party, and they furnished music for the occasion."[115]

In spite of border frictions and threats and counter-threats by both governments, relations between military commanders on both sides of the border were often cordial. In his memoirs, General Zenas R. Bliss, who commanded several forts on the frontier, wrote: "Occasionally there were pleasant dances in Piedras Negras given by the Mexicans to which we were invited. On other occasions some of the people from Piedras Negras were invited to our side."[116] Bliss recalled a social event hosted by the elderly Mexican military commander at Piedras Negras. Bliss and his fellow officers furnished the refreshments and the old captain "invited all the pretty señoritas in town and their mothers, as usual, came with them." These older women took their places at a long table. "As soon as we took our seats," writes Bliss, "one old Mexican woman took a red bandana from her pocket and reached over and took a whole chicken and wrapped it in her handkerchief and placed it under her chair. The others followed suit and in a few seconds we had nothing left on the table, but the old captain made them put it back."[117]

Bonds of solidarity and friendship between Anglos and Mexicans were probably more common than many histories would lead us to believe. Santleben writes of the many poor Mexican families that he transported to San Antonio free of charge because they could not pay the fare. He remembered giving such a ride to an elderly woman living on the Castroville Road near Leon Creek, and for the next thirty-five years she looked for ways to show her gratitude "under the belief that she never [could] do enough for me or my family."[118] Zenas Bliss recounts an anecdote about his friend, Darío Rodríguez, an ordinary, hard-working farmer of Presidio del Norte, who had children born on both sides of the border. Rodríguez made the long trek from Presidio del Norte to see Bliss, who wrote that he "was highly honored, for though [Rodríguez] was about sixty years old, it was the first time that he had ever been that far from home and his friends said that nothing but a desire to see me would have induced him to have taken the journey of one hundred miles."[119]

Trust and loyalty were characteristic of these relationships. Charles Schreiner, whose family migrated to Texas from the Alsace-Lorraine region between Germany and France in 1852, became a supplier to Camp Verde, south of Kerrville, where he eventually opened a store. He married María Magdalena Enderle of San Antonio and they had eight children. To transfer money to San Antonio,

Schreiner employed one of his ranch hands, Simón Ayala, a "peg-legged Mexican cowboy who carried his gold in the mor[r]al [pouch] that usually held the rider's lunch" so that thieves would not suspect he was carrying a fortune. Ayala had been born in Monterrey, part of a family of sixteen. He "quietly took Captain Schreiner's money to the bank in San Antonio, when he might just as easily have ridden to refuge and personal fortune in his native land." Ayala "possessed that ingredient of personal honor that is more valuable and lasting than capital in business."[120]

Friendship was often forged through adversity. Zenas Bliss wrote of his association with Jesús Aguilar, his "splendid guide and trailer," which began in 1856 while Bliss was commander at Fort Davis. Aguilar was then a boy of sixteen who had spent years as an Indian captive. Upon Aguilar's premature death in the 1870s, Bliss penned the following entry in his diary: "We traveled many a hundred miles together across the plains and mountains of western Texas. . . . We had shared our last rations, divided the last drink of water, slept under the same blankets and under the same bushes without blankets, hunted and scouted for hostiles together for several years and I always found him a faithful and trustworthy man and guide."[121]

A revealing testimony of frontier friendship and solidarity comes from George W. Baylor, whose correspondence with Vidaurri during the Civil War was mentioned earlier. An Indian fighter and Confederate officer decorated for bravery, Baylor wrote of his campaigns in West Texas and northern Mexico against the Apaches, fighting alongside Mexicans. He particularly admired Luz Villanueva, who had "probably killed more Indians in personal combat than any one on the frontier." He "was well versed in the use of fire arms and knowledge of woodcraft that gives the frontier men of Mexico as well as the United States confidence in themselves and keeps them ready for any emergency." On one occasion Villanueva ran into a party of nine Indians and engaged in a desperate fight for his life. He fired 150 rounds, killed two of the enemy, and received multiple wounds. The Indians fled and Villanueva spent three days in extreme pain without food, water, or medical attention. On being found by a detachment of U.S. cavalry, he asked them to put a bullet in his head to end his misery. Instead, they took him to a hospital where his wounds were dressed and where he spent six months recovering.[122]

In 1879 George Baylor, who declared that "some of [his] most intimate friends were Mexicans," was appointed to command a Texas Ranger frontier battalion in Ysleta, near Paso del Norte. There, he and his rangers joined Mexican settlers on both sides of the river to combat the Apaches. At San Elizario he came upon Captain Gregorio García, "that grand, brave old Mexican" who had served with George's brother, General John R. Baylor. He recalled that "Captain García, with some of the citizens of San Elizario, prevented the massacre of the United States troops in Dog Canyon by his skill and courage."[123]

In November 1879, Baylor was notified that the Apache chief Victorio and about 150 Indians were committing depredations in the region then taking refuge in the Candelaria Mountains, south of Paso del Norte. Two groups of Mexicans had been sent to the mountains after the Apaches, but they underestimated Victorio's force and were massacred. Twenty-nine men in all lost their lives. Baylor was asked to join a force of one hundred vecinos, and he and nine other rangers crossed the border to join in the search for Victorio. Francisco Escajeda was appointed commander of the expedition with Baylor second in command. The combined force headed for the mountains but found no Apaches, only the bodies of the twenty-nine Mexicans, scattered among the rocks. "The saddest scene that I ever witnessed," wrote Baylor, "was that presented as we gathered the bodies of the murdered men. As each fresh discovery of a loved friend, brother, or father was made, and the last hope fled that any had escaped, a wail of sorrow went up, and I doubt if there was a dry eye either of Texan or Mexican. It has been well said 'a touch of human nature makes all men akin.'"[124]

Race Relations in Northeast Mexico

The same dichotomy of hate and harmony that was observed in Texas was evident in northern Mexico, where Americans formed a very tiny minority. For example, a state government census taken in Nuevo León in 1879 listed thirty-eight Americans, ten of whom lived in Monterrey. The actual figure was probably closer to one hundred because many did not register with the government. Nevertheless, compared to the total native Mexican population of 178,872 (in 1873), the American presence was insignificant. The other states of Northeast Mexico probably had similar numbers.[125]

Even though Americans made up a miniscule minority, some U.S. consular agents believed that many if not most Mexicans hated them and sought to expel them from the country. William Schuchardt wrote to the U.S. ambassador to Mexico, Thomas H. Nelson, that "the feelings of the Mexicans here and in fact in the greater part of Coahuila against the Americans is bitter, and is shown on all occasions."[126] Consul Juan Weber of Monterrey wrote of the Mexicans' aversion to Americans: "This prejudice is so deeply rooted amongst all classes, that it will take several generations to mitigate it." He concluded "that the two races can never be amalgamated; their antagonism is innate."[127]

The preceding statements represent the views of U.S. representatives in Mexico, and one might assume that as diplomats they felt the pulse of the country. What was the origin of the hostility against Americans in the 1870s? For some it was the loss of Mexican territory during the war or the rigors and the humiliation of the occupation. These events had happened more than two decades earlier, however, and had been tempered somewhat by the willingness of the United States to aid Mexico in her struggle against the French. For others it originated in information they received or stories they were told about Anglo oppression of their compatriots in Texas. It is true that anti-American perceptions and sentiments were common among members of the ruling class and the different spheres of the government and military. It is however clear that these attitudes arose not from inherent racism, but rather as a result of internal conflicts or external provocations.

In a brief and unfortunate term as commercial agent at Camargo, John Kelsey went through a "terrible ordeal" when rebels against the Juárez government took the town in early 1870. They demanded a forced loan of two thousand pesos from each merchant. When Kelsey refused to pay, they confiscated his store and occupied his home. Kelsey finally agreed to pay five hundred pesos when his friend the alcalde assured him he would be repaid in twenty days. Kelsey wrote that his life was in danger and when he called on Ringgold Barracks for help, it was refused. Kelsey, who had been in the border region for four decades, knew and got along well with the Mexican people, who in turn liked and respected him and his wife. The Kelseys had chosen to stay in Camargo after the Civil War, instead of returning to Texas like most Union sympathizers. This incident moved Kelsey to talk about the "well-known Mexican duplicity" and the lack of "security for life or property in this country."[128] Kelsey's change of attitude was caused by his personal ordeal, the result of an internal conflict, not Mexican racism.

Joseph Ulrich, the U.S. consul at Monterrey, believed that forced loans were the greatest plague visited upon American residents because the loans were arbitrary and, given Mexico's propensity for revolts, frequent. Local and national revolts afflicted Nuevo León in 1871–72 and 1876–77, and forced loans were common. In turn, rebel leaders and military chiefs sent to crush the revolts levied special taxes and loans that were seldom repaid. In February 1870, a group of foreign merchants signed a letter of protest to the state government, which had levied a special tax in order to suppress a revolt. The merchants argued that the tax violated treaties between the two nations that exempted foreigners from taxes for war or military purposes. State officials responded that the tax was applicable to all the people and foreigners did not have special privileges and could not be exempted.[129]

Another American victim of an internal Mexican conflict was Henry Muller, a longtime German-American resident of Chihuahua who was kidnapped for ransom in 1876. Muller was a merchant and owner of the Bank of Chihuahua. The rebel leader Ángel Trías had declared war on the local government, and one of his henchmen abducted Muller to exact a ransom of $3,500. Governor Mariano Samaniego called the rebels a bunch of "horse thieves" and refused their demands. He "also asked Mose Kelly, a merchant, tax collector, notary public, and ladies' man at Spencer's Rancho near American Presidio to use his influence and do what he could." Should Kelly's efforts fail, Samaniego suggested that Kelly "should 'call on the United States to cross over [the border] and give those bandits a good thrashing.'" That a Mexican governor would suggest U.S. military intervention to crush an internal revolt seems strange enough, but even more bizarre was the way the affair ended. Muller was released, crossed the border, obtained the $3,500, and returned to Chihuahua to pay his own ransom.[130]

The abuse Kelsey and Muller suffered was caused not by hatred of Americans, but by circumstances related to internal conflicts. External events were another factor. In 1878, the entire Mexican North was inflamed with talk of war against the United States after Washington ordered General E. O. C. Ord to cross the border against predators with or without permission. American visitor R. B. Myers saw General Gerónimo Treviño leave Monterrey for the border with orders to kill any Americans who crossed the border without a proper passport. The orders, wrote Myers, were "hailed with the greatest joy by every Mexican North of the Siera Madra [sic]."[131]

Much of the animosity toward Americans came from government officials. Commercial agent James J. Haynes complained to Washington that "all foreigners coming to this part of the country are looked on as interlopers and all their movements are jealously watched. This is particularly the case when the foreigners are Americans."[132] Charles Winslow, the commercial agent at Guerrero, Tamaulipas, explained that Americans did not choose to live in the Villas del Norte because an 1856 decree by the government of Ignacio Comonfort prevented them from owning land within twenty leagues of the border. Exceptions were few and hard to obtain because of the deep distrust of Americans in government circles. Only a few Americans, wrote Winslow, were living in the Villas: "three or four live in

[Nuevo] Laredo, one in Guerrero, two in Mier, four in Camargo, and the rest in Matamoras; being mostly doctors and merchants."[133]

The anti-American attitudes of the governing classes usually filtered down to the lower classes. From Piedras Negras, Schuchardt wrote that bitterness against Americans was propagated by government officials in the government newspaper and "the lower classes are taught and encouraged in this spirit of enmity."[134] This was especially true in Nuevo León under Governor Genaro Garza García, who was passionately anti-American. The governor used the official newspaper to systematically attack the U.S. government and Americans in Mexico. In an editorial, he accused Americans of constantly complaining and provoking the authorities. He told U.S. consul Joseph Ulrich that foreigners had no special rights and if they did not like conditions in Mexico, they should leave.[135] Ulrich accused Garza García of wanting to shoot him. Believing that the consul was working to stage a U.S. intervention in Mexico, the governor warned that if American troops arrived at Monterrey the consul "won't be present to welcome them."[136]

It is a truism that hatred often leads to violence, yet there are few crimes against Americans in the record, and those reported from the consulate at Monterrey were associated with robbery rather than racial hatred. In June 1873, a man named Henderson from Kansas came down to Nuevo León to buy mules. Near Cerralvo he was murdered and two young men traveling with him were also attacked, but managed to escape. Arrests were made in this case. A month later, Agustín Morrell was murdered at Sabinas Hidalgo. He was a doctor about sixty years of age who was engaged in purchasing hides and wool for several individuals in Corpus Christi, and it was widely known he usually had money. He went to sleep in his house with the door open, and assassins entered, buried a knife in him, and stole everything they could carry off. Later that year, Alexander Saunders was killed about forty miles north of Monterrey. His death caused profound consternation because he had a large family in Rio Grande City, had lived in the region for twenty years, and was well known and liked in Northeast Mexico. He and his servant, who was wounded, were on their way to Mier with about $3,500 in gold. Ulrich reported that "the cause of these attacks . . . on foreigners is that they generally are known to have money or other property." Such crimes would continue, he wrote, because of "the almost certain assurance on the part of the criminals that they will neither be arrested nor punished."[137] There is no evidence that these and other similar crimes were motivated by racial hatred or a desire to rid the country of foreigners.

Mexico did not have a policy of rejecting foreigners. After the defeat of Maximilian in 1867, the country entered the decade-long Restored Republic. Its leaders, beginning with Benito Juárez, worked to change society "on the basis of certain abstract ideas and one concrete model: the United States."[138] Immigration was encouraged, especially from Europe, but also from the United States. Hardworking foreigners with technical skills were considered necessary for efficient exploitation of Mexico's abundant natural resources. The Mexican national congress passed a law in May 1875 "offering immigrants land at low prices and long-term payments; it made it easier to acquire Mexican citizenship and it offered economic assistance and other benefits." Religious freedom was guaranteed, which was a precondition of many potential immigrants.[139] In spite of these and other measures, immigration was meager. Historian Erika Pani estimates that "between 1821 and 1910 in Mexico, foreigners never made up more than 0.78 percent of the population, which was reached in 1910." In 1876, at the end of the Restored Republic, there were only 25,067 foreign residents in the country and Spaniards made up 52 percent of the total. Americans made up only 6 percent of the foreign population.[140]

In sum it is safe to say that despite the innate nationalism of many government officials, foreigners, even Americans, were generally welcome in Mexico. Certain groups of Americans were however viewed as a threat. Dr. Plutarco Ornelas, the Mexican consul in San Antonio, wrote in 1879 of a large floating population of adventurers and fortune hunters primed to go into Mexico at the least provocation. Ornelas's larger worry, however, was of a possible migratory invasion of blacks into Mexico. He wrote of the exodus of ten thousand blacks to Kansas, where they were living in misery because of lack of employment opportunities. Ornelas wrote that the Democratic Party hated blacks and wished to be rid of them, and it was not inconceivable that they would try to send them to the northern states of Mexico, a situation that Ornelas referred to as "deplorable" in the extreme. Mexico would be attractive to blacks, he concluded, because they would "not find [there] the aversion and rejection of all classes" that they suffered in the United States. Ornelas was probably not opposed to a small trickle of blacks entering Mexico, but he panicked at the thought of a flood.[141]

Notwithstanding Ornelas's reservations, Americans were well received in Mexico and it is clear that neither all members of the upper class nor all government and military officials disliked them. I have already noted that Evaristo Madero not only had many friends in Texas, but also admired Benjamin Franklin and espoused American values. In 1879 a new consular agent arrived in Nuevo

Laredo. James Haynes, who had written about the hostility of Mexican officials, departed, and John F. Jenne took his place. Either there were different Mexican authorities as well, or the new vice consul got along with the existing ones a lot better. Jenne wrote, "I can find no fault with the authorities here, they evidently desire to treat American Citizens fairly. I have had but two or three trivial complaints that have easily been rectified."[142] On another front, the jefe político of the Rio Grande District, Vicente Galán, let William Schuchardt know that he wanted to live in harmony with the American people and was anxious not to "provoke unjust claims or complaints."[143]

Americans who lived in or often visited Mexico referred at times to anti-American hostility. August Santleben acknowledged that there were "popular prejudices on both sides" and that the upper class in Mexico generally avoided sending their children to school in the United States, preferring Europe. His own personal experiences in the country had "always been pleasant," and he expressed his gratitude for "the liberal and courteous treatment that was received by me from the government and people on every occasion, when I visited that country on business or pleasure."[144] When Baptist missionary W. D. Powell was asked how he got along with the Mexican people, he replied: "Splendidly. The officials are at all times ready to give us every protection." He added that they resolved problems that arose; only once did he ask for intervention from President Díaz "and that was the outcome of trouble with another denomination." Powell then added, "We have perfect religious liberty, complete separation of church and state, and as an American I have nothing that I can complain of. I have been treated kindly, and no American who will attend to his own business will be molested."[145]

Some Americans adapted well to living among the Mexican people. One of these was Dr. William J. Howerton. His father had fought with Andrew Jackson at New Orleans and had managed one of Jackson's plantations in Mississippi. William had a better-than-average education, studying law and medicine. His family moved to Texas, and by 1850 he had settled in Lavaca County and was practicing law in the coastal region. Active in Democratic Party politics, he was elected to the Texas legislature in 1857 and fought for the Confederacy when the war broke out. After the conflict, Howerton chose exile and settled in Apodaca, Nuevo León, where he practiced medicine for the remainder of his life. Some of his descendants still live in Apodaca. A letter he sent to Consul Joseph Ulrich reveals some of the problems Americans faced in adjusting to Mexico. He wrote that the alcalde of Apodaca compelled him to vote in a local election even though he was an American and prohibited by law from voting. Ulrich told him not to worry, the alcalde's ignorance was to blame. The consul, who had a low opinion of Mexicans and especially of Mexican government officials, told Howerton: "it is a rare case to find one who understands his duties or his rights, or has any idea of the rights of others."[146]

Three other Confederate loyalists, Hamilton P. Bee, Dr. David McKnight, and Charles Russell, also settled in Northeast Mexico. They were united by friendship and family ties; Bee was married to the sister of McKnight's wife and Russell had been Bee's quartermaster at Brownsville. In 1866, Russell was in Monterrey looking for business opportunities while his family was with McKnight's family in Saltillo. Bee, also in Monterrey, promised to send McKnight several cases of medicine that had arrived from Matamoros. In the shipment was quinine, potassium sulfate, calomel, chloroform, and many other drugs with a total cost of $2,169.49.[147]

In July 1866, Bee wrote to McKnight that he had asked his wife, who was still in Texas, to join him in Monterrey. He also had exciting news. Russell had been offered a lucrative opportunity by Patricio Milmo, who wanted him to operate his insurance business. Milmo and Russell had collaborated in the Civil War cotton trade at Brownsville. Bee was happy for Russell, whom he believed had a great talent for business but was also a "correct man." Milmo, wrote Bee, "would trust his business to no other man in Mexico." Bee was happy because Russell had offered "to share his good fortune" with him. McKnight could now come to Monterrey and establish his drugstore with "Charlie [Russell]" with plenty of credit and "as large a scale as the trade will permit."[148]

The sunny future that the three friends anticipated during the bright summer grew dimmer upon the arrival of gloomy winter. In December Bee wrote McKnight that Russell's deal with Milmo had fallen through. Bee now faced uncertain prospects, but nothing was too daunting for a man who had been described by one Texas correspondent as "a man of unbounded resources, of large brain and one of the most successful diplomats" he had ever met.[149] Shortly thereafter, Bee moved with his family to Saltillo, where he undertook various business enterprises. His integration into the community was manifest in 1869 when he and his wife, Mildred Tarver, baptized their newborn son. Bishop Verea of Monterrey performed the ceremony. A Mexican newspaper reported that many foreign Protestants were present and were very respectful. "General Bee, although his face is furrowed with the vestiges of work and misfortune, reflected in those moments the disappearance of his misfortunes and the happiness in his countenance."[150] After a little more than a decade,

Bee and his family returned to Texas, though his association with Mexico continued throughout his life.

The lives of Dr. Frank Paschal and his wife, Ladie Napier, reveal the great capacity of some Anglos to settle in northern Mexico and mix easily with the native population and culture. Paschal spoke Spanish fluently, having spent part of his boyhood in Monterrey where his father operated a hotel during the Civil War. His family returned to San Antonio after the war and he studied medicine at Louisville Medical College, graduating as one of its most decorated students. He decided to practice in Chihuahua and quickly earned, in the words of August Santleben, "an enviable reputation as a physician and surgeon . . . where he was also highly esteemed by all classes for his talents and many excellent qualities."[151] He returned briefly to San Antonio in order to marry Ladie Napier, who returned to Mexico with her husband. Santleben writes that "in a short time the young wife was loved and admired by a large circle of acquaintances." Her husband performed surgeries that were beyond the expertise of most doctors and developed "an extensive and lucrative practice, but his services were not withheld from the poor, and he was greatly assisted in his charitable attentions by Mrs. Paschal. . . . Many indigent people were relieved by his skill as a surgeon, and quantities of medicine were generously distributed to them free of cost."[152]

Ladie Napier Paschal was renowned for her singing ability. In 1879, a Texas newspaper reported that she "sang the Mexican national hymn on . . . the occasion of the celebration of Mexican independence, before an assemblage of upwards of 3,000 persons in Chihuahua." "Her singing was received with rapturous applause."[153] The Paschals eventually returned to San Antonio, where Frank established an outstanding reputation as one of Texas's foremost medical doctors. A member of the American College of Surgeons who published in medical journals, he served as president of the Texas Medical Association. He also "founded the Associated Charities of San Antonio and aided in building the Physicians and Surgeons Hospital." He was a tireless fighter against tuberculosis and his record in public health and his contributions to the medical profession were widely admired.[154]

~

To characterize the 1870s in the Texas-Mexico border region as a period of violence does not tell the whole story. It was also a time of contact between Anglo-Americans and Mexicans in both Texas and Northeast Mexico. Mexicans migrated to Texas in greater numbers than ever before, motivated by labor opportunities and relatively better pay in a Texas economy that recovered quickly

Dr. Frank Paschal. An important number of Anglo-American doctors chose to practice their profession in northern Mexico. They were welcomed into a society that was perennially short of doctors. Paschal won the respect and admiration of the people of Chihuahua for his talent as a surgeon and his generosity in providing care to those who could not pay for his services. After almost two decades in Mexico he returned to San Antonio, Texas, and established a brilliant medical career. Dr. Frank Paschal Collection, Series 1, Box MS 8*1-1, Item 1, P. I. Nixon Medical Historical Library, University of Texas Health Science Center at San Antonio.

from the Civil War. Mexican labor was sought after in sheep and cattle ranching, transportation, railroad construction, and cotton cultivation.

Labor opportunities came with a cost as Mexicans were increasingly relegated to menial jobs within an exploitative labor system that converted many of them into dependent wage laborers. Nevertheless, their arrival in ever-increasing numbers ensured a constant reinforcement of Mexican culture and values and an injection of vitality into the Mexican communities of Texas. Mexican labor migration clearly demonstrates that Mexican and U.S. history cannot stop at each nation's borders. Historians Samuel Truett and Elliott Young argue that "any nation's borderlands cannot be understood solely within the framework of national history because forces from both sides of a border shape the lives of borderlands residents."[155]

Protestant missionaries spread their religions with greater insistence among the Mexican population of Northeast Mexico and South Texas. Religious freedom in Mexico began in the 1860s, allowing Protestant missionaries to carry out their work of evangelization. Their efforts were crowned with very modest success. The hundreds of missionaries who traveled to Mexico were like a small stream flowing into a vast Catholic ocean. Nevertheless, their religious practices and the educational institutions they founded played a role in changing traditional Mexican values. Protestants also worked to convert Mexican Catholics in Texas, and the major Protestant groups recruited Mexican converts from south of the Rio Grande to help them in their work.

In Northeast Mexico, the Catholic hierarchy faced the Protestant challenge while continuing its struggle against liberal national governments intent on reducing its power. In Texas, Catholicism had not changed significantly since the 1850s. Europeans continued to dominate the clergy, and their presence contributed to the region's multiethnic character even as it served as a buffer between Anglo-Americans and Mexicans. The Texas Catholic Church strengthened its contacts with Mexican Catholicism. Priests and nuns expelled from Mexico received refuge in Texas. Jesuits driven from the country established a seminary at Seguin with the support of the bishops of Monterrey and San Antonio. As was true for commerce, networks played a vital role in the spread of religion.

Mixed marriages are important evidence of integration among Anglos and Mexicans. Marriages between Anglo men and Mexican women produced families that were bilingual and bicultural, many of which have survived to the present generation. Interethnic fraternization occurred often, whether at parties, dances, celebrations, or spontaneous gatherings. Mexican-Anglo friendship and loyalty were not uncommon and were often forged in the adverse conditions of the frontier.

Anglo-Americans who made Northeast Mexico their home often faced an ambivalent attitude from the Mexican population. They were disliked by some, liked by others, and tolerated by most. Antipathy toward them, when it existed, arose less out of racial prejudice than of past experience arising from the war between the two countries; the way Mexicans had been treated in Texas; or, in the case of missionaries, religious differences. Nevertheless, American doctors and missionaries who sought to heal body and soul showed Mexicans another, more benevolent face of the United States than that displayed by politicians and military men. Americans usually found acceptance and lived in harmony among the Mexican people. Hamilton Bee and Frank Paschal are among the few whose stories are known. There are many others who lived and died in Mexico and remain unknown.

The increasing forms of cooperation throughout the Rio Grande frontier in the 1870s should come as no surprise. Its inhabitants were engaged in more than a Darwinian competition for survival; many discovered that cooperation best served their interests. This reality was captured by the Russian thinker Peter Kropotkin, who "argued that survival was fostered by cooperation within and among species rather than by murderous rivalries."[156]

CHAPTER 9

Pacification and Economic Integration

1868–1880

In August 1878, the Mexican commercial agent in the United States, Man-uel María de Zamacona, held a reception in Chicago for the Manufac-turers' Association of the Northwest. The meeting was part of a Mexican government campaign to change Mexico's negative image in the United States and attract investments with which to develop the country. The businessmen were curious about commerce with Mexico and were seeking more information. After speaking of the economic potential and many opportunities in Mexico, Zamacona invited them to visit the country and see for themselves. A fact-finding trip was planned, but in the interim the association received a response to the request for information they had sent to John W. Foster, the U.S. ambassador to Mexico. Claiming that Zamacona was not telling the truth about the reality in Mexico, Foster wrote a forty-four-page letter outlining the inconveniences, risks, and dangers for American investors. His letter was printed as a pamphlet and disseminated broadly in the United States. Foster stated that it was his "duty to speak frankly and not conceal that which may be unpleasant to some."[1]

Foster's letter covers central issues pertaining to the border region so it is worth quoting certain passages at length. The ambassador was well aware of the country's great potential. "No person can visit Mexico," he wrote, "without being struck with its marvelous natural resources, its fertility of soil, its genial climate, and its capacity to sustain a large population and extensive commerce."[2] He continued by saying that Mexico

> can produce all the coffee consumed in the United States. It has
> a greater area of sugar-producing lands than Cuba, and of equal

fertility. Its capacity for the production of vegetable textiles is equal
to any country in the world. Almost all the tropical dyes and drugs,
and all the fruits in the world can be cultivated successfully. Its varied
climate admits of the growth of all the cereals of all the zones. Its
ranges afford the wide scope and the best conditions for wool and
stock raising. And, most of all, skillful American mining engineers . . .
claim that its mineral wealth, yet hidden away in the recesses of
its mountain ridges, is superior to that of California, Nevada, or
Australia.[3]

Alas, that bright potential, Foster believed, was obscured by a dark reality.
The diplomat proceeded to deal "frankly" with the issues that most interested the
Chicago capitalists: railroad networks; tariff and trade regulations; and protection
of life and property. At the meeting with Zamacona, the manufacturers had
regarded the lack of railroad lines "as the chief obstacle to . . . increasing intimate
commercial relations between the United States and Mexico." Foster concurred,
but stated that Mexico could not afford to grant the subsidies necessary to attract
railroad builders. Secondly, many Mexicans opposed a railroad connecting their
country with the United States, believing that it would lead to the destruction
of its nationhood and hasten the annexation of Mexico by her neighbor. Foster
then turned to Mexican trade policy. The laws and regulations were byzantine
and constantly changing, which produced evasion and corruption.[4] Mining was
taxed heavily because the nation was desperate for funds to combat insurrections.
Tariffs on many items were prohibitive, encouraging smuggling, which was
"carried on . . . to such an extent as to almost bankrupt the national Treasury."
Chicago merchants, Foster concluded, could not compete with this illegal trade.[5]

The ambassador dedicated the longest part of his letter to the "protection
afforded to persons and property in Mexico," stating this was "the most important subject to be treated."[6] Reminding his readers that they should "not lose
sight of the half century of disorder and revolution in Mexico," he declared that
the Mexican people themselves "recognize this as its greatest evil and the chief
cause of its many disasters and embarrassments."[7]

Mexico's state of revolution, wrote Foster, "places itself in the way of all national
progress, of all enterprise, of all business and economic reforms." Forced loans
were the major curse accompanying the constant revolts. In Chihuahua during the
Tuxtepec revolt thirteen forced loans were imposed on the population—mostly
against merchants and mining companies—in a period of six months.[8] Added

to these calamities was the widespread lawlessness that characterized most of Mexico's countryside and the impunity with which the criminals operated. Foster cited cases of Americans being robbed or killed without arrests being made. The government was helpless to control this lawlessness: "It is almost impossible for a Government . . . which must be constantly on the alert for a new revolution threatening its existence, and with a scant Treasury, to suppress this brigandage."[9]

Much of Foster's letter described the problems of the Texas-Mexico border region and was motivated by the continuing troubles there, even though many of the cases he cited occurred before Porfirio Díaz rose to power. Contraband, forced loans, and lawlessness were part of the daily reality on the border, but so too were ongoing social, cultural, and religious exchanges and commercial intercourse. Hesitant Chicago capitalists were probably unaware that merchants of Texas and Northeast Mexico had been trading for decades, regardless of revolutionary conditions, interruptions, and forced loans. Smuggling was not a major problem because businessmen on both sides of the border engaged in it. It was a natural part of the landscape. These merchants understood that a strong government and a peaceful Mexico were in their best interests, but they did not wait around for these developments. Even before the pacification of the border, the subjugation of the Indians, and the coming of the railroad, merchants of Texas and Northeast Mexico were carrying out their commercial activities, and in the 1870s had begun to channel some of the enormous wealth generated by the cotton boom into other economic enterprises. Of course, this transition from commerce to investments in land, mining, banking, and manufacturing was hastened and facilitated by the pacification of the border and the construction of the railroads, but the process was beginning even without them.

COMMERCE AFTER THE CIVIL WAR

The end of the Civil War brought an end to the cotton boom, but trade continued at a lively pace all along the border from Matamoros to Paso del Norte. It involved many of the products and merchants present in an earlier period. The thriving trade was newsworthy in Texas. Just months after the end of the Civil War a Houston newspaper reported that "Mexican carts in large numbers . . . [were] loading with flour in the wheat regions of Texas." The report added that Texas-Mexico trade was "evidently on the increase, and, if a settled government obtain in Mexico . . . it will evidently become very large in time to come."[10] In Corpus Christi it was reported that "Mexican carts with wool and hides began to pour into the City and continued to arrive in large numbers."[11] Another newspaper reported that Galveston was now connected to Liverpool by steamer and "that nearly every steamer brings merchandise for Northern Mexico."[12] Indianola also profited from trade with Mexico, as a local newspaper stated: "The Mexican trade through Indianola is becoming one of much importance. The splendid three masted schooner Veto, now lying at our wharf, brought over as part of her cargo, machinery for a cotton factory that established at Monclova, Mexico. There are eighty Mexican carts in waiting for this freight, which they take as soon as landed."[13]

Commerce in cotton exemplifies the continuation of trade, even if on a modest scale. As was true in the Civil War, San Antonio was the conduit for East Texas cotton destined for Mexico. The destination was no longer Matamoros, but the growing textile factories of Nuevo León, Coahuila, Durango and San Luis Potosí. A San Antonio newspaper reported in 1872 that large numbers of Mexican carts were traversing the city, some bound for Victoria and others headed for East Texas. It concluded: "A large amount of the Texas cotton from that portion of the State not yet reached by railroads will be taken to Mexico."[14]

The textile factories of Nuevo León and Coahuila continued to rely on Texas cotton until the Laguna region around Torreón began to produce great quantities of the fiber in the late 1870s. There were three mills in Nuevo León: La Fama, (established 1854), El Porvenir (established 1872), and La Leona (established 1874). One of the most important textile plants, La Estrella, had produced Confederate uniforms during the Civil War. It was located in one of the finest haciendas in northern Mexico: El Rosario, just outside Parras, Coahuila. In 1869 Evaristo Madero bought Hacienda El Rosario and returned to Coahuila from Monterrey to concentrate on his myriad business operations, which now included textile mills, a flour mill that supplied the Texas market, and vineyards producing fine wines, all of which formed the base of the family's fortune. During his stay in Monterrey, Madero had partnered with his son-in-law Lorenzo González Tre-viño, a young businessman who also developed extensive contacts with Texas merchants and who brought dynamism and innovation to the firm.[15]

One of Madero's chief suppliers of Texas cotton was John Twohig. In Febru-ary 1867, he wrote that he had sent 283 bales to Madero and was having difficulty obtaining carts for additional shipments. Madero also received cotton from his friends and former partners William Stone of Eagle Pass and Charles Griesen-beck of San Antonio. Griesenbeck was another German who had fled to Mexico during the Civil War. He stayed in Monterrey with his family and developed a lifelong friendship with Madero. All three merchants sent their cotton through

Eagle Pass and Piedras Negras, where Twohig employed an agent to handle his operations.[16]

Madero continued to develop La Estrella mill. His partner, González Treviño, traveled to England in 1876 to purchase modern machinery, which was shipped to Coahuila in the midst of Díaz's Tuxtepec rebellion, which was convulsing the region. Producers in Texas competed to sell their cotton to La Estrella. P. K. Hawkins and Co. asked a good friend of Madero's in Austin to inform him that they could offer him better prices than he could obtain in San Antonio or Galveston. They even had an employee who could write and speak in Spanish to facilitate communication.[17]

Two other merchants associated with Madero who traded principally through Piedras Negras were William Schuchardt and Santiago Lincoln. Schuchardt, who had been a clerk in Madero's firm, was strongly recommended for the post of consular agent at Piedras Negras by fellow merchants who knew him well. One of these was Joseph Ulrich, who also served as U.S. consul in Monterrey. Ulrich wrote to Washington that the appointment was "essential for the interests of all the merchants at San Antonio and Eagle Pass, Texas, as Piedras Negras is the port of entry for all goods coming to Mexico from these points, and also for the greater portion of the goods from Mexico to Texas." He further stated that there was "no other place in Mexico where there [were] so many American residents as at Piedras Negras and vicinity." Ulrich wrote that he had known Schuchardt for ten years and considered him "a very suitable person. . . . He speaks Spanish well and understands the country and people thoroughly."[18]

Santiago Lincoln, merchant and freighter, traveled the dusty roads of northern Mexico, operating mainly in Coahuila and Nuevo León. Lincoln hauled cotton to Mexico for Wulfing and Company of San Antonio. Between April and August 1866, he carried 738 bales of cotton to Monterrey, Saltillo, and San Luis Potosí. He would often return loaded with hides. One of his suppliers in Mexico was Mariano de los Santos of Villaldama, Nuevo León. On one journey, Lincoln asked him for fifteen thousand goat hides.[19]

A broad range of products other than cotton and hides were exchanged along the border. Texas tobacco continued to find a ready market in Mexico. Schuchardt reported that more than four Mexican states used it "exclusively." Long-established border merchants such as Joseph Kleiber of Brownsville and John P. Kelsey of Rio Grande City continued to sell dry goods. Kleiber still depended on the Mexican market and was in Monterrey and Zacatecas in 1867 selling wines and other goods. Despite his profound antipathy toward Mexicans, in 1869 Kleiber made a three-month tour of the Mexican states on the Pacific coast in search of business opportunities. Salt was another item of exchange that was used primarily to cure meat. The salt lakes near the Nueces (unlike those at San Elizario where attempted privatization provoked an uprising) were open to anyone who wished to haul off the salt for private or commercial use.[20]

Another Texas export to northern Mexico was livestock. Independent of the vast clandestine market in stolen cattle, some Texas ranchers sought to sell their beeves to Mexico legally. This trend began during the Civil War, when the Union capture of Vicksburg closed off many Southern markets for Texas livestock. Ranchers such as John Chisholm began to look west and south to sell their cattle. Northern Mexico became one of their markets, despite the objections of Confederate authorities. General James E. Slaughter at Fort Brown ordered his commander at Eagle Pass to stop all cattle drives to Mexico. His orders were apparently largely disobeyed. General John David McAdoo of the Texas Rangers "called the traffic in Texas cattle 'notorious.' He observed that beeves were crossing unimpeded into Mexico every day after ranchers paid Confederate authorities bribes of one to two dollars per head."[21] In 1869, Jesse Sumpter, whose Mexican connections in the Eagle Pass–Piedras Negras region were extensive, sold 1,200 head of cattle at three and a half pesos each to Monterrey merchant Jesús González Treviño. Jesús, the brother of Madero's son-in-law Lorenzo, sought to stock his ranch in Coahuila with Texas cattle.[22]

Cattle drives to Mexico through the Big Bend country were common during the period. Historian Robert M. Utley writes that the "traffic reached a peak in 1868 and 1869, when thousands of Longhorns threaded Paisano Pass and dropped down the Alamito to the river crossing at Presidio." In 1868, Captain D. M. Poer drove 1,200 head of cattle from present-day San Angelo through Presidio to Chihuahua. He had a distinguished client. Luis Terrazas, who had lost much of his stock to Indian raiders and warring armies during the French Intervention, was seeking to rebuild his herds and he looked to Texas for help. On the grassy plains of Chihuahua he built a great cattle empire that became the source of his domination of the state during the Porfiriato. Poer later organized other stock drives, including taking sheep to Zacatecas in 1872 and 1873.[23] Texas sheep had been sold in northern Mexico at least since the Civil War. In the 1870s they were driven across the border in increasing numbers. An Austin newspaper reported that rancher Henry Burns had "sold 100 head of Vermont and 100 head of Michigan bucks to Santiago Sanchez of [Nuevo Laredo, Tamaulipas] Mexico."[24]

Throughout the 1870s a change occurred in the composition of American exports. Historian Richard Salvucci affirms that "Mexico began to import capital goods from the United States, and the share of steam engines, sewing machines, machinery, and builders' hardware grew." Joseph Ulrich, the U.S. consul at Monterrey, confirms this change, reporting that among the products entering the Mexican Northeast were machinery, agricultural implements, and hardware. American producers began to send agents to promote their products in Mexico. I. H. Hutton, for example, was sent to sell sewing machines in Monterrey. He was an early version of the traveling salesman, though his story ended not in humor but in tragedy. He was killed by an irate Frenchman who discovered the American sleeping with his wife.[25]

Exports from, or passing through, Mexico's Northeast consisted mainly of the same products that were traded in the 1830s: hides, skins, and silver. Much of the last was mined in Zacatecas and Chihuahua, though small quantities were also produced in Vallecillo and Villaldama, Nuevo León. The Vallecillo mines also began producing lead on a large scale. Lucius Avery reported that by the late 1870s they were sending about 2,000,000 pounds per year across the Texas border. The region around Piedras Negras prospered from sending many of its agricultural products to Texas, particularly corn, wheat, and piloncillo, the raw sugar that was widely used by Mexicans on both sides of the border. Much of the corn sent to Texas was consumed at U.S. Army posts on the frontier.[26]

As in an earlier period, the shipment of silver was vital to both countries and its transport was greatly facilitated by the consolidation of the Chihuahua Trail through Texas, which supplanted the old Santa Fe Trail and peaked in its volume of trade in the 1870s, before the arrival of the railroads. It connected the mines of Chihuahua with the northeastern United States and Europe by way of Presidio, San Antonio, and Indianola. Long lines of wagons set out from the city of Chihuahua toward Presidio del Norte. They continued through Forts Davis, Stockton, and Clark; proceeded through Uvalde and Castroville; then passed through San Antonio, Goliad, and Victoria before reaching the coast. Burr Duval, who was part of an expedition to explore West Texas in 1879, wrote that the trail was "the great highway for freights to the upper Rio Grande and Northern Mexico, as well as the U.S. military posts along the Western Frontier." He and his party "passed three or four hundred wagons going and coming" along the route.[27]

U.S. Commercial Agents

In response to the growth in commerce with Northeast Mexico, the U.S. government established commercial agencies in the Mexican towns of the border region. These agencies were at a level below consular posts, but they served to protect the interests of the growing number of merchants who traded with Mexico or lived in the country. The commercial agency at Piedras Negras was established in 1867 with William Schuchardt in charge. Agencies were opened in Camargo in 1870 and Guerrero and Nuevo Laredo (Tamaulipas) the following year. These border offices, under the supervision of the consulate at Matamoros, intensified the American diplomatic presence, which heretofore had been concentrated in that port city and Monterrey. The men who served as commercial agents were merchants, and most of them had been engaged in trade with Mexico for many years. They were familiar with the country and spoke the language. John P. Kelsey of Rio Grande City, who had been trading with Mexico since the Federalist War of 1840, was a natural choice to occupy the post at Camargo, across the river, although he occupied the post for only a few months in 1870 before being replaced by Lucius Avery. Charles Winslow, a former surgeon in the U.S. army who had lived in Mexico since 1866, was appointed to fill the post at Guerrero. James J. Haynes was the commercial agent at Nuevo Laredo through most of the 1870s. At one point he requested a leave of absence to join the delegation of Chicago capitalists who had accepted Zamacona's invitation to visit Mexico City in January 1879. As justification for the leave, Haynes explained he wanted to learn more about the commerce of Mexico in order to do a better job. He also felt that he could serve as interpreter for the visiting merchants.[28]

Monterrey was important enough to be a consular post, and two merchants served as consul throughout the 1870s: Joseph Ulrich and Juan Weber. Ulrich had been a printer in New York in his youth and declared himself an old abolitionist of the "Sumner and Greely school." In 1861, recognizing that Texas was not a place congenial to abolitionists, he moved to Monterrey. He was appointed consul in 1866 and played a vital role in Schuchardt's appointment at Piedras Negras the following year. Ulrich returned to San Antonio in 1875 and earned renown as a civic leader.

He was succeeded by Juan Weber, a native of Stuttgart, Germany, who arrived in Monterrey in the early 1850s. Weber had served in Santiago Vidaurri's army during the War of Reform. When the nomination was announced, Ulrich, a proud Union backer, protested confidentially to the State Department that

Weber had provided the Confederacy with powder and lead during the Civil War, was an "enthusiastic monarchist," and was a deserter from the U.S. army. These revelations did not prevent the State Department from naming Weber consul in 1876. He went on to have great commercial success and was one of the few American merchants to be accepted fully into the Monterrey ruling oligarchy during the Porfiriato. He would participate in the pacification of the border as a trusted intermediary between Generals E. O. C. Ord and Gerónimo Treviño.[29]

Commercial agents from Camargo to Piedras Negras concerned themselves with many issues, but their main focus was trade. They kept Washington policy makers well informed about vital issues related to commerce, such as contraband, the zona libre, and the competition between Americans and Europeans to win the Mexican market. They all agreed that contraband traffic was rife and that it flowed in both directions across the border. Schuchardt condemned the illegal trade from Mexico to Texas, whereby Mexican and European goods from the zona libre were smuggled into Texas from the ranches along the river and passed off as commodities produced in Texas. This rankled some Texas merchants, who demanded that their government pressure Mexico to abolish the free zone.[30]

It was almost impossible to stop contraband goods from entering Texas. The Nuevo Laredo agent, James Haynes, lamented: "The customs force on the Texas frontier is wholly inadequate to patrol and protect the passes and fords and all their movements are closely watched by the smugglers."[31] Moreover, smuggling was so pervasive, involving all social classes and racial groups, that it became, according to Joseph B. Wilkinson, "another of the respectable vocations outside the law, with many otherwise honest merchants participating." In consequence, prosecution for smuggling was rare. "The U.S. commissioner at Laredo had in his file complaints against many of the more prominent citizens of that community." These were not prosecuted because "he was pretty sure that juries would not convict—many of the potential jurors no doubt were engaged in similar enterprises." This remark could just as well have been made in the 1820s and every decade since.[32]

Commercial agents also wrote of the contraband taken to Mexico. Haynes reported that "nearly all the merchants from the villages of Tamaulipas, Nuevo Leon, Coahuila, and Chihuahua purchase their stocks of goods from the merchants in Texas and smuggle them into Mexico at the fords and passes to be found at nearly any point of the Rio Grande." His successor, John F. Jenne, concluded that "an immense trade is done surreptitiously of which no record reaches any office."[33] Smugglers in Mexico operated as they had before, except that now their challenge was to move goods from the zona libre to the interior. They met the challenge successfully. The governments of Juárez and Lerdo de Tejada were ineffective in patrolling such a vast expanse of land. Moreover, they were shaken by two major revolts in 1871 and 1876 led by Porfirio Díaz. The latter uprising toppled the Lerdo government. The *contraresguardo* was reorganized in 1870, but as in the 1850s, this provoked strong opposition and violent attacks. Nuevo León governor Viviano Villarreal complained that federal agents were disdainful of local authorities and the contraresguardo was hated by the common people. The clandestine economy was alive and well in the border region and continued to provoke friction with the national government.[34]

One of the main concerns of U.S. diplomats along the border was the commercial competition with Europe. Early in the decade, the European monopoly seemed complete, as U.S. ambassador Thomas H. Nelson stated. Mexican commerce, he wrote, was largely controlled by the European nations. One historian has argued that this was due to the antipathy between Mexicans and Americans after the border wars of the 1840s and 1860s.[35] Perhaps this was a factor, but it has been shown that national antipathies did not have the same weight as the law of supply and demand. Europeans knew the Mexican market, had cultivated it for half a century, and had tailored their products and prices in order to compete favorably, even though they were separated from that market by a great ocean. Many American producers and merchants somehow failed to understand the issue and blamed European competition on the zona libre, even though they had the same access and were much closer. Charles Winslow, the commercial agent at Guerrero, expressed the issue clearly: "the merchants in the United States can hardly complain of [the zona libre], as they have here one of the best markets for their goods, and if they made a better quality and sold at a more reasonable rate, they could easily compete with European goods." Conditions were equal for European and American merchants, "and the United States [merchants] have the advantage that they are nearer to Mexico than Europe is."[36]

Interestingly, as U.S. merchants began to compete more favorably with their European counterparts in the 1870s, their objections to the zona libre lessened. This is reflected in a note by commercial agent James J. Haynes of Nuevo Laredo: "In former years nearly all the goods used in Mexico were of European manufacture and could be sold in the towns in the Zona much cheaper than on the Texas side of the River, but that has changed very materially since 1874 or 1875." Haynes specified the American products that were gaining favor in Mexico, particularly cotton goods, machinery, and manufactured products. He concluded that the zona libre was not hostile to his government and its removal "would not materially benefit the United States or the towns situated opposite the ones in the Zona, but would certainly create trouble on the frontier and increase the bad feeling of the Mexicans toward Americans."[37]

Lucius Avery at Camargo also wrote in 1878 of growing U.S. commercial domination. Over the past few years, he wrote, American goods had been displacing European merchandise "until at present all the towns and villages along the Rio Grande and for a distance of one hundred miles or more in the interior depend entirely on the United States for their supplies." Notably, this process was underway even before the railroad extended its reach to northern Mexico in the early 1880s. It seems clear that irrespective of what policy makers in Washington and Mexico City thought, borderlanders on both sides of the river had accommodated themselves to the existence of the zona libre and worked within its legal and territorial structure to accomplish their aims.[38]

Commercial agents often wrote of corruption among Mexican authorities, but they were not oblivious to the dishonesty of some U.S. officials. When John Kelsey left his post at Camargo, he urged Washington to keep his office open and staff it with another capable person because it was necessary to have a commercial agent in areas where there were U.S. revenue collectors across the border. This, he noted, would keep them honest because otherwise they did not report all imports and were prone to tolerate smuggling. Joseph Ulrich of Monterrey claimed to have proof that U.S. customs inspectors in New Orleans were stealing merchandise bound for the capital of Nuevo León. Ulrich was embarrassed, he wrote, because most of the importers in Monterrey were Germans and they would likely get the wrong impression of the United States: "it is a very bitter pill for a Consul to swallow . . . that our Custom House officials in New Orleans have reached a point of demoralization hardly approached by those of Mexico, who, are sufficiently corrupt, but rarely descend to pilfer in this way." Apparently, Mexican officials did not have a monopoly on corruption.[39]

TRANSPORTATION BEFORE THE ARRIVAL OF THE RAILROAD

The growing commerce between Texas and Mexico was facilitated by advances in transportation. Even before the arrival of the railroad, sleek prairie schooners drawn by fast, sturdy mules had replaced the plodding ox-drawn carretas. These wagons weighed an average of seven thousand pounds and could carry ten thousand pounds of cargo. August Santleben, perhaps the single most important freighter in the region throughout the 1870s, wrote that "a train of twelve wagons, each drawn by fourteen mules . . . would transport one hundred and twenty thousand pounds of freight with ease over the roads in Mexico."[40] Santleben commented with regard to freight operators in the region: "The Mexican trains could not compare with those of Americans in general appearance, but in many respects they were far superior, and they were managed more successfully, because of the strictness with which they conducted the business." Perhaps for this reason, twenty of the twenty-nine freighting companies in San Antonio on the eve of the railroad's arrival were operated by Mexican Texans.[41]

Santleben relied on Mexican teamsters to man his wagons, but he also kept a sharp eye on his Mexican competitors. "The finest lot of mules I ever saw belonged to Rocke Garady [Roque Garay], who owned and ran a train of twelve wagons, with fourteen mules to each, that was known as the finest outfit in Mexico, and I am sure that their equal could not be found in the United States." Among his competitors he mentioned David and Daniel Sada of Monterrey, who carried freight between Coahuila and Texas, and the San Miguel brothers who arrived in the Alamo City in 1868 with ten carts from Mexico to haul freight to the frontier posts for the government. He also wrote of the González brothers of Saltillo, who, with a train of twenty-five carts and 125 mules, "passed through San Antonio, in 1867, on their way to New Braunfels, where they loaded each cart with eight bales of cotton . . . for the Mexican market."[42]

Santleben was one of many freighters who made San Antonio their base of operations. The city's strategic location made it a focal point for mail, passenger, and freight routes destined for Mexico. In the 1870s the Alamo, which would later be resurrected as the great shrine of Texas independence and the struggle for freedom, was, according to one observer, a "station for the mule and ox teams waiting to receive stores."[43] Bethel Coopwood, another veteran of the U.S.-Mexican War and Civil War and known more popularly as the promoter of camels for use in the arid climate of Texas and Northeast Mexico, announced in 1866 that he was about to start a mule train to connect San Antonio with El Paso and Chihuahua. Jesse Sumpter of Eagle Pass wrote that Coopwood lived in Coahuila for a time after the Civil War and used his camels to haul freight between Laredo and Piedras Negras. He kept his camel herd in a corral at the latter place.[44]

In May 1867, Santleben partnered with Adolph Muenzenberger to establish a stage line between San Antonio and Monterrey. The route would connect various towns and cross the border at Piedras Negras. Santleben requested that his passengers be allowed to pass the customhouse without a search of their luggage and offered to carry official and private mail for free. Narciso Dávila, the *oficial mayor* of Nuevo León, welcomed the stage line but stated that luggage had to be searched to prevent contraband. Yet Santleben managed to avoid the searches: "During the two years that the line was operated the contents of the coach was never investigated nor was it ever delayed on any occasion by government officials on either side of the Rio Grande." It turns out that he had made friends with the customs collectors at Piedras Negras, Nicolás Gresanta, and Pedro Morales.[45] The only item taxed was money. Santleben carried large sums in silver from Monterrey to the Alamo City, charging 3 percent for his services. He wrote that for San Antonio firms such as Halff & Bro., Goldfrank, Frank & Co., and F. Groos & Co., his stage "often brought for them as much as twenty thousand dollars from that country."[46]

Aside from passengers, Santleben transported just about everything in his stagecoach, from tropical fruit to weapons. He delivered oranges to San Antonio and Minié rifles for the Mexican government. During its brief existence, the stage facilitated not only commercial exchanges, but also growing integration between the populations of Texas and Northeast Mexico. This is evident in Santleben's account of the way he was received, the friendships he made, and the people who rode his coach. He perceived that after the U.S.-Mexican War and the filibustering expeditions of the 1850s, there was a residue of resentment against Americans that "lingered to some extent among the people; but it was never manifested in my case, because I was always treated with uniform courtesy in all my travels among them, and every facility was extended to me, both by the government and the people." Santleben names many prominent citizens of the towns through which he passed who expressed "their appreciation of our services. . . . Wherever the stage appeared a greater sensation was created than is usually expressed in a new railroad town."[47]

Americans, Europeans, and Mexicans shared experiences in Santleben's coaches. The passengers on one trip from San Antonio to Monterrey included "Mrs. Buss and her two children; Mrs. Dress[e]l, a sister of ex-Congressman Schleicher, and her child; three Robin children, of San Antonio; Charles Sada, Dr. Felix and Henry Rice, all citizens of Monterrey." Also aboard were "Colonel Morales, of the Mexican army, and several others whose names I cannot recall." They all had a harrowing experience crossing the Sabinas River when the coach sank, though they escaped unharmed. Santleben also wrote of his friends in Monterrey, including "Messrs. Weber and Ulrich, who did a large commission business . . . Mr. A. Buss, who conducted a large lumber business; Mr. Dress[e]l, a large hardware merchant; and Mr. George Paschal, ex-mayor of San Antonio, a brother of Dr. Frank Paschal." These friends and those in the many towns along the route "always took a great interest in the line because of the facility it gave them to communicate with their friends in Texas."[48] Regrettably, this happy state of affairs came to an end in 1869 when the customs officers at Eagle Pass and Piedras Negras were changed. Santleben had to close the line, because "the removal of our friends naturally affected our business." Borderlanders depended greatly on personal networks and friendships to survive and get ahead.[49]

The irrepressible German American quickly started a freighting business between San Antonio and Chihuahua through Presidio, and became one of the prime players in the shipment of silver when the mines were activated with the infusion of American capital in the 1870s. Santleben writes that he carried millions of dollars of cargo: "I hauled more money from Mexico during that period, on stages and wagons, than any other person, the greater part of which was consigned to parties in Europe."[50] His route began in Chihuahua, crossed the border at Presidio, and proceeded to Indianola by way of San Antonio, the same route used by Texas traders since the 1840s. On at least one occasion he had to change this route. During the revolt of 1876 led by Ángel Trías, Presidio had fallen into rebel hands and Santleben, fearing confiscation of his cargo, took a longer route through Paso del Norte. On that particular trip he carried "the largest amount of money and copper that was ever brought from Chihuahua. I carried three hundred and fifty thousand dollars in Mexican silver" and forty thousand pounds of copper, for which his commission totaled $17,500.[51] On dangerous trips, Santleben hired armed protection. On this occasion he employed Captain Máximo Aranda "who had made himself conspicuous in his opposition to the revolution." Santleben "paid him one thousand dollars to escort [his] train to El Paso with his thirty men, and he performed his duty faithfully." Out of the money earned, Santleben had to pay $14,000 in expenses so his profit was about $3,500 for a six-month trip filled with "hardships and disappointments."[52]

Those engaged in transportation of people or goods between Texas and Mexico inevitably also carried information and knowledge of how things were done in the two countries. On one of his trips to Chihuahua, Santleben brought back to San Antonio a rudimentary handmade *azadón* (hoe) that the natives used. His friends Norton and Deutz, who were hardware merchants, appealed to northern manufacturers and "arranged to have a better and more highly finished hoe made at a price that gave the retailer in Mexico a liberal profit when sold at three dollars each, consequently they supplanted the ruder implement and in a short time were in common use all over that country."[53] Sometimes information of a military nature was exchanged. In return for an armed escort on a trip to Fort Stockton, Santleben provided General Ord with valuable details of the Trías revolution in Chihuahua.[54]

On one of Santleben's most memorable trips he transported a huge meteorite that was found about ten miles from Chihuahua in 1875. The rock, wrote Santleben, "was composed of solid iron and weighed 5,400 pounds. It was shaped like a turtle, round on top and flat below" and had to be hauled in a special reinforced wagon. The German American freighter had an ambition of exhibiting the huge rock at the World's Fair, which was being held in Philadelphia. When the meteorite arrived at Luling, Texas, it was taken by rail to Philadelphia, where it "was placed in the Mexican exhibit and shown free" at the World's Fair. To the chagrin of Santleben and the authorities of Chihuahua "the meteorite was given to the British Museum."[55]

In 1877, realizing that his wagons had been superseded by the railroads, which "linked the two countries together with bonds of steel that will encourage friendship and assure perpetual peace," Santleben gave up freighting but continued to visit Mexico.[56] He calculated that he had traveled "over one hundred and twenty-six thousand miles, or about five times around the earth." These trips "were made through a wild and uninhabited country, over routes that were continually beset by savage Indians, who were inveterate enemies of the white race, and by equally lawless men who frequented the frontiers of Texas and Mexico."[57]

INVESTMENTS: THE NEW PATTERN OF COOPERATION

In various ways Santleben symbolizes the transition that was felt throughout the Texas-Mexico border region in the 1870s. His freighting operation using mule-drawn wagons gave way to fast, efficient trains. Moreover, the content of his cargo reflects a change in economic patterns. He concentrated on shipping silver and industrial metals because Mexican mines were being opened or rehabilitated by foreign and domestic capital. At the beginning of the decade commerce was still predominant. Toward the end, investments in land for ranching, agricultural, or mining purposes dominated economic activity in northern Mexico. This process was advanced in large part by men who had accumulated wealth in the region.

In April 1869, William Schuchardt wrote to Washington on mining prospects in Coahuila, which was reported to be "rich in silver and lead." He wrote, "efforts are now being made to develop some mines lying in the vicinity of Santa Rosa by companies of Americans, who have already procured machinery and commenced work, and are sanguine that the mineral will be both abundant and wonderfully rich." These mines had been mostly abandoned since independence, though American investors such as William Cazneau began extracting silver in the early 1850s and shipping it out of Mexico through Piedras Negras. The wars and revolts of the 1850s and 1860s produced constant disruptions that precluded further progress. Schuchardt wrote that many mining opportunities were available, but most American capitalists did not want to invest because of the risks and were hoping for the annexation of the region to the United States or the creation of a protectorate so that their investments would be secure.[58]

Despite talk in the United States of annexing northern Mexico, it appears that this was no longer a plausible option in the 1870s. Historian Thomas Schoonover argues that Lincoln's influential secretary of state, William H. Seward, was opposed to annexation and was "the man most responsible for establishing the ideological basis that encouraged U.S. economic involvement in Mexico." Seward was convinced "that his fellow citizens no longer desired outright territorial acquisition" because "they had learned to 'value dollars more, and dominion less.'" Mexico, they thought, could be conquered by U.S. capital without bloodshed.[59]

Capital for investment was abundant in the United States. It was the Gilded Age, the era of the robber barons when fortunes were being made by a few hard-driving and often rapacious capitalists. Historian W. Dirk Raat writes that economic growth produced huge amounts of capital that "needed an outlet. It was now time for the ever-expanding United States to invest in lands and resources . . . south of the Río Grande."[60] Leading the way were merchants of Texas and Northeast Mexico who were flush with cash, much of it obtained in the cotton trade of the Civil War. With their newfound wealth, San Antonio merchants such as John Twohig, Tom Frost, and Friedrich Groos followed in the steps of George Brackenridge, Charles Stillman's associate, and established banks in the Alamo City. The Groos brothers also established the Western Texas Life, Fire, and Marine Insurance Company, "the first such insurance undertaking in West Texas." Valley merchants such as Joseph Kleiber and José San Román invested in railroad construction. San Román returned to Spain in 1879, married, and died two years later. His nephews assumed control of the commercial establishment and invested in land in Tamaulipas. At one of their haciendas, Buenavista, they cultivated a variety of grains and raised livestock.[61]

A good illustration of Texas merchant capital in Northeast Mexico is provided by Jean Baptiste LaCoste. According to historian Arthur James Mayer, the French

American businessman made as much as one million dollars during the Civil War. Besides using his fortune to establish the first ice-making company in San Antonio, he invested in mining and ranching properties in northern Mexico.[62] LaCoste promoted mining and ranching properties in the Santa Rosa region of Coahuila. A pamphlet he printed for potential investors declared that the valley of Santa Rosa "is magnificent . . . a land unequal in the entire American continent. It is prolific in minerals such as silver, lead, copper, tin, iron, zinc, bituminous and anthracite coal." It was also ideal for stock raising and agriculture. A brief comment on the population assured readers that the upper class "is of the highest order of Mexicans and the laboring classes or peons work under the ancient system similar to Cuban slavery. By nature, the servants are inoffensive, obedient and submissive."[63] These words must have been like music to the ears of potential investors.

Vast quantities of land in Coahuila became available in the 1870s after the Sánchez Navarro and Leonardo Zuloaga latifundios were broken up. Their owners paid a heavy price for collaborating with the government of Maximilian. Most of their land became available to buyers eager to develop it. LaCoste was one of those buyers. He joined with Coahuila investors such as Miguel M. González and Evaristo Madero to buy and sell mining properties. In 1879, LaCoste purchased shares in the Esmeralda and Cruz de Oro mines in Coahuila. With González and another associate named Smith, LaCoste bought up mines in the region around Ramos Arizpe. One of his biggest purchases was 277 leagues of the Sánchez Navarro estate at a price of $174,467.17. From the Zuloaga estate he bought and promoted a section of the Hacienda El Coyote, located near the town of Lerdo on the border between Coahuila and Durango. These lands were producing 12,500 pounds of cotton per acre, but with American cotton seed, LaCoste assured readers, "the fertility of these lands may be estimated at from 22,500 to 25,000 pounds per acre." LaCoste also bought forty leagues of land along the Rio Grande above present-day Del Rio. Since Mexican law prohibited foreigners from owning land near the border or seacoast, the registered owner was M. M. González, LaCoste's business partner.[64]

Before the rush to the silver mines in the Sierra Mojada in the late 1870s, it was known that Coahuila was very rich in coal deposits. Coal was of crucial importance to fuel locomotives, and a massive belt of coal-bearing land overlapped the Rio Grande and extended north into Texas and south into Coahuila. It was so visible that it inspired the name Piedras Negras (Black Rocks). As early as 1874, LaCoste, in association with Evaristo Madero and others, sold to railroad magnate Collis P. Huntington, one-sixth of a parcel of 220 leagues of land per-taining to the Haciendas Encinas and Álamos in Coahuila.[65]

In the late 1870s Collis Huntington was busy building a southern route to the Pacific, extending his Southern Pacific Railroad from New Orleans to California. He obtained a concession from the government of Manuel González in 1881 to extend his line into Mexico. It would be called the Mexican International Railroad and would extend from Piedras Negras through Coahuila to Durango. Besides traversing the mineral-rich state of Coahuila, the Mexican International would connect with the Mexican Central Railroad, a line that cut through the center of the country from Paso del Norte to Mexico City. Aware of Coahuila's coal potential and needing to fuel his trains, Huntington wrote to Evaristo Madero, recently elected governor of the state, to inform him of his project. Huntington argued that his line would bring prosperity to Coahuila, but to make it profitable, his company required "certain advantages, such as the donation of land," for the construction of trunk lines.[66] Months earlier, John Twohig had already written to Madero, his "old, dear and esteemed friend." The cagey Irish American called on the newly elected governor to do everything in his power to facilitate construction of the Mexican International because it would promote prosperity and "contribute to establish harmony and peace as well as the continued friendship between the two countries." Left unsaid was that the railroad would pass through Twohig's land in the Eagle Pass region.[67]

LaCoste and Madero, who both owned large tracts of land in Coahuila, were eager to provide Huntington with the coal he needed. With four other investors, they formed the Compañía Carbonífera de Sabinas in Saltillo in March 1884. Their objective was to exploit nine leagues of coal lands along the Sabinas River in the region near Monclova, about seventy-three miles from the Rio Grande. Less than two months after its creation, the Sabinas Coal Company, as it was known in Texas, sold two-thirds of its land to a group headed by Huntington and Thomas Wentworth Pierce of Boston.[68] Huntington bought another property rich in coal along the Sabinas River from General Francisco Naranjo, who with Gerónimo Treviño, formed Nuevo León's duo of military leaders. Both men accumulated vast landholdings, Treviño as much as three million acres while Naranjo had about 850,000 acres. The property that Naranjo sold to Huntington was the Hacienda La Soledad, a 220,000-acre tract that had been part of the Sánchez Navarro estate. The now-wealthy general received 400,000 pesos and a share of profits from mining operations.[69]

The Sabinas Coal Company was one of many firms established with binational ownership. The composition of its board of directors and their shares in the company were as follows: President: Evaristo Madero (20 percent); Treasurer: J. B. LaCoste (20 percent); General Manager: R. H. McCracken (15 percent); Directors: M. M. González (15 percent); Francisco Sada (15 percent); and W. N. Monroe (15 percent).[70] The presence of Texas capitalists McCracken and Monroe on the board is indicative of an informal network of Texas businessmen with ties and investments in Mexico. Both directors joined with other U.S. capitalists to invest in mining properties in Mexico during the Porfiriato.[71]

Two other Texans with extensive contacts and knowledge of Northeast Mexico used them to launch diverse business ventures, though they were not investors in the usual sense. John Willett of Corpus Christi and Hamilton P. Bee of Laredo had several things in common. They had engaged in commerce and experimented with cotton cultivation in the sandy soil of the Gulf Coast region in the 1850s. They both served in the Confederate army, left Texas for Mexico in 1865, and married into the Tarver family, Bee to Mildred and Willett to Ellen. They engaged in various businesses and generated capital in Mexico, though Willett was far more successful. He first established a mercantile business in San Luis Potosí. Later he moved to Saltillo, where he claimed to have bought and sold between seventy and eighty thousand hides and to have "spent several thousand pesos in Saltillo, giving occupation to many hands."[72]

Before moving to Saltillo, Willett heard from Bee that he was engaged in commerce in Coahuila. By 1871 he was planting cotton on rented land and wrote to Willett in San Luis Potosí that he needed money to buy a plantation. It is not known whether Bee obtained the funds, but Willett's move to Saltillo enabled the two men to work together. By this time Willett had developed a very lucrative business. He advertised in a Mexico City newspaper as an exporter of Mexican products and offered "Exchange for Sale on London, N. Y., City of Mexico, San Luis, Zacatecas, Durango and Monterey."[73]

Bee, meanwhile, received an invitation from Governor Edmund J. Davis to return to Texas, but he chose to stay with his family in Saltillo, where they had found acceptance and where his tireless efforts were apparently starting to produce results. He had entered into a seven-year contract to produce cotton in the rich Laguna district of southwestern Coahuila and northeastern Durango. This region lies between the Nazas and Aguanaval Rivers and is equidistant from the cities of Saltillo and Durango. A Mexico City newspaper reported on

Bee's contract, describing the region as an "extensive basin embracing approximately 800 square leagues of four million acres of land." Only about twenty of
those leagues were under cultivation. The area was favorably compared to the
best agricultural districts of the United States and Mexico, and reportedly it
was perfect for cotton because of its fertility. The crop of 1874 produced about
50,000 bales, which were sent to Mexico City. Three years later La Laguna was
producing about one-fifth of the national output of cotton.[74]

Bee wrote about his experience at La Laguna and other aspects of his life in
Mexico in a letter to a Texas newspaper: "I have passed years of bitterness since
we parted at Monterey, in the spring of 1865; have been victimized, and sometimes
on the border of hunger for my children; but I have also had my bright days and
more than once have found strong and true friends to help me." He described
La Laguna as "the cotton country of the continent" and reported harvesting a
crop in 1874 of "two hundred and thirty bales, of five hundred pounds each." In
describing the economic potential of La Laguna, Bee, like LaCoste, became a
publicist for Mexican land: "The Laguna [on the Rio Nazas] . . . is the Nile of the
continent. The soil is the alluvial deposits of centuries of overflow, and the various
changes which time has made in the course of the river have left . . . the richest
of soils." As a Texan, he expressed the hope that a railroad would soon extend
from Laredo to Mazatlán through La Laguna. In anticipating the construction
of such a line and the vast resources it would make accessible, Bee seemed to
foretell the massive American investments during the Porfiriato.[75]

We do not know exactly when Bee returned to live in Texas, but he was in
San Antonio in 1879 when stories of fantastic silver and gold strikes in the Sierra
Mojada reached the city. Located in the extreme western edge of Coahuila, due
west from Cuatro Ciénegas and Monclova and bordering on Chihuahua and
Durango, this range is part of the eastern branch of the Sierra Madre. A local
prospector, Néstor Arreola, and two companions had discovered a rich vein
of silver in May 1878. Rumors of the discovery soon reached Texas and generated considerable excitement. In Matamoros and Brownsville, Daniel Sada,
who carried freight between Coahuila and Texas, confirmed the rumors. Sada,
described as "a gentleman of reliability," stated that the mines were "rich beyond
all expectation." According to Sada, the mines were on the borders of Coahuila,
Chihuahua, and Durango and were being disputed by the three states in a conflict that had already generated fighting and bloodshed. Texans learned that the
mines were within reach: only about 720 miles from Matamoros "to the field of
the greatest gold bonanza ever discovered."[76]

The *San Antonio Express* informed its readers that in the Sierra Mojada John Willett and two other men "in an hour dug out a lump [of silver] worth three thousand dollars." In a letter written for Texas readers, Willett wrote that they were standing "literally on a mountain of silver." An assayer from Parras also detected gold in the metal. The letter caused "a profound sensation," and parties of men began organizing to set out for the mines. With hyperbole, the newspaper exulted, "if half the stories in circulation are true, it is the richest discovery of precious metal in the world."[77] Among the men who left San Antonio for the Sierra Mojada was Hamilton P. Bee. He did not leave with the first rush, but instead was "waiting to take out crushers and amalgamatory machinery, and [would] not leave for some time."[78]

Willett also called attention to Coahuila's ranching and agricultural potential. He bought a huge tract of land along the Sabinas River on speculation and began to apportion parts of his property to individual investors. He published a circular promoting land "where sugar, cotton, wheat and all kinds of grain can be produced; as well as grapes, oranges, pears, etc." He offered for sale or rent "tracts of land of suitable size for cultivation." The land was also ideal for stock raising, he claimed.[79] Willett's promotion reached far places. In 1882 it was reported that David McKellar "with several assistants from New Zealand, arrived at Laredo . . . en route to his large estates purchased last year from Mr. John Willett, containing 250,000 acres of pastoral and agricultural lands in one body, near Santa Rosa, Mexico, about sixty miles from Eagle Pass." McKellar, who had been informed of the availability of this land by John Twohig of San Antonio, asked Willett to purchase for him another one million acres to be used for grazing sheep.[80]

There was however an obstacle to Willett's land deals. Part of his land was in Nacimiento, which was still being occupied by remnants of the Seminole and Kickapoo tribes. The Indians claimed the land had been granted to them in consideration for services they had rendered the nation in combating other hostile Indians and in fighting with the liberals against Maximilian's government. Willett informed Governor Evaristo Madero that one of his clients, Thomas Lamb of England, wanted to grow cotton and sugar near Nacimiento, but was impeded by these Indians. He called on the governor "to intervene in the matter so that I can occupy my property without being molested and that these Indians be removed or obligated to respect my rights." The Seminoles and Kickapoos, who had played a role in defending the region in a previous age, were now seen as obstacles to progress. They had suffered removal in the United States and now faced the same process and for the same reasons in Mexico. Moreover, what was occurring in Coahuila heralded the massive displacement of Indian and mestizo populations from their land during the Porfiriato, one of the driving factors in the outbreak of the Mexican Revolution of 1910.[81]

The fever generated by the Sierra Mojada strike subsided quickly when it became evident that gold and silver was not to be found on the surface waiting to be picked up. This was the conclusion of J. J. Sánchez, who had been sent by the government of Coahuila to report on the mines. He wrote that it would take a lot of work to dig out the silver. This was corroborated by an Englishman named Courtney, who reported to the *San Antonio Express* that in order to extract ores it "would cost hundreds of thousands of dollars to open the mines and furnish proper machinery to run them." The mines could "only be worked by a very large capital, and will produce only after months of labor."[82]

The zeal of Texan and other foreign capitalists to invest in Mexican mining properties and other ventures was more than matched by local capital. Monterrey merchants played a major role in the economic development of northern Mexico. Sometimes allied with foreign capital and at other times without it, they invested their wealth in land, financial institutions, mining, agriculture, ranching, and manufacturing.[83] This process is exemplified by three men: Jesús González Treviño, Patricio Milmo, and Evaristo Madero. González Treviño invested part of the capital he derived from commerce in the establishment in 1870 of El Porvenir, a textile manufacturing plant near Monterrey. He was joined in this venture by the Zambrano family and Valentín Rivero, whom we first encountered in the early 1840s as a young Spanish merchant involved in a judicial dispute over contraband. González Treviño acquired machinery for the plant from England even as he continued to import cotton from Texas in the early 1870s before fiber from La Laguna became available. He also had a mining interest in the Sierra Mojada and bought more land to raise livestock. He pooled his capital with his brother Lorenzo, Evaristo Madero's business partner, to buy a ranch at Aguaverde and an iron and lead mining venture in San Pablo. Through marriage and business associations, the two brothers became members of Monterrey's oligarchy.[84]

One of the most prosperous men in Northeast Mexico in the 1870s was Patricio Milmo. He had survived the demise of Vidaurri, his father-in-law and had overcome the stigma of supporting Maximilian and opposing Juárez. With the money he made in the Civil War he bought land, which he used to increase his fortune by renting it to other capitalists and raising livestock. By the time of his death in 1899, he and his family owned "two ranches and one hacienda in Nuevo León; three haciendas, two *estancias* and three ranches in Coahuila; and one hacienda and six ranches in Tamaulipas." His family was "one of the most powerful groups of landholders in Northeast Mexico."[85] In the 1880s Milmo allowed Collis Huntington to extract coal from one of his Coahuila properties and was paid twenty-five cents for every ton produced. He was also a member of a binational group that exploited mines near Monterrey. Among the stockholders were Gerónimo Treviño and Francisco Naranjo, Nuevo León's most prominent military generals, and Texas capitalists such as William H. Abrams of Dallas and George F. Alford of Galveston.[86]

Milmo continued to engage in commerce and with his brother, Daniel, formed Milmo Bros. and Co, which commercial agent James Haynes described as "the largest wholesale house on [the] frontier." In 1879, when the extension of rail lines to Laredo was imminent, he and Daniel moved their operations to that city and "built large store houses there for conducting their business."[87] By 1882, Laredo was "reached by the International and Great Northern Railroad from the interior of the state, and the Texas Mexican from Corpus Christi," and had become "the gateway to Mexico," according to one Texas newspaper.[88] Seeing greater business opportunities, Milmo established the Milmo National Bank in 1882. By the 1880s this man, who had been vilified in Texas as a "miscreant" for confiscating Confederate funds, had obtained respectability. He was now known as "the millionaire banker from Monterey, Mexico," whose opinions were respected by the Texas public. Wealth had purified his reputation in the same way that it whitened people's skin.[89]

Perhaps no other Mexican merchant reflects the diversification of wealth to other productive activities or had closer ties to Texas than Evaristo Madero. The number of enterprises in agriculture, ranching, mining, manufacturing, and banking that he established with his sons is astonishing. Their mining ventures alone covered eight states: Coahuila, Nuevo León, Tamaulipas, Chihuahua, Guanajuato, Durango, Zacatecas, and San Luis Potosí. These enterprises amassed a family fortune that allowed one of Evaristo's grandchildren, Francisco I. Madero, to build a political following and lead a revolution that toppled the thirty-four-year rule of Porfirio Díaz. The young Madero planned his revolution in San Antonio, where his family had had close ties since the 1820s when his great-grandfather José Francisco Madero had allied himself with the Bexareño elite.[90]

Madero had many friends and business connections in Texas. He joined Texan investors such as LaCoste and his friend Charles Griesenbeck in various business ventures and was constantly asked for advice on buying land and investing in Mexico. He was an exhibitor in at least three international fairs in

San Antonio, where he "secured premiums on a great variety of liquors of all kinds, including wines, brandy, etc. of his own manufacture." He felt at home in San Antonio. During his term as governor of Coahuila (1880–84) he continued to travel to that city. His presence at a Masonic reception in the Alamo City in 1883 was duly noted by a local paper, but without fanfare.[91]

As governor, he welcomed Texans to his state. Governor John Ireland of Texas visited Coahuila in September 1883 to celebrate the arrival of the Mexican National Railroad to Saltillo that month. A crowd received him with music and tolling bells, and a banquet was given in his honor in a great hall decorated with the flags of Mexico and the United States. Governor Ireland expressed his gratitude for the warm welcome, stating that "the American people identified totally with the Mexican Republic" and that Texas stood ready to defend Mexico's interests.[92] Ireland's visit put many people in Texas at ease about traveling to Mexico and doing business in the country. The *Houston Post* declared that "such interchange of official courtesy and the benefits that flow from personal conference do more to produce good feeling and confidence than a score of treaties or any amount of correspondence at long range."[93]

Governor Ireland's visit to Coahuila underscores the fundamental change brought about by the railroad. Northeast Mexico and Texas had been connected for decades by the tramping feet of animals and humans. Now the region was integrated with iron rails that joined the two countries with "hooks of steel." Three railroad companies built roads into Mexico: The Mexican Central Railroad at El Paso, Huntington's International Railroad at Piedras Negras, and Jay Gould's International and Great Northern Railroad, which entered Mexico at Laredo as the Mexican National Railroad; this was the line Ireland used to travel to Saltillo. In anticipation of the railroad's arrival in San Antonio a local paper rejoiced that its extension into Mexico "would restore all of our old commerce that brought in olden times such wealth and established general comity between the two neighboring peoples, but it would be increased a thousand fold."[94] The reference to a "general comity" in "olden times" was perhaps an acknowledgment that relations between northern Mexico and Texas had been much more than violent clashes and bitter hatred during the previous half century.

Railroad connections facilitated commerce and the extraction of Mexico's mineral wealth, as the Chicago capitalists had anticipated, but they also promoted a much greater movement of people: Americans traveling to Mexico and Mexicans—principally of the laboring classes—traveling to Texas and points beyond in search of opportunities. Railroads also altered trade patterns because

Matamoros was left without a train connection to northern Mexico. Thus the shift to interior routes—including those through Laredo and Piedras Negras—that had begun timidly in the 1830s and accelerated during the Civil War in the 1860s, was now complete. Brownsville and Matamoros were left behind. Even in Corpus Christi, Uriah Lott, Richard King, and Mifflin Kenedy had begun to build a spur that connected with the Mexican National at Laredo. William Purcell, a longtime English merchant at Saltillo, captured the significance with alacrity: "Matamoros, I am afraid, will go to the wall, as there is no chance, without a railway, of competing with Laredo."[95]

Interest in Mexico for its mineral wealth and as a market for U.S. products and capital grew steadily in the 1870s. Throughout the decade railroad lines crept closer and closer to the border in their inexorable drive to connect the two nations. A final element, which U.S. Ambassador John Foster had emphasized to the Chicago capitalists, was still pending: pacification of the country, and especially the border region.

The Difficult Road to Pacification

The violence that racked the Texas-Mexico border region in the 1870s threatened to provoke war between the United States and Mexico. Both nations were too occupied with the problems of reconstruction to pay much attention to their common border. Between 1875 and 1880 however, they consolidated their power sufficiently to address the violence on the border and began taking positive steps toward pacification. A review of the major events of this complex process, as seen from the border region, might make it more comprehensible.

The violence continued unabated in 1875. The Nuecestown raid in March and its terrible consequences for the Mexican Texan population was followed in April by a Mexican raid on Carrizo in Zapata County. Eleven men robbed the post office and killed Dr. D. D. Lowell, "an old citizen of Texas, and a most estimable gentleman."[96] Cortinistas continued to prey on the cattle ranches near the border. In June, Captain McNelly and his rangers discovered a group herding 265 head of cattle toward the Rio Grande. A battle ensued and sixteen rustlers were killed. McNelly ordered their bodies "stacked like cordwood on Market Square [in Brownsville] as a ghoulish display of Ranger bravado." When Cortina threatened to launch another border war, General E. O. C. Ord, a man of "average build, with well-defined features and iron-gray mustache," called for reinforcements from New Orleans. Ord, a decorated Civil War veteran who had fought Indians in Florida and in the Pacific Northwest, had just been named to head the Texas Military Department in April. Meanwhile, in Mexico City, U.S. Ambassador Foster pressed the Mexican government to remove Cheno from the border. President Lerdo acceded and ordered Cortina to Mexico City. When Cortina refused, he was arrested and taken to the capital under heavy guard in July 1875. He stayed there for one year until Díaz's Tuxtepec rebellion gave him the opportunity to return to the border region.[97]

Indian raiders, mainly Lipan Apaches based in Mexico, continued to prey on Texas ranches and towns. Colonel William R. Shafter's reaction to these raids gained him broad notoriety in Mexico. He was described in a Texas newspaper as "a square built soldier" with "side whiskers in English style." Shafter and his subordinate, First Lieutenant John Bullis, with Ord's backing, made several incursions into Mexico, often accompanied by black cavalrymen known as Buffalo Soldiers.[98]

The participation of black soldiers in the pacification of the border was not insignificant. Historian James N. Leiker writes that black soldiers made up between 3 and 7 percent of the total American population along the border during the 1870s. At one point they "outnumbered white soldiers by three to one." When Shafter called for reinforcements he was sent a regiment of black soldiers. In their new role as soldiers and figures of authority, African Americans no longer shared the affinity with Mexicans that had been evident in the 1850s when they were slaves. Relations were now less friendly and often conflictive.[99]

One historian writes that in 1876–77, "the U.S. Army made ten illegal cross-border incursions in order to exterminate the Lipan Apaches in Mexico." On only two occasions were the incursions made in "hot pursuit."[100] Shafter wrote to his superior that the Mexicans were making "'not the slightest attempt' to prevent the Indians from raiding into the United States, but on the contrary they were 'finding refuge in the towns when pursued and a market for their stolen plunder at all times.'"[101]

In addition to cattle rustlers and Indian raiders, the border region suffered from three major uprisings in the 1870s, two led by Porfirio Díaz and one by the followers of Sebastián Lerdo de Tejada, after he had been deposed by Díaz. The first of these revolts (La Noria) occurred in 1871–72 and served as a prelude to the second (Tuxtepec) in 1876. The first revolt was carried out mainly in the northern states. On November 8, 1871, Porfirio Díaz proclaimed his Plan de la Noria, accusing Juárez of violating the constitution by remaining in the presidency. There was little enthusiasm for the rebellion in most of the country—people were tired of war—but the two military chiefs of Nuevo León, Gerónimo

Treviño and Francisco Naranjo, were eager proponents. The revolt went nowhere. Zacatecas was taken by the rebels but quickly retaken by the government. In May 1872, Consul Joseph Ulrich wrote that Nuevo León was in ruins. "Twenty years will not be sufficient to enable this people to recover from the damages of the last eight months." So this revolt, which barely registered a blip on the national radar, had tremendous local impact. In July Díaz capitulated in Mexico City, ending the revolt.[102]

In the region of Piedras Negras, the revolt brought to the fore one of the most polemical military figures of the 1870s, Pedro Advíncula Valdés, who sided with the government against the rebels. Valdés was a longtime Indian fighter whose nickname, Huíncar (interpreted by American soldiers as "Winker"), was given to him by Indians who could not pronounce Advíncula. Originally from Allende, Coahuila, he spent his youth in San Antonio and spoke English. He was fighting Indians as a teenager and returned to Coahuila to head a rural police force at the tender age of eighteen.[103] In 1862, he joined the republican army to fight against the French, served until the fall of Maximilian in 1867, and was highly decorated for his service to the nation. After the war, Valdés returned to Coahuila as a colonel in the Mexican army and head of the National Guard, charged with combating Indian predators. His courage was unquestioned. General Zenas R. Bliss wrote that Valdés was "one of the bravest men I ever saw."[104]

Huíncar used his Texas connections extensively, recruiting men in San Antonio to fight the rebels. This action brought forth a barrage of criticism from William Schuchardt, who accused Valdés of violating the neutrality laws. Valdés and his men, wrote Schuchardt, were "roaming Mexicans who call themselves exiles, despise honest work, and have no means to support themselves." He called them "a scourge for this Texas frontier."[105] Valdés crossed back and forth across the Rio Grande as it suited him. At some point he married an American woman, Louisa Brown. He was wounded in battle in 1872 and fled to Texas. He returned to Mexico in July, but by then the revolt of La Noria was all but over. The central government was in the process of annihilating the last of the rebels when Juárez died suddenly on July 18, 1872. The new government, headed by Sebastián Lerdo de Tejada, declared an amnesty, the war ended, and Porfirio Díaz returned to Oaxaca to lick his wounds and await another opportunity.[106]

That opportunity came in the fall of 1875, when it was learned that Lerdo would seek reelection to the presidency. While his followers proclaimed the Plan de Tuxtepec in Oaxaca, Díaz arrived in Brownsville, where he launched his second revolt against the government in December. Díaz chose to launch his insurrection from the border region because he could obtain arms across the border and resources from the customhouses. He counted on the support of a number of northern caudillos, such as Gerónimo Treviño and Francisco Naranjo of Nuevo León, Hipólito Charles and Anacleto Falcón of Coahuila, and Cortina in Tamaulipas, who left his Mexico City prison and returned to the border region during the revolt. Díaz also selected Brownsville because it afforded refuge and the possibility of acquiring economic support from Texas merchants. All of these elements were crucial to his success.[107]

In search of funds, Díaz made contact with prominent Texas businessmen and public figures. He met with Rip Ford, who told him that resources for his movement could be had in Texas if he would promise to remove Cortina from the border once in power. "General Díaz," wrote Ford, "gave his word as requested." It was reported that Sabas Cavazos, Cortina's half-brother, obtained a $50,000 loan for Díaz. Díaz also met with Richard King, Mifflin Kenedy, Francisco Yturria, and Charles Sterling, a representative of James Stillman, who was based in New York and who had inherited the money and power of his father. (Charles Stillman had moved to New York in 1866 and died there in 1875.) They all offered to help him on condition that he rid the border of Cortina and that he open the country to investments.[108]

Historian John Hart estimates that by spring 1876 Díaz had received in excess of $130,000 in loans and donations from American interests. This allowed him to purchase arms on a large scale. Two known shipments totaled more than 1,000 rifles, 350 carbines, and more than 600,000 rounds of ammunition. He also obtained horses, mules, wagons, and uniforms.[109] For his operations, Díaz could also count on complicity or at least tolerance from military commanders such as General Ord, allowing him to carry out his activities without interference.[110]

By August 1876, most of Tamaulipas, Nuevo León, and Coahuila were under the control of the rebels. By keeping government forces occupied in the North, Díaz and his principal collaborator, General Manuel González, were able to deal a lethal blow in the center and south of the country. They headed south with arms, artillery, and ammunition obtained in the border region. On November 16 at the battle of Tecoac in Tlaxcala, Díaz was cornered and on the verge of defeat when González appeared suddenly with a force of 3,800 troops and routed the government forces. President Lerdo abandoned Mexico City on November 21, and Porfirio Díaz entered the city two days later.[111] The key to Diaz's victory, argues John Hart, was "his ability to conduct a prolonged guerilla war against the financially bankrupt Lerdo government throughout the states of Tamaulipas and

Nuevo León."[112] The triumph of Tuxtepec gave Díaz the reins of power in Mexico, which he held for a third of a century until he was toppled by the Revolution of 1910. Hart is convinced that Díaz's triumph can be traced to American support: "The alliance between Díaz and the Americans set the stage for thirty-five years of U.S. economic expansion into Mexico."[113]

On assuming the presidency, Díaz was faced with a host of problems. He inherited a country exhausted by political chaos, a stagnant economy, an empty treasury, a huge foreign debt, and a largely rural and uneducated population. His government faced insurrections in Sinaloa and Guerrero and uprisings over the seizure of village lands in many parts of the country. Understandably, he "was too busy organizing his government to concentrate on the capture of bandits, smugglers, and frontier cattle rustlers supposed to be Mexican."[114] These, however, were among the main issues on U.S. Ambassador John Foster's agenda when he met with Ignacio Vallarta, Díaz's foreign minister. Foster insisted Cortina's removal was a necessary step to pacify the border region. Díaz was interested in pacifying the entire country, not just the border region, as a precondition for attracting foreign investment and modernizing Mexico. He reorganized and strengthened the *rurales*, a tough police force, to control brigandage in the countryside; he reduced the National Guard in the states usually controlled by local caudillos, and strengthened the national army; he separated the roles of governor and military chief in the states so that local leaders could not concentrate their power; and he played off local leaders against each other, meddling shamelessly in the internal politics of the states.[115]

Díaz summoned Cortina to Mexico City in February 1877. When Cheno disobeyed the order, he was arrested. On April 8, Cortina was escorted to the capital under a heavy armed guard. Díaz had kept his commitment to his Texas backers. Except for a short visit in 1891, Cortina would not be allowed to return to the border region where he had held sway for almost two decades.[116] Cortina's removal did not satisfy the United States. The Hayes government insisted on the pacification of the border region and withheld recognition from the Diaz government, a position that continued to strain relations.

With lawlessness still endemic across the Rio Grande, Díaz sent one of his most trusted generals, Gerónimo Treviño of Nuevo León, to pacify the border region. Treviño had assumed the role of caudillo of Nuevo León in the vacuum left by Santiago Vidaurri's execution. With a vast knowledge of the border and its inhabitants, he had a long and distinguished military career fighting Indians, conservatives, and French soldiers. Treviño occupied the governorship of the state when it suited him or selected one of his cronies to keep the seat warm for him. He was also one of the region's most enterprising capitalists. Treviño began his task, but while he was organizing his forces word arrived that the Hayes government had issued the Order of June 1, 1877, known publicly as the Ord Order, which provoked a political storm in Mexico. Secretary of War George W. McCrary gave Ord authorization to use "his own discretion, when in pursuit of a band of [Mexican] marauders, and when his troops [were] in sight of them or upon a fresh trail, to follow them across the Rio Grande, and to overtake and punish them, as well as retake stolen property."[117]

Military men such as Mackenzie, Shafter, and Bullis had practiced a local version of the Ord Order since the early 1870s. The fact that the U.S. government made it official policy, however, provoked outrage and a fiery nationalist reaction in Mexico. In some American circles the Ord Order was viewed as the act of "a stronger power bullying a weaker one. Businessmen and developers wondered how they could invest in Mexican mines and ranches when the Order of June 1 had antagonized the population against Americans."[118]

The Ord Order damaged relations between the two countries. Foreign Minister Ignacio Vallarta warned Foster that Mexico "would never permit its territory to be violated by American troops" and were Ord to carry out his orders, there would be grave consequences. President Díaz ordered Treviño to continue toward the Texas border and repel with force any incursion of American troops.[119] The Mexican press carried out an intense anti-American campaign. An editorial in *El Pájaro Verde* is typical of many that appeared in Mexico City newspapers. It accused the U.S. government of provoking Mexico into a war for the purpose of annexing more territory and declared that national honor was at stake. "Every Mexican will be a soldier . . . and the entire nation will hurl itself into the fray, firm and unified as if a single man." Some might argue that Mexico was weak, divided, and ill prepared for war, the editorial continued, "but we contend, based on our history, that Mexico was never prepared for peace." This damning self-indictment was followed by a call to all Mexicans to lay aside their differences and rally around Díaz, who had valiantly ordered General Treviño to meet force with force.[120]

Regional newspapers repeated this bellicose narrative. Nuevo León's official organ asked rhetorically if American superiority was a substitute for justice. If Mexico were attacked, "it would defend itself in the same manner that the ancient Greeks resisted the powerful Xerxes and will show the United States that we are in a much better condition than in 1847." This, of course, ignores the fact that the United States was also in a much better condition, but what is interesting is that the editorial informed readers that U.S. President Rutherford B. Hayes had assumed power by a vote of Congress after a fraudulent election, which he lost, and that was why he was using Mexico as an issue to distract public opinion. It is revealing that in a Mexican province most Americans didn't even know existed, Hayes's legitimacy as leader of his country was being questioned.[121]

The violence on the border and the issue of recognition of Mexico continued to strain relations between the two countries throughout 1877 and 1878, but amidst the heated rhetoric and threats of war in the press of both countries, events on the border were moving haltingly toward pacification. Treviño headed toward the border in June 1877, with precise orders from the secretary of war and navy. He was instructed to oppose with force the entry of U.S. troops into Mexico, but also "to cooperate fully with General Ord in apprehending malefactors and in their extradition under terms of a treaty signed in 1862."[122] Another Mexican general headed for the border, but not for the purpose of pacification. Mariano Escobedo, the Nuevo León general who had defeated Maximilian at Querétaro, was intending to lead a revolt to restore to the presidency his former commander-in-chief, Lerdo de Tejada, who was in exile in New York. This was the third revolt to convulse the border region during the decade.[123]

Other than Escobedo, there were few Lerdo loyalists on the frontier. One of these was Pedro A. Valdés. Huíncar had supported the government against Díaz in 1872, but he had remained outside the stream of events during the rebellion of Tuxtepec that elevated Díaz to power. In early 1877, when the Lerdo revolt was picking up steam, Valdés joined the cause, recruiting men on both sides of the border in the region of Eagle Pass and Piedras Negras. It was believed that he commanded 150 troops and was waiting on the Texas side for an opportunity to capture Piedras Negras. In early June 1877, he made a foray into Mexico, but was chased back to Texas by government troops. In the meantime, Treviño reached the border and quickly sought a meeting with Ord, who traveled from San Antonio to meet with the Mexican general at Piedras Negras. They had a cordial meeting on June 17, after which they crossed the river and proceeded to Fort Clark, where they held a joint review of the troops. After the meeting, Ord was optimistic. He wrote that he and Treviño "had reached an understanding to suppress marauding raiders, achieve greater cooperation by both armies, and to pursue raiders on both sides of the Río Bravo."[124]

The Ord-Treviño meeting began to produce results immediately. Troops under Treviño's command crossed the border in pursuit of Valdés. Colonel Shafter reported this incursion to Ord, who instructed him to take no action. Valdés, wrote an American who was visiting Coahuila, had caused excitement along the border, but "he has no sympathy among the Mexicans further in from the river, nor a single one who would assume his cause." Apparently the wily Huíncar saw the handwriting on the wall. On July 27, a Texas newspaper reported that he and his followers had sought pardons and permission to return to Mexico.[125]

Escobedo was mostly left on his own to continue the revolt. However, in the Ord-Treviño spirit of cooperation, his actions were closely watched. He arrived in Rio Grande City in July to await a shipment of arms. The weapons, "eight cases of Remington breech-loading arms and ammunition," arrived on the steamer *Ackley* but were immediately seized, and Escobedo and fourteen of his officers arrested. They were charged with violating the laws of neutrality, but were quickly released.[126] It became clear that the followers of Lerdo would not receive the same considerations that Díaz and his adherents had during the earlier Tuxtepec revolt. Moreover, Escobedo had few contacts in Texas and nothing to promise Texas businessmen, since Cortina had already been removed from the border.

Cattle rustling had decreased with Cortina's departure but had not ceased completely. And, although Escobedo and his followers were largely kept in check, tension remained high in the border region. On August 12, 1877, an event occurred that ratcheted the tension even higher. In the dead of night eight armed Mexicans crossed the river at Camargo and attacked the Rio Grande City jail. They wounded one guard, killed another, brutally pistol-whipped a woman believed to be the wife of one of the jailers and wounded and left for dead Starr County District Attorney Noah Cox. They then released all the prisoners, including "the notorious Segundo Garza, a man who delighted in bragging that he had murdered twenty-seven Americans" and was facing trial for another murder. The Texas press was apoplectic, calling the raid an invasion and hurling threats at Mexico.[127]

While the Rio Grande City raid was still fresh in the collective memory of Texans, the Salt War erupted in October. Texas newspapers had a field day attacking Mexicans. The *Dallas Weekly Herald* echoed other newspapers when it referred to the "Mexican mob, four hundred strong [that] took possession of the towns of Pieta and San Elizario." The "infuriated rabble" shouted "Death to Gringos and Viva Mexico." The report warned of an impending race war: "The lives of all white men are threatened. There are no troops on the frontier, and a horrible massacre is imminent." All over Texas there was outrage: "a war feeling is being excited which will not be easily repressed," the article concluded.[128] Mexican newspapers were no less vitriolic in their invective against the U.S.

government for issuing the Ord Order and refusing to recognize Díaz. The *New York Times* editorialized that "on both sides of the boundary" there is "a deliberate determination to create the impression that war is imminent and that each Government is making active hostile preparations." It charged that this was a false image created by hotheads and adventurers on both sides.[129]

The heated rhetoric tended to eclipse genuine efforts by men of both countries to bring about peace. One of these men was U.S. Consul John Weber in Monterrey.[130] He established constant communication with both Ord and Treviño, who was a personal friend, and facilitated the meeting of the two military leaders. Weber also kept Ord informed of public opinion and military movements in northern Mexico. He shared letters from Mexican military commanders and translated official correspondence published in Nuevo León's *Periódico Oficial*. Ord wrote that he was making good use of the information. He added: "I am in hopes that the effort of Mexican officials on the frontier will, when they see that we are only working for the common good, cooperate with us in a friendly spirit."[131]

As 1877 came to a close, four issues continued to complicate relations between the two countries, all of them related to the border region: the question of U.S. recognition of Díaz's government, the continuation of the Ord Order, the Lerdo revolt, and the persistence of Indian raids into Texas. In December, in his message to Congress, President Hayes declared that "official recognition" of Díaz had "been deferred by the occurrences on the Rio Grande border." Ambassador Foster was summoned to Washington in January 1878 to testify on the recognition issue before the House Foreign Affairs Committee. The U.S. ambassador provided the committee with an extensive report and recommended recognizing the Díaz government. At the same time, Manuel María de Zamacona was carrying out his "public relations offensive," meeting with many different groups, especially businessmen, who began to apply pressure on the Hayes administration to recognize Díaz. Upon his return to Mexico in April, Foster was instructed to tender U.S. recognition of the government.[132]

Recognition was an important step, but other issues remained. The Lerdo revolt was more of a nuisance than a serious threat to the Díaz government, but its leader, Mariano Escobedo, continued to use the border to obtain refuge and arms, which strained relations between the two countries.[133] In June and July, Escobedo's small force made various incursions into Mexico, but was driven back each time. When he ventured farther into the interior in search of support, he was captured in mid-July near Cuatro Ciénegas, Coahuila. He was taken to Monterrey and stood before Treviño, his former subordinate, then transferred to Mexico City. Díaz was merciful with his former comrade in arms, who had rendered distinguished service to the nation during the French Intervention, and had him pardoned after he swore loyalty to the government.[134]

With the issues of recognition and the Lerdo revolt resolved, two other matters remained pending during 1878–79: the sporadic raids carried out by scattered groups of Lipan Indians and the Ord Order, which, although it posed no real threat to Mexican sovereignty, was galling to national pride. Though Indian forays from Mexico into Texas had decreased, they continued to generate conflict on the border. In April 1878, a band of Lipan Indians rode out of their refuge in Coahuila and carried out a raid in Texas. Several Texas newspapers reported that Kickapoos and Mexicans also formed part of the band. One report claimed that thirty men and boys were murdered by the raiders, a wild exaggeration. Upon their return to Coahuila, the raiders allegedly shared the spoils with the authorities of Santa Rosa. The Texas reading public believed the story because the source of the report was an American resident of Santa Rosa who supposedly witnessed these events. However, a group of American residents from the same Coahuila town sent a letter to General Ord denying the veracity of the report. They informed Ord that Mexican authorities, joined by Kickapoos, went after the Lipans and captured twenty-seven horses after killing and capturing several Indians. Only one horse had an American brand, which suggests that the horses may have been previously stolen in Mexico and taken across the border. A. Murdock, the commercial agent at Santa Rosa, who was one of the letter signers, wrote that the source had given false information "for the purpose of stirring up strife and fermenting the American heart." Other signers included James H. Duvall, Rufus James, and Alexander Warfield.[135]

Throughout the summer and early fall of 1878, tensions were high and the threat of war latent. In July an Austin newspaper reported, "Indian raids have been more frequent and destructive to life and property in the last few months than ever before in Texas. Scores of our frontier people have been massacred in cold blood."[136] War fever was also rife in Northeast Mexico. In July 1878 Weber wrote from Monterrey that "warlike feeling toward the United States" was "beginning to spread amongst all classes of the Mexican people." He told Ord that General Treviño had confided to him that American incursions into Mexico were complicating matters and "that public opinion and even many of his subordinate officers were severely criticizing and censuring him for not repelling . . . force by force."[137] In August, Weber wrote again that the situation on the frontier and in all of Mexico was critical and "our situation here is becoming daily more perilous."[138]

Then in September an event occurred in Mexico City that further exacerbated public opinion. U.S. Ambassador John Foster attended a ceremony at the National Theater to commemorate Mexican independence. One of the orators, Anselmo Alfaro, an impetuous youth fired with patriotic fervor, read a poem that Foster described as "a fierce diatribe against the Government of the United States." It was read "in a most excited manner," wrote Foster, "and it did not fail to stir up the audience to a state almost of frenzy." Hearing cries of "'Death to the Yankees' shouted from every part of the house," Foster remained composed and waited until calm was restored before leaving the theater with his family. Amidst the furor over the incident and rumors that Foster was about to abandon Mexico and break off diplomatic relations, the U.S. ambassador assured the Mexican government that he "had never for a moment considered the federal authorities in any way responsible for whatever had occurred in the national festival" and that "the demonstration could only be regarded as the unpremeditated expression of a miscellaneous audience in a time of popular excitement."[139]

With public opinion in Texas and Mexico so inflamed, Foster reported to Washington that there was a "prevailing belief" in Mexico that there would be war between the two countries. The U.S. consul in Monterrey, John Weber, confirmed that there was much excitement about the possibility of war and that many of Treviño's officers were itching to fight the United States.[140] In early October, Weber informed Ord that Treviño was headed for the border with a body of troops. Many believed that his mission was to face the Texans and defend the national honor. In fact, he was marching to the Rio Grande to begin his long-delayed campaign to rid the Mexican border of predators. Treviño wanted to meet again with Ord and asked Weber to communicate that desire to the American general. Weber transmitted the message and received Ord's assurances that he would be at Fort Duncan on October 7, awaiting Treviño's arrival at Piedras Negras.[141]

In November, Treviño's troops began to move vigorously against Indian and Mexican predators. It was reported that Mexican government forces were "engaged in dispersing the Lipan Indians who have been depredating in Texas."[142] These actions began to show results. Consul Weber informed Ord and Washington of the captured raiders that passed through Monterrey on their way to Mexico City. Fourteen raiders, including the notorious Apolonio Arreola, had been sent to the capital along with seventy-five Lipan and Mescalero braves, among them "Arzate, Capitan Colorado, and Oro Ballo." A large number of Kickapoos had also been rounded up and were being relocated to the mountains south of

Monterrey, far from the Rio Grande. "General Treviño," wrote Weber, was "trying to do his best to establish peace and order." By January 1879, Treviño reported that his campaign against the Lipan Apaches had been successful and that most of them had been removed from the border. A few scattered remnants remained, but they were rounded up in 1880–81 by Blas M. Flores and Pedro A. Valdés.[143]

Beginning in the winter of 1879, a positive change could be seen along the border and in U.S.-Mexico relations. The group of Chicago capitalists was in Mexico City in January 1879, and Zamacona wrote from Washington "that while the American merchants and manufacturers were paying tribute to Díaz in Mexico City, 'in Texas they do the same with General Treviño and in Washington they drown the humble representative of our republic with flattery.'"[144] Relations between Treviño and Ord were moving from cordiality to camaraderie as John Weber continued to facilitate contacts between the two men. In June 1879, Weber asked Ord if it was true that General Philip Sheridan would be making a tour of the Texas frontier and "if so, would it not be well to quietly prepare an accidental interview somewhere on the Rio-Grande between yourself, Gen. Sheridan and General Treviño?"[145] In February 1880, Weber wrote to Ord that Treviño had been appointed secretary of war and was "very anxious to have a talk with [Ord] so as to arrange matters in case he should have to go to the city of Mexico as a member of the Cabinet." Weber, who was becoming somewhat of a busybody, also suggested that Ord give Treviño a sword in a public ceremony in San Antonio and make a big splash in the city's newspapers. "General Treviño," wrote the consul, "highly appreciates all courtesies extended to him by the American People."[146]

Events on the border demonstrated Díaz's increasing grasp on state power. He was demonstrating to Mexicans and the world that his government was not another short-term operation but one that would last. Besides bringing predators to justice, his regime "was gradually eliminating armed opposition and thus most complaints of forced loans and seized property." Ord and Treviño not only shared intelligence, they agreed on joint patrols and some of Ord's representatives may have accompanied Treviño in his campaign against the Lipans.[147] Hayes's message to Congress in 1879 reflects the improved state of affairs on the border. He stated that "through the judicious and energetic action of the military commanders of the two nations on each side of the Rio Grande, under instructions of their respective governments, raids and depredations have greatly decreased."[148]

The final issue driving a wedge between the two countries was resolved on February 24, 1880, when the Ord Order was revoked. Secretary of State William

Evarts "expressed the satisfaction of President Hayes that 'the efforts of the Mexican military in guarding the frontier make the order no longer necessary' and hoped that 'no future occurrences on the border' would disturb cordial relations between the two countries."[149] In 1882, the two governments signed an agreement to allow reciprocal crossings in pursuit of predators. It had a number of limitations, such as the obligation to notify civil and military authorities on the other side of an impending incursion, but the accord was another step toward the cordial and mutually beneficial relations that developed between the two nations until the Mexican Revolution of 1910.[150]

An event that occurred in San Antonio in August 1880 seemed to symbolize the harmonious relations that had developed between the United States and Mexico. General Gerónimo Treviño married General Ord's daughter, Roberta Augusta Ord. The ceremony was lavish; American and Mexican flags and brilliant lights served as decoration and the cuisine was exquisite and abundant. The entire scene seemed to radiate "international friendship."[151] A San Antonio newspaper declared that the marriage would help in the "creation of . . . kindlier, more amicable feelings" between the people on both sides of the border. The marriage, continued the report, "bears an aspect of international importance that no one acquainted with the situation can fail to recognize."[152] After retiring in December 1880, Ord spent time in Monterrey in the home of his daughter and son-in-law. He received from Treviño a generous gift of ninety thousand acres of land in Coahuila. When the old warrior visited Mexico City in 1881 "he was hailed as a hero and welcomed as a relative, hardly the reception Mexicans had envisioned in 1877."[153]

The resolution of border problems was a major step in improving relations between Mexico and the United States. Border raids had largely ceased and were unlikely to revive given the spirit of cooperation that had developed between authorities on both sides of the Rio Grande. Forced loans had ended as Díaz consolidated his power and made rebellions extremely dangerous. Disputes over the zona libre had diminished as American products began to compete favorably with European goods, especially because rail transport lowered freight costs. "Very soon the distrust of the Northern Colossus gave way to the urgency of achieving economic progress and the inevitable conviction that it could only be done with foreign capital."[154]

~

Violence and increasing cooperation were two distinct features of the Texas-Mexican frontier in the 1870s. Yet, one other characteristic stands out with greater prominence: change. The 1870s was a decade of transition in which commerce began to lose its dominance to other economic activities such as mining and commercial ranching and agriculture. Transportation became faster and more secure with the arrival of the railroad at the end of the decade. For the first time in half a century the border region was pacified. These changes were driven by outside forces, including capitalist development. Meanwhile, the Mexican national government finally stabilized under the administration of Porfirio Díaz starting in 1877, and began to pursue vigorously its goal of pacifying the country, including the border region.

The winds of change blew over the border region, but continuity was also evident in the persistence of commercial patterns established in an earlier period. Cotton continued to flow to Northeast Mexico, though in smaller volumes and no longer bound for Europe but for the textile factories of northern Mexico. Cattle and sheep from Texas were driven south to stock Mexican ranches. Greater quantities of goods and manufactured products from the eastern and northern United States began to cross the Rio Grande, especially once the railroad extended its reach into Mexico. Mexican exports were mostly the same items that had been dominant fifty years earlier: hides and silver.

Trade, which was promoted by U.S. commercial agents, continued to be a factor in the integration of the region, but investments in land and mines also played an increasing role. Investment capital was plentiful in the expanding U.S. economy and large amounts flowed into Mexico during the last quarter of the nineteenth century. Merchants in Texas and Northeast Mexico, with decades of experience in the transborder trade and flush with cash from the cotton boom of the Civil War, led the way. With their experience and connections, they moved easily into other investment opportunities, from banking to railroad construction, mining, and commercial agriculture or ranching.

The extension of the railroad below the border was a major step in opening Mexico's economy to foreign investment. It made Mexico's mineral wealth more accessible, though it intensified Mexico's dependence on an extractive economy. It gave the United States an advantage in the competition with European nations for the Mexican market. In Northeast Mexico the transportation of goods accelerated, as did the movement of people: migrant workers drawn north to the expanding labor market in Texas and Americans attracted south by business opportunities in Mexico. The railroad tracks followed interior routes established decades earlier through Laredo, Eagle Pass, and El Paso, ending the half-century hegemony that Matamoros had enjoyed as the gateway to Mexico's

Northeast. The railroad was crucial in completing the integration of the region, a process initiated decades before by merchants and freighters with horses, mules, and oxcarts.

A precondition for the extension of the railroad and the arrival of significant foreign investment was the pacification of the countryside. This process reflected the two faces of the border region: conflict and cooperation. It can be argued that the pacification of Mexico began on the Rio Grande because it was there, with the support of American merchants, that Porfirio Díaz mounted a successful revolt that toppled the Lerdo government and imposed a highly centralized authoritarian regime that restored order to the region along with the rest of the nation. The new government removed Cortina from the border, which probably served notice to others that their raids into Texas would no longer go unpunished.

Violent events in the second half of the decade complicated relations between the two countries, and there was even talk of war after the Ord Order of June 1, 1877, was issued. Cooler heads prevailed. Porfirio Díaz sent General Gerónimo Treviño to the border region, where he met with the military commander in Texas, General E. O. C. Ord, and together they began to work to pacify the region. By 1879 conflict in the border region was largely extinguished and relations between the two countries had improved considerably. The wedding in August 1880 of General Ord's daughter, Augusta, to General Treviño symbolized the growing cooperation between the United States and Mexico.

~

At this point—1880—it is appropriate to say a few words about the evolution of this story that began half a century earlier, in 1830. Various trajectories are evident. One involves some of the actors and their families. Beardless young men in 1830, such as John Linn and Reuben Potter, were wizened old men by 1880. Other men, such as José Francisco Madero and Victor Blanco, had died in the interim, but by 1880 their sons were powerful men in the worlds of business and politics, and their family names are still prominent today.

The fifty-year period witnessed the creation and coalescence of a border. This was part of a larger story that was occurring throughout the Western Hemisphere during the hundred-year period after colonial domination. Border formation ran parallel to the consolidation of the nation-states on both sides of that new boundary. Both processes were crucial in defining the level of violence in the Rio Grande region. Before 1848 there was no border and little or no government presence. After 1848 there was a lawless border with weak governments beset by wars and reconstruction. By 1880, the two states were able to exercise a good measure of control over the violence.

In harmony with a coalescing border and the growing power of the nation-state, another trajectory became evident in the forging of identities. The lower Rio Grande region, both north and south of the border, was peopled mostly by Mexicans, so it is their identity that concerns me. The identity of a people is defined largely by their membership in a community and by those elements, such as language and culture, that distinguish them from others outside the community. According to historian Peter Sahlins, who studied the Pyrenean frontier of France and Spain, "it is this sense of difference—of 'us' and 'them'—which was so critical in defining an identity. Imagining oneself a member of a community or a nation meant perceiving a significant difference between oneself and the other across the boundary."[155]

After 1848, norteños had a clear boundary to differentiate themselves from their Anglo-Texan neighbors. However, their identity as Mexicans began to develop even before that boundary was fixed, due to their having lived through the separation of Texas, the incursions of Anglo adventurers, and the bitter war against the United States. After the establishment of the border, they were beset by filibusters and further threats of war and annexation from their foreign neighbor.

Mexicans who lived north the Rio Grande underwent a different experience. Before the arrival of Anglo-American colonists, they considered themselves norteños, but Texas independence left them adrift, separated from their national anchor. Under Anglo domination a new boundary was erected: a racial and ethnic divide that was unseen but definitely felt. Mexicans were constantly reminded that they were different when Anglos referred to them as "greasers," but they felt their difference more forcefully when they suffered abuse and despoliation in the 1830s, expulsions in the nativist 1850s, and oppression and killings in the 1870s. Consequently, Mexican communities on both sides of the Rio Grande felt intimately the "subjective experience of difference," to use Sahlins's phrase.[156]

For norteños the development of identity had another dimension. Sahlins states that "identity was a function of local interests." Norteños were willing to identify with a state that provided solutions to their problems and needs. Unfortunately, throughout much of the nineteenth century the Mexican state did not fit that description. Norteños could not feel loyalty to a state that imposed high tariffs while failing to defend them from Indian raids. That is why they did not embrace vigorous nationalism after Mexican independence. This sentiment gradually changed. It was the Mexican army and not local militias that bore the brunt of the battles in the U.S.-Mexican War. It was the national government that established the colonias militares in an attempt to combat Indian predators. It was to the same government that authorities in Coahuila turned when they sought resettlement for Mexicans fleeing Texas after 1836 and 1848. In these and other ways local communities "adopted national identities without losing their local ones," and by doing so, "brought the nation into the village."[157]

The physical presence in Northeast Mexico of the Mexican state in the charismatic figure of Benito Juárez, when Mexico was fighting the French Empire, went a long way toward aligning norteños with adherence to the nation. All of this occurred before Porfirio Díaz, a later incarnation of the Mexican state, took a firm hold of the nation's rudder and implemented policies of educational, cultural, and political unification.[158]

Afterword

Two visions have coexisted in the history of the Texas-Mexico border region: the negative one, oriented toward conflict, has been magnified by the popular press. Meanwhile, the one oriented toward cooperation, which reflected the lived experiences of many people, has received little attention. Reading only one vision of the history may lead readers to consider the Rio Grande frontier as a Hobbesian world where individuals who were unrestrained by the normal checks of an organized society preyed on their fellows, especially people who were not members of their clan, race, or nation. In fact, on the frontier everyone struggled to survive. That struggle sometimes led to violence, at other times to cooperation. This book focuses on cooperation, and especially interethnic relations involving Anglos and Mexicans.

During the period covered by this study, Anglos and Mexicans lived through dramatic events and changes: the separation of Texas from Mexico in the 1830s; the war between the United States and Mexico in the 1840s; revolts and wars in the 1850s and 1860s; and unrelenting violence in the 1870s. They emerged in 1880 into a far different world than the one they had known in 1830. In the process they gradually learned to coexist and, in many cases, to live together in peace. This issue has received scant attention. The historical literature is weighted in the other direction, replete with affirmations that Anglos and Mexicans could not share the same space. The comment by a lady in Texas who was interviewed by Frederick Law Olmsted is typical. She stated, "White folks and Mexicans were never made to live together." Mexicans were becoming uppity, so "the Americans would just have to get together and drive them all out of the country."[1] In fact, they were driven out of some counties in Texas in the 1850s, until it was discovered that their labor was needed for the state's expanding economy.

The sentiments expressed by the Southern lady cannot explain the many examples of peaceful interethnic coexistence that I have documented in this study, both in Texas and in Northeast Mexico. Most Americans in Mexico and Mexicans in Texas who went about their work and minded their own business usually found an atmosphere conducive to a mutually rewarding coexistence. The occasional crime committed against foreign residents in Mexico, as well as the violence perpetrated against Mexicans in Texas, were recorded in the headlines and the diplomatic correspondence. Then as now, the day-to-day business of life and work generates little interest and no headlines,[2] but this is undoubtedly what transpired in towns and villages of Northeast Mexico and in inclusive communities in Texas, such as Eagle Pass, Laredo, Brownsville, Corpus Christi, and Victoria, as well as on the many farms and ranches that dotted the region.

Cooperation and Conflict in the Balance

Cooperation largely depended on the attitudes that Anglos and Mexicans had about each other. We can begin with a simple truth: Not all Mexicans hated Anglos and not all Anglos were racists who detested Mexicans. Mexican antipathy toward Anglos resulted from their persecution in Texas, the loss of their land to acquisitive Anglos, the abuses of the American occupation during the U.S.-Mexican War, the murder of Mexicans in the Nueces Strip during the 1870s, or other events. It is safe to say that most Mexicans did not believe Anglos were inherently evil and did not consider them as enemies. They probably agreed with José Antonio Navarro, who reminded Juan Cortina that not all Texans were like his tormentors: "that class of infamous men has nothing in common with the law-abiding and honorable nature of the American people in general."[3]

Anglo attitudes toward Mexicans are more complicated because the issue is intimately bound up with race. Race relations go a long way toward explaining the scope and limits of cooperation, but these relations were contingent on many factors related to time and circumstance. Demography was one of these. Negative Anglo attitudes were tempered when the makeup of the population was overwhelmingly Mexican. According to David Weber, "Anglo newcomers, frequently hostile toward Mexicans at first, tended to develop tolerance and understanding when they were outnumbered."[4] Given these circumstances, they "had little choice but to adapt to their new human geography" and they "learned to know their Hispanic neighbors and judge them as individuals rather than prejudging them as a group."[5] This demographic reality was clearly at work in the lower Rio

Grande Valley, where Mexicans comprised 85 percent or more of the population throughout the second half of the nineteenth century. This was not a welcoming place for radical racists such as the one who was subdued after riding into the campsite of August Santleben's freighters with the intention to kill a Mexican.

Economic considerations played a crucial role in softening the hard edges of racial prejudice. Mexican workers, products, and markets were too essential to Texans to allow racial issues to derail a mutually beneficial relationship. James Crisp states that "interethnic alliances along class lines based on mutual economic interests at times proved stronger than the pride and prejudice of race."[6]

Other elements are worth mentioning. Wealthy or skilled Mexicans were accepted, even admired in Anglo society. Policarpo Rodríguez, Luz Villanueva, and Gregorio García were greatly respected for their bravery and proficiency as trackers and Indian fighters. Josefa Guajardo de Hewetson, Rita Alderete, and Petra Vela were admired, both for their ability to manage large business operations and for their basic decency and humanity.

The presence of so many Europeans in the border region and in positions of prominence in society—especially doctors, merchants, and religious people—was another factor. These groups were less conscious of race than their Anglo-American counterparts were, and often served as buffers between the Anglo and Mexican population.

The presence or absence of conflict between Americans and Mexicans also shaped interethnic relations. Relations were strained during the 1850s owing primarily to the flight of black slaves across the border and to the rise of the Know Nothing Party. They were tense in the 1870s because of cattle raids in the Nueces Strip and the protection that Indians received south of the Rio Grande after making forays into Texas. In contrast, conflict subsided between the two races during the U.S. Civil War in the 1860s. Both the Union and the Confederacy sought allies, soldiers, and workers among the Mexican population. Racism decreased, at least outwardly, and relations between the races improved due to one simple fact: Anglos and Mexicans needed each other. Historian Michael G. Webster writes that the cordial relations between Anglos and Mexicans during the Civil War were attributable "largely to necessity. . . . Each needed the other's trade."[7] The Civil War also redirected the hatred of many Texans away from Mexicans toward "Yankees."

As these factors demonstrate, racial attitudes were not permanent or immutable, but fluid and dependent on many variables. They were not a structural inevitability; neither were they an automatic source of conflict nor a major obstacle to cooperation. Even though the period between 1830 and 1880 is known mainly for conflict, a case can be made that cooperation was every bit as pervasive. The many examples of economic, social, and religious cooperation contained in this book confirm the observation of Malcolm McLean, one of the most respected scholars of Texas history, who stated that "the lives of the Anglo-Americans, the Mexicans, and the Indians became intimately intertwined, in a more humane, sympathetic, and understanding atmosphere than the usual Texas histories would lead us to believe ever existed."[8]

When viewed from a larger perspective, the Texas-Mexico border region mirrors the conclusion David Cannadine reached in his book *The Undivided Past*: "Whether envisaged individually or collectively, the reality of the human past has always been informed by dialogue, interaction, connection, borrowing, blending, and assimilation, at least as much as it has been by disagreement, hostility, belligerence, conflict, separation, or unlikeness." If we accept this premise as true, it follows that "to write about the past no less than to live in the present, we need to see beyond our differences, our sectional interests, our identity politics, and our parochial concerns to embrace and to celebrate the common humanity that has always bound us together . . . and that will continue to bind us together in the future."[9]

The Border Region after 1880

Pacification and the coming of the railroad brought change to the border region after 1880, but did not alter the basic patterns that had existed since the 1820s. Economic integration of the region, which had begun decades earlier, became stronger with more efficient systems of communication and transportation. San Antonio and Monterrey retained their role as vital centers on opposite sides of the border. Contraband continued to play an important role in the regional economy as neither country attained absolute control of its border. Labor migration accelerated as the Texas economy expanded and campesinos in Mexico were increasingly displaced from their land by regional oligarchs, often allied with foreign capital. The railroad expanded the scope of migration; after 1880 more people began the trek north from states such as Jalisco, Zacatecas, and Guanajuato.

The railroad also contributed to transforming the ranching economy of South Texas into an emporium of commercial agriculture with modern irrigation systems. This development and the arrival of thousands of Anglo farmers accelerated the loss of Mexican lands in the lower Rio Grande region, and many former landholders were now forced to work as farm laborers on land where their cows used to graze. This process, in turn, exacerbated racial attitudes and facilitated the establishment of a system of segregation, similar to the one imposed on African Americans.[10] This oppressive system required huge amounts of cheap labor, and recruiters were sent south of the Rio Grande in search of farm laborers, much as they had done during the Civil War era when they went in search of freighters to haul cotton.

Another connection with the past was the use of the border as a refuge for dissidents. Porfirio Díaz established a rigid authoritarian system that stifled personal freedom and regional autonomy. This provoked strong opposition from norteños who had revolted against governments since the 1830s to preserve these rights. The revolt of Catarino Garza against Diaz's despotic regime began in Texas in 1891. Like the revolts of Antonio Canales and José María Carvajal decades earlier, it failed. Díaz, who had engineered a successful revolt from his refuge in Brownsville, was not about to let the same thing happen to him. Besides his effective system of espionage, the dictator had another factor in his favor: Garza was also pursued by Texas authorities because his revolt incited Texas Mexicans to rise up against Anglo racism and oppression. His revolt ultimately failed and Garza fled Texas, only to die fighting another oppressive government in Colombia in 1895.[11] Catarino Garza became a folk hero in Texas for his fight against racial injustice, joining other figures such as Jacinto Treviño and Gregorio Cortez. Their trail had been blazed years earlier by Juan Cortina.

The Mexican Revolution (1910–20) shook the border region to its core and brought back memories of the nineteenth century when government authority, at least on the Mexican side, was largely absent. The threat to American lives and the destruction of their property raised cries for U.S. intervention and—reminiscent of the 1870s—even for annexation of part of Mexico. The violence produced a flood of immigrants, many of them fanning out from Texas and California to other parts of the United States. Once again, revolutionaries used Texas as a base of operations. Francisco Madero began his revolution against Porfirio Díaz in San Antonio, and later Bernardo Reyes, the ex-governor of Nuevo León, sought refuge in the Alamo City to plot against Madero. Events in the border region continued to dominate the diplomatic agendas of both nations, whether the issue was the harboring of rebels or the flow of arms to the various military factions.

The Mexican Revolution was deeply felt north of the Rio Grande, according to historians Don M. Coerver and Linda B. Hall. "So closely was South Texas linked to northern Mexico that a political upheaval in one was bound to have a major impact on the other."[12] San Antonio received scores of refugees and immigrants, many of whom were professional people and writers who gave considerable force to Mexican traditions and culture. South Texas was also greatly influenced by the ideals of social justice motivating the Revolution. Rural people's struggle to retain their land was appealing to people who were losing theirs. This was one of the causes of the 1915 revolt known as the Plan de San Diego.[13] The U.S. government was persuaded that one of Mexico's revolutionary factions was supporting the revolt, and this belief created a conflict between the two countries that threatened to escalate into a war. In one incident reminiscent of the 1870s, U.S. soldiers entered Mexico in pursuit of rebels and stayed overnight near Matamoros.[14]

The Plan de San Diego resurrected Anglo fear and hatred of Mexicans. The Texas Rangers committed unspeakable atrocities against the mostly innocent Mexican population of South Texas. The revolt also intensified the brutal system of segregation, which weakened the bonds of interethnic cooperation of an earlier age. According to historian Benjamin H. Johnson, "by 1930 some 90 percent of the region's school districts maintained separate facilities for 'Mexicans' and whites." It is interesting, however, that this South Texas version of apartheid did not prevail in cities such as Brownsville and Laredo, which had large Mexican populations and where the interests of Anglo merchants, unlike those of Anglo farmers, dictated benign treatment of Mexicans who formed the largest market for their products. This, too, recalls the many mid-nineteenth-century instances when economic considerations carried more weight than racial prejudice.[15]

Throughout the Porfiriato, the Mexican Revolution, and beyond, the border has facilitated transnational exchange. As Coerver and Hall pointed out, "Social, cultural, religious, and economic relationships transcended the international frontier."[16] Commerce, even when it suffered temporary interruptions during certain phases of the Mexican Revolution, always resumed. Arms and rebels moved freely across the boundary. Migrant labor, vital to economic development in Texas and other parts of the United States, continued to stream across a porous and open border well into the twentieth century, despite U.S. government efforts to control it.

This borderlands study, which is also a transnational study, shows that the histories of Texas and northern Mexico are interconnected, both with each other and with the greater world. These connections have taken many forms. Minié and Sharps rifles brought badly needed European and American weapons technology to Mexico's republican armies. Military men such as Edelmiro Mayer and Danish American John P. Encking (Eucking) brought to northern Mexico a military culture forged in Argentina and the United States. Physicians such as Charles

Linn and Frank Paschal brought to Northeast Mexico the latest innovations in European and American medical science. The mascogos brought to northern Mexico cultural practices that originated in Africa. Catholic priests from Europe and Protestant missionaries from New England brought their beliefs and values to the border region. Mexican hides and silver found their way to many corners of the United States and Europe. The abundant natural resources in northern Mexico spurred movements of capital not only in the cities of Texas, but also in Chicago, New York, and faraway New Zealand. The northern flow of Mexican labor contributed to the development of Texas and over time has substantially altered demographic patterns in many American communities. These workers did not journey alone. They carried with them their culture and their language. These and other examples presented in this study illustrate "experiences and processes that overflow the boundaries of the nation-state." They occur in a global context. In the words of historians Ramón A. Gutiérrez and Elliott Young, they demonstrate how "state borders and boundaries . . . fail to contain, to constrain, to delimit, or to fully define how humans live their lives."[17]

Abbreviations

AD	Archivo Diocesano
AE	Asuntos Eclesiásticos
AGEC	Archivo General del Estado de Coahuila
AGENL	Archivo General del Estado de Nuevo León
AHM	Archivo Histórico de Monterrey
AMS	Archivo Municipal de Saltillo
BCAH	Dolph Briscoe Center for American History
BL UCB	Bancroft Library, University of California at Berkeley
CD, C	Consular Despatches, Camargo
CD, G	Consular Despatches, Guerrero
CD, MAT	Consular Despatches, Matamoros
CD, MTY	Consular Despatches, Monterrey
CD, NL	Consular Despatches, Nuevo Laredo
CD, PN	Consular Despatches, Piedras Negras
CIT	Correspondencia con el Interior–Texas
DMP	David McKnight III Family Papers
EDHR	*Executive Documents Printed by Order of the House of Representatives*
EM	Estadísticas de Municipios
FCMO	Fondo Colonias Militares de Oriente
FCV	Fondo Correspondencia Santiago Vidaurri
FEM	Fondo Evaristo Madero
FJ	Fondo Justicia

FMNLC	Fondo Monterrey, Nuevo León y Coahuila

FPM	Fondo Presidencia Municipal

FRE	Fondo Relaciones Exteriores

FS	Fondo Siglo XIX

JL-C	Jueces de Letras–Contrabando

NARA	National Archives and Records Administration

OCP	Edward Otho Cresap Ord Correspondence and Papers

OR	U.S. War Department, *War of the Rebellion: A Compilation of the Official Records of the Union and Confederate Armies*

ORN	U.S. War Department, *Official Records of the Union and Confederate Navies in the War of the Rebellion*

P	Protocolos

SEDENA	Archivo Histórico, Secretaría de la Defensa Nacional

SMRE-C	Sección Ministerio de Relaciones Exteriores, Correspondencia

SMRE-IE	Sección Ministerio de Relaciones Exteriores, Informe de Extranjeros

SRMC	Santiago Roel Melo Collection (in possession of the Roel family)

TP	Twohig Papers

USDS	U.S. Department of State

UTA	University of Texas at Austin

VMC	Vallecillo Mining Company

Notes

Introduction

1. "Danger on the Border," *New York Times*, November 26, 1877, p. 4; Foster, *Diplomatic Memoirs*, 1:101.

2. The greatest obstacle "to friendly relations between the United States and Mexico for more than a decade subsequent to 1867," writes J. Fred Rippy, "was the state of affairs on the international frontier. During this period conditions on the border, and especially along the Rio Grande, were probably more unsettled and irritating than ever before or since." Rippy, *United States and Mexico*, 282 (quotation), 290. See also Dobie, *Vaquero of the Brush Country*, 58–68.

3. Examples include Collins, *Texas Devils* and *Crooked River*; Rippy "Border Troubles along the Rio Grande" and *United States and Mexico*; Paul Taylor, *American-Mexican Frontier*; Nance, *Attack and Counter-Attack*; Rayburn and Rayburn, *Century of Conflict*; Wilkinson, *Laredo and the Rio Grande Frontier*; Oscar Martínez, *Troublesome Border*; Metz, *Border*; McWilliams, *North from Mexico*; David Adams, "Embattled Borderland"; and Callahan, "Mexican Border Troubles." From a Mexican perspective, see Zorrilla, *Historia de las relaciones entre México y los Estados Unidos*; García Cantú, *Las invasiones norteamericanas en México*; Bosch García, *Historia de las relaciones entre México y los Estados Unidos*; Cosío Villegas, *Porfiriato*; Herrera Pérez, *Norte de Tamaulipas*.

4. According to David Cannadine, "A history that dwells only on divided pasts denies us the just inheritance of what we have always shared, namely a capacity to 'live together in societies sufficiently harmonious and orderly not to be constantly breaking apart.' Surely, then, it is at least as worthwhile to take as our starting point humanity's essential (but under-studied) unity as it is to obsess on its lesser (but over-studied) divisions." Cannadine, *Undivided Past*, 263. Cooperation is crucial to human progress, according to Yuval Noah Harari, who argues that *Homo sapiens* "rule the world because we alone can cooperate flexibly in large numbers." See Harari, *Homo Deus*, 138 (quotation), 132–44.

5. William Schuchardt to U.S. Department of State (hereafter cited as USDS), April 15, 1877, Record Group 59, U.S. Department of State, Consular Despatches,

Piedras Negras (hereafter cited as CD, PN), reel 1, National Archives and Records Administration (hereafter cited as NARA); Utley, "Range Cattle Industry," 423, 424; Brackenridge and García-Treto, *Iglesia Presbiteriana*, 17; Juan Martínez, *Sea la Luz*, 66.

6. Santleben, *Texas Pioneer*, 174; Pat Ireland Nixon, "Paschal, Frank," in *Handbook of Texas Online*, http://www.tshaonline.org/handbook/online/articles/fpa44; González-Quiroga, "Puerta de México."

7. Prominent examples of conflict in the 1830–80 period are the war for Texas independence in the 1830s, the U.S.-Mexican War in the 1840s, the filibustering expeditions of the 1850s, internal wars in Mexico and the United States that affected the borderlands in the 1860s, the cattle wars and racial violence that desolated the region in the 1870s, and the Indian transborder raids that characterized the entire period. These are in addition to random acts of violence, which were endemic.

8. Historians and other social scientists know that conflict and cooperation often co-occur. In *Sociobiology and Conflict*, J. van der Dennen and V. Falger argue that "conflict and cooperation are always intertwined" (1). In his extraordinary book *Captives & Cousins*, James F. Brooks asserts that relations between New Mexican villagers and nomadic and pastoral Indigenous neighbors were "both violently competitive and simultaneously mutualistic and cooperative" (82).

9. David J. Weber, whose work inspires this study, recognized that the historiography of the U.S.-Mexican borderlands was dominated by histories of conflict. He wrote:

> If we are to find a usable past for more harmonious relations between the nations of North America, we who work along "la frontera norte de México" must better understand those earlier times and places when Anglos, Hispanos, and Mexicanos found common ground through mutual accommodation and developed a sense of regional identity, even in times of conflict. That project, so contrary to the predominant historiographical and popular representations of the border region, still has far to go. (Weber, "Conflicts and Accommodations," 24–25)

Among historians working on that project, which stresses the cooperation and ties among people of the U.S.-Mexican borderlands, are Hinojosa, *Borderlands Town in Transition*; Alonzo, *Tejano Legacy*; Cerutti and González-Quiroga, *Norte de México y Texas*; Calderón, *Mexican Coal Mining Labor*; Crimm, *De León, a Tejano Family History*; Morgenthaler, *River Has Never Divided Us*; Truett and Young, *Continental Crossroads*; Young, *Catarino Garza's Revolution*; Truett, *Fugitive Landscapes*; John Adams, *Conflict and Commerce*; and Johnson and Graybill, *Bridging National Borders*.

10. Adam Smith, *Wealth of Nations*, 14.

11. Historiographical issues and much, though not all, of the analysis will be found in the reference notes. There are topics of interest for historians in these pages, such as the permeability of borders and the forging of identities. The study of relations among diverse groups in a border region also permits us to explore a wealth of topics, such as race relations, transculturation, factors that contribute to

violence and cooperation, and establishment of transborder social and economic networks.

12. Historians Michiel Baud and Willem van Schendel point out the advantages of such a history: "By taking both sides of the border as a starting point for research, it will be easier to understand the social, cultural, and economic dynamics of borderlands and the particular historical transformations that they have experienced. It is necessary to invest borderlands, and their population, with a more active historical role. . . . The crucial question is what borderlands can teach us about ways of conceptualizing social space and local identity, and the roles these have played in promoting or thwarting the development of modern states." Baud and Van Schendel, "Toward a Comparative History of Borderlands," 241. See also Truett, *Fugitive Landscapes*, 7.

13. Weber, *Mexican Frontier*, 277.

14. Traditionally, historians of the United States and Mexico, and of Texas and the northeastern Mexican states, have mainly written histories with little or no transnational connections, as if events and processes stopped at the border. This orientation is beginning to change among both U.S. and Mexican scholars (see examples in note 9). Additional works by U.S. scholars include Haynes, *Soldiers of Misfortune*; Mulroy, *Freedom on the Border*; Ralph Smith, *Borderlander*; Mora-Torres, *Making of the Mexican Border*; de la Teja, "St. James at the Fair"; Valerio-Jiménez, *River of Hope*; Gassner, "African American Fugitive Slaves"; Reséndez, *Changing National Identities*; Gallegos, "'Last Drop of My Blood'"; Thompson, *Cortina*; Hamalainen, *Comanche Empire*; DeLay, *War of a Thousand Deserts*; Robinson, *I Fought a Good Fight*; Minor, *Turning Adversity to Advantage*; Jacoby, *Shadows at Dawn*; Guidotti-Hernández, *Unspeakable Violence*; José Ángel Hernández, *Mexican American Colonization*; Dewey and Evans, *Pesos and Dollars*; Torget, *Seeds of Empire*; George Díaz, *Border Contraband*; Nichols, "Limits of Liberty." Works by Mexican scholars include Cerutti and González-Quiroga, "Guerra y comercio" and *El norte de México y Texas*; González-Quiroga, "Puerta de México"; Gurza Lavalle, *Una vecindad efímera*; Terrazas y Basante, "Colaboración y conflicto"; Guerra de Luna, *Los Madero*; Mendirichaga, *Colegio de San Juan*.

15. Bolton, "Wider Horizons of American History," 3. See also Gutiérrez and Young, "Transnationalizing Borderlands History."

16. I will only use "Tejano" in quotations from other sources. "Tejano," in reference to Mexicans of Texas, did not enter general usage until the 1960s and 1970s. Use of the term may have been a strategy of resistance employed mainly by academics of Mexican descent against the discursive violence of Anglos who used the word "Mexican" (usually preceded by an ugly adjective) in an insulting way. In the inaugural issue of *El Bejareño*, a Spanish-language newspaper published in San Antonio, Texas, Mexican-origin Texans are referred to as Mejico-Tejanos (the "j" in both terms reflects the editors' preference for traditional Spanish orthography). "Editorial," *El Bejareño*, February 7, 1855, p. 1.

17. Among the sources for this study are secondary works and documentary evidence from state, municipal, and private archives in northern Mexico and Texas. Other

archival sources include the Bancroft Collection at the University of California at Berkeley and the U.S. National Archives. In Mexico, archival sources include the Archivo Histórico of the Secretaría de Relaciones Exteriores and the Secretaría de la Defensa Nacional. Especially valuable is the vast wealth of information available on the Internet, particularly newspapers and digitized documents, as well as secondary sources from both countries. The Portal to Texas History, a collaborative venture by libraries, museums, archives, and other institutions administered by the University of North Texas in Denton contains a vast treasure of digitalized documents, photographs, books, and newspapers that are important sources for this book (see http://texashistory.unt.edu). Another valuable source is the digitized newspapers of Mexico's Hemeroteca Nacional, administered by the Universidad Nacional Autónoma de México.

Chapter 1. Attraction and Rejection

1. The Saltillo fair grew out of the feast day celebration of St. James the Greater in the seventeenth century and was an annual meeting of "regional merchants and small traders," according to De la Teja, "St. James at the Fair," 407, 415.

2. In the period before regional markets became fully integrated into commercial networks, fairs were common in frontier societies of North and South America and played a significant role in bringing people and products together at a single place. An annual rendezvous was common in many regions along the expanding U.S. frontier. In addition to trading, trappers, merchants, and Indian traders engaged in duels, games of chance such as cards and dice, and athletic competitions such as footraces and horse races. See Hine and Faragher, *American West*, 153–54.

3. Karras, "First Impressions of Mexico by Reuben Potter," 59, 61, 67.

4. Kearney and Knopp, *Boom and Bust*, 33; Sibley, "Charles Stillman," 229.

5. Lundy, *Life, Travels, and Opinions of Benjamin Lundy*, 62, 90 (quotation), 104.

6. Guerra de Luna, *Los Madero*, 67–69. Múzquiz was a member of a prominent Coahuilan family that included Melchor Múzquiz, who served briefly as Mexico's president in 1832. See Reséndez, "Ramón Múzquiz," 129–45. Trade with Louisiana is explored in Barrera Enderle, "Contrabando y liberalismo," 47–94.

7. Lundy, *Life, Travels, and Opinions of Benjamin Lundy*, 95.

8. Tijerina, *Tejanos and Texas*, 68; Campbell, *Gone to Texas*, 78.

9. Quoted in Galindo, *Provincialismo nuevoleonés*, 53. During the late colonial period these provinces sent livestock and agricultural products to the richer mining regions of San Luis Potosí and Zacatecas and served as an internal colony of New Spain, according to Barrera Enderle, "Contrabando y liberalismo," 29–33.

10. Historian Thomas D. Hall argues that "tradition is an adaptation by a group of people to a specific set of circumstances. As long as those circumstances continue, the tradition will continue. When circumstances alter, pressures for change are created." Hall, *Social Change in the Southwest*, 6. This is a good description of what occurred in Northeast Mexico and Texas in the 1820s and 1830s.

11. Baylies, "March to Saltillo," 306.

12. William H. Goetzmann, quoted in Thompson, *Wild and Vivid Land*, 2.

13. De León, *Mexican Americans in Texas*, 7–8; Alessio Robles, *Coahuila y Texas*, 1:513.

14. Herrera Pérez, *Breve historia de Tamaulipas*, 65, 66; Juan Zorrilla, *Historia de Tamaulipas*, 13, 14.

15. Arreola, *Tejano South Texas*, 36. See also Alonzo, "History of Ranching."

16. Valerio-Jiménez, "Neglected Citizens," 264; Alonzo, "History of Ranching," 206.

17. Tijerina, *Tejano Empire*, 4; Viele, "Frontiers of the United States," 177–78 (quotation), 181.

18. A calculus was clearly at work, wherein the population produced goods on which they could make a profit and imported goods that could be more effectively produced elsewhere. See Valerio-Jiménez, "Neglected Citizens," 265.

19. Smithwick, *Evolution of a State*, 47.

20. John Adams, *Conflict and Commerce*, 42; Guerra de Luna, *Los Madero*, 73–74.

21. Harris, *Sánchez Navarros*, 8.

22. The historiography on the Mexican hacienda is vast. For examples pertaining to northern Mexico see Harris, *Sánchez Navarros*; García Flores, *Ser ranchero*; Bazant, *Cinco haciendas mexicanas*; Chevalier, *Formación de los latifundios*.

23. For powerful elites and rural oligarchies in Coahuila; Tamaulipas; and the towns of Montemorelos, Linares, and Monterrey in Nuevo León, see Harris, *Imperio de la familia Sánchez Navarro*; Galindo, *Provincialismo nuevoleonés*, 156; and Valerio-Jiménez, "Neglected Citizens," 258, 279.

24. Juan Mora-Torres argues that in Nuevo León most rural people were landholders, although their holdings grew progressively smaller with each generation. In South Texas, Armando Alonzo states there was a tradition of "individually owned ranchos that were worked by the ranchero, by his sons, and occasionally by hired workers." Most of these settlers followed a pattern established in their native provinces of Nuevo León and Coahuila. Mora-Torres, *Making of the Mexican Border*, 20; Alonzo, *Tejano Legacy*, 275. See also Medina Peña, *Bárbaros del norte*, 195, 251.

25. The region's class structure is consistent with its condition as the periphery of a peripheral state of the capitalist world system, according to Hall, *Social Change in the Southwest*, 13, 24–25, 199.

26. De León, *Mexican Americans in Texas*, 20.

27. De León, *Mexican Americans in Texas*, 16. Contributing to this process was the captive exchange system that Apaches and Comanches practiced with captured Mexican women and children, who were often integrated into the Indian tribe. James F. Brooks cited an Indian agent who stated: "so intermingled amongst these tribes have most of the Mexican captives become that it is somewhat difficult to distinguish them." Brooks, *Captives & Cousins*, 322.

28. Weber, *Mexican Frontier*, 214 (first quotation), 215 (second quotation).

29. Downs, "History of Mexicans in Texas," 253 (quotation), 267; In contrast, Andrés Tijerina asserts that most Bexareños had an Indian-mestizo background, which made them more racially tolerant. Tijerina, *Tejanos and Texas*, 23.

30. According to James Brooks, some individuals "inhabited, or coexisted in, multiple social worlds, fluidly crossing back and forth between them." Brooks, *Captives & Cousins*, 5, 34, 68. See also Alonso, *Thread of Blood*, 69.

31. Salinas, *Indians of the Rio Grande Delta*, 140 (quotation), 164; Thompson, *Wild and Vivid Land*, 9, 13.

32. From *Siglo Diez y Nueve* newspaper, quoted in Vizcaya Canales, *Tierra de guerra viva*, 264. All translations from Spanish-language sources are by the author.

33. Quoted in Vizcaya Canales, *Tierra de guerra viva*, 73.

34. Weber, *Mexican Frontier*, 104. Randolph B. Campbell (*Gone to Texas*, 82) asserts that a treaty with Comanches in 1785 brought a forty-year peace, while Ana María Alonso (*Thread of Blood*, 27) claims that most Apache groups stopped raiding Chihuahua between 1790 and 1831. Karl Jacoby (*Shadows at Dawn*, 56, 57) writes that the same applies for Sonora.

35. Weber, *Mexican Frontier*, 111, 120 (quotation), 121; Brian DeLay states that many of the soldiers of the frontier "sold their weapons and animals out of desperation, and others fled." DeLay, *War of a Thousand Deserts*, 147–48.

36. DeLay, *War of a Thousand Deserts*, xv.

37. Cavazos Garza, "Características de los pobladores de Nuevo León," 477.

38. Quoted in Lucas Martínez, *Ejército del Norte*, 144. Cavazos Garza ("Características de los pobladores de Nuevo León," 477) asserts that children began to use firearms as young as the age of twelve.

39. Northern Mexico was a major supplier of people, particularly captive women and children, and animals that became commodities in commercial networks dominated by Indians of the southern plains, particularly Comanches and, to a lesser degree, Apaches. See these groundbreaking books: Brooks, *Captives & Cousins*; Hamalainen, *Comanche Empire*; and DeLay, *War of a Thousand Deserts*.

40. In the period when a tenuous peace existed, Comanches made regular visits to San Antonio and to towns along the Rio Grande "bringing mules loaded with commodities for barter." In the early 1830s, "the main exports of San Antonio district were hides and pelts, perhaps ten thousand annually, the great majority obtained from native peoples." DeLay, *War of a Thousand Deserts*, 58, 59.

41. DeLay, *War of a Thousand Deserts*, 103. DeLay states that the number of horses and mules that Comanches and their allies stole from the ranches and haciendas of northern Mexico between 1830 and 1846 "probably exceeded one hundred thousand" (95).

42. Brooks, *Captives & Cousins*, 181–82. Brian DeLay argues that in the 1830s and 1840s raiding into Mexico became an important part of the "collective livelihoods" of the southern plains Indians. Historians have attributed other, noneconomic factors to the raids; among them, the Mexican policy of disarming its citizens for fear of revolts after centralism was established in 1834. Revenge is also cited as a motive. See DeLay, *War of a Thousand Deserts*, 129, 135.

43. Weber, *Mexican Frontier*, 95.

44. Gallegos, "'Last Drop of My Blood,'" 59.

45. Barrera Enderle, "Contrabando y liberalismo," 68–78.

46. Rivaya Martínez, "Trespassers in the Land of Plenty," 21, 22 (quotation). Vizcaya Canales, *Incursiones de indios,* 26, 27; Robinson, *I Fought a Good Fight,* 319. More information on Mexican-Indian trade relations is provided in chapter 7. Many instances of Mexican-Indian collaboration are also cited in Vizcaya Canales, *Tierra de guerra viva.*

47. Davis, *Land!,* 197 (quotations); Martin Donell Kohout, "Magoffin, James Wiley," in *Handbook of Texas Online,* http://www.tshaonline.org/handbook/online/articles /fma13.

48. Kearney and Knopp, *Boom and Bust,* 29–32.

49. Hobart Huson, "Hewetson, James," in *Handbook of Texas Online.* http://www .tshaonline.org/handbook/online/articles/fhe36; Craig H. Roell, "Linn, John Joseph," in *Handbook of Texas Online,* http://www.tshaonline.org/handbook/online /articles/fli12.

50. Ministro de Relaciones Exteriores to Gobierno de Nuevo León, May 9 and 11, 1827, box 2, Fondo Relaciones Exteriores, Sección Ministerio de Relaciones Exteriores, Correspondencia, Archivo General del Estado de Nuevo León (hereafter cited as FRE, SMRE-C, AGENL); L. W. Kemp, "Cameron, John," in *Handbook of Texas Online,* http://www.tshaonline.org/handbook/online/articles/fca26. If Rougier was in Mexico in 1822 this might explain the absence of a passport. The first law that required foreigners to register and have a passport was passed on February 1, 1823. See Pani, "Ciudadanos precarios," 632.

51. Juicio civil, August 16, 1841, box 87, file (i.e., *expediente*) 12, Fondo Presidencia Municipal, Archivo Municipal de Saltillo (hereafter cited as FPM, AMS). See also October 22, 1844, box 89, file 25; and August 24, 1857, box 101, file 12, FPM, AMS. "Bork" may have been a Hispanicized version of Burke, but that is how it appears in multiple documents in the archives of Coahuila.

52. Causa criminal, box 6, file 26, Sección Concluidos, AGENL.

53. Spell, *Pioneer Printer,* 41, 91; Spell, "Samuel Bangs," 251, 258. Another American printer, Godwin B. Cotton, directed the government printing press in Tamaulipas in 1824. He printed the official newspaper, *Termómetro Político,* along with the first decrees, circulars, and broadsides of that government. See González Salas, *Diccionario biográfico de Tamaulipas,* 108; and Zorrilla, Miró Flaquer, and Herrera Pérez, *Tamaulipas, una historia compartida,* 1:138.

54. Garver, "Benjamin Rush Milam," (1934), 102, 103, 108–9, 111, 177.

55. Informe, 1828, box 73/2, file 110, FPM, AMS; Censo, March 14, 1832, box 1, Estadísticas de Municipios (hereafter cited as EM), Monterrey, AGENL.

56. Refugio García to Joaquín García, May 22, 1832, Ignacio Fernández to Joaquín García, May 27, 1832, and J. Ángel Gutiérrez de Lara to Joaquín García, May 31, 1831, all in box 10, FRE, SMRE-C, AGENL. A decree signed in Mexico City by Anastacio Bustamante and Lucas Alamán required that all persons who practiced medicine in the country pass an examination, complete three courses in the national school of surgery, and have a command of Spanish, but these requirements were largely

ignored on the frontier. See Decreto, December 23, 1830, box 7, FRE, SMRE-C, AGENL.

57. José Cayetano de Cárdenas to Joaquín García, May 26, 1832, box 10, FRE, SMRE-C, AGENL.

58. Juan Long to Santiago Vidaurri, April 6, 1856, July 24, 1857, and March 25, 1859 (quotation); Documento, March 21, 1863, all in Fondo Correspondencia Santiago Vidaurri, (hereafter cited as FCV), AGENL. Letters in the Vidaurri collection are generally ordered by the last name of the correspondent. See also Vizcaya Canales, *Tierra de guerra viva*, 153.

59. "Obituary," *The Two Republics*, December 25, 1869, p. 3; Linn, *Reminiscences*, 26–27; Franklin, "Memoirs of Annie P. Harris," 238 (quotations); Laura Gutiérrez, "Prolongado ocaso de un estado," 159–60.

60. Alcalde Primero de Monterrey to Governor, August 10, 1833, and Governor to Alcalde Primero, November 5, 1833, box 1, Sección Ministerio de Relaciones Exteriores, Informe de Extranjeros (hereafter cited as SMRE-IE), FRE, AGENL; Refugio García to Joaquín García, May 22, 1832, box 10, FRE, SMRE-C, AGENL.

61. Jorge Hernández, "Social Change in Mexico's Northeast," 61–62.

62. Quoted in Reséndez, *Changing National Identities*, 109.

63. Smithwick, *Evolution of a State*, 45.

64. Linn, *Reminiscences*, 26, 27.

65. Austin, "Affairs of Texas," 234. After his inspection trip to Texas in 1834, Juan Almonte wrote that Texas products could be sold at Veracruz and Matamoros for between 6 and 8 percent more, a figure far lower than Austin's but still attractive for Texan traders. Almonte, "Statistical Report," 193.

66. Escríbano Público Antonio Escobedo, Contrato de compraventa, March 11, 1833, box 20, book 1, file 21, Protocolos (hereafter cited as P), AMS; Alcalde Primero José Alberto Gutiérrez, Contrato de compraventa, January 19, 1833, box 20, book 1, file 5, P, AMS.

67. "The Mexican Trade," *Corpus Christi Star*, October 10, 1848, p. 1; *Centennial History of Corpus Christi*, 26; Jorge Hernández, "Social Change in Mexico's Northeast," 84.

68. Linn, *Reminiscences*, 11.

69. Linn, *Reminiscences*, 24.

70. Spell, *Pioneer Printer*, 81, 85; Leonardo de Llano to Gobierno del Estado, September 20, 1834, box 24, file 369, Sección Concluidos, AGENL.

71. Laura Gutiérrez, "Prolongado ocaso de un estado," 171; Gammel, *Laws of Texas*, 191, 193; Contrato, November 9, 1832, box 77/2, file 125, FPM, AMS.

72. Carta Poder, October 12, 1838, box 22, book 1, file 129, P, AMS. This is an example of the many operations registered in the notarial and municipal records of Coahuila.

73. Franklin, "Memoirs of Annie P. Harris," 240; Looscan, "Dugald McFarlane," 284 (quotation).

74. Ibarra Bellon, *Comercio y poder*, 259; Jorge Hernández, "Social Change in Mexico's Northeast," 75 (quotation); Weber, *Mexican Frontier*, 150.

75. Barrera Enderle, "Contrabando y liberalismo," 50–71; Baur, "Evolution of a Mexican Trade Policy," 244 (quotation); Ontiveros Ruiz, *Historia del comercio de México*, 51.

76. Ontiveros Ruiz, *Historia del comercio de México*, 53, 54; Baur, "Evolution of a Mexican Trade Policy," 245.

77. Weber, *Mexican Frontier*, 149; Ibarra Bellon, *Comercio y poder*, 262.

78. Memorias de Gobernadores, Manuel Gómez de Castro, 1827, p. 17; and 1828, pp. 42–43 AGENL. See also section on Ramo industria agrícola, mercantil y fabril in Memorias de Gobernadores, Joaquín García, 1829, AGENL.

79. Kearney and Knopp, *Boom and Bust*, 36.

80. Weber, *Mexican Frontier*, 151, 152 (quotation); Valerio-Jiménez, "Neglected Citizens," 282.

81. Weber, *Mexican Frontier*, 150.

82. "Sección Congreso del Estado," *Gaceta Constitucional*, February 19, 1829, p. 1. U.S. consul D. W. Smith wrote from Matamoros that "American citizens are not permitted by a number of the states to retail their goods but are compelled to sell by the original package." Smith to USDS, July 1, 1829, Consular Despatches, Matamoros (hereafter cited as CD, MAT), reel 1, NARA.

83. *Semanario Político*, August 13, 1840, pp. 304–5. Suspension of the tobacco monopoly in 1829 allowed Mexican producers to cultivate the crop until 1837, when the monopoly was reinstated with the establishment of centralism.

84. Valerio-Jiménez, "Neglected Citizens," 283–84.

85. Quoted in Ávila, Martínez, and Morado, *Santiago Vidaurri*, 242–43.

86. Garza González, *Cronista desconocido*, 24, 29, 30 (quotation), 31, 136–37, 157.

87. J. M. Camacho to Juez de Distrito, August 14, 1829, box 74/2, file 110, FPM, AMS; the Bork case can be found in "Embargo," August 16, 1841, box 87, file 1; and Juez de Hacienda to Gobierno del Estado, October 22, 1844, box 89, file 25, both in FPM, AMS.

88. Linn, *Reminiscences*, 11.

89. Juicio civil, April 5, 1830, box 1, Jueces de Letras, Contrabando, Fondo Justicia (hereafter cited as JL-C, FJ), AGENL.

90. Smithwick, *Evolution of a State*, 53.

91. Smithwick, *Evolution of a State*, 42, 44, 45.

92. Land speculation was rampant in the early history of the United States. Notorious land scams like that of the Ohio Company and the Yazoo scandal in Georgia "testified to the victory of speculators over actual settlers in the land policy of the early republic." Hine and Faragher, *American West*, 112–13.

93. Kimball, *Laws and Decrees of Coahuila and Texas*, 190. Randolph Campbell quotes one settler's eloquent statement on the powerful attraction of the Coahuila law: "What the discovery of gold was to California, the Colonization Act of 1825 was to Texas." Campbell, *Gone to Texas*, 107. See also Soto, "Agentes y socios del 'destino manifiesto,'" 95, 124–25; and Soto, "Texas en la mira," 26. Tamaulipas also passed attractive colonization legislation. A law in 1833 welcomed foreign settlers and offered "lands completely free" in the "unpopulated and vacant" lands of the state.

Throughout the 1830s and 1840s, the state government established agreements with German and Belgian entrepreneurs to bring in colonists, but these ventures failed. Zorrilla, Miró Flaquer, and Herrera Pérez, *Tamaulipas, una historia compartida*, 1:133–35, 137.

94. Soto, "Texas en la mira," 25, 41n, 42, 43. Fourteen years before his triumph at San Jacinto, Sam Houston had helped found the Texas Association with the hope of obtaining land in Texas. He later became involved with a number of New York businessmen who had speculative ventures in Texas. These ties and his proximity to Andrew Jackson would propel him into the center of events in Texas.

95. Soto, "Agentes y socios del 'destino manifiesto,'" 101; Soto, "Texas en la mira," 23, 33; Alessio Robles, *Coahuila y Texas*, 1:368; Henson, *Lorenzo de Zavala*, 46 (quotations).

96. Henson, *Lorenzo de Zavala*, 51–52. The Anglo-American and Mexican businessmen of the Galveston Bay Company were breaking both state and federal laws in Mexico that prohibited the sale or transfer of land granted for colonization. Soto, "Texas en la mira," 34.

97. Austin to Williams, August 21, 1833, in Barker, *Austin Papers*, 2:1000.

98. Hutchinson, "'General José Antonio Mexía," 121, 125. In Texas, Mejía's name was spelled Mexía, and he is the namesake of the city of Mexia. Chance, *Carvajal*, 18–19. Carvajal's name appears in many sources as "Carbajal." Carvajal to Austin, September 1, 1830, and Austin to Holley, January 30, 1832 (quotation), both in Barker, *Austin Papers*, 2:475, 745.

99. Speculation was rampant in New Orleans in the 1830s "and the ongoing political instability in Mexico and the revolution in Texas . . . fueled the hunger for more land." Edward Miller, *New Orleans and Texas Revolution*, 203–4, 209 (quotation).

100. Guerra de Luna, *Los Madero*, 190, 194. The Viesca brothers also favored fellow Masons Lorenzo de Zavala and José Antonio Mejía with generous grants and advantageous sales of Texas land. Reséndez, *Changing National Identities*, 65, 68.

101. Reséndez, *Changing National Identities*, 71.

102. Madero had his roots in Chihuahua, while Victoriana, his wife, whom he married in 1824, was from Nuevo León. Both maintained familial ties in those states, contributing to the multiple bonds that united Mexico's Northeast. Vasconcelos, *Evaristo Madero*, 38, 49.

103. Guerra de Luna, *Los Madero*, 250–51; Carta Poder, July 23, 1869, box 112, file 26, FPM, AMS. The date is when a petition was filed for the original document, which was dated April 28, 1832.

104. The vecinos of Parras were Diego Grant, Cesario Montaño, José María Borrego, José Luís Escobar, Buenaventura Reyes, Manuel Hurtado, Vicente Ortín, José María de la Fuente, Santos de Arco, Onofre Fernández, Nicolás Nava, and Miguel Ocadis. Carta Poder, May 17, 1834, box 20, book 8, file 30, P, AMS.

105. Cartas Poder, July 9, 1835, box 20, book 11, file 52, P, AMS; November 10, 1837, box 21, book 5, file 137, P, AMS; May 7, 1839, box 22, book 4, files 6 and 7, P, AMS.

106. Smith to Livingston, August 21, 1832, reel 1, CD, MAT, NARA.

107. Smithwick, *Evolution of a State*, 51.

108. De León, *Mexican Americans in Texas*, 40. American–Mexican marriages were the norm in some communities. The 1880 census of Presidio listed a population of 147. Only six Anglo men were listed, and all had Mexican wives. See Elam, "Aspects of Acculturation," 78.

109. Dysart, "Mexican Women in San Antonio," 372, 374, 375 (quotation).

110. Dysart, "Mexican Women in San Antonio," 372.

111. One of Craver's discoveries is that, contrary to the idea that mixed marriages were mainly the province of upper-class Mexicans and Anglos, many involved men and women who were not elite. "Many of these Anglos, because they did not become economically successful or politically well-known, remain historically obscure figures." Craver, *Impact of Intimacy*, 2, 45.

112. Crimm, *De León, a Tejano Family History*, 227.

113. Quoted in Zorrilla, Miró Flaquer, and Herrera Pérez, *Tamaulipas, una historia compartida*, 1:136.

114. Brister, "Johann von Racknitz," 79. Von Racknitz later became a captain in the Mexican army and fought for Mexico in the U.S.-Mexican War.

115. Weber, *Foreigners in Their Native Land*, 212.

116. Historian Marcela Terrazas y Basante ("Colaboración y conflicto," 155) argues that "there were groups that got along well and others that did not. Harmony and conflict were dynamic and constantly changing, as were the groups involved."

117. Quoted in Aboites Aguilar, "José Fuentes Mares," 480. Alonso argues the incessant struggle against hostile Indigenous tribes was a "key factor in the shaping of norteño society" that differentiated it from the rest of the country. Alonso, *Thread of Blood*, 17 (quotation), 28, 29, 43. Other authors who share this view are Jacoby, *Shadows at Dawn*, 209; Green, "República del Río Grande," 54; and Medina Peña, *Bárbaros del norte*.

118. Fehrenbach writes: "The Texan's attitudes, his inherent chauvinism, and the seeds of his belligerence, sprouted from his conscious effort to take and hold his land. It was the reaction of essentially civilized men and women thrown into new and harsh conditions, beset by enemies they despised." *Lone Star*, 256–57. See also Valerio-Jiménez, "Neglected Citizens," 262.

119. Campbell, *Gone to Texas*, 133. In Matamoros a faction of the local elite "dependent on the American connection to sustain the new commercial expansion . . . did all it could to succor and shield the American presence locally." Kearney and Knopp, *Boom and Bust*, 34–35.

120. Quoted in Weber, *Mexican Frontier*, 176 (also following quotation). The municipal governments of San Antonio, Goliad, and Nacogdoches expressed their views on December 19, 1832, in a document that "argued against the provision of the law of April 6, 1830, which closed the border to further immigration from the United States."

121. Torget, *Seeds of Empire*, 8.

122. Crisp, "José Antonio Navarro," 150–51; Campbell, *Gone to Texas*, 113; Vázquez, "Contexto nacional," 25. Coahuilan elites were not homogeneous in their affinities and support for the Texans. While a liberal faction in Monclova headed by the

Viesca family backed the colonists, a rival conservative group centered in Saltillo and allied politically with the Santa Anna government was wary of the Texans and sought to limit their growing influence. Laura Gutiérrez, "Prolongado ocaso de un estado," 180.

123. Tijerina, *Tejanos and Texas*, 114–15; José Ildefonso Díaz de León to Gobierno del Estado, October 1827, box 7, file 15, Fondo Siglo XIX (hereafter cited as FS), Archivo General del Estado de Coahuila (hereafter cited as AGEC).

124. Sherif, *In Common Predicament*, viii. In Arizona Mexicans and Anglo-Americans forged alliances to combat the common threat of Apache raiders. This theme is developed in Jacoby, *Shadows at Dawn*. See also Weber, *Foreigners in Their Native Land*, 211.

125. Lowrie, *Culture Conflict in Texas*, 116; DeLay, *War of a Thousand Deserts*, 72.

126. Weber, *Mexican Frontier*, 177 (quotation); Campbell, *Gone to Texas*, 159; De León, *Mexican Americans in Texas*, 19. Land was the principal incentive, but Andrew Torget argues that land was valuable if it could support cotton, so the cotton economy and slavery were central to the surge in immigration. Torget, *Seeds of Empire*, 7, 11.

127. Quoted in Sibley, *Travelers in Texas*, 92; Weber, *Foreigners in Their Native Land*, 104–5.

128. Vázquez, "Contexto nacional," 27.

129. James E. Crisp argues that many historians followed the lead of Eugene C. Barker in stating that racial prejudice "was the chief underlying cause of the Texan revolt against Mexico." Crisp, "Anglo-Texan Attitudes," 3.

130. Ronald Takaki argues that racism was not exclusive to the South; it was "both virulent and violent in the states above the Mason and Dixon Line during the years before the Civil War." Takaki, *Iron Cages*, 110.

131. Potter, "Texas Revolution," 18.

132. Crisp, "Race, Revolution, and the Texas Republic," 48 (first quotation); Crisp, "Anglo-Texan Attitudes," 97 (second quotation).

133. Austin, "Affairs of Texas," 241.

134. Quoted in Crisp, "Race, Revolution and the Texas Republic," 43–44.

135. Lack, "Occupied Texas," 36. J. van der Dennen and V. Falger sustain that "aggressive or hostile 'impulses' do not suffice to account for social conflict. It has often been pointed out . . . that hostile stereotypes, prejudice, threat perception, general hostility, and aggression (however conceptualized) are more likely to be the result of conflict than its cause." *Sociobiology and Conflict*, 6.

136. Crisp, "Race, Revolution and the Texas Republic," 46. Andrés Reséndez (*Changing National Identities*, 152) argues that "a classic federalist-centralist dispute affected the loyalties and identities of those involved and ultimately led to secessionism." These authors take their cue from David Weber's seminal work, *Mexican Frontier*. Historian Josefina Zoraida Vázquez has a different perspective. She argues that in 1834 the Coahuila y Texas state congress passed sweeping legislation that satisfied most Texan demands. Among other reforms Texas was granted greater representation and the English language was approved for judicial proceedings as well as

trial by jury. Texas, she states, "had no cause for complaint," but was moved toward separation by the annexationist goals of recent newcomers to the state. Vázquez, "Contexto nacional," 31.

137. Paschal, "Texas Must Be a Slave Country," iv. Andrew Torget makes the same argument forcefully in *Seeds of Empire*.

138. Foley, *White Scourge*, 18–19. Josefina Zoraida Vázquez argues that slavery was a major cause of Texas independence, which argument was confirmed when the Texans drafted a constitution patterned on those of the Southern states, which guaranteed slavery and forbade free blacks from residing in Texas without approval of the state congress. Vázquez, "Contexto nacional," 38.

139. Campbell, *Gone to Texas*, 133.

140. A revealing case of cooperative violence in which Anglos, Mexicans, and Tohono O'odham joined in the slaughter of Aravaipa and Pinal Apaches occurred at the Camp Grant Massacre of 1871 in southern Arizona. See Jacoby, *Shadows at Dawn*.

141. Anglos and Mexicans cooperated in collective acts of violence much earlier than the 1830s. An important example is the Gutiérrez-Magee expedition of 1813, in which a large force of Mexicans, Anglos, and Lipan Apaches fought royalist forces in Texas during Mexican independence. See Narrett, "Gutiérrez de Lara."

142. Campbell, *Gone to Texas*, 120.

143. Austin to Williams, January 9, 1831, in Barker, *Austin Papers*, 2:581–83.

144. Campbell, *Gone to Texas*, 125.

145. Austin to Perry, January 14 and August 25, 1834; Austin to Fisher, January 15, 1834; Austin to Williams, June 3, 1834, all in Barker, *Austin Papers*, 2:1033, 1037, 1060, 1062.

146. Quoted in Reséndez, *Changing National Identities*, 154.

147. Soto, "Disputa entre Monclova y Saltillo," 127.

148. Reséndez, *Changing National Identities*, 158 (quotation); Soto, "Agentes y socios del 'destino manifiesto,'" 105–8.

149. Alessio Robles, *Coahuila y Texas*, 1:413; Hutchinson, "General José Antonio Mexía," 121, 123.

150. Alessio Robles, *Coahuila y Texas*, 2:86, 87.

151. Edward Miller, *New Orleans and the Texas Revolution*, 98–99, 104 (quotation); Austin to Williams, August 21, 1833, in Barker, *Austin Papers*, 2:1000.

152. The Texans were not alone in believing there was a strong commitment to federalism among the population of the Northeast. One of Santa Anna's generals, José Urrea, wrote of the affinity between Texans and Mexican federalists. See Green, "Texas Revolution," 51–52.

153. Grant's motives have been the subject of speculation. Stuart Reid argues that Grant was defending British interests in the hope of thwarting American expansion. Reid, *Secret War for Texas*, 5, 116.

154. Campbell, *Gone to Texas*, 137.

155. Quoted in Weber, *Mexican Frontier*, 251.

156. Nance, *After San Jacinto*, 172; Weber, *Mexican Frontier*, 251.

157. Most of the people of Tamaulipas, including the ayuntamientos of Matamoros and Ciudad Victoria, favored the movement toward centralism, though many were unsure of its implications. In Nuevo León, political leaders accepted centralism because they were certain that only the educated could govern and most of the people did not fit that description. They also agreed that Mexico had made a mistake in adopting federalism as three hundred years of Spanish authoritarian rule had not prepared the people for republican institutions. See *Gaceta Constitucional*, January 1, 1835, pp. 3–4, and June 25, 1835, p. 3; *Semanario Político*, December 3, 1835, p. 11; Zorrilla, Miró Flaquer, and Herrera Pérez, *Tamaulipas, una historia compartida*, 1:107, 108. The failure of federalism is best summed up by Josefina Zoraida Vázquez: "The deplorable situation that surrounded its [federalism's] establishment and the radicalism in its interpretation . . . denied the national government fiscal authority over its citizens and made it dependent on the states, condemning it to extreme weakness that impeded its compliance with the obligations established in the constitution. Vázquez, "Contexto nacional," 39.

158. Alessio Robles, *Coahuila y Texas*, 2:93; Crisp, "Anglo-Texan Attitudes," 98.

159. Amberson, McAllen, and McAllen, *I Would Rather Sleep in Texas*, 72; Lack, "Occupied Texas," 37.

160. Walraven and Walraven, *Magnificent Barbarians*, 42, 45 (quotation); Downs, "History of Mexicans in Texas," 235; "Hispanic Texian Patriots in the Struggle for Independence," http://www.tamu.edu/ccbn/dewitt/tejanopatriots.htm; Alwyn Barr, "Siege of Bexar," in *Handbook of Texas Online*, http://www.tshaonline.org/handbook /online/articles/qeb01. Milam was killed in the battle and gained immortal fame.

161. Walraven and Walraven, *Magnificent Barbarians*, 44.

162. Quoted in Barker, "Tampico Expedition," 184; Vázquez, "Texas Question," 312.

163. Barr, "Siege of Bexar," *Handbook of Texas Online*; Alessio Robles, *Coahuila y Texas*, 2:80.

164. The other seven defenders were Andrés Nava, José Toribio Lozano, José María Guerrero, Antonio Fuentes, Carlos Espalier, Juan Antonio Badillo, and Juan Alamillo, according to Richard Bruce Winders, historian and curator of the Alamo, who kindly responded to my query.

165. Weber, *Mexican Frontier*, 252–53; Downs, "History of Mexicans in Texas," 245.

166. Walraven and Walraven, *Magnificent Barbarians*, 72.

167. Weber, *Mexican Frontier*, 254 (quotation); De León, *Mexican Americans in Texas*, 29, 32.

Chapter 2. Conflict and Cooperation

1. Tijerina, *Tejanos and Texas*, 138 (quotation); Ministro de Relaciones Exteriores to Gobierno de Coahuila, July 7, 1845, box 3, file 7, folio 3, Ministro de Relaciones Exteriores, FS, AGEC. Between 1837 and 1843, Anglo-Texans bought 1,386,574 acres of land from 358 Mexican landowners. Ridout, "Anti-national Disorder," 51. See also De León, *Mexican Americans in Texas*, 41.

2. Campbell, *Gone to Texas*, 167; Herring, "Córdova Rebellion," in *Handbook of Texas Online*, http://www.tshaonline.org/handbook/online/articles/jcc03.

3. Kendall, *Narrative of the Santa Fé Expedition*, 393–94; Alessio Robles, *Coahuila y Texas*, 2:224–26; H. Bailey Carroll, "Texan Santa Fe Expedition," in *Handbook of Texas Online*, http://www.tshaonline.org/handbook/online/articles/qyt03.

4. Kendall, *Narrative of the Santa Fé Expedition*, 393–94.

5. Nance, *Attack and Counter-Attack*, 7.

6. Jack W. Gunn, "Mexican Invasions of 1842," in *Handbook of Texas Online*, http://www.tshaonline.org/handbook/online/articles/qem02; Joseph Milton Nance, "Republic of Texas," in *Handbook of Texas Online*, http://www.tshaonline.org/handbook/online/articles/mzr02; Arthur Mayer, "San Antonio, Frontier Entrepot," 321.

7. Much of the ire was directed not against Mexicans personally but against their political system. One newspaper reported: "we are ... determined to make one powerful and united effort to burst asunder the chains of civil and religious despotism by which *our brethren* in Mexico have long been bound" (emphasis mine). There is no racial animosity in these words, only indignation at the way Mexicans had been treated by their government. It is hard to say how prevalent this view was, but it may reflect the thinking of more thoughtful people in Texas. Quoted in Nance, *Attack and Counter-Attack*, 59.

8. Haynes, *Soldiers of Misfortune*, 9.

9. Wilcox, "Laredo during the Texas Republic," 101–2 (quotation); Joseph Milton Nance, "Somervell Expedition," in *Handbook of Texas Online*. http://www.tshaonline.org/handbook/online/articles/qys03.

10. A detailed account of the Black Bean Episode is provided by Haynes, *Soldiers of Misfortune*, 122–27.

11. Crisp, "Race, Revolution, and the Texas Republic," 45. This contrasts with a certain tolerance toward Mexicans directly after the war for Texas independence. Mexicans were accepted in military and government positions and there was no serious obstacle to immigration from Mexico. See Crisp, "Anglo-Texan Attitudes," 366.

12. *Semanario Político*, June 9, 1836, p. 120.

13. *Siglo Diez y Nueve*, May 3, 1842, p. 2. The letter is dated October 30, 1841.

14. *Siglo Diez y Nueve*, May 3, 1842.

15. *Siglo Diez y Nueve*, May 3, 1842, and editorial, March 5, 1842, p. 4.

16. Proclama, Vicente Filisola, General en Jefe del Ejército del Norte, August 10, 1837, carton 2, Documents Relating to Nuevo León, Mexico, Bancroft Library, University of California, Berkeley (hereafter cited as BL UCB). These proclamations inveighing against trading with the Texans appeared frequently in official publications.

17. Nance, *After San Jacinto*, 154, citing the *Matagorda Bulletin* of December 6, 1838.

18. Quoted in Nance, *After San Jacinto*, 78.

19. Weber, *Mexican Frontier*, 13 (first quotation), 128 (second quotation); Fernandez, *United States–Mexico Border*, 48 (third quotation); Acuña, *Occupied America*, 56.

20. Weber, *Mexican Frontier*, 128–29.

21. Kohout, "Magoffin," in *Handbook of Texas Online* (quotation); Applegate and Hanselka, "Junta de los Rios," 30.

22. Weber, *Mexican Frontier*, 129; Acuña, *Occupied America*, 56.

23. Stephen Austin to Henry Austin, August 27, 1829, in Barker, *Austin Papers*, 2:253. See also Austin, "Affairs of Texas," 235.

24. Almonte, "Statistical Report on Texas," 192.

25. Linn, *Reminiscences*, 35; "Mexican Trade," *Corpus Christi Star*, October 10, 1848, p. 1.

26. Marshall, "Commercial Aspects," 244 (quotation), 245; Weber, *Mexican Frontier*, 130.

27. Swift and Corning, *Three Roads to Chihuahua*, 34–35.

28. Swift and Corning, *Three Roads to Chihuahua*, 36 (quotation); Morgenthaler, *River Has Never Divided Us*, 35.

29. Swift and Corning, *Three Roads to Chihuahua*, 40. According to Swift and Corning (42) Connelly "was a gentleman of refinement and intelligence," who worked to establish cordial relations between Anglo-Americans and Mexicans and used commerce to peacefully conquer new territories. In 1861 President Abraham Lincoln appointed him territorial governor of New Mexico.

30. Morgenthaler, *River Has Never Divided Us*, 37–38.

31. Graf, "Economic History," 129, 144, 147, 150–51 (quotation); Herrera Pérez, *Breve historia de Tamaulipas*, 128; Kearney and Knopp, *Boom and Bust*, 29–32.

32. Herrera Pérez, *Breve historia de Tamaulipas*, 128; Graf, "Economic History," 127, 136, 147, 150–51; Kearney and Knoop, *Boom and Bust*, 54.

33. Acta, May 7, 1842, box 87, file 12, FPM, AMS; Zorrilla, Miró Flaquer, and Herrera Pérez, *Tamaulipas, una historia compartida*, 1:181.

34. Quoted in Green, "Texas Revolution," 50.

35. Nance, *After San Jacinto*, 102.

36. Jorge Hernández, "Social Change in Mexico's Northeast," 97.

37. Quoted in Nance, *After San Jacinto*, 155–56.

38. Nance, "Republic of Texas," in *Handbook of Texas Online* (quotation); Fehrenbach, *Lone Star*, 252.

39. Swift and Corning, *Three Roads to Chihuahua*, 46 (quotation); Graf, "Economic History," 141.

40. Herrera Pérez, *Norte de Tamaulipas*, 29; Green, "República del Río Grande," 59; Nance, *After San Jacinto*, 156–57.

41. Quoted in Nance, *After San Jacinto*, 155. Alsbury, whom Nance refers to as Horatio, was married to Juana Navarro Pérez, a niece of José Antonio Navarro.

42. Jorge Hernández, "Social Change in Mexico's Northeast," 97; John Adams, *Conflict and Commerce*, 62 (quotation); Nance, *After San Jacinto*, 156.

43. *Centennial History of Corpus Christi*, 33; Huson, *Refugio*, 1:441, 442; Paul Taylor, *American-Mexican Frontier*, 15–16.

44. Alessio Robles, *Coahuila y Texas*, 2:322; Kearney and Knopp, *Boom and Bust*, 51; *Centennial History of Corpus Christi*, 35. Arista's mansion is described in Ferrell, *Monterrey Is Ours!*

45. Circular, April 13, 1841, vol. 38, p. 196, box 2Q275, Matamoros Archives, Dolph Briscoe
    Center for American History (hereafter cited as BCAH), University of Texas at
    Austin (hereafter cited as UTA). See also Nance, *After San Jacinto*, 441n. If Arista
    was leading a double life—publicly combating the Texans and their commerce while
    clandestinely engaging with them in the contraband trade—he would not be the
    first or last person in the borderlands to have multiple identities. Andrés Reséndez
    argues that with so many "contradictory forces swirling around them" border people
    had to decide on their loyalties. These "identity choices almost always follow[ed]
    a situational logic. A person was not a mission Indian *or* a Mexican, a black slave
    in Mexico *or* an American, a foreign-born colonist *or* a Texan, but could be either
    depending on who was asking." Reséndez, *Changing National Identities*, 3.
46. Green, "Texas Revolution," 66.
47. Quoted in Valerio-Jiménez, "Neglected Citizens," 295. See also Herrera Pérez,
    Norte de Tamaulipas, 29.
48. Wilkinson, *Laredo and the Rio Grande Frontier*, 184; Justin Smith, "Republica de
    Rio Grande," 663.
49. Caso de Miguel González Taméz, October 7, 1841, box 29, file 455, Sección Con-
    cluidos, AGENL; Borjas García, Alcalde Primero, to Gobernador, September 19,
    1828, box 1481, file 1/04, Sección Alcaldes, AGENL. This section was digitalized
    recently, so file and box numbers have changed. Researchers can easily find the
    source by its date.
50. Causa contra Luciano de la Garza y cómplices, March 27, 1845, box 1, JL-C, FJ,
    AGENL.
51. Informe, Administrador de Rentas, December 6, 1843, box 726, Jueces de Letras,
    Embargos, FJ, AGENL (quotation); Jorge Hernández, "Social Change in Mexico's
    Northeast," 108, 146–47, 151.
52. Cossío, *Historia de Nuevo León*, 6:163; Lorenzo Antonio de Melo contra V. Rivero,
    July 16, 1842 (quotation), box 1, JL-C, FJ, AGENL; Joseph Milton Nance, "Woll,
    Adrián," in *Handbook of Texas Online*, http://www.tshaonline.org/handbook/online
    /articles/fwoo3.
53. Green, "Texas Revolution," 58 (quotation); Herrera Pérez, *Norte de Tamaulipas*,
    49–50. For Arista's suspicions see Informe, April 15, 1841, box 1, file 7, folder 5, FS,
    AGEC; Nance, *After San Jacinto*, 434. In *Revolution Remembered* Seguín revealed
    Uribe's role in the contraband trade. Arthur Mayer, "San Antonio, Frontier
    Entrepot," 353.
54. Quoted in Green, "República del Río Grande," 59.
55. Cited in Ávila, Martínez, and Morado, *Santiago Vidaurri*, 242.
56. Nance, *After San Jacinto*, 63, 65; Graf, "Economic History," 143.
57. "The West," *Telegraph and Texas Register*, April 29, 1840, p. 3.
58. Lamar, *Papers of Mirabeau B. Lamar*, 3:564–65.
59. Lamar, *Papers of Mirabeau B. Lamar*, 4:212. See also Paul Taylor, *American-Mexican
    Frontier*, 19–20.
60. Graf, "Economic History," 123 (quotation), 143.

61. Herrera Pérez, *Norte de Tamaulipas*, 64; Lamar, *Papers of Mirabeau B. Lamar*, vol. 4, pt. 1, 212 (quotation).

62. Thompson, *Sabers on the Rio Grande*, 99, 101–2 (quotations); Tijerina, *Tejanos and Texas*, 90.

63. Fisher, *Sketches of Texas*, 46.

64. Nance, *After San Jacinto*, 432. Lamar was making these overtures to Arista at the same time as he was launching the Santa Fe expedition.

65. Graf, "Economic History," 144; Nance, *After San Jacinto*, 438 (quotation), 440, 443.

66. Quoted in Nance, *After San Jacinto*, 318–19.

67. Nance, *After San Jacinto*, 318–19.

68. Quoted in Nance, *After San Jacinto*, 490.

69. Nance, *After San Jacinto*, 490. Mexican producers and merchants and Texas consumers of the frontier region developed a relationship of overlapping interests, a "non-zero-sum dynamic" that allowed both sides to win. See Wright, *Nonzero*.

70. Weber, *Mexican Frontier*, 157. Thomas D. Hall (*Social Change in the Southwest*, 14) argues that "market articulation is a major mechanism of incorporation by which more advanced areas (core states) produce changes in less advanced peripheral areas."

71. Reséndez, *Changing National Identities*, 7–8.

72. Vázquez, *Supuesta República del Río Grande*, 6 (quotation); Vázquez ("Texas Question," 313) argues that "centralism became the principal cause of unrest in the decade from 1836 to 1846, paralyzing the nation and preventing an attempt to reconquer Texas."

73. Quoted in Gallegos, "'Last Drop of My Blood,'" 98; Herrera Pérez, *Norte de Tamaulipas*, 25.

74. For more on the Federalist War, see Vigness, "Republic of the Rio Grande"; Lindheim, *Republic of the Rio Grande*; Nance, *After San Jacinto*; Alessio Robles, *Coahuila y Texas*, vol. 2; Herrera Pérez, *Norte de Tamaulipas*; Zorrilla, Miró Flaquer, and Herrera Pérez, *Tamaulipas, una historia compartida*, vol. 1.

75. Green, "Texas Revolution," 63; Herrera Pérez, *Norte de Tamaulipas*, 36–37; Ridout, "Anti-national Disorder," 50; Vázquez, "Texas Question," 322.

76. "Parte Oficial," *Correo del Río Bravo del Norte*, February 16, 1840, p. 1 (quotation); Harrison, "Los federalistas mexicanos," 338, 339. Luis Medina Peña argues that the brand of federalism practiced by politicians of northern Mexico was learned not in books, but in the daily practice of defending their families and their properties. Medina Peña, *Bárbaros del norte*, 181, 252.

77. Nance, *After San Jacinto*, 214.

78. Gallegos, "'Last Drop of My Blood,'" 44; Nance, *After San Jacinto*, 216n.

79. Quoted in Vizcaya Canales, *Un siglo de Monterrey*, 39.

80. Nance, *After San Jacinto*, 148, 152, 160, 162.

81. Lindheim, *Republic of the Rio Grande*, 1 (quotation); Harrison, "Los federalistas mexicanos," 331, 332. Anaya's offer to the Texans was reported by a centralist newspaper, *La Gaceta* (Zacatecas), so its veracity is open to question.

82. Harrison, "Los federalistas mexicanos," 336–37, 341; Ridout, "Anti-national Disorder," 76, 100–101; Alessio Robles, *Coahuila y Texas*, 2:207.

83. Alessio Robles, *Coahuila y Texas*, 2:216; Nance, *After San Jacinto*, 218–19, 227–29.

84. Letter of December 11, published in *Semanario Político*, January 16, 1840, p. 187;
Nance, *After San Jacinto*, 232.

85. Nance, *After San Jacinto*, 235–36.

86. Nance, *After San Jacinto*, 246, 247.

87. *Semanario Político*, January 3, 1840, p. 2.

88. These events are described in Nance, *After San Jacinto*, 249–67. See also Alessio
Robles, *Coahuila y Texas*, 2:217.

89. Nance, *After San Jacinto*, 252–53; "Parte Oficial," *Correo del Río Bravo del Norte*,
February 16, 1840.

90. David M. Vigness has argued that the revolt of 1839–40 was a separatist movement
that culminated in the establishment of the Republic of the Rio Grande. Vigness,
"Republic of the Rio Grande." Other historians have followed his lead. See, for
example, Nance, *After San Jacinto*; Lindheim, *Republic of the Rio Grande*; and Ridout, "Anti-national Disorder." Josefina Z. Vázquez advanced the first serious and
authoritative critique of this interpretation. Vázquez, *Supuesta República del Río
Grande*. She argues that the supposed republic was a Texas invention promoted by
the press and that no official document that lends credence to such a view has ever
surfaced. She claims Juan Pablo Anaya stated explicitly that it was not a separatist
movement. In an incisive chapter of his master's thesis, Juan José Gallegos explores
the historiography and arguments surrounding the Republic of the Rio Grande
and concludes that the republic never existed. Gallegos, "'Last Drop of My Blood,'"
162–92. Octavio Herrera believes that Antonio Canales was playing a double game
with the Texans and led them to believe that his was a separatist movement so that
he could obtain their support. The flag, designed by the foreign mercenaries hired
by Canales, is now exhibited in a museum in Laredo dedicated to a republic that
perhaps never existed. See Herrera Pérez, *Norte de Tamaulipas*, 33n.

91. José Urrea to Gómez Farías, April 6, 1840, no. 625, folder 47ª, Gómez Farías Papers,
Benson Latin American Collection, UTA.

92. Quoted in Herrera Pérez, *Norte de Tamaulipas*, 71.

93. DeLay, *War of a Thousand Deserts*, 142.

94. Ridout, "Anti-national Disorder," 42–43; Hall, *Social Change in the Southwest*, 185
(quotation). The very conditions found in the border region fostered attitudes
that debilitated nationalism. "The isolation and hardship of the frontier fostered
a remarkable openness toward outsiders." Reséndez, *Changing National Identities*,
125.

95. Broadside, Arista to residents of Saltillo, December 12, 1839, no. 943, microfilm
reel 15, Mexican Imprints from the Streeter Collection, Mary and Jeff Bell Library,
Texas A&M University–Corpus Christi.

96. Broadside, Arista to residents of Saltillo. See also broadside, November 1839, General
Valentín Canalizo to residents of Matamoros, no. 945, microfilm reel 15, Streeter
Collection.

97. Nance, *After San Jacinto*, 206.

98. Ridout, "Anti-national Disorder," 81–82. Through various intermediaries, including Plummer and Juan Seguín, Canales was able to see Lamar. The Texas president publicly refused to support the rebels, but Seguín later wrote that Lamar had encouraged him to recruit men for the federalists and had provided him with arms. Nance, *After San Jacinto*, 281, 288, 328.

99. Nance, *After San Jacinto*, 294–95.

100. Nance, *After San Jacinto*, 206; Huson, *Refugio*, 1:444.

101. Huson, *Refugio*, 1:441, 442 (quotation).

102. Nance, *After San Jacinto*, 305.

103. Nance, *After San Jacinto*, 302.

104. Chance, *Carvajal*, 49, 53.

105. Gallegos, "'Last Drop of My Blood,'" 120.

106. Nance, *After San Jacinto*, 308; Haynes, *Soldiers of Misfortune*, 44 (quotation).

107. Nance, *After San Jacinto*, 338.

108. Nance, *After San Jacinto*, 343, 353–60; Lindheim, *Republic of the Rio Grande*, 8.

109. Alcance al *Semanario Político*, November 12, 1840; Nance, *After San Jacinto*, 362, 364, 373.

110. Nance, *After San Jacinto*, 275.

111. Nance, *After San Jacinto*, 172.

112. Herrera Pérez, *Norte de Tamaulipas*, 42.

113. Green, "Texas Revolution," 64.

114. A decade after the events, a Texas newspaper referred to Canales as the "betrayer of Jourdan [sic] and his Texans." See "Mexican Affairs," *Western Texan*, November 4, 1852, p. 2.

115. Quoted in Weber, *Mexican Frontier*, 105.

116. Quoted in Haynes, *Soldiers of Misfortune*, 156–57.

117. Broussard, "San Antonio," 33.

118. Kelsey, *Through the Years*, 18; Brown, *Indian Wars and Pioneers*, 759.

119. Neale served as mayor of Brownsville on two occasions and lived until 1896. John C. Rayburn, "Neale William," in *Handbook of Texas Online*, http://www.tshaonline.org/handbook/online/articles/fne03; Rayburn and Rayburn, *Century of Conflict*, 4, 10n; Kearney and Knopp, *Boom and Bust*, 52, 53.

120. Kelsey, *Through the Years*, 1–5; Garna L. Christian, "Rio Grande City, Texas," in *Handbook of Texas Online*, http://www.tsha.utexas.edu/handbook/online/articles/RR/hfr5.html.

121. *Centennial History of Corpus Christi*, 38 (first quotation), 29 (second quotation); Amelia W. Williams, "Kinney, Henry Lawrence," in *Handbook of Texas Online*, http://www.tshaonline.org/handbook/online/articles/fki29.

122. *Telegraph and Texas Register*, August 25, 1841, quoted in Nance, *After San Jacinto*, 464.

123. *Centennial History of Corpus Christi*, 45.

124. Quoted in Ávila, Martínez, and Morado, *Santiago Vidaurri*, 243.

125. Quoted in Herrera Pérez, *Norte de Tamaulipas*, 52–53.

126. Quoted in Payne, "Camp Life," 335–36.

127. Justin Smith, *War with Mexico*, 2:262, 484n (quotation).

128. Quoted in Green, "Texas Revolution," 67.

129. Other towns close to Monterrey posted similar figures. See EM-Montemorelos, boxes 2 and 3, AGENL; González-Quiroga, "Nuevo León ante la invasión norteamericana," 466–68.

130. Ford, *Rip Ford's Texas*, 102.

131. The Mexican press reported that these rural people were forced to work for the U.S. army or else suffer the destruction of their homes and fields. See *Semanario Político*, July 30, 1846, p. 562.

132. Justin Smith, "Republica de Rio Grande," 663 (first quotation), 664 (second quotation).

133. Ridout, "Anti-national Disorder," 136, 162 (quotations).

134. William Marcy to Zachary Taylor, July 9, 1846, *Messages of the President of the United States*, United States, President (1845–1849: Polk), United States War Department. Center for Digital Scholarship, Rice University, http://scholarship.rice.edu /bitstream/handle/1911/27059/aa00388a.xml?sequence=1.

135. Tilden, *Notes on Upper Rio Grande*, 14–15.

136. Tilden, *Notes on Upper Rio Grande*, 15 (first and second quotations), 16 (third and fourth quotations).

137. Quoted in Wilcox, "Laredo During the Texas Republic," 104.

138. Lamar, *Papers of Mirabeau B. Lamar*, vol. 4, part 1, 162 (quotation), 166.

139. Thomas W. Cutrer, "Bee, Hamilton Prioleau," in *Handbook of Texas Online*, http:// www.tshaonline.org/handbook/online/articles/fbe24.

140. Baylies, "March to Saltillo," 297, 298, 302, 303, 307 (first quotation), 308 (second quotation).

141. Baylies, "March to Saltillo," 297–98, 302–3, 303 (quotation). See also Laura Gutiérrez, "Prolongado ocaso de un estado," 189.

142. Pourade, *Sign of the Eagle*, 43 (first quotation), 29 (second quotation).

143. "The War Between the United States and Mexico," chap. 9, pp. 3–4, box 2E287, Kendall (George Wilkins) Papers, BCAH, UTA. Kendall's assertion of American protection from Indian raids is false. These raids continued to such a degree that prominent citizens met in Monclova, Coahuila, to organize a force of three hundred men to protect the towns. Laura Gutiérrez, "Prolongado ocaso de un estado," 163.

144. A few of the authors who deal with racial attitudes and abuses against the Mexican population during the war are Chance, *Mexican War Journal*; McCaffrey, *Army of Manifest Destiny*; and Foos, *Short, Offhand, Killing Affair*.

145. Ridout, "Anti-national Disorder," 156–57. Ridout cites Samuel E. Chamberlain, who witnessed or knew firsthand about many of the abuses, which he recorded in his memoir, *My Confession*.

146. Quoted in Justin Smith, "Republica de Rio Grande," 670.

147. Informe de Ayuntamiento, 1854-04-15, "Noticias estadísticas históricas de la Villa de Mier del año de [1]852." I thank Professor Stanley Green, formerly of Texas A&M International University of Laredo, for sharing this document.

148. *Semanario Político*, July 23, 1846, p. 558.

149. Ridout, "Anti-national Disorder," 156–57.

150. Ridout, "Anti-national Disorder," 157.

151. Quoted in Ferrell, *Monterrey Is Ours!* 152.

152. Quoted in Justin Smith, "Republica de Rio Grande," 670–71; Ridout, "Anti-national Disorder," 162, 187.

153. Meyer, "Evolución del nacionalismo defensivo mexicano," 431.

154. Harris, *Sánchez Navarros*, 5 (quotation), 14; Laura Gutiérrez, "Prolongado ocaso de un estado," 193.

155. According to historian Elliott Young, "The establishment of national borders changes the context within which borderlanders act and interact, but transnational linkages do not evaporate or even necessarily diminish over time." Young, *Catarino Garza's Revolution*, 14. Young (6–7) distinguishes borders from borderlands. Whereas "borderland" refers "to the cultural and ethnoracial community that remains unified across imperial or national boundary lines," the "border" is "the political and ideological boundary that produces differences that are then used to forge national identity." In this duality, "borderlands unite and borders divide." For the next three decades and even beyond, the region of South Texas and Northeast Mexico continued to be a borderland in the full meaning of the word.

Chapter 3. The Permeable Border

1. Grass, *Tin Drum*, 394–95.

2. Brown, *Indian Wars and Pioneers*, 230. Other merchants based in Matamoros did reach San Juan with their goods. The U.S. consul at that port reported in 1850 that "his fellow citizens controlled around half a million dollars' worth of inventory in the exposition at San Juan de los Lagos." Quoted in Jorge Hernández, "Social Change in Mexico's Northeast," 128.

3. "Eagle Pass Road," *Nueces Valley*, July 13, 1850, p. 2; "Mexican Trade," *Corpus Christi Star*, October 10, 1848, p. 1.

4. "De Laredo," *Corpus Christi Star*, September 26, 1848, p. 3; *Centennial History of Corpus Christi*, 54.

5. *Corpus Christi Star*, September 19, 1848, p. 1.

6. Frank Wagner, "Cazneau, William Leslie," in *Handbook of Texas Online* http://www.tshaonline.org/handbook/online/articles/fcaae.

7. *Corpus Christi Star*, September 19, 1848, p. 2.

8. *Centennial History of Corpus Christi*, 57.

9. Paul Taylor, *American-Mexican Frontier*, 69.

10. From the *Corpus Christi Star*, August 11, 1849, quoted in Paul Taylor, *American-Mexican Frontier*, 69.

11. Paul Taylor, *American-Mexican Frontier*, 69.

12. *Corpus Christi Star*, September 19, 1848, p. 1 (quotation); *Centennial History of Corpus Christi*, 55.

13. Applegate and Hanselka, "Junta de los Rios," 32 (quotation), 45; Bliss, *Reminiscences*, 114 n. 12.

14. Ben E. Pingenot, "Eagle Pass, Texas," in *Handbook of Texas Online*, http://www .tshaonline.org/handbook/online/articles/hee01.

15. Hudson, *Mistress of Manifest Destiny*, 132 (quotation); Kerrigan, "Race, Expansion, and Slavery," 278.

16. Kinsall, "Fort Duncan," 94 (quotation); Wood, *John Twohig*, 27, 28.

17. John Mason Hart, "Charles Stillman," in *Handbook of Texas Online*, http://www .tshaonline.org/handbook/online/articles/fst57. Cortina's resentment was also fueled by the loss of thousands of acres of his mother's land to pay lawyers to defend that land. He felt "that he had been cheated out of his heritage." See Amberson, McAllen, and McAllen, *I Would Rather Sleep in Texas*, 162.

18. Advertisement, *Corpus Christi Star*, September 1, 1849, p. 1.

19. "Texas," *Nueces Valley*, July 13, 1850, p. 2.

20. José María de la Garza to Secretario de Gobierno, March 7, 1850, box 5, file 94, folio 6, Fondo Colonias Militares de Oriente (hereafter cited as FCMO), AGEC.

21. Lister and Lister, *Chihuahua*, 136 (quotation); Guerra de Luna, *Los Madero*, 324–25; Juan Manuel Maldonado to Antonio María Jáuregui, March 7, 1850, box 5, folder 6, file 92, FCMO, AGEC.

22. Jorge Hernández, "Social Change in Mexico's Northeast," 185; Stemmons to USDS, February 12, 1849, reel 3, CD, MAT, NARA.

23. Quoted in Clarke, *Travels in Mexico and California*, xiii.

24. Arthur Mayer, "San Antonio: Frontier Entrepot," 358 (quotation). Leaton, a man "of dubious character and ambiguous background," had married Juana Pedrasa and "was actively engaged in trade with Indians and Mexicans." Elam, "Aspects of Acculturation," 77, 78.

25. Art Leatherwood, "Whiting, William Henry Chase," in *Handbook of Texas Online*, http://www.tshaonline.org/handbook/online/articles/fwhew; Bliss, *Reminiscences*, 188n.

26. Rodríguez, *José Policarpo Rodríguez*, 58.

27. Art Leatherwood, "Neighbors Expedition," in *Handbook of Texas Online*, http:// www.tshaonline.org/handbook/online/articles/upnse; Ford, *Rip Ford's Texas*, 114.

28. "Trade with Chihuahua," *Telegraph and Texas Register*, July 4, 1851, p. 2.

29. "For El Paso," *Nueces Valley*, March 18, 1854, p. 2.

30. "Smith's Train," *San Antonio Ledger*, March 11, 1852, p. 2.

31. Nicolás de Arredondo to Gobierno, September 16, 1848, folder 40, file 1564, vol. 43, pp. 53–99, Saltillo Archives, BCAH, UTA. A large part of the contraband entering Coahuila consisted of bales of cotton, which fed an incipient textile industry that had evolved since 1840, located mainly around Saltillo.

32. Quoted in Ávila, Martínez, and Morado, *Santiago Vidaurri*, 239 (quotation), 251.

33. Quoted in Jorge Hernández, "Trading across the Border," 437–38.

34. Quoted in Paul Taylor, *American-Mexican Frontier*, 51.

35. Domenech, *Missionary Adventures*, 268.

36. Horgan, *Great River*, 789–90; Herrera Pérez, *Norte de Tamaulipas*, 94.

37. Herrera Pérez, *Norte de Tamaulipas*, 101. According to historian George T. Díaz, "Government interference in free trade caused local resentment and rather than acquiesce to what they regarded as arbitrary trade regulations, borderlanders on both sides of the river developed a moral economy of illicit trade, a contrabandista community, which accepted some forms of smuggling as just." Díaz, *Border Contraband*, 1–2.

38. Sierra and Martínez Vera, "Contraresguardo," 270, 271. The formal name of this customs force was the Contraresguardo de Gendarmería Fiscal. Jorge Hernandez, "Social Change in Mexico's Northeast," 139. Political instability prevented the Contraresguardo from fulfilling its mission and it was suspended, only to be restored years later.

39. Quoted in Ávila, Martínez, and Morado, *Santiago Vidaurri*, 240.

40. Stemmons to USDS, June 18, 1849, reel 3, CD, MAT, NARA; Chance, *Carvajal*, 146.

41. Zorrilla, Miró Flaquer, and Herrera Pérez, *Tamaulipas: textos de su historia*, 1:274, 275 (quotation).

42. Quoted in Paul Taylor, *American-Mexican Frontier*, 29. John Hart argues that Stillman, King, and Kenedy "bankrolled the attempted invasion of Mexico by José María Carbajal for the purpose of setting up their own Republic of the Sierra Madre extending south from Matamoros to Tampico, west from Tampico to Monterrey and Saltillo, and north from Saltillo to Nuevo Laredo." Hart, *Revolutionary Mexico*, 111.

43. Quoted in Chance, *Carvajal*, 87.

44. "Another Revolution in Mexico," *Telegraph and Texas Register*, September 5, 1851, p. 2.

45. "From Laredo," *Texas State Times*, November 4, 1854, p. 2. In *Across the Rio*, Schwartz declares that "slavery stopped 150 miles short of the Rio Grande in Southwestern Texas. Realistic slave owners could not afford to lose their valuable property, and the Mexican border persistently beckoned Negro slaves toward freedom" (54).

46. Schwartz, *Across the Rio*, 34 (quotation). Chance (*Carvajal*, 161) writes that huge profits could be made by returning slaves who had fled to northern Mexico, estimating that bounties totaled about $3 million.

47. Ford, *Rip Ford's Texas*, 196, 203–4, 205.

48. Herrera Pérez, *Norte de Tamaulipas*, 86; Jorge Hernández, "Social Change in Mexico's Northeast," 54; García to Jáuregui, November 19, 1851, box 15, file 34, folio 5, FCMO, AGEC.

49. Quoted in Amberson, McAllen, and McAllen, *I Would Rather Sleep in Texas*, 138.

50. *Telegraph and Texas Register*, January 16, 1852, p. 2; Kerrigan, "Race, Expansion, and Slavery," 286.

51. Herrera Pérez, *Norte de Tamaulipas*, 87 (quotation); Chance, *Carvajal*, 142, 144.

52. For information on the trial of Carvajal and more than a dozen of his collaborators see Castillo to Gobierno de Nuevo León, June 6 and August 8, 1853, box 1, Cor-

respondencia con el Interior–Texas (hereafter cited as CIT), AGENL. See also Chance, *Carvajal*, 160, 166.

53. Zorrilla, Miró Flaquer, and Herrera Pérez, *Tamaulipas, textos de su historia*, 1:286, 287, 291.

54. Vidaurri's rise to power is recounted in Benavides Hinojosa, *Santiago Vidaurri*. Herrera Pérez (*Norte de Tamaulipas*, 96) explains that the Ávalos tariff, imposed during the Carvajal revolt, was abolished because "it was severely challenged by the merchants of Mexico City, Veracruz, and Tampico," as well as by powerful European groups in the country. This is another example of the northern frontier being sacrificed in favor of commercial interests in the center.

55. Juan Fidel Zorrilla, "Fuentes documentales del Movimiento de Ayutla en Tamaulipas," 295, 296, http://www.juridicas.unam.mx/publica/librev/rev/hisder/cont /3/doc/docii.pdf; Herrera Pérez, *Breve historia de Tamaulipas*, 157.

56. Lucas Martínez, *Ejército del norte*, 84; Lawrence Taylor, "Voluntarios extranjeros," 208; Guerra de Luna, *Los Madero*, 348, 349, 366, 368; "México," *El Bejareño*, July 31, 1855, p. 1; Benavides Hinojosa, *Santiago Vidaurri*, 52–53. Luis Medina Peña (*Bárbaros del norte*, 200) argues that the revolution of Ayutla triumphed because "Santa Anna lost the northern part of the country." The final santanista stronghold in the Northeast fell when the rebels captured Matamoros in September 1855.

57. Tyler, "Callahan Expedition of 1855," 577n.

58. Horace Alsbury to Bennett Riddells, June 29, 1855. I obtained a copy of this letter from Tom McDonald, who in turn obtained it from Ron Tyler. It forms part of the Vidaurri correspondence held by the Santiago Roel family in Monterrey.

59. Henry's proclamations were published in "Our Own Correspondence," *San Antonio Ledger*, July 21, 1855, p. 7. One rationale in support of an independent republic was that Mexican claims under article 11 of the Treaty of Guadalupe Hidalgo, which obligated the United States to stop Indian depredations from its territory into Mexico, now exceeded $15 million, according to the *Telegraph and Texas Register*, September 12, 1851, p. 2, and December 5, 1851, p. 2. If the separation of northern Mexico became a reality, "the United States [would] be released from the onerous provisions of this treaty, as there will be Anglo-Americans enough in these departments to keep the savages constantly in check." This, of course, assumes that Mexicans and Anglos would live collectively in the new republic and fight together against the Indian enemy.

60. According to Mario Cerutti, Vidaurri reduced tariffs by up to 60 percent, which "caused panic . . . among the middlemen located in Veracruz, Mexico [City], and even Tampico." In August 1855 Vidaurri opened several ports on the Rio Grande to foreign commerce, including Mier, Camargo, Monterrey-Laredo, and Piedras Negras, and two months later, Reynosa and Guerrero. See Cerutti, *Economía de guerra*, 70, 71, 78–79 (quotation); Zorrilla, Miró Flaquer and Herrera Pérez, *Tamaulipas, textos de su historia*, 1:319.

61. Benavides Hinojosa, *Santiago Vidaurri*, 55, 76; "Méjico. La recolocación en la frontera," *El Bejareño*, August 18, 1855, p. 3, and September 1, 1855, p. 2. "Nuevo Leon's

revenue averaged around 660,000 pesos per year between 1855 and 1859, 75 percent of it going directly to the Army of the North." Mora-Torres, *Making of the Mexican Border*, 48. The best work on Vidaurri's construction of regional power is Cerutti, *Economía de guerra*. Vidaurri's annexation of Coahuila is explained in Martha Rodríguez, "Odisea para instalar el progreso," 216–17; and Medina Peña, *Bárbaros del norte*, 215–26.

62. Henry to Vidaurri, August 12, 1856. This document is part of the Santiago Roel Melo Collection held by the Roel family of Monterrey (hereafter cited as SRMC).

63. Quoted in Acuña and Compean, *Voices of Latino Experience*, 1:128.

64. Vidaurri to Editor, *Southern Intelligencer*, February 28, 1859, file 1, vol. 45, Colección Principal, Sección Correspondencia, Fondo Monterrey, Nuevo León y Coahuila (hereafter cited as FMNLC), Archivo Histórico de Monterrey (hereafter cited as AHM). There are many contradictory sources on the creation of the Republic of the Sierra Madre. It was a subject of debate in San Antonio's two Spanish-language newspapers in the 1850s: *El Ranchero* and *El Bejareño*. A thick file on the "República de la Sierra Madre," which includes these debates, exists in Archivo Histórico, Secretaría de la Defensa Nacional (hereafter cited as SEDENA), file XI/1814/8535.

65. Jorge Hernández, "Trading across the Border," 435–36 (quotation); González-Quiroga, "Nuevo León ante la invasión norteamericana," 443.

66. Santos Benavides to Santiago Vidaurri, May 4, 1854; Ángel Navarro to Santiago Vidaurri, May 28 and June 26, 1860, both in FCV, AGENL; Jorge Hernández, "Social Change in Mexico's Northeast," 160–61.

67. Aviso, February 8, 1850, box 1, SMRE-IE, FRE, AGENL.

68. Juicio civil, Walsh vs. Wolf, November 4, 1856, box 93, Jueces de Letras, Asuntos Comerciales, FJ, AGENL.

69. An attempt to attract German immigrants to Tamaulipas in the 1830s was mentioned in chapter 1.

70. Miguel Blanco to Santiago Vidaurri, November 25, 1855, FCV, AGENL. Riotte and Vidaurri signed an agreement in which the German representative stated, "The spirit of hatred which has sprung up during the last two years . . . against the foreign settlers [in Texas] has given rise to the most lamentable manifestations of intolerance . . . and has even occasioned open conflict and bloodshed." See *New York Daily Times*, January 31, 1856, p. 4.

71. Langberg and Flores, *Dust, Smoke, and Tracks*, 19. Langberg himself reported an exception to the decorum of U.S. soldiers in a letter to his sister in which he wrote that "several American officers . . . helped celebrate my birthday. Most ended up under the table." Cunningham and Hewitt, "Lovely Land," 406.

72. "Movements of Germans from Texas to Mexico," *New York Daily Times*, November 30, 1855, p. 6.

73. *New York Daily Times*, January 31, 1856, p. 4 (quotation); "Colonización de Nuevo León," *El Bejareño*, January 19, 1856, p. 5; "Los alemanes en Nuevo León," *El Clamor Público*, March 29, 1856, p. 1.

74. Quoted in Paul Taylor, *American-Mexican Frontier*, 33; José de Garay to Nicanor Martínez, January 1, 1826, file 46, vol. 17, Colección Correspondencia, Sección Asuntos Legales, Fondo Capital del Estado, AHM; Nichols, "Limits of Liberty," 35, 40.

75. Ministro de Relaciones Exteriores to Gobierno de Coahuila, April 23, 1849, folio 8, file 3, box 2, FS, AGEC; Green, "Texas Revolution," 62.

76. Salinas, *Indians of the Rio Grande Delta*, 54, 136; Schwartz, *Across the Rio*, 26 (quotation); Nichols, "Limits of Liberty," 128. This is the second report of Ampudia serving as godfather to a non-Mexican (the other was William Peter Neale). This is a little-known facet of this Mexican general, so reviled in Texas.

77. Ford, *Rip Ford's Texas*, 214; Nichols, "Limits of Liberty," 52 (quotation).

78. Olmsted, *Journey through Texas*, 455.

79. Alberto Rodriguez "Ethnic Conflict in South Texas," 32–33. According to Rodriguez, "Many masters ran ads in the local Matamoros newspapers advertising slave labor for hire," so that "for some Blacks crossing the river did not mean freedom." This probably describes the arrangement that sent Kinchlow to Mexico.

80. Alberto Rodriguez, "Ethnic Conflict in South Texas," 38.

81. *Telegraph and Texas Register*, August 29, 1851, p. 2.

82. Ford, *Rip Ford's Texas*, 196; Gassner, "African American Fugitive Slaves," 105 (first quotation); Schwartz, *Across the Rio*, 33 (second quotation).

83. Quoted in Schwartz, *Across the Rio*, 42.

84. Manuel Flores to Secretario de Gobierno, June 27, 1851, folio 6, file 3, box 6, FS, AGEC; Juzgado de Paz to Juez de Primera Instancia, August 11, 1855, folio 5, file 9, box 4, FS, AGEC.

85. Quoted in Taylor, *American-Mexican Frontier*, 37.

86. Nichols, "Limits of Liberty," 98.

87. Nichols, "Limits of Liberty," 56–57, 425–26. Stewart and De León (*Not Room Enough*, 31) argue that the expulsions of the 1850s "took place at locations in the interstice, where the Mexican region touched those areas populated by white people, most of whom had migrated in an earlier era from the upper- and lower-southern states." The Mexican region is discussed below.

88. Green, "Texas Revolution," 62 (quotation); Tyler, "Callahan Expedition of 1855," 576.

89. Maldonado to Galán Falcón, January 28, 1850, folio 2, file 16, box 5, FCMO, AGEC.

90. Manuel Flores to Secretario de Gobierno, March 20, 1851, box 3, file 8, folio 8, FS, AGEC.

91. Kerrigan, "Race, Expansion, and Slavery," 286; Sumpter, *Paso del Aguila*, 70n; Lucas Martínez, *Ejército del Norte*, 351–52.

92. Quoted in a printed two-page document that accompanied the letter from Hanson Alsbury to Bennett Riddells of June 29, 1855, cited in n. 58. This document was detached from the letter and is in SRMC.

93. Quoted in "Invasion of Mexico," *New York Daily Times*, August 17, 1855, p. 6; and *National Era*, August 23, 1855.

94. Cunningham and Hewitt, "Lovely Land," 409.

95. Several historians have written on the Callahan expedition; see Rippy, "Border Troubles," 101; Mulroy, *Freedom on the Border*, 78; Nichols, "Limits of Liberty," 224, 225. In "The Callahan Expedition of 1855" (577–78) Ronnie Tyler argues that the primary intent was to recapture fugitive slaves. Tom McDonald, a researcher from Texas, has shared with me a draft manuscript which makes a compelling argument that the expedition was primarily designed to stop Indian raids into Texas from Mexico.

96. Santiago Vidaurri to Hamilton Bee, November 29, 1855, SRMC.

97. Bee to Vidaurri, January 20, 1856, SRMC.

98. Nichols, "Limits of Liberty," 149, 150, 152, 153 (quotation). Another motivation for inviting friendly Indians to Mexico to help defend the frontier was the high desertion rate among Mexican soldiers of the local militias. See Informe, November 2, 1849, box Q279, and Joaquín Arguelles to Comandancia General, May 24, 1859, box 2Q281, Matamoros Archives, BCAH, UTA.

99. Nichols, "Limits of Liberty," 156, 157, 166; Mulroy, *Freedom on the Border*, 3, 55, 68.

100. Nichols, "Limits of Liberty," 198, 199, 200, 201.

101. Jáuregui to Minister of War and Navy, July 27, 1850, file 620, box 36, Sección Concluidos, AGENL. The utilization of *indios mansos* (literally "tame Indians") to combat *indios salvajes* (savage Indians) was a longstanding practice in Mexico, first used by the Spanish Crown and later the Mexican government. Jacoby, *Shadows at Dawn*, 37.

102. Schwartz, *Across the Rio*, 40.

103. Nichols, "Limits of Liberty," 234, 241, 242, 245, 248 (quotation), 256; Minor, *Turning Adversity to Advantage*, 145. A good account of Lipan-Texan relations is provided by Robinson, *I Fought a Good Fight*, 174–250. The Lipan and other nomadic tribes inhabited what Samuel Truett (*Fugitive Landscapes*, 15) refers to as a fugitive landscape, "one characterized by mobility and flexibility, that survived by eluding the scrutiny of empire and resisting incorporation."

104. Minor, *Turning Adversity to Advantage*, 145, 169 (quotation); Nichols, "Limits of Liberty," 259–60.

105. Nichols, "Limits of Liberty," 259–60 (quotation), 262.

106. Nichols, "Limits of Liberty," 161, 163, 165, 169–70, 170.

107. Moseley, "Indians from the Eastern United States," 278.

108. Mulroy, *Freedom on the Border*, 81 (quotations); Moseley, "Indians from the Eastern United States," 277–79. Many people on the frontier opposed Vidaurri's plan to colonize the region with Indians. According to Nichols ("Limits of Liberty," 184), "the Tamaulipas paper, *Prisma*, warned against colonizing the frontier with yet more 'savages.'"

109. M. Christopher Nunley, "Kickapoo Indians," in *Handbook of Texas Online*, http://www.tshaonline.org/handbook/online/articles/bmk09; Martha Rodríguez, "Odisea para instalar el progreso," 208.

110. Bliss, *Reminiscences*, 163.

111. Gassner, "African American Fugitive Slaves," 110.

112. Nichols, "Limits of Liberty," 266, 267; Vizcaya Canales, *Tierra de guerra viva*, 309. Vidaurri launched his deadliest attack on Lipans five months after the Callahan expedition. See Minor, *Turning Adversity to Advantage*, 174.

113. Quoted in Vizcaya Canales, *Tierra de guerra viva*, 319.

114. Quoted in Vizcaya Canales, *Tierra de guerra viva*, 334. The twin massacre is described on pp. 333–34. See also Nichols, "Limits of Liberty," 270–75. On Vidaurri's supposed elimination of the Lipans, see Minor, *Turning Adversity to Advantage*, 175, 178, 180, 184–90. Even after these disastrous events, a few Lipans collaborated with Vidaurri in combating Comanches. See Vizcaya Canales, *Tierra de guerra viva*, 371, 372.

115. This exchange is included in the correspondence between Carranza and Vidaurri in Lucas Martínez, *De Monterrey a Cuatro Ciénegas*, 112–13, 124. Carranza was the father of Venustiano, the leader of the Constitutionalist Army and president during the Mexican Revolution. Martha Rodríguez quotes one government official who wrote that poisoning water holes frequented by Indians was necessary because "it is impossible to get rid of the barbarous tribes that desolate our fields by means of ordinary war." Rodríguez, "Odisea para instalar el progreso," 211. Shocking as this strategy may seem, Anglo settlers in Arizona "laced several bags of sugar with strychnine and then left them where they were sure to be found by local Indians." Jacoby, *Shadows at Dawn*, 122.

116. Herrera Pérez, *Norte de Tamaulipas*, 84. Martha Rodríguez, "Odisea para instalar el progreso," 205, 206. Santa Anna abolished the colonias in 1853.

117. Minister of Foreign Relations to Jáuregui, December 6, 1849, folio 3, file 9, box 9, FS, AGEC; DeLay, *War of a Thousand Deserts*, 302.

118. Maldonado to Jáuregui, March 11, 1850, folio 7, file 99, box 5, FCMO, AGEC.

119. "More Indian News," *San Antonio Ledger*, February 6, 1851, p. 2.

120. Maldonado to Jáuregui, June 23, 1851, folio 2, file 22, box 14, FCMO, AGEC. Many of the Mexican women and children captured by Comanches and Apaches were integrated into the Indian tribes and never returned. See Brooks, *Captives & Cousins*, 322.

121. Quoted in Minor, *Turning Adversity to Advantage*, 175.

122. Maldonado to Jáuregui, May 1, 1851, folio 11, file 68, box 13, FCMO, AGEC.

123. Vizcaya Canales, *Tierra de guerra viva*, 396; Sumpter, *Paso del Aguila*, 98n.

124. Anderson to Office of Adjutant General of Texas, May 28, 1872, U.S. Department of State, Foreign Relations of the United States, *Executive Documents Printed by Order of the House of Representatives* (hereafter cited as USDS, EDHR), 1872–73, p. 449.

125. Vidaurri's letters were published in *El Bejareño*, April 5 and 26, 1856, p. 2; Vizcaya Canales (*Tierra de guerra viva*) discovered abundant correspondence between the government of Nuevo León y Coahuila and Texas military authorities. Vidaurri had a point when he blamed U.S. officials for "shameful and inhuman traffic" with the barbarous Indians. Historian Joaquín Rivaya Martínez has documented the correspondence of Texas Indian agents such as Robert Neighbors who were well

aware of the traffic in stolen goods from Mexico. See Rivaya Martínez, "Trespassers in the Land of Plenty," 17.

126. David Adams, "Embattled Borderland," 219; Nichols, "Limits of Liberty," 179; Vizcaya Canales, *Tierra de guerra viva*, 373.

127. Poyo and Hinojosa, *Tejano Origins*, 29.

128. Informe, September 1, 1849, folio 1, file 3, box 6, FS, AGEC; Herrera Pérez, *Norte de Tamaulipas*, 107; Jorge Hernández, "Social Change in Mexico's Northeast," 218.

129. Quoted in Nance, *After San Jacinto*, 472.

130. Tijerina, *Tejanos and Texas*, 142 (quotation). See also Crimm, "Success in Adversity," 221. It should be noted that the pull of the Texas labor market was not yet strong in the 1830s and 1840s.

131. Nichols, "Limits of Liberty," 83.

132. José María Girón to Zachary Taylor, June 1, 1846, p. 165 vol. 55, box 2Q279, Matamoros Archives, BCAH, UTA.

133. *Telegraph and Texas Register*, October 7, 1846, p. 5.

134. González-Quiroga, "Nuevo León ante la invasión norteamericana," 439.

135. Ford, *Rip Ford's Texas*, 265; Thompson, *Cortina*, 17.

136. Sirvientes became "people in between," a phrase used by Adelman and Aron ("From Borderlands to Borders"). Through mobility they could negotiate better conditions, play "one state off of the other," and obtain "for themselves the best possible working conditions in the trade." Nichols, "Limits of Liberty," 70.

137. Quoted in Dávila and Rivera Saldaña, *Matamoros en la guerra*, 70.

138. Nichols, "Limits of Liberty," 62–63.

139. "Tropas para la frontera," *Corpus Christi Star*, September 26, 1848, p. 3.

140. *Informe de la Comisión Pesquisidora*, 62. There are various versions of the Mexican Commission's findings. I have chosen to use the report that was prepared in Monterrey and published in Mexico City in 1873. For a detailed and convincing account of Anglo racism against Mexicans in the nineteenth century, see De León, *They Called Them Greasers*.

141. Crews, "Know-Nothing Party in Texas," 48, 52.

142. Lack, "Slavery and Vigilantism in Austin," 4, 9 (first quotation), 10, 11 (second quotation).

143. Lack, "Slavery and Vigilantism in Austin," 12, 19 (quotation).

144. Many scholars have accepted the Mexican government's claim that Anglos killed seventy-five Mexican cartmen. See, for example, Montejano, *Anglos and Mexicans*, 29; De León, *They Called Them Greasers*, 82–83; and Rippy, "Border Troubles," 91–111. In "The Cart War" historian Larry Knight disputes this claim as greatly exaggerated. An official version of the attacks is included in Governor E. M. Pease, "Message in Regard to Mexican Carts," November 11, 1857, in the R. Niles Graham-Pease Collection, Austin Public Library.

145. Quoted in Knight, "Cart War," 324.

146. *San Antonio Daily Herald*, August 5, 1857, p. 2 (quotation); and September 26, 1857, p. 2.

147. Arthur Mayer, "San Antonio, Frontier Entrepot," 373, 379.

148. T. S. Paschal and S. A. Maverick to Pease, September 20, 1857, box 301–26, Governor's Papers, Elisha M. Pease, Texas State Archives.

149. The term "Mexican settlement region" appears in Stewart and De León, *Not Room Enough*, 23. Mexican migration is explored more fully in De León and Stewart, *Tejanos and the Numbers Game*, 15–29, where the authors utilize the Texas census to calculate statistically Mexican migration to the region in the second half of the nineteenth century. For example, in 1850, 62 percent of the Mexican population in the southern counties had been born in Texas. Ten years later, in 1860, 62 percent had been born in Mexico.

150. *Telegraph and Texas Register*, June 27, 1851, p. 2; Sumpter, *Paso del Aguila*, 41, 98n; Utley, "Range Cattle Industry."

151. Quoted in Benavides Hinojosa, *Santiago Vidaurri*, 62. Vidaurri also justified his annexation of Coahuila because the state was unable to defend itself from Indian raiders or Texas filibusters. Moreover, the majority of its inhabitants were in favor of incorporation. See Medina Peña, *Bárbaros del norte*, 215–26.

152. Juan Manuel Maldonado to Antonio María Jáuregui, October, 1852, folio 9, file 82, box 19, FCMO, AGEC; Valerio-Jiménez, *River of Hope*, 173 (quotation).

153. Zorrilla, Miró Flaquer, and Herrera Pérez, *Tamaulipas, textos de su historia*, 1:322.

154. Oscar Martínez, *Border Boom Town*, 11–12. Juan Mora-Torres states that "everyday goods such as sugar, coffee, shoes, and clothing cost two to four times less on the Texas side of the border than on the Mexican side." See Mora-Torres, *Making of the Mexican Border*, 62.

155. "Los Mejicanos," *Corpus Christi Star*, September 26, 1848, p. 4.

156. Zorrilla, Miró Flaquer, and Herrera Pérez, *Tamaulipas, textos de su historia*, 1:323.

157. Quoted in Nichols, "Line of Liberty," 422. Manuel Valdez, a chronicler of the War of Reform, was appalled at the condition of peons in the haciendas of San Luis Potosí. He had lived in Texas and declared that slaves there were better off. See Medina Peña, *Bárbaros del norte*, 397.

158. Jane Cazneau's book, published under the pseudonym Cora Montgomery, contains a section on debt peonage. See Montgomery, *Eagle Pass*, 59–81.

159. Nichols, "Limits of Liberty," 64 (quotation), 74.

160. Rudesindo Jiménez to Santiago Vidaurri, July 4, 1859, box 1, Sección Trabajo-Sirvientes, AGENL.

161. Kerrigan, "Race, Expansion, and Slavery," 296 (quotations); Nichols, "Limits of Liberty," 90.

162. Both Paul Taylor (*American-Mexican Frontier*, 36) and Juan Mora-Torres (*Making of the Mexican Border*, 27–28) utilize Comisión Pesquisidora data that 2,812 sirvientes and 2,572 family members left for Texas. They recognize, however, that not all of the towns of the Northeast responded to the commission's inquiry on escaped peons.

163. Quoted in "Informe Annual de 1850," EM-Montemorelos, AGENL; Nichols, "Limits of Liberty," 93. The problem of sirviente flight was much worse in Coahuila, where

haciendas dominated the agrarian structure, than in Nuevo León, where smaller properties were the norm. See Medina Peña, *Bárbaros del norte*, 183.

164. González Navarro, *Anatomía del poder en México*, 150–51.

165. Pingenot, "Great Wagon Train Expedition," 192, 194.

166. "The Mexicans," *Corpus Christi Star*, September 19, 1848, p. 1.

167. Sumpter, *Paso del Aguila*, 101n (quotation); Kinsall, "Fort Duncan," 94.

168. Monday and Vick, *Petra's Legacy*, 57 (quotations); Utley, "Range Cattle Industry," 423, 427.

169. Montejano, *Anglos and Mexicans*, 78; Paul Taylor, *American-Mexican Frontier*, 116; Harris, *Imperio de la familia Sánchez Navarro*, 255; Cross, "Living Standards in Zacatecas," 2; Memoria, February 23, 1843, box 2, EM-Montemorelos, AGENL.

170. Ford, *Rip Ford's Texas*, 149 (quotation), 163–64; Sumpter, *Paso del Aguila*, 17.

171. Quoted in Paul Taylor, *American-Mexican Frontier*, 33 (quotation), 34.

172. Crook, "San Antonio," 23; Arthur Mayer, "San Antonio, Frontier Entrepot," 342.

173. De León and Stewart, *Tejanos and the Numbers Game*, 34; Olmsted, *Journey through Texas*, 160.

174. Santleben, *Texas Pioneer*, 116; Arthur Mayer, "San Antonio, Frontier Entrepot," 378.

175. Spillman, *Historical Geography*, 44–46; Monday and Vick, *Petra's Legacy*, 57.

176. Woolford, "Burr G. Duval Diary," 493.

177. "Mexicans in Texas," *Daily Ranchero*, January 13, 1870, p. 2. The editor went on to vindicate most Mexicans, who "are numbered among our most honorable citizens, and we have every reason to feel that our community is more exalted by having them among us."

178. Valerio-Jiménez, *River of Hope*, 174 (quotation); Ford, *Rip Ford's Texas*, 466.

179. *Daily Ranchero*, August 2, 1870, p. 2.

180. Crimm, "Success in Adversity," 224.

181. Crimm, *De León, a Tejano Family History*, 225. The *Corpus Christi Star* (September 19, 1848, p. 1) reported that some of the wealthy Tamaulipas families that settled in Corpus Christi went back to Mexico to induce other families to come and live there.

182. Ignacio Mariscal to Hamilton Fish, January 30, 1875, USDS, EDHR, 1875–76, vol. 2, no. 452, pp. 954–79.

183. Juan Manuel Maldonado to Antonio María Jáuregui, March 7, 1850, box 5, file 92, folio 6, FCMO, AGEC.

184. Escobedo, "Iron Men and Wooden Carts," 53.

185. Brown, *Indian Wars and Pioneers*, 580.

186. Sumpter, *Paso del Aguila*, 40n, 41n (quotation); Tijerina, *Tejano Empire*, 19.

187. Crimm, *De León, a Tejano Family History*, 223.

188. Luz Escalera de León inherited 19,253.5 acres, as well as seventeen town lots, upon the death of Fernando de León, making her "the wealthiest widow in the county." Crimm, *De León, a Tejano Family History*, 216, 223, 225.

189. Crimm, "Success in Adversity," 289.

190. Document 50, Silver Mine of "Jesus María," New York, 1855, Vallecillo Mining Company (hereafter cited as VMC), BL UCB.

191. *El Bejareño*, February 7, 1855, p. 1.

192. Utley, "Range Cattle industry," 424; "Musquiz Creek," in *Handbook of Texas Online*, http://www.tshaonline.org/handbook/online/articles/rkm05.

193. De León, *Mexican Americans in Texas*, 37. David Montejano places these mechanisms, which included the use of physical force, within a conceptual framework that he calls a "peace structure," which is an "accommodation between the victorious Anglos and the defeated Mexican elite." The "concept focuses on the manner in which victors are able to exercise and establish authority over the defeated." See Montejano, *Anglos and Mexicans*, 34.

194. Ulrich to USDS, April 27, 1875, Consular Despatches, Monterrey (hereafter cited as CD, MTY), reel 3, NARA. Aside from proximity, which made interactions easier, it seems clear that the various groups in the region found cooperation to be mutually beneficial. This dynamic is explained in Sherif, *In Common Predicament*, 15.

195. As a proponent of slavery, Cazneau's notion of inclusion did not extend to blacks. Kerrigan, "Race, Expansion, and Slavery," 289 (quotations), 291, 292.

196. Viele, *Following the Drum*, 126 (first quotation), 155 (second quotation), 158.

197. Quoted in Thompson, *Wild and Vivid Land*, 81.

198. Bliss, *Reminiscences*, 124.

199. Thompson, *Sabers on the Rio Grande*, 184.

200. Sumpter, *Paso del Aguila*, x, 78, 80 (quotation).

201. Brown, *Indian Wars and Pioneers*, 587 (quotation); Sumpter, *Paso del Aguila*, 98n.

202. *El Bejareño*, February 7, 1855, p. 1.

203. *San Antonio Ledger*, April 24, 1858, p. 2; and July 5, 1856, p. 4; Advertisement, *San Antonio Ledger and Texan*, December 1, 1860, p. 3. Debray and Quintero also served as translators for the General Land Office.

204. Sonnichsen, *Roy Bean*, 49 (quotations), 57. Bean's affinity did not extend to all Mexicans. He killed one in a dispute, according to Arthur Mayer, "San Antonio, Frontier Entrepot," 505.

205. Nichols "Limits of Liberty," 7.

206. These concepts, which Sheila McManus used to describe the Alberta-Montana borderlands, are equally applicable to the Rio Grande region. See McManus, *The Line Which Separates*, xii.

207. Nobles, *American Frontiers*, 12.

208. Adelman, and Aron, "From Borderlands to Borders," 840. Among historians who differ with these authors are Elliott Young and James David Nichols. Young argues, "The U.S.-Mexico border established in 1848 cut straight through preexisting political, economic, and cultural communities. The nation-state project of severing these communities, however, remains even today only partially completed." Young, *Catarino Garza's Revolution*, 6. Nichols states emphatically, "Given the mobility that characterizes the borderlands of the Rio Grande/Bravo, and probably most

borders, the generalized historical trajectory from borderland to bordered land is
overblown. . . . Mobility has characterized the social history of the borderlands."
"Limits of Liberty," 300.

Chapter 4. Commercial and Religious Expansion

1. In the 1850s, Protestantism and Catholicism were engaged in fierce and sometimes
deadly competition in the United States. See, for example, Franchot, *Roads to Rome;*
and Noll, *God and Mammon.*
2. Quoted in Weber, *Mexican Frontier,* 81.
3. Petición, June 13, 1831, folio 6, file 3, box 6, FS, AGEC; Weber, *Mexican Frontier,* 72.
4. Quoted in Jorge Hernández, "Social Change in Mexico's Northeast," 223.
5. Hogan, *Texas Republic,* 192 (quotation); Campbell, *Gone to Texas,* 110.
6. The Cumberland branch of the Presbyterian Church emerged from the Second
Great Awakening in the first half of the nineteenth century. This more informal
and rustic strand of Presbyterianism developed from the revivals of the period. See
Rankin, *Twenty Years among the Mexicans,* x.
7. "Religious Operations in Texas," *Boston Recorder* 21, no. 11 (March 11, 1836), 41,
http://search.proquest.com/docview/124105952?accountid=6667. Bacon's work
was facilitated by the establishment, years earlier, of national organizations such
as the American Bible Society and the American Tract Society, in which various
religious sects attempted to cooperate in the publication of religious literature.
8. Hogan, *Texas Republic,* 218.
9. Rankin, *Texas in 1850,* 178; Rankin, *Twenty Years among the Mexicans,* 25 (quotations),
30 n.1.
10. Herrera Pérez, *Norte de Tamaulipas,* 108–9.
11. *Texas Presbyterian,* September 25, 1847, p. 2.
12. Brackenridge and García-Treto, *Iglesia Presbiteriana,* 9. Ill health forced McCullough
to leave his work incomplete.
13. "Sunday Schools, Pioneers of the Ministry: The Rio Grande Experiment," *Christian
Observer* 29, no. 18 (May 4, 1850): 72, http://search.proquest.com/docview/135968778
?accountid=6667.
14. "The Rising Race on the Rio Grande," *Christian Observer* 28, no. 31 (August 4, 1849):
124, http://search.proquest.com/docview/136092835?accountid=6667.
15. Rankin, *Texas in 1850,* 193 (quotation); "Christian Effort on the Rio Grande: Missionary Operations on the Rio Grande," *Christian Observer* 28, no. 30 (July 28,
1849): 118, http://search.proquest.com.proxy.libraries.smu.edu/docview/136110276
?accountid=6667.
16. Rankin, *Twenty Years among the Mexicans,* xii.
17. Rankin, *Twenty Years among the Mexicans,* xxxiii n. 11 (quotation), 27–29.
18. Rankin, *Twenty Years among the Mexicans,* xiii, xiv, 38 (quotation).
19. Rankin, *Twenty Years among the Mexicans,* xiv–xv.
20. Cruz, *Century of Service,* 16; Gilbert, *Archdiocese of San Antonio,* 7, 9; Wright,
"Pioneer Religious Congregations," 67, 67–68, 70.

21. Parisot, *Reminiscences of a Texas Missionary*, 85 (quotation); Cruz, *Century of Service*, 16.

22. *Galveston Weekly Journal*, December 20, 1850, p. 5 (quotation); Cruz, *Century of Service*, 17.

23. Quoted in Monday and Vick, *Petra's Legacy*, 101.

24. Wright, "Pioneer Religious Congregations," 73 (quotation); Wood, *John Twohig*, 37.

25. Moore, *Through Fire and Flood*, 98.

26. Amberson, McAllen, and McAllen, *I Would Rather Sleep in Texas*, 110; Parisot, *Reminiscences of a Texas Missionary*, 5.

27. Moore, *Through Fire and Flood*, 124 (quotation); Cruz, *Century of Service*, 17.

28. Monday and Vick, *Petra's Legacy*, 225.

29. Wood, *John Twohig*, 47.

30. Patrick Foley, "Odin, Jean Marie," in *Handbook of Texas Online*, http://www.tshaonline.org/handbook/online/articles/fod02.

31. Juan Manuel Maldonado to Antonio María Jáuregui, June 1 and 23, 1850, folios 3 and 7, files 33 and 93, box 7, FCMO, AGEC; Moore, *Through Fire and Flood*, 90. During a brief period after 1848 Nuevo Laredo was named Monterrey–Nuevo Laredo.

32. Mariano Arista to Jáuregui, July 1850, folio 9, file 125, box 7, FCMO, AGEC.

33. "From Laredo," *Texas State Times*, November 4, 1854, p. 2.

34. Moore, *Through Fire and Flood*, 90, 91 (quotation).

35. Moore, *Through Fire and Flood*, 97 (first three quotations), 98 (last quotation). Odin and Verea met at Rancho Las Tortillas, a border crossing notorious for smuggling. Parisot, *Reminiscences of a Texas Missionary*, 80.

36. Moore, *Through Fire and Flood*, 101–2.

37. Quoted in Parisot, *Reminiscences of a Texas Missionary*, 62–63.

38. Quoted in Ann Lozano, "Domenech, Emmanuel Henri Dieudonne," in *Handbook of Texas Online*, http://www.tshaonline.org/handbook/online/articles/fdo09.

39. Domenech, *Missionary Adventures*, 228.

40. Domenech, *Missionary Adventures*, 265–66. Due "to his distaste for the hardships of missionary life and his continuing poor health," Domenech left the Rio Grande in 1852 and returned to France. His health apparently improved, because he became a prolific writer and in 1864 took part in the French Intervention in Mexico, first as chaplain to the French troops and later as Maximilian's press secretary. He lived a full life and died in 1903 of apoplexy. Lozano, "Domenech."

41. Keralum finished the job that Verdet had started after the latter died "in a violent storm off the Louisiana coast." Wright, "Building Churches," 17.

42. Wright, "Building Churches," 17 (quotation), 18. Keralum "disappeared while traveling on horseback in 1872 in an especially remote and dense area of the brush country. The chance discovery of his undisturbed remains a full decade later confirmed that he had become lost."

43. Moore, *Through Fire and Flood*, 97–98.

44. Aníbal A. González, "Parisot, Pierre Fourrier," in *Handbook of Texas Online*, http://www.tshaonline.org/handbook/online/articles/fpa72 (quotations); Parisot, *Reminiscences of a Texas Missionary*, 39.

45. Parisot, *Reminiscences of a Texas Missionary*, 55.

46. Parisot, *Reminiscences of a Texas Missionary*, 43, 50 (quotation).

47. Jorge Hernández, "Social Change in Mexico's Northeast," 1–2.

48. From *Corpus Christi Ranchero*, February 9, 1861, p. 2, quoted in Stanley C. Green, "Popular Religion on the Texas-Tamaulipas Border: Revilla/Guerrero 1750–1861," 28, unpublished paper courtesy of the author.

49. Parisot, *Reminiscences of a Texas Missionary*, 47–49.

50. Parisot, *Reminiscences of a Texas Missionary*, 53 (quotations); Moore, *Through Fire and Flood*, 98; Benavides Hinojosa, *Santiago Vidaurri*, 111.

51. Parisot, *Reminiscences of a Texas Missionary*, 51–52.

52. Quoted in Lucas Martínez, *Ejército del norte*, 194–95.

53. Santiago Vidaurri to Santos Benavides, July 3, 1859, FCV, AGENL.

54. According to Jorge Hernández ("Trading across the Border," 435), in 1827 "the bullion from Zacatecas represented two-thirds of Mexican silver production."

55. Estadísticas de 1826 y 1827, box 1, EM, Cerralvo, AGENL; Censo y Estadística, December 22, 1833, box 1, EM, Vallecillo, AGENL; Estadística, December 31, 1832, box 1, EM, Villaldama, AGENL.

56. An internal report of the Vallecillo Mining Company in 1852 stated that the U.S.-Mexican War and "the subsequent incursions of the Comanches depopulated and impoverished the country to such a degree that the works [of the mine] could never be taken up again till now." Document 60, VMC, BL UCB.

57. Quoted in Reséndez, *Changing National Identities*, 206.

58. Memorias de Gobernadores, José María Parás, 1848, pp. 203–4, AGENL.

59. José Manuel Mendoza to Gobierno del Estado, May 12, 1849, box 1, Fondo Minas, AGENL; Document 1, VMC, BL UCB.

60. Documents 2, 6 (quotations), and 7, VMC, BL UCB.

61. Memorias de Gobernadores, Juan N. de la Garza y Evia, April 23, 1853, AGENL. See also Estadística, December 31, 1852, box 1, EM, Vallecillo, AGENL.

62. Prevost changed his given name from Grayson to Julio when he decided to stay in Mexico. With Mariana he would raise eleven children, nine of them girls. In 1856 he was appointed U.S. consul in Zacatecas, and in the 1860s and 1870s played a leading role in the expansion of Protestantism in Mexico. Martínez López, *Presbiterianismo en México*, 51; Documents 10 and 11, VMC, BL UCB.

63. Documents 48, 59 (quotation), and 72, VMC, BL UCB.

64. Hart, *Revolutionary Mexico*, 110.

65. Quoted in Thompson, *Fifty Miles and a Fight*, 12–13, 155, 165, 168 (quotation).

66. Diario, Denuncia de Minas, box 2, Fondo Minas, AGENL. John/Juan Weber also served as U.S. consul in Monterrey from 1876 to 1882.

67. "Later from the Rio Grande," *New York Daily Times*, December 12, 1855, p. 8.

68. Alonzo, *Tejano Legacy*, 11 (quotation), 12; Crimm, *De León, a Tejano Family History*, 224.

69. Quoted in Paul Taylor, *American-Mexican Frontier*, 75.

70. Hébert, *Forgotton Colony*, 359.

71. Solicitud, September 7, 1865, Colección Civil, vol. 285, Sección Ayuntamiento, Fondo Monterrey del Departamento en el Segundo Imperio, AHM.

72. Sumpter, *Paso del Aguila*, 98n.

73. Ávila, Martínez, and Morado, *Santiago Vidaurri*, 69–74.

74. Santiago Vidaurri to Santos Benavides, May 30, 1861, and Ángel Navarro to Vidaurri, March 30, 1860, FCV, AGENL.

75. *San Antonio Ledger and Texan*, June 30, 1860, p. 1.

76. Mahon and Kielman, "George H. Giddings," 225.

77. Quoted in Kilgore, "Two Sixshooters and a Sunbonnet," 60, 64 (quotation), 68.

78. Kilgore, "Two Sixshooters and a Sunbonnet," 60, 66, 68 (quotation); Huson, *Refugio*, 2:204–6.

79. Oficio del Gobernador, August 3, 1859, vol. 44, file 11, Colección Miscelánea, Sección Correspondencia, FMNLC, AHM; Circular 24, August 11, 1859, Colección Impresos, Sección Reglamentos, Decretos y Circulares, FMNLC, AHM.

80. Graf, "Economic History," 302.

81. Negrete Salas, "Frontera texana," 91.

82. *Informe de la Comisión Pesquisidora*, 14–15.

83. Joseph Kleiber to Casa Sepúlveda, March 6, 1861; and Kleiber to Wright, April 25, 1861, letterpress, box 2E293, Kleiber Papers, BCAH, UTA.

84. For information on San Román's contacts in Mexico, Cuba, the United States, and Europe, see Cerutti and González-Quiroga, *Norte de México y Texas*, 30, 58–62, 67–68, 94–99; *American Flag*, September 29, 1847, p. 4.

85. Francois Gilbeau to John Leyendecker, February 6, 1857, and January 2, 1859, box 2M315, folder 2, John Z. Leyendecker Papers, BCAH, UTA.

86. Belden to Leyendecker, February 9, and March 22, 1857; J. B. Mitchell to Leyendecker, November 21 and December 11, 1857, and Perkins to Leyendecker, February 24, 1859, all in box 2M315, folder 2, Leyendecker Papers, BCAH, UTA; John Adams, *Conflict and Commerce*, 79.

87. Miriam York, "Groos, Friedrich Wilhelm Carl," in *Handbook of Texas Online*, http://www.tshaonline.org/handbook/online/articles/fgr76; Brown, *Indian Wars and Pioneers*, 289. Other sources indicate that Groos and Gertrude had seven children.

88. "San Antonio," *Western Texan*, April 15, 1852, p. 3.

89. Bliss, *Reminiscences*, 255.

90. Corner, *San Antonio de Bexar*, 108 (quotation); Wood, *John Twohig*, 14, 16.

91. Among the Bexar merchants who were living in Chihuahua or had stores there were A. F. Wulff, S. Mayer, Emil Schetelig, and the Moye brothers. Sweet to LaCoste, March 16, May 16, and June 11, 1861, box 2E310, folder 2, LaCoste Papers, BCAH, UTA; advertisements in *Daily Ledger and Texan*, July 3, 1861, p. 4, and *San Antonio*

Ledger, July 1, 1852, p. 4 (quotation); Pease, "LaCoste, Jean Batiste," in *Handbook of Texas Online*; Arthur Mayer, "San Antonio, Frontier Entrepot," 433, 477.

92. Cavazos Garza, *Diccionario biográfico*, 2:317–18; Cerutti, *Burguesía, capitales e industria*, 57.

93. Vasconcelos, *Evaristo Madero*, 53, 93, 94, 97 (quotation); Guerra de Luna, *Los Madero*, 432; Cerutti, *Burguesía, capitales e industria*, 58.

94. Aduana Fronteriza to Alcalde de Guerrero, January 24, 1858 (quotation), folio 5, file 13, box 1, FS, AGEC; Cerutti and González-Quiroga, *Norte de México y Texas*, 84.

95. Garza González, *Cronista desconocido*, 19–20, 38–41, 47, 52, 53, 60, 74–75, 86–92, 98, 176.

96. There are exceptions to this general pattern. Joseph Kleiber eagerly sought the Mexican market, but in his correspondence he referred to Mexico as "greaserdom." He stated that he was "not disposed to have anything to do with any enterprise" involving Mexicans because "anything connected with them always ends badly." Kleiber to Ben Carter, March 27, 1866, and Kleiber to K. A. Carey, June 5, 1869, box 2R72, Kleiber Papers, BCAH, UTA.

97. Quoted in Jorge Hernández, "Trading across the Border," 438.

98. Bell and Smallwood, "Zona Libre," 123–24 (quotations); Haynes to USDS, September 28, 1879, Consular Despatches, Nuevo Laredo (hereafter cited as CD, NL), reel 1, NARA. The most comprehensive treatment of the creation of the zona libre is found in Herrera Pérez, *Zona libre*.

99. Zorrilla, Miró Flaquer, and Herrera Pérez, *Tamaulipas, una historia compartida*, 1:196, 197 (quotation).

100. Salvucci, "Origins and Progress of U.S.-Mexican Trade," 719. The author uses the example that draft animals were in such great demand in Mexico that it "drove their ordinarily large share of the border trade to zero." He has a point, but he examines only the registered legal trade.

101. Cerutti and González-Quiroga, *Norte de México y Texas*, 16 (quotation), 38. Martha Rodríguez argues that the "movement of men, soldiers, merchandise, animals, and beasts of burden through the state of Coahuila penetrated its previous isolation and dynamized its incipient local and regional market." Rodríguez, "Odisea para instalar el progreso," 220.

102. Harris, *Imperio de la familia Sánchez Navarro*, 313, 315.

103. Dionisio Meade to Pedro de Ampudia, June 11, 1853, folio 14, file 125, box 21, FCMO, AGEC. The same correspondence is found in folder 45, file 1720, vol. 44, pp. 192–219, Saltillo Archives, BCAH, UTA. The importance of American products in maintaining the morale of Mexican soldiers is illustrated by their predilection for tobacco. One officer in San Luis Potosí asked Santiago Vidaurri to send Virginia tobacco, "which is the one to which they are accustomed." Medina Peña, *Bárbaros del norte*, 411.

104. Juan Manuel Maldonado to Ampudia, June 11, 1853, folio 14, file 125, box 21, FCMO, AGEC.

105. Ministro de Guerra y Marina to Government of Coahuila, November 21, 1848, box 5, file 8, folio 9, FS, AGEC; Joaquín I. de Castillo to Government of Nuevo León, April 18, 1853, box 1, CIT, AGENL. See also Vizcaya Canales, *Tierra de guerra viva*, 194–95, 232.

106. Ávila, Martínez, and Morado, *Santiago Vidaurri*, 258. Vidaurri was the only regional caudillo who paid his soldiers regularly, according to Luis Medina Peña, *Bárbaros del norte*, 405–6.

107. Cerutti and González-Quiroga, *Norte de México y Texas*, 43, 49.

108. Lucas Martínez, *Ejército del norte*, 151, 212 (quotation), 348–49, 380. The money to pay for these arms was obtained through forced loans on merchants and producers or, in Vidaurri's case, by offering discounts on tariffs to merchants who traded across the border through the customhouses under his control.

109. Ignacio Galindo to Santiago Vidaurri, August 25, 1859, FCV, AGENL.

110. Medina Peña, *Bárbaros del norte*, 132, 257 (quotation), 282.

111. Fernández de Castro, "Comercio y contrabando," 26 (quotation); Cerutti and González-Quiroga, *Norte de México y Texas*, 30.

112. Ford, *Rip Ford's Texas*, 460.

113. Gilbert Kingsbury to Warren, June 1860, box 2R72 and box 2E290, Gilbert Kingsbury Papers and Memoirs, BCAH, UTA.

114. Vidaurri to Francisco Zarco, April 14, 1861, FCV, AGENL. After many years of combating the Indians, the norteños adopted many of the former's methods. One of his enemies declared that "when they entered into combat [Zuazua's troops] were not formed in a column, but were dispersed, dragging themselves on the ground and then jumping . . . and emitting screams and whoops like the Comanches." Benavides Hinojosa, *Santiago Vidaurri*, 127.

115. Quoted in Lucas Martínez, *Ejército del norte*, 95. Vidaurri often repeated this theme, usually with a heavy dose of racism toward the people in central and southern Mexico. On one occasion he wrote, "Nuevo León, unlike the states of the interior, is not populated by miserable Indians: we are aware of our duties, and at the same time of our power and rights, and with a strong feeling of the dignity of free men who will not allow themselves to be oppressed by force instead of ruled by just laws." Quoted in Benavides Hinojosa, *Santiago Vidaurri*, 30. Despite what Vidaurri said publicly about his army, he had great difficulty in recruiting citizens so he had to resort to conscriptions, which many rural people evaded. Desertions were also common. See García, *Guerra y frontera*, 64–66.

116. Lawrence Douglas Taylor devotes a section to this topic in his "Voluntarios extranjeros," 207–15.

117. "The War in Northern Mexico," *New York Times*, May 20, 1858, p. 2.

118. Lawrence Taylor, "Voluntarios extranjeros," 209–10, 213; Lucas Martínez, *Ejército del norte*, 263, 282, 293. Medina Peña (*Bárbaros del norte*, 312–22) analyzes the various factors that contributed to the defeat and places most of the blame on Vidaurri. Jordan was exonerated after an investigation.

119. Galindo to Vidaurri, July 6, 1859, FCV, AGENL.

120. Taylor, "Voluntarios extranjeros," 214 (first quotation), 215 (second quotation).

121. Thompson, *Cortina*, 39–45.

122. Thompson, *Cortina*, 44.

123. "Latest from the Rio Grande," *San Antonio Ledger and Texan*, December 10, 1859, p. 1.

124. Thompson, *Cortina*, 86.

125. Ford, *Rip Ford's Texas*, 264–65; Thompson, *Cortina*, 14; Hart, *Revolutionary Mexico*, 115. Mexican merchants of Brownsville and their circle opposed the Cortina War because it interrupted commerce with Mexico "worth millions of dollars."

126. López y Rivas, "Cortina y el conflicto fronterizo," 337 (quotations), 339, 342; Amberson, McAllen, and McAllen, *I Would Rather Sleep in Texas*, 167.

127. Brown to Arguelles and Arguelles to Brown, both September 28, 1859; Arguelles to Governor of the State, September 29 and October 3, 1859, and February 20, 1860, 1-15-1683 (1877), Fondo de Gaveta, Archivo Histórico Genaro Estrada, Secretaría de Relaciones Exteriores.

128. Thompson, *Cortina*, 48.

129. Chance, *Carvajal*, 170. One of the reasons why Brownsville was virtually defenseless is that months earlier General David E. Twiggs had decided to remove his troops from Fort Brown to Fort Duncan, a measure that angered Brownsville merchants. The absence of a military force in Brownsville facilitated Cortina's attack. Thompson, *Cortina*, 36–37.

130. Thompson, *Cortina*, 52–53, 82 (quotation).

Chapter 5. The U.S. Civil War and Its Impact on the Rio Grande

1. Bee to Quintero, November 9, 1863, in U.S. War Department, *War of the Rebellion* (hereafter cited as OR) ser. 1, vol. 26, pt. 2, 399–400, http://collections.library.cornell.edu/moa_new/waro.html. Bee was criticized in some quarters for his actions at Brownsville. R. Fitzpatrick, the Confederate commercial agent at Matamoros, believed the fire was intended to cover up shady dealings of Bee and quartermaster Charles Russell. See Fitzpatrick to Benjamin, March 8, 1864, in OR, ser. 1, vol. 34, pt. 2, 1030–32.

2. Some of the more important works on the Texas Civil War trade are Cowling, "Civil War Trade"; Diamond, "Imports of the Confederate Government"; Irby, *Back Door at Bagdad*; Tyler, "Santiago Vidaurri and the Confederacy"; and Owsley, *King Cotton Diplomacy*. These Spanish-language works focus on the Civil War trade: Gurza Lavalle, *Una vecindad efímera*; and Cerutti and González-Quiroga, *Frontera e historia económica*.

3. Montejano, "Mexican Merchants and Teamsters," 152 (first two quotations), 153 (third quotation). See also Ellis, "Maritime Commerce," 175, 205.

4. Russell to McNeill, May 4, 1863, in OR, ser. 1, vol. 15, 1072–74. The spelling of Matamoros with an "a" instead of an "o" at the end was common among American sources; similarly, Monterrey was commonly written with one "r." Those spellings are maintained in quotations.

5. Ford, *Rip Ford's Texas*, 458, 464 (quotation).

6. Magruder to Cooper, June 8, 1863, in OR, ser. 1, vol. 26, pt. 2, 57–65.

7. Couthouy to Welles, May 16, 1863, in U.S. War Department, *Official Records of the Navies* (hereafter cited as ORN), ser. 1, vol. 17, 441–42, http://collections.library .cornell.edu/moa_new/ofre.html.

8. Ellis, "Maritime Commerce," 208; Amberson, McAllen, and McAllen, *I Would Rather Sleep in Texas*, 207.

9. Couthouy to Welles, March 19, 1862, ORN, ser. 1, vol. 17, 191–92.

10. Couthouy to Welles, March 19, 1862.

11. Tables showing these shipments, compiled from information in the San Román correspondence, can be found in Cerutti and González-Quiroga, *Norte de México y Texas*, 99–103; and Cerutti and González-Quiroga, "Guerra y comercio," 271–74.

12. See González-Quiroga, "Trabajadores mexicanos en Texas," 62–68; and Cerutti and González-Quiroga, "Guerra y comercio," 281–88.

13. Houston to Vidaurri, April 20, 1863, SRMC. This collection contains several other letters of recommendation from Houston to Vidaurri.

14. Ford, *Rip Ford's Texas*, 369.

15. Amberson, McAllen, and McAllen, *I Would Rather Sleep in Texas*, 210.

16. Ellis, "Maritime Commerce," 209–10; Delaney, "Matamoros, Port of Texas," 483.

17. Windham, "Problem of Supply," 162. Much of the cargo that reached Matamoros came from the port of New York, the Union's largest city. In March 1865 a Texas newspaper reported that the value of shipments from that port averaged two million dollars per week and that "Matamoros merchants tremble at the sound of peace." *Texas State Gazette*, March 29, 1865, p. 1. The involvement of New York with the Confederate trade and the ways in which merchants such as Stillman camouflaged their transactions is explored by Ellis, "Maritime Commerce" and Montejano, "Mexican Merchants and Teamsters."

18. Brown to Wallace, January 13, 1865, in OR, ser. 1, vol. 48, pt. 1, 512–13.

19. Ellis, "Maritime Commerce," 224n. Customs receipts averaged some $2.4 million annually in legal trade during the Civil War, exceeding the receipts of Veracruz, Mexico's most important port. This figure does not account for the contraband that was introduced through the port. Zorrilla, Miró Flaquer, and Herrera Pérez, *Tamaulipas, una historia compartida*, 1:198.

20. Kimmey to USDS, May 11, 1864, reel 1, CD, MTY, NARA.

21. *Texas State Gazette*, November 10, 1860, p. 3. See also the obituary in the New Orleans *Daily Picayune*, September 8, 1885.

22. Quintero to Vidaurri, June 2 and October 27, 1860, FCV, AGENL; Tyler, "Cotton on the Border," 458.

23. Clark to Vidaurri, May 23, 1861, FCV, AGENL; Toombs to Vidaurri, May 22, 1861, in ORN, ser. 2, vol. 3, 101.

24. Browne to Quintero, September 3, 1861, in ORN, ser. 2, vol. 3, 253–55.

25. Quintero to Vidaurri, August 12, 1862, FCV, AGENL.

26. *El Ranchero*, July 19, 1856, p. 2; R. Curtis Tyler, "Vidaurri and the Confederacy," 66, 69; Schoonover, "Dollars over Dominion," 43.

27. R. Curtis Tyler, "Vidaurri and the Confederacy," 69. The best analysis of this issue is found in Gurza Lavalle, *Una vecindad efímera*, 74–77. Jefferson Davis had long been a proponent of Manifest Destiny, but a possible annexation of northern Mexico would complicate relations with potential European allies such as France and Britain. Whereas Quintero entertained hopes that Vidaurri would support the Confederacy, the caudillo expressed his view of the American Civil War to Mexico's minister of foreign relations, Francisco Zarco, as follows: "No honest man should hope for the calamity that threatens that flourishing nation, but if it should inflict it upon itself, our own nation may be compensated for what that nation did to ours, making it suffer unjustly by making war on it and dismembering her territory." These do not sound like the words of a leader eager to join his province to a nation facing a calamity. Zarco, "Información Europea," 323.

28. Quoted in Diamond, "Imports of the Confederate Government," 499.

29. Bee to Anderson, November 30, 1862, in OR, ser. 1, vol. 15, 881–83.

30. Tyler, "Cotton on the Border," 459.

31. Graf, "Economic History," 580; Browne to Quintero, December 9, 1861 (quotation), and January 14, 1862, in ORN, ser. 2, vol. 3, 308, 316–17; Diamond, "Imports of the Confederate Government," 499.

32. Milmo to Hart, December 11, 1863, OR, ser. 1, vol. 53, 936; and Howard to Hart, September 10, 1863, OR, ser. 1, vol. 53, 936–37 (quotation). The need for flour reflects Texas's dependence on Northeast Mexico. Flour was hard to come by in Texas in part because many planters had stopped growing wheat and were concentrating on cotton, which was more profitable. The region around Dallas continued to be an important wheat-producing area throughout the war, but it suffered from a transportation shortage. See also Cerutti, *Burguesía, capitales e industria*, 51; Sonnichsen, *Roy Bean*, 51.

33. Cerutti, *Burguesía, capitales e industria*, 47, 48; Martha Rodríguez, "Odisea para instalar el progreso," 221.

34. Quintero to Benjamin, September 16, 1863, OR, ser. 2, vol. 3, 899–902.

35. Quintero to Vidaurri, August 12, 1862, FCV, AGENL.

36. *Texas State Gazette*, June 7, 1862, p. 1.

37. "Bust of President Davis," *Fort Brown Flag*, April 17, 1862, p. 3.

38. Kimmey to USDS, October 29, 1862, reel 1, CD, MTY, NARA.

39. Kimmey to USDS, October 29, 1862.

40. Cerutti, *Burguesía, capitales e industria*, 47.

41. Fergusson to West, February 13, 1863, OR, ser. 1, vol. 15, 682–86. Vidaurri prohibited speculation in and excessive prices on corn. He also established stores of corn in each town to be sold to poor people at modest prices. These actions reflect the policies that made Vidaurri a popular hero to many of the vecinos of the Northeast.

42. Gurza Lavalle, *Una vecindad efímera*, 83–84.

43. Kimmey to West, October 14, 1863, OR, ser. 1, vol. 26, pt. 1, 916–17.

44. Kimmey to USDS, December 25, 1863, reel 1, CD, MTY, NARA.

45. *Texas State Gazette*, December 30, 1863, p. 1.

46. Hart to Seddon, November 18, 1863, OR, ser. 1, vol. 53, 913. The cotton routes are described in Tyler, "Cotton on the Border," 460–61. Travel time for the San Antonio–Eagle Pass–Monterrey–Matamoros route was about ten days by stagecoach and about thirty days by mule team. The distance was approximately 575 miles according to *The Standard*, January 16, 1864, p. 1. See also Arthur Mayer, "San Antonio, Frontier Entrepot," 449, 502.

47. Russell to Bloomfield, November 28, 1863, OR, ser. 1, vol. 53, 916–17.

48. Bee to Benavides, November 9, 1863, OR, ser. 1, vol. 26, pt. 2, 398–99.

49. Ford, *Rip Ford's Texas*, 357. This battle is described in chap. 6.

50. *Texas State Gazette*, December 30, 1863, p. 1.

51. *Weekly State Gazette*, July 6, 1864, p. 2; and August 10, 1864, p. 1. A downside to this trend was that prices rose for most products, a phenomenon that was affecting other towns—including San Antonio, Eagle Pass, and Matamoros—and was hitting the lower classes there especially hard. This issue will be discussed later in the chapter. Gilberto Hinojosa (*Borderlands Town in Transition*, 87) explains the effects of this commercial boom on Laredo.

52. This data is found in box 2M321, Leyendecker Papers, BCAH, UTA.

53. Kimmey to USDS, December 25, 1863, and May 21, 1864, reel 1, CD, MTY, NARA. The occupation of Brownsville had little effect on producers and merchants of Northeast Mexico. If anything, it provided them with a new market: the Union army General N. J. T. Dana informed Kimmey that his unit would "need many mules and horses for the army here, and are now buying all that are offered at fair prices." See Dana to Kimmey, November 16, 1863; and Dana to Banks, November 16, 1863, OR, ser. 1, vol. 26, pt. 1, 413–14.

54. Kimmey to USDS, May 11, 1864, reel 1, CD, MTY, NARA.

55. Advertisement, *Tri-Weekly Telegraph*, June 3, 1863, p. 2; Tyler, "Cotton on the Border," 463. The antagonism between Germans and the Confederate authorities is reflected in a notorious incident on August 10, 1862. A group of more than sixty pro-Union Germans on their way to Mexico were attacked by a Confederate force on the Nueces River. Between twenty-five and twenty-seven of them were killed at the site, and another nine were executed away from the battlefield in one of the most infamous events of the war in Texas. See McGowen, "Battle or Massacre?" Information on Groos can be found in York, "Groos, Friedrich," in *Handbook of Texas Online*.

56. Miriam York, "Groos, Carl Wilhelm August," in *Handbook of Texas Online*, http://www.tshaonline.org/handbook/online/articles/fgr88. Other merchants of Eagle Pass and Piedras Negras, such as William Stone and Adolfo Duclos, retooled their operations to handle the massive volume of trade, while San Antonio firms such as Guilbeau and Hermann moved part of their operations to the port. All competed vigorously to win the trade by offering lower freight rates and better service. *Weekly State Gazette*, February 1, 1865, p. 1; *San Antonio Daily Herald*, November 15, 1862, p. 1; Tyler, "Cotton on the Border," 463.

57. Santleben, *Texas Pioneer*, 5, 9, 15, 22, 25.

58. Their papers are found in the Dolph Briscoe Center for American History, University of Texas at Austin.

59. González-Quiroga, "Puerta de México," 221; Jaques, *Texan Ranch Life*, 233, 234.

60. "Stage Line to Chihuahua," *Daily Ledger and Texan*, April 26, 1861, p. 3. See also June 4, 1861, p. 4.

61. Kimmey to USDS, October 29, 1862, reel 1, CD, MTY, NARA.

62. Reports on Murphy's shipments are found in folder 11, box 3N1, Twohig Papers (hereafter cited as TP), BCAH, UTA.

63. Cavender to Twohig, August 23 and August 30, 1862, folder 9, box 3N1, TP, BCAH, UTA.

64. González-Quiroga, "Puerta de México," 221 n. 28. Much of this information comes from a table showing Twohig's operations in 1863, in Cerutti and González-Quiroga, "Guerra y comercio," 290–94.

65. Pease, "LaCoste, Jean Batiste," in *Handbook of Texas Online*; González-Quiroga, "Puerta de México," 221; *Texas State Gazette*, August 24, 1861, p. 2.

66. "Letter From Mexico," *Weekly Telegraph*, January 19, 1864, p. 1.

67. The story is convoluted and may have involved Confederate quartermaster Charles Russell, who it was believed, was out to make money for himself. The Confederate commercial agent at Matamoros, R. Fitzpatrick, believed that Russell and Milmo orchestrated the seizure of the Confederate notes. See Fitzpatrick to Benjamin, March 8, 1864, OR, ser. 1, vol. 34, pt. 2, 1030–32; and Tyler, "Cotton on the Border," 470–72. Some sources report the amount of Confederate money confiscated by Milmo as $16,000,000.

68. Quintero to Vidaurri, December 17, 1863 (quotation), FCV, AGENL; Gurza Lavalle, *Una vecindad efímera*, 85–86.

69. Quoted in Tyler, "Cotton on the Border," 472; Kimmey to Seward, February 12, 1864, OR, ser. 1, vol. 34, pt. 2, 627–28.

70. Tyler, "Cotton on the Border," 472; Russell to Johnson, January 1, 1864, OR, ser. 1, vol. 26, pt. 2, 566–70; "Letter From Mexico," *Tri-Weekly Telegraph*, January 15, 1864, p. 1.

71. Emigration to Mexico began even while the cannons were firing at Fort Sumter. In April 1861, Santiago Vidaurri wrote to Francisco Zarco, Mexico's minister of foreign relations that "many landowners were trying to immigrate to Mexico." Vidaurri added a rather astonishing statement. He told Zarco that through a mutual friend Governor Sam Houston, with whom he had struck up a friendship during his exile in Austin, "asked me for asylum in the event that he finds it necessary to flee from a war that he considers inevitable." A deeper search in Vidaurri's correspondence may offer more details of this interesting proposal, though Houston was too savvy to put anything of this nature in writing. It is interesting that only a year earlier Houston was proposing that the United States invade northern Mexico and establish a protectorate over that section of the country. See Vidaurri to Zarco, April 14, 1861 in Zarco, "Información Europea," 20:322; and Thompson, *Cortina*, 90, 91, 93.

72. Kimmey to Seward, October 29, 1862, OR, ser. 3, vol. 2, 950.

73. Quintero to Vidaurri, November 23, 1863, FCV, AGENL.

74. An account of the conflict in Tamaulipas and the battle for Matamoros can be found in Thompson, *Cortina*, 122–27.

75. Quintero to Santacilia, January 29, 1864, quoted in Ávila, Martínez, and Morado, *Santiago Vidaurri*, 291; Kimmey to USDS, February 23, 1864, reel 1, CD, MTY, NARA.

76. The revenues of the customhouses on the border, which Vidaurri appropriated, by law belonged to the national government. That government was strapped for money, but Vidaurri would not budge. When Juárez arrived in the region he marshaled his forces at Saltillo for an attack on Monterrey in early April 1864. Faced with confronting a far superior army, Vidaurri fled to Texas. He returned to Nuevo León after Juárez abandoned the city in August 1864, but by then the French were in control and he made the biggest mistake of his life, even greater than defying Juárez: he joined Maximilian's empire, for which many Mexican historians have labeled him as a traitor to his country. He was shot in Mexico City on orders from Porfirio Díaz days after Maximilian was executed at Querétaro. The dispute between Vidaurri and Juárez is explained in González-Quiroga, "Patria en peligro."

77. Quintero to Santacilia, January 29, 1864, in Ávila, Martínez, and Morado, *Santiago Vidaurri*, 290–92.

78. Gurza Lavalle, *Una vecindad efímera*, 108.

79. Kimmey to USDS, March 4, 1864, reel 1, CD, MTY, NARA.

80. Quoted in Tyler, "Cotton on the Border," 476. Quintero negotiated an agreement with General Castagny that abolished the 6 percent tax on all European goods passing through Northeast Mexico, although a tax on cotton remained. Castagny also promised Quintero that arms and other provisions would soon be sent to Texas. Gurza Lavalle, *Una vecindad efímera*, 109.

81. Sibley, "Charles Stillman," 231; Letters, vol. 1, p. 149, box 2R72, Kingsbury Papers, BCAH, UTA.

82. This development is explored in Cerutti, *Burguesía, capitales e industria*.

83. Quoted in Cerutti, *Burguesía, capitales e industria*, 52.

84. Hart to Seddon, November 18, 1863, OR, ser. 1, vol. 53, 913; Cerutti, *Burguesía, capitales e industria*, 50.

85. *Tri-Weekly Telegraph*, December 24, 1862, p. 4.

86. Irby, "Line of the Rio Grande," 100, 102. See also *Civilian and Gazette*, September 10, 1861, p. 3.

87. James to Murphy, September 25, 1863, box 3N1, TP, BCAH, UTA.

88. Cerutti and González-Quiroga, *Norte de México y Texas*, 138–39; see p. 140 for a list of these men.

89. Cerutti and González-Quiroga, *Norte de México y Texas*, 137. A list of these men appears in González-Quiroga, "Inicios de la migración laboral," pp. 357–58.

90. A small sample of nineteen teamsters and their places of origin is provided in Cerutti and González-Quiroga, *Norte de México y Texas*, 139.

91. Lang to San Román, February 19, 1863, box 2G63, José San Román Papers, BCAH, UTA.

92. Escobedo, "Iron Men and Wooden Carts," 56.

93. Serrano to San Román, January 7, 1863, box 2G62, San Román Papers, BCAH, UTA.

94. Quoted in Winsor, *Texas in the Confederacy*, 82; *Civilian and Gazette*, September 10, 1861, p. 3.

95. "Texas Items," *Weekly Telegraph*, October 20, 1863, p. 2.

96. Kleiber to Hale, February 18, 1862, letterpress, p. 120, box 2R72, Kleiber Papers, BCAH, UTA. Data on wages can be gleaned from a variety of sources. See Arthur Mayer, "San Antonio, Frontier Entrepot," 501–4; Irby, "Line of the Rio Grande," 76–77; *Semi-Weekly News*, July 27, 1863, p. 2; *Civilian and Gazette*, March 26, 1861, p. 1. See also September 3, 1863, and May 21, 1864, box 3N1, TP, BCAH, UTA. The wages paid by Leyendecker can be found in González-Quiroga, "Inicios de la migración laboral," 357–58.

97. "To My Countrymen," *Texas Almanac, Extra*, May 19, 1863, p. 1.

98. Ford to García, June 27, 1861, file XI/1814/8535, SEDENA. This file relates to the Republic of the Sierra Madre and includes letters in Spanish and English and copies of letters sent by Ford to the *Fort Brown Flag*.

99. Enclosures in Romero to Seward, July 9, 1864, USDS, EDHR, 1865–66, 497–98; Tyler, "Santiago Vidaurri and the Confederacy," 75–76.

100. Winsor, *Texas in the Confederacy*, 51.

101. "The San Antonio Mutual Aid Association," *San Antonio Daily Herald*, February 21, 1863, p. 2; *Tri-Weekly Telegraph*, December 22, 1862, p. 1.

102. Quoted in *Tri-Weekly Telegraph*, December 22, 1862, p. 1; "The Meat Supply Association," *San Antonio Herald*, May 2, 1863, p. 1. Arthur J. Mayer dedicates a section of his doctoral dissertation to these aid organizations. See "San Antonio, Frontier Entrepot," 520–26.

103. This case was reported in "Decision upon the Conscript Law," *San Antonio News*, May 14, 1864, p. 2.

104. "Later from Mexico," *Tri-Weekly Telegraph*, January 20, 1864, p. 2.

105. Navarro to Vidaurri, December 1, 1863, FCV, AGENL.

106. *San Antonio Ledger*, May 18, 1867, p. 2. See also *Southern Intelligencer*, February 1, 1866, p. 2.

107. Fergusson to West, February 13, 1863, OR, ser. 1, vol. 15, 682–86.

108. Navarro to Vidaurri, May 10, 1861, FCV, AGENL.

109. Autorizaciones, March 16, 1863, and October 29, 1863, files 62 and 64, box 106, FPM, AMS.

110. "From Matamoros, Monterrey," *Weekly Telegraph*, February 16, 1864, p. 1.

111. Quoted in *State Gazette*, September 24, 1862, p. 1. No one has tried to quantify the number of Texans who fled to Mexico during the Civil War. Some traveled to states in the Mexican interior. For example, in May 1861, M. J. Box led a group of twenty Texas families to Durango. See Vizcaya Canales, *Tierra de guerra viva*, 367.

112. Dana to Stone, December 18, 1863, OR, ser. 1, vol. 26, pt. 1, 864–65.

113. *Morning Star*, March 25, 1864, p. 2; emphasis mine.

114. Wahlstrom, "Southern Exodus to Mexico," 9; Nunn, *Escape from Reconstruction*, 30.

115. Sheridan to Rawlins, November 11, 1866, OR, ser. 1, vol. 48, pt. 1, 297–303.

116. Hanna and Hanna, "Immigration Movement," 238. The bibliography on the Confederate exodus to Mexico is extensive. A sample is provided in a blog by C. M. Mayo in "Confederates in Mexico: A Brief Bibliography," http://maximilian-carlota .blogspot.mx/2011/02/confederates-in-mexico-brief.html.

117. Maury, "American Colony in Mexico," 628; Hanna and Hanna, "Immigration Movement," 239–41. It would be interesting to explore the Catholic reaction to Maury's declarations, which must certainly have been known in Mexico. One of the factors in Maximilian's downfall was his conflict-ridden relationship with the Mexican Catholic Church.

118. *Tri-Weekly Telegraph*, August 28, 1865, p. 7; Nunn, *Escape from Reconstruction*, 31, 32. Murrah's sad tale is told in González-Quiroga, "Fuga y muerte de Murrah."

119. Sheridan to Rawlins, November 11, 1866, OR, ser. 1, vol. 48, pt. 1, 297–303.

120. Nunn, *Escape from Reconstruction*, 34; Sheridan to Grant, November 5, 1865, OR, ser. 1, vol. 48, pt. 2, 1252–53.

121. Rolle, *Lost Cause*, 80, 81; Nunn, *Escape from Reconstruction*, 30.

122. Hanna and Hanna, "Immigration Movement," 244 (quotation), 245; Wahlstrom, "Southern Exodus to Mexico," 11.

123. Quoted in Rippy, "Mexican Projects," 317.

Chapter 6. Cooperation in Times of War

1. For this decade, my task is made easier by the many works of border historian Jerry Thompson, among them *Cortina*; *Vaqueros in Blue and Gray*; and *Mexican Texans in the Union Army*, as well as Thompson and Jones, *Civil War and Revolution*. Also useful are specific chapters in Zorrilla, Miró Flaquer, and Herrera Pérez, *Tamaulipas, una historia compartida* and *Tamaulipas, textos de su historia*, both two-volume works; Herrera Pérez, *Breve historia de Tamaulipas*; and Santoscoy et al. *Breve historia de Coahuila*.

2. Thompson, *Cortina*, 84.

3. Quoted in Thompson, *Cortina*, 94, see also 95.

4. Ford, *Rip Ford's Texas*, 324 (quotation); Thompson, *Cortina*, 97.

5. Thompson, *Cortina*, 98.

6. Thompson, *Cortina*, 100 (quotation), 101. An account of the battle can be found in "From the Rio Grande," *Civilian and Gazette*, June 18, 1861, p. 1.

7. Quoted in Thompson, *Vaqueros in Blue and Gray*, 23.

8. Thompson, *Cortina*, 101; "Letters from the Rio Grande," *Galveston Weekly News*, June 18, 1861, p. 2.

9. Quoted in Thompson, *Cortina*, 101.

10. Thompson, *Cortina*, 325.

11. Jerry Thompson, "Baylor, John Robert," in *Handbook of Texas Online*, http://www .tshaonline.org/handbook/online/articles/fbaat.

12. Baylor to Vidaurri, in Quintero Correspondence, June 21, 1861, FCV, AGENL.

13. Baylor to Vidaurri.

14. Vidaurri to Baylor, in Quintero Correspondence, June 29, 1861, FCV, AGENL; "Secession in Diplomacy," *New York Daily Tribune*, October, 22, 1861, p. 4; Vizcaya Canales, *Tierra de guerra viva*, 371–72.

15. Valerio-Jiménez, *River of Hope*, 258.

16. Bee to Vidaurri, November 22, 1863, OR, ser. 1, vol. 26, pt. 1, 438–39.

17. A good overview of the conflict between rojos and crinolinos appears in Herrera Pérez, *Breve historia de Tamaulipas*, 172–75.

18. "The Siege of Matamoros," *Weekly Telegraph*, December 11, 1861, p. 2.

19. "Siege of Matamoros."

20. "Siege of Matamoros."

21. "Later from the Rio Grande," *Houston Telegraph*, March 17, 1862, p. 2 (quotation); Tyler, "Santiago Vidaurri and the Confederacy," 72; Zorrilla, Miró Flaquer, and Herrera Pérez, *Tamaulipas, una historia compartida*, 2:18, 19.

22. Tyler, "Santiago Vidaurri and the Confederacy," 72, 72–73; Zorrilla, Miró Flaquer, and Herrera Pérez, *Tamaulipas, una historia compartida*, 2:20.

23. *Fort Brown Flag*, April 17, 1862, p. 3; Special Order No. 84 from H. E. McCulloch, April 16, 1862, box 1, CIT, AGENL; Rippy, "Mexican Projects," 302 (quotation).

24. Bee to Vidaurri, April 25, 1862, box 1, CIT, AGENL.

25. Vidaurri to Quintero, May 23, 1862, FCV, AGENL.

26. Quoted in Ávila, Martínez, and Morado, *Santiago Vidaurri*, 162; Benavides to Vidaurri, May 8, 1862, FCV, AGENL; Gurza Lavalle, *Una vecindad efímera*, 93–94.

27. *Corpus Christi Ranchero*, April 30, 1863, p. 2 (quotation); Thompson, *Mexican Texans in the Union Army*, vii, 38; Thompson, *Vaqueros in Blue and Gray*, 10, 55–56. "Not only did Mexican Texans cross the physical international border to escape conscription but they also intentionally blurred the figurative border of citizenship. Like people living in national borderlands elsewhere, Tejanos embraced their ambiguous national identity to their advantage." Valerio-Jiménez, *River of Hope*, 255.

28. Quoted in Thompson *Vaqueros in Blue and Gray*, 56, 57 (quotation).

29. Thompson, *Vaqueros in Blue and Gray*, 26–30.

30. Thompson, *Vaqueros in Blue and Gray*, 7, 27 (quotation), 48, 58.

31. Thompson, *Vaqueros in Blue and Gray*, 43, 46 (quotation).

32. Thompson, *Vaqueros in Blue and Gray*, 45, 47.

33. Thompson, *Vaqueros in Blue and Gray*, 12, 13 (quotations).

34. Thompson, *Vaqueros in Blue and Gray*, 49.

35. Smyrl, "Texans in the Union Army," 235. For a biography on Davis, see Moneyhon, *Edmund J. Davis*.

36. Thompson, *Mexican Texans in the Union Army*, 10, 13 (quotation); Thompson, *Vaqueros in Blue and Gray*, 61; Bee to Anderson, November 30, 1862, OR, ser. 1, vol. 15, 881–83.

37. Thompson, *Mexican Texans in the Union Army*, 15–16, 16.

38. Thompson, *Mexican Texans in the Union Army*, 8 (quotation); Thompson, *Cortina*, 109.

39. Zapata to Pérez, n.d. 1863 (quotations), and July 24, 1863, in Zapata Correspondence, FCV, AGENL; Thompson, *Mexican Texans in the Union Army*, 8, 16, 17.

40. Thompson, *Vaqueros in Blue and Gray*, 50; James W. Daddysman, "Zapata, Octaviano," in *Handbook of Texas Online*, http://www.tshaonline.org/handbook/online /articles/fza12 (quotation); Rippy, "Mexican Projects," 303.

41. "From Texas," *Augusta Chronicle*, April 23, 1863, p. 2; Gurza Lavalle, *Una vecindad efímera*, 97–103; Rippy, "Mexican Projects," 303.

42. Smyrl, "Texans in the Union Army," 237–38 (quotations); Thompson, *Vaqueros in Blue and Gray*, 52. Bee's role is subject to debate. Michael Collins (*Crooked River*, 19, 20) claims that Bee was involved in the raid, though he denied it.

43. Bee to Turner, September 11, 1863 (quotations), OR, ser. 1, vol. 26, pt. 1, 284; Benavides to Yager, September 3, 1863, OR, ser. 1, vol. 26, pt. 1, 285; Thompson, *Vaqueros in Blue and Gray*, 61; Daddysman, "Zapata."

44. Smyrl, "Texans in the Union Army," 244 (quotation), 245; Thompson, *Mexican Texans in the Union Army*, 14–15.

45. Thompson, *Mexican Texans in the Union Army*, 15.

46. Thompson, *Cortina*, 136 (quotation), 152.

47. Thompson, "Vidal, Adrián J," in *Handbook of Texas Online*, http://www.tshaonline .org/handbook/online/articles/fvi14.

48. Russell to Bloomfield, November 28, 1863, OR, ser. 1, vol. 53, 916–17; Monday and Vick, *Petra's Legacy*, 105–7.

49. *State Gazette*, December 30, 1863, p. 1.

50. Thompson, "Vidal."

51. Thompson, "Vidal."

52. Thompson, *Mexican Texans in the Union Army*, 16, 42.

53. Davis to Ord, February 10, 1864, OR, ser. 1, vol. 34, pt. 2, 287–89.

54. Quoted in Thompson, *Mexican Texans in the Union Army*, 25.

55. Thompson, *Mexican Texans in the Union Army*, 25, 28. Desertion was also common among Anglo troops. Smyrl, "Texans in the Union Army," 247.

56. Control of the border region would further other Union objectives, such as providing refuge to fleeing Texas Unionists and hope to republican forces in Mexico in their war against the imperialists.

57. "Texas Items of Interest," *Weekly Telegraph*, December 22, 1863, p. 1, reprinted from the *San Antonio Herald*.

58. "Items of Interest," *Tri-Weekly Telegraph*, December 18, 1863, p. 2, reprinted from *State Gazette*; John Adams, *Conflict and Commerce*, 90.

59. Quoted in Carroll, "Texas Collection," 455.

60. Benavides to Vidaurri, February 7, 1862, FCV, AGENL.

61. Vidaurri to Benavides, February 16, 1862 (quotation); Benavides to Vidaurri, December 2, 1863, both in FCV, AGENL.

62. Quoted in Ford, *Rip Ford's Texas*, 357.

63. Benavides to Ford, March 21, 1864, OR, ser. 1, vol. 34, pt. 1, 648–49; Thompson, *Mexican Texans in the Union Army*, 24.

64. Ford, *Rip Ford's Texas*, 357.

65. Ford, *Rip Ford's Texas*, 358.

66. Thompson, *Vaqueros in Blue and Gray*, 23 (first quotation); Thompson, *Mexican Texans in the Union Army*, viii (second quotation).

67. Ford, *Rip Ford's Texas*, 359 (quotation), 360; González-Quiroga, "Patria en peligro," 482.

68. Herron to Dwight, June 26, 1864, OR, ser. 1, vol. 34, pt. 1, 1053–54.

69. Ford, *Rip Ford's Texas*, 364–68.

70. Rippy, "Mexican Projects," 293 (quotation); Lilia Díaz, "Liberalismo militante," 614.

71. Kimmey to USDS, May 9, 1864, reel 1, CD, MTY, NARA.

72. Thompson, *Cortina*, 136 (quotation); Zorrilla, Miró Flaquer, and Herrera Pérez, *Tamaulipas, una historia compartida*, 2:36.

73. Meyer and Sherman, *Course of Mexican History*, 397 (quotations); Kimmey to USDS, May 9, 1864, reel 1, CD, MTY, NARA.

74. Lilia Díaz, "Liberalismo militante," 618; Zorrilla, Miró Flaquer, and Herrera Pérez, *Tamaulipas, una historia compartida*, 2:33, 38.

75. Ford, *Rip Ford's Texas*, 370 (quotation); Thompson, *Cortina*, 138.

76. Ford, *Rip Ford's Texas*, 369.

77. Thompson, *Cortina*, 145 (quotation); Ford, *Rip Ford's Texas*, 376; Zorrilla, Miró Flaquer, and Herrera Pérez, *Tamaulipas, una historia compartida*, 2:38.

78. Ford, *Rip Ford's Texas*, 383.

79. Thompson, *Cortina*, 147.

80. Herrera Pérez, *Breve historia de Tamaulipas*, 182–83 (quotation); Zorrilla, Miró Flaquer, and Herrera Pérez, *Tamaulipas, una historia compartida*, 2:43, 44.

81. González-Quiroga, "Patria en peligro," 493.

82. Creel to Carleton, September 18, 1864, OR, ser. 1, vol. 41, pt. 3, 245–47.

83. Thompson, *Cortina*, 148 (quotation); Herrera Pérez, *Breve historia de Tamaulipas*, 181; Zorrilla, Miró Flaquer, and Herrera Pérez, *Tamaulipas, una historia compartida*, 1:2, 43.

84. Beall, "Military Occupation of the Lower Rio Grande," 205, 206, 207, 214, 220; Sheridan to Rawlins, November 11, 1866, OR, ser. 1, vol. 48, pt. 1, 297–303.

85. Beall, "Military Occupation of the Lower Rio Grande," 209.

86. Grant to Sheridan, October 22, 1865, OR, ser. 1, vol. 48, pt. 2, 1242–43.

87. Thompson, *Cortina*, 154 (quotations); Zorrilla, Miró Flaquer, and Herrera Pérez, *Tamaulipas, una historia compartida*, 2:42.

88. Rippy, "Mexican Projects," 296–97, 298; Ford, *Rip Ford's Texas*, 388. Historian Patrick Kelly argues that an "illiberal alliance between the slaveholding Confederate States of America and monarchical France against the sister republics of Mexico

and the United States" did exist. In an interesting formulation, he sees the Civil War and the War of French Intervention as parts of an ideological struggle waged by Napoleonic France and the Confederacy against republicanism and, as such, believes they should be viewed "within a North American framework." See Kelly, "North American Crisis," 337, 338, 339 (quotation), 343.

89. Sheridan to Rawlins, November 11, 1866 (quotation), OR, ser. 1, vol. 48, pt. 1, 297–303; Sheridan to Grant, November 5, 1865, OR, ser. 1, vol. 48, pt. 2, 1252–53.

90. Robert Miller, "American Legion of Honor," 229 (quotation); Beall, "Military Occupation of the Lower Rio Grande," 213.

91. Ford, *Rip Ford's Texas*, 401, 403, 405 (quotation).

92. Robert Miller, *Arms across the Border*, 47, 60 (quotation); Lawrence Taylor, "Voluntarios extranjeros," 221.

93. Robert Miller, *Arms across the Border*, 42 (quotation), 43, 44; Cohen, "Texas-Mexico Border," 164–65.

94. Miller, *Arms across the Border*, 43, 53 (first quotation), 57, 58, 60 (second quotation), 59 (third quotation). Sturm was forced to appeal to the United States and Mexican Mixed Claims Commission of 1868 for redress.

95. Robert Miller, "American Legion of Honor," 236 (quotations); Schoonover, "Dollars over Dominion," 41; Robert Miller, *Arms across the Border*, 46.

96. Quoted in Robert Miller, *Arms across the Border*, 47.

97. Robert Miller, "American Legion of Honor," 230; Lawrence Taylor, "Voluntarios extranjeros," 222, 223.

98. Robert Miller, "American Legion of Honor," 229. Lawrence Douglas Taylor ("Voluntarios extranjeros," 224) believes that the number was less, perhaps in the hundreds. In addition to Miller's article, see W. A. Cornwall, "Maximilian and the American Legion," *Overland Monthly and Out West Magazine* 7, no. 5 (November 1871): 445–48, https://quod.lib.umich.edu/m/moajrnl/ahj1472.1-07.005/441:11?rgn=full+text;view =image.

99. Cornwall, "Maximilian and the American Legion," 445–46.

100. "Californians at the Siege of Queretaro," *New York Times*, August 3, 1867, https:// www.nytimes.com/1867/08/03/archives/californians-at-the-siege-of-queretaro .html.

101. Gilbert, "Safe in No-Man's Land," 73 (quotation); Ford, *Rip Ford's Texas*, 360.

102. Lucas Martínez, *Coahuila durante la intervención*, 109 (quotation), 162n, 219.

103. "Personal Recollections of the late President Juarez of Mexico," *Catholic World* 16, no. 91 (November 1872): 280, (quotation); http://www.mirrorservice.org/sites /ftp.ibiblio.org/pub/docs/books/gutenberg/4/9/9/4/49948/49948.txt; Lilia Díaz, "Liberalismo militante," 626.

104. Herrera Pérez, *Breve historia de Tamaulipas*, 183; Lilia Díaz, "Liberalismo militante," 623, 626.

105. Cloue to Weitzel, November 6, 1865; and Weitzel to Cloue, November 10, 1865, EDHR, USDS, 1866–67, 40–41.

106. Weitzel to Mejía, November 13, 1865, EDHR, USDS, 1866–67, 39. See also Zorrilla, Miró Flaquer, and Herrera Pérez, *Tamaulipas, una historia compartida*, 2:42.

107. For accounts of the battle see Thompson, *Cortina*, 164; Herrera Pérez, *Breve historia de Tamaulipas*, 183.

108. Díaz, "El liberalismo militante," 627–28.

109. The Bagdad Raid, or Bagdad Affair as it became known, is best explained by Thompson, *Cortina*, 167–70. Other sources with often contradictory details are Cohen, "Texas-Mexico Border," 164; Rayburn and Rayburn, *Century of Conflict*, 92, 98; Beall, "Military Occupation of the Lower Rio Grande," 213; Miller, *Arms across the Border*, 45; Zorrilla, Miró Flaquer, and Herrera Pérez, *Tamaulipas, textos de su historia*, 1:376, 2:44–45; Herrera Pérez, *Breve historia de Tamaulipas*, 184.

110. Thompson, *Cortina*, 167, 168 (quotations).

111. Thompson, *Cortina*, 168–69. Mejía served the Mexican government in various capacities. Bilingual and bicultural, he was sent to the United States shortly after the Bagdad raid to work with Romero and Carvajal in the procurement of arms. After the French intervention, he participated in Mexican politics and invested in various enterprises during the Porfirian period. One of his daughters, Ynéz, became an eminent botanist at the University of California, Berkeley, and donated her father's papers to that university (archived as Mexía Family Papers in the Bancroft Library).

112. Thompson, *Cortina*, 169; Escobedo to Weitzel, January 7, 1866, box 1, folder M, Mexía Family Papers, BL UCB.

113. Rodríguez, "Odisea para instalar el progreso," 223; Ford, *Rip Ford's Texas*, xl, 405, 406.

114. Thompson, *Cortina*, 178 (first quotation), 179 (second quotation); Zorrilla, Miró Flaquer, and Herrera Pérez, *Tamaulipas, textos de su historia*, 1:378; Cohen, "Texas-Mexico Border," 164.

115. Quoted in Thompson, *Cortina*, 180.

116. Robert Miller, *Arms across the Border*, 52.

117. Quoted in Cohen, "Texas-Mexico Border," 164; Zorrilla, Miró Flaquer, and Herrera Pérez, *Tamaulipas, una historia compartida*, 1:378.

118. Mayer, *Campaña y guarnición*, 145, 166–67; Lawrence Taylor, "Voluntarios extranjeros," 220, 221n.

119. "Encking" is probably a Spanish version of Eucking. A John P. Eucking is listed in the index of the War of the Rebellion, and one document refers to his valor in battle. See McCook to Pratt, July 6, 1863, OR, ser. 1, vol. 23, pt. 1, 548–49.

120. Mayer, *Campaña y guarnición*, 160.

121. Mayer, *Campaña y guarnición*, 160–61.

122. "Further Mexican News," *Dallas Herald*, July 21, 1866, p. 1.

123. Colné to Bernard, included in a letter from Romero to Seward, July 10, 1866, USDS, EDHR, 1866–67, p. 181; Meyer and Sherman, *Course of Mexican History*, 399; Thompson, *Cortina*, 181.

124. Zorrilla, Miró Flaquer, and Herrera Pérez, *Tamaulipas, textos de su historia*, 2:11; "Further Mexican News," *Dallas Herald*, July 21, 1866, p. 1.

125. Thompson, *Cortina*, 185, 186; Zorrilla, Miró Flaquer, and Herrera Pérez, *Tamaulipas, textos de su historia*, 2:12–14.

126. Testimony of Juan de Dios Arias, November 25, 1866, doc. 44, in Sugawara, *Mariano Escobedo*, 212–13.

127. Thompson, *Cortina*, 186, 187, 188 (quotation); Escobedo to Sedgwick, November 27, 1866, doc. 45, in Sugawara, *Mariano Escobedo*, 213–15. Canales had boasted around town that the American force was there to help him defend the city. Subsequently, Sedgwick was stripped of command and arrested on orders from Secretary of War Edwin Stanton.

128. Thompson, *Cortina*, 188, 189; Herrera Pérez, *Breve historia de Tamaulipas*, 189–90.

129. Escobedo to Juárez, December 6, 1866, doc. 49, in Sugawara, *Mariano Escobedo*, 219.

130. Martínez (*Coahuila durante la intervención*, 196) writes that American arms were "a determining factor." This may be an overstatement, but his knowledge of the matter is vast.

131. Martha Rodríguez, "Odisea para instalar el progreso," 223; Lilia Díaz, "liberalismo militante," 630; González, "Liberalismo triunfante," 635.

132. The claims of soldiers who accepted the cash bonus were denied because they had signed a document renouncing all further claims. See Robert Miller, "American Legion of Honor," 230, 240; and Lawrence Taylor, "Voluntarios extranjeros," 227, 228.

133. Quoted in Robert Miller, "American Legion of Honor," 239.

134. Taylor, "Voluntarios extranjeros," 228; Sheridan to Rawlins, November 11, 1866, OR, ser. 1, vol. 48, pt. 1, 297–303; Meyer and Sherman, *Course of Mexican History*, 401.

Chapter 7. A Most Violent Decade

1. Wilkinson, *Laredo and the Rio Grande Frontier*, 331.

2. Avery to USDS, April 24, 1875, Consular Despatches, Camargo (hereafter cited as CD, C), reel 1, NARA.

3. Van der Dennen and Falger claim, "Competition of two species for the same resources is . . . more fatal than a predatory-prey relation. Competition eventually leads to the extermination of the species with the smaller growth capacity." *Sociobiology and Conflict*, 8.

4. Oscar J. Martínez and Manuel Ceballos Ramírez affirm that boundary violations were the most important cause of conflict between the United States and Mexico in the nineteenth century. "Conflict and Accommodation," 136–40. They are correct only insofar as boundary violations mainly concerned officials of the two governments.

5. Daniel Cosío Villegas has written that on the Mexican side of the river "the absence of an economic activity that would provide a stable occupation to its inhabitants [and] the evident weakness of the central government to make its influence felt" contributed to the violence. Cosío Villegas, *Porfiriato*, 34–35.

6. Quoted in Jacoby, *Shadows at Dawn*, 228. Vidaurri was all too aware that many Mexicans, whom he referred to as "vermin," crossed the border to commit crimes that brought discredit to Mexico and reprisals from the Anglo-American population. He declared that the problem should be faced decisively because systematic violation of the law would "produce the total demoralization" of the region. Vidaurri to Zarco, April 13, 1861, in Zarco, "Información Europea," 316.

7. Rippy, *United States and Mexico*, 282.

8. Quoted in Callahan, "Mexican Border Troubles,"138. Callahan argues that the daily life of the people of region was characterized by an "economy of violence" (10) that included racial and cultural animosity, national disputes, and local factors.

9. Lea, *King Ranch*, 261–62 (quotation); Brooks, *Captives & Cousins*, 341.

10. The report is included in Hamilton Fish to Thomas A. Nelson, April 13, 1872, USDS, EDHR, 1872–73, pp. 414–16.

11. Ford, *Rip Ford's Texas*, 308–9.

12. Thompson, *Cortina*, 211; Lea, *King Ranch*, 262 (quotation).

13. Thompson, *Cortina*, 202.

14. Rayburn and Rayburn, *Century of Conflict*, 116, 122n1 (quotation); Wilkinson, *Laredo and the Rio Grande Frontier*, 335.

15. Thompson, *Cortina*, 208; Amberson, McAllen, and McAllen, *I Would Rather Sleep in Texas*, 316.

16. Monday and Vick, *Petra's Legacy*, 196; Amberson, McAllen, and McAllen, *I Would Rather Sleep in Texas*, 317. In his doctoral dissertation, Manuel Callahan argues that this commission and others established by the U.S. government fed a growing historiographical narrative of frontier conquest that "glorified Anglos while vilifying everyone else." In this "representational machine," Mexicans and Indians were criminalized and deemed "unworthy of the land they occupied." Callahan, "Mexican Border Troubles," 310.

17. *Informe de la Comisión Pesquisidora*, 35, 37 (quotation), 99.

18. *Informe de la Comisión Pesquisidora*, 9, 10, 17 (quotation), 39.

19. Quoted in Paul Taylor, *American-Mexican Frontier*, 63.

20. Paul Taylor, *American-Mexican Frontier*, 63.

21. Santleben, *Texas Pioneer*, 52.

22. *Informe de la Comisión Pesquisidora*, 13, 15, 17.

23. *Informe de la Comisión Pesquisidora*, 12.

24. *Informe de la Comisión Pesquisidora*, 80, 82 (quotation).

25. *Informe de la Comisión Pesquisidora*, 49, 81 (quotation), 83. Even Rip Ford acknowledged that cattle losses of Texans "might have been greatly inflated." Collins, *Crooked River*, 136.

26. Wilkinson, *Laredo and the Rio Grande Frontier*, 334–35, 335 (quotation). Commercial agent William Schuchardt was also persuaded that much of the raiding from Mexico was done by professional cattle thieves. See Schuchardt to USDS, July 15, 1872, reel 1, CD, PN, NARA.

27. Avery to USDS, April 24, 1875, reel 1, CD, C, NARA.

28. *Informe de la Comisión Pesquisidora*, 42, 53 (quotation), 56, 60, 61.

29. *Informe de la Comisión Pesquisidora*, 65, 66, 67, 69, 71, 73, 74, 77.

30. *Informe de la Comisión Pesquisidora*, 30, 51, 52, 84, 86; Nichols, "Limits of Liberty," 95.

31. *Informe de la Comisión Pesquisidora*, 102, 103–6. I have chosen to write about the findings of the Comisión Pesquisidora in greater detail than is customary in histories of the border region because U.S. historians have ignored it, downplayed its findings, or equated it with the U.S. Robb Commission. It was much more comprehensive than the latter. Its authors undertook a serious investigation, much as modern researchers do, exploring multiple sources and attempting to corroborate their findings. It is also a dissenting response to American versions of frontier conquest that glorify Anglos and denigrate Mexicans.

32. Durham, *Taming the Nueces Strip*, 137.

33. "A Brush with Outlaws," *Dallas Daily Herald*, October 3, 1876, p. 1.

34. *Weekly State Gazette*, April 27, 1878, p. 1. Fisher eventually gained some respectability, becoming a lawman in Uvalde County, but he and the notorious Ben Thompson were gunned down in an incident at a theater in San Antonio.

35. William Schuchardt to USDS, October 15, 1872, and September 28, 1872, reel 1, CD, PN, NARA.

36. Schuchardt to USDS, October 15, 1872.

37. Schuchardt to USDS, October 15, 1872.

38. Schuchardt to USDS, July 11, 1875, reel 1, CD, PN, NARA.

39. Mariscal to Fish, January 30, 1875, USDS, EDHR, 1875–76, no. 452, vol. 2, p. 955 (quotation), 961.

40. Mariscal to Fish, January 30, 1875, pp. 956, 961 (quotation), 962.

41. Fish to Mariscal, February 19, 1875, USDS, EDHR, 1875–76, no. 453, vol. 2, p. 974.

42. "A Midnight Deed," *Goliad Guard*, June 13, 1874, p. 2.

43. Huson, *Refugio*, 2:206, 208 (first quotation), 211 (second and third quotations), 214 (fourth quotation).

44. "Telegraphic Summary," *Dallas Daily Herald*, November 17, 1875, p. 1. The reference to American marauders is probably a typographical error or a Freudian slip. At the end of the report the grand jury called on the state and federal governments to "punish the criminals and protect the inhabitants against Mexican banditti."

45. Rippy, *United States and Mexico*, 290.

46. "Current Topics," *Intelligencer-Echo*, April 12, 1875, p. 2.

47. Metz, *Border*, 159.

48. "The Mexican Raiders Continuing Their Depredations along the Rio Grande," *Dallas Daily Herald*, April 25, 1875, p. 1.

49. Cynthia E. Orozco, "Nuecestown Raid of 1875," in *Handbook of Texas Online*, http://www.tshaonline.org/handbook/online/articles/jcnnt.

50. Quoted in Thompson, *Cortina*, 224.

51. For more information on the Nuecestown Raid, see Orozco, "Nuecestown Raid."

52. Samora, Bernal, and Peña, *Gunpowder Justice*, 47, 48 (quotation). For information on the Las Cuevas raid, see Callahan, "Mexican Border Troubles," 188–90; Rippy, *United States and Mexico*, 290–92; Cosío Villegas, *Porfiriato*, 44; Wilkinson, *Laredo and the Rio Grande Frontier*, 343–45.

53. Avery to USDS, November 25, 1875, reel 1, CD, C, NARA.

54. Cool, *Salt Warriors*, 2, 3.

55. Quoted in Callahan, "Mexican Border Troubles," 229. Callahan deals with some of the complexities of this conflict, including the fact that Mexicans "played key roles on both sides of the battle lines" and "Anglo allies could be counted among each faction" (197).

56. Callahan, "Mexican Border Troubles," 261.

57. Tijerina, *Tejano Empire*, 125–26, 129.

58. "The Rio Grande Border, History of the Present Trouble," *New York Times*, October 22, 1877, p. 2.

59. "The Rio Grande Border, History of the Present Trouble," p. 4. U.S. ambassador to Mexico John Foster opined that some Washington politicians desired a war with Mexico in order to distract public opinion, prop up the shaky government of Rutherford B. Hayes, and take another slice of Mexican territory. See Cosío Villegas, *Porfiriato*, 64. See also Webster, "Texas Manifest Destiny."

60. Hogan, *Texas Republic*, 265. It is also likely that Texas's propensity for violence stemmed in part from its experience with slavery. James David Nichols argues that slavery was a "social relationship structured by violence" because it entailed the "brutal subjugation of one human being by another." Nichols, "Limits of Liberty," 25.

61. Morales to Secretaría de Relaciones Exteriores, June 5, 1875, "Revistas políticas y comerciales remitidas por el Consulado de San Antonio," 1875–78, file 2-14-3164, Fondo de Gaveta, Archivo Histórico Genaro Estrada, Secretaría de Relaciones Exteriores.

62. Quoted in Paul Taylor, *American-Mexican Frontier*, 58.

63. Egbert L. Viele, "The Rio Grande Frontier and Our Relations with Mexico," *Frank Leslie's Popular Monthly* 4 (April 1878), 2, http://search.proquest.com/docview/136545620?accountid=6667.

64. Quoted in Durham, *Taming the Nueces Strip*, 35.

65. Quoted in Paul Taylor, *American-Mexican Frontier*, 59.

66. Paul Taylor, *American-Mexican Frontier*, 57. Against innocent Mexicans these vigilante groups applied the concept of "defensive conquest," also practiced by Anglos against hostile Indians. They were shot on sight "on the assumption that such 'savages' were likely to be involved in past or future assaults on Americans." See Jacoby, *Shadows at Dawn*, 113.

67. Coke to Ord, May 24, 1875, Adjutant General, M 666, "Mexican Border Troubles," microfilm roll 197, NARA.

68. Acuña, *Occupied America*, 39–40.

69. Durham, *Taming the Nueces Strip*, 44 (quotation), 54–55; Rayburn and Rayburn, *Century of Conflict*, 117; Collins, *Crooked River*, 192–93.
70. Cosío Villegas, *Porfiriato*, 44.
71. Durham, *Taming the Nueces Strip*, 38.
72. Durham, *Taming the Nueces Strip*, 61–62.
73. Quoted in Wilkinson, *Laredo and the Rio Grande Frontier*, 341–42, 342n. McNelly's stint with the rangers was brief, from 1875 to 1876. He retired to his farm and died of tuberculosis in 1877.
74. Santleben, *Texas Pioneer*, 261.
75. Bliss, *Reminiscences*, 447. Charles Winslow, the consular agent at Guerrero, Tamaulipas, documented the constant Indian activity in the region. See, for example, Winslow to USDS, September 26, 1871, Consular Despatches, Guerrero (hereafter cited as CD, G), reel 1, NARA.
76. Robinson, *I Fought a Good Fight*, 286.
77. Utley, "Range Cattle Industry," 428–29; DeLay, *War of a Thousand Deserts*, 308, 309; Robinson, *I Fought a Good Fight*, 280–81; Vizcaya Canales, *Tierra de guerra viva*, 389; Martha Rodríguez, *Guerra entre bárbaros y civilizados*, 83–84. In the New Mexico–Chihuahua borderlands, raids with a north-to-south trajectory targeting Mexico continued into the 1870s.
78. Rippy, *United States and Mexico*, 288; Schuchardt to USDS, June 25, 1870, reel 1, CD, PN, NARA; Fuentes to Secretario de Gobierno de Coahuila, February 22, 1871, folio 3, file 9, box 3, FS, AGEC.
79. Schuchardt to USDS, April 12, 1869, reel 1, CD, PN, NARA.
80. Schuchardt to USDS, July 11, 1869, reel 1, CD, PN, NARA.
81. Schuchardt to USDS, April 12, 1869 (quotation), and July 11, 1869, reel 1, CD, PN, NARA.
82. Minor, *Turning Adversity to Advantage*, 177–78. Apaches were not particular about who they raided and with whom they traded on either side of the border. They made pacts with certain Mexican communities to deal in stolen goods from other Mexican towns. In the words of one observer: "what was stolen from one Mexican found ready sale to another." Quoted in Jacoby, *Shadows at Dawn*, 58.
83. Schuchardt to USDS, July 15, 1872, reel 1, CD, PN, NARA.
84. Minor, *Turning Adversity to Advantage*, 180.
85. Metz, *Border*, 161, 162; Minor, *Turning Adversity to Advantage*, 182. Metz described Mackenzie as an "eccentric officer" who developed mental illness "that would eventually force his retirement and early death in an insane asylum" (161).
86. Minor, *Turning Adversity to Advantage*, 182.
87. Mulroy, *Freedom on the Border*, 115 (first quotation), 117 (second quotation).
88. "Augur's Annual Report," September 30, 1873, in Wallace, *Mackenzie's Correspondence*, 62. Nichols ("Limits of Liberty," 296) states that Mackenzie's raid "represents a new willingness on the part of the U.S. government to appropriate the border-crossing practiced by mobile peoples who had long frustrated state efforts to assert sovereignty over the borderlands."

89. Schuchardt to USDS, February 13, 1874, reel 1, CD, PN, NARA.

90. U.S. Bureau of Indian Affairs, "Report of H. M. Atkinson," 170.

91. U.S. Bureau of Indian Affairs, "Report of H. M. Atkinson," 170; Schuchardt to USDS, April 12 and July 11, 1869, reel 1, CD, PN, NARA.

92. U.S. Bureau of Indian Affairs, "Report of H. M. Atkinson," 171; "The Kickapoos Moving," *Weekly Democratic Statesman*, September 25, 1873, p. 1.

93. U.S. Bureau of Indian Affairs, "Report of H. M. Atkinson," 172.

94. U.S. Bureau of Indian Affairs, "Report of H. M. Atkinson," 173.

95. Cepeda to Atkinson, September 10, 1873, folio 3, file 7, box 9, FS, AGEC.

96. Minor, *Turning Adversity to Advantage*, 184, 185; Robinson, *I Fought a Good Fight*, 295.

97. Steven Pinker, "We're Getting Nicer Every Day: A History of Violence," *New Republic Online*, http://www.tnr.com/docprint.mhtml?i=20070319&s=pinker031907.

Chapter 8. Between Hate and Harmony

1. Prospecto, September 1, 1873, box 1, CIT, AGENL.

2. *Houston Daily Mercury*, January 21, 1874, p. 2.

3. Campbell, *Gone to Texas*, 306, 472.

4. Viele, "Rio Grande Frontier," *Frank Leslie's Popular Monthly* 4: 7 (quotation), 11.

5. *Tri-Weekly State Gazette*, October 7, 1870, p. 3; advertisements for Mexican laborers also appeared in the *San Antonio Daily Herald*, February 17 and April 7, 1867, p. 3.

6. Quoted in González Navarro, *Colonización en México*, 126–27.

7. Schuchardt to USDS, January 3, 1872, and April 15, 1877, reel 1, CD, PN, NARA.

8. Francisco Rodríguez to Governor, October 27, 1868, folio 3, file 9, box 12, FS, AGEC; Valentín de los Santos to Secretario de Gobierno, April 25, 1873, folio 6, file 4, box 4, FS, AGEC. Josef Barton argues that increased land concentration in the second half of the nineteenth century deprived many rural people from owning land and they became "more dependent than ever on wages and migration for their living." Barton, "At the Edge of the Storm," 16n23.

9. Arellano, *Ignacio Ramírez*, 59 (quotation). Ramírez's hope became Harvard thinker Samuel Huntington's fear when he wrote in 2004 that with the increasing Hispanic presence and influence, the United States was in danger of losing "its cultural and linguistic unity and [becoming] a bilingual, bicultural society." Huntington, *Who Are We?* 20.

10. "Brady's Glimpse of Texas," *Houston Telegraph*, November 28, 1872, p. 3.

11. Montejano, *Anglos and Mexicans*, 54–55; De León, *Comunidad tejana*, 77; John Adams, *Conflict and Commerce*, 100.

12. Ramírez, "The Vaquero and Ranching," 105–7.

13. Alonzo, *Tejano Legacy*, 11, 279.

14. Paul Taylor, *American-Mexican Frontier*, 71; Calvert and De León, *History of Texas*, 163.

15. Arreola, *Tejano South Texas*, 112 (quotation), 114.

16. Carlson, *Texas Woollybacks*, 44, 179; "Texas Facts and Fancies," *Weekly Democratic Statesman*, June 24, 1880, p. 2 (quotation).

17. *Weekly Democratic Statesman*, November 10, 1881, p. 4.

18. John Adams, *Conflict and Commerce*, 101.

19. De León, *Comunidad tejana*, 82–83.

20. Ramírez, "The Vaquero and Ranching," 108, 134. The names and salaries of workers at El Rincon are found in the Coleman-Fulton Pasture Company Records, box 4ZE53, BCAH, UTA.

21. Santleben, *Texas Pioneer*, 227–28. A list of freighters employed by Twohig is located in box 3N1, TP, BCAH, UTA. Also see John Adams, *Conflict and Commerce*, 105.

22. Santleben, *Texas Pioneer*, 93 (first quotation), 95 (second quotation).

23. "Horrible Massacre of Nine Texans," *The Standard*, May 25, 1872, p. 2; Woolford, "Burr G. Duval Diary," 495n.

24. "Texas News," *Tri-Weekly State Gazette*, September 7, 1870, p. 1; *Houston Telegraph*, March 31, 1870, p. 4; De León, *Comunidad tejana*, 107–8.

25. Quoted in Paul Taylor, *American-Mexican Frontier*, 81; Foley, *White Scourge*, 25–26. The base salary for many farming and ranching operations in the 1870s was about $15 a month. For a discussion of various occupations and their salary structures, see De León, *Comunidad tejana*, 82–87.

26. De León, *Mexican Americans in Texas*, 35.

27. Barton, "At the Edge of the Storm," 59.

28. Stewart and De León, *Not Room Enough*, 28, 29 (quotation).

29. Montejano, *Anglos and Mexicans*, 104 (first quotation), 114 (second quotation). This process unfolded slowly because Mexican stock raisers were still the majority of landholders in the Nueces Strip in the 1870s and 1880s. Between 1885 and 1900 "most Tejanos became minority landholders in their own land." See Alonzo, *Tejano Legacy*, 12, 282, 283 (quotation).

30. Data on these immigrants appears in a series of tables in Cerutti and González-Quiroga, *Norte de México y Texas*, 168–70. The naturalization applications can be consulted in "Declarations of Intentions," Bexar County Naturalization Records, Texas State Archives.

31. De León, *Mexican Americans in Texas*, 43.

32. Smith and Smith. "Life of Valeriano Torres," 39, 43 (quotation), 44–45, 50.

33. Gómez, *Crossing the Rio Grande*, 2, 10 (quotation), 48, 84.

34. Elliott Young writes, "Culture, just like capital, has proven to be far more transnational than nationalist imaginations could have predicted." Young, *Catarino Garza's Revolution*, 16.

35. Consular offices were located in New York, New Orleans, San Francisco, Brownsville, Galveston, San Antonio, and Franklin (El Paso). Lafragua to Governor of Nuevo León, September 1, 1872, box 57, SMRE-C, AGENL; De León, *Mexican Americans in Texas*, 35 (quotation). The population figures for 1850 and 1880 are good estimates, arrived at by various historians. Terry G. Jordan discovered a lost

census of 1887 that records 78,878 Mexicans in Texas, giving credence to the 1880 estimate. Jordan, "1887 Census," 272.

36. Quoted in Barton, "At the Edge of the Storm," 50. In another example that defies Frederick Jackson Turner's frontier thesis that westward expansion shaped the American character, coming into a new environment did not greatly alter the conduct and character of Mexicans. Ray Allen Billington has written that "the bulk of the customs and beliefs of the pioneers were transmitted, and were only slightly modified by the changing culture in which they lived." Quoted in Weber, *Mexican Frontier*, 278.

37. Baez Camargo and Grubb, *Religion in Mexico*, 89.

38. Rankin, *Twenty Years among the Mexicans*, xviii, xix, 83, 84 (quotation).

39. Rankin, *Twenty Years among the Mexicans*, xxi. The state archive of Nuevo León contains complaints of harassment from Protestant converts and missionaries in various towns. See box 4, Asuntos Eclesiásticos (hereafter cited as AE), AGENL for complaints from the towns of Escobedo, Agualeguas, and Marín.

40. Rankin, *Twenty Years among the Mexicans*, xxii, xxiii (quotation), 105–6.

41. Rankin, *Twenty Years among the Mexicans*, xvii–xviii, xxxiv n. 28, 30. After Hickey's death a feud erupted among the Protestants in Monterrey between those who favored Rankin's Presbyterianism and those who preferred Westrup's Baptist Church. Accounts of this division are provided in Rankin's book and in Westrup, *Principios*.

42. Informe, December 31, 1880, box 8, EM-Monterrey, AGENL.

43. Ulrich to USDS, April 21, 1874 (quotation), and April 27, 1874, reel 3, CD, MTY, NARA.

44. Union Baptist Association, *Minutes*, 6–7 (quotation), 8–9, 58.

45. "The Baptist Excursion to Mexico," *Dallas Weekly Herald*, January 29, 1885, p. 5.

46. "In Mexico," *Fort Worth Daily Gazette*, August 15, 1890, p. 8.

47. "In Mexico." The liberals in charge of government policy believed that Protestantism's promotion of education would help to lift up the Indian population. This idea was summed up in a phrase attributed to Juárez in which declared that the Indians "need a religion that obligates them to read instead of spending their earnings on candles for their saints." Bastian, *Los disidentes*, 38.

48. Purdie and Purdie, "Correspondence," 139.

49. Quoted in Knowles, *Samuel A. Purdie*, 64, 66 (quotation). Purdie did however chide Mexicans for their affinity for "low amusements," such as the "lottery, the theatre, and cock fighting."

50. Knowles, *Samuel A. Purdie*, 66.

51. Knowles, *Samuel A. Purdie*, 68.

52. Holding, *Decade of Mission Life*, 65, 67; Ruiz Guerra, *Hombres nuevos*, 68; Rankin, *Twenty Years among the Mexicans*, 7n5. Also see the Instituto Laurens website: https://www.laurens.edu.mx/.

53. Bastian, *Los disidentes*, 141.

54. Bastian, "Las sociedades protestantes," 143.

55. Náñez, *Rio Grande Conference*, 42–45; Juan Martínez, *Sea la Luz*, 62.

56. Nail, *Texas Methodist Centennial Yearbook*, 183.

57. Náñez, *Rio Grande Conference*, 42–48. Juan Martínez, *Sea la Luz*, 63. Headen was another European-born man of the border region with close ties to Mexico. A native of Ireland, he was an admired civic leader in Corpus Christi, where he was a merchant and served several terms as mayor. He lived his last years in Mexico. See *Weekly Corpus Christi Caller*, September 18, 1908, p. 4, and "William Headen," *Weekly Corpus Christi Caller*, October 9, 1908, p. 5.

58. W. M. Sabin, "Methodism in San Antonio, Texas," *Western Christian Advocate* 48, no. 2 (1881): 14, American Periodicals Online, http://search.proquest.com/docview /1263512012accountid=6667.14 (quotation); American Tract Society, "Fifth Annual Report," 5.

59. Brackenridge and García-Treto, *Iglesia Presbiteriana*, 17 (quotations), 17–18.

60. Brackenridge and García-Treto, *Iglesia Presbiteriana*, 20 (quotations); Juan Martínez, *Sea la Luz*, 67.

61. Brackenridge and García-Treto, *Iglesia Presbiteriana*, 21.

62. Brackenridge and García-Treto, *Iglesia Presbiteriana*, 22.

63. This description is from a letter, dated February 11, 1874, which is quoted in Westrup, *Principios*, 14, 16 (quotation).

64. José Rodríguez, *José Policarpo Rodríguez*, 89, 90–91, 94 (quotation), 98.

65. José Rodríguez, *José Policarpo Rodríguez*, 111–13, 116 (quotations).

66. José Rodríguez, *José Policarpo Rodríguez*, 94 (quotation), 99, 100, 101.

67. *Periódico Oficial*, October 24, 1868, p. 1.

68. Autorización, February 10, 1867, box 4, AE, AGENL.

69. Examples of these requests can be found in petitions dated March 25, July 31, and November 13, 1862; November 19, 1863; and December 9, 14, and 23, 1864, box 3, AE, AGENL.

70. Cabildo Eclesiástico de Monterrey to Gobierno de la Mitra, February 6, 1867, no. 338, folder 56, box 5, Archivo Diocesano (hereafter cited as AD).

71. Document, no date, in folder Circulares y cartas pastorales de Francisco Paula Verea, box Circulares Obispos 1854–1892, AD.

72. Pastoral Letter, September 16, 1870, folder Circulares y cartas pastorales de Francisco Paula Verea, box Circulares Obispos 1854–1892, AD. Little evidence of the abuses committed by the Catholic clergy against the population is found in the Diocesan Archive, but much can be found in the state archives.

73. Sermon, September 8, 1884, no. 412, folder 64, box 5, AD.

74. Tapia, *Montes de Oca*, 84.

75. Guerra de Luna, *Los Madero*, 571–76; Tapia, *Montes de Oca*, 67, 68, 69.

76. Tapia, *Montes de Oca*, 50, 71 (quotation). W. D. Powell later reported that the state government had offered him monetary support, but he refused it in order to maintain his independence and observe the separation of church and state. See "In Mexico," *Fort Worth Daily Gazette*, August 15, 1890, p. 8.

77. Guerra de Luna, *Los Madero*, 570. Madero was among a long line of leaders in the Mexican border region who expressed admiration for American values. Others

were Bernardo Gutiérrez de Lara, Antonio Canales, Juan Pablo Anaya, and José María Carvajal.

78. Parisot, *Reminiscences of a Texas Missionary,* 115; M. J. Gilbert, *Archdiocese of San Antonio,* 14, 16.

79. Moore, *Through Fire and Flood,* 175.

80. M. J. Gilbert, *Archdiocese of San Antonio,* 15.

81. Parisot, *Reminiscences of a Texas Missionary,* 120.

82. Monday and Vick, *Petra's Legacy,* 320.

83. Monday and Vick, *Petra's Legacy,* 225 (quotation); Smith and Smith "Life of Valeriano Torres," 60–61n2.

84. Parisot, *Reminiscences of a Texas Missionary,* 130.

85. Vález, "Pilgrimage of Hispanics," 181, 182 (quotation).

86. Wright, "Pioneer Religious Congregations," 82.

87. Vález, "Pilgrimage of Hispanics," 183.

88. Vález, "Pilgrimage of Hispanics," 184.

89. Moore, *Through Fire and Flood,* 173.

90. Monday and Vick, *Petra's Legacy,* 287.

91. Tapia, *Montes de Oca,* 79.

92. Vález, "Pilgrimage of Hispanics," 187.

93. Neumann, *Centennial History of St. Joseph's Church,* 15.

94. Wright, "From Hispanic Gateway to Border Byway," 7, 10, 11.

95. Parisot, *Reminiscences of a Texas Missionary,* 77 (quotation), 177.

96. Moore, *Through Fire and Flood,* 173 (quotations); Mendirichaga, *Colegio de San Juan,* 84–87.

97. Mendirichaga, *Colegio de San Juan,* 88 (quotation), 90.

98. Mendirichaga, *Colegio de San Juan,* 92; Moore, *Through Fire and Flood,* 174.

99. Benavides to Vidaurri, March 10, 1863, FCV, AGENL.

100. Navarro to Madero, May 17, 1872, Fondo Evaristo Madero (hereafter cited as FEM), AGEC.

101. Santleben, *Texas Pioneer,* 301–2.

102. St. Pierre to Madero, July 30, 1884, FEM, AGEC.

103. Groos to Madero, August 6, 1898, FEM, AGEC; "San Antonio Academy," *San Antonio Daily Light,* April 28, 1886, p. 1. Some San Antonio schools advertised in Mexican newspapers. St. Mary's Catholic Institute advertised in a Monterrey newspaper that it offered business courses, as well as English, Spanish, German, art, and music. See *El Centinela,* July 18, 1869.

104. Examples are Schuchardt to Commanding Officer, Fort Duncan, October 11, 1876, reel 1, CD, PN, NARA; and Haynes to USDS, May 29, 1878, reel 1, CD, NL, NARA.

105. Sumpter, *Paso del Aguila,* 98–99n. The claimants asked for more than $11,000,000, a sum deemed ridiculous by almost everyone who was familiar with Piedras Negras. They eventually obtained $50,000.

106. Santleben, *Texas Pioneer,* 126.

107. Santleben, *Texas Pioneer,* 122.

108. "Obituary," *The Two Republics*, December 25, 1869, p. 3.

109. Amberson, McAllen, and McAllen, *I Would Rather Sleep in Texas*, 126, 175–76, 201, 361 (quotations).

110. Monday and Vick, *Petra's Legacy*, 3 (quotation), 43, 45, 47, 57, 80.

111. Monday and Vick, *Petra's Legacy*, 170.

112. Amberson, McAllen, and McAllen, *I Would Rather Sleep in Texas*, 341.

113. Limerick, *Legacy of Conquest*, 27.

114. Santleben, *Texas Pioneer*, 55.

115. Santleben, *Texas Pioneer*, 169–70.

116. Bliss, *Reminiscences*, 21, see also 428, 434.

117. Bliss, *Reminiscences*, 20.

118. Santleben, *Texas Pioneer*, 228–29.

119. Bliss, *Reminiscences*, 122n17, 466 (quotation).

120. Haley, *Charles Schreiner, General Merchandise*, 1, 5, 20–21 (quotation). Schreiner became a large landholder and banker and established the Schreiner Institute, which later became Schreiner College. See W. Eugene Hollon, "Schreiner, Charles Armand," in *Handbook of Texas Online*, http://www.tshaonline.org/handbook /online/articles/fsc15.

121. Bliss, *Reminiscences*, 489.

122. Baylor, *Into the Far, Wild Country*, 141 (quotations), 145–47.

123. Baylor, *Into the Far, Wild Country*, 276.

124. Baylor, *Into the Far, Wild Country*, 287, 288 (quotation).

125. Memorias de Gobernadores, Genaro Garza García, AGENL. See also Weber to USDS, September 30, 1879, reel 3, CD, MTY, NARA.

126. Schuchardt to Nelson, July 28, 1869, reel 1, CD, PN, NARA.

127. Juan Weber to USDS, June 15, 1880, reel 3, CD, MTY, NARA.

128. Kelsey to USDS, May 30, 1870, reel 1, CD, C, NARA.

129. Ulrich to USDS, February 18 and April 6, 1870, reel 2, CD, MTY, NARA.

130. Metz, *Border*, 166 (quotation), 167.

131. Myers to Mackenzie, October 9, 1878, in Wallace, *Mackenzie's Correspondence*, 222.

132. Haynes to USDS, July 11, 1878, reel 1, CD, NL, NARA.

133. Winslow to USDS, December 15, 1881, reel 1, CD, G, NARA. The prohibition against Americans buying land close to the border was ratified in 1876. See González Navarro, *Extranjeros en México*, 16. See also Pani, "Ciudadanos precarios," 635.

134. Schuchardt to Nelson, July 28, 1869, reel 1, CD, PN, NARA.

135. Ulrich to USDS, November 3, 1871, reel 2, CD, MTY, NARA.

136. Ulrich to USDS, April 13, 1872, reel 2, CD, MTY, NARA.

137. Ulrich to USDS, June 28, July 12, August 8, and December 22, 1873 (quotations), reel 2, CD, MTY, NARA.

138. González, "Liberalismo triunfante," 644.

139. González Navarro, *Extranjeros en México*, 2:16, 135; González, "Liberalismo triunfante," 649 (quotation).

140. Pani, "Ciudadanos precarios," 628 (quotation); González Navarro, *Extranjeros en México*, 2:20, 144.

141. Plutarco Ornelas to Gobierno de Coahuila, August 9, 1879, folio 2, file 8, box 5, FS, AGEC.

142. Jenne to USDS, December 20, 1879, reel 1, CD, NL, NARA.

143. Schuchardt to USDS, July 11, 1875, reel 1, CD, PN, NARA.

144. Santleben, *Texas Pioneer*, 294–95, 296 (quotation).

145. "In Mexico," *Fort Worth Daily Gazette*, August 15, 1890, p. 8.

146. Ulrich to USDS, July 31, 1873, reel 2, CD, MTY, NARA. Information about Howerton was provided by Sergio Javier García Zapata, one of his descendants.

147. Bee to McKnight, July 18, 1866, and Russell to McKnight, March 8, 1866, folder 1.2, box 3G141, David McKnight III Family Papers (hereafter cited as DMP), BCAH, UTA.

148. Bee to McKnight, July 25, 1866, folder 1.2, box 3G141, DMP, BCAH, UTA. McKnight traveled throughout northern Mexico providing medical services. He died tragically in a buggy accident in 1873. On the relationship between Russell and Milmo, see Arthur Mayer, "San Antonio, Frontier Entrepot," 453, 454.

149. "Letter from a Rebel," *Weekly Telegraph*, September 11, 1861, p. 4 (quotation); Bee to McKnight, December 2, 1866, folder 1.2, box 3G141, DMP, BCAH, UTA. Historian Michael L. Collins (*Crooked River*, 44, 102) writes that Bee, like other Confederate officials, profited from the cotton trade and made a "personal fortune." I have not seen evidence of this. While living in Monterrey he appeared to be almost destitute.

150. *Revista Universal*, October 16, 1869, p. 3. The son who was baptized in Saltillo was Carlos Bee. He went on to have a successful life as a lawyer in San Antonio and, like his father, was a member of the Democratic Party and served in the Texas house and senate. He became one of the most admired politicians in Texas.

151. Santleben, *Texas Pioneer*, 174.

152. Santleben, *Texas Pioneer*, 175.

153. *Weekly Democratic Statesman*, October 9, 1879, p. 2.

154. Nixon, "Paschal, Frank," *Handbook of Texas Online*.

155. Truett and Young, *Continental Crossroads*, ix.

156. Cited in Barber, "Lost Art of Cooperation." This idea is also embodied in Robert Wright's logic of non-zero-sum games. See also Pinker, "We're Getting Nicer," *New Republic Online*.

Chapter 9. Pacification and Economic Integration

1. Foster, *Trade with Mexico*, 6. Historian Janice Lee Jayes reports the pamphlet was also published in Spanish and it "infuriated Mexicans who responded angrily to the implication that Mexico was a land of banditry and corruption." Matías Romero, who had spent many years in the United States, responded with a stinging two-hundred-page rebuttal of Foster. "The Díaz administration, Romero assured Americans, was committed to safeguarding the property of investors and

securing the political and economic stability needed for trade." Jayes, *Illusion of Ignorance*, 48.

2. Foster, *Trade with Mexico*, 29.

3. Foster, *Trade with Mexico*, 30.

4. Foster, *Trade with Mexico*, 7, 8 (quotation), 11, 15, 21–23.

5. Foster, *Trade with Mexico*, 25, 41 (quotation).

6. Foster, *Trade with Mexico*, 28.

7. Foster, *Trade with Mexico*, 9, 28. Some Mexican historians have written critically of the nineteenth century. Luis González wrote that Europeans refused to come to Mexico because of the risk to their safety. Mexico, he added, was "famous for its crimes" and "had acquired in half a century of independence a vast discredit." González, "Liberalismo triunfante," 645.

8. Foster, *Trade with Mexico*, 31 (quotation), 35.

9. Foster, *Trade with Mexico*, 33 (quotation), 39–40. Despite Foster's reservations, Americans had already invested in Mexico. In the 1860s American businessmen channeled funds into mining and agricultural projects in Northwest Mexico, a region far from the civil wars raging in both countries. Several million dollars were invested in mines in Sonora and in cotton cultivation in Sinaloa. This history demonstrated that, because of its abundant natural resources, a peaceful Mexico would be attractive to American investors. See Schoonover, "Dollars over Dominion," 24, 26, 28, 39, 40–41, 44–45.

10. *Tri-Weekly Telegraph*, October 30, 1865, p. 4.

11. "Local News," *Nueces Valley*, January 27, 1872, p. 3.

12. *The Standard*, April 26, 1873, p. 1.

13. Quoted from the *Indianola Times* by the *Southern Intelligencer*, July 26, 1866, p. 2.

14. *Houston Telegraph*, September 5, 1872, p. 1, and September 12, 1872, p. 2 (quotation). These articles were originally published in the *San Antonio Herald*.

15. Guerra de Luna, *Los Madero*, 457, 498–504, 508, 511.

16. Wood, *John Twohig*, 46; Administrador de Aduana to Gobierno del Estado de Coahuila, May 28, 1866, folio 12, file 9, box 2, FS, AGEC; Twohig to Madero, February 2, 1867, p. 29, Letterpress #3, TP, BCAH, UTA.

17. Anderson to Madero, October 6, 1881, FEM, AGEC; Guerra de Luna, *Los Madero*, 524.

18. State Department document, October 27, 1867, reel 1, CD, PN, NARA; Guerra de Luna, *Los Madero*, 432.

19. Lincoln to De los Santos, July 22, 1866, box 2, James Lincoln Papers, Daughters of the Republic of Texas Library, San Antonio, Texas. A larger collection of James Lincoln's papers is housed at BCAH, UTA.

20. Untitled document, August 26, 1869, box 2R72, Kleiber Papers, BCAH, UTA; Schuchardt to USDS, October 15, 1870, reel 1, CD, PN, NARA.

21. Ely, "Gone from Texas," 461 (quotation); Amberson, McAllen, and McAllen, *I Would Rather Sleep in Texas*, 257.

22. Garza González, *Cronista desconocido*, 146.

23. Applegate and Hanselka, "Junta de los Rios," 39; Utley, "Range Cattle Industry," 426.

24. "The Great Range," *Weekly Statesman*, October 4, 1888, p. 12 (quotation); Carlson, *Texas Woollybacks*, 44.

25. Ulrich to USDS, October 8, 1874, and Weber to USDS, August 10, 1879, both in reel 3, CD, MTY, NARA; Salvucci, "Origins and Progress of U.S.-Mexican Trade," 720–21 (quotation).

26. Schuchardt to USDS, April 12, 1869, and July 15, 1872, reel 1, CD, PN, NARA; Avery to USDS, September 2, 1878, reel 1, CD, C, NARA; Jenne to USDS, October 5, 1880, reel 1, CD, NL, NARA; Weber to USDS, August 10, 1879, reel 3, CD, MTY, NARA.

27. Woolford, "Burr G. Duval Diary," 510 (quotation); Applegate and Hanselka, "Junta de los Rios," 39, 44. The demise of the Chihuahua Trail through Texas was brought about by the construction of the railroad between El Paso and San Antonio in 1883. Trade diminished even before this time because in 1875 Indianola was destroyed by a hurricane. The port recovered once, but was flattened again eleven years later and was not rebuilt.

28. Haynes to USDS, January 2, 1879, reel 1, CD, NL, NARA; Winslow to USDS, August 11, 1881, reel 1, CD, G, NARA; Kelsey to USDS, January 12, and May 13, 1870, reel 1, CD, C, NARA.

29. Ulrich to USDS, October 1, 1871, April 27, 1875, June 22, 1875, and January 17, 1876, and Weber to USDS, September 12, 1876, and January 12, 1879, reel 3, CD, MTY, NARA.

30. Cosío Villegas, *Porfiriato* 37; Wilkinson, *Laredo and the Rio Grande Frontier*, 336. One powerful voice in Mexico spoke out against the zona libre. Minister of Finance Matías Romero opposed it because it made smuggling easier, harmed legal commerce, and reduced government revenues.

31. Haynes to USDS, September 28, 1879, reel 1, CD, NL, NARA.

32. Wilkinson, *Laredo and the Rio Grande Frontier*, 336.

33. Haynes to USDS, September 28, 1879, and Jenne to USDS, July 2, 1880, reel 1, CD, NL, NARA. Richard J. Salvucci explains that although overland exports from the United States into Mexico went unrecorded until 1893, it is evident that "smuggling from Texas into the northern Free Zone was rampant in the middle and later 1870s." Salvucci, "Origins and Progress of U.S.-Mexican Trade," 725. His observation is based on the increase in Mexican silver exports (which *were* recorded as U.S. imports) to pay for smuggled goods.

34. Vizcaya Canales, *Orígenes de la industrialización*, 21–22.

35. Horgan, *Great River*, 869; Zorrilla, *Historia de las relaciones entre México y los Estados Unidos*, 472, Schuchardt to USDS, October 15, 1870, reel 1, CD, PN, NARA.

36. Winslow to USDS, January 21, 1883, reel 1, CD, G, NARA.

37. Haynes to USDS, September 28, 1879, reel 1, CD, NL, NARA. Cosío Villegas (*Porfiriato*, 182) writes that U.S. ambassador John Foster came to a similar conclusion after a trip to the border region in 1879.

38. Avery to USDS, October 1, 1878, reel 1, CD, C, NARA. Avery did not live to witness the full extent of U.S. commercial domination. After he left his post as commercial

agent, he was employed as superintendent of the Vallecillo mines and, in 1885, was killed by bandits while defending the company's strongbox. *Daily Cosmopolitan*, April 23, 1885, p. 2.

39. Ulrich to USDS, April 22, 1875, reel 3, CD, MTY, NARA; Kelsey to USDS, August 30, 1870, reel 1, CD, C, NARA.

40. Santleben, *Texas Pioneer*, 112–13 (quotation); Applegate and Hanselka, "Junta de los Rios," 41.

41. Santleben, *Texas Pioneer*, 112; Arthur Mayer, "San Antonio, Frontier Entrepot," 576–77.

42. Santleben, *Texas Pioneer*, 112–13 (first quotation), 113–14 (second quotation), 124–25.

43. "Glimpses of Texas—I: A Visit to San Antonio," *Scribner's Monthly* 7, no. 3 (1874), 322, http://search.proquest.com.proxy.libraries.smu.edu/americanperiodicals/docview /125530003/fulltextPDF/9D7B97F1C519424APQ/2?accountid=6667.

44. Sumpter, *Paso del Aguila*, 98–99; "Texas Items," *Tri-Weekly Telegraph*, February 12, 1866, p. 6.

45. Santleben, *Texas Pioneer*, 60; Santleben and Co. to Gómez, May 11, 1867, box 132, Fondo Concesiones y Permisos, AGENL.

46. Santleben, *Texas Pioneer*, 62, 62–63 (quotation), 73.

47. Santleben, *Texas Pioneer*, 71.

48. Santleben, *Texas Pioneer*, 91.

49. Santleben, *Texas Pioneer*, 95.

50. Santleben, *Texas Pioneer*, 227.

51. Santleben, *Texas Pioneer*, 200.

52. Santleben, *Texas Pioneer*, 201 (quotation), 206.

53. Santleben, *Texas Pioneer*, 146.

54. Santleben, *Texas Pioneer*, 203.

55. Santleben, *Texas Pioneer*, 40.

56. Santleben, *Texas Pioneer*, 296.

57. Santleben, *Texas Pioneer*, 227.

58. Schuchardt to USDS, April 12, 1869 (quotation), and July 15, 1872, reel 1, CD, PN, NARA.

59. Schoonover, "Dollars over Dominion," 26.

60. Raat, *Mexico and the United States*, 78.

61. Cerutti and González-Quiroga, *Norte de México y Texas*, 89–90; González-Quiroga, "Puerta de México," 227, n. 41. Arthur Mayer, "San Antonio, Frontier Entrepot," 492 (quotation), 495.

62. Arthur Mayer, "San Antonio, Frontier Entrepot," 488.

63. "Report on Santa Rosa," pamphlet, November 12, 1882, folder 7, box 2E311, LaCoste Papers, BCAH, UTA.

64. "San Antonio del Coyote," pamphlet, folder 14, box 2E311, LaCoste Papers, BCAH, UTA. An extensive letter in folder 10 documents many of LaCoste's transactions. It was written by his partner M. M. González and directed to Lucien LaCoste after the death of his father. A table of LaCoste's transactions in Mexico, compiled

from his correspondence, appears in González-Quiroga, "Puerta de México," 230–32. For information on the breakup of the Coahuilan latifundios, see Martha Rodríguez, "Odisea para instalar el progreso," 216, 223, 241; and Plana, *Reino del algodón*, 33, 53, 73–74.

65. Memorial de Convenio, March 7, 1874, folder 5, box 2E311, LaCoste Papers, BCAH, UTA; Calderón, *Mexican Coal Mining Labor*, 31–33.

66. Huntington to Madero, November 25, 1881, FEM, AGEC.

67. Twohig to Madero, January 13, 1881, box 3N3, TP, BCAH, UTA.

68. González-Quiroga, "Puerta de México," 231.

69. Calderón, *Mexican Coal Mining Labor*, 66; Cerutti, "Militares, terratenientes y empresarios," 108, 114, 123.

70. González-Quiroga, "Puerta de México," 231; "Coal for Texas," *San Antonio Light*, September 26, 1883, p. 1.

71. For information on these directors see "Monterey Items," *The Two Republics*, May 21, 1891, p. 1, and January 19, 1892, p. 3; Brownsville *Daily Herald*, January 5, 1893, p. 3, April 13, 1895, p. 7, April 19, 1895, p. 7, and July 7, 1896, p. 7; "Minas denunciadas," *Siglo Diez y Nueve*, June 24, 1892, p. 3; "News by Specials," *Dallas Weekly Herald*, December 7, 1882, p. 7; *Weekly Democratic Statesman*, January 4, 1883, p. 3.

72. Solicitud de Juan Willett, May 29, 1873, file 52, box 116, FPM, AMS.

73. Willett's advertisements appeared in *The Two Republics* throughout the 1870s. See, for example, December 23, 1874, p. 3.

74. "The Lands of Tlahualilo," *The Two Republics*, May 26, 1875, p. 2; Bee to McKnight, n.d. [March 1871?], folder 1.3, box 3G141, DMP, BCAH, UTA; Mildred T. Bee to her sister, November 24, 1872, folder 1.6, box 3G141, DMP, BCAH, UTA. The transformation of La Laguna into a cotton-producing powerhouse is examined in Plana, *Reino del algodón*.

75. The letter, originally published in the *Dallas Herald*, was reprinted in the *Weekly Democratic Statesman*, March 11, 1875, p. 2.

76. Román Jáquez, *Del Aguanaval a Sierra Mojada*, 53. This author provides information on the territorial dispute over the mines. "The Old Mexico Bonanza," *Fort Griffin Echo*, October 4, 1879, p. 1 (quotations); *Brenham Weekly Banner*, October 17, 1879, p. 1.

77. Quoted in "The Mojada Mines," *Denison Daily News*, September 21, 1879, p. 1. The paper misspelled John Willett's name as "Millett."

78. "The Rush to Mojada," *San Marcos Free Press*, November 1, 1879, p. 2.

79. "Emigration to Mexico," *The Two Republics*, April 11, 1880, p. 2.

80. "Laredo Items," *The Two Republics*, July 6, 1882, p. 1; González-Quiroga, "Puerta de México," 224.

81. Willet to Madero, January 9, 1882, FEM, AGEC. Other buyers of Willet's land at Nacimiento faced the same problem. A. E. and John Nobles of Victoria bought land near Santa Rosa and shipped by rail about 1,500 head of cattle to Eagle Pass with the intention of driving them down to their new ranch. They were prevented from

taking possession by the Seminoles and Kickapoos. See "Uncertainty of Mexican Land Titles," *Victoria Advocate*, August 9, 1884, p. 4.

82. Quoted in "Sierra Mojada Mines," *Denison Daily News*, December 23, 1879, p. 1; Román Jáquez, *Del Aguanaval a Sierra Mojada*, 54. Willett continued to promote the Sierra Mojada because he owned land there and because he became involved with a long-term project that would tie Corpus Christi's development to Mexico's economic potential. He envisioned the construction of a deep-water port at Padre Island with a rail connection to the rest of the United States and to the "Mexican National [Railroad] with its connections to bring us the products of the mines and the riches of Mexico." Information on his project is found in various newspaper reports, including "Going to Deep Water," *Fort Worth Daily Gazette*, December 17, 1886, p. 2; and "The Texas Harbor," *Fort Worth Daily Gazette*, July 29, 1884, p. 3.

83. Mario Cerutti has studied this process at length in various books analyzing the business activities of a number of Monterrey families that made their fortune in commerce and expanded to other areas, becoming in the process among Mexico's most powerful oligarchies. See, for example, Cerutti, *Burguesía y capitalismo en Monterrey; Burguesía, capitales e industria;* and *Propietarios, empresarios y empresa.* This regional oligarchy is also explored in Zaragoza, *Monterrey Elite.*

84. Garza González, *Cronista desconocido*, 146, 148–49, 151, 158, 159. Lorenzo González Treviño is known as Evaristo Madero's junior partner and husband of one of Madero's daughters, but he had multiple land, mining, and manufacturing interests in his own right. A list of his activities is found in Cerutti, *Burguesía y capitalismo en Monterrey*, 74–75.

85. Cerutti, *Propietarios, empresarios y empresa*, 56.

86. "Silver Mines," *Dallas Herald*, March 14, 1887, p. 2; Calderón, *Mexican Coal Mining Labor*, 64.

87. Haynes to USDS, September 28, 1879, reel 1, CD, NL, NARA.

88. "Laredo, the Gateway to Mexico," *Weekly Democratic Statesman*, May 3, 1883, p. 5.

89. *San Antonio Light*, November 6, 1883, p. 2; *Brenham Weekly Banner*, November 4, 1880, p. 1.

90. An ample discussion of the Madero family's vast economic interests is provided by Cerutti, *Burguesía y capitalismo en Monterrey*, 76–106. See also Guerra de Luna, *Los Madero.*

91. Santleben, *Texas Pioneer*, 301 (quotation); Griesenbeck to Madero, February 10, 1884, and B. F. Fly to Madero, March 22, 1884, FEM, AGEC; "The San Antonio Club," *San Antonio Light*, April 18, 1883, p. 1.

92. Quoted in Guerra de Luna, *Los Madero*, 620.

93. Quoted in *San Antonio Light*, October 4, 1883, p. 2.

94. Hart, *Revolutionary Mexico*, p. 117, quoted from the *San Antonio Express*, January 13, 1876.

95. Purcell to Bagnall, May 19, 1882, in Purcell, *Frontier Mexico*, 74–75.

96. "Mexican Raiders," *Dallas Daily Herald*, April 25, 1875, p. 1 (quotation); *Weekly Democratic Statesman*, April 29, 1875, p. 3.

97. Thompson, *Cortina*, 226 (first quotation), 227, 228–30; Wooster, "Army and the Politics of Expansion," 157 (second quotation).

98. Rippy, *United States and Mexico*, 294–95; "Colonel Shafter," *Dallas Weekly Herald*, January 5, 1878, p. 4.

99. Leiker, *Racial Borders*, 13, 14, 28 (quotation); "Texas Facts and Fancies," *Weekly Democratic Statesman*, June 17, 1880, p. 4.

100. Minor, *Turning Adversity to Advantage*, 186 (quotation). Rippy ("Some Precedents of the Pershing Expedition," 303) writes that in the decade after 1873, Mexico documented twenty-three such violations of its territory.

101. Quoted in Rippy, *United States and Mexico*, 294–95.

102. Ulrich to USDS, March 11, 1872, and May 24, 1872 (quotation), reel 2, CD, MTY, NARA.

103. Lucas Martínez, *Coahuila durante la intervención*, 99n; Ben E. Pingenot, "Valdés, Pedro Advíncula," in *Handbook of Texas Online*, http://www.tshaonline.org /handbook/online/articles/VV/fvapp.html.

104. Quoted in Pingenot, "Colonel 'Winker' Valdés," 41; Valdés to Minister of War, March 6, 1868, file XI/III/4-8498, in Pedro Valdés, Coronel de Caballería, 2nd. vol., SEDENA; Pingenot, "Valdés," in *Handbook of Texas Online*.

105. Schuchardt to USDS, July 21, 1872, reel 1, CD, PN, NARA.

106. Zorrilla, Miró Flaquer, and Herrera Pérez, *Tamaulipas, una historia compartida*, 2:68; Valdés to Minister of War, March 21, 1872, file XI/III/4-8498, in Pedro Valdés, Coronel de Caballería, vol. 2, SEDENA; Lucas Martínez, *Coahuila durante la intervención*, 99n.

107. Herrera Pérez, *Breve historia de Tamaulipas*, 198–99.

108. Ford, *Rip Ford's Texas*, 412 (quotation); Miró Flaquer, "Revuelta de Tuxtepec," 27.

109. Hart, *Revolutionary Mexico*, 106, 107, 109, 122, 123.

110. Zorrilla, Miró Flaquer, and Herrera Pérez, *Tamaulipas, una historia compartida*, 2:83–84.

111. Luis González, "Liberalismo triunfante," 653, 654; Zorrilla, Miró Flaquer, and Herrera Pérez, *Tamaulipas, una historia compartida*, 2:80, 81; Herrera Pérez, *Breve historia de Tamaulipas*, 201, 202.

112. Hart, *Revolutionary Mexico*, 125.

113. Hart, *Revolutionary Mexico*, 106.

114. Zorrilla, Miró Flaquer, and Herrera Pérez, *Tamaulipas, una historia compartida*, 2:91 (quotation); Meyer and Sherman, *Course of Mexican History*, 434.

115. Zorrilla, Miró Flaquer, and Herrera Pérez, *Tamaulipas, una historia compartida*, 2:94; Cosío Villegas, *Porfiriato*, 20, 26, 32–33.

116. Thompson, *Cortina*, 237; Herrera Pérez, *Breve historia de Tamaulipas*, 203.

117. Quoted in Wilkinson, *Laredo and the Rio Grande Frontier*, 355.

118. Metz, *Border*, 178.

119. Rippy, *United States and Mexico*, 300, 301 (quotation), 302; Cosío Villegas, *Porfiriato*, 76.

120. "Editorial, Partido Nacional," *El Pájaro Verde*, June 22, 1877, p. 2. For other editorials critical of the Ord Order and consequently the United States, see "Editiorial," *Siglo Diez y Nueve*, June 18, 1877, p. 1; "Deberes hacia la patria," June 22, 1877, *Siglo Diez y Nueve*, p. 3. See also "Opinión de una parte de la prensa americana a favor de México," *El Monitor Republicano*, June 19, 1877, p. 4.

121. *Periódico Oficial*, June 27, 1877, included in Weber to USDS, June 27, 1877, reel 3, CD, MTY, NARA.

122. Wilkinson, *Laredo and the Rio Grande Frontier*, 356.

123. "La Frontera," *Siglo Diez y Nueve*, June 20, 1877, p. 4.

124. Quoted in Case, "Frontera texana," 436–37; Metz, *Border*, 167–68; *Dallas Daily Herald*, July 19, 1877, p. 2.

125. *Weekly Democratic Statesman*, July 5, 1877, p. 4 (quotation); "Mexican Border Troubles," *Dallas Daily Herald*, July 27, 1877, p. 2; Case, "Frontera texana," 439–40.

126. Wilkinson, *Laredo and the Rio Grande Frontier*, 358 (quotation); Metz, *Border*, 168.

127. Michael Smith, "General Rafael Benavides," 235, 236 (quotation). For an example of the aggressive posture of the Texas press, see "Texas Invaded," *Weekly Democratic Statesman*, August 16, 1877, p. 3.

128. "First Installment of Troops on the Rio Grande," *Dallas Weekly Herald*, December 29, 1877, p. 1.

129. "The Danger on the Border," *New York Times*, November 26, 1877, p. 4; Jayes, *Illusion of Ignorance*, 30.

130. Another was General Rafael Benavides, who was sent by Díaz to complement Treviño's work and write a report on the border violence. He made a favorable impression on Ord and the Texas press. His was a voice of moderation in an atmosphere poisoned by racial and nationalist jingoism. See Michael Smith, "General Rafael Benavides."

131. Weber to Ord, November 11, 1877, Incoming Letters, U.S. C-Z, C-B 479, folder U.S. Consulate, Monterrey, Mexico, box 6, Ord Correspondence and Papers (hereafter cited as OCP), BL UCB.

132. Jayes, *Illusion of Ignorance*, 43, 44; Cosío Villegas, *Porfiriato*, 148; Raiser, "Frontera y el Reconocimiento de Díaz," 52, 53; "President's Message. Our Relations with Mexico," *San Marcos Free Press*, December 15, 1877, p. 3 (quotation).

133. Zorrilla, Miró Flaquer, and Herrera Pérez, *Tamaulipas, una historia compartida*, 2:97; Cosío Villegas, *Porfiriato*, 73. To combat Escobedo, Díaz had established a network of spies in the border region, coordinated by the Mexican consul in San Antonio, Dr. Plutarco Ornelas. His spies kept Díaz informed of all lerdista movements. Information on Díaz's espionage system is found in file 1-14-1601, 1878–1886, Archivo Histórico Genaro Estrada, Secretaría de Relaciones Exteriores.

134. Weber to Ord, July 27, 1878, Incoming Letters, U.S. C-Z, C-B 479, folder U.S. Consulate, Monterrey, Mexico, box 6, OCP, BL UCB; Dressel to USDS, June 15, 1878, reel 3, CD, MTY, NARA; Case, "Frontera texana," 446, 447.

135. American residents of Santa Rosa to Ord, December 3, 1878, folio 1, file 11, FS, box 8, AGEC. See also "From Mexico," *Denison Daily News*, June 8, 1878, p. 1; and "Mexican Collusion," *Texas Sentinel*, August 16, 1878, p. 2.

136. *Weekly State Gazette*, July 13, 1878, p. 1.

137. Weber to Ord, July 27, 1878, Incoming Letters, U.S. C-Z, C-B 479, folder U.S. Consulate, Monterrey, Mexico, box 6, OCP, BL UCB.

138. Weber to USDS, August 4, 1878, reel 3, CD, MTY, NARA.

139. Foster, *Diplomatic Memoirs*, 1:102; Lewis, "Hayes Administration and Mexico," 149.

140. Weber to Ord, September 28, 1878, Incoming Letters, U.S. C-Z, C-B 479, folder U.S. Consulate, Monterrey, Mexico, box 6, OCP, BL UCB; Foster, *Diplomatic Memoirs*, 1:101.

141. Weber to Ord, October 2, 1878, Incoming Letters, U.S. C-Z, C-B 479, folder U.S. Consulate, Monterrey, Mexico, box 6, OCP, BL UCB.

142. *Brenham Weekly Banner*, November 8, 1878, p. 1.

143. Martha Rodríguez, *Guerra entre bárbaros y civilizados*, 232, 238; Minor, *Turning Adversity to Advantage*, 190, 191; Weber to USDS, January 10 and February 16, 1879; Weber to Ord, February 16, 1879 (quotation), all in Incoming Letters, U.S. C-Z, C-B 479, folder U.S. Consulate, Monterrey, Mexico, box 6, OCP, BL UCB. While Treviño and Ord were collaborating to pacify South Texas, Tamaulipas, and Coahuila, farther west U.S. and Mexican military men were working together to combat a band of Apaches led by Chief Victorio in the Chihuahua–New Mexico border region. See Baylor, *Into the Far, Wild Country*, 21–23, 286; and Dinges, "Victorio Campaign," 93.

144. Quoted in Jayes, *Illusion of Ignorance*, 49.

145. Weber to Ord, June 11, 1879, Incoming Letters, U.S. C-Z, C-B 479, folder U.S. Consulate, Monterrey, Mexico, box 6, OCP, BL UCB.

146. Weber to Ord, February 8, 1880, Incoming Letters, U.S. C-Z, C-B 479, folder U.S. Consulate, Monterrey, Mexico, box 6, OCP, BL UCB.

147. Jayes, *Illusion of Ignorance*, 50.

148. Quoted in Lewis, "Hayes Administration and Mexico," 153.

149. Quoted in Dinges, "Victorio Campaign," 87–88.

150. Sayles, "Romero-Frelinghuysen Convention," 307–8.

151. Cosío Villegas, *Porfiriato*, 222–23.

152. Copy of *San Antonio Express* in Weber to USDS, July 30, 1880, reel 3, CD, MTY, NARA.

153. Jayes, *Illusion of Ignorance*, 50 (quotation); Hart, *Revolutionary Mexico*, 124.

154. Cosío Villegas, *Porfiriato*, 229–31, 231–32 (quotation).

155. Sahlins, *Boundaries*, 9.

156. Sahlins, *Boundaries*, 271. In *Beyond the Alamo* historian Raúl A. Ramos analyzes identity formation among Mexicans in San Antonio during the first half of the nineteenth century, a complex process given the changing conditions and sovereignties endured by the Bexareños.

157. Quotations from Sahlins, *Boundaries*, 291, 274, 9.

158. In the case of the Pyrenean frontier, Sahlins (*Boundaries*, 9, 274) affirms that national identity emerged on the periphery before it was imposed there from the center of power. In the Rio Grande border region formation of a national identity appears to have been a dual process because early on the nation had at its disposal not only common language and customs, but "an impressive and overlapping patronage network that included the civil administration and the military and Church apparatuses." These institutions served as the glue that kept the frontier tied to the nation. Reséndez, *Changing National Identities*, 4.

Afterword

1. Quoted in Olmsted, *Journey through Texas*, 245.

2. In *The Undivided Past*, David Cannadine writes that cooperation and common humanity among people "tend to be to historians what good news is to journalists: the default mode of human activity, a quotidian reality that rarely merits headlines, being somehow either unworthy or uninteresting" (262).

3. Quoted in Crisp, "José Antonio Navarro," 159.

4. Weber, *Foreigners in Their Native Land*, 212.

5. Weber, "Conflicts and Accommodations," 19.

6. Crisp, "Race, Revolution, and the Texas Republic," 41.

7. Webster, "Texas Manifest Destiny," 30.

8. Quoted in Crisp, "Race, Revolution, and the Texas Republic," 38.

9. Quotations in Cannadine, *Undivided Past*, 260, 264, respectively.

10. For more on this process see, for example, Montejano, *Anglos and Mexicans*; Young, *Catarino Garza's Revolution*; and Johnson, *Revolution in Texas*.

11. Young, *Catarino Garza's Revolution*.

12. Coerver and Hall, *Texas and the Mexican Revolution*, 6.

13. The "intellectual inspiration for the Plan de San Diego," writes Benjamin H. Johnson, had its roots in the teachings of the Flores Magón brothers, whose newspaper, *Regeneración*, was widely read in South Texas. Johnson, *Revolution in Texas*, 60.

14. Johnson, *Revolution in Texas*, 141. The Mexican Revolution was heavily influenced by the United States, beginning with the machinations of Ambassador Henry Lane Wilson, followed by the occupation of Veracruz and the Pershing Expedition. See Hart, *Revolutionary Mexico*.

15. Johnson, *Revolution in Texas*, 3, 150, 178 (quotation), 180.

16. Coerver and Hall, *Texas and the Mexican Revolution*, 6.

17. Gutiérrez and Young, "Transnationalizing Borderlands History," 29. These authors argue for a transnational approach to historical studies. This approach is reviewed in Simon Macdonald, "Transnational History: A Review of Past and Present Scholarship," https://www.ucl.ac.uk/cth/objectives/simon_macdonald_tns_review."

Bibliography

Primary Sources
Austin, Texas
R. Niles Graham-Pease Collection, Austin Public Library
University of Texas at Austin (UTA)
    Benson Latin American Collection, Gómez Farías Papers
    Dolph Briscoe Center for American History (BCAH)
        Gilbert Kingsbury Papers and Memoirs
        Kendall (George Wilkins) Papers
        Kleiber Papers
        LaCoste Papers
        John Z. Leyendecker Papers
        Matamoros Archives
        David McKnight III Family Papers (DMP)
        Saltillo Archives
        José San Román Papers
        Twohig Papers (TP)
Texas State Archives
    Bexar County Naturalization Records
    Governor's Papers, Elisha M. Pease

Berkeley, California
Bancroft Library, University of California at Berkeley (BL UCB)
    Documents Relating to Nuevo León, Mexico
    Mexía Family Papers
    Edward Otho Cresap Ord Correspondence and Papers (OCP)
    Vallecillo Mining Company (VMC)

Corpus Christi, Texas
Mexican Imprints, Streeter Collection, Mary and Jeff Bell Library, Texas A&M
    University–Corpus Christi

México

Archivo Histórico Genaro Estrada, Secretaría de Relaciones Exteriores (AHGE SRE)

Archivo Histórico, Secretaría de la Defensa Nacional (SEDENA)

Monterrey, Nuevo León

Archivo Diocesano (AD)

Archivo General del Estado de Nuevo León (AGENL)
    Asuntos Eclesiásticos (AE)
    Correspondencia con el Interior–Texas (CIT)
    Estadísticas de Municipios (EM)
    Fondo Concesiones y Permisos
    Fondo Correspondencia Santiago Vidaurri (FCV)
    Fondo Justicia (FJ)
        Jueces de Letras–Asuntos Comerciales
        Jueces de Letras–Contrabando (JL-C)
        Jueces de Letras–Embargos
    Fondo Minas
    Fondo Relaciones Exteriores, Sección Ministerio de Relaciones Exteriores (FRE, SMRE)
        Correspondencia (SMRE-C)
        Informe de Extranjeros (SMRE-IE)
    Memorias de Gobernadores
        Juan N. de la Garza y Evia
        Joaquín García (1829)
        Genaro Garza García
        Manuel Gómez de Castro (1827, 1828)
        José María Parás (1848)
    Sección Alcaldes
    Sección Concluidos
    Sección Trabajo-Sirvientes

Archivo Histórico de Monterrey (AHM)
    Fondo Capital del Estado, Sección Asuntos Legales, Colección Correspondencia
    Fondo Monterrey del Departamento en el Segundo Imperio, Sección Ayuntamiento, Colección Civil
    Fondo Monterrey, Nuevo León y Coahuila (FMNLC), Sección Correspondencia
        Colección Miscelánea
        Colección Principal
        Sección Reglamentos, Decretos y Circulares; Colección Impresos II

Santiago Roel Melo Collection (in possession of the Roel family) (SRMC)

Saltillo, Coahuila

Archivo General del Estado de Coahuila (AGEC)
    Fondo Colonias Militares de Oriente (FCMO)

Fondo Evaristo Madero (FEM)
Fondo Siglo XIX (FS)
Archivo Municipal de Saltillo (AMS)
Fondo Presidencia Municipal (FPM)
Protocolos (P)

San Antonio, Texas
James Lincoln Papers, Daughters of the Republic of Texas Library,
   Texas A&M University, San Antonio

Washington, D.C.
Executive Documents, House of Representatives, U.S. Department of State (EDHR,
   USDS)
National Archives and Records Administration (NARA)
   U.S. Department of State, Record Group 59, Consular Despatches (CD)
      Camargo (C)
      Guerrero (G)
      Matamoros (MAT)
      Monterrey (MTY)
      Nuevo Laredo (NL)
      Piedras Negras (PN)
   U.S. Department of State, Record Group 94, Adjutant General

Newspapers
American Flag (Matamoros)
Augusta Chronicle
El Bejareño (San Antonio, Texas)
Brenham Weekly Banner
El Centinela (Monterrey)
The Civilian and Gazette (Galveston)
Corpus Christi Ranchero
Corpus Christi Star
Correo del Río Bravo del Norte (Cd. Guerrero)
Daily Cosmopolitan (Brownsville)
Daily Herald (Brownsville)
Daily Ledger and Texan (San Antonio)
Daily Picayune (New Orleans)
Daily Ranchero (Brownsville)
Dallas Daily Herald and *Dallas Weekly Herald*
Denison Daily News
El Clamor Público (Los Angeles, California)
Fort Brown Flag
Fort Griffin Echo

Fort Worth Daily Gazette
Gaceta Constitucional (Nuevo León)
Galveston Weekly Journal
Galveston Weekly News
Goliad Guard
Houston Daily Mercury
Houston Telegraph
Intelligencer-Echo (Austin)
El Monitor Republicano (México)
The Morning Star (Monterrey)
National Era (Washington, D.C.)
New York Daily Times
New York Daily Tribune
New York Times
The Nueces Valley (Corpus Christi)
El Pájaro Verde (México)
Periódico Oficial (Nuevo León)
El Ranchero (San Antonio, Tex.)
Revista Universal (México)
San Antonio Daily Herald
San Antonio Daily Light
San Antonio Ledger
San Antonio Ledger and Texan
San Antonio Light
San Antonio News
San Marcos Free Press
Semanario Político (Nuevo León)
Semi-Weekly News (San Antonio)
Siglo Diez y Nueve (Mexico)
Southern Intelligencer (Austin)
The Standard (Clarksville, Texas)
Telegraph and Texas Register (Houston)
Texas Almanac (Austin)
Texas Presbyterian (Houston)
The Texas Sentinel (Brenham)
Texas State Gazette (Austin)
Texas State Times (Austin)
Tri-Weekly State Gazette (Austin)
Tri-Weekly Telegraph (Houston)
The Two Republics (México)
Victoria Advocate
Weekly Corpus Christi Caller
Weekly Democratic Statesman (Austin)

Weekly State Gazette (Austin)
Weekly Statesman (Austin)
Weekly Telegraph (Houston)
Western Texan (San Antonio)

Books, Book Chapters, and Articles

Aboites Aguilar, Luis. "José Fuentes Mares y la historiografía del norte de México. Una aproximación desde Chihuahua (1950–1957)." *Historia Mexicana* 49, no. 3 (2000): 477–507.

Acuña, Rodolfo. *Occupied America: A History of Chicanos.* 3rd ed. New York: Harper & and Row, 1988.

Acuña, Rodolfo, and Guadalupe Compean, eds. *Voices of the U.S. Latino Experience*, vol. 1. Westport, Conn: Greenwood Press, 2008.

Adams, David B. "Embattled Borderland: Northern Nuevo León and the Indios Bárbaros, 1686–1870." *Southwestern Historical Quarterly* 95, no. 1 (1991): 205–20.

Adams, John A. Jr. *Conflict and Commerce on the Rio Grande: Laredo, 1755–1955.* College Station: Texas A&M University Press, 2008.

Adelman, Jeremy, and Stephen Aron. "From Borderlands to Borders: Empires, Nation-States, and the Peoples in between in North American History." *American Historical Review* 104, no. 3 (1999): 814–41.

Alessio Robles, Vito. *Coahuila y Texas desde la consumación de la independencia hasta el Tratado de Paz de Guadalupe Hidalgo.* 2 vols. México: Talleres Gráficos de la Nación, 1945.

Almonte, Juan N. "Statistical Report on Texas, 1835." Translated by Carlos E. Castañeda. *Southwestern Historical Quarterly* 28, no. 3 (1925): 177–222.

Alonso, Ana María. *Thread of Blood: Colonialism, Revolution, and Gender on Mexico's Northern Frontier.* Tucson: University of Arizona Press, 1995.

Alonzo, Armando. "A History of Ranching in Nuevo Santader's Villas del Norte, 1730s–1848." In *Coastal Encounters, The Transformation of the Gulf South in the Eighteenth Century*, edited by Richmond F. Brown, 187–209. Lincoln: University of Nebraska Press, 2007.

———. *Tejano Legacy: Rancheros and Settlers in South Texas, 1734–1900.* Albuquerque: University of New Mexico Press, 1998.

American Tract Society. "Fifth Annual Report of the Texas Agency of the American Tract Society," 1879. DeGolyer Library, Southern Methodist University.

Amberson, Mary Margaret McAllen, James A. McAllen, and Margaret H. McAllen. *I Would Rather Sleep in Texas: A History of the Lower Rio Grande Valley and the People of the Santa Anita Land Grant.* Austin: Texas State Historical Association, 2003.

Applegate, Howard G., and C. Wayne Hanselka. "La Junta de los Rios del Norte y Conchos." Southwestern Studies Monograph 41. El Paso: Texas Western Press, 1974.

Arellano, Emilio. *Ignacio Ramírez, El Nigromante. Memorias prohibidas.* México: Planeta, 2009.

Arreola, Daniel D. *Tejano South Texas: A Mexican American Cultural Province.* Austin: University of Texas Press, 2002.

Austin, Stephen F. "Explanation to the Public Concerning the Affairs of Texas." Translated by Ethel Zivley Rather. *Texas Historical Association Quarterly* 8, no. 3 (1905):
232–58.

Ávila, Jesús, Leticia Martínez, and César Morado. *Santiago Vidaurri. La formación de un
liderazgo regional desde Monterrey (1809–1867)*. Monterrey: Universidad Autónoma
de Nuevo León, 2012.

Baez Camargo, Gonzalo, and Kenneth G. Grubb, *Religion in the Republic of Mexico*.
London and New York: World Dominion Press, 1935.

Barber, Benjamin R. "The Lost Art of Cooperation." *Wilson Quarterly* 31, no. 4 (2007):
56–61.

Barker, Eugene C., ed. *The Austin Papers*. 2 vols. Washington, D.C.: American Historical
Association, 1919–1928.

———. "The Tampico Expedition." *Quarterly of the Texas State Historical Association*
6, no. 3 (1903): 169–86.

Barrera Enderle, Alberto. "Contrabando y liberalismo. La transformación de la cultura
política en las Provincias Internas de Oriente, 1808–1821." PhD diss., University of
California at Irvine, 2013.

Barton, Josef. "At the Edge of the Storm: Northern Mexico's Rural Peoples in a New
Regime of Consumption, 1880–1940." In *Land of Necessity: Consumer Culture in the
United States–Mexico Borderlands*, edited by Alexis McCrossen, 217–47. Durham,
N.C.: Duke University Press, 2009.

Bastian, Jean Pierre, "Las sociedades protestantes y la oposición a Porfirio Díaz en México,
1877–1911." In *Protestantes, liberales y francmasones. Sociedades de ideas y modernidad
en América Latina, siglo XIX*, edited by Jean Pierre Bastian, 132–64. México: Fondo
de Cultura Económica, 1990.

———. *Los disidentes. Sociedades protestantes y revolución en México, 1872–1911*. México:
Fondo de Cultura Económica; Colegio de México, 1989.

Baud, Michiel, and Willem van Schendel. "Toward a Comparative History of Borderlands." *Journal of World History* 8, no. 2 (1997): 211–42.

Baur, John E. "The Evolution of a Mexican Foreign Trade Policy, 1821–1828." *The Americas*, 19, no. 3 (1963): 225–61.

Baylies, Francis. "The March of the United States Troops, under the Command of
General John E. Wool, from San Antonio, Texas, to Saltillo, Mexico, in the Year
1846." *Stryker's American Register and Magazine* 4 (July 1850): 297–312. http://
sacweb03.sac.alamo.edu:2066/americanperiodicals/docview/126131279/fulltextPDF
/E065A09465D14BFFPQ/1?accountid=7151.

Baylor, George Wythe. *Into the Far, Wild Country: True Tales of the Old Southwest*. Edited
with an introduction by Jerry D. Thompson. El Paso: Texas Western Press of the
University of Texas at El Paso, 1996.

Bazant, Jan. *Cinco haciendas mexicanas. Tres siglos de vida rural en San Luís Potosí, 1600–
1910*. México: El Colegio de México, 1975.

Beall, Jonathan A. "The Military Occupation of the Lower Rio Grande Valley, 1865–1866."
Journal of South Texas 16, no. 2 (2003): 195–236.

Bell, Samuel E., and James M. Smallwood. "Zona Libre: Trade & Diplomacy on the Mexican Border, 1858–1905." *Arizona and the West* 24, no. 2 (1982): 119–52.

Benavides Hinojosa, Artemio. *Santiago Vidaurri. Caudillo del noreste mexicano (1855–1864)*. México: Tusquets, 2012.

Bliss, Zenas R. *The Reminiscences of Major General Zenas R. Bliss, 1854–1876*. Edited by Thomas T. Smith, Jerry D. Thompson, Robert Wooster, and Ben E. Pingenot. Austin: Texas State Historical Association, 2007.

Bolton, Herbert E. "Wider Horizons of American History." In *The Appleton-Century Historical Essays*, edited by William E. Lingelbach. New York: D. Appleton-Century, 1939.

Bosch García, Carlos. *Historia de las relaciones entre México y los Estados Unidos, 1819–1848*. México: Secretaría de Relaciones Exteriores, 1974.

Brackenridge, R. Douglas, and Francisco O. García-Treto. *Iglesia Presbiteriana: A History of Presbyterians and Mexican Americans in the Southwest*. 2nd ed. San Antonio: Trinity University Press, 1987.

Brister, Louis E. "Johann von Racknitz: German Empresario and Soldier of Fortune in Texas and Mexico, 1832–1848." *Southwestern Historical Quarterly* 99, no. 1 (1995): 48–79.

Brooks, James F. *Captives & Cousins: Slavery, Kinship, and Community in the Southwest Borderlands*. Chapel Hill: University of North Carolina Press, 2002.

Broussard, Ray F. "San Antonio during the Texas Republic." Southwestern Studies 5, no. 2, Monograph 18 (1967): 16–67.

Brown, John Henry. *Indian Wars and Pioneers of Texas*. Austin: L. E. Daniell, 1880.

Calderón, Roberto R. *Mexican Coal Mining Labor in Texas and Coahuila, 1880–1930*. College Station: Texas A&M University Press, 2000.

Callahan, Manuel. "Mexican Border Troubles: Social War, Settler Colonialism, and the Production of Frontier Discourses, 1848–1880." PhD diss., University of Texas at Austin, 2003.

Calvert, Robert A., and Arnoldo de León. *The History of Texas*. Arlington Heights, Ill.: Harlan Davison, 1990.

Campbell, Randolph B. *Gone to Texas: A History of the Lone Star State*. New York and Oxford: Oxford University Press, 2003.

Cannadine, David. *The Undivided Past: Humanity Beyond Our Differences*. New York: Knopf, 2013.

Carlson, Paul H. *Texas Woollybacks, the Range Sheep and Goat Industry*. College Station: Texas A&M University Press, 1982.

Carroll, H. Bailey. "Texas Collection." *Southwestern Historical Quarterly* 49, no. 3 (1946): 432–62.

Case, Robert. "La frontera texana y los movimientos de insurrección en México, 1850–1900." In *Historia Mexicana* 30, no. 3 (1981): 415–52.

Cavazos Garza, Israel. "Algunas características de los pobladores de Nuevo León, en el siglo XVII." *Humanitas* 1, no. 1 (1960): 467–79.

———. *Diccionario Biográfico de Nuevo León*. 2 vols. Monterrey: Universidad Autónoma de Nuevo León, 1984.

Centennial History of Corpus Christi. Corpus Christi: Corpus Christi Caller Times, n.d.

Cerutti, Mario. *Burguesía, capitales e industria en el norte de México. Monterrey y su ámbito regional (1850–1910)*. Monterrey: Universidad Autónoma de Nuevo León, 1989.

———. *Burguesía y capitalismo en Monterrey, 1850–1910*. México: Claves Latinoamericanas, 1983.

———. *Economía de guerra y poder regional en el siglo XIX. Gastos militares, aduanas y comerciantes en años de Vidaurri (1855–1864)*. Monterrey: Archivo General del Estado de Nuevo León, 1983.

———. "Militares, terratenientes y empresarios en el noreste. Los generales Treviño y Naranjo (1880–1910)." In *Monterrey, Nuevo León, el noreste. Siete estudios históricos*, edited by Mario Cerutti. Monterrey: Universidad Autónoma de Nuevo León, 1987.

———. *Propietarios, empresarios y empresa en el norte de México*. México: Siglo Veintiuno, 2000.

Cerutti, Mario, and Miguel A. González-Quiroga, comps. and eds. *Frontera e historia económica. Texas y el norte de México (1850–1865)*. México: Instituto Mora, Universidad Autónoma Metropolitana, 1993.

———. *El norte de México y Texas (1848–1880)*. México: Instituto Mora, Universidad Autónoma Metropolitana, 1999.

———. "Guerra y comercio en torno al Río Bravo (1855–1867). Línea fronteriza, espacio económico común." *Historia Mexicana* 40, no. 2 (1991): 217–97.

Chance, Joseph E. *Jose Maria De Jesus Carvajal: The Life and Times of a Mexican Revolutionary*. San Antonio, Tex.: Trinity University Press, 2006.

———. *The Mexican War Journal of Captain Franklin Smith*. Jackson: University of Mississippi Press, 1991.

Chevalier, François. *La formación de los latifundios en México. Haciendas y sociedad en los siglos XVI, XVII y XVIII*. México: Fondo de Cultura Económica, 1999.

Clarke, A. B. *Travels in Mexico and California*. Edited by Anne M. Perry. College Station: Texas A&M University Press, 1988.

Coerver, Don M., and Linda B. Hall. *Texas and the Mexican Revolution: A Study in State and National Border Policy, 1910–1920*. San Antonio, Tex.: Trinity University Press, 1984.

Cohen, Barry M. "The Texas-Mexico Border, 1858–1867." *Texana* 6, no. 2 (1968): 153–65.

Collins, Michael L. *A Crooked River: Rustlers, Rangers, and Regulars on the Lower Rio Grande, 1861–1877*. Norman: University of Oklahoma Press, 2018.

———. *Texas Devils: Rangers and Regulars on the Lower Rio Grande, 1846–1861*. Norman: University of Oklahoma Press, 2008.

Cool, Paul. *Salt Warriors: Insurgency on the Rio Grande*. College Station: Texas A&M University Press, 2008.

Corner, William, comp and ed. *San Antonio de Bexar: A Guide and History*. San Antonio: Bainbridge and Corner, 1890. http://texashistory.unt.edu/ark:/67531/metapth143549.

Cosío Villegas, Daniel. *El Porfiriato, la vida política exterior*, vol. 6, pt. 2. of *Historia moderna de México*. México: Editorial Hermes, 1974.

Cossío, David Alberto. *Historia de Nuevo León. Evolución política y social*. In *Obras completas*, compiled by Adalberto A. Madero Quiroga, vol. 6. Monterrey: Congreso del Estado de Nuevo León, 2000.

Cowling, Annie. "The Civil War Trade of the Lower Rio Grande Valley." Master's thesis, University of Texas at Austin, 1926.

Craver, Rebecca McDowell. *The Impact of Intimacy: Mexican-Anglo Intermarriage in New Mexico, 1821–1846.* Southwestern Studies Monograph no. 66. El Paso: Texas Western Press, 1982.

Crews, Litha. "The Know-Nothing Party in Texas." Master's thesis, University of Texas at Austin, 1925.

Crimm, Ana Carolina Castillo. *De León: A Tejano Family History.* Austin: University of Texas Press, 2003.

———. "Success in Adversity: The Mexican Americans of Victoria County, Texas, 1800–1880." PhD diss., University of Texas at Austin, 1994.

Crisp, James E. "Anglo-Texan Attitudes toward the Mexican, 1821–1845." PhD diss., Yale University, 1976.

———. "José Antonio Navarro: The Problem of Tejano Powerlessness." In *Tejano Leadership in Mexican and Revolutionary Texas,* edited by Jesús F. de la Teja, 146–68. College Station: Texas A&M University Press, 2010.

———. "Race, Revolution, and the Texas Republic: Toward a Reinterpretation." In *The Texas Military Experience from the Texas Revolution through World War II,* edited by Joseph G. Dawson III, 32–48. College Station: Texas A&M University Press, 1995.

Crook, Carland Elaine. "San Antonio, Texas, 1846–1861." Master's thesis, Rice University, 1964.

Cross, Harry E. "Living Standards in Rural Nineteenth-Century Mexico: Zacatecas, 1820–1880." *Journal of Latin American Studies* 10, no. 1 (1978): 1–19.

Cruz, Gilbert. *A Century of Service: The History of the Catholic Church in the Lower Rio Grande Valley.* Harlingen, Tex.: United Printers & Publishers, 1979.

Cunningham, Bob, and Harry P. Hewitt. "A 'Lovely Land Full of Roses and Thorns': Emil Langberg and Mexico, 1835–1866." *Southwestern Historical Quarterly* 98, no. 3 (1995): 387–425.

Dávila, Rosaura Alicia, and Oscar Rivera Saldaña. *Matamoros en la guerra con los Estados Unidos.* Matamoros, Tamps.: Ediciones Archivo Histórico, 1996.

Davis, Graham. *Land! Irish Pioneers in Mexican and Revolutionary Texas.* College Station: Texas A&M University Press, 2002.

Delaney, Robert W. "Matamoros, Port of Texas during the Civil War." *Southwestern Historical Quarterly* 58, no. 4 (1955): 473–87.

De la Teja, Jesus F. "St. James at the Fair: Religious Ceremony, Civic Boosterism, and Commercial Development on the Colonial Mexican Frontier." *The Americas* 57, no. 3 (2001): 395–416.

DeLay, Brian. *War of a Thousand Deserts: Indian Raids and the U.S.-Mexican War.* New Haven, Conn.: Yale University Press, 2008.

De León, Arnoldo. *La comunidad tejana, 1836–1900.* México: Fondo de Cultura Económica, 1988.

———. *Mexican Americans in Texas: A Brief History.* Arlington Heights, Ill.: Harlan Davidson, 1993.

———. *They Called Them Greasers: Anglo Attitudes toward Mexicans in Texas, 1821–1900.* Austin: University of Texas Press, 1983.

De León, Arnoldo, and Kenneth L. Stewart. *Tejanos and the Numbers Game: A Socio-historical Interpretation from the Federal Censuses, 1850–1900.* Albuquerque: University of New Mexico Press, 1989.

Dewey, Alicia M., and Sterling D. Evans. *Pesos and Dollars: Entrepreneurs in the Texas-Mexico Borderlands, 1880–1940.* College Station: Texas A&M University Press, 2014.

Diamond, William. "Imports of the Confederate Government from Europe and Mexico." *Journal of Southern History* 6, no. 4 (1940): 470–503.

Díaz, George T. *Border Contraband: A History of Smuggling across the Rio Grande.* Austin: University of Texas Press, 2015.

Díaz, Lilia. "El liberalismo militante." In *Historia general de México,* edited by Ignacio Bernal. México: Colegio de México, 2000.

Dinges, Bruce J. "The Victorio Campaign of 1880: Cooperation and Conflict on the United States–Mexico Border." *New Mexico Historical Review* 62, no. 1 (January 1987): 81–94.

Dobie, J. Frank. *A Vaquero of the Brush Country.* Boston: Little, Brown & Co., 1943.

Domenech, Abbé [Emmanuel]. *Missionary Adventures in Texas and Mexico: A Personal Narrative of Six Years' Sojourn in Those Regions.* London: Longman, Brown, Green, Longmans, and Roberts, 1858.

Downs, Fane. "The History of Mexicans in Texas, 1820–1845." PhD diss., Texas Tech University, 1970.

Durham, George. *Taming the Nueces Strip: The Story of McNelly's Rangers.* As told to Clyde Wantland. 7th printing. Austin: University of Texas Press, 2003.

Dysart, Jane. "Mexican Women in San Antonio, 1830–1860." *Western Historical Quarterly* 7, no. 4 (1976): 365–75.

Elam, Earl H. "Aspects of Acculturation in the Lower Big Bend Region of Texas, 1848–1943." *Journal of Big Bend Studies* 12 (2000): 71–91.

Ellis, L. Tuffly. "Maritime Commerce on the Far Western Gulf, 1861–1865." *Southwestern Historical Quarterly* 77, no. 2 (1973): 167–226.

Ely, Glen Sample. "Gone from Texas and Trading with the Enemy: New Perspectives on Civil War West Texas." *Southwestern Historical Quarterly* 110, no. 4 (2007): 439–63.

Escobedo, Santiago. "Iron Men and Wooden Carts: Tejano Freighters during the Civil War." *Journal of South Texas* 17, no. 2 (2004): 51–60.

Fehrenbach, T. R. *Lone Star: A History of Texas and the Texans.* New York: Macmillan, 1968.

Fernandez, Raul A. *The United States–Mexico Border: A Politico-economic Profile.* Notre Dame, Ind.: University of Notre Dame Press, 1977.

Fernández de Castro, Patricia. "Comercio y contrabando en la frontera noreste, 1861–1865." *Frontera Norte* 6, no. 11 (1994): 23–39.

Ferrell, Robert H., ed. *Monterrey Is Ours! The Mexican War Letters of Lieutenant Dana, 1845–1847.* Lexington: University of Kentucky Press, 1990.

Fisher, Orceneth. *Sketches of Texas in 1840.* Springfield, Ill.: Walters and Weber, 1841.

Foley, Neil. *The White Scourge: Mexicans, Blacks, and Poor Whites in Texas Cotton Culture.* Berkeley: University of California Press, 1997.

Foos, Paul. *A Short, Offhand, Killing Affair: Soldiers and Social Conflict during the Mexican-American War.* Chapel Hill: University of North Carolina Press, 2002.

Ford, John Salmon. *Rip Ford's Texas.* Edited by Stephen B. Oates. 1987. Repr., Austin: University of Texas Press, 2004.

Foster, John W. *Diplomatic Memoirs.* Vol 1. Boston and New York: Houghton Mifflin,, 1909. http://www.archive.org/details/diplomaticmemoir027725mbp.

———. *Trade with Mexico: Correspondence between the Manufacturers' Association of the Northwest, Chicago.* Chicago, 1878.

Franchot, Jenny. *Roads to Rome: The Antebellum Protestant Encounter with Catholicism.* Berkeley: University of California Press, 1994.

Franklin, Ethel Mary, ed. "Memoirs of Mrs. Annie P. Harris." *Southwestern Historical Quarterly* 40, no. 3 (1937): 231–46.

Galindo. Benjamín. *El provincialismo nuevoleonés en la época de Parás Ballesteros, 1822–1850.* Monterrey: Universidad Autónoma de Nuevo León, 2005.

Gallegos, Juan José. "'Last Drop of My Blood': Col. Antonio Zapata: A Life and Times on Mexico's Rio Grande Frontier, 1797–1840." Master's thesis, University of Houston, 2005.

Gammel, Hans Peter Mareus Neilsen. *The Laws of Texas, 1822–1897.* Vol. 1. Austin, Tex.: Gammel Book Co., 1898. http://texashistory.unt.edu/ark:/67531/metapth5872.

García, Luis Alberto. *Guerra y frontera. El Ejército del Norte entre 1855 y 1858.* Anuario del Archivo General del Estado de Nuevo León. Monterrey: Fondo Editorial de Nuevo León, Archivo General del Estado de Nuevo León, 2007.

García Cantú, Gastón. *Las invasiones norteamericanas en México.* México: Serie Popular Era, 1971.

García Flores, Raúl. *Ser ranchero, católico y fronterizo. La construcción de identidades en el sur de Nuevo León durante la primera mitad del siglo XIX.* México: Instituto Nacional de Antropología e Historia, 2008.

Garver, Lois. "Benjamin Rush Milam." *Southwestern Historical Quarterly* 38, no. 2 (1934): 79–121.

———. "Benjamin Rush Milam." *Southwestern Historical Quarterly* 38, no. 3 (1935): 177–202.

Garza González, Virgilio, ed. *Tras las huellas de un cronista desconocido. Memorias de Jesús González Treviño.* Monterrey: Universidad Autónoma de Nuevo León, 2012.

Gassner, John C. "African American Fugitive Slaves and Freemen in Matamoros, Tamaulipas, 1820–1865." Master's thesis, University of Texas–Pan American, 2003.

Gilbert, M. J., ed. *Archdiocese of San Antonio, 1874–1949; an illustrated record of the foundation and growth of parishes, missions, and religious institutions in that part of Texas under the spiritual jurisdiction of the See of San Antonio.* San Antonio, Tex.: Archdiocese of San Antonio, 1949.

Gilbert, Minnie. "Safe in No-Man's Land." In *Roots by the River: A Story of Texas Tropical Borderland,* 69–76. Valley By-Liners Book 2. Canyon, Tex.: Staked Plains Press, 1978.

Gómez, Luis G. *Crossing the Rio Grande: An Immigrant's Life in the 1880s*. Edited by
    Guadalupe Valdez Jr. and Thomas H. Krenneck. Translated by Guadalupe Valdez Jr.
    College Station: Texas A&M University Press, 2006.
González, Luis. "El liberalismo triunfante." In *Historia general de México*, edited by
    Ignacio Bernal. México: Colegio de México, 2000.
González Navarro, Moisés. *Anatomía del poder en México, 1848–1853*. México: Colegio
    de México, 1977.
———. *La colonización en México, 1877–1910*. México: Talleres de Impresión de Estampil-
    las y Valores, 1960.
———. *Los extranjeros en México y los mexicanos en el extranjero*. 2 vols. México: Colegio
    de México, 1993.
González Quiroga, Miguel A. "Conflict and Cooperation in the Making of Texas-
    Mexico Border Society, 1840–1880." In *Bridging National Borders in North America:
    Transnational and Comparative Histories*, 33–58, edited by Benjamin H. Johnson and
    Andrew R. Graybill, 33–58. Durham, N.C.: Duke University Press, 2010.
———. "Fuga y muerte de Murrah." *Atisbo* 3, no. 14 (2008): 15–22.
———. "La patria en peligro: Juárez en Monterrey." In *Juárez, historia y mito*, edited by
    Josefina Zoraida Vázquez, 459–93. México: Colegio de México, 2010.
———. "La puerta de México, los comerciantes texanos y el noreste mexicano, 1850–1880."
    Estudios Sociológicos 11, no. 31 (1993): 209–36.
———. "Los inicios de la migración laboral mexicana a Texas." In *Encuentro en la frontera.
    Mexicanos y norteamericanos en un espacio común*, edited by Manuel Ceballos Ramírez,
    345–72. México: Colegio de México; Tijuana: Colegio de la Frontera Norte; Ciudad
    Victoria: Universidad Autónoma de Tamaulipas, 2001.
———. "Nuevo León ante la invasión norteamericana, 1846–1848." In *México en guerra
    (1846–1848). Perspectivas regionales*, edited by Laura Herrera Serna, 425–71. México:
    Museo Nacional de las Intervenciones; Consejo Nacional para la Cultura y las Artes,
    1997.
———. "Trabajadores mexicanos en Texas (1850–1865). Los carreteros y el transporte
    de carga." *Siglo XIX, Cuadernos de Historia* 3, no. 9 (1994): 51–81.
González Salas, Carlos. *Diccionario biográfico de Tamaulipas*. Ciudad Victoria: Univer-
    sidad Autónoma de Tamaulipas, 1984.
Graf, LeRoy. "The Economic History of the Lower Rio Grande Valley, 1820–1875." PhD
    diss., Harvard University, 1942.
Grass, Gunter. *The Tin Drum*. New York: Pantheon Books, 1961.
Green, Stanley C. "La República del Río Grande y Nuevo León." In *El noreste, reflex-
    iones*, edited by Isabel Ortega Ridaura, 53–59. Monterrey: Fondo Editorial de Nuevo
    León, 2006.
———. "The Texas Revolution and the Rio Grande Border." In *The Texas Revolution
    on the Rio Grande: Bi-National Conference proceedings, March 25, 2005*. San Antonio:
    Daughters of the Republic of Texas Library at the Alamo, 2005.
Guerra de Luna, Manuel. *Los Madero. La saga liberal*. México: Editorial Siglo Bicen-
    tenario, 2009.

Guidotti-Hernández, Nicole M. *Unspeakable Violence: Remapping U.S. and Mexican National Imaginaries*. Durham, N.C.: Duke University Press, 2011.

Gurza Lavalle, Gerardo. *Una vecindad efímera: Los Estados Confederados de América y su política exterior hacia México, 1861–1865*. México: Instituto Mora, Universidad Autónoma Metropolitana, 2001.

Gutiérrez, Laura. "El prolongado ocaso de un estado y la gestación de otro." In *Breve Historia de Coahuila*, edited by María Elena Santoscoy, Laura Gutiérrez, Martha Rodríguez, and Francisco Cepeda, 91–199. México: Colegio de México; Fondo de Cultura Económica, 2000.

Gutiérrez, Ramón A., and Elliott Young. "Transnationalizing Borderlands History." *Western Historical Quarterly* 41, no. 1 (2010): 26–53.

Haley, J. Evetts. *Charles Schreiner, General Merchandise: The Story of a Country Store*. Austin: Texas State Historical Association, 1944.

Hall, Thomas D. *Social Change in the Southwest, 1350–1880*. Lawrence: University Press of Kansas, 1989.

Hamalainen, Pekka. *The Comanche Empire*. New Haven, Conn.: Yale University Press, 2008.

Hanna, Alfred J., and Kathryn Abbey Hanna. "The Immigration Movement of the Intervention and Empire as Seen through the Mexican Press." *Hispanic American Historical Review* 27, no. 2 (1947): 220–46.

Harari, Yuval Noah. *Homo Deus: A Brief History of Tomorrow*. New York: Harper Perennial, 2017.

Harris, Charles H. III. *El imperio de la familia Sánchez Navarro, 1765–1867*. Monclova, Coah.: Sociedad Monclovense de Historia, 1989.

———. *The Sánchez Navarros: A Socio-economic Study of a Coahuilan Latifundio 1846–1853*. Chicago: Loyola University Press, 1964.

Harrison, Horace V. "Los federalistas mexicanos de 1839–40 y sus tanteos diplomáticos en Texas." *Historia Mexicana* 6, no. 3 (1957): 321–49.

Hart, John M. *Revolutionary Mexico: The Coming and Process of the Mexican Revolution*. Berkeley: University of California Press, 1987.

Haynes, Sam W. *Soldiers of Misfortune: The Somervell and Mier Expeditions*. Austin: University of Texas Press, 1990.

Hébert, Rachel Bluntzer. *The Forgotten Colony: San Patricio de Hibernia: The History, the People and the Legends of the Irish Colony of McMullen-McGloin*. Burnet, Tex.: Eakin Press, 1981. http://texashistory.unt.edu/ark:/67531/metapth61113.

Henson, Margaret Swett. *Lorenzo de Zavala: The Pragmatic Idealist*. Fort Worth: Texas Christian University Press, 1996.

Hernández, Jorge A. "Social Change in Mexico's Northeast and the Rise of Pedro Rojas, 1821–1860." PhD diss., Texas Christian University, 1995.

———. "Trading across the Border: National Customs Guards in Nuevo León." *Southwestern Historical Quarterly* 100, no. 4 (1997): 433–50.

Hernández, José Angel. *Mexican American Colonization during the Nineteenth Century: A History of the U.S.-Mexico Borderlands*. New York: Cambridge University Press, 2012.

Herrera Pérez, Octavio. *Breve historia de Tamaulipas*. México: Colegio de México; Fondo de Cultura Económica, 1999.

———. *El norte de Tamaulipas y la conformación de la frontera México–Estados Unidos, 1835–1855*. Ciudad Victoria: Colegio de Tamaulipas, 2003.

———. *La zona libre. Excepción fiscal y conformación histórica de la frontera norte de México*. México: Secretaría de Relaciones Exteriores, 2004.

Hine, Robert V., and John Mack Faragher. *The American West: A New Interpretive History*. New Haven, Conn.: Yale University Press, 2000.

Hinojosa, Gilberto M. *A Borderlands Town in Transition: Laredo, 1755–1870*. College Station: Texas A&M University Press, 1983.

Hogan, William Ransom. *The Texas Republic: A Social and Economic History*. 1946. Repr., Austin: Texas State Historical Association, 1984.

Holding, Nannie Emory. *A Decade of Mission Life in Mexican Mission Homes*. Nashville, Tenn.: Methodist Episcopal Church, South, Barbee & Smith, Agents, 1895.

Horgan, Paul. *Great River: The Rio Grande in North American History*. Vol 2. New York: Rinehart & Co, 1954.

Hudson, Linda S. *Mistress of Manifest Destiny: A Biography of Jane McManus Storm Cazneau, 1807–1878*. Austin: Texas State Historical Association, 2001.

Huntington, Samuel. *Who Are We? The Challenges to America's National Identity*. New York: Simon and Schuster, 2004.

Huson, Hobart. *Refugio: A Comprehensive History of Refugio County from Aboriginal Times to 1953*. 2 vols. Woodsboro, Tex.: Rooke Foundation, 1953.

Hutchinson, C. Alan. "General José Antonio Mexía and His Texas Interests." *Southwestern Historical Quarterly* 82, no. 2 (1978): 117–42.

Ibarra Bellon, Araceli. *El comercio y el poder en México, 1821–1864. La lucha por las fuentes financieras entre el estado central y las regiones*. México: Fondo de Cultura Económica; Guadalajara: Universidad de Guadalajara, 1998.

Informe de la Comisión Pesquisidora de la Frontera del Norte al Ejecutivo de la Unión. México: Imprenta de Ignacio Cumplido, 1873.

Irby, James A. *Back Door at Bagdad: The Civil War on the Rio Grande*. El Paso: University of Texas Press, 1977.

———. "Line of the Rio Grande: War and Trade on the Confederate Frontier, 1861–1865." PhD diss., Southern Methodist University, 1969.

Jacoby, Karl. *Shadows at Dawn: An Apache Massacre and the Violence of History*. New York: Penguin Books, 2008.

Jaques, Mary J. *Texan Ranch Life; with Three Months through in a "Prairie Schooner."* 1894. Repr., College Station: Texas A&M University Press, 1989.

Jayes, Janice Lee. *The Illusion of Ignorance: Constructing the American Encounter with Mexico, 1877–1929*. Lanham, Md.: University Press of America, 2011.

Johnson, Benjamin H. *Revolution in Texas: How a Forgotten Rebellion and Its Bloody Suppression Turned Mexicans into Americans*. New Haven, Conn.: Yale University Press, 2003.

Johnson, Benjamin H., and Andrew R. Graybill, eds. *Bridging National Borders in North America: Transnational and Comparative Histories*. Durham, N.C.: Duke University Press, 2010.

Jordan, Terry G. "The 1887 Census of Texas' Hispanic Population." *Aztlan, International Journal of Chicano Studies* 12, no. 2 (1981): 271–78.

Karras, Bill, ed. "First Impressions of Mexico, 1828, by Reuben Potter." *Southwestern Historical Quarterly* 79, no. 1 (1975): 55–68.

Kearney, Milo, and Anthony Knopp. *Boom and Bust: The Historical Cycles of Matamoros and Brownsville*. Austin: Eakin Press, 1991.

Kelly, Patrick J. "The North American Crisis of the 1860s." *Journal of the Civil War Era* 2, no. 3 (2012): 337–68.

Kelsey, Anna Marieta. *Through the Years: Reminiscences of Pioneer Days on the Texas Border*. San Antonio, Tex.: Naylor, 1952.

Kendall, George Wilkins. *Narrative of the Santa Fé Expedition*. Vol 1. New York: Harper and Brothers, 1844.

Kerrigan, William T. "Race, Expansion, and Slavery in Eagle Pass, Texas, 1852." *Southwestern Historical Quarterly* 101, no. 3 (1998): 275–301.

Kilgore, Dan. "Two Sixshooters and a Sunbonnet. The Story of Sally Skull." In *Legendary Ladies of Texas*, edited by Francis Edward Abernethy, 59–70. Nacogdoches: Texas Folklore Society, 1994. http://texashistory.unt.edu/ark:/67531/metadc38860.

Kimball, J. P., *Laws and Decrees of the State of Coahuila and Texas, in Spanish and English*. Houston, Tex.: Telegraph Power Press, 1839.

Kinsall, Al. "Fort Duncan: Frontier Outpost on the Rio Grande." *Journal of Big Bend Studies* 11 (1999): 93–107.

Knight, Larry. "The Cart War: Defining American in San Antonio in the 1850s." *Southwestern Historical Quarterly* 109, no. 3 (2006): 319–35.

Knowles, James Purdie. *Samuel A. Purdie, His Life and Letters: His Work as a Missionary and Spanish Writer and Publisher in Mexico and Central America*. Plainfield, Ind.: Publishing Association of Friends, 1908. http://openlibrary.org/books/OL23331263M/Samuel_A._Purdie_his_life_and_letters.

Lack, Paul D. "Occupied Texas: Bexar and Goliad, 1835–1836." In *Mexican Americans in Texas History: Selected Essays*, edited by Emilio Zamora, Cynthia Orozco, and Rodolfo Rocha, 35–49. Austin: Texas State Historical Association, 2000.

———. "Slavery and Vigilantism in Austin, Texas, 1840–1860." *Southwestern Historical Quarterly* 85, no. 1 (1981): 1–20.

Lamar, Mirabeau Buonaparte. *The Papers of Mirabeau Buonaparte Lamar*, vol. 3. Edited by Charles Adams Gulick Jr. Austin: A. C. Baldwin & Sons, 1922.

———. *The Papers of Mirabeau Buonaparte Lamar*. Edited by Charles Adams Gulick Jr. Vols. 3–4. Austin, Tex.: Von Boeckmann–Jones, 1922–24.

Langberg, Emilio, and Blas Flores. *Dust, Smoke, and Tracks: Two Accounts of Nineteenth-Century Mexican Military Expeditions to Northern Coahuila and Chihuahua*. Edited by

Solveig A. Turpin and Herbert H. Eling. Jr. Center for Big Bend Studies Occasional Papers no. 11. Alpine, Tex.: Sul Ross State University, 2009.

Lea, Tom. *The King Ranch*. Vol. 1. Boston: Little, Brown, 1957.

Leiker, James N. *Racial Borders: Black Soldiers along the Rio Grande*. College Station: Texas A&M University Press, 2002.

Lewis, William Ray. "The Hayes Administration and Mexico." *Southwestern Historical Quarterly* 24, no. 2 (1920): 140–53.

Limerick, Patricia Nelson. *The Legacy of Conquest: The Unbroken Past of the American West*. New York: W. W. Norton, 1987.

Lindheim, Milton. *The Republic of the Rio Grande: Texans in Mexico, 1839–40*. Waco, Tex.: W. M. Morrison, 1964.

Linn, John J. *Reminiscences of Fifty Years in Texas*. 1883. Facsimile, Austin, Tex.: Steck, 1935.

Lister, Florence C., and Robert H. Lister. *Chihuahua: Storehouse of Storms*. Albuquerque: University of New Mexico Press, 1966.

López y Rivas, Gilberto. "Cortina y el conflicto fronterizo entre Estados Unidos y México." In *Tamaulipas. Textos de su historia, 1810–1921*, edited by Juan Fidel Zorrilla, Maribel Miró Flaquer, and Octavio Herrera Pérez, 1:332–43. México: Instituto Mora, Universidad Autónoma Metropolitana; Ciudad Victoria: Gobierno del Estado de Tamaulipas, 1990.

Looscan, Adele B. "Dugald McFarlane." *Southwestern Historical Quarterly* 16, no. 3 (1913): 284–90.

Lowrie, Samuel Harman. *Culture Conflict in Texas, 1821–1835*. New York: Columbia University Press, 1932.

Lundy, Benjamin. *The Life, Travels, and Opinions of Benjamin Lundy; including his journeys to Texas and Mexico, with a sketch of contemporary events, and a notice of the revolution in Hayti*. Philadelphia: William D. Parrish, 1847.

Mahon, Emmie Giddings W., and Chester V. Kielman. "George H. Giddings and the San Antonio–San Diego Mail Line." *Southwestern Historical Quarterly* 61, no. 2 (1957): 220–39.

Marshall, Thomas Maitland. "Commercial Aspects of the Texas Santa Fe Expedition." *Southwestern Historical Quarterly* 20, no. 3 (1917): 242–59.

Martínez, Juan Francisco. *Sea la Luz: The Making of Mexican Protestantism in the American Southwest, 1829–1900*. Denton: University of North Texas Press, 2006.

Martínez, Lucas. *Coahuila durante la intervención francesa, 1862–1867*. Saltillo: Gobierno del Estado de Coahuila, 2008.

———., comp. *De Monterrey a Cuatro Ciénegas: Los senderos de Santiago Vidaurri y Jesús Carranza*. 2nd ed. Monterrey, N.L.: Ayuntamiento de Monterrey, 2007.

———. *El Ejército del Norte. Coahuila durante la Guerra de Reforma, 1858–1860*. Saltillo: Gobierno del Estado de Coahuila, 2012.

Martínez, Oscar J. *Border Boom Town: Ciudad Juarez since 1848*. Austin: University of Texas Press, 1975.

———. *Troublesome Border*. Tucson: University of Arizona Press, 1988.

Martínez, Oscar J., and Manuel Ceballos Ramírez. "Conflict and Accommodation on the U.S.-Mexican Border, 1848–1911." In *Myths, Misdeeds, and Misunderstandings:*

The Roots of Conflict in U.S.-Mexican Relations, edited by Jaime E. Rodríguez and Kathryn Vincent, 135–58. Wilmington, Del.: SR Books, 1997.

Martínez López, Joel. *Orígenes del Presbiterianismo en México*. Matamoros: Self-published, 1972.

Maury, M. F. "The American Colony in Mexico." *DeBow's Review: Devoted to the Restoration of the Southern States* 1, no. 6 (1866): 623–30. http://search.proquest.com .proxy.libraries.smu.edu/americanperiodicals/docview/89633266/fulltextPDF /AEAE59F10AF54135PQ/1?accountid=6667.

Mayer, Arthur James. "San Antonio, Frontier Entrepot." PhD diss., University of Texas at Austin, 1976.

Mayer, Edelmiro. *Campaña y guarnición. Memorias de un militar argentino en el ejército republicano de Benito Juárez*. México: Secretaría de Hacienda y Crédito Público, 1972.

McCaffrey, James M. *Army of Manifest Destiny: The American Soldier in the Mexican War, 1846–1848*. New York: New York University Press, 1992.

McGowen, Stanley S. "Battle or Massacre?: The Incident on the Nueces, August 10, 1862." *Southwestern Historical Quarterly* 104, no. 1 (2000): 64–86.

McManus, Sheila. *The Line Which Separates: Race, Gender, and the Making of the Alberta-Montana Borderlands*. Edmonton: University of Alberta Press, 2005.

McWilliams, Carey. *North from Mexico: The Spanish-Speaking People of the United States*. Updated by Matt S. Meier. New York: Praeger, 1990.

Medina Peña, Luis. *Los bárbaros del norte. Guardia Nacional y política en Nuevo León, siglo XIX*. México: Fondo de Cultura Económica; Centro de Investigación y Docencia Económicas, 2014.

Mendirichaga, José Roberto. *El Colegio de San Juan en Saltillo, 1878–1914*. Saltillo: Gobierno del Estado de Coahuila, 2010.

Metz, Leon C. *Border: The U.S.-Mexico Line*. El Paso, Tex.: Mangan Books, 1989.

Meyer, Lorenzo. "Estados Unidos y la evolución del nacionalismo defensivo mexicano." *Foro Internacional* 46, no. 3 (2006): 421–64.

Meyer, Michael C., and William L. Sherman. *The Course of Mexican History*. 3rd ed. New York: Oxford University Press, 1987.

Miller, Edward L. *New Orleans and the Texas Revolution*. College Station: Texas A&M University Press, 2004.

Miller, Robert Ryal. "The American Legion of Honor in Mexico." *Pacific Historical Review* 30, no. 3 (1961): 229–41.

———. *Arms across the Border: United States Aid to Juárez during the French Intervention in Mexico*. Transactions of the American Philosophical Society, n.s., vol. 63, pt. 6. Philadelphia: American Philosophical Society, 1973.

Minor, Nancy McGown. *Turning Adversity to Advantage: A History of the Lipan Apaches of Texas and Northern Mexico, 1700–1900*. New York: University Press of America, 2009.

Miró Flaquer, Maribel. "La Revuelta de Tuxtepec en Tamaulipas." In *Tamaulipas. Textos de su historia, 1810–1921*, edited by Juan Fidel Zorrilla, Maribel Miró Flaquer, and Octavio Herrera Pérez, 2:26–43. México: Instituto Mora, Universidad Autónoma Metropolitana; Ciudad Victoria: Gobierno del Estado de Tamaulipas, 1990.

Monday, Jane Clements, and Frances Brannen Vick. *Petra's Legacy: The South Texas Ranching Empire of Petra Vela and Mifflin Kenedy*. College Station: Texas A&M University Press, 2007.

Moneyhon, Carl H. *Edmund J. Davis: Civil War General, Republican Leader, Reconstruction Governor*. Fort Worth: Texas Christian University Press, 2010.

Montejano, David. *Anglos and Mexicans in the Making of Texas, 1836–1986*. Austin: University of Texas Press, 1986.

———. "Mexican Merchants and Teamsters on the Texas Cotton Road." In *Mexico and Mexicans in the Making of the United States*, edited by John Tutino. Austin: University of Texas Press, 2012.

Montgomery, Cora [Jane McManus Cazneau]. *Eagle Pass, or Life on the Border*. Edited by Robert Crawford Cotner. Austin, Tex.: Pemberton Press, 1966.

Moore, James Talmadge. *Through Fire and Flood: The Catholic Church in Frontier Texas, 1836–1900*. College Station: Texas A&M University Press, 1992.

Mora-Torres, Juan. *The Making of the Mexican Border*. Austin: University of Texas Press, 2001.

Morgenthaler, George J. *The River Has Never Divided Us: A Border History of La Junta de los Rios*. Austin: University of Texas Press, 2004.

Moseley, Edward H. "Indians from the Eastern United States and the Defense of Northeastern Mexico: 1855–1864." *Southwestern Social Science Quarterly* 46, no. 3 (1965): 273–80.

Mulroy, Kevin. *Freedom on the Border: The Seminole Maroons in Florida, the Indian Territory, Coahuila, and Texas*. Lubbock: Texas Tech University Press, 1993.

Nail, Olin W., ed. *Texas Methodist Centennial Yearbook: The Story of Methodism during the Last One Hundred Years in Texas*. Elgin, Tex.: Self-published, 1934. http://texashistory .unt.edu/ark:/67531/metapth46841.

Nance, Joseph M. *After San Jacinto: The Texas-Mexican Frontier, 1836–1841*. Austin: University of Texas Press, 1963.

———. *Attack and Counter-Attack: The Texas-Mexican Frontier, 1842*. Austin: University of Texas Press, 1964.

Náñez, Alfredo, *History of the Rio Grande Conference of the United Methodist Church*. Dallas, Tex.: Bridwell Library, Southern Methodist University, 1980.

Narrett, David E. "José Bernardo Gutiérrez de Lara: Caudillo of the Mexican Republic in Texas." *Southwestern Historical Quarterly* 106, no. 2 (2002): 195–228.

Negrete Salas, Martaelena. "La frontera texana y el abigeato, 1848–1872." *Historia Mexicana* 31, no. 1 (1981): 79–100.

Neumann, Ray. *A Centennial History of St. Joseph's Church and Parish, 1868 to 1968*. San Antonio, Tex.: Clemens, 1968.

Nichols, James David. "The Limits of Liberty: African Americans, Indians, and Peons in the Texas-Mexico Borderlands, 1820–1860." PhD diss., Stony Brook University, 2012.

———. "The Line of Liberty: Runaway Slaves and Fugitive Peons in the Texas-Mexico Borderlands." *Western Historical Quarterly* 44, no. 4 (2013): 413–33.

Nobles, Gregory H. *American Frontiers: Cultural Encounters and Continental Conquest.* New York: Hill and Wang, 1997.

Noll, Mark, ed. *God and Mammon: Protestants, Money and the Market, 1790–1860.* Oxford: Oxford University Press, 2002.

Nunn, W. C. *Escape from Reconstruction.* Fort Worth: Leo Potishman Foundation, Texas Christian University, 1956.

Olmsted, Frederick Law. *A Journey through Texas: or, A Saddle-trip on the Southwestern Frontier: With a Statistical Appendix.* 1857. Repr., Austin: University of Texas Press, 1978.

Ontiveros Ruiz, G. *Historia del comercio de México con los Estados Unidos durante los primeros 25 años de vida independiente (1821–1846).* N.p.: Eumed.net, 2005. http://www.eumed.net/libros-gratis/2005/gor-his/.

Owsley, Frank L. *King Cotton Diplomacy.* Chicago: University of Chicago Press, 1931.

Pani, Erika. "Ciudadanos precarios. Naturalización y extranjería en el México decimonónico." *Historia Mexicana* 62, no. 2 (2012): 627–74.

Parisot, P. F. *The Reminiscences of a Texas Missionary.* San Antonio, Tex.: St. Mary's Church, 1899.

Paschal, Kristopher B. "'Texas Must Be a Slave Country': The Development of Slavery in Mexican Texas and the Institution's Role in the Coming of Revolution, 1821–1836." Master's thesis, Southern Methodist University, 2010.

Payne, Darwin. "Camp Life in the Army of Occupation: Corpus Christi, July 1845 to March 1846." *Southwestern Historical Quarterly* 73, no. 3 (1970): 326–42.

Pingenot, Ben E. "Colonel 'Winker' Valdés: 'El Azote de los Indios.'" *Journal of Big Bend Studies* 9 (1997): 33–43.

———. "The Great Wagon Train Expedition of 1850." *Southwestern Historical Quarterly* 98, no. 2 (1994): 183–225.

Plana, Manuel. *El reino del algodón en México. La estructura agraria de la Laguna (1855–1910).* 2nd ed. Monterrey: Universidad Autónoma de Nuevo León; Universidad Iberoamericana; Centro de Estudios Sociales y Humanísticos de Saltillo, 1996.

Potter, Reuben M. "The Texas Revolution. Distinguished Mexicans who took part in the revolution of Texas, with glances at its early events." *Magazine of American History,* October 1878.

Pourade, Richard F. *The Sign of the Eagle: A View of Mexico, 1835–1855.* San Diego, Calif.: Union Tribune, 1970.

Poyo, Gerald E., and Gilberto M. Hinojosa, eds. *Tejano Origins in Eighteenth-Century San Antonio.* Austin: University of Texas Press, 1991.

Purcell, Anita, ed. *Frontier Mexico, 1875–1894: Letters of William L. Purcell.* San Antonio, Tex.: Naylor, 1963.

Purdie, Samuel A., and Gulielma M. Purdie. "Correspondence." *Friends' Review: A Religious, Literary and Miscellaneous Journal* 26, no. 9 (1872): 139. http://search.proquest.com.proxy.libraries.smu.edu/americanperiodicals/docview/91096996/fulltextPDF/6E7EF2956C5E4297PQ/2?accountid=6667.

Raiser, Chester C. "La frontera y el reconocimiento de Díaz por Estados Unidos." *Historia Mexicana* 7, no. 3 (1958): 442–59.

Ramírez, Nora E. "The Vaquero and Ranching in the Southwestern United States, 1600–1970." PhD diss., Indiana University, 1979.

Ramos, Raúl A. *Beyond the Alamo: Forging Mexican Ethnicity in San Antonio, 1821–1861.* Chapel Hill: University of North Carolina Press, 2008.

Rankin, Melinda. *Texas in 1850.* Boston: Damrell & Moore, 1852. http://texashistory .unt.edu/ark:/67531/metapth6107.

———. *Twenty Years among the Mexicans: A Narrative of Missionary Labor.* Edited by Miguel A. González-Quiroga and Timothy Bowman. Dallas, Tex.: DeGolyer Library and William P. Clements Center for Southwest Studies, 2008.

Raat, W. Dirk. *Mexico and the United States: Ambivalent Vistas.* Athens: University of Georgia Press, 1992.

Rayburn, John C., and Virginia Kemp Rayburn, eds. *Century of Conflict, 1821–1913: Incidents in the Lives of William Neale and William A. Neale, Early Settlers in South Texas.* Waco, Tex.: Texian Press, 1966.

Reid, Stuart. *The Secret War for Texas.* College Station: Texas A&M University Press, 2007.

Reséndez, Andrés. *Changing National Identities at the Frontier: Texas and New Mexico, 1800–1850.* Cambridge: Cambridge University Press, 2005.

———. "Ramón Múzquiz, The Ultimate Insider." In *Tejano Leadership in Mexican and Revolutionary Texas,* edited by Jesús F. de la Teja, 129–45. College Station: Texas A&M University Press, 2010.

Ridout, Joseph B. "'An Anti-national Disorder': Antonio Canales and Northeastern Mexico, 1836–1852." Master's thesis, University of Texas at Austin, 1994.

Rippy, J. Fred. "Border Troubles along the Rio Grande, 1848–1860." *Southwestern Historical Quarterly* 23, no. 2 (1919): 91–111.

———. "Mexican Projects of the Confederates." *Southwestern Historical Quarterly* 22, no. 4 (1919): 291–317.

———. "Some Precedents of the Pershing Expedition into Mexico." *Southwestern Historical Quarterly* 24, no. 1 (1920): 292–316.

———. *The United States and Mexico.* Rev. ed. New York: F. S. Crofts and Co., 1971.

Rivaya Martínez, Joaquín. "Trespassers in the Land of Plenty: Comanche Raiding across the U.S.-Mexican Border, 1846–1853." Paper presented at the International Symposium on Violence in the U.S.-Mexican Borderlands, Clements Center for Southwest Studies, April 16, 2016.

Robinson, Sherry. *I Fought a Good Fight: A History of the Lipan Apaches.* Denton: University of North Texas Press, 2013.

Rodriguez, Alberto. "Ethnic Conflict in South Texas, 1860–1930." Master's thesis, University of Texas–Pan American, 2005.

Rodríguez, José Policarpo. *José Policarpo Rodríguez, the Old Guide: Surveyor, Scout, Hunter, Indian Fighter, Ranchman, Preacher: His Life in His Own Words.* Nashville, Tenn., and Dallas, Tex.: Publishing House of the Methodist Episcopal Church South, n.d.

Rodríguez, Martha. *La guerra entre bárbaros y civilizados. El exterminio del nómada en Coahuila, 1840–1880.* Saltillo, Coah.: Centro de Estudios Sociales y Humanísticos, 1998.

———. "La odisea para instalar el progreso." In *Breve Historia de Coahuila*, edited by María Elena Santoscoy, Laura Gutiérrez, Martha Rodríguez, and Francisco Cepeda, 201–88. México: Colegio de México; Fondo de Cultura Económica, 2000.

Rolle, Andrew F. *The Lost Cause: The Confederate Exodus to Mexico.* Norman: University of Oklahoma Press, 1965.

Román Jáquez, Juana Gabriela. *Del Aguanaval a Sierra Mojada. El conflicto de límites entre Durango y Coahuila.* Saltillo, Coah.: Centro de Estudios Sociales y Humanísticos, 2001.

Ruiz Guerra, Rubén, *Hombres nuevos. Metodismo y modernización en México, 1873–1930.* México: Centro de Comunicación Cultural CUPSA, 1992.

Sahlins, Peter. *Boundaries: The Making of France and Spain in the Pyrenees.* Berkeley: University of California Press, 1989.

Salinas, Martín. *Indians of the Rio Grande Delta: Their Role in the History of Southern Texas and Northeastern Mexico.* Austin: University of Texas Press, 1990.

Salvucci, Richard J. "The Origins and Progress of U.S.-Mexican Trade, 1825–1884: 'Hoc opus, hic labor est.'" *Hispanic American Historical Review* 71, no. 4 (1991): 697–735.

Samora, Julian, Joe Bernal, and Albert Peña. *Gunpowder Justice: A Reassessment of the Texas Rangers.* Notre Dame, Ind.: University of Notre Dame Press, 1979.

Santleben, August. *A Texas Pioneer: Early Staging and Overland Freighting Days on the Frontiers of Texas and Mexico.* Edited by I. D. Affleck. New York and Washington: Neale, 1910. Facsimile: Waco, Tex.: W. M. Morrison, 1967.

Santoscoy, Elena, et al. *Breve historia de Coahuila.* México: Colegio de México; Fondo de Cultura Económica, 2000.

Sayles, Stephen. "The Romero-Frelinghuysen Convention: A Milestone in Border Relations." *New Mexico Historical Review* 51, no. 4 (1976): 295–311.

Schoonover, Thomas. "Dollars over Dominion: United States Economic Interests in Mexico, 1861–1867." *Pacific Historical Review* 45, no. 1 (1976): 23–45.

Schwartz, Rosalie. *Across the Rio to Freedom: U.S. Negroes in Mexico.* Southwestern Studies Monograph no. 44. El Paso: Texas Western Press, 1975.

Seguín, Juan Nepomuceno. *A Revolution Remembered: The Memoirs and Selected Correspondence of Juan N. Seguín.* Edited by Jesús F. de la Teja. Austin: Texas State Historical Association, 2002.

Sherif, Muzafer. *In Common Predicament: Social Psychology of Intergroup Conflict and Cooperation.* Boston: Houghton Mifflin, 1966.

Sibley, Marilyn McAdams. "Charles Stillman: A Case Study of Entrepreneurship on the Rio Grande, 1861–1865." *Southwestern Historical Quarterly* 77, no. 2 (1973): 227–40.

———. *Travelers in Texas, 1761–1860.* Austin: University of Texas Press, 1967.

Sierra, Carlos J., and Rogelio Martínez Vera. "El Contraresguardo de Nuevo León y Tamaulipas." In *Tamaulipas. Textos de su historia, 1810–1921*, edited by Juan Fidel Zorrilla, Maribel Miró Flaquer, and Octavio Herrera Pérez, 1:269–73. México:

Instituto Mora, Universidad Autónoma Metropolitana; Ciudad Victoria: Gobierno del Estado de Tamaulipas, 1990.

Smith, Adam. *An Inquiry into the Nature and Causes of the Wealth of Nations.* Edited by Edwin Cannan with an introduction by Max Lerner. New York: Random House, 1937.

Smith, Anita Torres, and Donald E. Smith. "The Life and Times of Valeriano Torres, 1844–1898." *Journal of Big Bend Studies* 13 (2001): 37–64.

Smith, Justin H. "La Republica de Rio Grande." *American Historical Review* 25, no. 4 (1920): 660–75.

———. *The War with Mexico.* Vol. 2. New York: Macmillan, 1919.

Smith, Michael M. "General Rafael Benavides and the Texas-Mexico Border Crisis of 1877." *Southwestern Historical Quarterly* 112, no. 3 (2009): 235–60.

Smith, Ralph Adam. *Borderlander: The Life of James Kirker, 1793–1852.* Norman: University of Oklahoma Press, 1999.

Smithwick, Noah. *The Evolution of a State, or Recollections of Old Texas Days.* Compiled by his daughter, Nanna Smithwick Donaldson. Austin, Tex.: Gammel Book Co. Facsimile, Steck: Austin, Tex.: 1900.

Smyrl, Frank H. "Texans in the Union Army, 1861–1865." *Southwestern Historical Quarterly* 65, no. 2 (1961): 234–50.

Sonnichsen, C. L. *Roy Bean: Law West of the Pecos.* Old Greenwich, Conn.: Devin-Adair, 1943.

Soto, Miguel. "Agentes y socios del 'destino manifiesto': negocios y política en los despojos territoriales de México." In *En busca de una nación soberana. Relaciones internacionales de México, siglos XIX y XX*, edited by Jorge A. Schiavón, Daniela Spenser, and Mario Vázquez Olivera, 91–126. México: Secretaría de Relaciones Exteriores; Centro de Investigación y Docencia Económicas, 2006.

———. "La disputa entre Monclova y Saltillo y la independencia de Texas." *Tempos, Revista de Historia* 1 (1993): 123–74.

———. "Texas en la mira. Política y negocios al iniciarse la gestión de Anthony Butler." In *Ensayos sobre la relación entre México y los Estados Unidos en el siglo XIX*, edited by Ana Rosa Suárez Argüello and Marcela Terrazas y Basante, 19–63. México: Universidad Nacional Autónoma de México; Instituto Mora, Universidad Autónoma Metropolitana, 1997.

Spell, Lota M. *Pioneer Printer: Samuel Bangs in Mexico and Texas.* Austin: University of Texas Press, 1963.

———. "Samuel Bangs: The First Printer in Texas." *Hispanic American Historical Review* 11, no. 2 (1931): 248–58.

Spillman, Robert C. *A Historical Geography of Mexican American Population Patterns in the South Texas Hispanic Borderland, 1850–1970.* Hattiesburg: University of Southern Mississippi, 1977.

Stewart, Kenneth L., and Arnoldo de León. *Not Room Enough: Mexicans, Anglos, and Socio-economic Change in Texas, 1850–1900.* Albuquerque: University of New Mexico Press, 1993.

Sugawara, Masael, comp. *Mariano Escobedo, Documentos*. http://biblio.juridicas.unam .mx/libros/libro.htm?i=2676.

Sumpter, Jesse. *Paso del Aguila: A Chronicle of Frontier Days on the Texas Border as Recorded in the Memoirs of Jesse Sumpter*. Compiled by Harry Warren. Edited by Ben E. Pingenot. Austin, Tex.: Encino Press, 1969.

Swift, Roy L., and Leavitt Corning Jr. *Three Roads to Chihuahua: The Great Wagon Roads That Opened the Southwest, 1823–1883*. Austin, Tex.: Eakin Press, 1989.

Takaki, Ronald T. *Iron Cages: Race and Culture in Nineteenth-Century America*. Seattle: University of Washington Press, 1979.

Tapia Méndez, Aureliano. *El diario de don José Ignacio Montes de Oca y Obregón—Ipandro Acaico*. Monterrey, N.L.: Producciones Al Voleo-El Troquel, 1988.

Taylor, Lawrence Douglas. "Voluntarios extranjeros en los ejércitos liberales mexicanos, 1854–1867." *Historia Mexicana* 37, no. 2 (1987): 205–37.

Taylor, Paul S. *An American-Mexican Frontier: Nueces County, Texas*. Chapel Hill: University of North Carolina Press, 1934.

———. "Historical Note on Dimmit County, Texas." *Southwestern Historical Quarterly* 34, no. 2 (1930): 79–90.

Terrazas y Basante, Marcela. "Colaboración y conflicto. Relaciones transfronterizas en el noreste mexicano." In *En busca de una nación soberana. Relaciones internacionales de México, siglos XIX y XX*, edited by Jorge A. Schiavón, Daniela Spenser, and Mario Vázquez Olivera, 127–56. México: Secretaría de Relaciones Exteriores; Centro de Investigación y Docencia Económicas, 2006.

Thompson, Jerry. *Cortina: Defending the Mexican Name in Texas*. College Station: Texas A&M University Press, 2007.

———., ed. *Fifty Miles and a Fight: Major Samuel Peter Heintzelman's Journal of Texas and the Cortina War*. Austin: Texas State Historical Association, 1998.

———. *Mexican Texans in the Union Army*. El Paso: Texas Western Press, 1986.

———. *Sabers on the Rio Grande*. Austin, Tex.: Presidial Press, 1974.

———. *Vaqueros in Blue and Gray*. Austin, Tex.: Presidial Press, 1976.

———. *A Wild and Vivid Land: An Illustrated History of the South Texas Border*. Austin: Texas State Historical Association, 1997.

Thompson, Jerry, and Lawrence T. Jones III. *Civil War and Revolution on the Rio Grande Frontier*. Austin: Texas State Historical Association, 2004.

Tijerina, Andrés. *Tejano Empire: Life on the South Texas Ranchos*. College Station: Texas A&M University Press, 1998.

———. *Tejanos and Texas under the Mexican Flag, 1821–1836*. College Station: Texas A&M University Press, 1994.

Tilden, Bryant P. *Notes on the Upper Rio Grande*. Philadelphia: Lindsay and Blakiston, 1847.

Torget, Andrew J. *Seeds of Empire: Cotton, Slavery, and the Transformation of the Texas Borderlands, 1800–1850*. David J. Weber Series in the New Borderlands History. Chapel Hill: University of North Carolina Press, 2015.

Truett, Samuel. *Fugitive Landscapes: The Forgotten History of the U.S.-Mexico Borderlands.* New Haven, Conn.: Yale University Press, 2006.

Truett, Samuel, and Elliott Young, eds. *Continental Crossroads: Remapping U.S.-Mexico Borderlands History.* Durham, N.C.: Duke University Press, 2004.

Tyler, R. Curtis. "Santiago Vidaurri and the Confederacy." *The Americas* 26, no. 1 (1969): 66–76.

Tyler, Ronnie C. "The Callahan Expedition of 1855." *Southwestern Historical Quarterly* 70, no. 4 (1967): 574–85.

———. "Cotton on the Border, 1861–1865." *Southwestern Historical Quarterly* 73, no. 4 (1970): 456–77.

———. *Santiago Vidaurri and the Southern Confederacy.* Austin: Texas State Historical Association, 1973.

Union Baptist Association (Texas). *Minutes of the Thirty-Sixth Annual Session of the Union Baptist Association.* San Antonio: Times Job Printing House, 1883. http://texashistory .unt.edu/ark:/67531/metapth253208.

U.S. Bureau of Indian Affairs. "Report of H. M. Atkinson and T. G. Williams, Special Commissioners to Visit the Kickapoos in Mexico, with the View of Inducing Them to Come and Remain in the Indian Territory." October 8, 1873. In *Annual Report, Commissioner of Indian Affairs to the Secretary of the Interior for the Year 1873.* Washington, D.C.: Government Printing Office, 1874. http://quod.lib.umich.edu/m/moa /AAG6455.0001.001?rgn=main;view=fulltext.

U.S. Department of State. *Executive Documents Printed by Order of the House of Representatives, during the First Session of the Thirty-Ninth Congress, 1865–66.* Pt. 3. U.S. Government Printing Office, 1865–66. http://digital.library.wisc.edu/1711.dl/FRUS .FRUS186566p3.

———. *Executive Documents Printed by Order of the House of Representatives, during the Second Session of the Thirty-Ninth Congress, 1866–67.* Washington, D.C.: U.S. Government Printing Office, 1866–67. http://digital.library.wisc.edu/1711.dl/FRUS.FRUS186667.

———. *Executive Documents Printed by Order of the House of Representatives, 1872–73.* U.S. Government Printing Office, 1872–73. http://digital.library.wisc.edu/1711.dl /FRUS.FRUS187273.

———. *Executive Documents Printed by Order of the House of Representatives, 1875–76.* Vol. 2. Washington, D.C.: U.S. Government Printing Office, 1875–76. http://digital .library.wisc.edu/1711.dl/FRUS.FRUS187576v02.

U.S. War Department. *Official Records of the Union and Confederate Navies in the War of the Rebellion.* Washington, D.C.: U.S. Government Printing Office, 1894–1922, http://collections.library.cornell.edu/moa_new/ofre.html.

———. *War of the Rebellion: A Compilation of the Official Records of the Union and Confederate Armies.* Washington, D.C.: Government Printing Office, 1880–1901, http://collections.library.cornell.edu/moa_new/waro.html.

Utley, Robert M. "The Range Cattle Industry in the Big Bend of Texas." *Southwestern Historical Quarterly* 69, no. 4 (1966): 419–41.

Valerio-Jiménez, Omar S. "Neglected Citizens and Willing Traders: The Villas del Norte (Tamaulipas) in Mexico's Northern Borderlands, 1749–1846." *Mexican Studies/ Estudios Mexicanos* 18, no. 2 (2002): 251–96.

———. *River of Hope: Forging Identity and Nation in the Rio Grande Borderlands.* Durham, N.C.: Duke University Press, 2013.

Vález, María Luisa. "The Pilgrimage of Hispanics in the Sisters of Charity of the Incarnate Word." *U.S. Catholic Historian* 9, nos. 1–2 (1990): 181–94.

Van der Dennen, J., and V. Falger. *Sociobiology and Conflict: Evolutionary Perspectives on Competition, Cooperation, Violence, and Warfare.* London: Chapman and Hall, 1980.

Vasconcelos, José. *Don Evaristo Madero (Biografía de un patricio).* México: Impresiones Modernas, 1958.

Vázquez, Josefina Zoraida. "Contexto nacional del primer federalismo mexicano." In *Práctica y fracaso del primer federalismo mexicano (1824–1835),* edited by Josefina Zoraida Vázquez and José Antonio Serrano Ortega. México: Colegio de México, 2012.

———. *La supuesta República del Río Grande.* 2nd ed. Ciudad Victoria: Instituto de Investigaciones Históricas, Universidad Autónoma de Tamaulipas, 1995.

———. "The Texas Question in Mexican Politics, 1836–1845." *Southwestern Historical Quarterly* 89, no. 3 (1986): 309–44.

Viele, Egbert L. "The Frontiers of the United States: First the Rio Grande Frontier." *Journal of the American Geographical Society of New York* 14 (January 1, 1882): 166. http://search.proquest.com/docview/125737085?accountid=6667.

Viele, Teresa. *Following the Drum: A Glimpse of Frontier Life.* Austin, Tex.: Steck-Vaughn, 1968.

Vigness, David M. "The Republic of the Rio Grande: An Example of Separatism in Northern Mexico." PhD diss., University of Texas at Austin, 1951.

Vizcaya Canales, Isidro. *Incursiones de indios al noreste en el México independiente (1821– 1855).* Monterrey: Archivo General del Estado de Nuevo León, 1995.

———. *Los orígenes de la industrialización de Monterrey.* 3rd ed. Monterrey: Archivo General del Estado de Nuevo León, 2001.

———. *Tierra de guerra viva. Invasión de los indios bárbaros al noreste de México, 1821–1885.* Monterrey, N.L.: Academia de Investigación Humanística, 2001.

———. *Un siglo de Monterrey. Desde el grito de Dolores hasta el Plan de San Luis, 1810–1910.* Monterrey, N.L.: Academia de Investigación Humanística, 1998.

Wahlstrom, Todd William. "The Southern Exodus to Mexico: Migration across the Borderlands after the U.S. Civil War." PhD diss., University of California at Santa Barbara, 2009.

Wallace, Ernest, ed. *Ranald S. Mackenzie's Official Correspondence Relating to Texas, 1873–1879.* Lubbock: West Texas Museum Association, 1968.

Walraven, Bill, and Marjorie K. Walraven. *The Magnificent Barbarians: Little-Told Tales of the Texas Revolution.* Austin, Tex.: Eakin Press, 1993.

Weber, David J. "Conflicts and Accommodations: Hispanic and Anglo-American Borders in Historical Perspective, 1670–1853." *Journal of the Southwest* 39, no. 1 (Spring 1997): 1–32.

———., ed. *Foreigners in Their Native Land: Historical Roots of the Mexican Americans.* Albuquerque: University of New Mexico Press, 1973.

———. *The Mexican Frontier, 1821–1846: The American Southwest under Mexico.* Albuquerque: University of New Mexico Press, 1982.

Webster, Michael G. "Texas Manifest Destiny and the Mexican Border Conflict, 1865–1880." PhD diss., Indiana University, 1972.

Westrup, Thomas M. *Principios. Relato de la introducción del Evangelio en México.* Edited by Enrique Tomás Westrup. Monterrey, N.L.: Enrique Tomás Westrup, 1948.

Wilcox, Seb. S. "Laredo during the Texas Republic." *Southwestern Historical Quarterly* 42, no. 2 (1938): 83–107.

Wilkinson, Joseph B. *Laredo and the Rio Grande Frontier.* Austin, Tex.: Jenkins, 1975.

Windham, William T. "The Problem of Supply in the Trans-Mississippi Confederacy." *Journal of Southern History* 27, no. 2 (1961): 149–68.

Winsor, Bill. *Texas in the Confederacy: Military Installations, Economy, and People.* Hillsboro, Tex.: Hill Junior College Press, 1978.

Wood, Robert D. *John Twohig: An Extraordinary Irish Immigrant.* San Antonio, Tex.: Pecan Grove Press, 2009.

Woolford, Sam, ed. "The Burr G. Duval Diary." *Southwestern Historical Quarterly* 65, no. 4 (1962): 487–511.

Wooster, Robert. "The Army and the Politics of Expansion: Texas and the Southwestern Borderlands, 1870–1886." *Southwestern Historical Quarterly* 93, no. 2 (1989): 151–68.

Wright, Robert. *Nonzero: The Logic of Human Destiny.* New York: Pantheon Books, 2000. www.nonzero.org.

Wright, Robert. E. "Building Churches and Communities in Nineteenth-Century South Texas," *Heritage* 17, no. 1 (1999): 16–20. http://texashistory.unt.edu/ark:/67531 /metapth45393.

———. "From Hispanic Gateway to Border Byway: The Catholic Church in the Middle Rio Grande District of Coahuila/Texas up to 1884." *Catholic Southwest: A Journal of History and Culture* 22: 3–20.

———. "Pioneer Religious Congregations of Men in Texas before 1900." *Journal of Texas Catholic History* 5 (1994): 65–89.

Young, Elliott. *Catarino Garza's Revolution on the Texas-Mexico Border.* Durham, N.C.: Duke University Press, 2004.

Zaragoza, Alex M. *The Monterrey Elite and the Mexican State, 1880–1940.* Austin: University of Texas Press, 1988.

Zarco, Francisco. "Información Europea. Secretaría de Relaciones Exteriores. Cartas." In *Obras completas de Francisco Zarco,* vol. 20. Compiled by Boris Rosen Jélomer. México: Centro de Investigación Científica Ing. Jorge L. Tamayo, 1992.

Zorrilla, Juan Fidel. *Historia de Tamaulipas.* 2nd ed. Ciudad Victoria: Instituto de Investigaciones Históricas, Universidad Autónoma de Tamaulipas, 1977.

Zorrilla, Juan Fidel, Maribel Miró Flaquer, and Octavio Herrera Pérez, comps. *Tamaulipas, textos de su historia, 1810–1921.* 2 vols. México: Instituto Mora, Universidad

Autónoma Metropolitana; Ciudad Victoria: Gobierno del Estado de Tamaulipas, 1990.

———. *Tamaulipas, una historia compartida, 1810–1921.* 2 vols. Ciudad Victoria: Instituto de Investigaciones Históricas, Universidad Autónoma de Tamaulipas, 1993.

Zorrilla, Luis G. *Historia de las relaciones entre México y los Estados Unidos de América, 1800–1958.* México: Editorial Porrúa, 1965.

Index

References to illustrations appear in italic type.

Printed in the USA
CPSIA information can be obtained
at www.ICGtesting.com
LVHW051311131023
760935LV00002B/240

9 780806 190952